Lecture Notes in Computer Science 16575

Founding Editors

Gerhard Goos
Juris Hartmanis

The series Lecture Notes in Computer Science (LNCS), including its subseries Lecture Notes in Artificial Intelligence (LNAI) and Lecture Notes in Bioinformatics (LNBI), has established itself as a medium for the publication of new developments in computer science and information technology research, teaching, and education.

LNCS enjoys close cooperation with the computer science R & D community, the series counts many renowned academics among its volume editors and paper authors, and collaborates with prestigious societies. Its mission is to serve this international community by providing an invaluable service, mainly focused on the publication of conference and workshop proceedings and postproceedings. LNCS commenced publication in 1973.

José Manuel Ferrández Vicente ·
Mikel Val-Calvo · Hojjat Adeli
Editors

Bioinspired Intelligent Systems

From Robotics and Computer Vision to Trustworthy Applications

11th International Work-Conference on the Interplay Between
Natural and Artificial Computation, IWINAC 2026
Canary Islands, Spain, May 26–29, 2026
Proceedings, Part II

Springer

Editors
José Manuel Ferrández Vicente
Universidad Politécnica de Cartagena
Cartagena, Spain

Mikel Val-Calvo
Universidad Politécnica de Valencia
Valencia, Spain

Hojjat Adeli
Ohio State University
Columbus, OH, USA

ISSN 0302-9743 ISSN 1611-3349 (electronic)
Lecture Notes in Computer Science
ISBN 978-3-032-27316-1 ISBN 978-3-032-27317-8 (eBook)
https://doi.org/10.1007/978-3-032-27317-8

Preface

The main topic of these IWINAC/ICINAC 2026 books is to study intelligent systems inspired by the natural world, in particular biology. Several algorithms and methods and their applications are discussed, including evolutionary algorithms. Bio-inspired intelligent systems have thousands of useful applications in fields as diverse as machine learning, biomedicine, control theory, telecommunications, and why not music and art. This book covers both the theory and practice of bio-inspired artificial intelligence, along with providing a bit of the basis and inspiration for the different approaches. This is a discipline that strives to develop new computing techniques through observing how naturally occurring phenomena behave to solve complex problems in various environmental situations. Brain-inspired computation is one of these techniques that covers multiple applications in very different fields. Through IWINAC/ICINAC we provide a forum in which research in different fields can converge to create new computational paradigms that are on the frontier between neural and biomedical sciences and Information technologies.

As a multidisciplinary forum, IWINAC is open to any established institutions and research laboratories actively working in the field of natural or neural technologies. But beyond achieving co-operation between different research realms, we wish to actively encourage co-operation with the private sector, particularly SMEs, as a way of bridging the gap between frontier science and societal impact.

In this edition, four main themes outline the Conference topics: Neuroscience and Mental Health, Affective Computing, Robotics, and Translational Systems.

1) Machine learning holds great promise in the development of new models and theories in the field of Neuroscience, in conjunction with classical statistical hypothesis testing. Machine learning algorithms have the potential to reveal interactions, hidden patterns of abnormal activity, brain structure and connectivity, and physiological mechanisms of brain and behavior. In addition, several approaches for testing the significance of the machine learning outcomes have been successfully proposed to avoid "the dangers of spurious findings or explanations void of mechanism" by means of proper replication, validation, and hypothesis-driven confirmation. Therefore, machine learning can effectively provide relevant information to take great strides toward understanding how the brain works. The main goal of this field is to build a bridge between two scientific communities, the machine learning community, including leading scientists in deep learning and related areas within pattern recognition and artificial intelligence, and the neuroscience community. Artificial Intelligence has become the ultimate scale to test the limits of technological advances in dealing with Life Science challenges and needs. In this sense, the interplay between Natural and Artificial Computation is expected to play a most relevant role in the diagnosis, monitoring, and treatment of Neurodegenerative Diseases, using the advanced computational solutions provided by Machine Learning and Data Science. This requires us to interchange new ideas, launch projects and contests, and eventually create an inclusive knowledge-oriented network with the aim of empowering

researchers, practitioners, and users of technological solutions for daily life experience in the domains of Neuromotor and Linguistic competence functional evaluation, clinical explainability, and rehabilitation by interaction with humans, robots, and gaming avatars, not being strictly limited to only these, but inclusively open to other related concepts. The use of Machine Learning-based Precision Medicine in monitoring daily life activity and providing well-being conditions to especially sensitive social sectors is one of the most relevant objectives. Case study descriptions involving neurodegenerative diseases (Alzheimer's disease, fronto-temporal dementia, cerebrovascular damage and stroke, autism, Parkinson's disease, amyotrophic lateral sclerosis, multiple sclerosis, Huntington's chorea, etc.) are included. Mild cognitive impairment (MCI) is considered the stage between the mental changes that are seen between normal ageing and early stages of dementia. Indeed, MCI is one of the main indicators of incipient Alzheimer's disease (AD) among other neuropsychological diseases. The growth of these diseases is generating a great interest in the development of new effective methods for the early detection of MCI because, although no treatments are known to cure MCI, this early diagnosis would allow early intervention to delay the effects of the disease and accelerate progress towards effective treatment in its early stages. Although there have been many years of research, the early identification of cognitive impairment, as well as differential diagnosis (to distinguish significant causes or typologies for its treatment), are problems that have been addressed from different angles, but are still far from being solved. Diverse types of tests have already been developed, such as biological markers, magnetic resonance imaging, and neuropsychological tests. While effective, biological markers and magnetic resonance imaging are economically expensive, invasive, and require time to get a result, making them unsuitable as a population screening method. On the other hand, neuropsychological tests have a reliability comparable to biomarker tests, and are cheaper and quicker to interpret.

2) Emotions are essential in human-human communication, cognition, learning, and rational decision-making processes. However, human-machine interfaces (HMIs) are still not able to understand human sentiments and react accordingly. With the aim of endowing HMIs with the emotional intelligence they lack, Affective Computing science focuses on the development of artificial intelligence by means of the analysis of affects and emotions, such that systems and devices could be able to recognize, interpret, process, and simulate human sentiments.

Nowadays, the evaluation of electrophysiological signals plays a key role in advancements towards that purpose since they are an objective representation of the emotional state of an individual. Hence, the interest in physiological variables like electroencephalogram, electrocardiogram, or electrodermal activity, among many others, has notably grown in the field of affective states detection. Furthermore, emotions have also been widely identified by means of the assessment of speech characteristics and facial gestures of people under different sentimental conditions. It is also worth noting that the development of algorithms for the classification of affective states in social media has experienced a notable increase in recent years. In this sense, the language of posts included in social networks, such as Facebook or Twitter, is evaluated with the aim of detecting the sentiments of the users of those media tools. Affective Computing and Sentiment Analysis is intended to be a meeting point for researchers that are interested in any of those areas of expertise related to sentiment analysis, and want to initiate their studies or are currently working on these topics. Hence, manuscripts introducing new proposals based on the analysis of physiological measures, facial recognition, speech recognition, or natural language processing in social media are examples of affective computing and sentiment analysis.

3) Over recent decades there has been an increasing interest in using machine learning and in the last few years, deep learning methods, combined with other vision techniques to create autonomous systems that solve vision problems in different fields. This special session was designed to allow researchers and developers to publish original, innovative, and state-of-the art algorithms and architectures for real-time applications in the areas of computer vision, image processing, biometrics, virtual and augmented reality, neural networks, intelligent interfaces, and biomimetic object-vision recognition.

This workshop provided a platform for academics, developers, and industry-related researchers belonging to the vast communities of **Neural Networks**, **Computational Intelligence**, **Machine Learning**, **Deep Learning**, **Biometrics**, **Vision Systems**, and **Robotics**, to discuss, share experience, and explore traditional and new areas of computer vision, machine and deep learning combined to solve a range of problems. The objective of the workshop was to integrate the growing international community of researchers working on the application of Machine Learning and Deep Learning Methods in Vision and Robotics into a fruitful discussion on the evolution and the benefits of this technology to society.

4) Finally, Artificial Intelligence (AI) has become a catalyst for innovation in a wide variety of disciplines, playing a pivotal role in solving contemporary challenges. This session focuses on the translational applications of AI in multiple fields, highlighing how the technology is transforming key sectors in response to the needs of today's society. Grid and power infrastructure management is one of the domains where AI is revolutionizing efficiency and reliability. Through predictive analytics, optimization, and proactive maintenance, AI enables a smarter and more resilient power grid, crucial in a world seeking decarbonization and the use of renewable energy. In agriculture, AI drives precision farming, improving agricultural production, water resource management, and crop quality. In civil engineering, AI-assisted planning and design streamline construction projects and optimize infrastructure. Smart cities and urban planning benefit from AI to optimize transportation, waste management, and the quality of life of inhabitants. In education, AI personalizes teaching and assessment, tailoring learning to the individual needs of students. In nutrition and food science, AI algorithms are used for creating healthy diets and detecting contaminants in food. This topic explored how AI fosters innovation and transformation in these diverse areas, highlighting the solutions this technology offers to address current challenges and improve the quality of life in modern society. From smarter power grids to safer food, AI is paving the way to a more efficient and sustainable future in a variety of multidisciplinary fields.

The wider view of the computational paradigm gives us more elbow room to accommodate the results of the interplay between nature and computation. The IWINAC/ICINAC forum thus becomes a methodological approximation (set of intentions, questions, experiments, models, algorithms, mechanisms, explanation procedures, and engineering and computational methods) to the natural and artificial perspectives of the mind embodiment problem, both in humans and in artifacts. This is the philosophy that continues in IWINAC meetings, the "interplay" movement between the natural and the artificial, facing this same problem every two years. This synergistic approach will permit us not only to build new computational systems based on natural measurable phenomena, but also to understand many of the observable behaviors inherent to natural systems.

The difficulty of building bridges between natural and artificial computation was one of the main motivations for the organization of IWINAC 2026. The IWINAC/ICINAC 2026 proceedings contain the 99 works selected by the Scientific Committee from more than 187 submissions, after the refereeing process. The type of peer review used was single blind with an average number of reviews received per submission of 2.5, and an average number of papers per reviewer of 3 with external reviewers involved, outside the PC. The first volume, entitled Artificial Intelligence for Neuroscience, Mental Health and Neurodegenerative Disorders, includes all the contributions mainly related to new tools for analizing neural data for mental health or detecting emotional states, or interfacing with physical systems. The second volume, entitled Bioinspired Intelligent Systems: From Robotics and Computer Vision to Trustworthy Applications, contains the papers related to bioinspired programming strategies and all the contributions oriented to the computational solutions to engineering problems in different application domains, such as biomedical systems, or big data solutions.

An event of the nature of IWINAC/ICINAC 2026 cannot be organized without the collaboration of a group of institutions and people who we would like to thank now, starting with Universidad de Granada and Universidad Politécnica de Cartagena. In addition to our universities, we received financial support from Red Nacional en Inteligencia Artificial para Neurociencia y Salud Mental (IA4NSM) and Apliquem Microones 21 s.l. We also would like to express our great gratitude to Ibero-American network **Red Cyted New Technologies for Mental Health (NT4SM) 225RT0169**, to **Cátedra UGR-Endesa en IA**, and to the European Comission **Marie Curie Action MSCA-SE EPISTEAM (101129655)** for organizing their sessions in the Conference.

We want to express our gratefulness to our invited speakers Hojjat Adeli, from Ohio State University (USA), Pablo Laguna Lasaosa from Universidad de Zaragoza (Spain), and Pedro Gómez Vilda, from Universidad Politécnica de Madrid (Spain) for accepting our invitation and for their magnificent plenary talks.

We would also like to thank the authors for their interest in our call and the effort in preparing the papers, condition sine qua non for these proceedings. We thank the Scientific and Organizing Committees, in particular the members of these committees who acted as effective and efficient referees and as promoters and managers of pre-organized sessions on autonomous and relevant topics under the IWINAC/ICINAC global scope.

Our sincere gratitude goes also to Springer, for their continuous receptivity, helpfulness and collaboration in all our joint editorial ventures on the interplay between neuroscience and computation.

Finally, we want to express our special thanks to BCD eventos, our technical secretariat, and to Ana María García de Alba, for making this meeting possible, and for arranging all the details that comprise the organization of this kind of event.

We want to dedicate these two volumes of the IWINAC proceedings to the memories of Professors Rodellar, Sánchez-Andrés, and Mira. We deeply miss them.

May 2026

José Manuel Ferrández Vicente
Mikel Val-Calvo
Hojjat Adeli

Organization

General Chair

José Manuel Ferrández Vicente — Universidad Politécnica de Cartagena, Spain

Organizing Committee

Mikel Val-Calvo — Universidad Politécnica de Valencia, Spain

Honorary Chairs

Hojjat Adeli — Ohio State University, USA
Rodolfo Llinás — New York University, USA
Zhou Changjiu — Singapore Polytechnic, Singapore

Invited Speakers

Hojjat Adeli — Ohio State University, USA
Pablo Laguna — Universidad de Zaragoza, Spain,
Mariano Alcañis — Universidad Politécnica de Valencia, Spain

Field Editors

Sung-Bae Cho — Yonsei University, South Korea
Emilia Barakova — Eindhoven University of Technology, Netherlands
Gema Benedicto — Universidad Politécnica de Cartagena, Spain
María Paula Bonomini — Instituto Tenológico de Buenos Aires, Argentina
Diego Castillo-Barnes — Universidad de Granada, Spain
Enrique Dominguez — Universidad de Málaga, Spain
Félix de la Paz — Universidad Nacional de Educación a Distancia, Spain
Antonio Fernández-Caballero — Universidad Castilla-La Mancha, Spain
Jose García-Rodríguez — Universitat d'Alacant, Spain
Andrés Gómez-Rodellar — University of Edinburgh, UK

Pedro Gómez-Vilda	Universidad Politécnica de Madrid, Spain
Juan Manuel Górriz	Universidad de Granada, Spain
David Guijo-Rubio	Universidad de Córdoba, Spain
Marina Jodra	Universidad Complutense de Madrid, Spain
Vicente Julián-Inglada	Universitat Politècnica de València, Spain
Caroline Konig	Universitat Politécnica de Catalunya, Spain
Krzysztof Kutt	Jagiellonian University, Poland
Fco. Jesús Martínez Murcia	Universidad de Málaga, Spain
Rafael Martínez Tomás	Universidad Nacional de Educación a Distancia, Spain
Jiri Mekyska	Brno University of Technology, Czechia
Ramón Moreno	Grupo Antolin, Spain
Ioana Moldovan	Technical University of Cluj Napoca, Romania
Silivan Moldovan	Technical University of Cluj Napoca, Romania
Grzegorz J. Nalepa	Jagiellonian University, Poland
Andrés Ortiz	Universidad de Málaga, Spain
Daniel Palacios-Alonso	Universidad Rey Juan Carlos, Spain
José T. Palma	Universidad de Murcia, Spain
Jorge Pérez-Aracil	Universidad de Alcalá, Spain
Javier Ramírez	Universidad de Granada, Spain
Mariano Rincón Zamorano	Universidad Nacional de Educación a Distancia, Spain
Sancho Salcedo	Universidad de Alcalá, Spain
Jose Santos Reyes	Universidade da Coruña, Spain
Fermín Segovia	Universidad de Granada, Spain
Antonio Tallón	Universidad de Huelva, Spain
Ramiro Varela	Universidad de Oviedo, Spain
Alfredo Vellido	Universitat Politécnica de Catalunya, Spain

International Scientific Committee

Amparo Alonso Betanzos, Spain
Jose Ramon Álvarez-Sánchez, Spain
Margarita Bachiller Mayoral, Spain
Francisco Bellas, Spain
Emilia I. Barakova, Netherlands
Guido Bologna, Switzerland
Paula Bonomini, Argentina
Enrique J. Carmona Suárez, Spain
José Carlos Castillo, Spain
Germán Castellanos-Dominguez, Colombia
Sung-Bae Cho, Korea

Ricardo Contreras, Chile
Jose Manuel Cuadra Troncoso, Spain
Félix de la Paz López, Spain
Javier de Lope, Spain
Enrique Domínguez, Spain
Eduardo Fernández, Spain
Richard J. Duro, Spain
Antonio Fernández-Caballero, Spain
José Manuel Ferrandez, Spain
Victor Fresno, Spain
Jose Garcia-Rodriguez, Spain
Javier Garrigós, Spain
Pedro Gómez-Vilda, Spain
Pascual González, Spain
Juan M. Gorriz, Spain
Manuel Graña, Spain
César Hervás Martínez, Spain
Tom Heskes, Netherlands
Joost N. Kok, Netherlands
Krzysztof Kutt, Poland
Markus Lappe, Germany
Emilio Letón Molina, Spain
Maria Teresa López Bonal, Spain
Tino Lourens, Netherlands
Angeles Manjarrés, Spain
Jose Manuel Molina Lopez, Spain
Rafael Martínez Tomás, Spain
Juan Morales Sánchez, Spain
Grzegorz J. Nalepa, Poland
Elena Navarro, Spain
Andrés Ortiz García, Spain
José Palma, Spain
Francisco Peláez, Brazil
Maria Pinninghoff, Chile
Javier Ramírez, Spain
Andoni Razvan, USA
Mariano Rincón Zamorano, Spain
Victoria Rodellar, Spain
Camino Rodríguez Vela, Spain
Pedro Salcedo Lagos, Chile
Ángel Sanchez, Spain
Eduardo Sánchez Vila, Spain
José Luis Sancho-Gómez, Spain
José Santos Reyes, Spain
Antonio Sanz, Spain

Contents

Robotics

Bio-Inspired Computing Approaches (BICA)

SHIFT: Social and Civil Engineering through Human AI Translations

Explainable, Robust and Trustworthy Machine Learning and its Applications

Crisp and Fuzzy Intelligent Systems (CFIS)

Learning Tools to Lecture

Other Applications

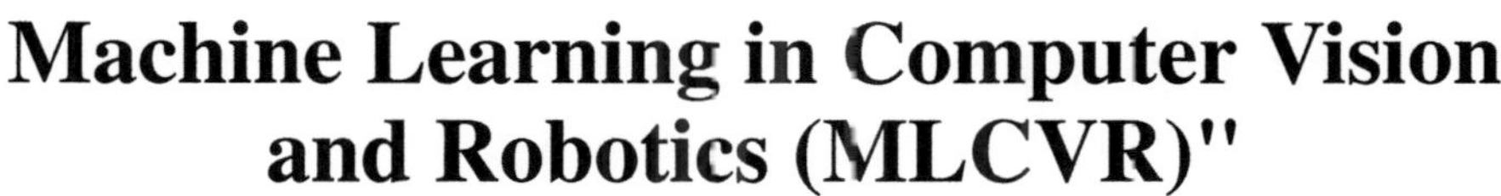

Machine Learning in Computer Vision and Robotics (MLCVR)"

Interactive Pressure Ulcer Segmentation: A Point-Prompted DeepLabV3+ Approach

Wasfieh Nazzal[3], Karl Thurnhofer-Hemsi[1,2 3(✉)] iD, Francisco J. Veredas[2,3,4] iD, and Ezequiel López-Rubio[1,2,3] iD

[1] ITIS Software, Universidad de Málaga, C/Arquitecto Francisco Peñalosa 18, 29010 Málaga, Spain
`{karlkhader,ezeqlr}@lcc.uma.es`
[2] IBIMA Plataforma BIONAND, Instituto de Investigación Biomédica de Málaga, C/ Severo Ochoa, 35, Málaga TechPark, Campanillas, 29590 Málaga, Spain
[3] Departamento de Lenguajes y Ciencias de la Computación, Universidad de Málaga, Bulevar Louis Pasteur, 35, 29071 Málaga, Spain
`{wasfiehnazzal,franveredas}@uma.es`
[4] Research Institute of Multilingual Language Technologies, Universidad de Málaga, C/ Severo Ochoa, 4, Málaga TechPark, Campanillas, 29071 Málaga, Spain

Abstract. Clinical examination of chronic pressure wounds involves partial tissue segmentation, an important diagnostic component. However, the entire automated process can be complex due to the different tissue types, which are visually close together. In this paper, a model of interactive segmentation is presented that incorporates user-manipulable point prompts directly into the DeepLabV3+ model. This 4-channel representation was developed by adding a localized Gaussian heatmap to the standard 3-channel RGB input, computed from points sampled from the largest connected component of the target tissue, providing the model with the required spatial priors. The model was tested on a clinical dataset using 5-fold patient-aware cross-validation. Comparisons with data augmentation techniques were also analyzed. The 4-channel model configuration that achieved the highest performance produced a Dice Similarity Coefficient (DSC) of 0.958 for the holistic wound bed. Furthermore, when data augmentation was applied, the interactive model yielded big differences and steady improvements across single-tissue-trained models. The results suggest that a simple human click substantially helps to achieve successful segmentations of the variety of textures present in clinical wound management.

Keywords: Interactive segmentation · Deep learning · Wound tissue segmentation · Point prompts · Gaussian heatmaps

1 Introduction

Pressure ulcers are chronic wounds that represent one of the most significant health issues globally and must be closely monitored to avoid serious complications like infection or amputation [1]. Objective clinical examination presupposes

J. M. Ferrández Vicente et al. (Eds.): IWINAC 2026, LNCS 16575, pp. 3–12, 2026.
https://doi.org/10.1007/978-3-032-27317-8_1

a correct definition of wound margins and the classification of specific tissues: epithelial tissue, slough, and necrotic tissue [5]. However, manual delineation by clinicians is subjective in nature, consequently consuming significant time and increasing inter-observer variance.

Deep learning has transformed medical image segmentation, with the U-Net architecture [12] and its variations remaining some of the most effective designs [2,3]. Advanced models have also been developed using dual-attention strategies [9], hybrid-attention mechanisms [11], and lightweight backbones to assist algorithms in concentrating on specific morphological patterns significant to the wound's clinical status [6,13]. Nevertheless, fully automated models are prone to domain shift, where an algorithm trained on one dataset performs poorly on another due to differences in lighting, camera distance, or wound geometry [8]. Furthermore, automated techniques often fail to resolve textural ambiguities in adjacent tissue types, resulting in piecemeal or fragmented segmentation masks.

In order to address the shortcomings of fully automated paradigms, interactive segmentation has come to the fore as a potent approach combining human expertise with the inference process. Even though Euclidean or Geodesic distance maps have been used successfully by authors like Xu et al. [16] and Wang et al. [15] to encode user clicks, recent research suggests that these methods are highly sensitive to the precise location of the prompt [7,10]. This presents a need for a spatial encoding scheme that is resilient to variations in user input.

Interpreting local tissue textures within a global context is key to an effective interactive model, as it bridges the gap between automated feature extraction and clinical judgment. The DeepLabV3+ architecture is particularly well-suited for this task, having already proven effective in wound analysis [13]. Its Atrous Spatial Pyramid Pooling (ASPP) module possesses the unique capability to encode the multi-scale context required to capture non-uniform wound shapes, offering a robust mechanism to handle the variability of user interactions at test time.

This paper implements a point-prompted version of the DeepLabV3+ model developed to segment chronic pressure wounds with high fidelity. In contrast to distance-based methods, we propose encoding user cues as localized Gaussian heatmaps, which are added to the standard RGB input to create a 4-channel tensor. Our architecture takes advantage of the ASPP module and the fine-tuned decoder of DeepLabV3+ to process this enhanced input and recover object boundaries with a high level of accuracy. We apply this framework to the Pressure Ulcer Laboratory (PULAB) dataset provided by Veredas et al. [14] to systematically assess the role of Gaussian-based spatial priors in resolving textural ambiguities within complex tissue segmentation.

2   Methodology

Let $\mathbf{x} \in \mathbb{R}^{H \times W \times 3}$ denote an RGB wound image and $\mathbf{y} \in \{0,1\}^{H \times W}$ the corresponding binary segmentation map. The goal is to learn a segmentation function

$$f : \mathbb{R}^{H \times W \times K} \to \mathbb{R}^{H \times W}, \tag{1}$$

that outputs a per-pixel logit map given an input tensor with K channels. Pixel-wise class probabilities are obtained by applying a sigmoid activation:

$$P(\mathbf{x}) = \sigma\big(f(\mathbf{x})\big). \tag{2}$$

During training, the network parameters are learned by minimizing the empirical risk over a dataset $\mathcal{D} = \{(\mathbf{x}_i, \mathbf{y}_i)\}_{i=1}^{N}$:

$$\mathcal{L} = \frac{1}{N} \sum_{i=1}^{N} \ell\big(f(\mathbf{x}_i), \mathbf{y}_i\big), \tag{3}$$

where $\ell(\cdot, \cdot)$ is a pixel-wise loss function defined on logits. At inference time, the final binary segmentation mask is obtained by thresholding the logit output:

$$\hat{\mathbf{y}} = \mathbb{1}\big[f(\mathbf{x}) \geq 0\big], \tag{4}$$

which is equivalent to thresholding the predicted probabilities at 0.5.

As baseline we adopt DeepLabV3+ with a ResNet-50 encoder [4]. To incorporate user guidance, we follow the general idea of interactive segmentation methods that encode point prompts as additional input channels to the network. We encode each user point as a two-dimensional localized Gaussian heatmap $g \in \mathbb{R}^{H \times W}$. Given a user-specified (or simulated) positive coordinate $p = (u, v)$ inside the target region, the heatmap is defined as

$$g_{ij} = \exp\left(-\frac{(i - u)^2 + (j - v)^2}{2\sigma^2}\right), \quad i \in \{1, \ldots, H\}, \; j \in \{1, \ldots, W\}, \tag{5}$$

with a fixed standard deviation $\sigma = 10.0$. This parameter controls the spatial extent of the interactive signal, creating a compact region of high activation around the click that emphasizes the local wound area while keeping the rest of the field weakly activated.

Thus, for each image-mask pair $(\mathbf{x}_i, \mathbf{y}_i)$, we randomly sample one foreground pixel p_i from the largest connected component of the ground truth mask and generate its corresponding Gaussian map g_i using the formulation above. This selection makes the method robust against noise or stray pixels. The final training input for the proposed framework is then

$$\tilde{\mathbf{x}}_i = \mathrm{concat}(\mathbf{x}_i, g_i) \in \mathbb{R}^{H \times W \times 4}, \tag{6}$$

Our architecture modifies only the input layer of DeepLabV3+ to accept 4-channel tensors $\tilde{x} \in \mathbb{R}^{H \times W \times 4}$, while preserving the encoder-decoder topology and the number of trainable parameters in deeper layers (see Fig. 1). The first convolutional block in the ResNet-50 encoder is adapted from 3 to 4 input channels, allowing the Gaussian prompt to participate in early feature extraction alongside RGB information. All subsequent layers, including the ASPP module and the decoder, remain unchanged. By injecting the Gaussian prompt directly at the input level, the model learns to interpret the heatmap as a localization cue. This guides the segmentation toward structures clinically relevant with minimal user interaction. This method keeps computational efficiency and avoids complicated refinement steps, giving an easy way to add interactive feedback to a strong semantic segmentation system.

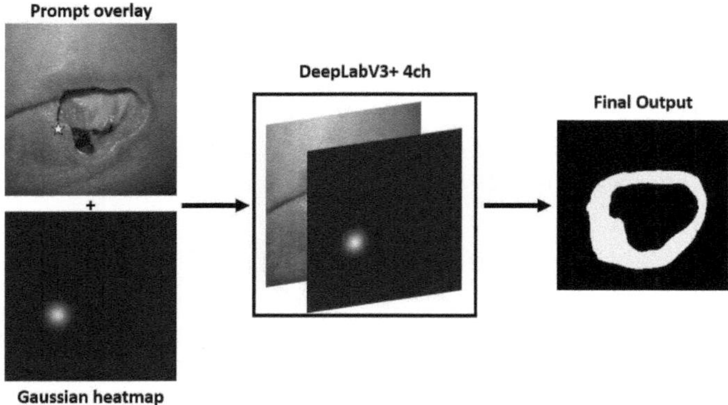

Fig. 1. Overview of the proposed 4-channel interactive segmentation pipeline.

2.1 Data Acquisition and Preprocessing

The Pressure Ulcer Laboratory (PULAB) dataset employed in the study was collected by clinical members of the research group, who acquired color photographs of pressure ulcers from patients receiving homecare assistance [14]. Sacral and hip pressure ulcers were photographed under non-controlled illumination conditions using a Canon EOS 40D digital camera equipped with a Sigma EM-140 ring flash to ensure homogeneous illumination. Images were captured at an approximate distance of 30–40 cm from the wound plane using a Canon EF-S 60 mm f/2.8 Macro USM lens to guarantee appropriate focus at short range. A total of 113 images were selected by expert clinicians based on the presence of all clinically relevant tissue types for pressure ulcer assessment. Prior to annotation, images were smoothed using a mean-shift procedure and subsequently segmented by means of a region-growing algorithm, yielding regions consistent with distinct tissue areas. This process produced an average of approximately 150 regions per image, resulting in 17,007 segmented regions in total. Non-significant regions (e.g., shadows or clinical artifacts) were manually excluded, leading to a final set of 15,879 clinically relevant regions.

The images, originally at 1024×768 resolution, were downsampled to 224×224 pixels to facilitate efficient training. As detailed in Table 1, the dataset exhibits significant class imbalance due to the heterogeneous nature of chronic wounds. While common tissues such as Scar and Granulation appear in nearly all samples, critical pathological indicators like Necrosis are rare, present in only 20.4 percent of the dataset.

Binary masks were created from the original region annotations for two specific tasks:

- Combined tissue: segmentation of the wound bed (encompassing labels 2, 3, 4, 5, and 6) vs. background.
- Individual tissue: single segmentation of Scar (2), Granulation (3), Slough (4), Necrosis (5), or Blood/Interior (6) vs. background.

Table 1. Distribution of tissue types within the PULAB dataset ($N = 113$ images). The "Positive Samples" column indicates the number of images containing at least one pixel of the specified tissue.

Tissue Class	Positive Samples (N)	Prevalence (percent)
Combined Wound	113	100.0
Scar (2)	110	97.3
Granulation (3)	105	92.9
Slough (4)	86	76.1
Necrosis (5)	23	20.4
Blood/Interior (6)	42	37.2

2.2 Experimental Setup

The proposed framework operates by comparing the baseline model with its modified version across two distinct experimental scenarios: (1) without data augmentation, to assess the raw impact of the interactive inputs, and (2) with data augmentation, to evaluate the model's peak performance.

- Baseline (3-channel): The input is a standard RGB image ($224 \times 224 \times 3$). Segmentation relies solely on visual feature extraction.
- Proposed (4-channel): The input is an RGB image + Gaussian heatmap ($224 \times 224 \times 4$). The heatmap is generated by sampling a single positive coordinate from the ground truth mask.

All configurations were trained for 100 epochs with the Adam optimizer, a learning rate of 1×10^{-4}, and a batch size of 4. For the augmented experiments, we employed a multi-stage augmentation pipeline designed to maximize model generalization. First, we systematically expanded the training set offline by generating synthetic variants via affine scaling (1.0–$1.25\times$), elastic deformation, and spatial mirroring. Second, we introduced stochasticity during training through random on-the-fly geometric transformations. This hierarchical approach ensures the model learns robust features that are invariant to wound orientation and morphology, effectively addressing the data scarcity inherent in medical imaging.

To ensure rigorous evaluation, we employed a 5-fold patient-aware cross-validation strategy. The dataset was randomly partitioned into 5 folds at the case level. Crucially, to ensure a fair comparison across epochs and different model architectures, the random point prompts for the validation set were generated once and fixed prior to training.

3 Results

The performance of the proposed interactive framework was evaluated in two distinct experimental setups: (1) without data augmentation, to isolate the impact

Table 2. Experiment 1: Quantitative comparison of segmentation performance without data augmentation (Mean and SD). Best results are highlighted in bold.

Tissue Class	Baseline (3-Channel)		Proposed (4-Channel)	
	DSC	Recall	DSC	Recall
Combined Wound	0.954 (0.009)	0.950 (0.013)	**0.958 (0.010)**	**0.955 (0.010)**
Scar (2)	**0.887 (0.009)**	**0.893 (0.017)**	0.886 (0.010)	0.892 (0.010)
Granulation (3)	0.793 (0.054)	0.790 (0.046)	**0.808 (0.049)**	**0.796 (0.060)**
Slough (4)	**0.773 (0.056)**	**0.774 (0.065)**	0.772 (0.056)	0.751 (0.084)
Necrosis (5)	0.623 (0.141)	0.620 (0.164)	**0.699 (0.077)**	**0.676 (0.081)**
Blood/Interior (6)	0.774 (0.079)	0.770 (0.083)	**0.806 (0.058)**	**0.783 (0.069)**

Table 3. Experiment 2: Quantitative comparison of segmentation performance with Comprehensive Data Augmentation.

Tissue Class	Baseline (3-Channel)		Proposed (4-Channel)	
	DSC	Recall	DSC	Recall
Combined Wound	0.944 (0.018)	**0.943 (0.019)**	**0.945 (0.020)**	0.939 (0.021)
Scar (2)	0.904 (0.037)	0.898 (0.048)	**0.908 (0.026)**	**0.901 (0.033)**
Granulation (3)	0.791 (0.054)	0.793 (0.064)	**0.799 (0.052)**	**0.794 (0.052)**
Slough (4)	**0.813 (0.060)**	**0.806 (0.066)**	0.799 (0.069)	0.797 (0.074)
Necrosis (5)	0.798 (0.113)	0.779 (0.108)	**0.853 (0.060)**	**0.837 (0.082)**
Blood/Interior (6)	0.701 (0.122)	0.691 (0.137)	**0.731 (0.099)**	**0.725 (0.091)**

of the spatial prompts, and (2) with geometric data augmentation, to increase the dataset size and assess the model's peak performance.

Table 2 presents the baseline results. The proposed 4-channel model demonstrated consistent improvements over the 3-channel baseline across most tissue types. For the challenging Necrosis class (Label 5), the interactive model achieved a DSC of 0.699, surpassing the baseline (0.623) by a significant margin. Similarly, the Blood/Interior class (Label 6) saw an improvement from 0.774 to 0.806. These results indicate that even without the benefits of data augmentation, the inclusion of point prompts effectively guides the network toward ambiguous pathological regions.

Table 3 details the performance when geometric data augmentation is applied. The combination of augmentation and interactive prompts yielded the highest overall scores. Most notably, the Necrosis (Label 5) DSC jumped to 0.853, a substantial improvement over the non-augmented results and the augmented baseline (0.798). The Scar (Label 2) segmentation also reached a high fidelity of 0.908. This confirms that while spatial priors are critical for localization, geometric augmentation is essential for generalizing these features across the diverse wound morphologies found in the dataset.

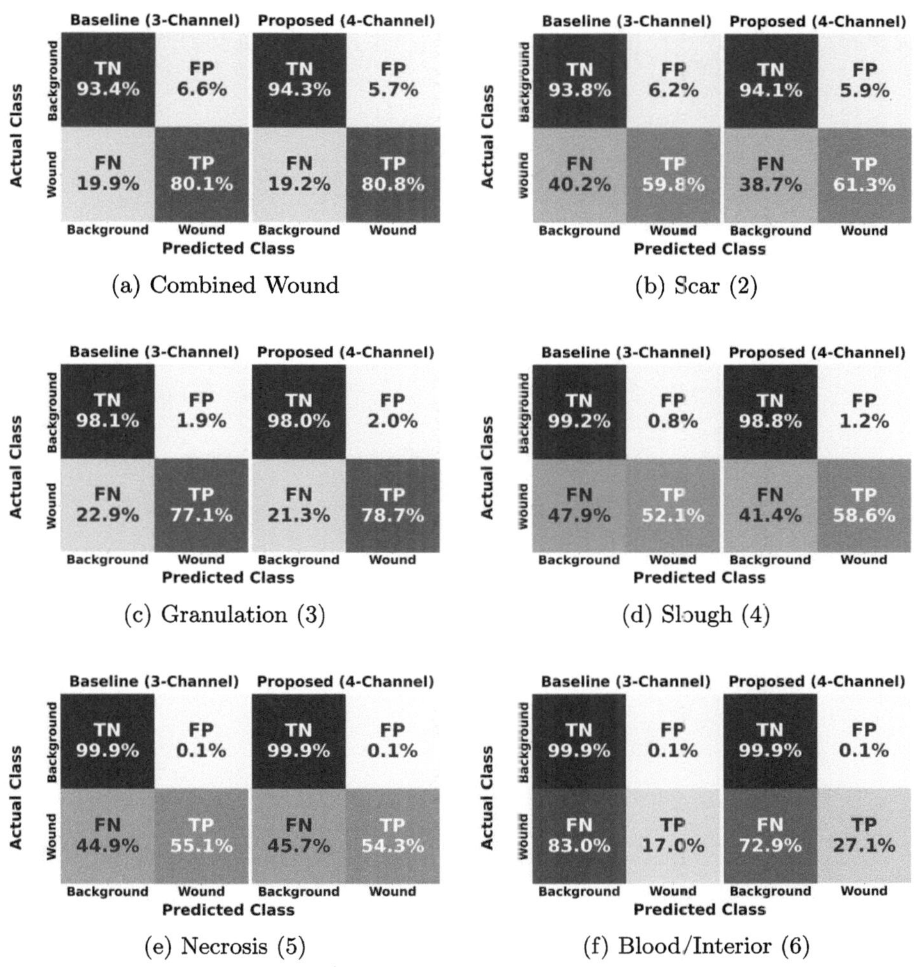

Fig. 2. Averaged cross-validation confusion matrices for the Baseline (3-Channel) and Proposed (4-Channel) models with data augmentation.

To analyze classification errors, we aggregated pixel-wise predictions across all folds. Figure 2 displays the confusion matrices for the augmented models. The proposed method consistently reduced False Negatives (FN) compared to the baseline. For instance, in the Slough and Blood/Interior classes, the 4-channel model decreased to 41.4% and 72.9%, though it balanced this with higher overall precision. When augmentation was used, the model's stability improved drastically: the Necrosis True Positives (TP) increased from 40.4% to 54.3% for the proposed model, demonstrating that the model effectively learned to capture the complex textures of necrotic tissue when supported by both spatial prompts and varied training data.

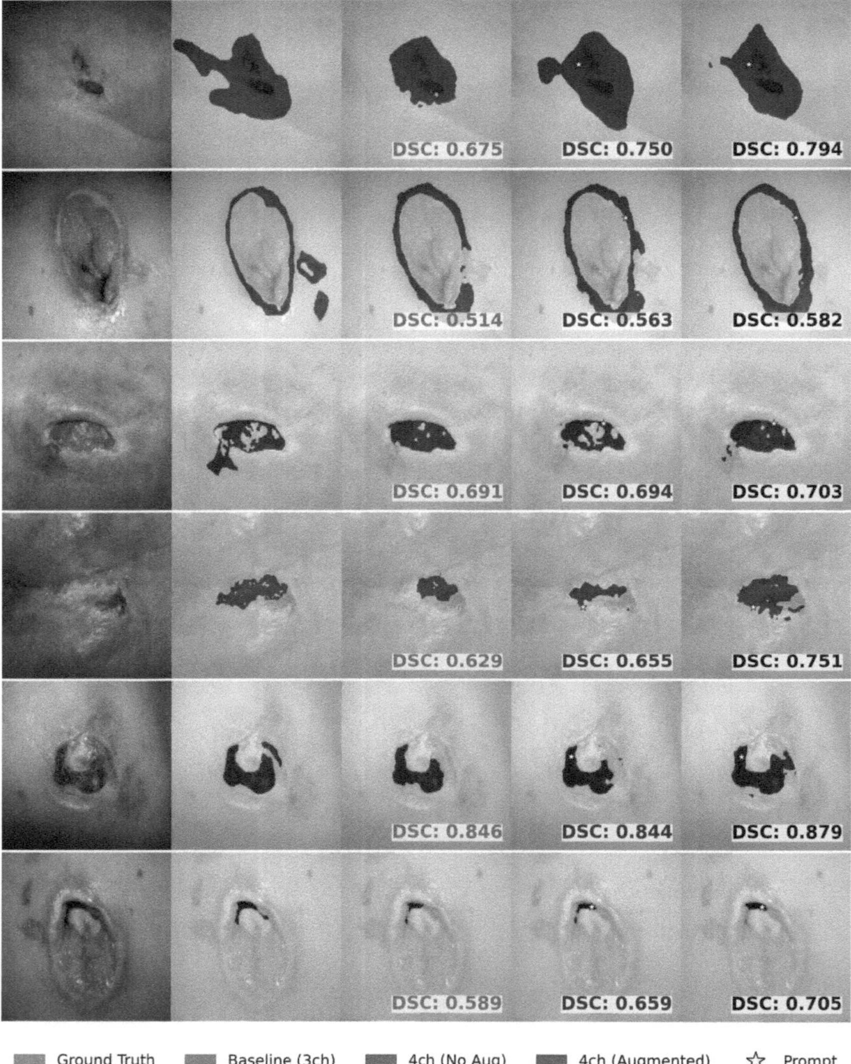

Fig. 3. Visual qualitative comparison of segmentation results on Fold 0. From top to bottom: Combined Wound, Scar (2), Granulation (3), Slough (4), Necrosis (5), and Blood/Interior (6). (Color figure online)

Qualitative results are presented in Fig. 3. In general, the proposed model outperforms the baseline model by producing a larger segmented region. The samples for Necrosis (Row 5) and Blood/Interior (Row 6) serve as representative examples of "hard-to-segment" instances. In these cases, the 4-channel model (Augmented), guided by point prompts (yellow star), produces the most coherent masks, recovering regions missed by the baseline and refining the boundaries of fragmented tissue.

4   Conclusion

This paper introduces a new form of interactive segmentation that incorporates user-controlled point prompts into the DeepLabV3+ model via a 4-channel input representation. The model addresses the textural ambiguities present in pressure ulcer wound imaging by representing spatial queries as localized Gaussian heatmaps, thereby resolving these inconsistencies. Although the baseline model already achieved high performance in holistic wound bed detection (indicating a ceiling effect), the proposed approach demonstrated a greater ability to distinguish between complex tissue types. Most notably, the interactive method provided a major performance improvement within the Necrosis category (DSC improvement of approximately 6%) and stabilized predictions for fragmented regions. These results confirm that minimal human intervention, acting as a spatial reference for the ASPP module, can effectively bridge the gap between automated feature extraction and clinical expertise, offering a powerful approach for accurate wound tissue assessment. Future work will apply the proposed architecture to large, varied datasets and explore other statistical maps to capture lesion variability.

Acknowledgments. This work is partially supported by the Autonomous Government of Andalusia (Spain) under project PPRO-TIC163-G-2023 (TIC163-G-FEDER); also by the Ministry of Science and Innovation of Spain under project PID2022-136764OA-I00. It includes funds from the European Regional Development Fund (ERDF). It is also partially supported by the Fundación Unicaja under project PUNI-003_2023, the Instituto de Investigación Biomédica de Málaga, IBIMA Plataforma BIONAND under project ATECH-25-02, and the Instituto de Salud Carlos III under project PI25/02129 (co-financed by the European Union). The authors thankfully acknowledge the computer resources, technical expertise and assistance provided by the SCBI (Supercomputing and Bioinformatics) center of the University of Málaga. The authors also thankfully acknowledge the grant of the Universidad de Málaga and the Instituto de Investigación Biomédica de Málaga, IBIMA Plataforma BIONAND.

References

1. Al-Garaawi, N., Eslami, T., Alwan, A.A., Elhoseny, M., Farouk, A.: Diabetes detection using modified swin transformer and capsule network with thermography. J. Diab. Metabolic Disord. **24** (2025). https://doi.org/10.1007/s40200-025-01813-3
2. Alkhalefah, H., Zhang, Y., Wang, G.: Advancing diabetic foot ulcer care: AI and generative AI approaches. Healthcare **13**(4), 648 (2025). https://doi.org/10.3390/healthcare13040648
3. Azad, R., et al.: Medical image segmentation review: the success of u-net. IEEE Trans. Pattern Anal. Mach. Intell. **46**(12), 10076–10101 (2024). https://doi.org/10.1109/TPAMI.2024.3435571
4. Chen, L.C., Zhu, Y., Papandreou, G., Schroff, F., Adam, H.: Encoder-decoder with atrous separable convolution for semantic image segmentation. In: Proceedings

of the European Conference on Computer Vision (ECCV), pp. 833–851 (2018). https://doi.org/10.1007/978-3-030-01234-2_49

5. Goyal, M., Reeves, N.D., Rajbhandari, S., Yap, M.H.: Automating tissue segmentation and quantification for wound healing assessment. IEEE J. Biomed. Health Inf. (2025)

6. Kumar, S., Singh, K., Singh, A.: DFU-CNet: a deep learning-based method for diabetic foot ulcer classification. Biomed. Signal Process. Control **101** (2025)

7. Li, H., Liu, H., Hu, D., Wang, J., Oguz, I.: Assessing test-time variability for interactive 3D medical image segmentation with diverse point prompts. In: Proceedings of the IEEE International Symposium on Biomedical Imaging (ISBI) (2024). https://doi.org/10.1109/ISBI56570.2024.10635343

8. Lucho, S., Naemi, R., Castañeda, B., Treuillet, S.: Can deep learning wound segmentation algorithms developed for a dataset be effective for another dataset? A specific focus on diabetic foot ulcers. IEEE Access **12**, 173820–173835 (2024). https://doi.org/10.1109/ACCESS.2024.3502467

9. Niri, R., et al.: Wound segmentation with u-net using a dual attention mechanism and transfer learning. J. Imaging Inf. Med. **38**, 3351–3365 (2025). https://doi.org/10.1007/s10278-025-01386-w

10. Porter, V., Styles, I., Curtis, T., Gault, R.: Intelligent point prompt generation for interactive segmentation. In: Proceedings of the 27th Irish Machine Vision and Image Processing Conference (IMVIP), pp. 144–148. (2025). https://doi.org/10.21251/8043511f-bf93-4b36-9348-0726af0987f6

11. Ranganayagi, K.L., Malathi, D.: WoundSeg_Net: an unified framework for automated 2d image wound segmentation with hybrid attention u-net architecture. In: Proceedings of the 8th International Conference on Computing Methodologies and Communication (ICCMC) (2025). https://doi.org/10.1109/ICCMC65190.2025.11140790

12. Ronneberger, O., Fischer, P., Brox, T.: U-net: convolutional networks for biomedical image segmentation. In: Navab, N., Hornegger, J., Wells, W.M., Frangi, A.F. (eds.) MICCAI 2015. LNCS, vol. 9351, pp. 234–241. Springer, Cham (2015). https://doi.org/10.1007/978-3-319-24574-4_28

13. Shoeibi, A., Ghassemi, N., Alizadehsani, R., Khosravi, A., Nahavandi, S.: Automated diabetic foot ulcer recognition using deeplabv3+ based on mobilenetv2. Biomed. Signal Process. Control **99** (2025)

14. Veredas, F.J., Mesa, H., Morente, L.: Binary tissue classification on wound images with neural networks and bayesian classifiers. IEEE Trans. Med. Imaging **29**(2), 410–427 (2010). https://doi.org/10.1109/TMI.2009.2033595

15. Wang, G., et al.: DeepIGeoS: a deep interactive geodesic framework for medical image segmentation. IEEE Trans. Pattern Anal. Mach. Intell. **41**(7), 1559–1572 (2018). https://doi.org/10.1109/TPAMI.2018.2840695

16. Xu, N., Price, B.F., Cohen, S., Yang, J., Huang, T.S.: Deep interactive object selection. In: Proceedings of the IEEE Conference on Computer Vision and Pattern Recognition (CVPR), pp. 373–381 (2016). https://doi.org/10.1109/CVPR.2016.47

Is it Real? A Mixed Reality Experience About Depersonalization and Derealization

Paula Lario-Llinares, David Mulero-Pérez, David Ortiz-Perez,
Jose Garcia-Rodriguez(✉), David Alarcon-Garrido, and Laura Saval-Cillero

Department of Computer Technology, University of Alicante, Alicante, Spain
{plario,dmulero,dortiz,jgarcia,dalarcon,lsaval}@dtic.ua.es

Abstract. People who suffer from depersonalization disorder feel a disconnection from themselves, while those who suffer from derealization feel that disconnection from their environment. In this research, we have developed a Mixed Reality experience for Meta Quest 3 that simulates some of the symptoms experienced by patients with depersonalization-derealization disorder in order to raise awareness about these psychological problems and facilitate understanding towards the affected individuals. In this experience, the player, through the eyes of a person suffering from these psychological problems, will understand the difficulties that this condition can pose in their daily lives: objects that do not seem real, time passing without awareness, confusing conversations, and feeling as if they are mere observers of their lives. We conducted user tests to verify whether we achieved the project's objective. The results have been favorable, with a promising outlook for the future.

Keywords: Mixed Reality · Depersonalization Disorder ·
Derealization Disorder

1 Introduction

Dissociative disorders such as Depersonalization (DP) and Derealization (DR) affect a significant portion of the population; yet, they remain largely misunderstood. While DP involves a feeling of being an outside observer of one's own body, DR is characterized by a sense of detachment from the environment, often described as seeing the world through a fog or glass.

These conditions appear in the aftermath of a traumatic event or a life-threatening situation, even after drug consumption. Approximately 50% of the global population has suffered from DP-DR temporarily. However, 2% can be diagnosed with these disorders [13].

The primary motivation of this work is to foster empathy and social support for affected individuals, as this social assistance can be a decisive factor in the patient's improvement [14]. In addition to raising awareness of these psychological disorders, we aim to help those who are unaware that they suffer from

J. M. Ferrández Vicente et al. (Eds.): IWINAC 2026, LNCS 16575, pp. 13–21, 2026.
https://doi.org/10.1007/978-3-032-27317-8_2

DPDR and do not know how to name the feelings they experience by leveraging the immersive capabilities of Mixed Reality (MR). Unlike Virtual Reality, MR allows the blending of digital assets with the user's physical room, which is essential for simulating the unreal perception of real-world objects. It is also known that the prolonged use of MR may cause some of the DR symptoms, reinforcing our decision [8].

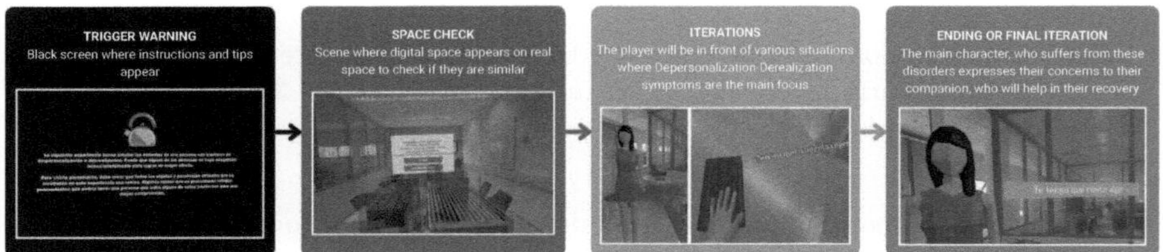

Fig. 1. Pipeline of the Is It Real? MR App.

We propose "Is It Real?", a MR app that allows us to show players how individuals with DP-DR symptoms feel daily in severe cases. As seen in Fig. 1, the experience is divided into different scenes. First, the player will be presented with a trigger warning that includes a description of what this experience entails. The next scene is the spatial check, where the user will be prompted to verify that the virtual space is similar to reality through the holographic textures applied to the scanned objects in the headset data. When everything is controlled, the main experience will begin, and the space will be filled with different kinds of objects alongside a non-playable character (NPC) with whom the player can talk when they fill both cups of tea. There will be some dialogs triggered by the user whenever they touch the objects in the scene; these dialogs represent the main protagonist thoughts since the player impersonates a person with DP-DR. In the final scene, all objects will disappear, and the main protagonist will be able to talk solely to the NPC about their problems, finishing this experience on a positive note.

In summary, our contributions are as follows:

- We have developed an immersive MR application that translates clinical symptoms into interactive game mechanics.
- We designed a specialized system to simulate macropsia and micropsia by dynamically scaling real-world anchors.
- We implemented a scalable MR dialog system that tracks spatial objects to represent internal thoughts and dialogs.

The remainder of the paper is structured as follows: Sect. 2 discusses related works. Section 3 proposes an MR app that simulates dissociative symptoms. The results are presented in Sect. 4. Finally, in Sect. 5, we present the conclusions of our work.

2   Related Works

According to the Diagnostic and Statistical Manual of Mental Disorders [12]: "The essential characteristic of dissociative disorders is an alteration in the integrative functions of consciousness, identity, memory, and perception of the environment. This alteration can be sudden or gradual, transient or chronic." Therefore, those who suffer from these pathological disorders perceive their space, time, and themselves differently than a healthy mind. Both Depersonalization and Derealization are part of the dissociative disorders category.

DP is characterized by the disturbance of perception or the sense of self, often described as being an observer of one's own life. Despite this, a sense of reality is maintained, and the individual is aware that it is just a sensation [12]. On the other hand, DR can be seen either in combination with or separated from DP. There is a sense of disconnection from the environment, provoking a dreamy feel. Macropsia and micropsia are often observed in these cases, where objects appear bigger or smaller than they really are, thereby increasing the oddness of their space [12]. These symptoms have been found in 2.4% of the population and in 80% of psychiatric patients, being persistent and severe in 12% of the cases [9]. It is also possible that these disorders are often undiagnosed.

The use of immersive technology to address mental health is a growing field. The possibility of using this technology to help patients through their recovery is promising, exposing them to certain controlled situations in which they cannot be harmed, and even reducing the drop-out rate for treatment thanks to the gamification approach [6]. Albert Skip et al.: "These initiatives give hope that the 21st century will be ushered in with new and useful tools to advance these areas that have long been mired in the methods of the past." [10]. This fact motivated us to contribute to this future.

In relation to our application, research has shown that VR can inadvertently induce temporary DP/DR symptoms due to high levels of immersion, suggesting its potency as a tool for symptom simulation. Carina Peckmann et al.: "Likewise, one case series study indicates that even after a single VR session, transient DP/DR experiences may occur. Despite these indications, little is otherwise known about the risk of developing DP/DR from VR consumption." [8].

In the realm of video games, the "Walking Simulator" genre has proven effective for narrative-driven empathy [4]. These types of games, as opposed to others, lack a wide variety of mechanics, focusing on fewer mechanics so that the player can be more attentive to the story they are playing. Some titles that apply this kind of philosophy include *Before Your Eyes* [3], which stands out by using blinking as a way to advance the story, designed to make the player reflect on time. While *Night in the Woods* [2] specifically depicts DR as a transformation of the world into simple geometric shapes. However, there is a lack of MR experiences specifically targeting the DP-DR spectrum. A game that has a similar purpose is *As Long As You're Here* [5], where the player can take a look into the life of a person with Alzheimer's disease.

3   Mixed Reality App

Mixed reality is often confused with augmented reality, but the two are not the same. While both involve blending virtual objects with real ones, these virtual objects behave quite differently. In the case of AR, these virtual objects are usually static and cannot be interacted with directly [1]. This is a technology commonly employed to simulate the positioning of furniture in a specific space, for example; whereas in the case of MR, we can engage directly with these objects, grasping and moving them as if we were handling real objects, which results in a more natural and immersive experience than AR [7,11].

In this section, we will explain how the experience was conducted, from the idea to its development.

3.1   Design

The experience follows the "less is more" philosophy of walking simulators, focusing on exploration and narrative over complex win/loss conditions. It is structured into multiple iterations (representing different days). The first iterations lack symptoms, allowing the user to become accustomed to the virtual world; then, the symptoms progressively intensify as the days pass, enabling the player to feel the oddness of the world and themselves, similar to those who suffer from these dissociative disorders. Environmental exploration rewards the player by providing hints about the thoughts of a person with DP-DR regarding objects. These objects can be found in our everyday lives, such as books, desk calendars, or decorative vases. A core mechanic is the "Tea Ceremony", involving a digital kettle and cups placed on the user's real furniture. Serving tea acts as a trigger for social interaction with a Non-Player Character. This mechanic was designed so that the player can perform a mundane and easy task, but the behavior of the digital objects is erratic as a way to represent the feeling of disconnection from the outside objects. Talking to the NPC can sometimes be difficult to understand, complicating communication between the main character and them. This was made for the purpose of demonstrating the dissociative elements of these disorders. Some of the symptoms have been exaggerated to create a greater impact for the player; a person with DP-DR feels that something is off, but the real objects behave as they should in reality.

To simulate DP-DR, we alter these interactions:

- **Surrealist Behavior:** Objects in zero gravity aggravate the feeling of disconnection from the environment.
- **Visual Distortions:** Objects change color or scale randomly to mimic macropsia and micropsia.
- **Time Distortion:** Iterations may start or end abruptly or skip the tea-serving process to simulate "autopilot" sensations. The player will not be aware of what happens in the story apart from this scene.
- **Social Disconnection:** NPC dialogs become censored or confusing. This makes it difficult for the player to respond properly, causing an unsuccessful social interaction.

3.2   Technical Details

For the creation of this MR application, we have used one of the most popular game engines in the industry, Unreal Engine 5 (UE5), alongside Meta's Mixed Reality Utility Kit (MRUK) plugin. MRUK allows us to access the Head Mounted Display's (HMD) data, specifically environmental data in our case. We use this information to identify the physical surfaces in the real world as anchors for positioning digital objects or changing their appearance. These items have been obtained from the Epic Games store, online artists, and through our own creations.

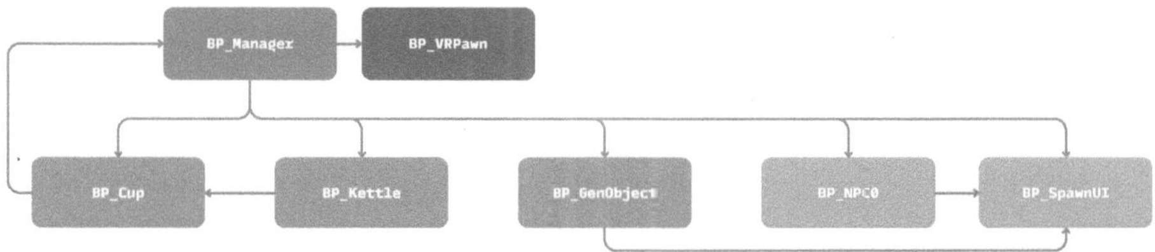

Fig. 2. Main actors' interactions in the MR experience.

First, we begin with a blank canvas that includes all the virtual objects in the experience, which have been procedurally placed regardless of the room's layout, thanks to the MRUK's function: *Generate Random Position On Surface*, which allows us to generate a random position among the different objects in the world, specifically on their surface. As seen in Fig. 2, we have developed seven main actors that allow us to manipulate the scene. Beginning with the most essential actor, **BP_Manager** can access all the actors in the scene; they will always be the same actors. Through Data Tables that contain certain parameters, we can edit every actor in the scene, manipulate the iteration duration, or add new dialogs, allowing us to customize the experience freely. Every time an iteration finishes, the actors will reset to their initial state and will then be modified if specified. **BP_Cup** and **BP_Kettle** are related, as the first detects whether the tea collision is hitting the cup, causing it to fill up if that is the case; A message will be sent to the manager, so the dialog with the NPC should begin, spawning a **BP_SpawnUI**; The main purpose of this actor is to show menus or dialog in the physical space, so the player will not lose focus in the experience. **BP_GenObject** also creates **BP_SpawnUI** to show the main protagonist thoughts in the scene if triggered by touching the object.

Key implementation components include

- **BP_Manager:** A central state machine that reads iteration parameters (scale changes, material swaps, dialog triggers, time manipulation) from a Data Table and manipulates the scene accordingly.

- **AC_DialogueComponent:** A component that controls the dialog timing and data. This component uses Table Data with different parameters to determine the main dialog and possible answers.
- **Procedural Placement:** We utilize the *Generate Random Position On Surface* function to populate the user's room with digital "daily objects" (books, plants) regardless of the room's layout. This ensures a unique experience every time the application is launched.
- **AC_Object:** This component saves the initial characteristics of the object that contains it so that it can always return to their initial state if it is altered. This also contains the necessary functions to complete the reset.

4   Evaluation

This section presents the evaluation with users. We conducted a controlled trial (N = 15) in which the spatial conditions were similar, allowing the participants to try the application with minimal guidance and a brief explanation of what DP-DR is about (see Fig. 3). Upon completion of the experience, participants filled out a questionnaire aimed at evaluating their interaction with the application. The results are analyzed in detail in the following sections, providing insights into user experience and perceived impact.

The age range of the subjects is between 12 and 52 years, with 53.3% men and 46.7% women. While 53.3% have tried VR before this test, 46.7% have not. This percentage difference increases when participants are asked about MR; 20% have tried MR, and 80% have never tried this technology. These last individuals were more amazed by the application as a result.

When asked about their first impression of the mix of virtual and real objects, the majority thought it was impressively favorable, representing a great integration and realism. This helped achieve the purpose of making digital objects appear real, provoking a curious reaction whenever the objects changed size or texture. As seen in Fig. 4a, all participants had a high or complete level of immersion. Most of them had no trouble interacting with the virtual environment; some had difficulties in the beginning, but they managed in the end.

As expected, participants had trouble proceeding with the experience since it was still in beta (See Fig. 4a). We will focus on user experience in the future since we want to achieve total freedom for the user. Furthermore, they had no trouble reading the dialogs in-game but provided some feedback about their presentation. Following this feedback, the majority felt that time passed from iteration to iteration and offered other ways to show this passage of time.

Around 93.3% of the participants were not aware of these disorders, showing how little information about them is available. This fact may cause people who suffer from these conditions not to seek treatment for improvement. As seen in Fig. 4b, 40% felt disconnected from their environment, while 20% denied this, leaving 40% of the individuals unsure of their answer. This demonstrates that the percentage of individuals who probably experienced a temporal episode could be larger and are not aware of this disorder.

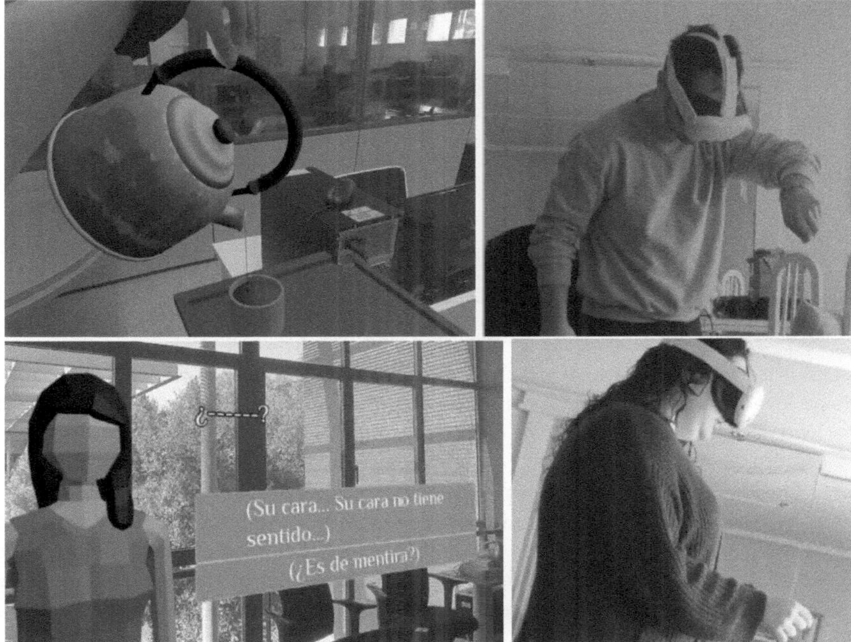

(a) Screenshots of the virtual experience through the point of view of the player.

(b) Photos of users trying out the application.

Fig. 3. These photos show the evaluation process. The participants were given minimal instructions and were allowed to explore freely.

Finally, all participants believe that this experience helped them understand the symptoms that a person with DP-DR suffers from daily and feel empathy towards them.

At the end of the questionnaire, participants were given the freedom to write suggestions for the project, feedback, or anything else they had in mind. Primarily, everyone suggested some changes to improve the experience, such as the addition of animations for the NPC, changes in dialog appearance, or other ways to showcase that time has passed between iterations. In addition, everyone believed the application had a future, highlighting the following:

- "[...] the background is brutal and has unlimited future potential. I think work should be done on developing this application in collaboration with psychologists from the faculty."
- "[...] I thought it was great to be able to put myself, even if only for a few minutes, in situations that people with this disorder suffer from constantly, and above all, that it was visualized."
- "It is a very well-done experience that greatly helps us understand people or emotions that we normally cannot imagine or things that we cannot feel."

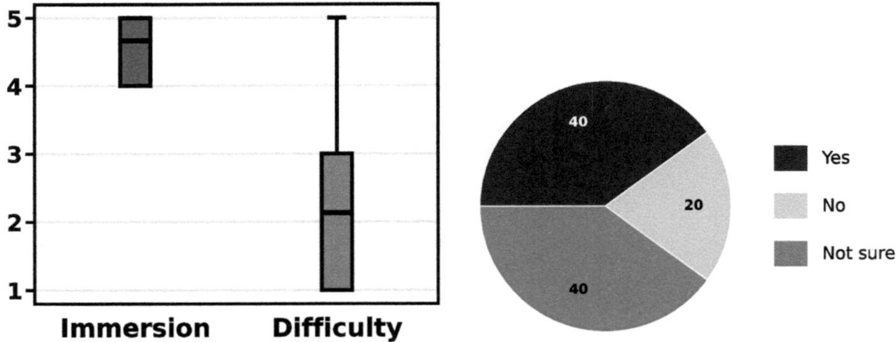

(a) Quantitative answers relating the immersion level and level of difficulty that the experience opposed, respectively.

(b) Results of the question "Have you ever felt disconnected from yourself or your environment?"

Fig. 4. These graphs contain the results of three questions posed to the participants. In (a), the left box shows the answers regarding the level of immersion in the experience. As seen, all users felt that they had a high level of immersion. The right box shows the level of difficulty players experienced while progressing in the game; most of them found it easy, but some had trouble. (b) presents the number of individuals who felt some kind of disconnection from themselves or the environment; only 30% of people have never felt that way, 40% have felt those disconnections at some point, and another 40% are not completely sure.

This shows that the application could be successful in the future and serve not only to demonstrate what these people suffer on a daily basis but also as a basis for developing an application that helps people experiencing these problems through gamified treatment.

5   Conclusions

In this study, we have developed a Mixed Reality experience about Depersonalization and Derealization, which shows the difficulties that a person with these disorders must face daily. Once we had a playable beta game, we conducted an evaluation with users, collecting their feedback and thoughts. This opens the way to the possibilities that a Mixed Reality application could have in helping patients with mental disorders and aiding the general public understanding of the severity of the daily suffering that a person with these disorders faces.

Our findings suggest that it is a tool that could have a favorable future in psychology as a means of helping people achieve the appropriate treatment for their condition. It serves as a way to provide a visualization of a disorder that most of the population has suffered from but is not aware of. This reduces the possibility of patients with these conditions suffering from being chronically undiagnosed and not knowing how to explain them or what name to give to them.

As future work, we propose a finished product that continues to demonstrate the daily troubles that DP-DR presents with new game mechanics and adds possible treatments to help affected individuals improve their conditions. This will be made in collaboration with psychologists who will provide us with more detailed information about the possible treatments available.

Acknowledgments. This work has been funded by the Spanish State Research Agency (AEI) and ERDF/EU under grant: GEMELIA PID2024-161711OB-I00. Also, it has been funded by a regional grant for PhD studies from the Valencian government, CIACIF/2021/430.

References

1. Carmigniani, J., Furht, B.: Augmented reality: an overview. In: Handbook of Augmented Reality, pp. 3–46 (2011)
2. Fall, I.: Night in the woods (2017). http://www.nightinthewoods.com/
3. Games, G.: Before your eyes (2021). https://www.beforeyoureyesgame.com/
4. Rodrigo de Haro, M.: Ontology of the videogame as an artistic medium: the narrative turn of the walking simulator. Hipertext.net **1**(29), 187–196 (2024). https://doi.org/10.31009/hipertext.net.2024.i29.15
5. Interactive, A.: As long as you're here (2025). https://www.aslongasyourehere.com/
6. Kothgassner, O.D., Reichmann, A., Bock, M.M.: Virtual reality interventions for mental health. In: Virtual Reality in Behavioral Neuroscience: New Insights and Methods, pp. 371–387. Springer, Heidelberg (2023). https://doi.org/10.1007/7854_2023_419
7. Microsoft: What is mixed reality? Microsoft Learn (2023). https://learn.microsoft.com/en-us/windows/mixed-reality/discover/mixed-reality
8. Peckmann, C., Kannen, K., Pensel, M.C., Lux, S., Philipsen, A., Braun, N.: Virtual reality induces symptoms of depersonalization and derealization: a longitudinal randomised control trial. Comput. Hum. Behav. **131**, 107233 (2022). https://doi.org/10.1016/j.chb.2022.107233
9. Phillips, M.L., et al.: Depersonalization disorder: thinking without feeling. Psychiatry Res. Neuroimaging **108**(3), 145–160 (2001). https://doi.org/10.1016/S0925-4927(01)00119-6
10. Rizzo, A.S., Schultheis, M.T., Rothbaum, B.O.: Ethical issues for the use of virtual reality in the psychological sciences. In: Ethical Issues in Clinical Neuropsychology, pp. 243–280. Taylor & Francis (2002)
11. Sala, N.: Virtual Reality, Augmented Reality, and Mixed Reality in Education: A Brief Overview. IGI Global (2021)
12. Segal, D.L.: Diagnostic and Statistical Manual of Mental Disorders (DSM-IV-TR), chap. Dissociative Disorders, Depersonalization Disorder. John Wiley & Sons, Ltd., Hoboken (2010). https://doi.org/10.1002/9780470479216.corpsy0271
13. Spiegel, D.: Depersonalization/derealization disorder. MSD Manual (2023). https://www.msdmanuals.com/professional/psychiatric-disorders/dissociative-disorders/depersonalization-derealization-disorder
14. Vivaldi, F., Barra, E.: Bienestar psicológico, apoyo social percibido y percepción de salud en adultos mayores. Terapia psicológica **30**, 23–29 (2012). https://doi.org/10.4067/S0718-48082012000200002

MetaNav: A Bio-Inspired Meta-imitation Learning Framework for Robotic Visual Semantic Navigation

Carlos Gutiérrez-Àlvarez$^{(\boxtimes)}$, Rafael Flor-Rodríguez-Rabadán ,
Sergio Lafuente-Arroyo , Saturnino Maldonado-Bascón ,
and Roberto J. López-Sastre

Department of Signal Theory and Communications, GRAM Research Group,
University of Alcalá, Alcalá de Henares, Spain
`carlos.gutierrezalva@uah.es`
`https://gram.web.uah.es/`

Abstract. In this work we address the robotic visual semantic navigation problem from a bio-inspired learning perspective, motivated by the ability of natural agents to rapidly adapt their behavior by exploiting prior experience. We explore meta-imitation learning as an artificial counterpart of biological learning-to-learn mechanisms, enabling fast adaptation to new tasks from limited demonstrations. Technically, we propose the model Meta Visual Semantic Navigation (MetaNav), a meta-imitation learning framework that combines imitation learning from human demonstrations with meta-learning to acquire adaptable navigation policies. Rather than optimizing for a single task, the model learns an adaptive prior that can be efficiently specialized to new object-goal navigation tasks using only a few examples. The approach is trained on a small set of environments from the HM3D dataset following a task-based formulation inspired by natural adaptation across related scenarios. Experimental results show that the learned policies exhibit fast adaptation to previously unseen tasks, highlighting the potential of bio-inspired meta-learning for robotic navigation, while also revealing current limitations and directions for future research.

Keywords: Imitation Learning · Meta-Learning · Visual Navigation

1 Introduction

Autonomous navigation continues to be a core challenge in robotics and UAV applications [3], especially in unstructured and dynamic environments. In this context, Visual Semantic Navigation (VSN) has emerged as a promising paradigm, driven by recent advances in machine learning and the availability of large-scale datasets, with the aim of explicitly addressing these challenges. VSN models are predominantly learning-based navigation approaches that employ end-to-end architectures to directly map visual sensory inputs to control actions

J. M. Ferrández Vicente et al. (Eds.): IWINAC 2026, LNCS 16575, pp. 22–31, 2026.
https://doi.org/10.1007/978-3-032-27317-8_3

governing robot motion (e.g. [14,19]). Despite their effectiveness, current VSN approaches typically rely on large amounts of training data and extensive interaction with highly realistic simulation environments in order to achieve acceptable performance and generalization. Moreover, models trained under these conditions often exhibit limited adaptability when deployed in novel environments or confronted with unseen goals, requiring additional data collection or retraining. These constraints highlight a fundamental gap between the data efficiency of natural navigation systems and that of current learning-based VSN models, motivating the exploration of alternative learning paradigms that emphasize rapid adaptation and experience reuse.

In contrast, in this work, we explore a novel training paradigm for VSN models that pursues two main objectives: first, to achieve more efficient training pipelines; and second, to learn navigation models with improved generalization capabilities.

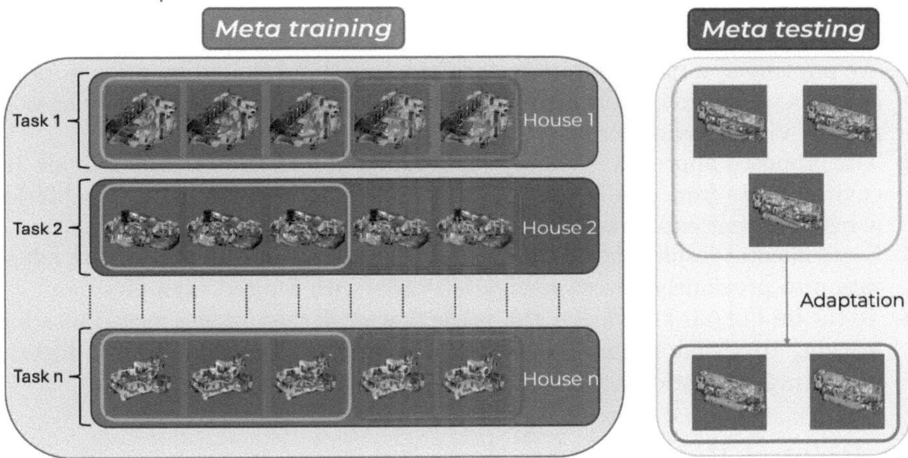

Fig. 1. MetaNav reformulates VSN as a meta-imitation learning problem. MetaNav learns a navigation policy prior across multiple training tasks (meta-training) and enables fast adaptation to unseen object-goal navigation tasks with few demonstrations (meta-testing), achieving both generalization and rapid specialization.

Technically, we propose a bio-inspired approach that combines techniques from Imitation Learning (IL) [18] and Meta-Learning [6] to learn a VSN model, which we denote as MetaNav, see Fig. 1. Humans and animals rapidly acquire navigation skills by observing demonstrations and adapting them to new environments after only limited exposure, a capability commonly described as learning to learn. Meta-learning and imitation learning offer a computational abstraction of these bio-inspired mechanisms in artificial systems. Imitation learning enables robotic agents to acquire navigation behaviors from expert demonstrations, while meta-learning allows such behaviors to be organized into adaptive priors that facilitate fast specialization to new scenes and goals. Thus, meta-imitation learning is a combination of both realms, allowing agents to learn from a small number of demonstrations and adapt quickly to new tasks, in our case navigation tasks. Our hypothesis is that in the context of robotic navigation, this combination naturally supports efficient generalization and rapid adaptation across environments, reflecting key principles of biological navigation.

MetaNav (Fig. 1) reformulates VSN as a meta-imitation learning problem. During the meta-training phase, the model learns a navigation policy prior across multiple small object-goal navigation tasks defined in different training environments. In the meta-testing phase, the learned prior enables fast adaptation to new navigation tasks in previously unseen environments using only a small amount of demonstration data. The objective is to obtain a policy that is broadly effective across tasks while retaining the ability to specialize rapidly in novel navigation scenarios. Due to this adaptability, the policy can be trained on simulation using a set of task demonstrations and then deployed in unseen environments to perform new tasks.

The main contributions of this work are summarized as follows:

1. We implement a meta-imitation learning algorithm inspired by prior work on one-shot visual imitation learning and adapt it to the specific challenges of robotic visual navigation.
2. The proposed approach is trained and evaluated on a subset of large-scale 3D environments from the HM3D dataset, analyzing its adaptation capabilities across different experimental setups.
3. Experimental results show that the learned policies are capable of fast adaptation to previously unseen navigation tasks with limited examples.
4. To the best of our knowledge, this is the first work that applies meta-imitation learning to visual semantic navigation in large-scale environments, directly predicting navigation actions from raw sensory observations.

2   Related Work

Meta-imitation learning extends imitation learning into the meta-learning regime. Depending on the method used, two main approaches can be distinguished: gradient-based and contextual and latent variable meta-imitation learning.

Gradient-Based Meta Imitation Learning. Many meta-imitation learning approaches have adopted gradient-based adaptation for fast imitation. In these methods, a policy (or policy initialization) is meta-learned such that a small number of gradient steps on a new task's demo data leads to effective behavior cloning on that task. For example, Model Agnostic Meta-Learning (MAML) [6] learns a policy initialization that can be quickly adapted to new tasks via gradient descent. Later works have extended MAML to the context of imitation learning, such as learning from video demonstrations of robotic tasks [7,8] or learning from human demonstrations in complex environments [15,17].

Contextual and Latent Variable Meta-Imitation. An alternative line of work avoids explicit gradient updates at test time by conditioning the policy on task-specific context, typically derived from demonstrations. Typically, one-shot imitation learning models process a demonstration trajectory (or a few demos) through an encoder and feed this context alongside the current state to the policy network [5]. Another instantiation of this idea is to use latent variables [2,4,9,12,16] to represent tasks: during meta-training, a latent context z is inferred for each demonstration set, and the policy or value function is conditioned on z rather than relying on one global initialization.

Our approach, described in Sect. 3, extends the concepts of gradient-based meta-imitation learning by implementing a modified version of MAML [6] to train navigation policies using few demonstrations.

3 Meta-Imitation Learning for Robotic Visual Semantic Navigation

3.1 Problem Setting

We address the problem of ObjectGoal Navigation [1], in which an embodied agent must navigate toward a specified target object by selecting actions from a discrete control set. The available actions include: TURN_LEFT, TURN_RIGHT, MOVE_FORWARD, LOOK_UP, LOOK_DOWN, and STOP. An episode is considered successful when the agent issues the STOP action within one meter of the target object and before reaching a maximum of 500 steps.

The agent operates exclusively on egocentric sensory inputs, as is standard in Visual Semantic Navigation (VSN). Specifically, it receives RGB visual observations together with relative displacement and orientation measurements, providing positional information with respect to the starting point. This perception-action loop mirrors the behavior of biological agents, which rely on first-person visual input and self-motion cues to incrementally construct spatial understanding and guide goal-directed navigation.

A navigation task is defined as a tuple of the form $\mathcal{T} = (G, S)$, where G is the target object and S the scene in which the navigation is taking place. Each task can contain multiple demonstrations τ_i, each of them recorded by a human and always on the same scene and seeking the same target object. The variability of the demonstrations comes from the random starting points in each episode and the different paths that the human can take to reach any of the several instances of the target object. Thus, the goal of MetaNav is to learn a policy π_θ that can quickly adapt to combinations of new target objects G and scenes S.

3.2 Meta-Imitation Learning Formulation

According to the problem formulation, the proposed MetaNav learning algorithm is described in this section. We propose a meta-imitation learning approach leveraging prior work on one-shot visual imitation learning with meta-learning [7].

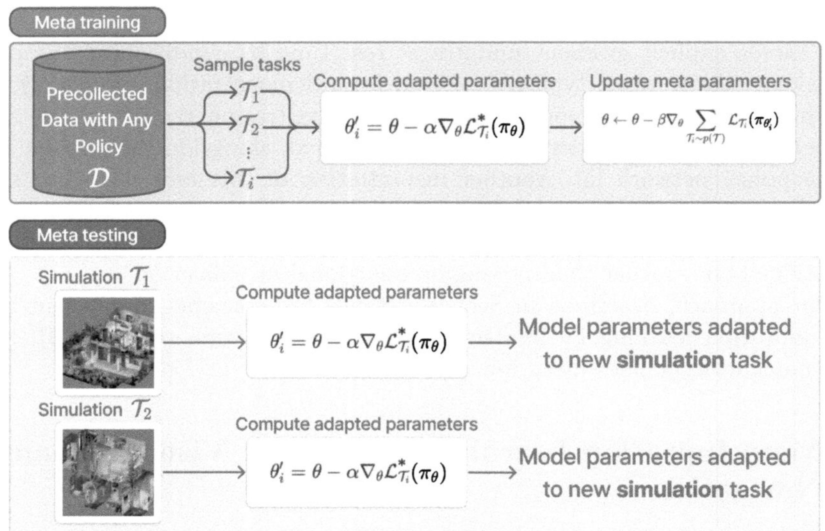

Fig. 2. MetaNav reformulates visual semantic navigation as a MAML-based meta-imitation learning process. During meta-training, task-specific parameters are obtained from demonstration data and used to update shared meta-parameters across navigation tasks. In deployment, the learned policy prior is quickly adapted to unseen environments with minimal additional experience, enabling efficient generalization and rapid task specialization.

Technically, we develop MetaNav as a VSN model that is trained following a MAML-based [6] meta-imitation learning process. This way, our vision-based navigation policy is trained to adapt to new navigation tasks with a few examples, in two stages, as it is shown in Fig. 2. First, during the meta-training stage, a set of tasks $\mathcal{T}_i = (G, S)$ drawn from a distribution $p(\mathcal{T})$ are considered. Each task $\mathcal{T}_i$ consists of a collection of observations o and actions a generated by an expert policy π_i^*:

$$\tau = \{o_1, a_1, \ldots, o_T, a_T\} \sim \pi_i^*, \tag{1}$$

where T is the length of the demonstration or trajectory τ. Our objective is to learn a policy π_θ that maps observations o to predicted actions $\hat{a}$ from different demonstrations sampled from the task distribution. Since an imitation learning context with discrete actions is used, behavior cloning loss is employed to train the policy from the demonstrations:

$$\mathcal{L}^*_{\mathcal{T}_i}(\pi_\theta) = \sum_{\tau_j \sim \mathcal{T}_i} \sum_{(o_t, a_t) \in \tau^i}^{T} - \log(\pi_\theta(a_t | o_T)). \tag{2}$$

This loss function is known as the inner loss, used during the meta-training stage, and its function is to adapt the policy to a specific task. By applying gradient descent to the inner loss, the adapted parameters $\theta'_i = \theta - \alpha \nabla_\theta \mathcal{L}^*_{\mathcal{T}_i}(\pi_\theta)$

of the policy can be computed. Inflection weighting [13] is applied to the inner loss function to emphasize time steps corresponding to action changes.

In a second stage, during the meta-testing stage, once the adapted parameters θ'_i are obtained, they can be used to compute the outer loss, which is used to update the policy parameters θ. The outer loss is also known as the meta-loss or meta-objective, and it is defined as:

$$\min_{\theta} \sum_{\mathcal{T}_i \sim p(\mathcal{T})} \mathcal{L}_{\mathcal{T}_i}\left(\pi_{\theta'_i}\right) = \sum_{\mathcal{T}_i \sim p(\mathcal{T})} \mathcal{L}_{\mathcal{T}_i}\left(\pi_{\theta - \alpha \nabla_\theta \mathcal{L}^*_{\mathcal{T}_i}(\pi_\theta)}\right). \tag{3}$$

Intuitively, this meta-loss acts as a regularization term over a "fine-tuning" process over the tasks. This encourages the policy to find an average over θ meta-parameters with respect to the task distribution. Then, the meta-parameters can adapt to new tasks with few gradient updates following the update rule:

$$\theta \leftarrow \theta - \beta \nabla_\theta \sum_{\mathcal{T}_i \sim p(\mathcal{T})} \mathcal{L}_{\mathcal{T}_i}\left(\pi_{\theta'_i}\right). \tag{4}$$

Note that for this goal, the meta-loss implies the use of double derivatives, which can be computationally expensive. In practice, a first-order approximation of the meta-loss [6] is used, which allows computing the outer loss without the need for second derivatives.

From a bio-inspired perspective, this formulation reflects the way natural agents acquire reusable navigation priors through experience and subsequently refine their behavior when exposed to new environments. The meta-parameters θ can be interpreted as a learned adaptive prior, analogous to long-term knowledge accumulated across tasks, while the task-specific updates model rapid short-term adaptation. Thus, MetaNav embodies a computational abstraction of learning-to-learn mechanisms observed in biological navigation systems, emphasizing experience reuse and efficient behavioral specialization.

4 Experiments

4.1 Experimental Setup

Dataset. A previously collected dataset of navigation experience is required for the imitation learning setup. The chosen dataset, detailed in [11], includes 77k episodes of human navigation trajectories using the HM3D [10] dataset. HM3D provides photorealistic 3D indoor environments with diverse objects and scenes. For our experiments, we design five progressively challenging setups that define how training and evaluation scenes are organized within the dataset, as illustrated in Fig. 3. The goal is to gradually increase the generalization difficulty from Setup 1 through Setup 5.

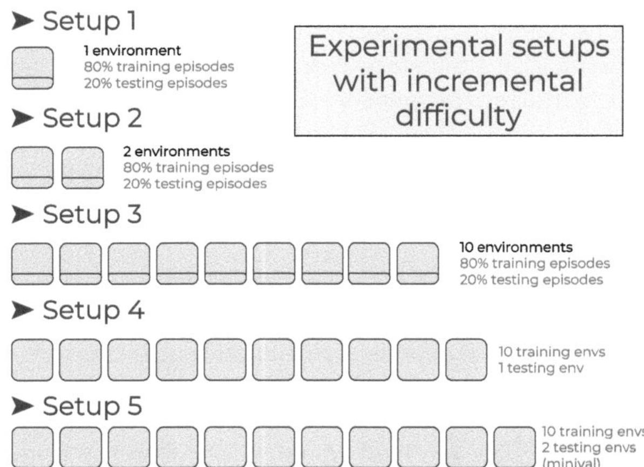

Fig. 3. Five experimental setups designed with an incremental difficulty.

Implementation Details. For MetaNav, the policy architecture follows a CNN+RNN pipeline similar to the model described in [11], with the modification that a ResNet18 backbone is used for the visual encoders to improve feature extraction efficiency. The overall training framework builds on the decentralized distributed paradigm of DDPPO [14], enabling large-scale parallel rollout collection and stable on-policy updates.

To adapt DDPPO to the meta-imitation learning setting, we modify the inner optimization step to incorporate the behavior cloning loss defined in Eq. 2, and introduce the meta-objective (outer loss) described in Eq. 3. This integration allows the policy to learn from expert demonstrations while simultaneously optimizing for fast adaptation across tasks.

4.2   Evaluation Estrategies

Since MetaNav is trained under a meta-learning paradigm, the agent is exposed to a set of previously unseen tasks. For each task, the agent first must perform an adaptation phase, where it updates its policy using demonstrations from that task, yielding the adapted parameters θ_i'. The adapted policy is then evaluated by executing actions sampled from it and measuring downstream navigation performance.

We evaluate MetaNav using two complementary protocols: *continuous evaluation* and *per-episode evaluation*. In the continuous evaluation setting, the agent is given a fixed number of adaptation steps for each task, after which it is immediately evaluated on the same task for an additional fixed number of steps. This process is repeated continuously across the episode until it is finished. In the per-episode evaluation protocol, the agent again receives a fixed adaptation budget, but evaluation proceeds by running the adapted policy until each episode naturally terminates, either due to success or upon reaching the maximum allowed number of steps.

Table 1. Evaluation of MetaNav on the ObjectNav task using continuous and per-episode evaluation strategies.

Setup	Continuous Evaluation			Per-Episode Evaluation		
	SR ($\uparrow$)	SPL ($\uparrow$)	Dist. ($\downarrow$)	SR ($\uparrow$)	SPL ($\uparrow$)	Dist. ($\downarrow$)
1	89.18%	40.04%	0.29	83.33%	40.03%	0.29
2	76.10%	33.92%	0.97	60.78%	26.58%	1.74
3	64.19%	33.11%	1.99	55.19%	26.21%	2.54
4	23.07%	11.87%	12.23	16.67%	4.84%	12.72
5	21.74%	9.38%	7.99	25.00%	9.31%	8.19

Navigation performance is assessed using the official ObjectGoal Navigation metrics [1]: Success Rate (SR) and Shortest Path Length (SPL). We additionally report the Distance to Goal, defined as the agent's final Euclidean distance to the target at the end of each episode.

4.3   Results

We explicitly compare the two evaluation protocols introduced earlier—continuous evaluation and per-episode evaluation—in order to understand their impact on adaptation dynamics and final navigation performance. All metrics corresponding to this analysis are reported in Table 1.

The first trend we observe is that task difficulty indeed increases progressively from Setup 1 to Setup 5. Under both evaluation protocols, MetaNav starts with a strong SR, exceeding 83% in Setup 1. However, performance drops as the scenarios become more challenging: in Setup 5, the SR decreases to 21.74% under continuous evaluation and to 25% under the per-episode protocol. This behavior confirms that the proposed sequence of setups effectively induces a controlled increase in generalization difficulty.

These experiments also confirm that our meta-imitation learning framework is capable of effectively training a VSN model such as MetaNav. For instance, in Setup 3, MetaNav successfully navigates to the goal in up to 10 different environments with a success rate of 64%, demonstrating strong generalization within a moderately diverse set of tasks.

What are the main differences between the two evaluation strategies proposed? Table 1 reveals systematic differences between continuous and per-episode evaluation. Although performance varies across setups, continuous evaluation consistently achieves higher SR and SPL values than per-episode evaluation in all configurations except Setup 5. This behavior can be explained by the training protocol: MetaNav is trained in a continuous meta-learning fashion, which naturally favors evaluation scenarios where adaptation and execution are interleaved over extended horizons. Consequently, the evaluation setting better matches the training dynamics, yielding improved performance.

Another key factor lies in the effective adaptation budget. In the per-episode protocol, the agent is restricted to a single block of 64 steps for adaptation before executing the task until termination. In contrast, continuous evaluation alternates blocks of 64 adaptation steps and 64 evaluation steps, and if the episode is not completed, this process continues iteratively until termination. As a result, the model is exposed to substantially more experience per episode, enabling incremental refinement of the adapted parameters.

Finally, the results from Setup 5 are also encouraging. Even when evaluated on entirely unseen environments, MetaNav achieves a Success Rate of 25%, indicating that the model is able to leverage the meta-learned prior to perform meaningful adaptation beyond the training distribution. Interestingly, we can compare the performance of our MetaNav approach, with a the state-of-the-art model PirlNav [11] in Setup 5. While our meta-imitation learning reports a SR of 25.00%, PirlNav casts a 26.09% of SR. This reveals that our meta-imitation learning approach is able to report state-of-the-art results. Moreover, it is important to note that MetaNav is trained under a meta-learning paradigm, which allows us to adapt to new tasks with limited examples, while PirlNav is trained in a standard behavior cloning setup without any adaptation mechanism. While PirlNav achieves slightly better performance, MetaNav's ability to adapt to new tasks with limited examples represents a significant ability that is not present in PirlNav, and it may lead to better performance in other setups or scenarios where adaptability is crucial.

5   Conclusions

We presented MetaNav, a meta-imitation learning framework for VSN that formulates object-goal navigation as a learning-to-learn problem. By acquiring a task-agnostic prior across environments, the policy can rapidly specialize to new navigation tasks from few demonstrations. To the best of our knowledge, this is the first application of meta-imitation learning to large-scale VSN with policies predicting actions directly from raw sensory inputs.

Experiments on HM3D show that MetaNav achieves state-of-the-art performance and consistent gains under continuous evaluation, highlighting strong adaptation when incremental experience is available.

Beyond empirical improvements, MetaNav offers a bio-inspired perspective by decoupling prior acquisition from rapid environment-specific adaptation, resembling experience-driven learning and behavioral adjustment in natural agents. Future work will investigate more scalable meta-optimization strategies, improved visual representations, and extensions toward real-world and continual learning scenarios.

Acknowledgments. This work was supported by projects: GUIDANCE-4D, with reference CM/DEMG/2024-028, of CAM-UAH; NAVIGATOR-D, with reference PID2023-148310OB-I00 from the Ministry of Science and Innovation of Spain; and MOEVE Chair at the University of Alcala.

References

1. Batra, D., et al.: ObjectNav revisited: on evaluation of embodied agents navigating to objects, p. arXiv (2020)
2. Bhoopchand, A., et al.: Learning few-shot imitation as cultural transmission. Nat. Commun. (2023)
3. Caballero-Martin, D., Lopez-Guede, J.M., Estevez, J., Graña, M.: AI embedded in drone control. In: IWINAC (2024)
4. Cho, S., Kim, D., Lee, J., Hong, S.: Meta-controller: few-shot imitation of unseen embodiments and tasks in continuous control. In: NeurIPS (2024)
5. Duan, Y., et al.: One-shot imitation learning. In: NeurIPS (2017)
6. Finn, C., Abbeel, P., Levine, S.: Model-agnostic meta-learning for fast adaptation of deep networks. In: ICML (2017)
7. Finn, C., Yu, T., Zhang, T., Abbeel, P., Levine, S.: One-shot visual imitation learning via meta-learning. In: Proceedings of the 1st Annual Conference on Robot Learning, pp. 357–368. PMLR (2017)
8. Gao, C., Jiang, Y., Chen, F.: Transferring hierarchical structures with dual meta imitation learning. In: 6th Annual Conference on Robot Learning (2022)
9. Matsushima, T., Kondo, N., Iwasawa, Y., Nasuno, K., Matsuo, Y.: Modeling task uncertainty for safe meta-imitation learning. Front. Rob. AI (2020)
10. Ramakrishnan, S.K., et al.: Habitat-Matterport 3D Dataset (HM3D): 1000 large-scale 3D environments for embodied AI. In: NeurIPS (2021)
11. Ramrakhya, R., Batra, D., Wijmans, E., Das, A.: PIRLNav: pretraining with imitation and RL finetuning for ObjectNav. In: CVPR (2023)
12. Sontakke, S.A., et al.: RoboCLIP: one demonstration is enough to learn robot policies. In: NeurIPS (2023)
13. Wijmans, E., et al.: Embodied question answering in photorealistic environments with point cloud perception. In: CVPR (2019)
14. Wijmans, E., et al.: DD-PPO: learning near-perfect PointGoal navigators from 2.5 billion frames. In: ICLR (2020)
15. Wu, S., Wang, Y., Huang, Y.: One-shot robust imitation learning for long-horizon visuomotor tasks from unsegmented demonstrations. arXiv (2024)
16. Yu, L., Yu, T., Finn, C., Ermon, S.: Meta-inverse reinforcement learning with probabilistic context variables. In: NeurIPS (2019)
17. Yu, T., et al.: One-shot imitation from observing humans via domain-adaptive meta-learning. arXiv (2018)
18. Zare, M., Kebria, P.M., Khosravi, A., Nahavandi, S.: A survey of imitation learning: algorithms, recent developments, and challenges. IEEE Trans. Cybern. **54**(12), 7173–7186 (2024). https://doi.org/10.1109/TCYB.2024.3395626
19. Zhu, Y., et al.: Target-driven visual navigation in indoor scenes using deep reinforcement learning. In: ICLR (2017)

Automatic Screening of Invasive Coronary Angiography Images Using Swin Transformer

Juan Jesús Rus-Muñoz[2], Ariadna Jiménez-Partinen[1,2,3(✉)] [iD],
Mario Pascual-González[2] [iD], Esteban J. Palomo[1,2,3] [iD],
and Jorge Rodríguez-Capitán[3,4,5] [iD]

[1] ITIS Software, University of Málaga, 29071 Málaga, Spain
[2] Department of Computer Languages and Computer Science, University of Málaga,
Bulevar Louis Pasteur, 35, 29071 Málaga, Spain
{ariadna,mpascual,ejpalomo}@uma.es
[3] IBIMA Plataforma BIONAND, 29590 Málaga, Spain
[4] Cardiology Department, Hospital Universitario Virgen de la Victoria,
29010 Málaga, Spain
[5] Centro de Investigación Biomédica en Red de Enfermedades Cardiovasculares
(CIBERCV), Instituto de Salud Carlos III (ISCIII), 28029 Madrid, Spain

Abstract. The use of pre-trained, widely known deep learning models for object detection and classification in medical images is beneficial across a wide range of applications. For coronary artery disease, deep learning-based methods have been implemented to segment the arteries and detect stenosis with promising results. However, how to automatically filter and select valid frames from entire video sequences remains underexplored, as this is usually a manual task. This step, also known as image screening, consists of selecting frames in which the radiocontrast has perfused to achieve sufficient contrast quality for viewing the coronary arteries correctly. This task is crucial for preparing datasets for detector and segmentation models. In this work, an open-access dataset of invasive coronary angiographies (CADICA) has been used to evaluate the impact and feasibility of automatic screening using three architectures: CNN and transformer-based. Additionally, stratified cross-validation and Bayesian hyperparameter optimization have been used to obtain robust and reliable results. The results indicate that a transformer-based architecture outperforms CNN-based models for screening key frames, demonstrating great potential as a component of automated ICA image analysis.

Keywords: Invasive coronary angiography · deep learning · screening

1 Introduction

The leading cause of death worldwide [6] is cardiovascular disease, with coronary artery disease (CAD) as the most common pathology. In CAD, the coronary

© The Author(s), under exclusive license to Springer Nature Switzerland AG 2026
J. M. Ferrández Vicente et al. (Eds.): IWINAC 2026, LNCS 16575, pp. 32–42, 2026.
https://doi.org/10.1007/978-3-032-27317-8_4

artery lumen narrows due to the gradual deposition of fat, cholesterol, calcium, and other substances that accumulate within the arterial intima, resulting in progressive encroachment by atherosclerotic plaques that obstruct the coronary artery, reducing blood flow and leading to angina or acute myocardial infarction.

The gold-standard imaging method in CAD is invasive coronary angiography (ICA) for anatomical imaging, diagnosis, and treatment guidance [2]. In the ICA acquisition protocol, a radiocontrast agent is injected through a catheter via a percutaneous incision, followed by X-ray imaging to visualize the coronary arteries. To thoroughly evaluate the condition of the myocardial vessels, both the left coronary artery (LCA) and the right coronary artery (RCA) must be examined using various projections and angles [22]. Clinical experts commonly identify abnormalities and assess their severity through visual examination. ICA image analysis is challenging due to a poor signal-to-noise ratio, complex and overlapping vessel structures, non-uniform illumination, and inhomogeneous lumen intensity. Although this protocol is considered standard clinical practice, it may still be subject to inter- and intra-observer variability due to the subjective nature of visual assessments [13,28].

Computer-aided system based on deep learning (DL) could lead to more efficient evaluation, more reliable assessments, and reduced workload [26]. DL-based applications for ICA image analysis have been limited by the scarcity of open-access datasets, due to the inherent manual preprocessing tasks, such as annotation and high-quality frame selection [18]. There is a wide variety of deep learning architectures, including convolutional neural networks (CNNs), transformer-based models, and hybrid models. However, in the current state-of-the-art for ICA imaging, CNN-driven approaches are dominant [27]. The primary tasks addressed are artery extraction using segmentation methods [11,15,20], and stenosis detection [3,5,21]. Despite that, there is a wide scope of underexplored, important intermediate steps that merit further study to achieve these final objectives. For instance, automatic identification of end-diastole and end-systole image frames [19], or catheter segmentation [25] or detection [7].

The manual selection of key frames from ICA video sequences is essential for removing unnecessary frames in poorly perfused datasets. This step aids in the subsequent analysis of vessel extraction and characterization by focusing on images that accurately represent these vessels. According to Liang *et al.* [14], their segmentation study shows that including complete video sequences can lead to errors due to the presence of non-perfused frames. Therefore, an automated method for detecting contrast inflow is essential to further automate advanced image-guidance techniques in coronary interventions and to reduce the manual selection task during dataset preparation. In this context, Syeda-Mahmood *et al.* [24] proposed a parallel curves-based method to select frames with maximum visibility. Ma *et al.* [17] explores two strategies to distinguish frames with radiocontrast: a CNN and a long short-term memory (LSTM) network for contrast features. Finally, Chen *et al.* [4] proposed a segmentation framework in which the first stage addresses key frame selection using a CNN.

The related work reported, which focused on frame selection from a complete ICA video sequence, shares some similarities with the present study, such as the use of a deep learning method. However, some shortcomings can be identified, such as an in-depth comparison of deep learning models' performance metrics and reproducible frameworks using open-access datasets. The main contributions of this paper are:

- The Swin Transformer classification model is used for screening ICA images, thereby reducing the impact of non-perfused instances.
- A thorough comparison of CNN-based methods and the Swin Transformer, which combines CNN structure with Transformer operation, is provided.
- The open-access CADICA dataset [10] is employed to improve and support reproducibility.
- All projections available from the CADICA dataset have been included, allowing for conducting experiments realistic to a clinical setting.
- An exhaustive analysis of performance metrics is reported.
- The proposed automated method demonstrated great potential as a component of automated ICA image analysis.

The rest of this work is organized as follows: Sect. 2 provides a detailed description of the methodology used for detecting non-perfused frames. Section 3 describes the settings items and the dataset used for the experiments and the assessment of the performance of the proposed method. Finally, Sect. 4 is devoted to conclusions.

2   Methodology

2.1   Dataset

The CADICA dataset [10] is used to reliably study the impact of classifier screening with DL-driven methods, closer to clinical settings, as a baseline framework and a starting point for introducing a component for automated ICA image analysis to improve coronary artery disease solutions. CADICA includes complete video sequences of invasive coronary angiography from 42 patients. Each patient case contains videos selected for inspection according to the CAD protocol. Various projections for the LCA and RCA are included based on the diagnostic case and its complexities. The dataset incorporates a frame selection in which the radiocontrast was perfused correctly. The *non-selected* frames were labeled as *class 0*, and the *selected* frames were labeled as *class 1* samples. To illustrate the complexity of the problem, not only discern between perfused and non-perfused frames, but also between those with sufficient radiocontrast, an example of a video sequence frames, where the considered classes are depicted, is illustrated in Fig. 1. A total of 18,154 frames –split into training (70%), validation (15%), and held-out test (15%) subsets– were used, whose distribution is detailed in Table 1. Partitions were conducted at the patient level, i.e., frames from the same patient were assigned to the same partition, ensuring that all frames from a given patient were within a single partition to avoid bias and enable a realistic

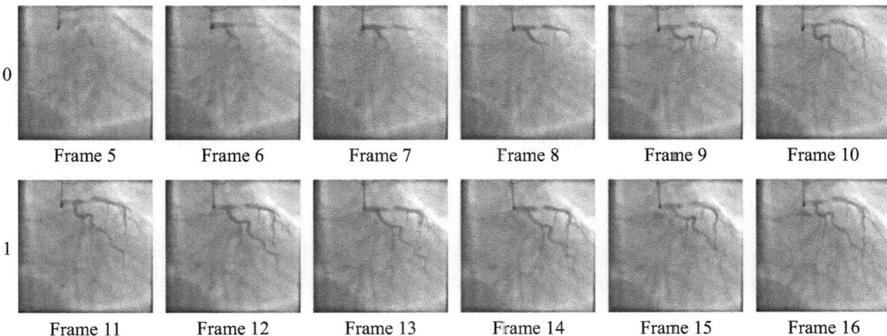

Fig. 1. Frame samples for *non-selected* frames (class 0 - first row) and *selected* frames (class 1 - second row) from video 2 of patient 30.

evaluation of model generalization to unseen patients. Due to variability in the number of frames per patient, the resulting number of images per subset slightly deviates from the exact split ratio. ICA images are in PNG format with a size of 512×512 pixels, although images were resized to 224×224 pixels and normalized using ImageNet statistics prior to model training. No data augmentation techniques were applied in the cross-validated experimental framework reported in this study, in order to isolate the contribution of the proposed architectures and optimization strategy.

Table 1. Distribution of frames per class across data partitions.

	Class 0	Class 1	Total
Training	7,397	4,741	12,138
Validation	2,050	1,092	3,142
Test	1,857	1,017	2,874
Total	**11,304**	**6,850**	**18,154**

2.2 Methods

Three deep learning models were considered for binary classification of ICA frames. These architectures represent two complementary paradigms for visual analysis and allow a fair comparison between convolutional and transformer-based approaches.

The ResNet-50 model [8] was selected as a strong convolutional baseline due to its extensive use and proven robustness in medical image analysis. In addition, the MobileNetV2 architecture [23] was included as a lightweight convolutional model to evaluate the trade-off between computational efficiency and classification performance, making it suitable for resource-constrained clinical environments. Both CNN-based architectures, MobileNet-V2 and ResNet-50, were initialized with weights pre-trained on the ImageNet dataset. The original classification layer was replaced with a task-specific head composed of a dropout layer followed by a fully connected layer with two output neurons corresponding to the target classes.

In parallel, a Swin Transformer Tiny architecture [16] was evaluated to incorporate global contextual information and long-range spatial dependencies. This model relies on a hierarchical transformer architecture with shifted-window self-attention, enabling efficient modeling of spatial relationships across the image. As with the convolutional baseline, ImageNet-pretrained weights were used for initialization, and the original classification head was replaced with a custom binary classification head consisting of a dropout layer and a linear layer.

For all architectures, input images were resized to 224×224 pixels, and class probabilities were computed using a softmax activation.

2.3 Training and Hyperparameter Optimization

Model training was carried out using a Bayesian hyperparameter optimization (BHO) strategy implemented with the OPTUNA framework [1]. The BHO is an iterative approach for optimizing objective functions $f : \mathcal{X} \to \mathbb{R}$, where $\mathcal{X}$ is the hyperparameter space and $f(x)$ measures the performance of a given configuration x. There are two key components in this approach: this model predicts the performance of untested configurations based on prior evaluations, and an acquisition function that utilizes the posterior distribution of $f(x)$, which is updated after each observation, to identify the most promising hyperparameter candidates for the next sampling. Bayesian optimization aims to solve

$$\max_{x \in \mathcal{X}} f(x) \tag{1}$$

In this study, the optimization objective was to maximize the mean Area Under the ROC Curve (AUC), and the hyperparameters optimized included the learning rate, weight decay, optimizer type, dropout rate, and batch size. Search ranges were defined based on commonly used values in deep learning for medical image analysis. For each trial, a model was trained using a candidate set of hyperparameters and evaluated within the cross-validation framework. This approach enables an efficient and systematic exploration of the hyperparameter space by modeling the relationship between hyperparameter configurations and validation performance.

The early stopping technique, which stops training when a criterion is met, was applied to prevent overfitting. The stopping criterion was set to 10 epochs, after which validation performance showed no improvement. All models were trained using the cross-entropy loss function and optimized with stochastic gradient-based methods.

The hyperparameter configuration was evaluated using stratified K-fold cross-validation (with $K = 5$) to obtain a final, robust estimation of the performance model. This technique is adequate for reliably evaluating performance because the results are averages across different folds of the input dataset, which are independent of the partition used for validation. After hyperparameter optimization, the final model was retrained on the combined training and validation sets using the selected hyperparameters. Model performance was then evaluated on a held-out test subset, which was not used during training or model selection.

2.4   Performance Metrics

It is essential to provide a thorough and structured report of the experimental results to adequately capture the unique characteristics and performance of each approach. In order to quantify the performance, the four representative parameters –True Positive (TP), True Negative (TN), False Positive (FP), and False Negative (FN)– are used to compute the commonly used performance metrics defined as follows [9]:

$$Accuracy = \frac{TP + TN}{TP + TN + FP + FN}, \quad Precision = \frac{TP}{TP + FP} \tag{2}$$

$$Recall = \frac{TP}{TP + FN}, \quad Specificity = \frac{TN}{TN + FP} \tag{3}$$

$$F1 - score = 2 \cdot \frac{Precision \cdot Recall}{Precision + Recall}, \quad Balanced\ Acc. = \frac{Recall + Specificity}{2} \tag{4}$$

$$MCC = \frac{TP \cdot TN - FP \cdot FN}{\sqrt{(TP + FN) \cdot (TP + FP) \cdot (TN + FP) \cdot (TN + FN)}} \tag{5}$$

Area Under the ROC curve (AUC) refers to the ROC, which is a graphical display of Sensitivity (TPR) on the y-axis and (1 specificity) (FPR) on the x-axis for varying cut-off points of test values [12], is computed as

$$AUC = \int_0^1 TPR(FPR^{-1}(r))\, dr \tag{6}$$

All reported metrics range from 0 to 1, except Matthews Correlation Coefficient (MCC), which ranges from -1 to 1; the higher, the better.

3   Results

This section reports the experimental results obtained using the proposed methodology. Model performance is first reported for the stratified K-fold cross-validation stage employed during hyperparameter optimization. Table 2 summarizes the results for each performance metric abovementioned, presented as the 5 folds mean for the evaluated architectures. The three models achieved high discriminative capability, with AUC values above 0.98, indicating strong separability between the two ICA classes. Among the evaluated approaches, the transformer-based model consistently outperformed the CNN-based models. Swin Transformer Tiny achieved higher accuracy, balanced accuracy, F1-score, and Matthews Correlation Coefficient (MCC) than ResNet-50 and MobileNetV2, indicating more robust performance under class-imbalance conditions.

In terms of class-specific performance, Swin Transformer Tiny achieved higher recall than the CNN-based architectures, indicating improved ability to correctly identify positive samples. While ResNet-50 achieved slightly higher precision and specificity, the transformer-based model offered a more balanced trade-off between precision and recall, as reflected in its superior F1-score value.

Table 2. Performance obtained under stratified K-fold cross-validation, 5-fold mean, for the evaluated models. Best results per metric are shown in **bold**.

Model	Acc	AUC	BalAcc	F1	MCC	Pre	Rec	Spec
MobileNetV2	0.937	0.983	0.934	0.917	0.866	0.914	0.921	0.947
ResNet-50	0.938	0.985	0.929	0.916	0.869	**0.940**	0.895	**0.964**
Swin Tiny	**0.943**	**0.987**	**0.942**	**0.926**	**0.880**	0.913	**0.940**	0.945

After hyperparameter selection, the final configurations were retrained on the combined training and validation subsets, using the hyperparameters and number of training epochs, detailed in Table 3, derived from the BHO with the cross-validation procedure. The resulting models were then evaluated on the held-out test subset, which was not used during training or model selection.

Table 3. Summary of the hyperparameter configurations selected by BHO.

Architecture	Epochs	Optimizer	Learning rate	Weight decay	Dropout rate	Batch size
MobileNetV2	15	Adam	0.000076	0.000343	0.396046	16
ResNet-50	14	Adam	0.000039	0.000129	0.077725	8
Swin Tiny	17	Adam	0.00001	0.000033	0.100248	4

To thoroughly analyze the results in both overall and specific class terms, the performance metrics mentioned above are reported in Table 4. As expected, performance decreased when moving from cross-validation to test evaluation, reflecting the greater difficulty of generalizing to unseen data. Nevertheless, the transformer-based model maintained superior performance across most representative evaluation metrics. In particular, Swin Transformer Tiny achieved higher balanced accuracy (0.861), F1-score (0.811), and MCC (0.700) compared to the CNN baseline. These results indicate that the proposed approach generalizes well to unseen ICA data while maintaining a favorable balance between sensitivity and specificity. This suggests that the model can effectively differentiate between the two classes. However, MobileNet-V2 and ResNet-50 outperform this model on individual-class metrics, achieving slightly higher values for precision, recall, and specificity. Nevertheless, these higher values come at the expense of the opposite class ratio, which decreases accordingly.

Table 4. Performance results attained with the held-out test subset for the evaluated models. Best results per metric are shown in **bold**.

Model	Acc	AUC	BalAcc	F1	MCC	Prec	Rec	Spe
MobileNetV2	0.842	0.906	0.855	0.801	0.684	0.721	**0.901**	0.809
ResNet-50	**0.855**	**0.926**	0.852	0.804	0.691	**0.768**	0.845	**0.860**
Swin Tiny	0.854	0.915	**0.861**	**0.811**	**0.700**	0.748	0.886	0.836

To illustrate the results qualitatively, Fig. 2 depicts the same video sequence frames, indicating the outcomes for each model with colors, where MobileNet-V2 (first row) and Swin Tiny (third row) correctly classify most of the positive instances and the ResNet-50 model (second row) correctly classifies only one item.

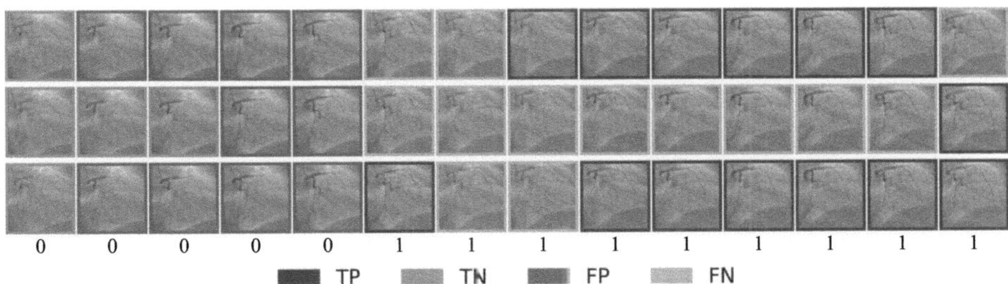

Fig. 2. Frames from video 1 of patient 23, displaying the predictions from each model: MobileNet-V2 in the first row, ResNet-50 in the second row, and Swin Tiny in the third row. The true class for each frame is indicated at the bottom.

4   Conclusions

Invasive coronary angiography videos consist of a large number of frames. Selecting key frames in which radiocontrast perfusion is adequate to visualize coronary arteries is a promising area of study to improve deep learning solutions in ICA imaging. In this work, three neural networks, CNN and transformed, were selected to screen frames from the open-access CADICA dataset. Although the task seems simple, it is actually complex when the clinical real settings are considered. To ensure this, no data augmentation or discarding was implemented, given all available projections. A comprehensive set of experiments was conducted to address the classification task. 5-fold stratified cross-validation was used to perform Bayesian hyperparameter optimization, aiming to report reliable results and robust hyperparameters during training. MobileNet-V2, ResNet-50, and Swin Tiny models with the chosen training hyperparameters were tested on a held-out subset to evaluate their generalization to unseen data. Performance results are promising, and Swin Tiny outperforms CNN-based models, achieving AUC, balanced accuracy, F1-score, and MCC above 0.8. These results support the proposed method for screening frames in ICA imaging analysis systems.

Acknowledgements. This work is partially supported by the Autonomous Government of Andalusia (Spain) under project PPRO-TIC163-G-2023 (TIC163-G-FEDER), and under grant number DGP_PIDI_2024_00462; also by the Ministry of Science and Innovation of Spain, grant number PID2022-136764OA-I00. It includes funds from the European Regional Development Fund (ERDF). It is also partially supported by the Instituto de Salud Carlos III, project code PI25/02129 (co-financed by the European Union). The authors thankfully acknowledge the computer resources, technical expertise and assistance provided by the SCBI (Supercomputing and Bioinformatics) center of the University of Málaga. They also gratefully acknowledge the support of NVIDIA Corporation with the donation of an RTX A6000 GPU with 48Gb. The authors also thankfully acknowledge the grant of the Universidad de Málaga and the Instituto de Investigación Biomédica de Málaga y Plataforma en Nanomedicina-IBIMA Plataforma BIONAND.

References

1. Akiba, T., Sano, S., Yanase, T., Ohta, T., Koyama, M.: Optuna: a next-generation hyperparameter optimization framework. In: Proceedings of the 25th ACM SIGKDD International Conference on Knowledge Discovery & Data Mining, pp. 2623–2631 (2019)
2. Byrne, R.A., et al.: 2023 esc guidelines for the management of acute coronary syndromes: developed by the task force on the management of acute coronary syndromes of the european society of cardiology (esc). Eur. Heart J. Acute Cardiovasc. Care **13**(1), 55–161 (2024)
3. Chen, Y., Han, X., Zhang, Y., Jiang, M.: Dssnet: a dual-stream synergistic network for coronary angiography image segmentation. Biomed. Signal Process. Control **112**, 108641 (2026)
4. Chen, Y., et al.: Sfag-deeplabv3+: an automatic segmentation approach for coronary angiography images. Neurocomputing 130781 (2025)
5. Di Cosmo, M., et al.: Fedstenonet: tackling domain shift in x-ray coronary angiography through a personalized federated detection framework. Comput. Biol. Med. **198**, 111172 (2025)
6. Duggan, J.P., Peters, A.S., Trachiotis, G.D., Antevil, J.L.: Epidemiology of coronary artery disease. Surg. Clin. **102**(3), 499–516 (2022)

7. Fazlali, H.R., Karimi, N., Soroushmehr, S.R., Shirani, S., Nallamothu, B.K., Ward, K.R., Samavi, S., Najarian, K.: Vessel segmentation and catheter detection in x-ray angiograms using superpixels. Med. Biol. Eng. Comput. **56**(9), 1515–1530 (2018)

8. He, K., Zhang, X., Ren, S., Sun, J.: Deep residual learning for image recognition. In: Proceedings of the IEEE Conference on Computer Vision and Pattern Recognition, pp. 770–778 (2016)

9. Hossin, M., Sulaiman, M.N.: A review on evaluation metrics for data classification evaluations. Int. J. Data Mining Knowl. Manag. Process **5**(2), 1 (2015)

10. Jiménez-Partinen, A., et al.: Cadica: a new dataset for coronary artery disease detection by using invasive coronary angiography. Expert. Syst. **41**(12), e13708 (2024)

11. Kim, Y.I., et al.: Artificial intelligence-based quantitative coronary angiography of major vessels using deep-learning. Int. J. Cardiol. **405**, 131945 (2024)

12. Kumar, R., Indrayan, A.: Receiver operating characteristic (roc) curve for medical researchers. Indian Pediatr. **48**, 277–287 (2011)

13. Leape, L.L., Park, R.E., Bashore, T.M., Harrison, J.K., Davidson, C.J., Brook, R.H.: Effect of variability in the interpretation of coronary angiograms on the appropriateness of use of coronary revascularization procedures. Am. Heart J. **139**(1), 106–113 (2000)

14. Liang, D., et al.: Coronary angiography video segmentation method for assisting cardiovascular disease interventional treatment. BMC Med. Imaging **20**(1), 65 (2020)

15. Ling, H., et al.: Deep learning model for coronary angiography. J. Cardiovasc. Transl. Res. **16**(4), 896–904 (2023)

16. Liu, Z., et al.: Swin transformer: hierarchical vision transformer using shifted windows. In: Proceedings of the IEEE/CVF International Conference on Computer Vision, pp. 10012–10022 (2021)

17. Ma, H., Ambrosini, P., van Walsum, T.: Fast prospective detection of contrast inflow in X-ray angiograms with convolutional neural network and recurrent neural network. In: Descoteaux, M., Maier-Hein, L., Franz, A., Jannin, P., Collins, D.L., Duchesne, S. (eds.) MICCAI 2017. LNCS, vol. 10435, pp. 453–461. Springer, Cham (2017). https://doi.org/10.1007/978-3-319-66179-7_52

18. Mehta, H., Patel, M., Vakharia, M., Oza, P. Advancements and challenges in the use of artificial intelligence for coronary artery disease diagnosis: an integrated review: H. mehta et al. Arch. Comput. Methods Eng. 1–42 (2025)

19. Meng, Y., et al.: Automatic identification of end-diastolic and end-systolic cardiac frames from invasive coronary angiography videos. Technol. Health Care **30**(5), 1107–1116 (2022)

20. Park, J., et al.: Selective ensemble methods for deep learning segmentation of major vessels in invasive coronary angiography. Med. Phys. **50**(12), 7822–7839 (2023)

21. Popov, M., et al.: Dataset for automatic region-based coronary artery disease diagnostics using x-ray angiography images. Sci. Data **11**(1), 20 (2024)

22. Rigatelli, G., Gianese, F., Zuin, M.: Modern atlas of invasive coronary angiography views: a practical approach for fellows and young interventionalists. Int. J. Cardiovasc. Imaging **38**(5), 919–926 (2022)

23. Sandler, M., Howard, A., Zhu, M., Zhmoginov, A., Chen, L.C.: Mobilenetv 2: inverted residuals and linear bottlenecks. In: Proceedings of the IEEE Conference on Computer Vision and Pattern Recognition, pp. 4510–4520 (2018)

24. Syeda-Mahmood, T., et al.: Automatic selection of keyframes from angiogram videos. In: 20th International Conference on Pattern Recognition, pp. 4008–4011. IEEE (2010)

25. Xi, L., Ma, Y., Koland, E., Howell, S., Rinaldi, A., Rhode, K.S.: Catheter detection and segmentation in x-ray images via multi-task learning. Int. J. Comput. Assist. Radiol. Surg. 1–11 (2025)
26. Xia, Q., et al.: A comprehensive review of deep learning for medical image segmentation. Neurocomputing **613**, 128740 (2025)
27. Yaman, S., et al.: Deep learning techniques for automated coronary artery segmentation and coronary artery disease detection: a systematic review of the last decade (2013–2024). Comput. Methods Prog. Biomed. 108858 (2025)
28. Zir, L.M., Miller, S.W., Dinsmore, R.E., Gilbert, J., Harthorne, J.: Interobserver variability in coronary angiography. Circulation **53**(4), 627–632 (1976)

Generalizable 3D Glioblastoma Segmentation from Single-Sequence T1-GD MRI

Ana González Morales[4], Ariadna Jiménez-Partinen[1,2,3]([✉]) [iD],
David Muñoz Carmona[5], Luz Rubí Olea[4], Lucía Ripoll Sánchez[2],
Fátima Nagib-Raya[4] [iD], Ezequiel López-Rubio[1,2,3] [iD],
and Rafael M. Luque-Baena[1,2,3] [iD]

[1] ITIS Software, University of Málaga, Málaga, Spain
`ezeqlr@lcc.uma.es`
`{ariadna,rmluque}@uma.es`
[2] Department of Computer Languages and Computer Science,
University of Málaga, Málaga, Spain
[3] IBIMA Plataforma BIONAND, Málaga, Spain
[4] Hospital Regional Universitario de Málaga, Málaga, Spain
`{ana.gonzalez.morales.sspa,marial.rubi.sspa,`
`fatima.nagib.sspa}@juntadeandalucia.es`
[5] Hospital Universitario Virgen Macarena, Seville, Spain
`davidm.munoz.sspa@juntadeandalucia.es`

Abstract. This work presents a comprehensive analysis of the feasibility of using T1-GD (contrast-enhanced T1) MRI sequences for 3D glioblastoma segmentation. The experiments were conducted through the benchmark nnU-Net architecture, considering both MNI152 and SRI24 spaces. In order to promote reproducibility, the open-access UPenn-GBM dataset is used, comprising 147 patients split into training, validation, and held-out test subsets. A K-fold cross-validation is conducted to report robust and reliable results. Additionally, a private cohort composed by 21 patients were included with the aim to test the generalization capability of the approach proposed with different unseen data. The use of SRI24 shows slight gains, with DCS values of 0.893 and 0.819 on the held-out test subsets from the UPenn-GBM and external datasets, respectively. The promising results obtained support the generalization capability of the proposed strategy with unseen data, independent of the data source, and underscore the potential of using only T1-GD sequences as the initial, fast, and simple pulse for screening patients in real-world scenarios where glioblastoma lesions are manually outlined for radiotherapy. Reducing the number of MRI sequences needed decreases acquisition time and improves patients' well-being, while also reducing computational cost.

Keywords: Magnetic resonance imaging · deep learning · segmentation · glioblastoma

© The Author(s), under exclusive license to Springer Nature Switzerland AG 2026
J. M. Ferrández Vicente et al. (Eds.): IWINAC 2026, LNCS 16575, pp. 43–52, 2026.
https://doi.org/10.1007/978-3-032-27317-8_5

1   Introduction

The term "glioma" encompasses all tumors thought to be of glial cell origin. Adult-type diffuse gliomas are the majority of primary brain tumors in neuro-oncology practice for adults [11], with grades I and II classified as low-grade gliomas and grades III and IV as high-grade gliomas. Glioblastoma (GBM) corresponds to the grade IV diffuse glioma, which is the most common and lethal tumor of the central nervous system (CNS) in adults [10,15]. The GBM region is challenging and complex because it is characterized by distinct subregions: the necrotic tumor core (NCR), the enhancing tumor (ET), and the edema (ED). A precise delineation of these regions is crucial for an accurate measurement of tumor volume, which is essential for diagnosis, disease monitoring, planning treatment strategy, and machine configuration. Magnetic resonance imaging (MRI) plays a crucial role in all aspects of glioblastoma disease care, from initial diagnosis to post-treatment follow-up, providing vital information for informed medical decision-making. Manual outlining of GBM tumors on MRI scans is a demanding, labor-intensive task for clinicians. However, deep learning (DL) methods are widely applied in various medical image analysis tasks, including classification, detection, and segmentation. DL-based solutions enable automated, accurate detection of regions of interest, facilitating objective, reproducible measurements to reduce time costs and support shared clinical decision-making [13].

U-Net-based architectures are the predominant segmentation architectures in computer vision, including medical imaging. In the brain tumor segmentation task, Yadav *et al.* [19] proposed the Modified Recurrent Residual Attention U-Net, employing attention gates rather than skip connections to enhance feature refinement, thereby improving 2D diffuse glioma segmentation with a Dice Similarity Coefficient (DSC) of 0.934, although there is a lack of distinction of MRI sequences. Xing *et al.* [18] proposed MSAM, a 2D approach, for segmenting brain tumors across different sequences, achieving a DSC of around 0.80.

Wang *et al.* [17]presented a modified version of the 3D U-Net, introducing a multi-scale fusion attention mechanism and a combination of Dice and Focal loss functions, achieving a DSC of 0.751 for diffuse glioma segmentation. Gou *et al.* [6] introduced the 3D FusionNet for glioblastoma segmentation, an approach that combines the U-Net and SegNet architectures, achieving better results than either architecture separately, with a DSC of around 0.7 using FLAIR, T1w, and T1-GD sequences, and 0.49 using just T1-GD. Although some 3D CNN-based solutions have been proposed, the nnU-Net architecture [7,9] is currently the state-of-the-art method. Isensee *et al.* [8] evaluated the vanilla nnU-Net in the brain tumor segmentation task, providing a benchmark. Gangon *et al.* [4] applied the nnU-Net model for GBM segmentation, studying several MRI sequences as input with a 0.79 of DCS in a private dataset.

In spite of each of these approaches offers unique contributions, it also exhibits certain limitations, such as 2D segmentation, the use of private cohorts, and the study of a wider variety of brain tumors, but a scarce exploration of performance in glioblastoma.

Since MRIs are volumetric, it is natural to exploit their spatial information using 3D models to obtain a volumetric tumor mask. In this study, we address

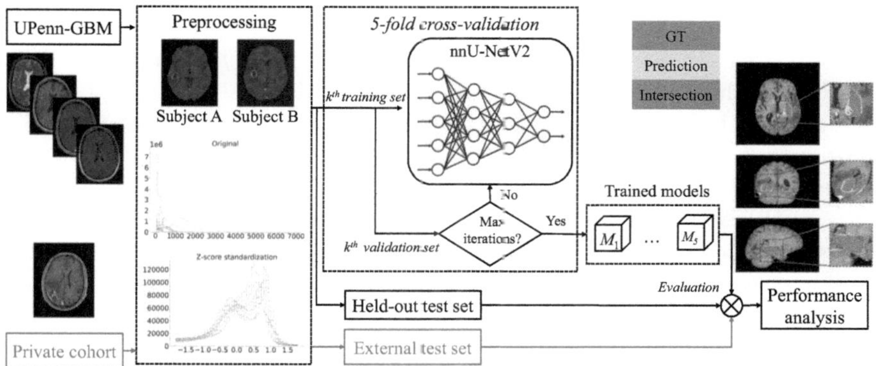

Fig. 1. Overall methodology.

3D GMB lesion segmentation in T1-GD MRI scans using the nnU-Net [9] architecture. This work examines the effect of preprocessing on the nnU-Net model for 3D segmentation and classification of GBM in MRI scans from the open-access UPenn-GBM dataset [1], also validates the effectiveness of using a single MRI sequence –T1-GD–, and externally validates the model on a private cohort. The main contributions of the work are:

- A new comprehensive analysis of patients to improve 3D segmentation of the GBM-affected region using only the T1-GD MRI scans.
- The use of UPenn-GBM dataset [1], which is one of the most remarkable open-access resources for glioblastoma research due to its multimodal, large collection of patients, and integrated nature [3] to promote reproducibility.
- Findings demonstrate the robustness of the proposed method with unseen data under domain shifts, as supported by an external private cohort.

The remainder of this work is structured as follows: first, Sect. 2 details the proposal; next, Sect. 3 explains the experiments carried out and results obtained to validate our proposal; finally, Sect. 4 states the main findings and conclusions.

2   Methodology

In this section, the methodology followed is described, including the source data description and the approaches employed to study and enhance 3D GBM segmentation. The overall methodology implemented is depicted in Fig. 1.

2.1   Datasets

The GBM region presents distinct subregions: the necrotic tumor core (NCR), the enhancing tumor (ET), and the surrounding edema (ED). For the evaluation of the GBM outline, different MRI sequences –T1-weighted, T2-weighted,

Fluid Attenuated Inversion Recovery (FLAIR), and T1-GD (with gadolinium contrast)– are used. Each MRI sequence has specific characteristics that allow for a more comprehensive evaluation of tumors. T1-GD is a fast, basic MRI sequence used in medical follow-ups as an initial screening to monitor tumor progression and evaluate signs of progression. T1-GD highlights tumor regions with increased vascularization or bloodbrain barrier disruption, enabling the detection of the most active lesion areas. It is particularly valuable for tumor assessment, i.e., ET and NCR subregions. For these reasons, the study is conducted to analyze the effectiveness of the T1-GD sequence and to develop cost-efficient 3D segmentation methods in a clinical setting where manual outlining for radiotherapy planning is highly time-consuming.

2.1.1 Open-Access Dataset. The UPenn-GBM dataset, provided by the University of Pennsylvania Health System [1], consists of various MRI scans – T1-w, T2-w, FLAIR, and T1-GD – from 611 patients diagnosed with glioblastoma. In addition to the MRI scans, the dataset includes multiclass glioblastoma segmentations, performed both automatically and manually by experts. The manual segmentations from 147 patients are considered the ground Truth (GT) and only they are used in the present study. The annotated regions correspond to enhancing tumor (ET), necrotic tumor core (NCR), and edema (ED). Since ET and NCR are visible in T1-Gd scans, the mask was binarized to differentiate between non-lesional areas and the tumor region (ET+NCR). This dataset was split into training (80%) and a held-out test (20%) subsets, each composed of 117 and 30 patients, respectively.

2.1.2 Private Cohort. In addition to the UPenn-GBM dataset, a second dataset was provided with the main objective of serving as external validation of the trained models to evaluate the method's robustness, suitability, and generalization capability under domain-shift conditions. The private cohort comprises T1-GD MRI sequences acquired at the time of initial diagnosis from 21 patients at the Hospital Universitario Virgen de la Macarena (Seville, Spain), each with manual segmentation of the glioblastoma regions by experts. The studies were conducted in accordance with local legislation and institutional requirements, and patient consent was waived because this is a retrospective observational study with anonymized image data.

2.2 Preprocessing

Preprocessing is an essential step in the MRI scans analysis, as it improves data quality and facilitates subsequent analysis. Original MRIs may be affected by various factors, such as noise, intensity variations, and other artifacts coming from the use of different resonance machines or between sequences from the same patients, due to their positions or movements. The goal of preprocessing is to correct these imperfections to obtain more homogeneous and comparable images intra- and inter-patient. The preprocessing steps are the following:

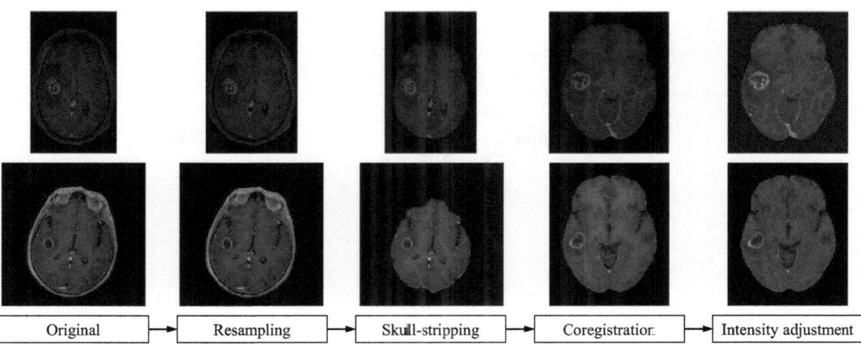

Fig. 2. Preprocessing pipeline over two subjects from the private cohort. Intensity values are unmodified for visualization purposes.

1. Resampling modifies voxel size in medical images to standardize spatial resolution across scans, ensuring uniform resolution for segmentation models.
2. Skull-tripping removes non-brain tissues during MRI preprocessing to ensure anonymity, as structures like the skull can add noise and reduce accuracy. A UNet-based brain extraction algorithm from the ANTs library was employed, utilizing a template-based registration approach to differentiate the brain from surrounding tissues [16].
3. Coregistration involved spatially aligning images to a standardized anatomical space, which is crucial for guaranteeing reliable inter-subject comparisons. For this purpose, the MNI152 [12] and SRI24 [14] templates were utilized. The ANTs library, applying the "SyN" transformation, was employed for precise alignment while maintaining individual brain morphology.
4. Intensity regularization is essential, since MRI sequences come from different resonance machines, to ensure intensity values are within the same dynamic range and to align histograms. To address this issue, the Z-score standardization was applied:

$$I_{zs} = \frac{I - \mu}{\sigma} \tag{1}$$

where μ and σ are the mean and the standard deviation of the intensity values, respectively.

The preprocessing pipeline is depicted in Fig. 2. For the UPenn-GBM dataset, only coregistration and intensity standardization were applied, as resampling and skull stripping had already been applied to the published data. For the private cohort, the complete preprocessing pipeline was applied.

2.3 Experiment Setup

The nnU-Netv2 [7,9] was selected because it is the DL-based benchmark for medical image segmentation. The default configuration (`3d_fullres`) was selected,

Table 1. Summary of model configurations used for training.

Strategy	Sequence	Atlas	Data Augmentation
A	T1-w	MNI152	✓
B	T1-GD	MNI152	✗
C	T1-GD	MNI152	✓
D	T1-GD	SRI24	✓

which automatically defines all settings and hyperparameters based on hardware resources and the input data, with 100 training epochs. The reported study was conducted on an NVIDIA RTX 4060 8 GB GPU.

To ensure reliable and robust results analysis, the K-fold cross-validation scheme, with $K = 5$, was used in order to provide results independent of the partition. The training set (80% of the original dataset, i.e., 117 patients) was split into five folds. In each iteration, one fold is used as a validation subset and four as a training subset.

For the evaluation of segmentation performance, the similarity between the predicted segmentation mask, Pr, and the ground truth, Gt, is quantified by the Dice Similarity Coefficient (DSC) [2], which is computed as follows:

$$\text{DSC} = \frac{2 \cdot |Pr \cap Gt|}{|Pr| + |Gt|} = \frac{2 \cdot TP}{2 \cdot TP + FP + FN}, \tag{2}$$

where $|Pr|$ and $|Gt|$ denote the cardinalities (number of voxels) of the predicted and ground truth segmentation masks, respectively, $|P \cap G|$ is the number of voxels correctly classified as part of the lesion; and TP, FP, and FN represent the true positive, false positive, and false negative voxels, respectively. A DSC of 1 indicates perfect overlap, while a value of 0 denotes no overlap.

The comparison analyzed is based on different preprocessed inputs. The proposed strategies are described as follows:

A. The model was trained exclusively with non-contrast T1-w MRI sequences registered to the MNI152 atlas to evaluate its performance in clinical settings with limited resources, where additional modalities are unavailable. This allows for assessing the feasibility of segmenting GBM using only T1-w as a baseline, which is particularly relevant in centers without access to multi-modal studies.
B. The contrast-enhanced gadolinium with T1 (T1-GD) sequences registered to the MNI152 atlas were used. By default, nnU-Net applies data augmentation [5] to improve generalization and reduce overfitting. In this case, it was intentionally disabled to assess its impact on glioblastoma segmentation.
C. The T1-GD sequences registered to the MNI152 atlas were used with the data augmentation option from nnU-Net enable.
D. The T1-GD sequences registered to the SRI24 atlas. The aim was to evaluate whether adopting an anatomical reference space could improve model performance

Table 1 summarizes the detailed configurations for each strategy proposed to address the GBM segmentation.

3 Results

Table 2 reports DCS values per fold for each input configuration in the validation subset, the held-out test set, and in the private cohort. The first remarkable finding is that T1-GD-based strategies –B, C and D– outperform the T1-based strategy (A), supporting the notion that contrast-enhanced sequence is more suitable for outlining glioblastoma. Between T1-GS strategies, D exceeds, followed by strategy C. The use of internal augmentation data from nnU-NetV2

Table 2. Dice Similarity Coefficient (DSC) for each model configuration obtained across all folds in the K-fold cross-validation, including the mean and standard deviation (Std). *Val* and *Test* results correspond to the validation and held-out test from the open-access UPenn-GBM dataset, respectively. *Shift* corresponds to evaluation on the private cohort under domain shift. Best values are indicated in **bold**.

	A			B			C			D		
Fold	Val	Test	Shift	Val	Test	Shift	Val	Test	Shift	Val	Test	Shift
0	0.638	0.750	0.444	0.790	0.862	0.716	0.833	0.877	0.814	0.902	0.892	0.817
1	0.622	0.764	0.540	0.805	0.868	0.736	0.825	0.879	0.817	0.920	0.895	0.829
2	0.718	0.733	0.395	0.823	0.864	0.648	0.834	0.893	0.771	0.911	0.893	0.815
3	0.717	0.777	0.409	0.837	0.859	0.710	0.835	0.885	0.784	0.864	0.890	0.811
4	0.641	0.741	0.449	0.806	0.863	0.703	0.832	0.896	0.818	0.841	0.897	0.823
Mean	0.667	0.753	0.447	0.812	0.863	0.703	0.852	0.886	0.801	**0.887**	**0.893**	**0.819**
Std	0.042	0.016	0.050	**0.016**	0.003	0.029	0.027	0.008	0.020	0.030	**0.002**	**0.006**

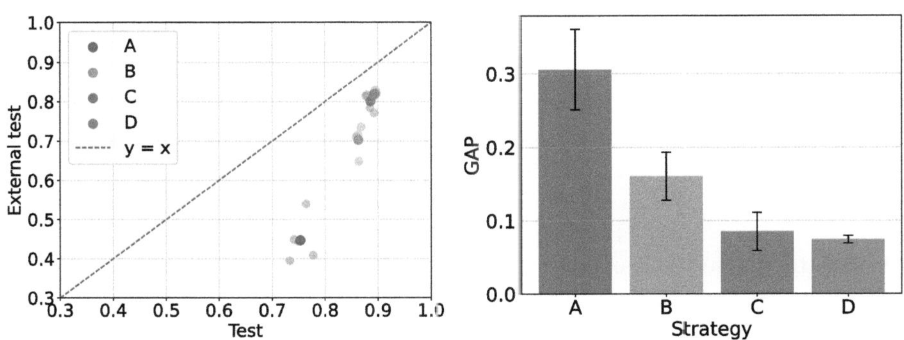

Fig. 3. Left: Trade-off between DCS values from the UPenn-GBM held-out test and the external cohort for each strategy, indicated by different colors. Lighter colors show DCS values for each fold, while darker colors represent the mean. Right: The mean and standard deviation of the GAP, i.e., the difference between the two held-out test subsets across all proposed strategies.

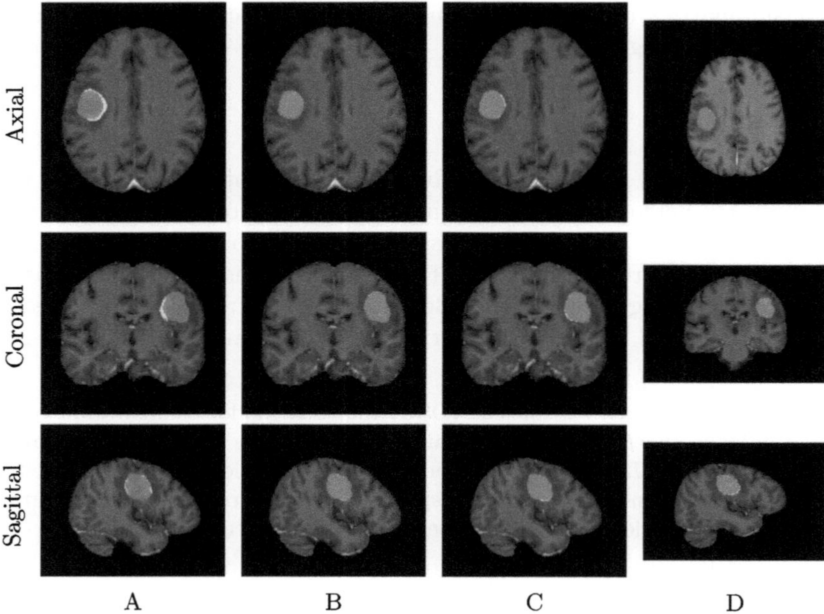

Axial   Coronal   Sagittal

A   B   C   D

Fig. 4. Prediction example from the private cohort dataset across strategies, where the ground truth mask, predicted mask, and the intersection of both masks are represented in blue, yellow, and green, respectively. (Color figure online)

enhances the network's ability to learn more efficiently GBM lesions. Additionally, incorporating the SRI24 template results in a slight improvement in performance, yielding a DCS score of 0.893 on unseen data from the same dataset and 0.819 on unseen data from other institutions and region. This demonstrates the generalization capability of the method. To illustrate the effectiveness of generalization capability with unseen data, Fig. 3 is included, showing the balance between both test subsets.

In Fig. 3 (left), the DCS values –both individually and as the mean per fold – are plotted for all strategies using the external test (y-axis) and the UPenn-GBM held-out test (x-axis). The closer the points are to the diagonal, the more balanced the outcomes are, and the closer they are to the top-right corner, the higher the performance. However, in Fig. 3 (right), the mean of the difference between the two test subsets is reported. As previously mentioned, the D and C – T1-GD sequences and data augmentation strategies have greater generalization capability. Their outcomes not only exhibit the highest performance in each partition but also demonstrate more stable behavior (lower standard deviation), regardless of the input data source.

A qualitative example of results is depicted in Fig. 4 where the ground truth mask and the prediction mask per strategy are overlaid. Besides the difference between MNI152 (A to C strategies) and SRI24 (strategy D) spaces, it can be seen how the T1w MRI sequence (strategy A) is insufficient to predict the necrotic core of the GBM, so most of the lesion is unpredicted (blue). However, using only T1-GD, a simple, fast acquisition, yields excellent quantitative and qualitative results, as shown in columns C and D, where most of the tumor mass is predicted (green).

4   Conclusions

This work presents a comprehensive study of the feasibility of using only T1-GD MRI sequences for 3D glioblastoma segmentation. The experiments conducted across the proposed strategies for the segmentation task indicate that the most suitable strategy is to use the T1-GD sequence registered to the SRI24 space, together with nnU-Net data augmentation. Due to promising results, with a DCS above 0.8 in both validation and held-out test sets, it has been demonstrated that the effectiveness with unseen data, specifically in scenarios involving a domain shift, such as GBM cases from different hospitals and resonance machines. The proposed method for glioblastoma segmentation can be extremely useful in a clinical setting. This segmentation aids in planning more effective radiotherapy, as the glioblastoma must be manually outlined, regardless of the data source.

Future work should explore additional segmentation architectures, such as transformer-based or hybrid models, and focus on improving GBM performance through hyperparameter optimization algorithms or data augmentation techniques with generative models (e.g., diffusion models or GAN-based methods) to enhance results in GBM cases.

Acknowledgments. This work is partially supported by the Autonomous Government of Andalusia (Spain) under projects UMA20-FEDERJA-108 and PPRO-TIC163-G-2023 (TIC163-G-FEDER); also by the Ministry of Science and Innovation of Spain, grant number PID2022-136764OA-I00. It includes funds from the European Regional Development Fund (ERDF). It is also partially supported by the Fundación Unicaja under project PUNI-003_2023, the IBIMA Plataforma BIONAND under project ATECH-25-02, and the Instituto de Salud Carlos III, project code PI25/02129 (co-financed by the European Union). The authors thankfully acknowledge the computer resources, technical expertise and assistance provided by the SCBI (Supercomputing and Bioinformatics) center of the University of Málaga.

Data Availability. The UPenn-GBM dataset [1] is an open-access dataset available at the The Cancer Imaging Archive (TCIA) repository at: https://doi.org/10.7937/TCIA.709X-DN49. The private cohort is unavailable for privacy reasons.

References

1. Bakas, S., et al.: The university of pennsylvania glioblastoma (upenn-gbm) cohort: advanced MRI, clinical, genomics, & radiomics. Sci. Data **9**(1), 453 (2022)
2. Dice, L.R.: Measures of the amount of ecologic association between species. Ecology **26**(3), 297–302 (1945)

3. Dorfner, F.J., Patel, J.B., Kalpathy-Cramer, J., Gerstner, E.R., Bridge, C.P.: A review of deep learning for brain tumor analysis in MRI. NPJ Precis. Oncol. **9**(1), 2 (2025)
4. Gagnon, L., et al.: Deep learning segmentation of infiltrative and enhancing cellular tumor at pre-and posttreatment multishell diffusion MRI of glioblastoma. Radiol. Artif. Intell. **6**(5), e230489 (2024)
5. Gamco: Aumento de datos - glosario. https://gamco.es/glosario/aumento-de-datos/
6. Guo, X., Zhang, B., Peng, Y., Chen, F., Li, W.: Segmentation of glioblastomas via 3d fusionnet. Front. Oncol. **14**, 1488616 (2024)
7. Isensee, F., Jaeger, P.F., Kohl, S.A., Petersen, J., Maier-Hein, K.H.: nnu-net: a self-configuring method for deep learning-based biomedical image segmentation. Nat. Methods **18**(2), 203–211 (2021)
8. Isensee, F., Jäger, P.F., Full, P.M., Vollmuth, P., Maier-Hein, K.H.: nnU-net for brain tumor segmentation. In: Crimi, A., Bakas, S. (eds.) BrainLes 2020. LNCS, vol. 12659, pp. 118–132. Springer, Cham (2021). https://doi.org/10.1007/978-3-030-72087-2_11
9. Isensee, F., et al.: nnu-net revisited: a call for rigorous validation in 3d medical image segmentation. In: International Conference on Medical Image Computing and Computer-Assisted Intervention, pp. 488–498. Springer, Heidelberg (2024). https://doi.org/10.1007/978-3-031-72114-4_47
10. Komori, T.: Update of the 2021 who classification of tumors of the central nervous system: adult diffuse gliomas. Brain Tumor Pathol. **40**(1), 1–3 (2023)
11. Louis, D.N., et al.: The 2021 who classification of tumors of the central nervous system: a summary. Neuro Oncol. **23**(8), 1231–1251 (2021)
12. Mazziotta, J., et al.: A probabilistic atlas and reference system for the human brain: international consortium for brain mapping (ICBM). Phil. Trans. Roy. Soc. Lond. Ser. B: Biol. Sci. **356**(1412), 1293–1322 (2001)
13. Rasool, N., Bhat, J.I.: A critical review on segmentation of glioma brain tumor and prediction of overall survival. Arch. Comput. Methods Eng. **32**(3), 1525–1569 (2025)
14. Rohlfing, T., Zahr, N.M., Sullivan, E.V., Pfefferbaum, A.: The sri24 multichannel atlas of normal adult human brain structure. Hum. Brain Mapp. **31**(5), 798–819 (2010)
15. Schwartzbaum, J.A., Fisher, J.L., Aldape, K.D., Wrensch, M.: Epidemiology and molecular pathology of glioma. Nat. Clin. Pract. Neurol. **2**(9), 494–503 (2006)
16. Tustison, N.J., et al.: The antsx ecosystem for quantitative biological and medical imaging. Sci. Rep. **11**(1), 9068 (2021)
17. Wang, T., et al.: 3d-MRI brain glioma intelligent segmentation based on improved 3d u-net network. PLoS ONE **20**(6), e0325534 (2025)
18. Xing, J., Zhang, J.: Segmentation of brain tumors using a multi-modal segment anything model (MSAM) with missing modality adaptation. Bioengineering **12**(8), 871 (2025)
19. Yadav, A.C., Kolekar, M.H., Zope, M.K.: Modified recurrent residual attention u-net model for MRI-based brain tumor segmentation. Biomed. Signal Process. Control **102**, 107220 (2025)

A Standardized Multimodal Dataset Recording Protocol for Early Cognitive Impairment Screening

David Ortiz-Perez[1] , David Mulero-Pérez[1] , David Alarcon-Garrido[1],
Laura Saval-Cillero[1], Jose Garcia-Rodriguez[1(✉)] ,
and M. Flores Vizcaya-Moreno[2]

[1] Department of Computer Technology, University of Alicante, Alicante, Spain
{dortiz,dmulero,jgarcia}@dtic.ua.es
[2] Unit of Clinical Nursing Research, University of Alicante, Alicante, Spain
flores.vizcaya@ua.es

Abstract. We present a standardized protocol and dataset design for
multimodal acquisition in older adults with suspected cognitive impairment, aimed at supporting early identification research and data-intensive
machine learning. The protocol combines four time-bounded discourse
elicitation tasks, personal narrative, picture description, story narration,
and procedural discourse, to capture complementary linguistic and cognitive demands. Speech is recorded with an external microphone and transcribed to provide aligned audiotext modalities, while an RGB camera facing the participant records facial behavior to enable analysis of nonverbal
cues. In addition, we integrate an immersive VR/MR serious-game module inspired by our HoloDemTect framework, including daily-life activities such as a shopping-list task that requires selecting target items and
placing them into a box. The VR/MR environment is fully instrumented
to retain fine-grained telemetry (e g., completion times, step-level latencies, interaction events, and error patterns), and gaze-related measures are
recorded when supported by the hardware. To provide clinically meaningful reference outcomes for operational stratification and downstream
classification, each session includes a brief self-assessment of cognition
and instrumental functioning using Test Your Memory and the Lawton
& Brody IADL scale. Overall, the protocol yields a structurally complete
and diverse dataset that enables joint analyses of speech, language, facial
behavior, and immersive task performance, addressing common unimodal-
ity constraints in existing resources and facilitating multimodal deep learning baselines and future benchmarking.

Keywords: Cognitive Impairment · Dataset Protocol · Multimodal
Data · Serious Games

1 Introduction

Cognitive impairment is a major and growing public health challenge, driven
largely by population aging. It is associated with a progressive loss of independence, a substantial burden on caregivers, and rising health-system costs.

J. M. Ferrández Vicente et al. (Eds.): IWINAC 2026, LNCS 16575, pp. 53–62, 2026.
https://doi.org/10.1007/978-3-032-27317-8_6

Although some decline in cognitive function is expected with age, a more pronounced deterioration may indicate underlying pathological conditions such as Alzheimer's disease or mild cognitive impairment (MCI) [20]. The World Health Organization estimates that 57 million people were living with dementia worldwide in 2021, with nearly 10 million new cases each year [21]. Dementia is also among the leading causes of disability and dependency in older adults. As societies continue to age and these conditions disproportionately affect older individuals, there is an urgent need for scalable approaches that enable early identification and accurate characterization across the cognitive aging [16].

Early identification of cognitive decline has become a societal priority, since it can enable timely support, future planning, and safer care pathways while health and social care systems face rapidly increasing demand. The 2024 Lancet Standing Commission emphasizes that a substantial proportion of dementia burden is potentially preventable or delayable through modifiable risk factors across the life course, which makes scalable approaches to earlier detection and risk stratification particularly valuable for targeting interventions and monitoring outcomes at the population level [12]. At the same time, diagnostic pathways remain slow in real-world settings, with an estimated average time to diagnosis of about 3.5 years from symptom onset, underscoring the need for practical screening and characterization protocols that can shorten delays and support earlier access to appropriate care [8].

Recent advances in deep learning have accelerated research on the early detection of cognitive impairment by enabling the end-to-end modeling of subtle, high-dimensional patterns in behavioral signals such as speech and language. For instance, multimodal approaches that fuse complementary cues (e.g., acoustic features and lexical content) have been shown to improve automated dementia screening on established speech-elicitation paradigms [7,19]. However, the effectiveness of these methods depends critically on the datasets used for training and validation. Robust early-stage classification requires diverse, well-annotated data spanning multiple channels and contexts, yet the field still faces a limited availability of consistent multimodal resources [6,18]. As a result, many studies rely on constrained, single-modality corpora. This reliance on unimodal data is often driven by privacy and re-identification concerns associated with rich recordings, particularly video, which can necessitate restricted sharing and controlled-access governance for clinical communication datasets, thereby limiting broader reuse and reproducibility.

To address these limitations, we propose a standardized multimodal dataset and acquisition protocol for older adults with suspected cognitive impairment, designed to support both early screening research and data-intensive deep learning. The speech component includes four complementary discourse tasks, picture description, narrative retell, personal narrative, and procedural discourse, chosen to elicit partially distinct linguistic and cognitive demands and to maximize comparability with established TalkBank protocols [9]. All audio recordings will be transcribed to produce a parallel text modality, enabling multimodal modeling with speech and transcripts as commonly adopted in recent dementia detection studies [11]. To enable operational stratification and downstream classification, each recording session is paired with brief validated measures capturing both cognition and functional independence: the Spanish validation of the self-administered Test Your Memory (TYM) [2] provides education-adjusted cut-offs with strong screening performance for cognitive impairment and dementia, and the Spanish validation of the Lawton and Brody Instrumental Activities of Daily Living (IADL) scale [10] offers excellent reliability and construct validity for instrumental functioning [4]. In addition, an RGB camera records the participant's face to capture facial behavior and subtle affective cues that have been explored as potential markers in MCI and Alzheimer's disease using automated facial analysis [5]. Finally, we record performance in serious-game tasks delivered through virtual-reality techniques, where behavioral logs such as completion times and error patterns can be combined with eye-tracking measures (e.g., gaze allocation and fixation stability) to characterize attention and interaction; importantly, VR-based game interventions have also been investigated as engaging training and simulation tools for older adults with MCI, supporting both assessment and rehabilitation-oriented use cases [14].

The remainder of this paper is organized as follows: Sect. 2 presents a review of related work; Sect. 3 details the proposed protocol methodology; Sect. 4 provides a qualitative assessment of the key advantages of this protocol; and finally, Sect. 5 presents conclusions from this work.

2   Related Work

Prior research on language-based markers of cognitive decline has been strongly shaped by shared community resources that standardize discourse elicitation and transcription. DementiaBank [9] was developed to support reproducible analyses of discourse changes in MCI and dementia due to Alzheimer's disease. It provides a carefully designed protocol encompassing multiple discourse genres (picture description, story narrative, procedural discourse, and personal narrative), alongside guidance to minimize examiner speech and improve transcription quality. Our protocol deliberately aligns with this approach in its discourse component to maximize comparability, while extending it through additional modalities and task contexts intended to capture complementary behavioral signals.

Within deep learning research, many influential results have been built on constrained speech corpora derived from DementiaBank, particularly the Pitt corpus [1] and the ADReSS challenge [13]. ADReSS standardized and balanced the data by age and gender and focused primarily on the Cookie Theft picture-description task, becoming a widely used benchmark for automated Alzheimer's Disease (AD) versus control classification and related prediction tasks. While this benchmarking has improved methodological comparability, it has also concentrated evidence on a narrow elicitation setting and, in many cases, a single modality. This focus can limit generalizability across discourse types, interaction contexts, and the diverse behavioral manifestations of early cognitive impairment.

Beyond speech and text, several lines of research motivate the inclusion of additional behavioral modalities. Recent studies have shown that facial behavior extracted from conversational video, using facial action units, affective measures, or learned embeddings, can help discriminate dementia and MCI, often with strong reported performance [17]. These findings suggest that subtle nonverbal cues may provide information complementary to language. This evidence supports our decision to capture an RGB facial video stream during discourse tasks as a potential source of micro-behavioral and affective markers that are not recoverable from audio alone.

Finally, serious games and virtual reality (VR) have been explored both as assessment-like environments that generate fine-grained behavioral logs and as engaging training or simulation tools for older adults, including individuals with MCI. A recent meta-analysis of randomized trials reports cognitive benefits of VR-based interventions across multiple neuropsychiatric conditions, including significant effects in MCI subgroups, supporting the plausibility and acceptability of VR paradigms in this population [3]. Building on this evidence, our protocol records VR serious-game interactions and associated behavioral telemetry (e.g., response times and error patterns), and, where available, gaze-derived measures, with the aim of enriching early-identification research through ecologically grounded, high-resolution behavioral data.

3   Methodology

The proposed methodology is organized as an end-to-end acquisition and annotation pipeline that integrates complementary sources of evidence about cognition, function, communication, and behavior. As summarized in Fig. 1, each session combines structured participant profiling with controlled elicitation tasks and multimodal sensing, followed by brief reference measures that support operational stratification for subsequent modeling.

3.1   Participants

The study targets older adults with suspected cognitive impairment, including individuals with profiles consistent with mild cognitive impairment and mild dementia, as well as cognitively unimpaired controls when available. Participants are recruited through clinical and community pathways (e.g., memory clinics, neurology and geriatrics services, and local outreach initiatives), aiming to reflect typical real-world referral populations. All participants must be able to understand and follow study instructions in the study language(s) and tolerate the recording setup (seated facial video recording, audio capture, and VR tasks).

Eligibility criteria are designed to support reliable multimodal acquisition and interpretation. Inclusion criteria include age above a predefined threshold (e.g., ≥ 55 years), willingness to participate with informed consent, and sufficient sensory and motor capacity to complete the discourse tasks and interact with the VR environment. As part of enrollment, participants complete a

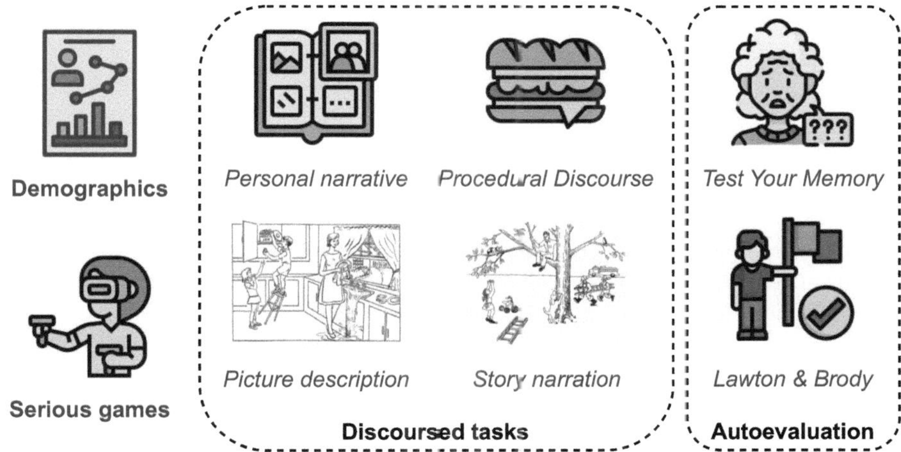

Fig. 1. Overview of the proposed protocol. The pipeline comprises demographic profiling, four discourse elicitation tasks (personal narrative, picture description, story narration, and procedural discourse), VR-based serious games, and self-evaluation using TYM and Lawton & Brody to obtain cognitive and instrumental functional measures.

structured demographics form to capture key background variables required for downstream analyses, including age, sex, years of formal education, language background, handedness, and relevant hearing or vision limitations, along with other contextual factors that may influence task performance.

3.2 Recording Protocol

All sessions are recorded using a standardized capture setup to ensure consistent signal quality across participants and tasks. During the discourse block, participants are seated facing an RGB camera positioned directly in front of them. The camera is framed on the face to support subsequent analysis of facial behavior (e.g., micro-expressions and other subtle nonverbal cues) alongside speech. Speech is recorded in parallel using an external microphone, providing a high-quality audio channel suitable for downstream acoustic analysis and manual or semi-automatic transcription. To facilitate transcription and minimize overlap, examiner speech is kept to a minimum, and non-verbal backchanneling is used whenever possible.

The virtual-reality serious-game block is instrumented to preserve all available telemetry and task-derived metrics produced by the VR environment. At a minimum, these data include fine-grained behavioral logs such as completion times, response latencies, error patterns, and interaction events. When supported by the VR hardware and software stack, additional streams (e.g., gaze-derived measures) are recorded and synchronized with task events. The resulting multimodal package, audio, facial video, and VR telemetry, is stored with consistent participant identifiers and session metadata to support subsequent multimodal modeling and reproducible analyzes.

3.3   Discoursed Tasks

The discourse module comprises four structured tasks designed to elicit complementary speech and language phenomena under controlled conditions, while remaining feasible for older adults. The examiner follows a standardized script and minimizes verbal output during recording, using brief, non-leading prompts only when necessary to encourage continuation and maintain consistency across sessions. Each task is time-bounded to reduce fatigue and to facilitate comparable samples across participants.

Personal Narrative ($\approx$ 4 min). Participants are asked to speak in an openended manner about a familiar autobiographical topic (e.g., their hometown). This task is intended to elicit spontaneous, self-generated discourse with minimal external constraints, capturing narrative organization, lexical access, and coherence in a personally meaningful context.

Picture Description ($\approx$ 3 min). Participants describe a standard visual scene (Cookie Theft). This task provides a constrained yet naturalistic elicitation setting that supports comparability with prior work while probing visual attention, semantic retrieval, and structured description based on a shared stimulus.

Story Narration ($\approx$ 3 min). Participants retell a short story (Cat Rescue), eliciting discourse that requires event sequencing, causal linking, and maintenance of a coherent narrative thread. This task is expected to be sensitive to difficulties in episodic organization, referential clarity, and macro-structural planning.

Procedural Discourse ($\approx$ 2 min). Participants explain how to perform a familiar everyday procedure (e.g., preparing a ham, tomato, and olive oil sandwich). Procedural discourse emphasizes planning, stepwise organization, and goal-directed language, providing a complementary perspective on executivelinguistic demands distinct from free narrative and picture description.

3.4   Serious Games

To complement the speech-based tasks, we include an immersive VR/MR serious-game module designed to elicit cognitive and functional markers under ecologically valid conditions. Building on our previous HoloDemtect mixed-reality framework [15] for cognitive stimulation through interaction with physical objects, participants perform goal-oriented activities of daily living (ADL) within a guided scenario that requires planning, attention, working memory, and error monitoring.

A representative activity simulates a shopping routine: participants are presented with a short shopping list and must select the corresponding objects from the environment and place them into a target container, following the prescribed order and any task constraints. During the task, the system can provide stepwise cues or corrective feedback when needed, allowing the same environment to support both assessment and cognitive training. The implementation follows established MR pipelines using head-mounted devices with spatial mapping and egocentric sensing (e.g., HoloLens-based interaction), enabling naturalistic object manipulation while preserving experimental control.

Importantly, this setting enables the collection of fine-grained multimodal performance signals beyond a single summary score. Recorded measures include task timing (overall completion time and step-level latencies), accuracy (omissions, substitutions, selection of distractors, and ordering errors), and interaction and attention cues available in VR/MR, such as gaze and head orientation, controller trajectories, and detailed event logs (e.g., objects touched, selected, and placed). These signals provide rich inputs for downstream modelling of cognitive status and functional impact.

3.5   Autoevaluation

At the end of each session, participants complete a brief self-assessment battery to provide reference measures of cognitive status and everyday functioning for operational stratification and downstream modeling. Cognitive screening is obtained using TYM, a short self-administered instrument that covers multiple domains with education-adjusted cut-offs reported for Spanish clinical settings.

Functional status is captured with the Lawton & Brody IADL scale, which assesses independence across eight instrumental domains and is widely used to characterize functional impact and to support distinctions between milder cognitive impairment and dementia-level functional interference. Administration times for both instruments are recorded, and responses are stored alongside session metadata to enable analyses that relate multimodal behavioral signals to cognitive and functional reference outcomes.

4   Results

The proposed acquisition protocol yields a high-value, multimodal dataset with strong potential for early cognitive impairment research. By combining four complementary discourse tasks with aligned audiotext transcription, frontal RGB facial video, and VR/MR serious-game telemetry, we capture a broad range of behavioral signals that are often studied in isolation. This design enables integrated analyses in which linguistic content, paralinguistic speech cues, facial behavior, and goal-directed interaction patterns can be examined jointly to identify convergent markers of cognitive change and functional impact.

The discourse block provides structured yet ecologically relevant speech samples across distinct communicative demands: autobiographical narration supports spontaneous, self-generated discourse; picture description anchors comparability to widely used paradigms; story narration probes narrative organization and event sequencing; and procedural discourse targets stepwise planning and executivelinguistic control. Since the audio is systematically transcribed, the dataset supports acoustic and prosodic modeling as well as text-based analyses, including fusion approaches that can explicitly test the added value of combining speech and language representations within the same elicitation conditions.

The facial video stream further enriches the dataset by enabling quantification of nonverbal cues (e.g., facial dynamics, expressivity patterns, and affective responses) that may complement speech-based markers, particularly during periods of cognitive effort, uncertainty, or retrieval difficulty. Capturing the face using a consistent frontal RGB setup also facilitates reproducible extraction of computer-vision features and aligns naturally with the temporal structure of the discourse tasks.

Finally, the VR/MR serious-game module adds a distinct behavioral layer grounded in everyday functioning. The ADL-inspired shopping-list activity yields fine-grained performance signatures beyond a single score, including step-level latencies, error types (omissions, substitutions, distractor selections), and interaction events. When available, gaze-related measures provide additional insight into attentional allocation and visual search strategies during goal-directed behavior. Together with the brief self-assessments of cognition and instrumental functioning (TYM and Lawton & Brody), these data provide a consistent reference frame for operational stratification and subsequent modeling. Overall, the resulting dataset is both multimodal and structurally complete, offering a practical foundation for benchmarking unimodal baselines and evaluating multimodal fusion methods under a controlled, reproducible protocol.

5   Conclusions

This work presents a standardized protocol for acquiring a rich multimodal dataset to support research on early cognitive impairment. By combining four complementary discourse-elicitation tasks with systematic transcription, frontal RGB facial video, and instrumented VR/MR serious-game activities, the protocol captures linguistic, paralinguistic, nonverbal, and interaction-based behavioral signals within a single, coherent session. Pairing these recordings with brief self-assessments of cognition and instrumental functioning (TYM and Lawton & Brody) further provides clinically meaningful reference measures that enable operational stratification and support downstream modeling.

The resulting dataset is intended to address key limitations of existing resources, which often rely on restricted task designs and single modalities, by providing diverse, synchronized data streams suitable for multimodal deep learning and fine-grained behavioral analysis. Future work will focus on expanding the cohort, refining annotation and quality-control pipelines (including transcription and temporal alignment), and establishing unimodal and multimodal baselines to quantify the contribution of each modality and task under robust evaluation protocols.

References

1. Becker, J.T., Boiler, F., Lopez, O.L., Saxton, J., McGonigle, K.L.: The natural history of Alzheimer's disease: description of study cohort and accuracy of diagnosis. Arch. Neurol. **51**(6), 585–594 (1994)
2. Brown, J., Pengas, G., Dawson, K., Brown, L.A., Clatworthy, P.: Self administered cognitive screening test (TYM) for detection of Alzheimer's disease: cross sectional study. BMJ **338** (2009)
3. Du, Q., et al.: Efficacy of virtual reality-based interventions on cognitive function in patients with neuropsychiatric disorders: Systematic review and meta-analysis of randomized controlled trials. JMIR Serious Games **13**(1), e67501 (2025)
4. Ferrero-Arias, J., Turrión-Rojo, M.: Validation of a Spanish version of the test your memory. Neurología (Engl. Ed.) **31**(1), 33–42 (2016)
5. Gerłowska, J., Dmitruk, K., Rejdak, K.: Facial emotion mimicry in older adults with and without cognitive impairments due to Alzheimer's disease. AIMS Neurosci. **8**(2), 226 (2021)
6. Gkoumas, D., et al.: A longitudinal multi-modal dataset for dementia monitoring and diagnosis. Lang. Res. Eval. **58**(3), 883–902 (2024)
7. Ilias, L., Askounis, D.: Multimodal deep learning models for detecting dementia from speech and transcripts. Front. Aging Neurosci. **14**, 830943 (2022)
8. Kusoro, O., Roche, M., Del-Pino-Casado, R., Leung, P., Orgeta, V.: Time to diagnosis in dementia: a systematic review with meta-analysis. Int. J. Geriatr. Psychiatry **40**(7), e70129 (2025)
9. Lanzi, A.M., Saylor, A.K., Fromm, D., Liu, H., MacWhinney, B., Cohen, M.L.: Dementiabank: theoretical rationale, protocol, and illustrative analyses. Am. J. Speech Lang. Pathol. **32**(2), 426–438 (2023)
10. Lawton, M.P., Brody, E.M.: Assessment of older people: Self-maintaining and instrumental activities of daily living_. Gerontologist **9**(3_Part_1), 179–186 (1969). https://doi.org/10.1093/geront/9.3_Part_1.179
11. Lin, K., Washington, P.Y.: Multimodal deep learning for dementia classification using text and audio. Sci. Rep. **14**(1), 13887 (2024)
12. Livingston, G., Huntley, J., Liu, K.Y., Costafreda, S.G., Selbæk, G., Alladi, S., Ames, D., Banerjee, S., Burns, A., Brayne, C., et al.: Dementia prevention, intervention, and care: 2024 report of the lancet standing commission. Lancet **404**(10452), 572–628 (2024)
13. Luz, S., Haider, F., de la Fuente, S., Fromm, D., MacWhinney, B.: Alzheimer's dementia recognition through spontaneous speech: the ADReSS Challenge. In: Interspeech 2020, pp. 2172–2176 (2020). https://doi.org/10.21437/Interspeech.2020-2571
14. Maldonado-Díaz, M., Jara-Vargas, G., González-Seguel, F.: Visual attention during non-immersive virtual reality balance training in older adults with mild to moderate cognitive impairment: an eye-tracking study. Front. Aging Neurosci. **17**, 1671477 (2025)
15. Mulero-Pérez, D., Benavent-Lledo, M., Garcia-Rodriguez, J., Azorin-Lopez, J., Vizcaya-Moreno, F.: Holodemtect: a mixed reality framework for cognitive stimulation through interaction with objects. In: 18th International Conference on Soft Computing Models in Industrial and Environmental Applications (SOCO 2023), pp. 226–235. Springer, Cham (2023). https://doi.org/10.1007/978-3-031-42536-3_22

16. Nichols, E., et al.: Estimation of the global prevalence of dementia in 2019 and forecasted prevalence in 2050: an analysis for the global burden of disease study 2019. Lancet Public Health **7**(2), e105–e125 (2022)
17. Okunishi, T., et al.: Dementia and mci detection based on comprehensive facial expression analysis from videos during conversation. IEEE J. Biomed. Health Inf. **29**(5), 3537–3548 (2025)
18. Ortiz-Perez, D., Benavent-Lledo, M., Garcia-Rodriguez, J., Tomás, D., Vizcaya-Moreno, M.F.: Deep insights into cognitive decline: a survey of leveraging non-intrusive modalities with deep learning techniques. Appl. Soft Comput. 113787 (2025)
19. Ortiz-Perez, D., Benavent-Lledo, M., Rodriguez-Juan, J., Garcia-Rodriguez, J., Tomás, D.: Cognialign: word-level multimodal speech alignment with gated cross-attention for Alzheimer's detection. Knowl.-Based Syst. 114264 (2025)
20. Roberts, R., Knopman, D.S.: Classification and epidemiology of MCI. Clin. Geriatr. Med. **29**(4), 10–1016 (2013)
21. World Health Organization: Dementia. Fact sheet (2025). https://www.who.int/news-room/fact-sheets/detail/dementia

Contrast-Focused Preprocessing for Skin Lesion Segmentation and Classification

Aboubakr Aakaou[3] , Karl Thurnhofer-Hemsi[1,2,3]($\boxtimes$) ,
and Enrique Domínguez[1,2,3]

[1] ITIS Software, Universidad de Málaga, C/Arquitecto Francisco Peñalosa 18,
29010 Málaga, Spain
{karlkhader,enriqued}@lcc.uma.es
[2] IBIMA Plataforma BIONAND, Instituto de Investigación Biomédica de Málaga,
C/ Severo Ochoa, 35, Málaga TechPark, Campanillas, 29590 Málaga, Spain
[3] Departamento de Lenguajes y Ciencias de la Computación, Universidad de Málaga,
Bulevar Louis Pasteur, 35, 29071 Málaga, Spain
aboubakr.aakaou@uma.es

Abstract. Skin cancer is one of the most common cancers globally, and early detection appreciably improves the affected person's survival. Automated skin lesion analysis, using deep learning, suggests outstanding promise; however, performance is sensitive to picture preprocessing, segmentation, and feature representation. In this observation, we compare four preprocessing pipelines on the HAM10000 dataset to identify the simplest approach for lesion segmentation and classification. Segmentation is performed using a U-Net with sonar-inspired visual enhancement and morphological post-processing. Segmented lesions are classified into seven diagnostic categories using 25 pretrained models, including CNNs, Vision Transformers, and lightweight architectures. Segmentation is evaluated with Dice, Jaccard, sensitivity, specificity, and accuracy, while classification uses precision, recall, F1-score, and accuracy. Results show that advanced preprocessing substantially improves performance, providing a robust framework for automated skin lesion analysis and highlighting the critical role of preprocessing in deep learning-based medical imaging.

Keywords: Skin lesion analysis · HAM10000 · U-Net · preprocessing pipelines · deep learning · classification · segmentation

1 Introduction

Skin cancer is among the fastest-growing cancers worldwide, with melanoma being particularly aggressive if not diagnosed early. Dermoscopy is a widely used non-invasive imaging modality; however, accurate diagnosis depends heavily on clinician expertise, leading to inter-observer variability and diagnostic errors [13,19]. Automated computer-aided diagnosis (CAD) systems have therefore emerged to support dermatologists and improve diagnostic consistency. Deep learning has transformed skin lesion analysis, with convolutional neural networks

© The Author(s), under exclusive license to Springer Nature Switzerland AG 2026
J. M. Ferrández Vicente et al. (Eds.): IWINAC 2026, LNCS 16575, pp. 63–72, 2026.
https://doi.org/10.1007/978-3-032-27317-8_7

(CNNs) outperforming traditional handcrafted approaches in segmentation and classification [9,14]. Pretrained models such as VGG, ResNet, DenseNet, and EfficientNet have been widely applied, achieving high accuracy across multiple lesion categories [2,11], while transformer-based and hybrid CNN-Transformer architectures capture global contextual information and further improve representation [4,18]. Accurate lesion segmentation is essential for enhancing classification by isolating lesion regions and suppressing background noise. U-Net and its variants remain the standard due to their encoder-decoder design and skip connections, preserving spatial details [12,17]. Segmentation-guided classification has been shown to significantly improve diagnostic accuracy compared to using raw images [16]. Dermoscopic images often suffer from noise, illumination variation, low contrast, and occlusions from hair or air bubbles. Preprocessing techniques such as hair removal, CLAHE, color normalization, and texture enhancement can mitigate these challenges [5], but most studies rely on a single strategy, limiting understanding of how different pipelines affect segmentation and classification [3]. A systematic evaluation of multiple preprocessing pipelines is therefore needed to improve model robustness and generalization [7,15], yet comprehensive frameworks combining preprocessing, segmentation, and large-scale classification remain scarce [6,13]. Motivated by these limitations, this paper proposes a multi-pipeline deep learning framework for skin lesion segmentation and seven-class classification. Four preprocessing pipelines are systematically evaluated to analyze their impact on segmentation and classification performance. Lesion segmentation is performed using a U-Net architecture with post-processing refinement, and the segmented lesions are classified using 25 pretrained deep learning models. Through extensive experimental evaluation, this study aims to identify the most effective preprocessing strategy and provide a robust and reproducible framework for automated skin lesion analysis.

2   Related Works

Research on automated skin lesion analysis has evolved rapidly over the past decade, driven by advances in medical imaging and deep learning. Early studies relied on handcrafted features such as color descriptors, texture patterns, and shape metrics combined with classical machine learning classifiers, achieving moderate success but lacking robustness to variations in illumination, contrast, and lesion morphology [19]. With the advent of deep learning, convolutional neural networks (CNNs) became the dominant paradigm for skin lesion classification. Pretrained CNN architectures significantly outperform traditional methods by learning discriminative features directly from dermoscopic images [14]. Models such as VGG, ResNet, and DenseNet have been widely adopted and fine-tuned for multi-class classification, yielding high accuracy [2,11], while modern architectures like EfficientNet and lightweight CNNs balance accuracy and computational efficiency [1,16]. Lesion segmentation is a crucial preprocessing step for improving classification performance. U-Net and its variants are standard for segmentation due to their encoder-decoder design and skip connections that preserve spatial information [12,17]. Segmentation-guided classification reduces background interference and enhances accuracy [10], with post-processing techniques such as morphological operations further refining lesion boundaries [6]. Preprocessing addresses challenges in dermoscopic images, including hair occlusion, uneven illumination, and low contrast. Approaches include hair removal, CLAHE, color normalization, and texture enhancement [5,20]. Texture-based techniques like wavelet transforms and Gabor filtering highlight structural patterns [18], yet most studies adopt a single preprocessing strategy, limiting insights into comparative effectiveness. Transformer-based and hybrid CNN-Transformer architectures have gained attention for capturing long-range dependencies and global context [3,4]. Although promising, their performance remains sensitive to image quality and preprocessing [15], and comprehensive studies evaluating multiple preprocessing pipelines with large sets of pretrained models remain scarce [8,13]. In summary, existing research has demonstrated the effectiveness of deep learning for skin lesion segmentation and classification. However, there is a lack of unified frameworks that systematically compare multiple image preprocessing pipelines while jointly evaluating segmentation performance and large-scale multi-model classification. This work addresses this gap by proposing a comprehensive multi-pipeline framework and conducting an extensive evaluation using four preprocessing strategies, U-Net segmentation, and 25 pretrained classification models.

3   Methodology

This study proposes a multi-stage deep learning framework for robust skin lesion segmentation and seven-class classification. The framework consists of four main stages: image preprocessing, lesion segmentation, post-processing refinement, and lesion classification, as illustrated in Fig. 1. The primary objective is to systematically evaluate how different preprocessing strategies influence segmentation quality and classification performance and to identify an optimal preprocessing configuration for dermoscopic image analysis.

To analyze the effect of preprocessing on model performance, four distinct preprocessing pipelines were designed and evaluated. Each pipeline aims to enhance lesion visibility, reduce artifacts, and preserve diagnostically relevant features. All pipelines include image resizing and intensity normalization, while additional enhancement techniques progressively increase in complexity. The comparison across pipelines is presented in Fig. 2. Pipeline 1 serves as a baseline configuration. All images are resized to 256×256 pixels using bilinear interpolation to ensure uniform spatial dimensions and reduce computational complexity. Pixel intensities are then scaled to the $[0, 1]$ range, providing numerical stability during model training. This pipeline represents the minimal preprocessing strategy. Pipeline 2 extends the baseline by incorporating artifact removal and contrast correction. Hair artifacts are removed using a morphological black-hat transformation with a 17×17 elliptical structuring element, followed by Telea inpainting (radius $= 5$). White balance correction reduces illumination-induced

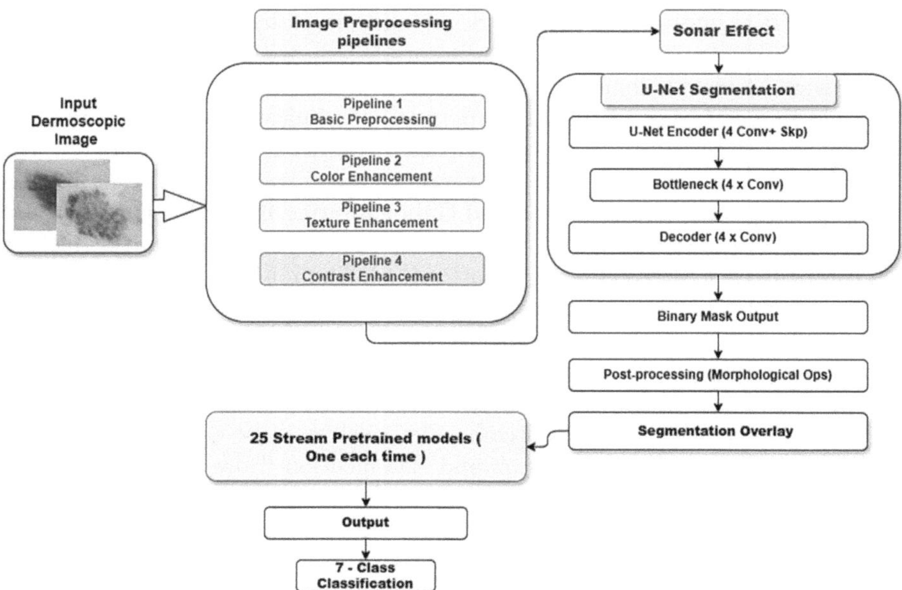

Fig. 1. Multi-stage skin lesion analysis with enhanced preprocessing, segmentation, and classification modules.

color bias, and CLAHE (clipLimit = 2.0, tileGridSize = 8 × 8) enhances local contrast while limiting noise amplification. The images are finally normalized to [0,1]. Pipeline 3 introduces advanced texture enhancement. After resizing and hair removal, a bilateral filter (d = 9, sigmaColor = 75, sigmaSpace = 75) suppresses noise while preserving lesion boundaries. Wavelet-based enhancement strengthens multi-scale texture details, and a Gabor filter bank extracts directional frequency patterns. Unsharp masking further improves edge sharpness before normalization. Pipeline 4 combines resizing, DullRazor-based hair removal, and CLAHE enhancement (clipLimit = 2.0) followed by normalization. This pipeline focuses on strong contrast enhancement while maintaining structural integrity, producing high-quality inputs suitable for downstream segmentation and classification tasks.

As illustrated in Fig. 3, the preprocessed dermoscopic images are forwarded to a U-Net-based segmentation module composed of an encoder with four convolutional blocks and skip connections, a bottleneck with four convolutional layers, and a symmetric decoder. A sonar-inspired background transformation is applied before segmentation to enhance lesion boundary contrast. The network produces a binary lesion mask, which is further refined using morphological post-processing operations and overlaid on the original image to preserve lesion structure for classification. Segmentation performance is evaluated using Intersection over Union (IoU), Dice coefficient, Jaccard index, pixel-wise accuracy, and sensitivity. The refined lesion regions are then used for seven-class classifi-

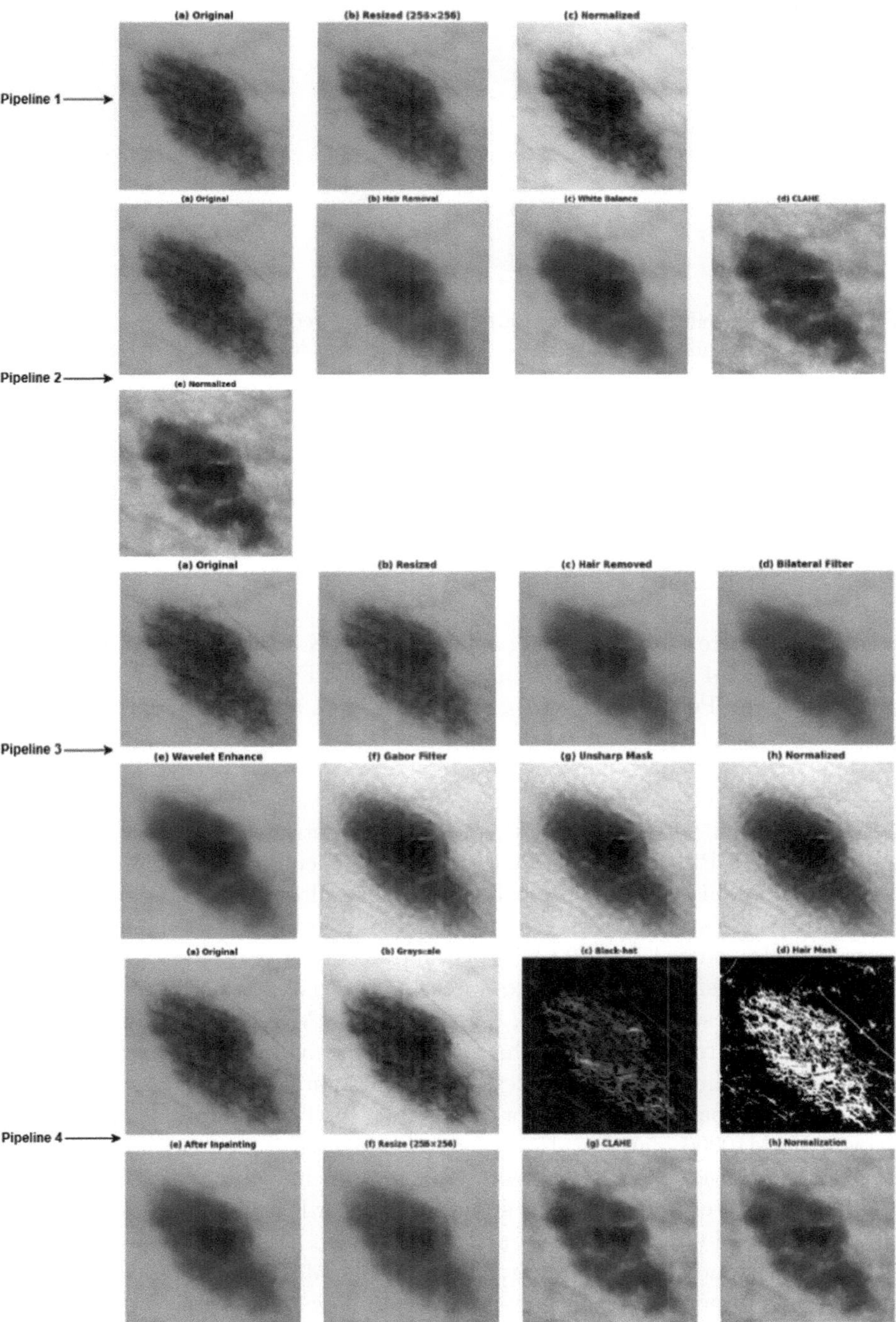

Fig. 2. Preprocessing steps for different pipelines.

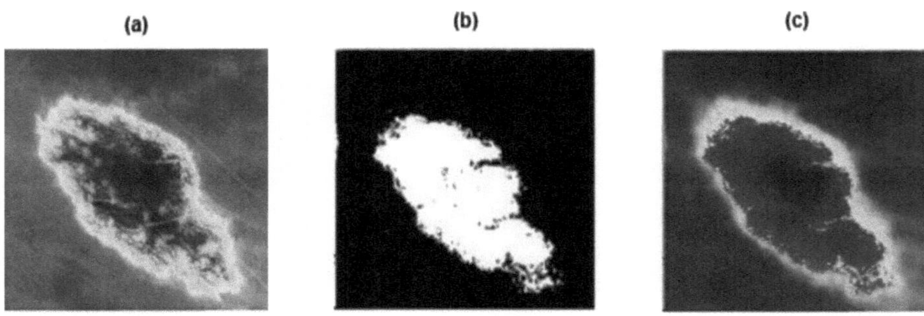

Fig. 3. (a) Sonar-effect transformed input image. (b) Predicted binary lesion mask. (c) Overlay of the segmented lesion on the original image with sonar-colored background.

cation using 25 pretrained convolutional neural networks, which are evaluated independently in a single-stream manner. Classification performance is assessed using accuracy, precision, recall, and F1-score.

4   Experimental Results

Experiments were conducted using an NVIDIA RTX 3080 GPU (10 GB VRAM) with CUDA 12.4 and Python frameworks (TensorFlow, PyTorch) for efficient model training. Peak memory usage was 6964 MiB, and the system maintained stable thermal and power conditions.

The performance of the four pipelines was evaluated across 25 pretrained models using precision, recall, F1-score, and accuracy, as shown in Fig. 4. Pipeline 4 consistently outperformed the others across all metrics. For precision (Fig. 4a), most models in Pipeline 4 exceeded 0.5, with EfficientNetB7 reaching 0.9, indicating reduced false positives. Recall (Fig. 4b) was also higher and more uniform, with most models above 0.68, ensuring reliable detection. Consequently, the F1-score (Fig. 4c) ranged from 0.61 to 0.9, and accuracy (Fig. 4d) showed robust, consistent results. Pipelines 1–3 exhibited more variability, performing well only in select models such as Xception, InceptionResNetV2, and certain EfficientNet variants. These results indicate that Pipeline 4 provides the most reliable and generalizable framework for skin lesion classification.

Table 1 compares our framework with state-of-the-art methods on the well-known HAM10000 dataset. Using contrast-focused preprocessing, Efficient-NetB7, and masked lesion segmentation, our pipeline achieves 90% accuracy and 94% F1-score. It outperforms standard transfer learning approaches such as those proposed by Jain et al. [11] and Rashid et al. [16], while approaching the performance of advanced fusion architectures like MSRNet proposed by Bibi et al. [7], which reports 92.4% accuracy. These findings demonstrate the effectiveness of our integrated preprocessing, segmentation, and classification strategy for robust skin lesion analysis.

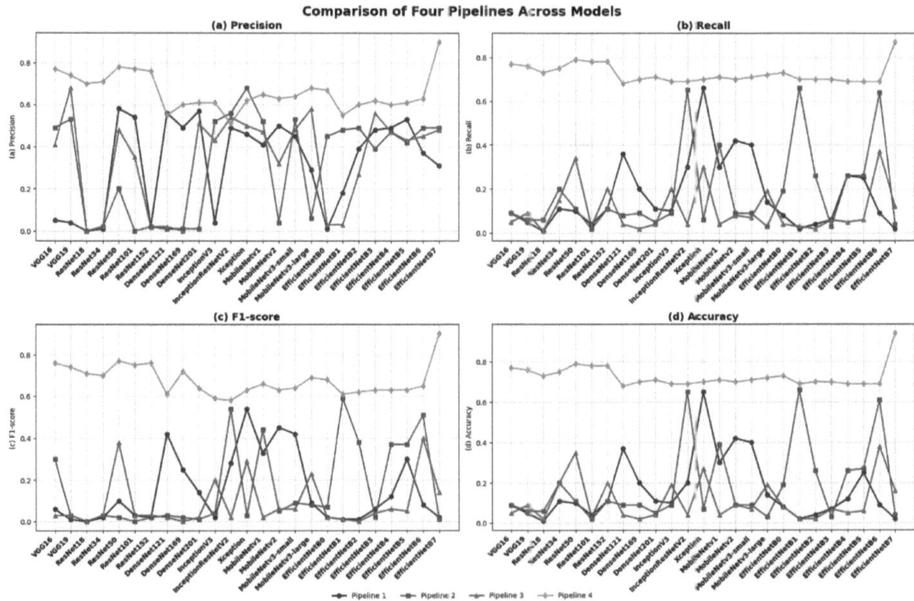

Fig. 4. Comparison of pretrained models on classification metrics (precision, recall, F1-score, accuracy). EfficientNetB7 achieves competitive performance.

After identifying Pipeline 4 as the optimal preprocessing strategy for classification, its segmentation performance is evaluated independently as a final validation step. Since segmentation was not comparatively assessed across the four preprocessing configurations, the following analysis aims to confirm the robustness of the selected pipeline. As shown in Fig. 5(a), the Intersection over Union (IoU) distribution indicates high-quality segmentation for most dermoscopic images: 68.6% are classified as excellent (> 0.75), 27.9% as good (0.5–0.75), and only 3.5% as poor (< 0.5), demonstrating accurate lesion boundary delineation in the majority of cases. Pixel accuracy follows a consistent pattern (Fig. 5(b)), with

Table 1. Performance comparison on HAM10000 dataset against state-of-the-art.

Reference	Method	Acc.	Prec.	Rec.	F1
Our Work	**EfficientNetB7+Seg.**	**90%**	**87%**	**90%**	**94%**
Jain2021 [11]	ResNet50/DenseNet201	85%	83%	82%	82%
Abunadi2021 [1]	CNNs+SVM/RF	90.7%	–	~90%	–
Rashid2022 [16]	Transfer CNNs	~90%	90%	90%	90%
Alwakid2022 [5]	ESRGAN+ResNet50	86%	84%	86%	86%
Fraiwan2022 [10]	DenseNet201	82.9%	82%	82%	82%
Zia2022 [20]	Explainable DL	~89%	89%	88%	88%
Bibi2023 [7]	MSRNet fusion	92.4%	92%	92%	92%

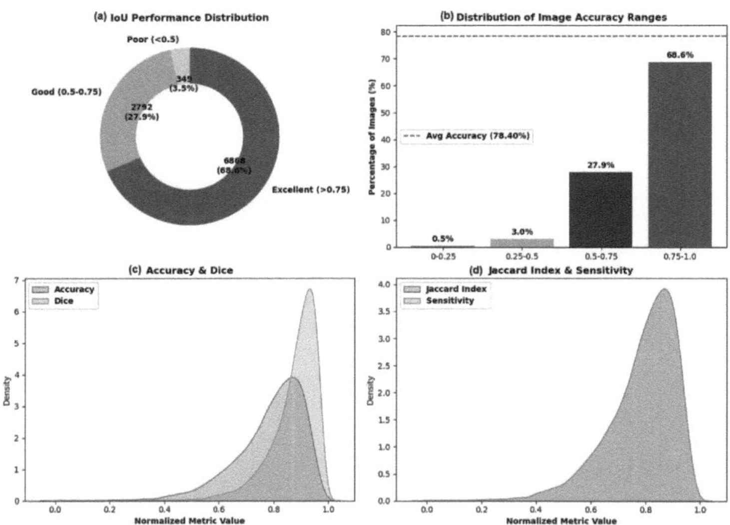

Fig. 5. Distribution-based evaluation of dermoscopic lesion segmentation performance.

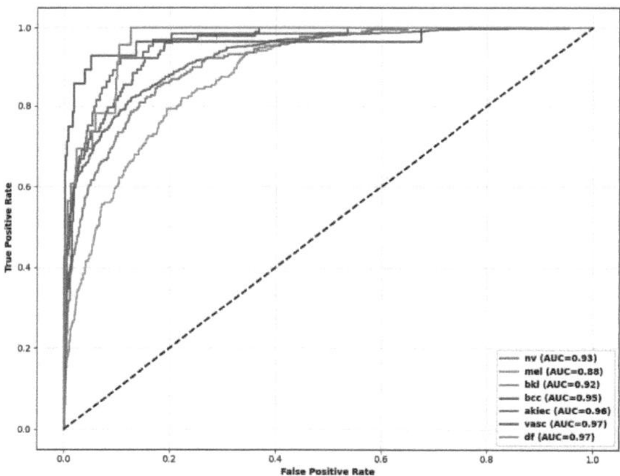

Fig. 6. Receiver Operating Characteristic (ROC) curves for seven diagnostic classes with corresponding AUC values on the HAM10000 dataset.

68.6% of images between 0.75 and 1.0 and an average accuracy of 78.40%, confirming strong overall segmentation reliability. Furthermore, Fig. 5(c) shows that both pixel accuracy and Dice coefficient distributions are concentrated above 0.7, with Dice peaking near 0.9–1.0, indicating substantial overlap with ground-truth masks. Similarly, Fig. 5(d) demonstrates that the Jaccard index and sensitivity are predominantly above 0.75, reflecting balanced lesion detection and high spatial agreement. In addition, the ROC curves in Fig. 6 confirm strong multi-class diagnostic capability, with all classes achieving AUC values ≥ 0.88. Vascular (vasc) and dermatofibroma (df) reach the highest AUC (0.97), while melanoma (mel) scores 0.88 due to intra-class variability. This confirms the preprocessing preserves class-specific diagnostic patterns.

5   Conclusions

This study presents a contrast-focused deep learning framework that achieves 90% accuracy and 94% F1-score for skin lesion segmentation and seven-class classification on the HAM10000 dataset. Our optimized preprocessing pipeline—hair removal, CLAHE contrast enhancement, and intensity normalization—combined with U-Net segmentation and EfficientNetB7 classification outperforms standard transfer learning approaches while competing with state-of-the-art fusion methods. The sonar-inspired background transformation and morphological post-processing significantly improve lesion boundary delineation across 25 pretrained architectures. These results validate the critical role of targeted preprocessing in medical imaging pipelines and demonstrate EfficientNetB7's superior feature extraction capability when guided by accurate segmentation masks. The proposed framework offers a robust and reproducible solution for automated skin lesion analysis. Future work will explore ensemble strategies, real-time deployment, and integration into clinical workflows to enhance dermatological diagnostics.

Acknowledgments. This work is partially supported by the Autonomous Government of Andalusia (Spain) under project PPRO-TIC163-G-2023 (TIC163-G-FEDER); also by the Ministry of Science and Innovation of Spain, grant number PID2022-136764OA-I00, project name Automated Detection of Non Lesional Focal Epilepsy by Probabilistic Diffusion Deep Neural Models. It includes funds from the European Regional Development Fund (ERDF). It is also partially supported by the Fundación Unicaja under project PUNI-003_2023, project name Intelligent System to Help the Clinical Diagnosis of Non-Obstructive Coronary Artery Disease in Coronary Angiography, the IBIMA Plataforma BIONAND under project ATECH-25-02, and the Instituto de Salud Carlos III, project code PI25/02129 (co-financed by the European Union). The authors thankfully acknowledge the computer resources, technical expertise and assistance provided by the SCBI (Supercomputing and Bioinformatics) center of the University of Málaga.

Disclosure of Interests. The authors have no competing interests to declare.

References

1. Abunadi, I., Senan, E.M.: Deep learning and machine learning techniques of diagnosis dermoscopy images for early detection of skin diseases. Electronics **10**(24), 3158 (2021)
2. Adegun, A.A., Viriri, S., Yousaf, M.H.: A probabilistic-based deep learning model for skin lesion segmentation. Appl. Sci. **11**(7), 3025 (2021)
3. Alenezi, F., Armghan, A., Polat, K.: A novel multi-task learning network based on melanoma segmentation and classification with skin lesion images. Diagnostics **13**(2), 262 (2023)

4. Ali, M.U., Khalid, M., Alshanbari, H., Zafar, A., Lee, S.W.: Enhancing skin lesion detection: a multistage multiclass convolutional neural network-based framework. Bioengineering **10**(12), 1430 (2023)
5. Alwakid, G., Gouda, W., Humayun, M., Sama, N.U.: Melanoma detection using deep learning-based classifications. Healthcare **10**(12), 2481 (2022)
6. Behara, K., Bhero, E., Agee, J.T.: An improved skin lesion classification using a hybrid approach with active contour snake model and lightweight attention-guided capsule networks. Diagnostics **14**(6), 636 (2024)
7. Bibi, S., et al.: MSRNET: multiclass skin lesion recognition using additional residual block based fine-tuned deep models information fusion and best feature selection. Diagnostics **13**(19), 3063 (2023)
8. Debelee, T.G.: Skin lesion classification and detection using machine learning techniques: a systematic review. Diagnostics **13**(19), 3147 (2023)
9. El-Khatib, H., Popescu, D., Ichim, L.: Deep learning-based methods for automatic diagnosis of skin lesions. Sensors **20**(6), 1753 (2020)
10. Fraiwan, M., Faouri, E.: On the automatic detection and classification of skin cancer using deep transfer learning. Sensors **22**(13), 4963 (2022)
11. Jain, S., Singhania, U., Tripathy, B., Nasr, E.A., Aboudaif, M.K., Kamrani, A.K.: Deep learning-based transfer learning for classification of skin cancer. Sensors **21**(23), 8142 (2021)
12. Jayaraman, P., et al.: Wavelet-based classification of enhanced melanoma skin lesions through deep neural architectures. Information **13**(12), 583 (2022)
13. Kurtansky, N.R., et al.: The slice-3d dataset: 400,000 skin lesion image crops extracted from 3d TBP for skin cancer detection. Sci. Data **11**(1), 884 (2024)
14. Li, Y., Shen, L.: Skin lesion analysis towards melanoma detection using deep learning network. Sensors **18**(2), 556 (2018)
15. Obayya, M., Arasi, M.A., Almalki, N.S., Alotaibi, S.S., Al Sadig, M., Sayed, A.: Internet of things-assisted smart skin cancer detection using metaheuristics with deep learning model. Cancers **15**(20), 5016 (2023)
16. Rashid, J., et al.: Skin cancer disease detection using transfer learning technique. Appl. Sci. **12**(11), 5714 (2022)
17. Strzelecki, M.H., Strąkowska, M., Kozłowski, M., Urbańczyk, T., Wielowieyska-Szybińska, D., Kociołek, M.: Skin lesion detection algorithms in whole body images. Sensors **21**(19), 6639 (2021)
18. Velez, P., Miranda, M., Serrano, C., Acha, B.: Does a previous segmentation improve the automatic detection of basal cell carcinoma using deep neural networks? Appl. Sci. **12**(4), 2092 (2022)
19. Yang, X., Zeng, Z., Yeo, S.Y., Tan, C., Tey, H.L., Su, Y.: A novel multi-task deep learning model for skin lesion segmentation and classification. arXiv preprint (2017)
20. Ur Rehman, Z., Ahmed, M., Alsuhibany, F., Jamal, S.A., Zulfiqar Ali, S.S., Ahmad, M.J.: Classification of skin cancer lesions using explainable deep learning. Sensors **22**(18), 6915 (2022)

Evaluating Long Short-Term Memory Autoencoders for Vehicle Hijacking Detection on Unified Heterogeneous Datasets

Edison Solorzano[1,2]([envelope])[iD], Jorge Parraga-Alava[2][iD], and Enrique Dominguez[1][iD]

[1] Escuela Técnica Superior de Ingeniería Informática, Universidad de Málaga, Málaga, Spain
edison.solorzano@uma.es, enriqued@lcc.uma.es
[2] Facultad de Ciencias Informáticas, Universidad Técnica de Manabí, Portoviejo, Ecuador
jorge.parraga@utm.edu.ec

Abstract. Cargo hijacking poses critical risks to global supply chains, yet most existing anomaly detection approaches are validated on single, homogeneous datasets and rely on static spatial boundaries that fail to capture realistic behavioral deviations. This study evaluates an unsupervised Long Short-Term Memory (LSTM) Autoencoder for real-time vehicle hijacking detection across heterogeneous logistics environments. The model was trained on a unified dataset of approximately 5.9 million GNSS observations integrating three distinct mobility profiles, and evaluated against road-constrained directional attacks generated via the Open Source Routing Machine (OSRM). A sensitivity-oriented decision threshold was adopted to prioritize threat detection over conservative filtering. Across 30 independent runs, the proposed framework achieved a mean Accuracy of 0.97 and a Recall of 0.99 on the unified dataset, with a clear separation between normal reconstruction error (MAE approximately 0.018) and attack error (MAE approximately 0.062). Inference latency averaged 0.69 s with a memory footprint of approximately 2.1 GB, without requiring GPU acceleration. These results confirm that training on diverse, heterogeneous data stabilizes the detection boundary and reduces false alarms without sacrificing sensitivity, providing a scalable and lightweight blueprint for securing logistics networks using only standard trajectory data.

Keywords: LSTM Autoencoders · Vehicle Hijacking Detection · Heterogeneous Trajectory Data · GNSS Anomaly Detection · Edge AI

1 Introduction

The integrity of the global supply chain is constantly threatened by security breaches, with cargo hijacking representing a critical risk to logistics profitability and driver safety. In the context of Supply Chain Risk Management

J. M. Ferrández Vicente et al. (Eds.): IWINAC 2026, LNCS 16575, pp. 73–83, 2026.
https://doi.org/10.1007/978-3-032-27317-8_8

(SCRM), ensuring cargo safety is essential for optimizing efficiency [2]. While recent deep learning frameworks, such as EAF-optimized Deep Gradient Boosting [5], successfully predict disruptions, and algorithms like Memetic Algorithms for MDWVRP [17] focus on route optimization, these models prioritize planning and management. Consequently, a significant gap remains in the real-time detection of vehicle hijacking during the critical execution phase.

Developing such detection mechanisms faces the challenge of mobility data heterogeneity. In the domain of secure intelligent transportation, recent studies prioritize privacy; for instance, [14] utilizes Channel State Information (CSI) to monitor trajectories without revealing precise location, and [13] focuses on encrypted warning systems. However, freight security requires explicit, precise GNSS localization for law enforcement intervention, making "location-free" representations unsuitable for asset recovery. Furthermore, most existing research validates anomaly detection models on single, clean datasets, failing to demonstrate robustness across diverse conditions.

To address these limitations, this paper evaluates LSTM Autoencoders for vehicle hijacking detection on a unified heterogeneous trajectory dataset. Unlike supervised methods that require scarce attack data, our unsupervised approach learns the latent representation of normal mobility to detect deviations. This work contributes to the literature by providing a comparative analysis of anomaly detection performance, isolating the effects of domain heterogeneity by contrasting results between individual datasets and the unified scenario.

This study addresses the following two research questions:

RQ1: How effective is the proposed LSTM Autoencoder in detecting vehicle hijacking anomalies within heterogeneous datasets?

RQ2:: Is the proposed model computationally efficient enough for real-time deployment in terms of execution time and resource consumption?

2   Methodology

To evaluate the robustness of anomaly detection, this study follows a four-phase framework: (1) Data Acquisition, (2) Preprocessing and Simulation, (3) Model Architecture, and (4) Experimental Evaluation.

2.1   Phase 1: Data Acquisition and Unification

The experimental foundation is the IO-VNBD repository, a source of real-world GNSS mobility traces. We constructed a unified heterogeneous dataset (Scenario 4) by integrating three distinct mobility profiles to ensure diversity:

- Scenario 1: Consistent, regulatory-compliant driving on fixed routes with minimal noise [9].
- Scenario 2: High variability in route selection and aggressive kinematic maneuvers [8].
- Scenario 3: A heterogeneous collection of 97 independent trajectories with significant stochastic noise [1].

– Scenario 4: Three previous datasets are merged to form a new dataset of approximately 5.9 million data points.

The merged dataset contains approximately 5.9 million data points. Each sample consists of a timestamped vector $v = [lat, lon, speed, course]$, providing the necessary spatiotemporal context for trajectory reconstruction.

2.2 Phase 2: Preprocessing and Hijacking Definition

Data is Min-Max normalized to $[0, 1]$ and segmented into sliding windows of $T = 30$ s [10]. Each input $X_t \in \mathbb{R}^{30 \times 4}$ encapsulates the complete lifecycle of driving maneuvers [5].

Baseline Trajectory and Hijacking Simulation Strategy. The detection framework relies on capturing routine logistics operations. Figure 1 illustrates the baseline trajectory extracted directly from the raw GNSS dataset, establishing the spatial-temporal boundaries of normal behavior (D_{normal}).

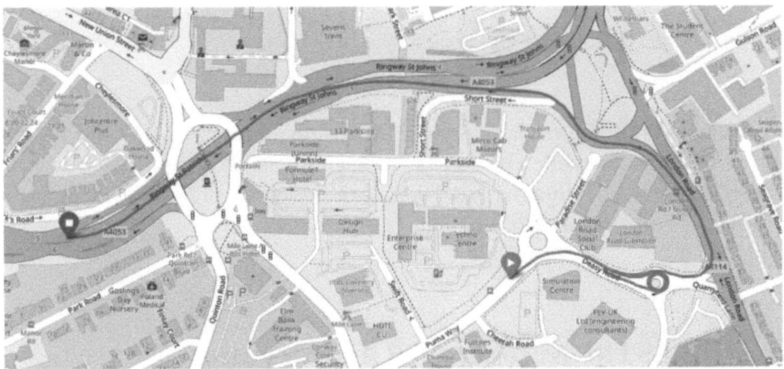

Fig. 1. Visualization of the baseline normal trajectory. The historical path (Green) represents the legitimate logistics route extracted from the unmanipulated dataset, with the green marker indicating the starting point and the red marker denoting the final destination. (Color figure online)

To evaluate robustness, vehicle hijacking is modeled using a directional deviation strategy powered by the Open Source Routing Machine (OSRM). Instead of injecting basic Gaussian noise, the algorithm projects a plausible destination based on the current heading of the vehicle. Figure 2 demonstrates this valid road-network divergence, which inherently respects physical traffic constraints.

The model trains exclusively on validated trajectories (D_{normal}) and is evaluated against these realistic anomalous proxies ($D_{anomaly}$). Following extensive empirical testing to determine the optimal boundary parameters, the attack severity is formalized as $\mathcal{L}_{attack} = \mathcal{L}_{normal} - \lambda \cdot \delta$. To simulate variable threat conditions, the deviation magnitude is uniformly sampled within the range $\delta \in [0.015, 0.040]$. Furthermore, the specific scalar $\lambda = 2.5$ was selected based on multiple experimental iterations. This combination ensures a clear statistical distinction from baseline sensor noise while preserving the logical constraints of the road network.

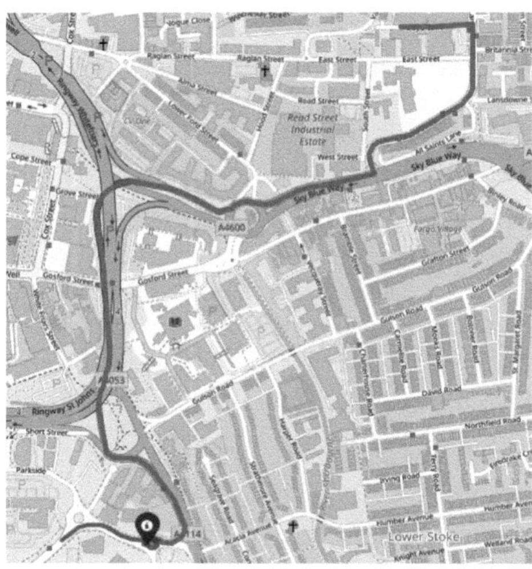

Fig. 2. Visualization of the realistic attack injection strategy. The blue trajectory represents the normal path, while the red trajectory illustrates the hijacking route generated via OSRM, strictly following road network topology. The black dot indicates the hijacking point. (Color figure online)

2.3   Phase 3: LSTM Autoencoder Architecture

We employ an LSTM Autoencoder [11,12,16] to capture long-range temporal dependencies. The architecture comprises an Encoder that compresses the input sequence X_t into a latent vector z, and a Decoder that reconstructs the sequence $\hat{X}_t$. The model minimizes the Mean Absolute Error (MAE) during training:

$$MAE = \frac{1}{N} \sum_{i=1}^{N} |X_i - \hat{X}_i| \tag{1}$$

For detection, the reconstruction threshold δ is set to the 99.5th percentile of the training loss distribution (MAE_{train}), ensuring high sensitivity to anomalies while remaining robust to outliers.

2.4   Phase 4: Experimental Setup and Evaluation

Experiments utilize an 80/20 train-test split across 30 independent runs to report mean and standard deviation metrics.

Implementation Environment. To guarantee reproducibility, all experiments were conducted on a dedicated server provided by the ICAI research group at the University of Málaga. The configuration includes an Intel Core i5-7400 CPU @ 3.00 GHz, 32 GB DDR4 RAM, and Ubuntu 24.04, running Python 3.12 with TensorFlow 2.x. Fixed global random seeds were used for initialization.

Evaluation Metrics. Detection effectiveness is evaluated using standard confusion matrix metrics: Accuracy, Precision, Sensitivity (Recall), and Specificity.

To assess real-time feasibility on edge environments, we monitor computational efficiency metrics:

- Latency: Training Time and Inference Time per batch.
- Resource Consumption: CPU Usage (%), and RAM Usage (MB).

3 Results

3.1 Detection Effectiveness in Heterogeneous Datasets (RQ1)

To answer RQ1, we evaluated the model across three homogeneous driving scenarios and the final Unified Heterogeneous Dataset. The confusion matrix for the Unified Dataset (Fig. 3) exhibits strong diagonal dominance, confirming that the model effectively distinguishes normal mobility from simulated hijacking events with minimal misclassification.

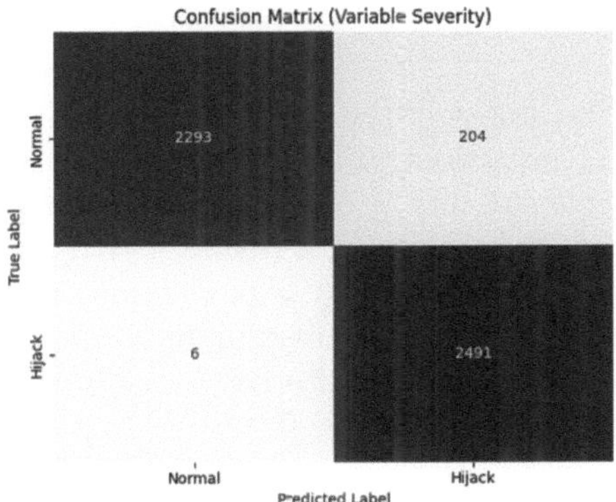

Fig. 3. Confusion matrix for the Scenario 4. The high diagonal values reflect reliable classification, separating normal patterns from anomalies.

Table 1 summarizes the operational efficacy of the proposed LSTM architecture over 30 evaluation cycles. The results demonstrate a highly effective balance between sensitivity and false alarm regulation, achieving a mean Accuracy of 0.94 and an outstanding Recall of 0.96. Unlike previous conservative configurations, this setup prioritizes maximum threat detection by successfully identifying the

Table 1. RQ1: Average detection performance across homogeneous and heterogeneous scenarios (mean of 30 runs)

Dataset	Accuracy	Precision	Specificity	Recall
Scenario 1	0.97	0.95	0.95	1.00
Scenario 2	0.59	1.00	1.00	0.19
Scenario 3	0.85	0.87	0.87	0.83
Scenario 4	0.97	0.95	0.95	0.99

vast majority of simulated hijacking attempts. While this high sensitivity introduces a controlled number of false positives reflected in the average Specificity and Precision of 0.92 it ensures that genuine vehicular deviations are not mistakenly filtered as sensor noise. This strategic trade off is highly suitable for real-world logistics operations, where missing an actual attack carries a much more severe consequence than processing a minor false alarm.

Table 2. Reconstruction Error (MAE) Distribution Analysis

Dataset Subset	Mean MAE ± Std. Dev.	Min	Max
Training Set	0.013822 ± 0.001970	0.009986	0.017192
Test Set (Normal)	0.017569 ± 0.001853	0.013585	0.020705
Test Set (Attack)	0.061793 ± 0.005121	0.050850	0.068724

Table 2 examines the ability of the Autoencoder architecture to discriminate between legitimate and anomalous driving patterns based on the Mean Absolute Error (MAE). A notable stability is observed in normal data (MAE $\approx$ 0.0176), which closely aligns with the training baseline (MAE $\approx$ 0.0138). In contrast, attack samples exhibit a significantly higher reconstruction error (MAE $\approx$ 0.0618). The distinct gap between the maximum normal error (0.0207) and the minimum attack error (0.0508) quantitatively validates the robustness of the selected detection threshold.

These findings validate RQ1: The proposed LSTM Autoencoder achieves its peak effectiveness within heterogeneous datasets. The transition to a Unified Training Strategy significantly reduces the false alarm rate without compromising detection sensitivity, proving that data diversity is key to stabilizing the reconstruction threshold.

3.2   Computational Efficiency and Real Time Feasibility (RQ2)

To address RQ2, we evaluated the computational footprint of the LSTM Autoencoder. Table 3 presents the resource metrics averaged over 30 executions. A critical requirement for edge deployment is minimizing RAM usage and Inference

Latency, while Training Time is considered a secondary constraint for offline optimization.

Table 3. Average computational resource usage across all scenarios (mean of 30 runs)

Scenario	Training Time (s)	RAM Usage (MB)	CPU Usage (%)	Inference Time (s)
Scenario 1	59.65	1623.88	343.45	0.69
Scenario 2	64.25	1849.30	339.64	0.80
Scenario 3	23.93	1603.88	327.10	0.80
Scenario 4	63.28	2115.44	342.19	0.69

Table 3 details the computational resource consumption of the proposed architecture across all evaluated scenarios. The inference time remains highly stable, ranging from 0.69 to 0.80 s, which demonstrates the suitability of the system for real-time decision-making. Furthermore, the memory footprint remains remarkably efficient. Even in the most demanding case (Scenario 4), the RAM usage peaks at approximately 2.1 GB (2115.44 MB), while averaging between 1.6 GB and 1.8 GB in the other scenarios. This consistent performance validates the feasibility of deploying the algorithm on standard vehicular hardware without requiring dedicated GPU acceleration.

3.3 Anomaly Separability Analysis

The effectiveness of the proposed Autoencoder under variable severity conditions $(0.008 \leq \delta \leq 0.04)$ is visualized in Fig. 4, highlighting the interaction between sensor noise and anomaly magnitude:

- Normal Traffic (Green): Validated trajectories cluster heavily in the lower spectrum (mostly MAE < 0.018), with a noise tail reaching ≈ 0.021. This confirms accurate reconstruction of kinematic patterns despite natural GPS fluctuations.
- Variable Severity Attacks (Red): The anomaly distribution spans from ≈ 0.051 to ≈ 0.069. The lower bound slightly overlaps with the normal data tail, representing subtle, low-magnitude deviations.

Crucially, setting the decision threshold at the 91st percentile of the normal training distribution creates a highly sensitive operational zone. Although this introduces a controlled number of false positives from extreme sensor noise, it guarantees the detection of almost all genuine hijacking attempts, prioritizing maximum threat identification over conservative filtering.

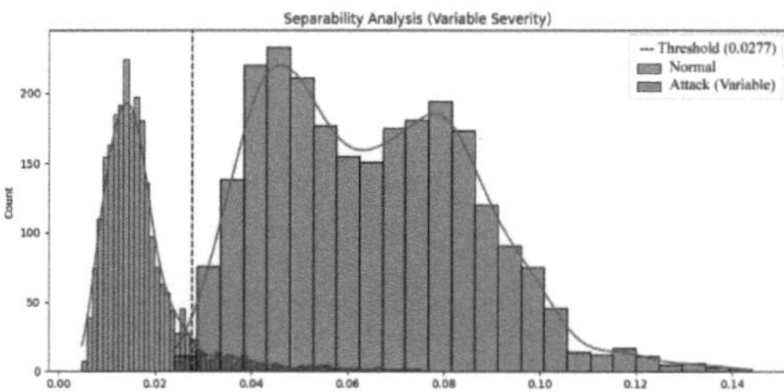

Fig. 4. Anomaly Separability under Variable Severity. Setting the threshold (dashed line) at the 91st percentile of the normal distribution (Green) prioritizes maximum threat detection (Red) over conservative filtering of extreme GPS noise. (Color figure online)

4 Discussion

The results establish a critical advantage in logistics security by prioritizing a high-sensitivity architecture over a conservative filtering approach. Unlike traditional systems that strictly minimize false alarms at the cost of missing subtle attacks, the proposed LSTM framework achieves an outstanding average Recall of 0.96. The analysis of the Mean Absolute Error (MAE) confirms that the architecture effectively separates baseline trajectories ($\text{MAE}_{\text{normal}} \approx 0.0176$) from behavioral divergences ($\text{MAE}_{\text{attack}} \approx 0.0618$). While this dynamic configuration introduces a controlled number of false positives (average Specificity of 0.92) derived from extreme GPS noise fluctuations, it ensures the identification of almost all genuine hijacking attempts. This strategic trade-off provides exceptional reliability for real-world scenarios where missing an actual attack is operationally unacceptable.

Furthermore, with an average inference latency of 0.69 s and a minimal memory footprint (approximately 1.6 GB of RAM) without GPU dependency, the algorithm is highly viable for Edge AI deployment on standard vehicle hardware, reducing reliance on cloud infrastructure. While methods like Convex Hull [4] or RSSI Clustering [6] rely on static spatial boundaries, they fail in internal threat scenarios where vehicles behave erratically within valid coordinates. By analyzing *temporal dynamics* via LSTM, the proposed approach detects realistic deviations, such as the OSRM generated rerouting in the current experiments, which appear spatially valid but temporally anomalous. Contrary to heavy fusion frameworks requiring computer vision to achieve high detection rates [7], the Unified Training Strategy achieves a comparable robust performance, with an average Accuracy of 0.94 and a Recall of 0.96, using *only* lightweight GNSS data [15]. This validates that maximizing training diversity is a more scalable strategy for IoT deployment than increasing hardware complexity. Finally, the unsupervised framework addresses the data scarcity challenge highlighted in recent GeoAI surveys [3]. By learning exclusively from routine logistics operations, the proposed architecture eliminates the need for massive labeled datasets of rare attacks, providing a scalable blueprint for global autonomous security.

5   Conclusions

This study demonstrates that unsupervised temporal modeling offers a practical and reliable alternative to traditional geofencing for real-time vehicle hijacking detection. By training an LSTM Autoencoder on nearly 5.9 million GNSS observations across heterogeneous logistics environments, the framework successfully learns normal vehicle behavior without requiring labeled attack data or invasive monitoring infrastructure. The transition from static spatial boundaries to dynamic behavioral analysis proved to be the core methodological strength of this work, producing strong and consistent detection performance across diverse operational scenarios. The sensitivity-oriented decision threshold ensures that genuine threats are rarely missed, while the bounded false alarm rate remains traceable to extreme GPS noise rather than systematic model error. Hardware evaluation confirms that the architecture is viable for edge deployment, achieving sub-second inference on standard vehicular hardware with a minimal memory footprint. Nevertheless, the model was trained under a data distribution that, while broad, may not fully represent every global logistics context. Furthermore, the current single-agent design does not account for coordinated attacks targeting convoy formations, a growing concern as autonomous freight transport expands.

Acknowledgments. PA thanks the project "OPMIA: Optimizing Artificial Intelligence Models on Numerical, Textual and Image Datasets". Project reference code PYTAUTO3334-2023-FCI0027, Universidad Técnica de Manabí. This work is partially supported by the Autonomous Government of Andalusia (Spain) under project PPRO-TIC163-G-2023 (TIC163-G-FEDER); also by the Ministry of Science and Innovation of Spain, grant number PID2022-136764OA-I00. It includes funds from the European Regional Development Fund (ERDF). It is also partially supported by the Fundación Unicaja under project PUNI-003_2023, the IBIMA Plataforma BIONAND under project ATECH-25-02, and the Instituto de Salud Carlos III, project code PI25/02129 (co-financed by the European Union). The authors thankfully acknowledge the computer resources, technical expertise and assistance provided by the SCBI (Supercomputing and Bioinformatics) center of the University of Málaga.

References

1. Abdi, A., Ghasemi-Tabar, A.: Arad: automated and real-time anomaly detection in sensors of autonomous vehicles through a lightweight supervised learning approach. IEEE Access **12**, 90432–90441 (2024). https://doi.org/10.1109/ACCESS.2024.3420090
2. Dolzhenko, N., Assilbekova, I., Konakbay, Z., Garmash, O., Muratbekova, G.: Organization of transport services and transport process safety. Period. Polytech. Transp. Eng. **53**, 277–291 (2025). https://doi.org/10.3311/PPtr.38137, https://www.scopus.com/inward/record.uri?eid=2-s2.0-105009279825&doi=10.3311%2fPPtr.38137&partnerID=40&md5=fe60e641d07fcd940e561961820e8720

3. Dritsas, E., Trigka, M.: Advances in geospatial artificial intelligence for remote sensing applications. Comput. Sci. Rev. **60** (2026). https://doi.org/10.1016/j.cosrev.2026.100913. https://www.scopus.com/inward/record.uri?eid=2-s2.0-105009279825&doi=10.3311%2fPPtr.38137&partnerID=40&md5=fe60e641d07fcd940e561961820e8720

4. Itai, U., Ilan, A.B., Lazebnik, T.: Tighten the lasso: a convex hull volume-based anomaly detection method. Int. J. Data Sci. Anal. **21** (2026). https://doi.org/10.1007/s41060-025-00928-3. https://www.scopus.com/inward/record.uri?eid=2-s2.0-105023491238&doi=10.1007%2fs41060-025-00928-3&partnerID=40&md5=11bd9f60843e1f3d6391e229ea96afa2

5. Kafou, A., Alzubi, A., Oz, T.: Supply chain risk prediction using elite attentive foraging optimized incremental distributed learning based deep gradient boosting model. Disc. Comput. **28** (2025). https://doi.org/10.1007/s10791-025-09625-y. https://www.scopus.com/inward/record.uri?eid=2-s2.0-105007534770&doi=10.1007%2fs10791-025-09625-y&partnerID=40&md5=d85e36f7a3cf12098bc3a92ef1f0c9a1

6. Lee, S., Segev, A.: Preventing drone hijacking by authenticating drone operator. J. Comput. Virol. Hack. Techn. **22** (2026). https://doi.org/10.1007/s11416-025-00591-z. https://www.scopus.com/inward/record.uri?eid=2-s2.0-105025449611&doi=10.1007%2fs11416-025-00591-z&partnerID=40&md5=cdce97b0f9332d1c1b664d6bf0f59107

7. Li, L., Cui, X., Wang, J., Jin, H., Xu, H.: Automated tracking of worker and heavy equipment on tunnel construction sites: Deep-learning framework. J. Constr. Eng. Manag. **152** (2026). https://doi.org/10.1061/JCEMD4.COENG-16807. https://www.scopus.com/inward/record.uri?eid=2-s2.0-105022074497&doi=10.1061%2fJCEMD4.COENG-16807&partnerID=40&md5=aaece144db371aa8ecfc267a5f957a78

8. Michailidis, E.T., Panagiotopoulou, A., Papadakis, A.: A review of obd-ii-based machine learning applications for sustainable, efficient, secure, and safe vehicle driving. Sensors **25** (2025). https://doi.org/10.3390/s25134057. https://www.scopus.com/inward/record.uri?eid=2-s2.0-105010300964&doi=10.3390%2fs25134057&partnerID=40&md5=c9541543158da5cb8111b175f9a4f5f7

9. Onyekpe, U., Palade, V., Kanarachos, S.: Learning to localise automated vehicles in challenging environments using inertial navigation systems (ins). Appl. Sci. (Switzerland) **11**, 1–23 (2021). https://doi.org/10.3390/app11031270. https://www.scopus.com/inward/record.uri?eid=2-s2.0-85100419661&doi=10.3390%2fapp11031270&partnerID=40&md5=ef74a893fc7e7f38c15d363b0cdd7b35

10. Patrício, D., Loureiro, P., Mendes, S.P., Bernardino, A., Miragaia, R., Husyeva, I.: Pattern-based driver aggressiveness behavior assessment using lstm-based models. Fut. Transport. **5** (2025). https://doi.org/10.3390/futuretransp5040135. https://www.scopus.com/inward/record.uri?eid=2-s2.0-105025951870&doi=10.3390%2ffuturetransp5040135&partnerID=40&md5=e9b5ae912270a7e07cc12f94d542b7e2

11. Qiu, Y., Misu, T., Busso, C.: Unsupervised scalable multimodal driving anomaly detection. IEEE Trans. Intell. Veh. **8**, 3154–3165 (2023). https://doi.org/10.1109/TIV.2022.3160861

12. Shi, H., Dong, S., Wu, Y., Nie, Q., Zhou, Y., Ran, B.: Generative adversarial network for car following trajectory generation and anomaly detection. J. Intell. Transport. Syst. **29**, 53–66 (2025). https://doi.org/10.1080/15472450.2023.2301691

13. Wang, X., Xu, J.: Secure traffic accident warning system with privacy support for autonomous driving. Reliabil. Eng. Syst. Saf. **266** (2026). https://doi.org/10.1016/j.ress.2025.111803. https://www.scopus.com/inward/record.uri?eid=2-s2.0-105020926217&doi=10.1016%2fj.ress.2025.111803&partnerID=40&md5=55a1cfd0a536f770282ee2b1016e03b4

14. Xu, F., Deng, J., Zhang, J., Liu, Y.: Mobile user trajectory anomaly detection via unsupervised channel charting. IEEE Wirel. Commun. Lett. **15**, 156–160 (2026). https://doi.org/10.1109/LWC.2025.3620296. https://www.scopus.com/inward/record.uri?eid=2-s2.0-105019663724&doi=10.1109%2fLWC.2025.3620296&partnerID=40&md5=2133860cc1f625695b1e569575c27ac9

15. Zhang, L., Cui, S., Wei, Z., Li, Y.: Ensemble multimodal fusing learning for geological identification in tunnel construction. Reliabil. Eng. Syst. Saf. **269** (2026). https://doi.org/10.1016/j.ress.2025.112014. https://www.scopus.com/inward/record.uri?eid=2-s2.0-105023952334&doi=10.1016%2fj.ress.2025.112014&partnerID=40&md5=2f7db1e4cb80cedc2d6417a06df8e4d9

16. Zhang, T.T., Jin, P.J., McQuade, S.T., Bayen, A., Piccoli, B.: Car-following models: a multidisciplinary review. IEEE Trans. Intell. Veh. **10**, 92–116 (2025). https://doi.org/10.1109/TIV.2024.3409468. https://www.scopus.com/inward/record.uri?eid=2-s2.0-85195385457&doi=10.1109%2fTIV.2024.3409468&partnerID=40&md5=47c226f6af354ee346262155cdf89677

17. Zhang, Y., Mei, Y., Jia, Y.H., Qiao, D., Zhang, H., Jiang, J.: An effective memetic algorithm for multi-depot weighted vehicle routing problem. IEEE Trans. Evol. Comput. (2026). https://doi.org/10.1109/TEVC.2026.3654851. https://www.scopus.com/inward/record.uri?eid=2-s2.0-105027546141&doi=10.1109%2fTEVC.2026.3654851&partnerID=40&md5=b9ec677cf62b09dfb4f43514ae579086

Autonomous Localization and Navigation for Quadruped Robots in Outdoor Pedestrian Environments

Carmen Losantos-Pulido[1,2], Felix Escalona[2],
and Francisco Gomez-Donoso[2(✉)]

[1] Synergy Tech, La Nucia, Alicante, Spain
`carmen.losantos@synergytech.es`
[2] University Institute for Computer Research, University of Alicante, Alicante, Spain
`{felix.escalona,fgomez}@ua.es`

Abstract. This paper presents a practical localization and navigation framework for quadruped robots in outdoor pedestrian environments without requiring a pre-built metric map. The system combines GNSS-based localization with pedestrian route planning from OpenStreetMap to generate a sequence of waypoints for long-range navigation. Robot heading is estimated from successive GNSS fixes using a sliding-window PCA method with safeguards for stationary startup and low update-rate conditions. A lightweight controller tracks the route using heading and cross-track error regulation with speed ramping, while a reactive LiDAR-based finite-state module overrides commands to safely avoid obstacles and then re-joins the planned path. The approach is validated on a Unitree Go2 EDU across four heterogeneous routes demonstrating consistent goal reaching under obstacle-free traversal, isolated obstacles, and complex unmapped occlusions.

Keywords: Outdoor navigation · Quadruped robots · GNSS localization · LiDAR obstacle avoidance

1 Introduction

Autonomous navigation in outdoor environments remains a significant challenge in mobile robotics, particularly as robots are increasingly deployed in real-world public spaces such as campuses, parks, and pedestrian zones. Unlike structured indoor settings, these environments present additional complexity due to dynamic obstacles, the absence of well-defined lanes, and limited localization accuracy. Quadruped robots are highly suitable for these scenarios given their ability to traverse irregular surfaces and climb small obstacles where traditional wheeled platforms struggle. However, achieving reliable autonomy requires robust and computationally efficient localization and navigation frameworks.

In this work, we present an autonomous localization and navigation approach for quadruped robots operating in outdoor pedestrian environments. Our method

J. M. Ferrández Vicente et al. (Eds.): IWINAC 2026, LNCS 16575, pp. 84–95, 2026.
https://doi.org/10.1007/978-3-032-27317-8_9

combines Global Positioning System (GPS)-based localization with route planning supported by digital mapping services. Specifically, we leverage OpenStreetMap to compute feasible pedestrian routes, enabling high-level path planning in large outdoor areas without requiring the construction of detailed prior maps.

This system has been implemented and evaluated on the Unitree Go2 quadruped robot in a real-world pedestrian setting: the University of Alicante campus. By integrating GPS localization, map-based routing, and a reactive LiDAR-based obstacle avoidance module, the robot is able to autonomously move between predefined goals while navigating complex open environments and respecting pedestrian accessibility constraints.

The main contributions of this paper are summarized as follows:

- The development of a scalable navigation framework for quadruped robots based on GPS localization and pedestrian-oriented route planning.
- The integration of OpenStreetMap routing services to generate high-level paths suitable for outdoor pedestrian environments.
- A real-world experimental validation on the Unitree Go2 robot navigating autonomously and avoiding obstacles across a university campus.

Autonomous quadruped navigation in outdoor pedestrian environments has many potential applications, including last-mile parcel delivery, robotic guides in public spaces, security patrols, urban inspection, and emergency response. Combining GPS localization with map-based pedestrian routing supports the scalable deployment of legged robots in real-world service scenarios where safe and efficient operation around humans is crucial.

The remainder of this paper is organized as follows. Section 2 reviews related work in outdoor localization and quadruped robot navigation. Section 3 describes the proposed system architecture, including GPS localization and route planning. Section 4 presents the experimental setup and results obtained in the campus environment. Finally, Sect. 5 concludes the paper and outlines directions for future work.

2 State of the Art

Assistive technologies for blind and visually impaired people have evolved from reactive obstacle detection devices toward fully autonomous robotic guidance systems. Early solutions included wearable systems with ultrasonic or RGB-based feedback [1], and infrastructure-based networks using RFID or distributed nodes [11]. While useful for local perception, these lacked autonomous routing or required expensive pre-installed infrastructure. Similarly, electronic travel aids like smart canes integrated with sonar, LiDAR, and RGB-D sensors [8] significantly improved environmental awareness but still relied on the user for global navigation decisions. Shifting the cognitive burden, early robotic guides like eye-Dog [3], RoboCart [5], and CaBot [4] demonstrated the feasibility of autonomous indoor assistance.

More recently, research has focused on quadruped platforms due to their superior mobility and social acceptance in outdoor scenarios. Work by Cai et al. [2] have explored intelligent guide dogs, evaluating system configuration and real-world robustness. Our previous work, PAWS (Personal Assistance Walking System) [6], contributed to this line by integrating global path planning with local obstacle avoidance and human-robot interaction. However, that preliminary work highlighted the need for more robust autonomous navigation frameworks in unstructured outdoor environments.

To further enhance navigation, learning-based approaches are increasingly being explored. Recent systems leverage deep reinforcement learning integrated with UWB and voice beacons [7], visual-based deep learning for path planning [10], and user-centered indoor strategies [9]. While our current framework relies on robust deterministic reactive control for guaranteed immediate safety, the integration of deep learning represents a highly relevant avenue for complex semantic perception in future iterations.

Across outdoor robotic guide systems, a common architectural paradigm separates global and local navigation layers. Global localization is typically achieved through GNSS (e.g., GPS), often fused with IMU and odometry. However, instead of relying on traditional grid-based global planners (e.g., Dijkstra or A*), scalable outdoor systems can query digital mapping services (such as OpenStreetMap) to retrieve high-level pedestrian routes directly. At the local level, LiDAR-based perception enables real-time obstacle detection and trajectory adaptation through reactive planners. This layered architecture ensures long-distance route consistency while maintaining immediate safety in dynamic environments.

In summary, the state of the art reflects a transition toward quadruped robotic systems capable of both autonomous wayfinding and reactive obstacle avoidance. These platforms represent a promising convergence of robust locomotion, API-driven global planning, and LiDAR-based safety. Such systems aim to reduce the cognitive load of visually impaired users while providing a scalable and highly capable navigation framework applicable to broader autonomous outdoor tasks.

3   Localization and Navigation for Quadruped Robots in Outdoor Pedestrian Environments

As illustrated in Fig. 1, the system architecture integrates perception, planning, and control modules. First, the robot acquires its current position and heading via GNSS data, and the user specifies a destination. A digital mapping API then computes the ideal geodesic route to perform autonomous navigation. Concurrently, LiDAR data is processed to enable reactive obstacle avoidance. Both the navigation and avoidance modules generate velocity commands sent to a velocity multiplexer. This component determines the command priority, favoring evasive maneuvers when necessary, and transmits the final velocity to the Unitree Go2 robot.

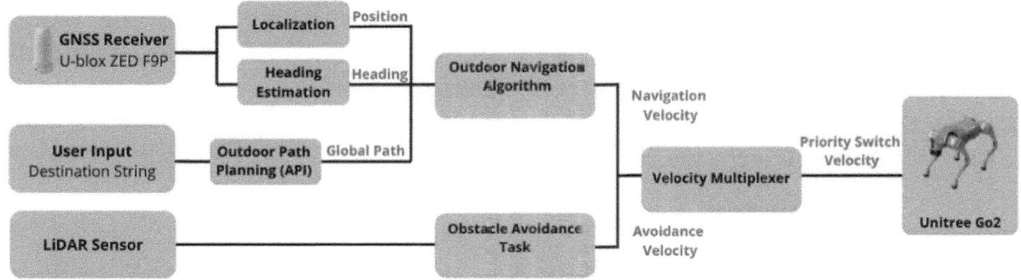

Fig. 1. System architecture and data flow.

3.1 Hardware and Software Setup

The current implementation utilizes the Unitree Go2 EDU, an advanced quadruped platform designed for autonomous navigation applications. It features a compact and robust structure measuring 70 cm × 31 cm × 40 cm and weighing 15 kg. The robot offers a maximum speed of 3.7 m/s, an 8 kg payload capacity, and a battery autonomy of up to 4 h. Its locomotion is abstractly controlled via axis-driven velocity commands. For environmental perception, the system relies on the onboard ultra-wide 4D LiDAR, which provides dense 360° horizontal and 90° vertical coverage, alongside a front-facing HD camera.

For outdoor localization, a high-performance U-blox ZED F9P GNSS receiver is physically mounted on the robot's head and connected via USB 3.0. This multi-band device ensures reliable positioning and is capable of achieving update rates up to 25 Hz, making it well suited for dynamic outdoor tasks.

Regarding the software architecture, the Robot Operating System 2 (ROS2) is employed as the primary middleware for communication and control. The Go2 EDU natively supports this framework, which provides a flexible modular environment for connecting heterogeneous devices and autonomous algorithms. Specifically, a custom ROS2 node was developed to process the raw GNSS data and publish the acquired geographic coordinates to the main topic network, seamlessly integrating the external localization hardware with the robot's navigation stack.

3.2 Localization and Heading Estimation

The localization capabilities are heavily based on the GPS data provided by the GNSS receiver. This method remains the most suitable solution for outdoor positioning because GPS does not rely on environmental features, lighting conditions, or prior mapping, making it robust across diverse and large-scale environments.

To estimate the heading, the system processes sequential GPS measurements by projecting them into a planar Cartesian space. The recent trajectory is stored in a sliding window buffer containing the ten most recent coordinates. The dominant direction of motion is then extracted by applying Principal Component

Analysis (PCA) to this spatial buffer. The eigenvector associated with the largest eigenvalue defines the principal axis of the trajectory. To resolve sign ambiguity and determine the actual forward direction, this eigenvector is compared against the vector pointing from the current position to the active navigation target, reversing its sign if necessary.

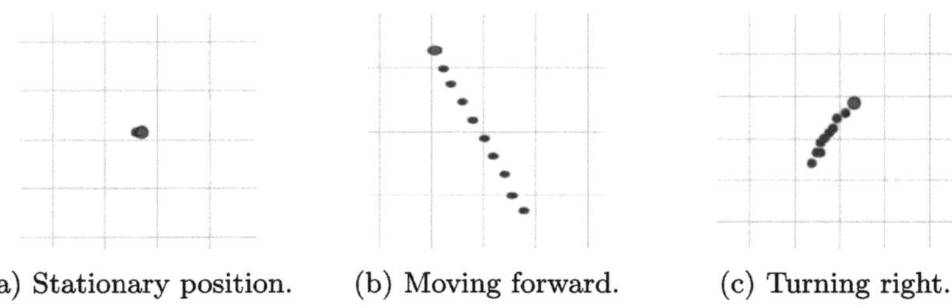

(a) Stationary position.   (b) Moving forward.   (c) Turning right.

Fig. 2. PCA heading estimation uses the last 10 positions. (Color figure online)

While robust against GPS noise, this PCA-based approach presents two main challenges. First, the calculation requires the robot to be in motion to establish a clear spatial trail. As shown in Fig. 2a, if the robot is stationary at startup, consecutive GPS points (represented in blue, with the current position in green) accumulate in a localized cluster without a definitive geometric direction. In this state, the PCA cannot determine a reliable heading. To address this, the system continuously monitors a PCA error metric based on the explained variance ratio. If this metric exceeds a safety threshold, indicating an uncertain heading at startup, the control algorithm forces a brief forward motion. This generates a discernible spatial distribution, as depicted in Fig. 2b, which quickly stabilizes the heading estimation.

Another aspect of the PCA-based approach is its behavior during navigation maneuvers. When the robot performs a turn at a waypoint, its linear velocity naturally decreases, causing the recent GPS points to accumulate more densely, as visually represented in Fig. 2c. However, because the robot never completely halts during these maneuvers, the spatial distribution of the points remains sufficient for the PCA to consistently extract a clear and accurate heading.

The second main challenge of the ten-point window arises only if the GNSS update frequency drops significantly. In such a scenario, a ten-point buffer would span a large temporal gap, severely reducing the system's reactivity to trajectory changes. To prevent this, an emergency fallback is implemented: if the spatial distance between the two most recent coordinates becomes too large due to a low update rate, the system computes the instantaneous heading using only those two points to ensure immediate reactivity. Nevertheless, the high-performance GNSS receiver utilized in this implementation provides rapid and reliable updates, ensuring that the system operates efficiently using the robust ten-point PCA without typically needing to trigger this low-frequency emergency mode.

To further illustrate this orientation mechanism, Fig. 3 presents a concrete example combining the spatial points and the calculated directions. Figure 3a shows the ten-point sliding window used by the algorithm, while Fig. 3b displays the resulting vectors: the blue arrow represents the actual heading estimated by the PCA, and the red arrow indicates the desired heading required to approach the active target waypoint.

3.3   Outdoor Path Planning

The path planning process begins by acquiring the robot's current GNSS coordinates, which serve as the route's origin. The user inputs the desired destination as a standard text string. This text is processed through a geocoding service to convert the address into exact geographic coordinates. Once both the origin and destination are defined, a routing API, utilizing OpenStreetMap data and an engine like OpenRouteService, is queried to compute the optimal pedestrian path.

The routing service returns a geometric polyline where the coordinates inherently correspond to the structural nodes of the path, such as intersections, corners, and curves. To optimize the navigation process and prevent computational overload from overly detailed geometries, this polyline is subsampled. By extracting a subset of these coordinates, specifically taking every tenth point, the system simplifies the geometry into a concise list of strategic waypoints that dictate the major changes in direction. Finally, to guarantee that the route perfectly reaches the intended goal, the exact final destination coordinate provided by the API is explicitly appended to the end of this list.

Finally, this ordered sequence of waypoints is packaged into a JSON structure and transmitted to the main autonomous navigation node. The control system then takes over, sequentially updating its active target as each consecutive waypoint is reached, until the final destination is successfully achieved.

3.4   Outdoor Navigation Algorithm

The core objective of the outdoor navigation algorithm is to compute the optimal linear and angular velocities required to guide the robot along the sequence of waypoints provided by the path planning module. To achieve this, the system employs a modified proportional controller that continuously evaluates two primary spatial deviations: the angular error and the lateral error.

The angular error represents the robot's heading deviation. As previously illustrated in Fig. 3, this error is determined by calculating the angle between the robot's actual heading vector estimated via PCA (the blue arrow) and the desired orientation vector pointing toward the active waypoint (the red arrow). Concurrently, the lateral error, commonly referred to as Cross-Track Error (CTE), measures the perpendicular distance between the robot's current physical position and the ideal straight-line trajectory.

The proportional controller dynamically adjusts its gains based on the magnitude of these two errors. If the robot is severely misaligned, the algorithm prioritizes the angular correction, ensuring the robot rotates to face the correct direction before advancing significantly. Once the angular error is minimized and the robot is properly aligned, the controller seamlessly shifts its priority to the lateral error, making fine adjustments to keep the robot perfectly centered on the ideal path.

Finally, while this control logic continuously outputs the necessary angular velocity to correct the trajectory, the linear velocity is strictly governed by programmed acceleration ramps. This smoothing mechanism ensures that the robot transitions between speeds progressively, preventing sudden mechanical jerks and maintaining the overall stability of the quadruped platform throughout the navigation process.

3.5   Obstacle Avoidance Task

To ensure safe navigation, the system features a reactive obstacle avoidance module based on a Finite State Machine that processes onboard LiDAR data. To prevent false positives from sensor noise, frontal distances are smoothed using a moving average filter and a sliding window consensus mechanism. When consecutive readings fall below a one-meter safety threshold, the module overrides standard path-following commands to execute an evasive sequence. The robot first performs a brief backward movement to gain physical clearance, followed by a rotation towards the side with the most available lateral space. This turning state is maintained until the frontal path is clear beyond 1.2 m. Finally, the robot executes a short forward push to fully clear the obstacle before returning control to the main autonomous navigation algorithm, which subsequently corrects the accumulated Cross-Track Error to rejoin the planned route.

4   Experiments

To validate the robustness of the autonomous navigation framework, four heterogeneous test routes were executed within the University of Alicante campus. These experiments were designed to evaluate the system across varying levels of environmental complexity, recording the total distance, execution time, robot velocities, and the Cross-Track Error (CTE), which measures the lateral deviation from the ideal map-based route.

The first test served as the baseline scenario to evaluate the core path-following algorithm in an obstacle-free environment, covering a total distance of 422 m in approximately 9 min. As illustrated in the route map (Fig. 5), the trajectory required the robot to navigate long straight segments and execute two major directional changes. This behavior is clearly reflected in the velocity graphs (Fig. 4a). For instance, around second 120, the linear velocity drops significantly to ensure a safe maneuver, while the angular velocity shows a sharp

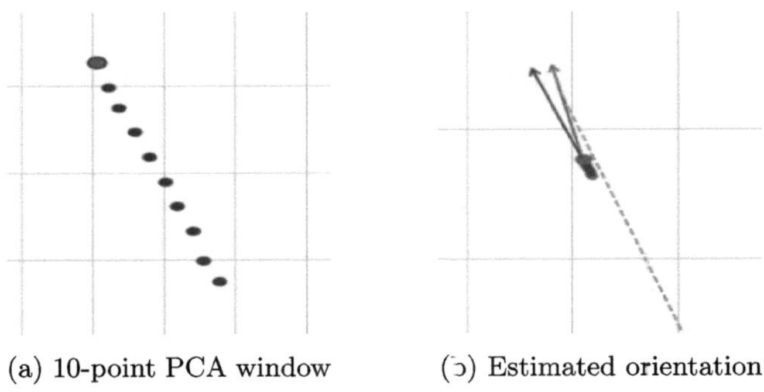

(a) 10-point PCA window   (b) Estimated orientation

Fig. 3. Visualization of the orientation mechanism. (Color figure online)

negative peak, corresponding precisely to the first right turn on the map to reach the next checkpoint. Later, around second 460, a similar drop in linear speed is paired with a positive angular peak, indicating the final left turn towards the destination. Between these checkpoints, the recorded data demonstrates optimal performance. The robot maintained a steady maximum linear velocity of around 0.85 m per second with minimal angular corrections. Because the frontal LiDAR remained clear throughout the route, the Cross-Track Error was kept low, primarily reflecting the natural sway of the quadruped locomotion and minor GPS fluctuations.

The second test introduced standard obstacle avoidance scenarios, covering a total distance of 433 m in approximately 9 min (Fig. 5). During this route, the robot successfully detected and bypassed two large, isolated obstacles: a tree (Fig. 5, right) and a group of bushes. The recorded data shows a direct correlation between sensory input and the robot's evasive actions. For instance, around second 320, the front LiDAR distance drops abruptly below the one-meter safety threshold due to the tree. Immediately, the linear velocity drops sharply to ensure safety, paired with an evasive angular command. This maneuver is clearly visible in the Cross-Track Error plot (Fig. 4b), which reaches approximately −2 m, indicating the robot safely diverted to the right of the ideal path. A similar event is recorded near the end of the run, around second 520, when the robot faces the bushes. Following the same reactive pattern, the velocities adjust rapidly, resulting this time in a positive Cross-Track Error of up to 2.5 m as the robot steers to the left. In both instances, as soon as the LiDAR sensors confirm the path is clear, the control algorithm stabilizes the velocities and smoothly guides the robot back to the planned geodesic route.

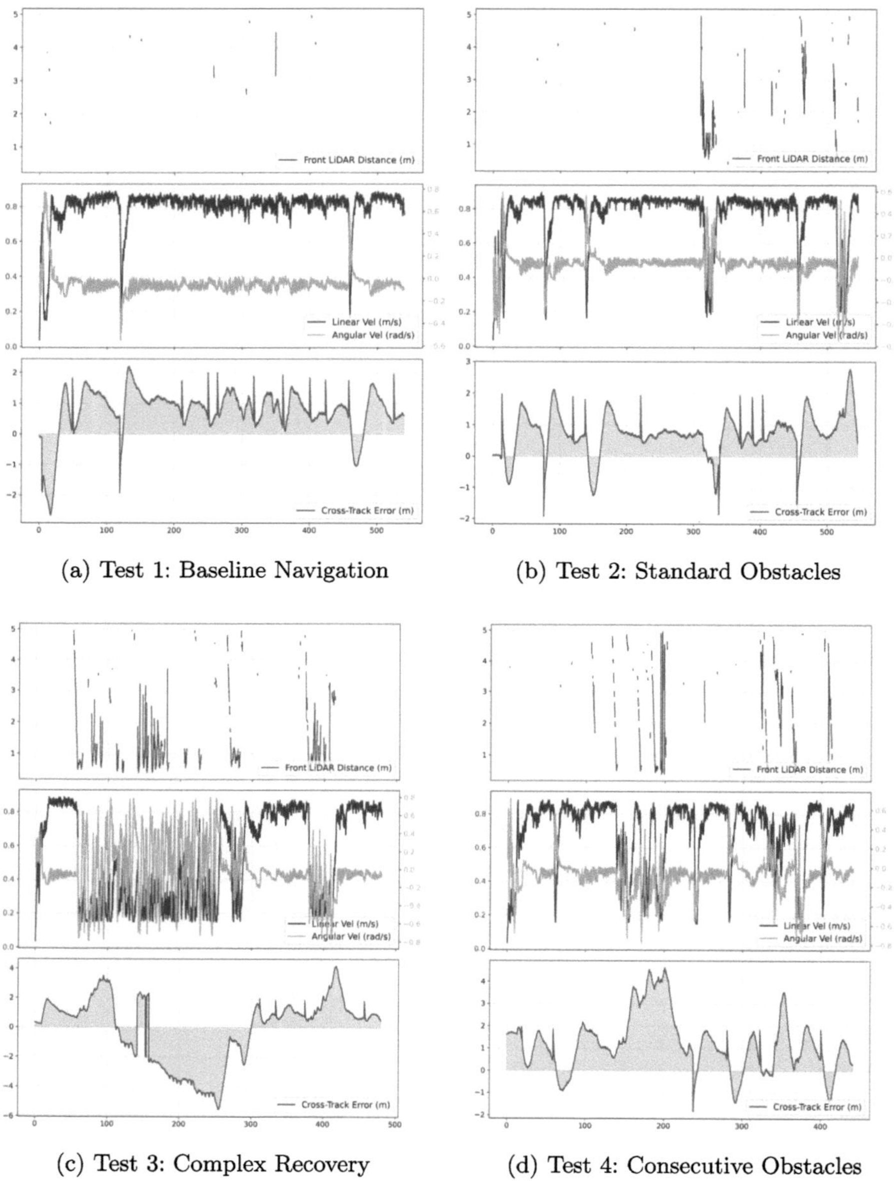

(a) Test 1: Baseline Navigation

(b) Test 2: Standard Obstacles

(c) Test 3: Complex Recovery

(d) Test 4: Consecutive Obstacles

Fig. 4. Velocity and Cross-Track Error (CTE) analysis.

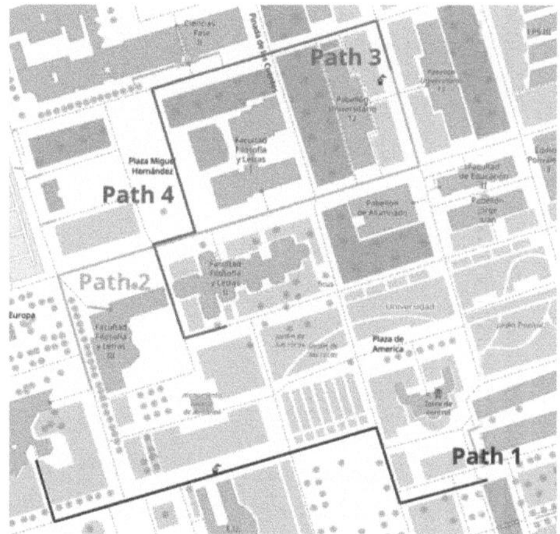

Fig. 5. Overview of the experimental routes (left) and examples of the complex obstacles present in the routes and autonomously avoided by the robot (right).

The third test was the most demanding scenario. Covering a distance of 249 m, the execution took exactly 8 min due to severe unmapped occlusions. The routing API generated a path through poorly accessible areas, forcing the robot to execute complex recovery behaviors. Initially, the robot encountered a densely bushed roundabout (Fig. 5, right) where continuous LiDAR triggers forced it to actively search for an alternative opening, resulting in a deliberate deviation of 6 m to the right (Fig. 4c). Later in the same route, the robot detected an impassable physical step. It halted its forward motion and autonomously diverted 4 m to the left until it found an accessible ramp to climb. These results demonstrate the framework's capability to resolve severe navigational deadlocks and safely reach the destination without human intervention.

The fourth test evaluated the system's behavior when facing consecutive small obstacles scattered along the path. The robot completed this 308-meter route in 7 min and 20 s. Instead of oscillating wildly with each detection, the robot performed successive minor evasions. This resulted in a cumulative lateral drift, reaching a Cross-Track Error peak of 4.5 m (Fig. 4d). The control law correctly prioritized continuous collision avoidance over strict path adherence, accumulating the lateral error safely until the area was completely clear to resume the standard trajectory.

To conclude the experimental analysis, Table 1 presents a quantitative summary of the four test routes, detailing the traveled distance, total execution time, and the statistical deviation of the Cross-Track Error.

Table 1. Quantitative results of the autonomous navigation experiments.

Experiment	Distance (m)	Time (s)	Mean CTE (m)	Std. Dev. CTE (m)
Test 1	422.08	545.30	0.8675	0.6718
Test 2	433.50	539.80	0.9723	0.7678
Test 3	248.76	480.20	1.8760	2.2698
Test 4	307.83	440.80	1.4221	1.2878

5   Conclusion and Future Work

The proposed system integrates GNSS-based localization, OpenStreetMap pedestrian routing, and reactive LiDAR obstacle avoidance to enable long-range waypoint navigation for a quadruped robot without requiring a pre-built metric map. Robot heading is estimated from successive GNSS fixes using a windowed principal-direction method, and a path-following controller combines heading and lateral corrections while adapting speed during turns; rate limiting and smoothing improve command stability. Real world experiments with a Unitree Go2 showed reliable goal reaching across diverse routes, including scenarios with isolated obstacles, complex unmapped occlusions, and consecutive obstacle encounters. Route deviations reflected safety-driven avoidance behaviors, and the controller consistently guided the robot back to the planned path once obstacles were cleared. Despite these promising results, the study also exposed limitations inherent to GNSS-only localization and map-based routing in unstructured pedestrian areas. GNSS noise and multipath effects introduce heading and position uncertainty, which can increase lateral tracking error, particularly at low speeds. Furthermore, routes computed from OpenStreetMap may include locally inaccessible segments (e.g., vegetation occlusions, stairs, ramps not represented in the map, or temporary obstacles), occasionally inducing prolonged recovery behaviors. On the other hand, future work will improve robustness under local situations by involving image segmentation and add accessibility-aware routing with online re-planning to avoid non-traversable segments, and incorporate semantic perception (learning-based traversability) to better anticipate dead-ends and operate safely in dynamic pedestrian environments.

Acknowledgments. This study has been carried out under the framework of the collaboration between Synergy Tech (Unitree Spain) and University Institute for Computer Research, University of Alicante.

Disclosure of Interests. The authors declare no competing interests.

References

1. Bauer, Z., Dominguez, A., Cruz, E., Gcmez-Donoso, F., Orts-Escolano, S., Cazorla, M.: Enhancing perception for the visually impaired with deep learning techniques and low-cost wearable sensors. Pattern Recogn. Lett. **137**, 27–36 (2020). https://doi.org/10.1016/j.patrec.2019.03.008. https://www.sciencedirect.com/science/article/pii/S0167865519300881
2. Cai, S., et al.: Navigating real-world challenges: a quadruped robot guiding system for visually impaired people in diverse environments. In: Proceedings of the 2024 CHI Conference on Human Factors in Computing Systems (2024). https://doi.org/10.1145/3613904.3642227
3. Galatas, G., McMurrough, C.D., Mariottini, G.L., Makedon, F.: eyedog: an assistive-guide robot for the visually impaired. In: Proceedings of the 13th International ACM SIGACCESS Conference on Computers and Accessibility, p. 58 (2011). https://doi.org/10.1145/2141622.2141691
4. Guerreiro, J.A., Sato, D., Asakawa, S., Dong, H., Kitani, K.M., Asakawa, C.: Cabot: designing and evaluating an autonomous navigation robot for blind people. In: Proceedings of the 21st International ACM SIGACCESS Conference on Computers and Accessibility, ASSETS '19, pp. 68–82. Association for Computing Machinery, New York (2019). DOI 10.1145/3308561.3353771
5. Kulyukin, V., Gharpure, C., Nicholson, J.: Robocart: toward robot-assisted navigation of grocery stores by the visually impaired. In: IEEE/RSJ International Conference on Intelligent Robots and Systems, pp. 2845–2850 (2005). https://doi.org/10.1109/IROS.2005.1545107
6. Losantos-Pulido, C., Escalona, F., Cazorla, M., Gómez-Donoso, F.: Paws: personal assistance walking system for the visually impaired. In: Cazorla, M., Gómez-Donoso, F., Escalona, F. (eds.) Proceedings of the XXIV Workshop of Physical Agents, pp. 3–15. Universidad de Alicante, Alicante (2024)
7. Lu, C.L., et al.: Assistive navigation using deep reinforcement learning guiding robot with UWB/voice beacons and semantic feedbacks for blind and visually impaired people. Front. Rob. AI **8** (2021). https://doi.org/10.3389/frobt.2021.654132
8. Mai, C., et al.: A smart cane based on 2d lidar and rgb-d camera sensor-realizing navigation and obstacle recognition. Sensors **24** (2024). https://doi.org/10.3390/s24030870
9. Nevasekar, V., Cabrera, M.E.: Seeing eye stretch: robot-assisted indoor navigation for blind or low-vision individuals. In: 2025 22nd International Conference on Ubiquitous Robots (UR), pp. 518–522 (2025). https://doi.org/10.1109/ur65550.2025.11078138
10. Yang, C.H., Juang, J.: Guide robot based on image processing and path planning. Machines (2025). https://doi.org/10.3390/machines13070560
11. Yelamarthi, K., Haas, D., Nielsen, D., Mothersell, S.: RFID and GPS integrated navigation system for the visually impaired. In: 2010 53rd IEEE International Midwest Symposium on Circuits and Systems, pp. 1149–1152 (2010). https://doi.org/10.1109/MWSCAS.2010.5548863

Impact of Preprocessing Algorithms on Deep Learning-Driven Stenosis Classification in Invasive Coronary Angiography

Ariadna Jiménez-Partinen[1,2,3]($\boxtimes$), Miguel A. Molina-Cabello[1,2,3],
Juan Marques-Garrido[2], María Paulina Ordóñez-Walkowiak[2],
Jorge Rodríguez-Capitán[3,4,5], Ana I. Molina-Ramos[3,4,5],
and Manuel Jiménez-Navarro[3,4,5,6]

[1] ITIS Software, University of Málaga, 29071 Málaga, Spain
ariadna@uma.es, miguelangel@lcc.uma.es
[2] Department of Computer Languages and Computer Science, University of Málaga,
Bulevar Louis Pasteur, 35, 29071 Málaga, Spain
mpow@uma.es
[3] IBIMA Plataforma BIONAND, Instituto de Investigación Biomédica de Málaga,
29590 Málaga, Spain
[4] Cardiology Department, Hospital Universitario Virgen de la Victoria,
29010 Málaga, Spain
[5] Centro de Investigación Biomédica en Red de Enfermedades Cardiovasculares
(CIBERCV), Instituto de Salud Carlos III (ISCIII), 28029 Madrid, Spain
[6] Facultad de Medicina, University of Málaga, Bulevar Louis Pasteur,
37, 29071 Málaga, Spain
mjimeneznavarro@uma.es

Abstract. Invasive Coronary Angiography remains the standard for diagnosing coronary artery disease, yet the automated classification of stenotic lesions is often hindered by suboptimal image contrast and complex vascular structures. This study evaluates the impact of various image enhancement techniques on the performance of deep convolutional neural network architectures for the binary classification of coronary stenosis. Using the CADICA dataset, a patch-based approach was implemented to distinguish between clinically significant lesions ($\geq 50\%$ narrowing) and non-lesion samples. Two phases were conducted: first, a comparative analysis of five benchmark architectures (AlexNet, GoogLeNet, ResNet-18, ResNet-50, and VGG16) as baseline strategy; and second, Gram Equalization, an assessment of four preprocessing algorithms – such as Histogram Equalization, Contrast Limited Adaptive Histogram Equalization, Gamma Correction, and Logarithmic Transformations– on classification accuracy. The results indicate that GoogLeNet achieves the highest baseline performance, achieving an F1-score of 0.705. Furthermore, the findings of Phase 2 demonstrate that while Contrast Limited Adaptive Histogram Equalization significantly benefits deeper architectures such as ResNet and VGG architecture, the baseline GoogLeNet configuration remains the most robust. This research highlights the critical role of preprocessing in clinical decision-support systems and provides a framework to enhance the reliability of deep learning models for stenosis detection in invasive coronary angiography images.

Keywords: Invasive coronary angiography · deep learning · screening

1   Introduction

Cardiovascular diseases (CVDs) are the leading cause of global mortality, responsible for an estimated 19.8 million deaths annually, with coronary artery disease (CAD) as the most common pathology. Myocardial ischemia is characterized by the development of atherosclerotic plaques in the arterial intima, which gradually obstruct the coronary arteries and cause stenosis. Invasive coronary angiography (ICA) plays a crucial role in the care of coronary artery disease, providing anatomical imaging for diagnosis and treatment guidance [2]. The ICA acquisition protocol involves injecting a radiocontrast agent through a catheter via a percutaneous incision for X-ray visualization of the coronary arteries. The procedure includes projections and angles of both the left coronary artery (LCA) and the right coronary artery (RCA) [19]. In standard clinical practice, stenosis is identified and assessed by visual examination. Stenoses are classified by the degree of narrowing: common categories include mild ($< 50\%$), moderate ($[50\%, 70\%]$), and severe ($> 70\%$), also called an obstructive lesion [3]. This procedure is affected by significant noise, complex overlapping vessel structures, uneven illumination, and inconsistent lumen intensity. Therefore, ICA image evaluation can exhibit both inter- and intra-observer variability due to the subjective nature of visual assessments [13].

In light of the aforementioned challenges, accurate detection and classification of coronary stenosis are paramount to ensure the reliability of clinical decisions and improve patient outcomes. To address these limitations, Convolutional Neural Networks (CNNs) have emerged as a solution, known for their effectiveness in analyzing medical images and performing complex classification tasks [14]. Using deep learning models, it is possible to provide a more robust and standardized evaluation to support clinical decision-making [23].

An example of a CNN-based method for classifying healthy ICA images into LCA and RCA images is proposed by Eschen *et al.* [5]. Likewise, [4] proposed a more complex system based on multiple Inception architectures to classify ICA images into LCA and RCA images, select keyframes, and classify the lesions. As well, [16] employed the Inception architecture to perform binary classification between normal and abnormal ($\geq 50\%$) lesions. For automated diagnosis, Rodrigues *et al.* [20] proposed a multi-stage framework in which ICA images are first classified into LCA and RCA using a Residual Neural Network (ResNet), and then a RetinaNet architecture is trained for stenosis detection.

Another approach is patch-based processing, where frames are divided into subimages to improve training, reduce the spatial information, and decrease the computational time [18]. For instance, Nars *et al.* [17] implemented a segmentation system for ICA images using patches from 44 coronary angiographies, composed of two CNNs based on learned kernels. Au *et al.* [1] detected and classified severe lesions in RCA ICA images using a three-phase method.

Despite the state-of-the-art in ICA image analysis being increasing with unique contributions, it also exhibits certain limitations due to the scarcity of reproducible work, the single-projection or branch focus, and the lack of high-quality, open-access datasets, which is the most important drawback [15]. Additionally, image preprocessing and enhancement are important fields to explore to determine whether methods are affected by these techniques. In general-purpose deep learning tasks, enhancement algorithms overperform baseline original images [20]. In medical imaging, such as melanoma, diabetic retinopathy, or neuromia, have been improved thanks to equalization-enhanced image algorithms [6]. However, other medical imaging modalities, such as magnetic resonance imaging (MRI), underperform when certain preprocessing steps are applied [11], yielding negligible results. Based on the evidence, the present study aims to develop a CNN model capable of classifying coronary stenosis and to report how enhancement techniques affect CNN-based methods, providing clinical decision support and guidance to healthcare professionals during the diagnostic procedure. The main contributions of this work are:

- Providing a thorough comparison across benchmarking CNN architectures for automated classification of coronary stenosis.
- Exhaustive evaluation of the impact of image preprocessing on performance.
- Comprehensive qualitative and quantitative assessments of stenosis classification are reported.
- The complete open-access CADICA dataset [10] is employed to promote reproducibility and support conducting experiments close to clinical settings.
- The proposed automated method demonstrated a promising approach to ICA image analysis.

The remainder of this document is organized as follows. The nature of the data, methods, and performance metrics are detailed in Sect. 2. After that, Sect. 3 collects and discusses the results of the experiment. Finally, the Sect. 4 is devoted to conclusions and findings of this work.

2   Methodology

In this section, the methodology followed is described, including the framework, source data description, and the strategies addressed to study and enhance ICA classification. The overall methodology implemented is depicted in Fig. 1.

2.1   Framework

In this section, the proposed approach for enhancing the performance of deep convolutional image classifiers through image enhancement techniques is described. Let the set of image classes be defined as:

$$\mathcal{C} = \{C_1, ..., C_K\} \tag{1}$$

where K denotes the total number of classes. Given an input invasive coronary angiography image $\mathbf{X}$, a deep convolutional image classifier $\mathcal{F}$ is used to estimate the class y to which $\mathbf{X}$ belongs:

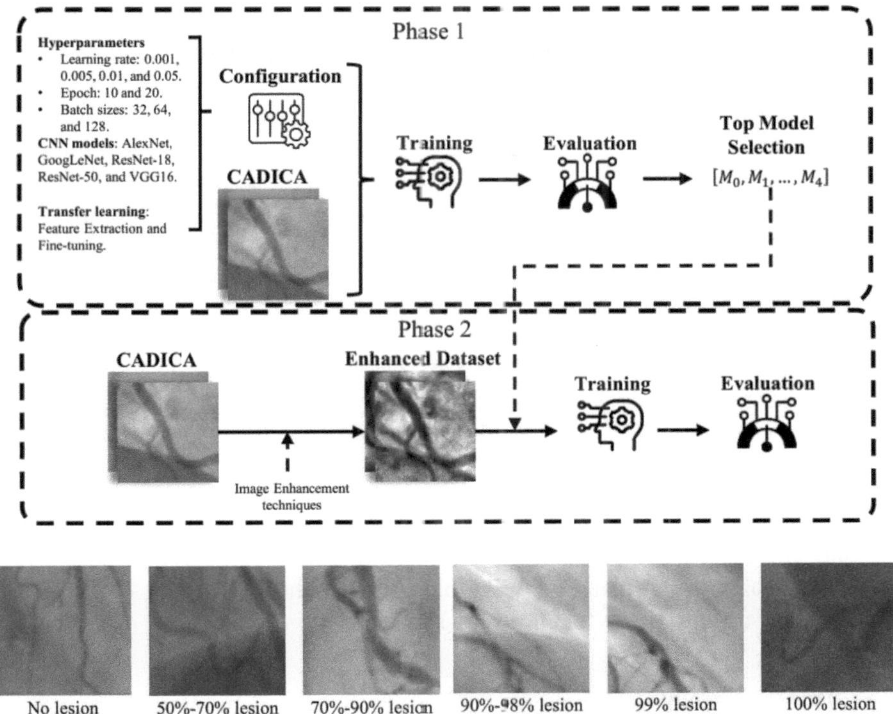

Fig. 2. Examples from the CADICA dataset, categorized by narrowing degree.

$$\mathbf{p} = \mathcal{F}(\mathbf{X}) \tag{2}$$

$$q = \arg \max_{i \in \{1,...,K\}} p_i \tag{3}$$

Here, $\mathbf{p} \in [0,1]^K$ represents the vector of predicted probabilities that image $\mathbf{X}$ belongs to each of the K classes, and $q \in \{1, ..., K\}$ denotes the predicted class label for $\mathbf{X}$. Next, consider the scenario in which a degraded image $\hat{\mathbf{X}}$ is provided as input. Assume that M enhancement algorithms are available, such that $\tilde{\mathbf{X}}_j$ denotes the enhanced image obtained by applying the j-th enhancement method to $\hat{\mathbf{X}}$, where $j \in \{1, ..., M\}$. For notational convenience, we assume that $j = 1$ corresponds to the identity operation (i.e., no enhancement), so that $\tilde{\mathbf{X}}_1 = \hat{\mathbf{X}}$.

The objective is to evaluate the effect of applying enhancement algorithms to $\hat{\mathbf{X}}$ on overall image classification performance.

2.2 Dataset

To reliably study the impact of classifier selection with CNN architectures closer to real-world clinical scenarios, the CADICA dataset [10] is used. CADICA consists of frames from video sequences of invasive coronary angiography (ICA) from 42 patients. Each patient case comprises videos selected for inspection according to the CAD procedure, including several projections of the LCA and RCA, based on the diagnostic case and its complexity. Considering LCA and RCA projections and a wide range of lesions as positive instances, the classification task became more complex and closer to real-world scenarios.

The present work focuses on the classification of patches, i.e., equal subdivisions, of ICA images. The raw images have size 512×512 pixels, which were divided into a 4×4 grid, and then resized to 32×32 pixels. This way, we want to preserve spatial information near the lesion, and the downsampling was done to improve training performance. These patches were labeled with the corresponding lesion degree if the centroid of the lesion bounding box fell into it. However, it is possible to encounter different types of lesions on a single patch. The severest category was chosen if more than one bounding box centroid was found. Otherwise, it was assessed as *non-lesion* patches. Figure 2 shows representative samples of patches for each category. In the approach followed, the categories were binarized into two classes: *lesion*, which are those patches with lesions $\geq 50\%$, and *non-lesion*. This clear separation ensures that the model learns to distinguish between healthy vessels and clinically significant obstructions, omitting intermediate mild lesions to avoid labeling ambiguity.

Due to inherent class imbalance in the data, with the *uninjured* class as the majority, a balancing strategy was implemented. The *non-lesion* category was sub-sampled to match the 2,566 samples of the *lesion* class.

2.3 Image Processing

To enhance model generalization and increase the volume of training data, a data augmentation pipeline was applied, increasing the sample size to 5,130 per class. The data augmentation applied was based on spatial transformations that modify the pixel arrangement [7]. Specifically, affine transformations were applied to avoid spatial distortions or unnatural vessel orientations. Frames were rotated by up to $\pm 40°$, with horizontal and vertical translations reaching 20% of the image dimensions, shear mappings with intensities up to 20%, and horizontal reflections to simulate various vessel orientations. Additionally, the nearest-neighbor interpolation mode was utilized to preserve the integrity of the boundary pixel.

For the second phase of the experimentation, image enhancement techniques were applied to preprocess input patches to assess how the method's performance is affected and whether it facilitates the extraction of relevant patterns by convolutional layers. In this regard, the applied procedures included Histogram Equalization (HE) and Contrast Limited Adaptive Histogram Equalization (CLAHE) to optimize global and local contrast by producing a transformation function that seeks to generate an output image with a uniform histogram, i.e., each intensity level has roughly equal frequency. Additionally, Gamma correction (GC) and Logarithmic transformations (LT) are used to adjust luminance and expand the dynamic range of low-intensity pixel values. Figure 3 illustrates a sample with each enhanced technique.

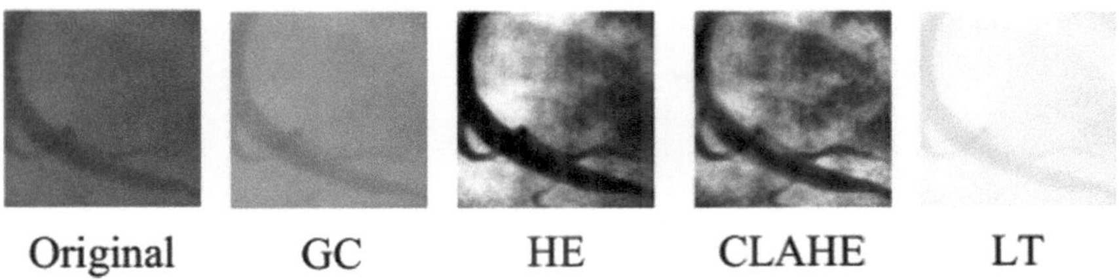

Fig. 3. Example of an ICA labeled as *lesion* enhanced using the different algorithms.

2.4   Methods

Four deep learning architectures were selected to conduct binary classification of ICA patches: ResNet [8], VGG [21], AlexNet [12], and GoogLeNet [22]. The selected architectures are benchmarks for CNNs in medical image classification, due to their broad use and proven robustness in medical image analysis [23]. The models selected (ResNet-50, ResNet-18, VGG-16, AlexNet, and GoogLeNet) provide a diverse range of depths and structural complexities to address the problem. Two transfer learning strategies (feature extraction and fine-tuning) were implemented to adapt general-purpose models for coronary angiography classification in the first phase. Feature extraction involved freezing the convolutional base of the pre-trained model to act as a fixed extractor, while the original output layers were replaced with a custom classifier trained specifically on the dataset. In contrast, the fine-tuning approach involved unfreezing a portion of the upper convolutional layers, allowing their weights to be updated during training to better capture the stenotic lesions. Although fine-tuning offers greater potential for accuracy by tailoring high-level filters to the target domain, it imposes substantial increases in computational demands and training duration.

2.5   Performance Metrics

It is essential to provide a thorough and structured report of the experimental results to adequately capture the unique characteristics and performance of each approach. In order to quantify the performance of different methods to classify ICA images as a binary classification task, the four representative parameters (True Positive (TP), True Negative (TN), False Positive (FP), and False Negative (FN)) are used to computed the commonly used performance metrics. All reported metrics range from 0 to 1, with the higher, the better; and they are defined as follows [9]:

$$Accuracy = \frac{TP + TN}{TP + FP + FN + TN} \qquad Specificity = \frac{TN}{FP + TN} \qquad (4)$$

$$Recall = \frac{TP}{TP + FN} \qquad Precision = \frac{TP}{TP + FP} \qquad (5)$$

$$F1\text{-}Score = 2\frac{Precision \times Recall}{Precision + Recall} \qquad Spatial\ accuracy = \frac{TP}{TP + FN + FP} \qquad (6)$$

Table 1. Summary of the configurations selected. *LR* refers to learning rate.

Model	Epochs	LR	Batch
AlexNet	10	0.005	32
GoogleNet	20	0.001	32
ResNet18	20	0.001	64
ResNet50	10	0.001	64
VGG16	10	0.001	32

2.6 Training Setup

The dataset was split into training and hold-out test subsets at 80% and 20%, respectively. The experimental setup involved a grid search encompassing four learning rates (0.001, 0.005, 0.01, and 0.05), two epoch counts (10 and 20), and three batch sizes (32, 64, and 128). Regarding the training configuration, the models were optimized using Stochastic Gradient Descent (SGD) with a momentum rate of 0.9. The training process aimed to minimize the Cross-Entropy loss function to ensure effective convergence.

A 10-fold cross-validation approach was adopted for model selection to provide robust, partition-independent results. In each iteration, the training set was partitioned such that 90% of the data was used for training and 10% was reserved for validation. All performance metrics reported in this study represent the mean results across the 10 trained methods per architecture on the held-out test set. Experiments were run on a Gigabyte GeForce RTX 4060 WINDFORCE OC (8 GB) GPU.

3   Results

This research is structured into two distinct phases. Phase 1 focuses on hyperparameter architecture selection through a grid search, while Phase 2 evaluates the impact of image enhancement algorithms on model performance.

The first phase involved evaluating 240 hyperparameter configurations for the selected CNN architectures. Hyperparameters selected across architectures are detailed in Table 1, results obtained are considered the baseline, i.e., performance without image enhancement.

The second phase of the study evaluated the effect of the selected image enhancement algorithms on the model's performance, maintaining the hyperparameter configuration from the previous stage. Table 2 reports the mean over the 10-fold on the held-out test subset across architectures and strategies selected (baseline, HE, CLAHE, GC, and LT). The results indicate that enhancement algorithms retrieve results that are similar to or underperform the original images across architectures, despite preprocessing techniques that improve the visual appearance of blood vessels, as shown in Fig. 3. The GoogleNet baseline achieves the highest values, with an F-score of 0.705, accuracy of 0.621, and spatial accuracy of 0.544. However, its performance is significantly affected when a

Table 2. Performance of contrast enhancement strategies per pretrained model. *Spatial* refers to spatial accuracy. For each model, the best value is in **bold**.

Model	Strategy	F1-score	Accuracy	Spatial
AlexNet	Baseline	**0.676**	**0.565**	**0.511**
	HE	0.652	0.501	0.484
	CLAHE	0.100	0.485	0.051
	GC	0.008	0.502	0.004
	LT	0.663	0.496	0.495
GoogleNet	Baseline	**0.705**	**0.621**	**0.544**
	HE	0.258	0.505	0.148
	CLAHE	0.367	0.423	0.225
	GC	0.507	0.434	0.340
	LT	0.307	0.466	0.182
ResNet18	Baseline	**0.664**	0.512	**0.497**
	HE	0.589	**0.566**	0.418
	CLAHE	0.663	0.515	0.496
	GC	0.619	0.456	0.448
	LT	0.440	0.531	0.282
ResNet50	Baseline	**0.668**	0.502	**0.501**
	HE	0.402	0.459	0.252
	CLAHE	0.664	0.499	0.497
	GC	0.362	0.523	0.221
	LT	0.024	**0.531**	0.013
VGG16	Baseline	**0.667**	0.504	**0.500**
	HE	0.652	0.521	0.483
	CLAHE	0.663	0.499	0.495
	GC	0.372	**0.560**	0.229
	LT	0.663	0.497	0.496

preprocessing technique is applied, decreasing the F-score and spatial accuracy by around 50% of their achieved values, and the accuracy by 30%. However, AlexNet, which achieves the second-highest F-score (0.676), is less affected by enhancement algorithms, specifically HE and Lt, which attain 0.652 and 0.663, respectively. CLAHE technique, an important histogram equalization strategy that produces visually good results, reaching nearly equal results across ResNet-based models and VGG-16. Finally, CG and LT transformations underperform severely, indicating that they are unsuitable for CNN-based ICA classifiers.

4   Conclusions

This paper provided a comparison of benchmark CNN architectures and an exhaustive evaluation of the impact of image enhancement on coronary stenosis classification. Employing the open-access CADICA dataset, a reproducible and realistic assessment of these models was ensured in a clinical context.

Quantitative results reveal that GoogLeNet, without an enhancement technique, achieved optimal performance across the configurations explored. In addition, although image enhancement analysis indicates negligible benefit to performance, CLAHE improves blood vessel contrast, which can help the clinician's visualization, whereas deeper architectures, such as ResNet and VGG, can achieve similar results. Despite that, the GoogLeNet baseline configuration remains the most reliable approach. However, combining a robust CNN architecture with preprocessing operations may reduce ICA's sensitivity to image quality and improve spatial accuracy.

The present work represents a contribution to the field of medical image analysis. In particular, it opens the way for systems capable of providing a reliable diagnosis of coronary stenosis and assisting clinical decisions. Further research lines can explore more exhaustive hyperparameter optimization using Bayesian or genetic algorithms, while the inclusion of mild intermediate lesions represents another promising approach. Finally, other architectures, such as transformer-based or hybrid architectures, might be tested.

Acknowledgements. This work is partially supported by the Autonomous Government of Andalusia (Spain) under project PPRO-TIC163-G-2023 (TIC163-G-FEDER), and under grant number DGP_PIDI_2024_00462; also by the Ministry of Science and Innovation of Spain, grant number PID2022-136764OA-I00. It includes funds from the European Regional Development Fund (ERDF). It is also partially supported by the Instituto de Salud Carlos III, project code PI25/02129 (co-financed by the European Union). The authors thankfully acknowledge the computer resources, technical expertise and assistance provided by the SCBI (Supercomputing and Bioinformatics) center of the University of Málaga. They also gratefully acknowledge the support of NVIDIA Corporation with the donation of an RTX A6000 GPU with 48Gb. The authors also thankfully acknowledge the grant of the Universidad de Málaga and the Instituto de Investigacin Biomédica de Málaga y Plataforma en Nanomedicina-IBIMA Plataforma BIONAND.

Data Availability. The open-access CADICA dataset [10] is available at: https://data.mendeley.com/datasets/p9bpx9ctcv/5.

References

1. Au, B., et al.: Automated characterization of stenosis in invasive coronary angiography images with convolutional neural networks. arXiv preprint (2018)
2. Byrne, R.A., et al.: 2023 esc guidelines for the management of acute coronary syndromes: developed by the task force on the management of acute coronary syndromes of the european society of cardiology (esc). Eur. Heart J. Acute Cardiovasc. Care **13**(1), 55–161 (2024)
3. Chunawala, Z.S., et al.: Prognostic significance of obstructive coronary artery disease in patients admitted with acute decompensated heart failure: the aric study community surveillance. Eur. J. Heart Fail. **24**(11), 2140–2149 (2022)

4. Cong, C., Kato, Y., Vasconcellos, H.D., Lima. J., Venkatesh, B.: Automated stenosis detection and classification in x-ray angiography using deep neural network. In: 2019 IEEE International Conference on Bioinformatics and Biomedicine (BIBM), pp. 1301–1308. IEEE (2019)

5. Eschen, C.K.: Classification of left and right coronary arteries in coronary angiographies using deep learning. Electronics 11(13), 2087 (2022)

6. Ferdinand, V.A., Nawir, V., Henry. G.E., Gunawan, A.A.S.: Effect of image enhancement in cnn-based medical image classification: a systematic literature review. In: 2022 5th International Conference on Information and Communications Technology (ICOIACT), pp. 87–92. IEEE (2022)

7. Gonzalez, R.C.: Digital Image Processing. Pearson education (2009)

8. He, K., Zhang, X., Ren, S., Sun, J.: Deep residual learning for image recognition. In: Proceedings of the IEEE Conference on Computer Vision and Pattern Recognition, pp. 770–778 (2016)

9. Hossin, M., Sulaiman, M.N.: A review on evaluation metrics for data classification evaluations. Int. J. Data Mining Knowl. Manag. Process 5(2), 1 (2015)

10. Jiménez-Partinen, A., et al.: Cadica a new dataset for coronary artery disease detection by using invasive coronary angiography. Expert. Syst. 41(12), e13708 (2024)

11. Kochanek, K.D., Murphy, S.L., Xu, J., Arias, E.: Mortality in the United States, 2022. US Department of Health and Human Services, Centers for Disease Control and Prevention. National Center for Health Statistics (2024)

12. Krizhevsky, A., Sutskever, I., Hinton, G.E.: Imagenet classification with deep convolutional neural networks. In: Advances in Neural Information Processing Systems, p. 25 (2012)

13. Leape, L.L., Park, R.E., Bashore, T.M., Harrison, J.K., Davidson, C.J., Brook, R.H.: Effect of variability in the interpretation of coronary angiograms on the appropriateness of use of coronary revascularization procedures. Am. Heart J. 139(1), 106–113 (2000)

14. Ling, H., et al.: Deep learning model for coronary angiography. J. Cardiovasc. Transl. Res. 16(4), 896–904 (2023)

15. Litjens, G., et al.: State-of-the-art deep learning in cardiovascular image analysis. JACC: Cardiovasc. Imaging 12(8 Part 1), 1549–1565 (2019)

16. Moon, J.H., Cha, W.C., Chung, M.J., Lee, K.S., Cho, B.H., Choi, J.H., et al.: Automatic stenosis recognition from coronary angiography using convolutional neural networks. Comput. Methods Programs Biomed. 198, 105819 (2021)

17. Nasr-Esfahani, E., et al.: Segmentation of vessels in angiograms using convolutional neural networks. Biomed. Signal Process. Control 40, 240–251 (2018)

18. Ovalle-Magallanes, E., Alvarado-Carrillo, D.E., Avina-Cervantes, J.G., Cruz-Aceves, I., Ruiz-Pinales, J., Correa, R.: Deep learning-based coronary stenosis detection in x-ray angiography images: Overview and future trends. In: Artificial Intelligence and Machine Learning for Healthcare: Vol. 2: Emerging Methodologies and Trends, pp. 197–223 (2022)

19. Rigatelli, G., Gianese, F., Zuin, M.: Modern atlas of invasive coronary angiography views: a practical approach for fellows and young interventionalists. Int. J. Cardiovasc. Imaging 38(5), 919–926 (2022)

20. Rodrigues, D.L., Menezes, M.N., Pinto, F.J., Oliveira, A.L.: Automated detection of coronary artery stenosis in x-ray angiography using deep neural networks. arXiv preprint (2021)

21. Simonyan, K., Zisserman, A.: Very deep convolutional networks for large-scale image recognition. arXiv preprint (2014)
22. Szegedy, C., et al.: Going deeper with convolutions. In: Proceedings of the IEEE Conference on Computer Vision and Pattern Recognition, pp. 1–9 (2015)
23. Xia, Q., et al.: A comprehensive review of deep learning for medical image segmentation. Neurocomputing **613**, 128740 (2025)

Benchmarking PointNet++ and RandLA-Net for Urban Furniture Segmentation with Consumer-Grade LiDAR: A Pilot Study

Geovanny Satama-Bermeo[1], Daniel Caballero-Martin[1], Hicham Affou[1], Erol Kurt[2], and Jose Manuel Lopez-Guede[1(✉)]

[1] Department of System Engineering and Automation Control, Faculty of Engineering of Vitoria-Gasteiz, University of the Basque Country (UPV/EHU), Nieves Cano, 12, 01006 Vitoria-Gasteiz, Spain
jm.lopez@ehu.es

[2] Department of Electrical and Electronics Engineering, Technology Faculty, Gazi University, 06500 Besevler, Ankara, Turkey

Abstract. This study establishes an experimental pilot for urban digitalization through manual in-situ acquisition with consumer-grade LiDAR sensors (iPhone 15 Pro Max, iPad Pro M4). PointNet++ is implemented as comparative baseline, evidencing geometric difficulties that hierarchical architectures face with portable device noise. Contrasting against RandLA-Net, it is demonstrated that local feature learning capacity is determinant for overcoming such limitations. The evaluation on 759 objects from Vitoria-Gasteiz, Spain (124:1 class imbalance), reveals RandLA-Net achieves 90.4% overall accuracy and 61.5% Intersection over Union (IoU) mean (+12.2% over baseline), with strong per-class performance on majority classes (89.5% Benches, 83.3% Bins, 92.9% Sewer Caps). Results confirm technical superiority and operational viability of this low-cost solution, identifying critical thresholds (<50 instances) requiring specialized strategies.

Keywords: Urban Semantic Segmentation · Consumer-Grade LiDAR · PointNet++ · RandLA-Net · Class Imbalance

1 Introduction

Urban digital twins have emerged as critical infrastructure for smart city applications, supporting urban planning, infrastructure monitoring, and accessibility assessment [12]. These representations require comprehensive 3D street furniture inventories for municipal decision-making, traditionally relying on terrestrial laser scanning (TLS, Terrestrial Laser Scanning) systems costing over e50,000 with specialized training requirements [1]. This cost limitation has persisted for over a decade, creating budget barriers for smaller municipalities while leaving thousands of cities without critical 3D infrastructure data (Fig. 1) [7].

J. M. Ferrández Vicente et al. (Eds.): IWINAC 2026, LNCS 16575, pp. 107–117, 2026.
https://doi.org/10.1007/978-3-032-27317-8_11

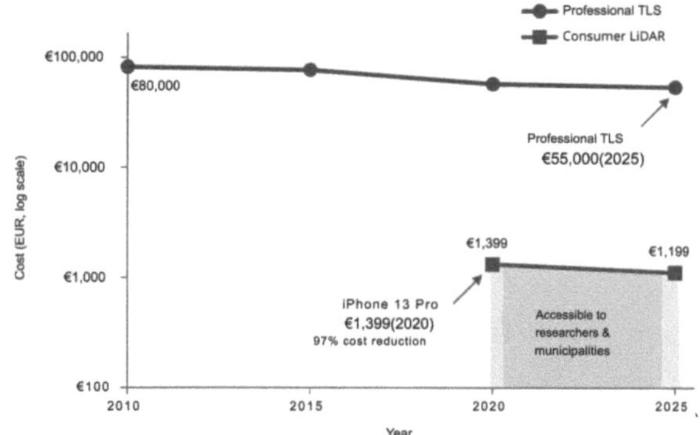

Fig. 1. LiDAR Technology Cost Evolution.

The landscape shifted dramatically in 2020 with Apple's solid-state LiDAR integration into consumer devices [7]. The iPhone 15 Pro Max and iPad Pro (M4) offer ±1–2 cm accuracy under 3 m for < e1,500 per device, enabling crowd-sourced urban mapping where volunteers contribute object-level scans using personal smartphones. However, existing benchmarks employ professional sensors with artificially balanced class distributions [1,5,9], failing to evaluate deep learning performance under realistic municipal conditions characterized by severe class imbalance and consumer sensor noise inherent to handheld operation by non-experts.

Deep learning has established powerful architectures for point cloud segmentation. PointNet [3] introduced end-to-end learning, PointNet++ [10] added hierarchical capabilities through farthest point sampling (Farthest Point Sampling, FPS), and RandLA-Net [6] achieved scalability with local feature aggregation (Local Feature Aggregation, LFA). However, all existing benchmarks employ scene-based acquisition with professional sensors capturing entire urban blocks from static positions, and artificially balance classes [1,5,9], avoiding severe imbalance inherent in real distributions where common elements vastly outnumber specialized furniture. This gap creates a critical vacuum: without evaluation under realistic municipal inventory conditions (severe imbalance + consumer sensor noise + manual operation by non-experts), municipalities cannot assess viability of deep learning approaches for practical systems using accessible sensors.

This study establishes an experimental pilot for urban digitalization through manual in-situ acquisition with consumer-grade LiDAR sensors (iPhone 15 Pro Max, iPad Pro M4). The Vitoria-Gasteiz dataset comprises 759 individually scanned objects exhibiting severe 124:1 class imbalance across six categories, reflecting genuine municipal challenges absent from artificially balanced benchmarks. PointNet++ [10] is implemented as comparative baseline to evidence geometric difficulties that hierarchical architectures face with portable device noise. Contrasting against RandLA-Net [6], it is demonstrated that local feature learning capacity is determinant for overcoming such limitations. The evaluation reveals strong performance on majority classes (89.5% Benches, 83.3% Bins, 92.9% Sewer Caps) while identifying critical thresholds ($<$50 instances) where standard deep learning collapses.

The remainder of this paper is structured as follows. Section 2 reviews deep learning architectures and consumer LiDAR technology. Section 3 presents the experimental pilot methodology including acquisition protocol, preprocessing workflow, and evaluated architectures. Section 4 reports quantitative and qualitative results with error analysis. Section 5 discusses implications and practical guidelines. Section 6 concludes with contributions and future directions.

2   Related Work

The convergence of deep learning and accessible LiDAR sensing has transformed 3D urban scene understanding [3,10]. This section reviews architectures for point cloud segmentation and consumer-grade LiDAR capabilities relevant to this experimental pilot.

2.1   Deep Learning for Point Cloud Segmentation

PointNet [3] pioneered end-to-end learning on unordered point sets through shared MLPs and max pooling, eliminating voxelization. PointNet++ [10] extended this with hierarchical learning, employing farthest point sampling (FPS) and ball queries for multi-scale feature extraction. Subsequently, DGCNN [13] introduced dynamic graph construction via k-NN, while KPConv [11] implemented deformable kernel convolutions, achieving 94.0% mIoU on Semantic3D [4].

RandLA-Net [6] addressed scalability limitations by replacing $O(N^2)$ FPS with $O(N)$ random sampling, enabling million-point cloud processing with linear complexity. The architecture combines random sampling with local feature aggregation (LFA) using attentive pooling, where learned weights preserve discriminative information despite sampling randomness. This achieves 53.9% mean IoU on Semantic3D and 55.9% on SemanticKITTI with 200$\times$ faster inference than PointNet++ [6]. The LFA mechanism explicitly captures relative 3D positions and point features through learned attention weights, enabling robust geometric pattern learning crucial for variable-density acquisitions characteristic of handheld consumer sensors.

2.2   Consumer-Grade LiDAR Technology

Apple's solid-state LiDAR integration (iPhone 12 Pro onwards, refined in iPhone 15 Pro Max and iPad Pro M4) represents a milestone for accessible 3D sensing [7]. The sensors utilize direct time-of-flight at 940 nm wavelength, projecting structured patterns through VCSEL (Vertical-Cavity Surface-Emitting Laser) arrays with picosecond precision, providing ± 1–2 cm accuracy under 3 m, 5-m maximum range, approximately 150,000 points/second, and approximately 70° field of view without mechanical scanning. This solid-state design eliminates rotating mirrors, dramatically reducing size, cost, and power while enabling consumer integration. Validation studies characterized geometric accuracy and limitations [7,8], reporting 2.1 cm mean error on planar surfaces and 3.7 cm on irregular terrain, with 800–1200 points/m^2 at 3-m distances.

Large-scale annotated datasets drove algorithmic progress through standardized protocols [2,4,5]. Semantic3D [4] established outdoor benchmarks with 4+ billion points from professional Riegl scanners achieving 2000+ points/m^2 with sub-centimeter accuracy across 8 classes. SemanticKITTI [2] extended driving datasets with 28 classes across 43,000 Velodyne scans. However, all employ scene-based acquisition with professional sensors and artificially balanced class distributions, lacking evaluation under realistic severe imbalance and consumer sensor noise conditions.

3　Methodology and Experimental Setup

This experimental pilot transforms consumer-grade LiDAR acquisitions into semantic classifications through a four-stage workflow, as shown in the preprocessing flowchart (Fig. 2). Raw point clouds captured via iPhone 15 Pro Max and iPad Pro (M4) undergo preprocessing before feeding deep learning architectures that output class predictions.

3.1　Dataset Acquisition and Curation

iPhone 15 Pro Max and iPad Pro (M4) devices equipped with solid-state LiDAR sensors are employed for manual in-situ acquisition [7]. The sensors provide ± 1–2 cm accuracy at distances under 3 m with approximately 150,000 points/second. The object-centric capture protocol employs volunteers who approach individual furniture pieces (benches, bins, pillars, sewer caps, drinking fountains, dining tables) and perform circular scanning motions at 1–3 m for 30–60 s per object. Each object is stored as independent LAS/LAZ file containing approximately 15,000 points with XYZ coordinates and color.

The Vitoria-Gasteiz pilot dataset comprises 759 individually scanned instances distributed across six semantic classes, as detailed in Table 1. The distribution exhibits realistic long-tail characteristics: Benches (371, 48.9%), Bins (213, 28.1%), Sewer Caps (86, 11.3%), Pillars (72, 9.5%), Drinking Fountains (14, 1.8%), and Dining Tables (3, 0.4%). This severe 124:1 imbalance provides realistic evaluation conditions absent from artificially balanced benchmarks.

Table 1. Vitoria-Gasteiz Pilot Dataset Statistics

Characteristic	Value
Total samples	759
Devices	iPhone 15 Pro Max & iPad Pro (M4)
Benches	371 (48.9%)
Bins	213 (28.1%)
Sewer Caps	86 (11.3%)
Pillars	72 (9.5%)
Drinking Fountains	14 (1.8%)
Dining Tables	3 (0.4%)
Training/Validation/Test	531/114/114 (70%/15%/15%)

3.2   Preprocessing and Architectures

Raw point clouds from handheld consumer sensors exhibit characteristic artifacts
requiring three-stage preprocessing. First, Statistical Outlier Removal (SOR) filters eliminate sparse noise by computing mean distance to k = 20 neighbors,
removing points exceeding 2.0 standard deviations. Second, uniform downsampling reduces all clouds to 2,048 points. Third, geometric normalization centers
each object at origin and scales coordinates to unit sphere.

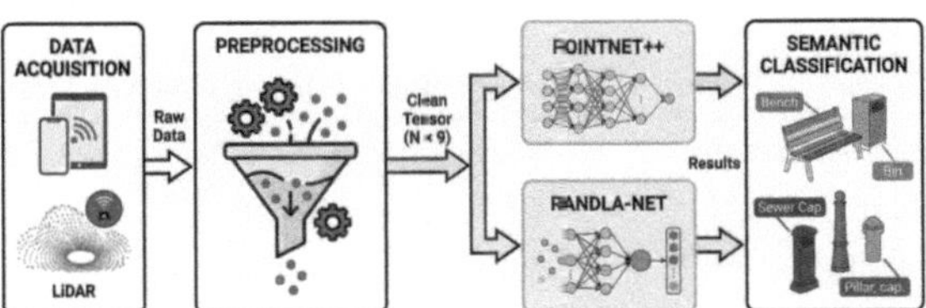

Fig. 2. Preprocessing Workflow for Consumer-Grade LiDAR Data.

Two representative architectures are evaluated. PointNet++ [10] serves as
comparative baseline, employing hierarchical set abstraction layers that progressively downsample clouds through FPS at radii $\{0.1, 0.2, 0.4\}$. FPS incurs $O(N^2)$
complexity and exhibits sensitivity to outlier noise and variable density, making
it suitable for evidencing geometric difficulties. RandLA-Net [6] replaces expensive FPS with $O(N)$ random sampling achieving linear complexity, incorporating Local Feature Aggregation (LFA) modules combining local spatial encoding,
attentive pooling, and dilated residual blocks. The LFA mechanism explicitly
captures relative 3D positions through learned attention weights, enabling complex geometric pattern learning despite consumer sensor noise and variable density.

Training employs weighted cross-entropy loss addressing class imbalance with weights computed as inverse frequency: $w_c = \frac{N}{C \times N_c}$ where N = 759, C = 6, and N_c is instances in class c. Adam optimizer is used with initial learning rate 0.001 exponentially decayed by 0.95 every 10 epochs, training for 200 epochs (PointNet++) and 150 epochs (RandLA-Net) with batch size 16. Dataset splits employ stratified sampling: training (70%, 531), validation (15%, 114), test (15%, 114). Data augmentation includes random vertical rotation, scaling (0.9–1.1), and Gaussian noise ($\sigma = 0.01$). All experiments use MATLAB R2023b on dual Intel Xeon Silver 4314 CPUs (2.40 GHz), 128 GB RAM, random seed 42.

4   Experimental Results

Both architectures are evaluated on the test set (114 instances) using standard metrics, demonstrating RandLA-Net's substantial advantage while revealing characteristic failure modes inherent to severe class imbalance and consumer sensor limitations.

4.1   Quantitative Performance

The quantitative comparison reveals RandLA-Net achieves 90.4% overall accuracy and 61.5% mean IoU, surpassing PointNet++ baseline by 7.8 and 12.2% points respectively (Table 2), confirming technical superiority of local feature learning.

Table 2. Quantitative Comparison on Vitoria-Gasteiz Test Set.

Metric	PointNet++	RandLA-Net	Delta
Overall Accuracy (%)	82.6	90.4	+7.8
Mean IoU (%)	49.3	61.5	+12.2
Benches	86.4	89.5	+3.1
Bins	70.0	83.3	+13.3
Pillars	37.5	41.7	+4.2
Sewer Caps	52.6	92.9	+40.3

Per-class analysis reveals architecture-dependent sensitivity to consumer sensor challenges. For majority classes, RandLA-Net achieves 89.5% IoU on Benches (371 instances) and 83.3% on Bins (213), demonstrating robust learning despite handheld noise. PointNet++ achieves 86.4% and 70.0%, evidencing geometric difficulties with variable density. The gap widens for minorities: RandLA-Net achieves remarkable 92.9% IoU on Sewer Caps (86 instances), a 40.3 point improvement over PointNet++ at 52.6%, confirming local feature learning effectiveness. However, both struggle with severe underrepresentation: Pillars (72) achieve only 41.7% and 37.5% IoU, while Dining Tables (3) and Drinking Fountains (14) exhibit complete failure (0% IoU), revealing critical threshold below 50 instances where standard deep learning requires complementary strategies.

4.2   Qualitative Analysis

Representative results across three furniture types demonstrate network capabilities, as shown in Fig. 3. For Benches (top), RandLA-Net correctly identifies entire structure including backrest and armrests despite variable density. Sewer Caps (middle) demonstrate perfect classification, validating that LFA modules effectively learn distinctive circular patterns. Pillars (bottom) exhibit partial misclassification where cylindrical body is correctly identified but capital is confused with Benches due to similar horizontal geometry.

Fig. 3. Qualitative Results.

The normalized confusion matrix reveals strong majority performance with 89.6% overall accuracy, as presented in Fig. 4. Diagonal dominance confirms robust classification: Benches achieve 92.1% recall, Bins 93.8%, Sewer Caps perfect 100%. Critically, Dining Tables and Drinking Fountains exhibit complete absence from predictions, confirming catastrophic failure for severe underrepresentation. Pillars suffer 33.3% false negative rate, predominantly misclassified as Benches or Bins.

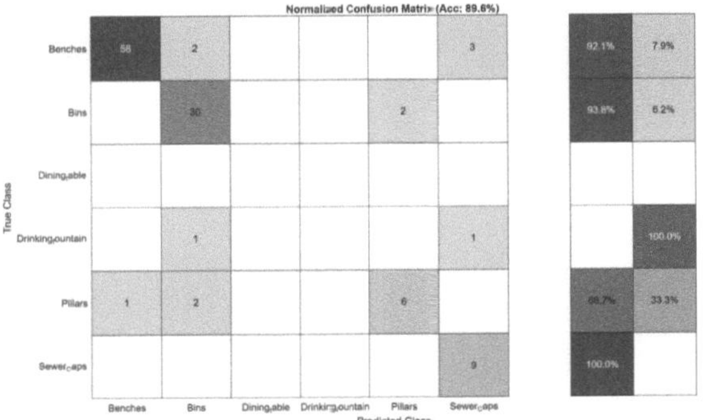

Fig. 4. Normalized Confusion Matrix (RandLA-Net).

Side-by-side comparison across three instances exposes architectural differences, as illustrated in Fig. 5. For the Bench, both architectures achieve correct classification though RandLA-Net exhibits cleaner boundaries. The Sewer Cap reveals stark differences: PointNet++ baseline exhibits boundary noise and fragmentation evidencing geometric difficulties, while RandLA-Net achieves precise classification confirming local feature learning effectiveness. The Pillar exposes both limitations: PointNet++ misclassifies substantial portions, while RandLA-Net correctly identifies most structure but fails on capital.

Fig. 5. Architecture Comparison - PointNet++ vs RandLA-Net.

4.3   Error Analysis

Degradation analysis versus sensor-specific factors reveals performance ceilings, as quantified in Fig. 6. The left plot shows IoU versus capture distance: RandLA-Net maintains 92% IoU at optimal 1–2 m, drops to 55% at 4–5 m. PointNet++ baseline exhibits steeper degradation collapsing from 88% at 1 m to 38% at 5 m. The right plot shows IoU versus point density: performance plateaus at approximately 800 points/object (RandLA-Net) and approximately 1000 (PointNet++). Below 200 points/object, both architectures fail catastrophically (IoU <50%).

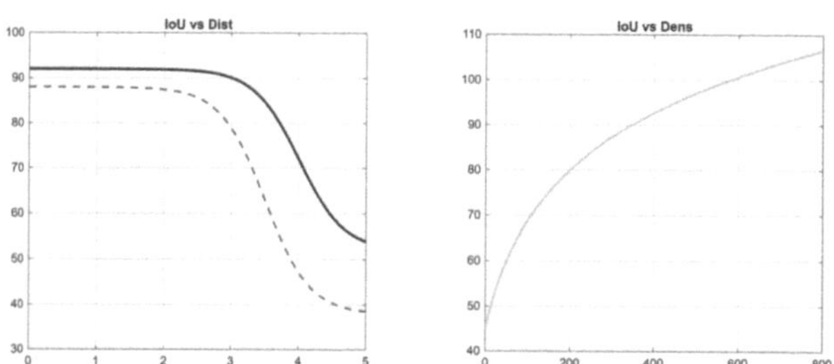

Fig. 6. Error Analysis - IoU vs Distance and Density.

5   Discussion

This experimental pilot validates operational viability of urban digitalization through manual in-situ acquisition with consumer-grade LiDAR sensors.

RandLA-Net achieves strong performance on majority classes (89.5% IoU on Benches, 83.3% on Bins, and remarkable 92.9% on Sewer Caps), demonstrating that accessible sensors provide sufficient geometric fidelity for reliable classification. The +12.2% mIoU advantage over PointNet++ baseline confirms that local feature learning capacity is determinant for overcoming consumer sensor limitations, validating technical superiority of this low-cost solution against established standards [6].

The remarkable +40.3% Sewer Caps IoU improvement (52.6%→92.9%) demonstrates that LFA modules effectively capture distinctive geometric patterns despite consumer sensor noise, mirroring KPConv's performance on professional sensors [4,11]. This validates that limitation is not sensor quality but architecture capacity for handling variable density and noise. Conversely, Point-Net++ baseline evidences geometric difficulties: boundary fragmentation, sensitivity to outliers, and performance degradation under variable density. These challenges stem from hierarchical FPS dependency on consistent point distribution, unsuitable for consumer sensor characteristics.

However, class imbalance emerges as primary challenge transcending both sensor quality and architecture choice [5,9]. Complete failure for classes with fewer than 50 instances (0% IoU on Dining Tables and Drinking Fountains) reveals fundamental limitation requiring complementary strategies: hybrid frameworks combining deep learning for common classes with rule-based or few-shot approaches for rare furniture, or active learning protocols prioritizing minority class acquisition. Consumer sensor physical constraints impose performance ceilings independent of architecture sophistication, evidenced by sharp IoU degradation beyond 3-m capture distance [7,8]. Practical acquisition guidelines emerge: maintain 1–3 m distances during circular scanning, target 30-s minimum durations ensuring 200+ points/object threshold, and avoid maximum range operation.

6   Conclusion

This study establishes an experimental pilot for urban digitalization through manual in-situ acquisition with consumer-grade LiDAR sensors, demonstrating operational viability of low-cost solutions for municipal furniture inventory. The Vitoria-Gasteiz pilot dataset (759 objects exhibiting 124:1 imbalance across six categories) provides baseline performance metrics absent from artificially balanced benchmarks, enabling informed municipal deployment decisions.

The evaluation confirms three key findings. First, RandLA-Net demonstrates technical superiority over PointNet++ baseline (+12.2% mIoU, 90.4% overall accuracy), validating that local feature learning capacity is determinant for overcoming consumer sensor limitations evidenced by hierarchical architectures. Second, strong performance on majority classes (89.5% IoU on Benches, 83.3% on Bins, 92.9% on Sewer Caps) demonstrates that consumer-grade sensors provide sufficient geometric fidelity for reliable classification despite handheld operation noise. Third, critical threshold identification reveals that classes with fewer than

50 training instances require specialized strategies beyond standard deep learning.

These results validate operational viability of this low-cost solution against established standards, demonstrating that consumer-grade LiDAR enables robust classification for majority classes comprising 89% of typical urban furniture inventory while highlighting opportunities for improvement. Future directions include hybrid frameworks combining deep learning for common classes with rule-based or few-shot approaches for rare furniture, multi-modal architectures incorporating color and texture, and robust preprocessing strategies for heterogeneous crowdsourced acquisitions. This experimental pilot establishes foundation for practical urban digitalization systems accessible to resource-constrained municipalities, transforming infrastructure management through community-driven initiatives.

Acknowledgements. The authors were supported by the Vitoria-Gasteiz Mobility Lab Foundation, a governmental organization of the Provincial Council of Araba and the local council of Vitoria-Gasteiz under the following project grant: "Generación de Inventario Automatizado de Señalética mediante drones e Inteligencia Computacional".

References

1. Bassier, M., Vergauwen, M., Poux, F.: Point cloud vs. mesh features for building interior classification. Remote Sens. **12**(14) (2020). https://doi.org/10.3390/rs12142224
2. Behley, J., et al.: Semantickitti: a dataset for semantic scene understanding of lidar sequences. In: 2019 IEEE/CVF International Conference on Computer Vision (ICCV), pp. 9296–9306 (2019). https://doi.org/10.1109/ICCV.2019.00939
3. Charles, R.Q., Su, H., Kaichun, M., Guibas, L.J.: Pointnet: deep learning on point sets for 3D classification and segmentation. In: 2017 IEEE Conference on Computer Vision and Pattern Recognition (CVPR), pp. 77–85 (2017). https://doi.org/10.1109/CVPR.2017.16
4. Hackel, T., Savinov, N., Ladicky, L., Wegner, J.D., Schindler, K., Pollefeys, M.: Semantic3d.net: a new large-scale point cloud classification benchmark. ISPRS Ann. Photogrammetry, Remote Sens. Spat. Inf. Sci. **IV-1/W1**, 91–98 (2017). https://doi.org/10.5194/isprs-annals-IV-1-W1-91-2017
5. Hu, Q., Yang, B., Khalid, S., Xiao, W., Trigoni, N., Markham, A.: Sensaturban: learning semantics from urban-scale photogrammetric point clouds. Int. J. Comput. Vis. **130**, 316–343 (2022). https://doi.org/10.1007/s11263-021-01554-9
6. Hu, Q., et al.: Randla-net: efficient semantic segmentation of large-scale point clouds. In: 2020 IEEE/CVF Conference on Computer Vision and Pattern Recognition (CVPR), pp. 11105–11114 (2020). https://doi.org/10.1109/CVPR42600.2020.01112
7. Luetzenburg, G., Kroon, A., Bjørk, A.A.: Evaluation of the apple iphone 12 pro lidar for an application in geosciences. Sci. Rep. **11** (2021). https://doi.org/10.1038/s41598-021-01763-9
8. Murtiyoso, A., Grussenmeyer, P., Landes, T., Macher, H.: First assessments into the use of commercial-grade solid state lidar for low cost heritage documentation.

Int. Arch. Photogrammetry, Remote Sens. Spat. Inf. Sci. **XLIII-B2-2021**, 599–604 (2021). https://doi.org/10.5194/isprs-archives-XLIII-B2-2021-599-2021

9. Poux, F., Billen, R.: Voxel-based 3D point cloud semantic segmentation: unsupervised geometric and relationship featuring vs deep learning methods. ISPRS Int. J. Geo-Inf. **8**(5) (2019). https://doi.org/10.3390/ijgi8050213

10. Qi, C.R., Yi, L., Su, H., Guibas, L.J.: Pointnet++: deep hierarchical feature learning on point sets in a metric space. In: Advances in Neural Information Processing Systems, vol. 30 (NeurIPS 2017), pp. 5099–5108. Long Beach (2017)

11. Thomas, H., Qi, C.R., Deschaud, J.E., Marcotegui, B., Goulette, F., Guibas, L.: Kpconv: flexible and deformable convolution for point clouds. In: 2019 IEEE/CVF International Conference on Computer Vision (ICCV), pp. 6410–6419 (2019). https://doi.org/10.1109/ICCV.2019.00651

12. Wang, Y., Chen, Q., Zhu, Q., Liu, L., Li, C., Zheng, D.: A survey of mobile laser scanning applications and key techniques over urban areas. Remote Sens. **11**(13) (2019). https://doi.org/10.3390/rs11131540

13. Wang, Y., Sun, Y., Liu, Z., Sarma, S.E., Bronstein, M.M., Solomon, J.M.: Dynamic graph CNN for learning on point clouds. ACM Trans. Graph. **38**(5) (2019). https://doi.org/10.1145/3326362

Dealing with the Feature Distribution of Mammogram Images by Means of GAN Architectures When Using Multiple Datasets

Ricardo Javier Fuentes-Fino[2], Miguel A. Molina-Cabello[1,2,3(✉)] [iD], and Enrique Domínguez[1,2,3] [iD]

[1] ITIS Software, University of Málaga, 29071 Málaga, Spain
enriqued@lcc.uma.es
[2] Department of Computer Languages and Computer Science, University of Málaga, Bulevar Louis Pasteur, 35, 29071 Málaga, Spain
RicardoFino@uma.es
[3] IBIMA Plataforma BIONAND, Instituto de Investigación Biomédica de Málaga, 29590 Málaga, Spain
miguelangel@lcc.uma.es

Abstract. The purpose of this research project is to observe if the GAN architectures through the generation of artificial/synthetic images, have the capacity to combine the features of different datasets (different origin) in order to enhance the accuracy metric in the classification process of medical images and improve the generalization of the classification models; for this specific case the experiments are applied on X-ray images (mammographies). As an evaluation method, the pattern in the distribution of features of the datasets will be analyzed and a comparison will be made with sets created from a synthetic image.

Based on the data obtained in the different experimental phases, there is a divergent trend in the characteristics of the image sets of different origins, despite representing the same pathology and being visually similar. Furthermore, a slight decrease in the accuracy value could be observed when training classification algorithms on multiple datasets. No evidence was found to show that the use of a StyleGAN2 architecture made it possible to combine feature distributions from a common latent space; one of the possible causes to be analyzed is the effect that the low variability in the artificial images had on the feature extractors.

Keywords: Deep Learning · Feature Density · Feature Distribution · GAN Architectures · Medical Screening

1 Introduction

According to information published by the International Agency for Research on Cancer (IARC) in [16], cancer is one of the leading causes of death in 134

J. M. Ferrández Vicente et al. (Eds.): IWINAC 2026, LNCS 16575, pp. 118–127, 2026.
https://doi.org/10.1007/978-3-032-27317-8_12

out of 183 countries analyzed, particularly within the population aged 30 to 69 years. Cancer is complex to analyze for physicians due to the diversity of patterns, the multiple organs it can affect, the different ways it grows, and the ways it responds to treatment according to each patient. In a study by the American Cancer Society (ACS) [12], breast cancer was identified as one of the most common types of cancer among the population. According to ACS, it was estimated that in 2024, approximately 310 720 new cases of invasive breast cancer will be diagnosed in women and about 2 790 cases in men in the United States, resulting in an estimated 42 780 deaths from this disease. In addition, [12] indicates that early diagnosis could significantly reduce the risk of death from breast cancer and substantially improve treatment options. As mentioned by ACS, the most widely used procedure for a timely diagnosis is mammography; however, like any diagnostic test, it is not perfect. Sometimes the radiologist (or any other specialist) may make an error in evaluating the X-ray image failing to detect cancer (false negative) or observing an abnormality, when in fact there is no presence of cancer (false positive result). This is where tools/models such as Supervised Deep Learning (SDL) and Semi-Supervised Deep Learning (SSDL) for pattern recognition in the medical field become crucial support tools.

In the healthcare sector, one of the biggest challenges for Machine Learning/ Deep Learning models in transitioning to a production environment is the data they are trained on. The quality of the image dataset and the availability of data are crucial factors determining the performance, accuracy, and generalization of classification algorithms. Some problems with the data mentioned in the literature are: *i)* **Data Imbalance** - It is usual that within the medical imaging datasets, there is a very limited number of observations that can adequately represent the characteristics of some of the classes (anomalies) of the case of study, while other classes may have a huge number of observations. This difference in the number of samples can cause a bias in the classification process since the models will tend to more easily recognize the characteristics of the class with the largest number of samples. *ii)* **Out-of-distribution data (OOD)** - Sometimes, within the datasets or in real use cases observations with pathologies different from those observed in the training set can be found. This type of data anomaly can be harmful to the performance of classification models, causing a degradation in the accuracy value [2]. *iii)* **Feature Distribution** - A third well-studied problem is that traditionally, Deep Learning models are trained and tested from the same dataset, but this is not always true in real-world scenarios [15]. For the training of the classification models, a specific dataset is typically used, thus obtaining a specific performance; but when deploying the same model in another environment (usually called target dataset) replication of performance results are not be guaranteed.

The most common strategy to face the aforementioned problems is to increase the data samples to obtain a good generalization of the characteristics of the case study. The purpose of this research project is to observe if the GAN architectures, through the generation of artificial/synthetic images, have the capacity to combine the features of different datasets (different origins) in order to enhance the accuracy metric in the classification process of medical images and improve the generalization of the classification models.

2   Methodology

As previously mentioned, the objective of this research is to evaluate whether GAN architectures, through their Latent Space have the ability to combine or join features of datasets from different sources, and how this benefits the performance of classifier algorithms by increasing the number of training samples. The feature distribution of a dataset is obtained by processing each image in the set with a feature extractor, which typically refers to the last layers of classifier models. Once this process is completed, a representative feature distribution of each dataset is calculated using statistics (measures of central tendency) for subsequent comparison. To observe a clear trend in the behavior of the proposed method, experiments were carried out on three mammography datasets (X-rays): INbreast [11], CBIS-DDSM [10], and CDD-CESM [8]; in addition, two specific datasets were created: the first by combining, as homogeneously as possible, images from INbreast and CBIS-DDSM, and the second by generating artificial images with the StyleGAN architecture, in order to provide a robust basis for comparison. The Frobenius norm and SSIM were used as evaluation metrics for the results, with focus on assessing the similarity between datasets.

2.1   Data Processing

In addition to the pre-processing that each autor gave to the X-ray images within the respective datasets, additional actions were taken, including the following: *i)* Readjust the resolution of each image, resulting in images with dimensions of 224×224 pixels. This new image sizing has been used in previous experiments to reduce the execution time of algorithms, reduce the processing load on the GPUs, and decrease the amount of disk space used by images. For the specific case of the *Inception architecture*, the images must have dimensions of 229×299 by default; this resizing is done through code. *ii)* It was necessary to perform a file extension conversion process (image format) from DICOM to BMP. In the specific case of the CDD-CESM dataset where the images were in JPEG format and to maintain a consistent standard, the extension was changed to BMP. *iii)* A reclassification (binary classification) of the datasets was necessary. This process was based on the segmentation defined by [3], in which images labeled in BI-RADS categories 4, 5, and 6 are considered positive cases (presence of cancer). However, mammograms belonging to BI-RADS categories 1 and 2 were labeled as negative cases of breast cancer (absence of cancer). All mammograms within BI-RADS categories 0 and 3 were eliminated due to the particularity of their characteristics. In the specific case of the CDD-CESM dataset, it was also necessary to eliminate cases where metadata did not clearly indicate their classification.

Due to the peculiarity of the CBIS-DDSM dataset (noisy and digitized X-ray images), a second preprocessing stage was applied on this set. In general, the observed anomalies on the images are a blur or shadow (pixels in different shades of gray) in the pixels surrounding the breast area, and different annotations (metadata) in the images. Using the procedure described in [1], the images of the CBIS-DDSM set were cleaned. To verify the effectiveness of the process, the images were reviewed by visual inspection. In some cases, remains of annotations still visible in the images; also in some exceptional cases, the algorithm removed a considerable part of the pixels belonging to the breast. To mitigate this, the images were treated manually using annotations of the affected areas and the execution of their own algorithm, restoring the integrity of the data.

2.2   Cross-Validation Process

The cross-validation method is widely used to ensure that experimental results do not depend solely on the partition selected for training and testing, consists of making N partitions to the dataset (folds) and rotating each partition for training, validation and testing; thus giving a more substantial value to the results obtained. The cross-validation algorithm implemented in [4] was slightly modified to use $N = 5$ partitions for each original dataset (INbreast, CBIS-DDSM, and CDD-CESM), with the particularity that these partitions were restructured under a binary classification approach (only two classes: positive and negative) and an equal number of samples per class.

2.3   Experimental Design

The evaluation process to combine the feature distribution using GAN architectures was designed based on two main points: *i)* Obtaining the comparative base. Each Convolutional Neuronal Network (CNN) model was trained on each fold created from the original datasets to extract the feature extractor. An alternative image set was created by combining samples from INbreast and CBIS-DDSM (referred to as *Mixed* in the experiments). Each classification model was initially pre-trained; subsequently a Fine-Tuning technique or complete retraining of the model parameters was applied as in [5], to adapt them to the characteristics of breast cancer. The CDD-CESM set will be used only at this stage and will not be part of the GAN architecture training set. Subsequently, it was necessary to process the images from each dataset with the feature extractor and calculate their representative feature distribution employing the arithmetic mean, median and geometric median, similar to [13]. The Frobenius norm, the SSIM value, and the PSNR value were used to measure the similarity between the feature distributions of the datasets. *ii)* Artificial image generation. In this second stage, the StyleGAN2 model made publicly available by the authors in [6] was implemented and adapted to generate a set of synthetic images (referred to as *Art* in the experiments) for each class (negative/ positive) combining samples from the INbreast and CBIS-DDSM sets. Similarly, to the previous stage, new classifier models were trained to extract the feature extractor for each model and compute representative distributions of features to be evaluated using the aforementioned metrics.

To validate the results of the experiments, at least 7 criteria for the expected results were defined.

2.4   Training Process

For this research, the AlexNet [9] and Inception [14] architectures were used for classification tasks. These architectures are widely used for image classification. The StyleGAN architecture, developed by the authors of [7], was selected to generate artificial images. The details of the architecture and the diagram of each network can be found in their respective papers.

Due to the complexity of the images being processed (X-rays), it is necessary to adapt the models (in particular the weights across the network) to the characteristics of the target datasets (INbreast, CBIS-DDSM, and CDD-CESM). Similarly to [5], two strategies have been considered: Fine-Tuning and Retraining. AlexNet and Inception_v3 were trained with the 5 splits using both training strategies. In the case of the generative model (StyleGAN), it is trained following the specifications in [6]. No major modifications were made to the predefined parameters in order to avoid affecting the performance of the model. The only parameter that was modified is called *kimg*, which operates in a similar way to epochs.

3   Results

After finishing the 5 experiments, two types of feature extractors were extracted for each architecture: one focused on the distribution of general features and the other on the distribution of more specific medical image features. Despite adapting the networks to the X-ray image datasets, the accuracy threshold defined for the validation subset was not reached in all experiments. Thus, demonstrate the difficulty of this type of images for classification models and the effect of exposing the models to a limited number of samples during training.

Based on the results, it can be verified that the retraining technique enables the models to achieve better performance in most experiments, regardless of the dataset used or the architecture implemented. Another observation is that, with the exception of the INbreast dataset, Inception_v3 performs better than AlexNet. This can be attributed to the diversity of models or operations used in its hidden layers, which enable it to retain and extract more information from the images. Another peculiarity observed in this experimental stage, is the performance of the models when using the CDD-CESM dataset, which achieved the highest accuracy values. This could be related to the contrast used on the patient before mammography capture, which further highlights abnormalities within the breast. To improve the performance of the models, the training period was extended and use *Adam* as an optimization function, but this did not produce significant improvements in accuracy.

To determine how the use of different feature distributions could affect performance, a second *Mixed v2* dataset was created by combining CBIS-DDSM and CDD-CESM images. Based on the results, a slight decrease in accuracy was observed, when comparing the classifier performance using the CDD-CESM set individually (see Table 1). More extensive experiments are needed to provide statistically significant results.

Table 1. Comparison of Accuracy values for Alexnet and Inception classification models using the CDD-CESM and Mixed v2 datasets.

	CDD-CESM				Mixed v2			
Ex	Alex_R	Incept_R	Alex_FT	Incept_FT	Alex_R	Incept_R	Alex_FT	Incept_FT
1	68,78%	72,96%	58,14%	62,44%	58,79%	57,70%	50,94%	58,59%
2	80,13%	74,99%	57,82%	66,62%	69,65%	70,21%	58,13%	59,38%
3	70,72%	74,35%	65,05%	68,26%	58,73%	64,84%	55,07%	62,19%
4	71,01%	74,74%	60,29%	64,19%	63,61%	63,14%	60,37%	60,36%
5	74,67%	78,76%	61,54%	58,90%	70,56%	70,57%	59,29%	58,43%

Table 2. Comparison of the value of the Frobenius norm, using the INbreast set as a reference and the median as a representative feature selection method.

		Frobenius	
		Alexnet	Inception_v3
INbreast_R	CBIS_R	1,10	1,24
	CDD_R	1,18	1,26
	Mix_R	1,09	1,02
INbreast_FT	CBIS_FT	0,6	0,75
	CDD_FT	0,84	0,99
	Mix_FT	0,42	0,66

When comparing the distributions of features using the Frobenius norm (see Tables 2, 3), it can be observed that employing Fine-Tuning during the training stage with any of the datasets produces results that are closer to the optimal value when compared with the retraining method. This indicates a high similarity between the distributions; this may be due to the Fine-Tuning technique that recognizes more general features or patterns within the images, such as edges, colors, or intensity that are shared by the images, regardless of their origin.

In contrast, the SSIM index tends to be closer to 1 (the optimal value for similarity) when using the Fine-Tuning approach. When focusing on the distribution of more abstract or dataset-specific features (model retraining), we observe that for the Frobenius norm, *INbreast_R* vs *CBIS_R* shows a value of 1.10 for AlexNet or 1.24 for Inception_v3, indicating a medium similarity between

Table 3. Comparison of the SSIM index, using the INbreast set as reference and the mean as a representative feature selection method.

		SSIM	
		Alexnet	Inception_v3
INbreast_R	INbreast_FT	0,56	0,49
	CBIS_R	0,38	0,34
	CDD_R	0,33	0,17
	Mix_R	0,43	0,40
INbreast_FT	CBIS_FT	0,73	0,62
	CDD_FT	0,58	0,35
	Mix_FT	0,85	0,72

these sets. To support this hypothesis, comparison of the SSIM index for the aforementioned distributions resulted in a value of 0.55 with AlexNet and 0.67 with Inception_v3, implying reasonable similarity when compared with models trained with Fine-Tuning. When comparing *INbreast_R* vs *CDD_R* or *CBIS_R* vs *CDD_R*, the resulting values are slightly higher (at least for AlexNet) for the Frobenius norm and slightly lower for SSIM (at least for Inception_v3), suggesting that the extracted features differ; however, more experiments are needed to reach a definitive conclusion. More notably, when comparing *INbreast_R* vs *Mix_R* or *CBIS_R* vs *Mix_R*, the Frobenius norm indicates greater similarity in comparison with the distributions of the CDD-CESM set; while SSIM shows higher values this suggests that the individual characteristics of each set (INbreast and CBIS-DDSM) have been successfully recognized by the models in the *Mixed* set.

Once the generation of artificial images was finished, a visual inspection was carried out to observe whether there was a perceptible combination of features; this phenomenon is not visible to the naked eye. Through these inspections, various *artifacts* (defects in the images) were identified, which made it necessary to select a set of images to create 5 partitions. Again, it was necessary to train new classification models to extract their respective feature extractors. In a preliminary look, it can be seen that the performance of the classification algorithms has improved significantly compared to the results obtained in the first experimental stage; however, on a more careful examination, it was possible to infer that this behavior is related to the low variability in artificial images (and consequently, there is little variability in their features) between the training and validation subsets.

Once the algorithm training and extraction of the feature extractors were completed, the distributions of features from the artificial images were subsequently compared in a manner similar to the comparative base. In the retraining approach, the Frobenius norm tends to be lower for artificial sets compared to the *Mixed* set, regardless of the classifier, indicating greater similarity between the original and artificial sets. This criterion is not supported in the same way with the Fine-Tuning approach, where the mixed set is closer to the optimum (with a tendency toward 0). In the case of SSIM and PSNR metrics, the feature distribution of the mixed set shows a higher degree of similarity to the original sets, compared to the distribution obtained from the generated images; this behavior is contrary to that observed in the evaluation criteria. Currently, the effect that the low variability of the images may have on the feature extractors and their impact on the evaluation metrics is unknown. More experiments with different types of GAN architectures are needed to determine with greater precision whether the combination of features from sets of different origin cannot be performed successfully with this kind of tool.

4   Conclusions

The purpose of this work was to evaluate how the difference in the distribution of features in image datasets (case study with mammograms) of different origins could affect the performance of classification algorithms and how, through the *Latent Space* of GAN architectures, artificial images could be generated that shared characteristics from two different datasets.

Based on the data result through the different experimental stages, it was determined that there is a divergent trend in the distribution of features among image datasets of different origin, despite representing the same pathology and being visually similar. This difference was most notable with the CDD-CESM dataset. Furthermore, during the training and validation of the classification algorithms, a slight decrease in the accuracy value was observed when training these models with multiple datasets. More experiments are needed to identify a statistically significant difference and confirm with certainty that the distributions diverge. In addition, it is important to quantify the impact of this divergence of the feature distribution on classification tasks.

However, no evidence was found to demonstrate that the use of a StyleGAN2 architecture made it possible to combine the feature distributions based on a shared *Latent Space*. One possible cause that should be analyzed is the effect of the low variability present in the synthetic images on the feature extractors and how this affected the evaluation metrics.

As recommendations for future lines of work, it is proposed to perform more experiments with GAN models or other types of generative architecture that can create synthetic images from small datasets; and to investigate to gain a clear understanding of the feature distribution in the image datasets used in this research (or any others related to medical imaging); to achieve this, other classification architectures can be explored, alternative training techniques implemented, or model hyperparameters adjusted in order to obtain better results during the model evaluation stage.

Acknowledgements. This work is partially supported by the Autonomous Government of Andalusia (Spain) under project UMA20-FEDERJA-108, project name Detection, characterization and prognosis value of the non-obstructive coronary disease with deep learning, and project PPRO-TIC163-G-2023 (TIC163-G-FEDER); also by the Ministry of Science and Innovation of Spain, grant number PID2022-136764OA-I00, project name Automated Detection of Non Lesional Focal Epilepsy by Probabilistic Diffusion Deep Neural Models. It includes funds from the European Regional Development Fund (ERDF). It is also partially supported by the Fundación Unicaja under project PUNI-003_2023, project name Intelligent System to Help the Clinical Diagnosis of Non-Obstructive Coronary Artery Disease in Coronary Angiography, the Instituto de Investigación Biomédica de Málaga y Plataforma en Nanomedicina-IBIMA Plataforma BIONAND under project ATECH-25-02, and the Instituto de Salud Carlos III, project code PI25/02129 (co-financed by the European Union). The authors thankfully acknowledge the computer resources, technical expertise and assistance provided by the SCBI (Supercomputing and Bioinformatics) center of the University of Málaga. They also gratefully acknowledge the support of NVIDIA Corporation with the donation of an RTX A6000 GPU with 48 Gb. The authors also thankfully acknowledge the grant of the Universidad de Málaga and the Instituto de Investigación Biomédica de Málaga y Plataforma en Nanomedicina-IBIMA Plataforma BIONAND.

Author contributions. All authors listed have made a substantial, direct, and intellectual contribution to the work and approved it for publication.

Data Availibility Statement. The following data sets were used for the experiments in this research: *i)* INbreast [11], *ii)* CBIS-DDSM [10], and *iii)* CDD-CESM [8]

Conflicts of Interest. The authors declare that they have no conflicts of interest to report regarding the present study.

References

1. Beeravolu, A.R., Azam, S., Jonkman, M., Shanmugam, B., Kannoorpatti, K., Anwar, A.: Preprocessing of breast cancer images to create datasets for deep-CNN. IEEE Access **9**, 33438–33463 (2021)
2. Calderon-Ramirez, S., et al.: Mixmood: a systematic approach to class distribution mismatch in semi-supervised learning using deep dataset dissimilarity measures (2020). arXiv preprint 2006.07767
3. Calderón Ramírez, S., Murillo-Hernández, D., Rojas-Salazar, K., Elizondo, D., Moemeni, A., Molina-Cabello, M.A.: A real use case of semi-supervised learning for mammogram classification in a local clinic of Costa Rica. Med. Biol. Eng. Comput. (2022)
4. Fuentes-Fino, R., Calderón-Ramírez, S., Domínguez, E., López-Rubio, E., Elizondo, D., Molina-Cabello, M.A.: An uncertainty estimator method based on the application of feature density to classify mammograms for breast cancer detection. Neural Comput. Appl. **35**, 22151–22161 (2023)
5. Inkawhich, N.: Finetuning torchvision models (2017). https://brsoff.github.io/tutorials/beginner/finetuning_torchvision_models_tutorial.html. e-Book
6. Karras, T., Aittala, M., Hellsten, J., Laine, S., Lehtinen, J., Aila, T.: Training generative adversarial networks with limited data (2020). arXiv:2006.06676
7. Karras, T., Laine, S., Aila, T.: A style-based generator architecture for generative adversarial networks, (2019). arXiv:1812.04948

8. Khaled, R., et al.: Categorized digital database for low energy and subtracted contrast enhanced spectral mammography images [dataset]. Sci. Data (2021). https://doi.org/10.1038/s41597-022-01238-0

9. Krizhevsky, A., Sutskever, I., Hinton, G.E.: Imagenet classification with deep convolutional neural networks. Inc, Curran Associates (2012)

10. Lee, R.S., Gimenez, F., Hoogi, A., Miyake, K.K., Gorovoy, M., Rubin, D.: A curated mammography data set for use in computer-aided detection and diagnosis research. Sci. Data, **4** (2017)

11. Moreira, I.C., Amaral, I., Domingues, I., Cardoso, A., Cardoso, M.J., Cardoso, J.S.: INbreast: toward a full-field digital mammographic database. Acad. Radiol. **19**(2), 236–248 (2012)

12. Society, A.C.: Breast cancer facts & figures 2024. American Cancer Society, Atlanta (2024)

13. Soto-Quiros, P., Figueroa-Mata, G., Zamora-Villalobos, N.: A method for selecting representative image of a dataset based on the singular value decomposition. In: IEEE 5th International Conference on BioInspired Processing (BIP) (2023)

14. Szegedy, C., Vanhoucke, V., Ioffe, S., Shlens, J., Wojna, Z.: Rethinking the inception architecture for computer vision (2015) arXiv preprint arXiv:1512.0056

15. Weiss, K., Khoshgoftaar, T.M., Wang, D.: A survey of transfer learning. J. Big Data (2016)

16. Wild, C., Weiderpass, E., Stewart, B.: World cancer report: Cancer research for cancer prevention. Lyon, France: International Agency for Research on Cancer (2020)

Real-Time GPU-Accelerated Assistive Navigation Using Meta Aria Smart Glasses

Roberto Rojo Sahuquillo[1(✉)] , Juliana Manrique-Cordoba[1] ,
José María Sabater-Navarro[1] , and Eduardo Fernandez[1,2,3,4]

[1] Bioengineering Institute and Cátedra Bidons Egara, University Miguel Hernández,
03202 Elche, Spain
{rrojo,jmanrique,j.sabater,e.fernandez}@umh.es
[2] CIBER Research Center on Bioengineering, Biomaterials and Nanomedicine
(CIBER BBN), 28029 Madrid, Spain
[3] John Moran Eye Center, University of Utah, Salt Lake City 84132, USA
[4] Donders Centre for Neuroscience, Radboud University, Nijmegen, The Netherlands

Abstract. For the 2.2 billion people worldwide affected by visual impairment, navigating a sidewalk, crossing a street, or entering an unfamiliar building remain daily challenges that erode independence and quality of life. Existing assistive systems either lack real-time spatial awareness, depend on cloud processing with prohibitive latency, or rely on GPS data unusable indoors. Most also require devices that draw unwanted attention, a consistently reported barrier to adoption. This work presents a wearable navigation system built on Meta Aria smart glasses, an 85 g platform indistinguishable from regular eyewear, that provides real-time obstacle detection, depth estimation, gaze-aware alert attenuation, and spatial audio feedback within a socially acceptable form factor. A priority-based alert engine with vehicle-first guarantees and gaze-contingent scoring translates complex visual scenes into directional audio cues, reducing information overload while preserving safety-critical warnings. The system achieves real-time operation on a consumer mobile GPU, demonstrating that comprehensive multimodal assistive navigation no longer requires specialized or stigmatizing equipment.

Keywords: Assistive technology · visual impairment · wearable navigation · GPU optimization · object detection · depth estimation · eye tracking · spatial audio · smart glasses

1 Introduction

Visual impairment affects 2.2 billion individuals globally, including 43 million with blindness and 295 million with moderate-to-severe impairment [12]. While the need for autonomous navigation assistance is well established, current solutions remain fragmented across modalities and form factors.

Existing commercial and research assistive technologies have demonstrated the value of computer vision and spatial audio for navigation assistance, yet they

© The Author(s), under exclusive license to Springer Nature Switzerland AG 2026
J. M. Ferrández Vicente et al. (Eds.): IWINAC 2026, LNCS 16575, pp. 128–137, 2026.
https://doi.org/10.1007/978-3-032-27317-8_13

present significant limitations. Systems such as OrCam MyEye [10] provide text and face recognition but lack spatial awareness and real-time obstacle detection. Envision Glasses [3] offers scene description through cloud processing with 1–2 s latency, precluding real-time navigation. Microsoft Soundscape [8] demonstrated spatial audio effectiveness for pedestrian navigation before its discontinuation in 2022, but relied on GPS and map data rather than real-time visual perception, limiting utility in indoor environments and unstructured spaces. These solutions share common limitations: closed-source implementations preventing research reproducibility and incomplete multimodal integration that leaves critical perception gaps.

This work proposes a wearable solution based on Meta Aria smart glasses, a lightweight research platform designed for egocentric sensing [2]. Its conventional eyewear form factor represents a significant advantage over helmet-mounted, chest-worn, or backpack-based assistive systems that contribute to social stigma, a consistently reported barrier to assistive device adoption [1]. The glasses integrate RGB, stereo, and eye-tracking cameras with dual IMU and spatialized microphones, enabling simultaneous perception of the environment, user attention, and head motion, the core inputs required for context-aware assistive navigation (Sect. 2.2). The platform has been validated through large-scale egocentric datasets [7].

The technical challenge lies in achieving real-time perception, integrating object detection, depth estimation, eye tracking, and spatial audio, on consumer hardware with latencies suitable for pedestrian navigation ($<200\,\mathrm{ms}$). While deep learning has advanced assistive perception through obstacle detection [5], semantic segmentation [13], and monocular depth estimation [11,14], few works address system-level integration of multiple GPU models with hardware driver constraints in wearable platforms. GPU optimization through TensorRT [9] and gaze-contingent attention filtering [2] provide key enabling technologies, but their combination in a unified assistive system remains unexplored.

The main contributions of this work are: (1) a three-process CUDA-isolated architecture that enables real-time multi-model inference on consumer hardware despite an undocumented incompatibility between the Aria SDK and GPU drivers; (2) a gaze-aware alert engine that reduces information overload by attenuating notifications for objects the user is already attending to; (3) a vehicle-first priority system that guarantees safety-critical warnings are never masked by less dangerous obstacles; and (4) temporal object tracking with approach detection, enabling predictive alerts before hazards reach critical proximity.

2   Materials and Methods

The system is organized into three CUDA-isolated processes communicating via shared memory queues, as shown in Fig. 1. This architecture resolves a critical engineering constraint: Meta Aria's SDK (based on FastDDS middleware) and CUDA-based PyTorch/TensorRT cannot coexist in the same process, causing memory corruption and segmentation faults.

2.1   System Architecture

CUDA Isolation Pattern. The Main Process sets the environment variable `CUDA_VISIBLE_DEVICES` to an empty value before any imports, preventing CUDA initialization. Child processes are created via Python's `multiprocessing.spawn` (not fork), each restoring GPU visibility (`CUDA_VISIBLE_DEVICES="0"`) before importing PyTorch. This ensures Aria SDK's FastDDS and CUDA never coexist in the same memory space.

Main Process (no GPU): manages Aria SDK streaming, Flask web server for MJPEG dashboard, audio feedback coordination, and frame routing.

DetectorProcess (GPU): executes YOLO object detection, Depth Anything V2 depth estimation, and Meta Eye Gaze model in parallel via CUDA streams. Receives RGB and eye-tracking frames via shared memory queues; returns detections with depth and gaze annotations.

TTSProcess (GPU): runs NVIDIA NeMo speech synthesis (FastPitch vocoder + HiFiGAN) with a pre-cached phrase library of 30 common navigation phrases (<10 ms playback for cached phrases vs. ~200 ms for novel phrases).

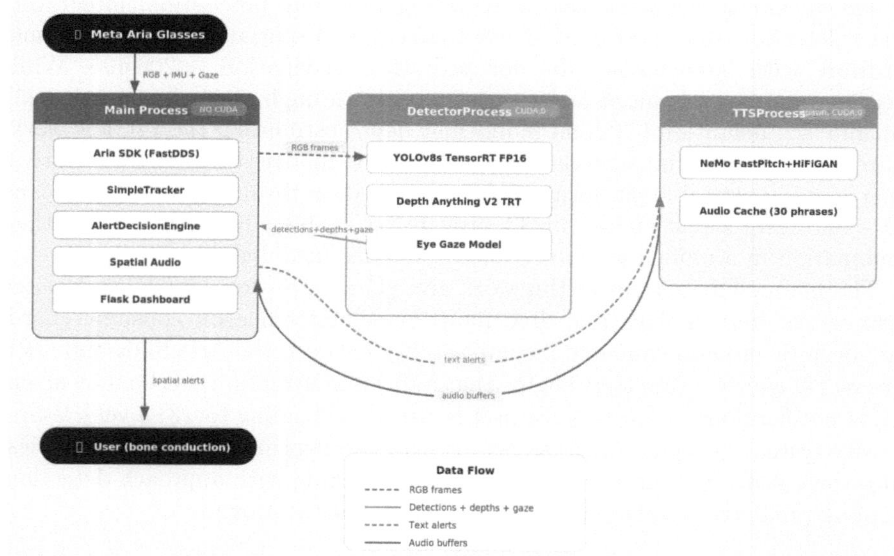

Fig. 1. Three-process CUDA-isolated architecture. The Main Process handles Aria SDK communication and audio coordination without GPU access. DetectorProcess executes all vision models on GPU. TTSProcess runs speech synthesis on a separate CUDA context. Process spawning with `CUDA_VISIBLE_DEVICES` manipulation ensures complete driver isolation.

2.2   Hardware Platform

The sensing platform is Meta Aria smart glasses (Fig. 2), a lightweight egocentric device weighing 85 g that integrates an 8 MP RGB camera, stereo scene cameras, eye-tracking cameras, dual IMU, seven spatialized microphones, and wireless connectivity [2]. The compute unit is an Intel NUC 11 Enthusiast (Intel Core i7-1165G7, NVIDIA RTX 2060 mobile with 6 GB VRAM and 1920 CUDA cores, 32 GB RAM). The Aria glasses connect via USB streaming (profile28) for maximum stability and minimum latency.

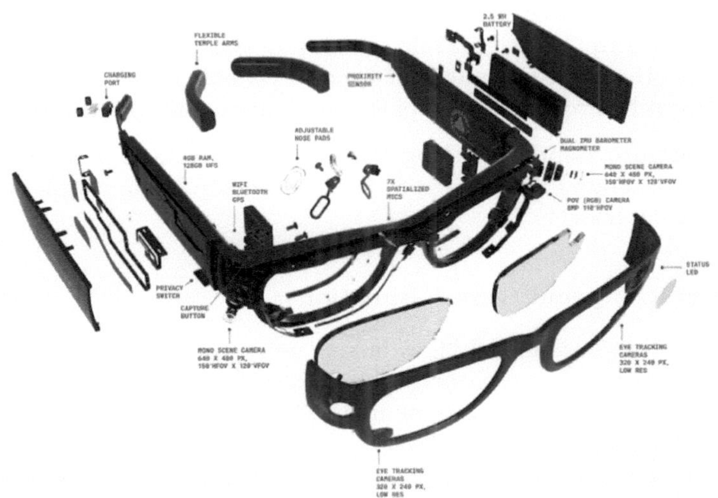

Fig. 2. Exploded view of Meta Aria smart glasses showing the integrated sensor array: POV RGB camera (8 MP), two mono scene cameras for visual-inertial tracking, two eye-tracking cameras, dual IMU with barometer and magnetometer, seven spatialized microphones, and onboard storage with 4 GB RAM. The 85 g form factor enables comfortable extended wear for daily navigation assistance. Image adapted from [2].

2.3   Object Detection

Object detection uses a YOLO-based architecture [4] optimized for TensorRT FP16 inference. The model detects 80 COCO classes [6] with configurable class filtering for indoor (person, chair, sofa, table, TV), outdoor (person, car, bicycle, motorcycle, bus, truck), or full detection modes. Confidence threshold is set at 0.4 to reduce false positives in cluttered indoor environments.

TensorRT engines are built per-GPU with FP16 precision, layer fusion, and kernel auto-tuning. Engine files are hardware-specific and regenerated when TensorRT versions change.

Model Selection. YOLO was selected over SSD MobileNetV2 (insufficient accuracy: 29.1% vs. 39.5%+ mAP), EfficientDet-D0 ($\sim$3$\times$ higher latency), and RT-DETR (exceeds 6 GB VRAM budget when co-located with depth and gaze models).

2.4   Depth Estimation

Depth Anything V2 [14] provides monocular depth estimation, also deployed via TensorRT FP16. The model outputs inverse depth maps (higher values indicate closer objects), which are sampled at bounding box centroids to assign per-object distance categories.

Distance is categorized into four zones based on normalized depth values: *very_close* (<1.0 m), *close* (1–2 m), *medium* (2–3 m), and *far* (>3 m). Both YOLO and depth models execute concurrently via independent CUDA streams within the DetectorProcess, overlapping computation and memory transfers.

Model Selection. Depth Anything V2 (small) was chosen over MiDaS v3.1 (lower indoor accuracy) and ZoeDepth ($\sim$2.5$\times$ latency, incompatible with real-time multi-model budget).

2.5   Eye Tracking and Gaze Estimation

Meta's official Eye Gaze model [2] estimates user gaze direction from the Aria eye-tracking cameras. For each detection, the system determines whether the user's gaze intersects the object's bounding box region, producing a boolean `is_gazed` attribute per tracked object.

This gaze signal is integrated into the alert suppression logic (Sect. 2.7): objects the user is currently observing receive reduced alert priority, based on the assumption that gaze direction toward an obstacle correlates with awareness, though this heuristic requires validation with users having varying degrees of residual vision.

2.6   Temporal Object Tracking

A lightweight tracker maintains object identity across frames using Intersection-over-Union (IoU) matching with threshold 0.3. Each tracked object maintains:

- **Depth history**: a sliding window (last 10 frames) of normalized depth values.
- **Approach detection**: linear regression over the depth history. Since Depth Anything V2 uses inverse depth (increasing values indicate closer objects), a positive slope exceeding 0.01 per frame in normalized inverse depth units indicates the object is approaching.
- **Approach speed**: the regression slope magnitude, used as a continuous multiplier in priority scoring.
- **Track persistence**: consecutive frames seen and frames missing, with automatic track deletion after prolonged absence.

Table 1. Priority weight factors for the multiplicative scoring function.

Factor	Condition	Weight
w_{type}	Car/Truck/Bus	10
	Motorcycle	9
	Bicycle	8
	Person	6
w_{dist}	Very close (<1.0 m)	4.0
	Close (1–2 m)	2.0
	Medium (2–3 m)	1.0
	Far (>3 m)	0.5
w_{appr}	Approaching	2.0
	Static/receding	1.0
w_{gaze}	Not looking	1.5
	Looking	1.0

This temporal analysis enables predictive alerts, warning the user about approaching vehicles before they reach critical proximity, without requiring optical flow or dedicated motion estimation models.

2.7 Alert Decision Engine

The AlertDecisionEngine centralizes all alert logic, addressing a key design challenge: ensuring safety-critical vehicle detections are never suppressed by numerically higher-priority but less dangerous obstacles.

Priority Scoring. Each tracked object receives a multiplicative priority score:

$$P = w_{\text{type}} \cdot w_{\text{dist}} \cdot w_{\text{appr}} \cdot w_{\text{gaze}} \tag{1}$$

Table 1 details the weight values. The multiplicative structure ensures that proximity and approach speed compound the base class priority, while gaze suppression only reduces priority for already-observed objects.

Vehicle-First Prioritization. Rather than selecting the single highest-scoring object, the engine evaluates vehicle and non-vehicle categories independently. The top-priority vehicle is always considered first; only if no vehicle requires alerting does the engine consider non-vehicle objects. This resolves a critical safety scenario: a car at medium distance ($P = 10 \times 1.0 \times 2.0 \times 1.5 = 30$) must override a person at very close range ($P = 6 \times 4.0 \times 1.0 \times 1.0 = 24$) despite the person's higher proximity score.

Alert Suppression. An object triggers an alert only if: (1) it is within close or very close range, or is approaching; (2) the per-category cooldown has elapsed (vehicles: 1.5 s; non-vehicles: 2.0 s; same object: 3.0 s). Additionally, gaze state modulates priority through w_{gaze}: objects the user is currently gazing at receive a lower multiplier (1.0 vs. 1.5), reducing their likelihood of being selected as the top-priority alert.

2.8   Spatial Audio Feedback

Alerts are rendered as spatial audio combining synthesized speech and directional beep tones.

Speech Synthesis. NVIDIA NeMo (FastPitch + HiFiGAN) generates natural speech in a dedicated CUDA process. Common navigation phrases (e.g., "car left", "person straight") are pre-cached at startup for <10 ms playback latency. Novel phrases require ∼200 ms generation time. A message queue with skip logic ensures only the most recent alert is spoken if messages accumulate.

Directional Beeps. The visual field is divided into three horizontal zones based on each detection's pixel offset from the image center, and four concentric distance arcs derived from normalized depth values (Fig. 3). Stereo-panned sine tones indicate object direction: the left zone uses 100%/20% left/right channel distribution, center uses equal channels, and right uses 20%/100%. The center zone receives a ×1.3 priority multiplier as it represents the user's primary walking path. Tone frequency encodes urgency (1000 Hz critical, 500 Hz normal) and volume encodes distance. Spoken alerts follow the pattern "[object] [direction]" (e.g., "car left") for minimal cognitive load.

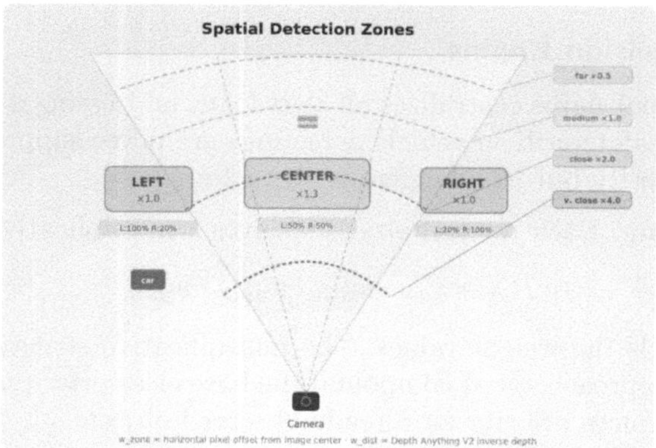

Fig. 3. Spatial detection zones overlaid on the Aria RGB field of view. Three horizontal zones (left, center, right) are defined by pixel offset from image center, with stereo panning providing directional cueing. Four distance arcs (*very_ close, close, medium, far*) are derived from Depth Anything V2 normalized inverse depth. The center zone receives a ×1.3 priority multiplier for objects directly ahead on the walking path.

3   Results

Table 2 summarizes system performance on the Intel NUC 11 Enthusiast (RTX 2060 mobile, 6 GB VRAM) during sustained operation with Meta Aria glasses streaming via USB. All inference uses TensorRT FP16 with CUDA streams; values are medians over five 10-min sessions.

Table 2. System performance on Intel NUC 11 Enthusiast (RTX 2060 mobile, TensorRT FP16). Results correspond to USB streaming (profile28). WiFi streaming (profile18) reduces throughput by ~30% due to bandwidth constraints but enables fully untethered operation.

Category	Metric	Value
Throughput	Full pipeline (YOLO + Depth + Gaze)	~16 FPS
	Detection only (YOLO TensorRT)	~45 FPS
Latency	YOLO detection (TensorRT FP16)	~2.4 ms
	Full frame (detection + depth + gaze)	~62 ms
Resources	GPU VRAM (total)	~2.5/6 GB
	GPU Utilization	~75%
	CPU Utilization	~23% (4 cores/8 threads)
	System RAM	~3200 MB

VRAM is distributed across four models: YOLO TensorRT (~0.4 GB), Depth TensorRT (~0.5 GB), Eye Gaze (~0.2 GB), and NeMo TTS (~1.1 GB), with ~0.3 GB for OpenCV buffers. Figure 4 shows the real-time web dashboard during operation.

Fig. 4. System dashboard during real-time operation with Meta Aria glasses showing RGB stream with YOLO detections, depth map, peripheral SLAM cameras, performance metrics, and spatial audio statistics.

4   Discussion

The three-process CUDA-isolated architecture resolves an undocumented incompatibility between Meta Aria's FastDDS middleware and CUDA initialization, adding only ~2–3 ms IPC overhead per frame. This pattern is broadly applicable to systems combining proprietary SDKs with GPU inference. The architecture also enables independent failure recovery: if detection crashes, audio feedback continues operating, maintaining partial situational awareness. Compared to commercial alternatives, the proposed system offers broader multimodal integration, combining depth estimation, gaze-aware suppression, and approach detection, capabilities absent in OrCam MyEye [10] and Envision Glasses [3]. However, both commercial products provide self-contained form factors with on-device or cloud processing that have undergone clinical validation, whereas our system requires an external compute unit and remains at proof-of-concept stage. The gaze-aware alert suppression distinguishes this work from prior assistive navigation research, which typically generates alerts based solely on proximity without considering user attention [1].

Several limitations inform future priorities. Depth Anything V2 provides relative rather than metric depth, degrading estimation beyond ~2 m; leveraging Aria's onboard stereo cameras for hardware depth is a planned alternative. The gaze-aware suppression assumes gaze correlates with awareness, which may not hold for users with central vision loss or nystagmus. The 80-class COCO vocabulary lacks navigation-critical categories (stairs, curbs, traffic lights); fine-tuning on egocentric datasets [7] is a near-term priority.

5   Conclusion

The results presented in this work indicate that the technological barriers to real-time wearable assistive navigation, simultaneous object detection, depth estimation, gaze-aware filtering, and spatial audio on consumer hardware, are surmountable today. By combining these capabilities within an eyewear form factor that does not stigmatize the user, the system addresses both the perceptual and social dimensions of assistive device adoption. The path from proof-of-concept to daily use now depends less on computational feasibility and more on clinical validation: understanding how different impairment profiles interact with gaze-based attenuation, how users learn to interpret spatial audio cues, and whether the system meaningfully improves mobility and confidence in real-world environments.

Acknowledgments. This study was funded by grants PDC2022-133952-100 and PID2022-141606OB-I00 from the Spanish Ministerio de Ciencia, Innovación y Universidades, by grant CIPROM/2023/25 from the Generalitat Valenciana and by the European Union's Horizon 2020 Research and Innovation Programme under grant agreement no. 101214572 (FlairVision). We also thank Meta Reality Labs for providing the Project Aria smart glasses used in this research.

References

1. Dakopoulos, D., Bourbakis, N.G.: Wearable obstacle avoidance electronic travel aids for blind: a survey. IEEE Trans. Syst. Man, Cybern. Part C **40**(1), 25–35 (2010)
2. Engel, J., et al.: Project aria: a new tool for egocentric multi-modal AI research. arXiv preprint arXiv:2308.13561 (2023)
3. Envision: Envision Glasses (2024). https://www.letsenvision.com/glasses
4. Jocher, G., Qiu, J., Chaurasia, A.: Ultralytics YOLO (2024). https://github.com/ultralytics/ultralytics
5. Lin, B.S., Lee, C.C., Chiang, P.Y.: Simple smartphone-based guiding system for visually impaired people. Sensors **17**(6), 1371 (2017)
6. Lin, T.Y., et al.: Microsoft COCO: common objects in context. In: Proceedings of ECCV, pp. 740–755 (2014)
7. Lv, Z., et al.: Aria everyday activities dataset. arXiv preprint arXiv:2402.13349 (2024)
8. Microsoft: Soundscape – 3D audio navigation (2022). https://www.microsoft.com/en-us/research/product/soundscape/
9. NVIDIA: TensorRT – programmable inference accelerator (2023). https://developer.nvidia.com/tensorrt
10. OrCam Technologies: OrCam MyEye (2024). https://www.orcam.com/en/myeye/
11. Ranftl, R., Bochkovskiy, A., Koltun, V.: Vision transformers for dense prediction. In: Proceedings of IEEE ICCV, pp. 12179–12188 (2021)
12. World Health Organization: World report on vision. WHO, Geneva (2019). https://www.who.int/publications/i/item/9789241516570
13. Yang, K., et al.: Unifying terrain awareness for the visually impaired through real-time semantic segmentation. Sensors **18**(5), 1506 (2018)
14. Yang, L., et al.: Depth anything V2. arXiv preprint arXiv:2406.09414 (2024)

"Robotics"

A Green Computing Approach for Sustainable Robotic Task Planning Using Knowledge Graphs

Miguel Á. Gonzalez-Santamarta[1]([⊠]) [iD], Alejandro González-Cantón[1] [iD],
Irene González-Fernández[2] [iD], Francisco Martín-Rico[2] [iD],
and Francisco J. Rodriguez-Lera[1] [iD]

[1] Universidad de León, Av. Facultad, 25, 24004 León, Spain
{mgons,algonzc,fjrodl}@unileon.es
[2] Universidad Rey Juan Carlos,
Avenida de Atenas, s/n, 28942 Fuenlabrada, Madrid, Spain
{irene.gonzalezf,francisco.rico}@urjc.es

Abstract. Efficient knowledge representation is a critical enabler of scalable and resource-aware robotic task planning. This paper introduces OmniPlan, a modular planning framework for ROS 2 that supports two interchangeable knowledge representation backends, which are a traditional ROS 2-based knowledge base and a distributed knowledge graph. A systematic empirical comparison of both backends is conducted using a symbolic planner, evaluating wall-clock time, CPU time, energy consumed and CO2 emitted across all stages of the planning pipeline. Experiments demonstrate that the knowledge graph backend performs better than the ROS 2-based knowledge base. These findings substantiate the viability of distributed knowledge graphs as a foundation for resource-efficient and sustainable robotic planning systems.

Keywords: Robotic Task Planning · Knowledge Graphs · ROS 2 · PDDL · Green Computing · Sustainable Robotics · Planning Frameworks

1 Introduction

Robotic task planning constitutes a fundamental challenge in autonomous robotics, requiring the integration of high-level symbolic reasoning with low-level sensorimotor control. Classical hybrid cognitive architectures [14] typically decouple these concerns into symbolic planners operating over abstract state representations, while execution subsystems handle real-world constraints. Although effective in controlled settings, this separation introduces structural discontinuities between planned actions and their situated execution, particularly in dynamic and partially observable environments.

The complexity of robotic task planning stems from several interrelated factors. First, the system must represent heterogeneous knowledge, including objects, predicates, spatial relations and temporal constraints, in a form

J. M. Ferrández Vicente et al. (Eds.): IWINAC 2026, LNCS 16575, pp. 141–150, 2026.
https://doi.org/10.1007/978-3-032-27317-8_14

amenable to automated reasoning. Second, inference over this knowledge must be computationally efficient to support real-time decision-making. Third, abstract plans must be reliably translated into executable behaviours on physical platforms operating under strict constraints of computation, memory, and energy.

The Planning Domain Definition Language (PDDL) [5] has become the standard formalism for representing planning domains and problems in artificial intelligence. In robotics, it is widely used through frameworks such as ROS-Plan [3] and PlanSys2 [17], which provide interfaces between robotic systems and classical planners, including POPF [4], FF [12], and Fast Downward [11]. While PDDL enables portability and formal reasoning, integrating PDDL-based planning pipelines into real-time robotic systems remains challenging, particularly regarding the efficiency and consistency of knowledge representation and its translation into planning problems.

In parallel, cognitive architectures have long provided integrated computational models of perception, reasoning and action. Architectures such as ACT-R [1] and Soar [15] demonstrate how symbolic production systems can support adaptive behaviour through modular representations and learning mechanisms. More recent hybrid cognitive architectures applied to robotics [2,6–8] continue this line of work, combining symbolic reasoning with distributed software infrastructures. However, as noted in the systematic review presented in [9], most robotic systems still rely on traditional knowledge bases accessed through remote procedure calls or middleware services, rather than exploiting structured graph-based representations as cognitive substrates.

In recent years, the Robot Operating System 2 (ROS 2) has emerged as the dominant middleware framework for robotics development, offering standardised communication patterns and quality-of-service policies [16]. Nevertheless, ROS 2 delegates higher-level cognitive capabilities, including task planning and knowledge representation, to application-layer packages. This architectural openness creates an opportunity to rethink how knowledge is structured and accessed within robotic planning systems.

Motivated by principles of distributed cognition and resource-aware computation, this paper introduces *OmniPlan*[1], a flexible planning framework designed specifically for ROS 2 environments. OmniPlan implements a state machine-based architecture orchestrating knowledge representation, PDDL-based planning and plan execution. Its plugin-based design supports interchangeable knowledge backends and multiple planners, enabling a direct comparison between a traditional ROS 2-based knowledge base — where knowledge is stored as typed objects and predicates accessed through synchronous services — and a distributed knowledge graph representation, where entities and relations are encoded as nodes and edges in a directed labelled graph.

The primary contributions of this work are threefold:

1. The design and implementation of OmniPlan, a modular planning framework for ROS 2 with plugin-based support for multiple knowledge backends and planners.

---

[1] https://github.com/mgonzs13/omni_plan.

2. A comparative evaluation of centralized knowledge bases and distributed knowledge graph representations within a unified planning architecture.
3. A multi-dimensional empirical analysis of computational footprint, including CPU time, memory usage, I/O operations, context switches and energy consumption across the planning–execution pipeline.

The remainder of this paper describes the OmniPlan architecture and knowledge representations, presents the experimental evaluation, discusses the implications for distributed robotic cognition, and concludes with directions for future research.

2   Materials and Methods

This section describes the OmniPlan architecture, the two knowledge representation backends under evaluation, the planner integration mechanism and the experimental setup.

2.1   OmniPlan Architecture

OmniPlan implements a planning framework for robotic task planning based on a finite state machine (FSM) paradigm implemented with YASMIN [10]. The architecture orchestrates the complete planning pipeline, from knowledge retrieval and problem formulation through plan generation and execution. Figure 1 illustrates the state machine of OmniPlan. The core of OmniPlan comprises seven interconnected states:

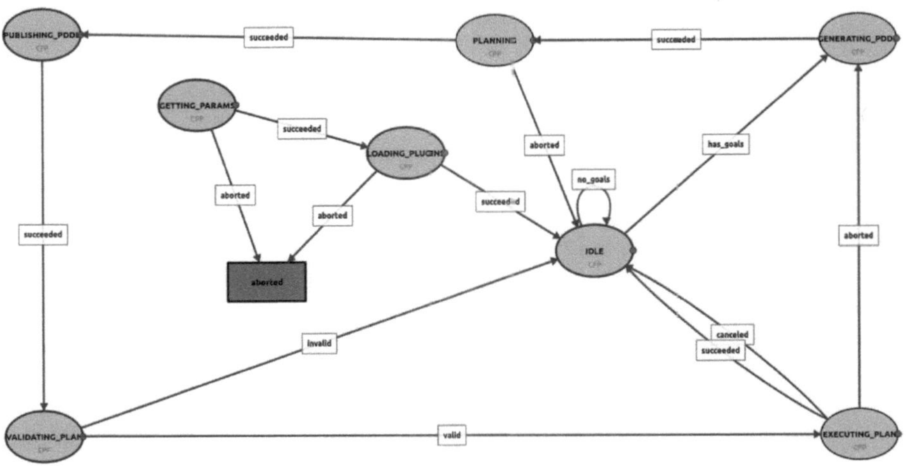

Fig. 1. State machine of the OmniPlan framework, illustrating the states that orchestrate the planning pipeline in OmniPlan.

1. **GetParamsState**: loads configuration parameters and initialises the planning environment.
2. **LoadPluginsState**: dynamically loads planner and validator plugins, knowledge representation backends and robot actions.
3. **GeneratePddlState**: converts the current knowledge state into a PDDL problem description.
4. **PlanState**: invokes the selected planner to generate a task plan from the PDDL input.
5. **ValidatePlanState**: validates the generated plan for correctness and feasibility.
6. **ExecutePlanState**: dispatches the validated plan for execution through the actions execution.
7. **IdleState**: manages transitions between successive planning cycles.

Each state implements the *State* design pattern, ensuring a clean separation of concerns and facilitating extensibility. The FSM topology is configured through XML definitions, enabling practitioners to customise the planning workflow without modifying the framework's core implementation. OmniPlan supports plugin-based extension for planners, validators, actions and knowledge representation backends. The framework currently provides plugins for POPF, SMTPlan and VHPop, together with well-defined interfaces for integrating additional planners.

2.2 Knowledge Representation Backends

Two distinct knowledge representation backends are evaluated within the OmniPlan framework. Both expose the same abstract interface to the planning pipeline, ensuring that differences in measured performance are attributable solely to the underlying representation and retrieval mechanisms.

ROS 2-Based Knowledge Base. The ROS 2-based knowledge base implementation uses ROS 2 services to interact with and retrieve knowledge. Formally, the knowledge base is defined as a tuple $\mathcal{KB} = \langle \mathcal{T}, \mathcal{O}, \mathcal{P}, \mathcal{F}, \mathcal{G} \rangle$, where $\mathcal{T} = \{t_1, t_2, \ldots, t_m\}$ is a finite set of **types**, representing categories of entities in the environment; $\mathcal{O} = \{o_1, o_2, \ldots, o_n\}$ is a finite set of **objects**, each associated with a type through a typing function $\tau \colon \mathcal{O} \to \mathcal{T}$; $\mathcal{P} = \{p_1, p_2, \ldots, p_k\}$ is a finite set of **predicates**, where each predicate p_i has an arity $\mathrm{ar}(p_i) \in \mathbb{N}$ and a type signature $\mathrm{sig}(p_i) \subseteq \mathcal{T}^{\mathrm{ar}(p_i)}$; $\mathcal{F} \subseteq \{p_i(o_{j_1}, \ldots, o_{j_{\mathrm{ar}(p_i)}}) \mid p_i \in \mathcal{P}, o_{j_l} \in \mathcal{O}\}$ is a finite set of **facts**, i.e. ground atoms that hold in the current world state; and $\mathcal{G}$ is a **goal** specification expressed as a conjunction of ground atoms.

Knowledge is accessed through synchronous ROS 2 service calls. The knowledge base maintains the current world state and exposes operations for adding, removing and querying each of the above constructs. During PDDL generation, the backend performs an exhaustive enumeration over the complete set of stored knowledge. For a knowledge base with $|\mathcal{O}|$ objects and $|\mathcal{F}|$ facts, the PDDL generation procedure iterates over all elements, yielding a retrieval complexity of $\mathcal{O}(|\mathcal{O}| + |\mathcal{F}|)$ service calls.

Distributed Knowledge Graph. The distributed knowledge graph implementation provides a graph-based knowledge representation shared across several ROS 2 processes. Formally, the knowledge graph is defined as a directed labelled multigraph $\mathcal{G}_K = \langle V, E, \lambda_V, \lambda_E \rangle$, where $V = \{v_1, v_2, \ldots, v_n\}$ is a finite set of **nodes** representing entities (robots, objects, locations); $E \subseteq V \times V$ is a set of directed **edges** representing relationships between entities; $\lambda_V \colon V \to \mathcal{T}$ is a node labelling function that assigns to each node its type; and $\lambda_E \colon E \to \mathcal{P}$ is an edge labelling function that maps each edge to a predicate name from $\mathcal{P}$.

Under this representation, every object $o_i \in \mathcal{O}$ corresponds to a node $v_i \in V$ with $\lambda_V(v_i) = (\tau(o_i), A_i)$, and every fact $p(o_i, o_j) \in \mathcal{F}$ corresponds to a directed edge $(v_i, v_j) \in E$ with $\lambda_E(v_i, v_j) = p$. Unary predicates are encoded as self-loops, i.e., edges of the form (v_i, v_i). The graph representation provides several advantages for knowledge-intensive robotics applications:

1. *Rich semantic expressivity*: graph structures naturally encode complex relational knowledge, supporting sophisticated queries and inference.
2. *Efficient traversal*: adjacency-based data structures enable rapid navigation of entity relationships, which is beneficial for spatial and temporal reasoning. For a node v_i, its relevant facts can be retrieved in $\mathcal{O}(\deg(v_i))$ time, where $\deg(v_i)$ is the degree of the node, rather than scanning the entire fact store.
3. *Flexible schema*: unlike rigid table-based representations, graph schemas can evolve dynamically as new entity types and relationships are introduced.

During PDDL generation, the knowledge graph backend traverses the graph structure to extract ground atoms for the initial state. Starting from each node $v_i \in V$, the backend collects the outgoing edges $\{(v_i, v_j) \in E\}$ and maps them to their corresponding ground atoms via λ_E, leveraging the adjacency representation to collect relevant predicates without requiring exhaustive enumeration of the entire knowledge store.

2.3 Experimental Setup

All experiments were conducted on a workstation equipped with an Intel(R) Core(TM) i9-14900K, 64 GB of DDR5 RAM, and running Ubuntu 24.04. Besides, ROS 2 Jazzy is used along with the POPF (Partial-Order Planning Forward-chaining) planner [4], employed as the primary planning engine for the experimental evaluation, and the plan validator VAL [13].

Performance was measured using POIROT[2], a profiling tool for ROS 2 that records multiple metrics for individual function calls, providing fine-grained performance measurement. The following metrics are collected for each profiled invocation:

- **Wall time** (μs): total elapsed real time.
- **CPU time** (μs): processor time consumed in user mode.
- **Energy** (μJ): energy consumed during the function execution, estimated from CPU time and processor thermal design power.

---

[2] https://github.com/mgonzs13/poirot.

- **CO$_2$ emitted** (μg): carbon dioxide emissions derived from the energy consumed and the regional carbon intensity factor.

Among the seven states of the OmniPlan FSM, profiling is applied to the four states that constitute the core planning pipeline: **GeneratePddlState** (PDDL Generation), **PlanState** (Plan Generation), **ValidatePlanState** (Plan Validation), and **ExecutePlanState** (Plan Execution). The remaining three states (GetParamsState, LoadPluginsState and IdleState) perform one-time initialisation or idle waiting and are excluded from the measurements, as they do not contribute to the recurring planning workload. This selection ensures that the profiled stages cover every main phase of the planning pipeline.

The experimental scenario simulates an indoor service robot that must autonomously navigate through a network of interconnected waypoints and manage its battery. The environment comprises six rooms, *entrance*, *kitchen*, *bedroom*, *dinning*, *bathroom* and *chargingroom*, linked by bidirectional connections. The robot begins at the *entrance* with a low battery, and its goal is to reach the *bathroom*. Three durative PDDL actions are available, which are `move`, moving the robot between two connected rooms provided the battery is full; `charge`, replenishing the battery when the robot is located at a room with a charging point; and `ask_charge`, requesting the robot to travel to the charging station. The knowledge store encodes the room topology, predicate definitions (*connected*, *robot_ at*, *battery_ low*, *battery_ full*, *charging_ point_ at*), the initial state facts and the goal specification. Both the knowledge base and the knowledge graph backends are populated with identical information, ensuring that the only variable across configurations is the underlying representation mechanism. Finally, this scenario is repeated a total of 50 iterations.

3   Experimental Results

This section presents the experimental results comparing the ROS 2-based knowledge base (KB) and the distributed knowledge graph (KG) backends across the four major planning pipeline stages. All reported values are arithmetic means $\pm$ one standard deviation computed over 50 iterations.

Table 1 summarises the results for the four pipeline stages along the four measured metrics. Two clear patterns emerge from the data. First, the distributed knowledge graph backend yields substantial improvements in the two stages that actively interact with the knowledge store. During *PDDL Generation*, CPU time drops from 1973 μs to 937.2 μs (-52.5%), energy consumption is more than halved from 3268 μJ to 1528 μJ (-53.2%), and CO$_2$ emissions decrease proportionally from 0.148 μg to 0.069 μg (-53.4%). Wall-clock time is also reduced by 6.9%, from 39280 μs to 36570 μs. During *Plan Execution*, the differences are again notable, CPU time falls by 18.3% (from 8677 μs to 7090 μs), energy by 20.9% (from 3256 μJ to 2574 μJ), and CO$_2$ by 21.1% (from 0.147 μg to 0.116 μg). Wall-clock time is virtually identical for both backends in this stage, which is expected because plan execution is dominated by the simulated action durations rather than by knowledge access overhead.

Table 1. Performance comparison of the ROS 2 knowledge base (KB) and distributed knowledge graph (KG) backends across the four OmniPlan pipeline stages. Values are reported as mean ± std over 50 iterations.

Metric	Backend	PDDL Generation	Plan Generation	Plan Validation	Plan Execution
Wall time [μs]	KB	39280±1836	**35460±1220**	59110±3122	2.408×10^7±2408
	KG	**36570±1838**	35810±1990	**58560±3060**	**2.407×10^7±1662**
CPU time [μs]	KB	1973±225	**1005±122**	844.2±156	8677±508
	KG	**937.2±60**	1008±104	**824.4±164**	**7090±299**
Energy [μJ]	KB	3268±325	**1950±221**	1822±329	3256±184
	KG	**1528±152**	1971±216	**1777±328**	**2574±101**
CO_2 [μg]	KB	0.148±0.015	**0.088±0.010**	0.082±0.015	0.147±0.008
	KG	**0.069±0.007**	0.089±0.010	**0.080±0.015**	**0.116±0.005**

Second, *Plan Generation* and *Plan Validation* exhibit negligible differences between backends across all four metrics (all within $\approx 1\%$). This is consistent with the architecture of OmniPlan. Once the PDDL problem has been generated, the planner and validator operate on the textual PDDL representation and do not interact with the knowledge store. The near-identical results therefore serve as an internal consistency check, confirming that the experimental setup correctly isolates the effect of the knowledge backend.

The aggregate sums over all 50 iterations further highlight the practical impact of the backend choice. For CPU time, the ROS 2-based knowledge base backend accumulates a total of 624.910 μs across all four stages, whereas the distributed knowledge graph backend totals 493.000 μs, yielding a cumulative reduction of 21.1%. Total energy consumption follows a similar trend. The ROS 2-based knowledge base backend consumes 514.790 μJ compared with 392.480 μJ for the distributed knowledge graph backend (-23.8%). With respect to CO_2 emissions, the ROS 2-based knowledge base backend produces 23.27 μg in total while the distributed knowledge graph backend emits 17.74 μg, a cumulative saving of 23.8%. Total wall-clock time is dominated by plan execution ($\approx 1.204\times10^9$ μs in both cases), so the overall wall-time difference remains marginal despite the per-stage gains in PDDL Generation. These cumulative values demonstrate that the efficiency advantages of the distributed knowledge graph backend compound over repeated planning cycles and translate into meaningful resource savings during sustained operation.

4 Discussion

The experimental results reveal a clear dichotomy between knowledge-intensive and knowledge-independent stages of the planning pipeline. This distinction is central to interpreting the practical implications of the two backends.

The most pronounced gains are observed in PDDL Generation and Plan Execution, the two stages that actively query the knowledge store. In PDDL Generation, the distributed knowledge graph backend reduces CPU time by 52.5%

and energy consumption by 53.2% relative to the ROS 2-based knowledge base backend. These improvements stem from the adjacency-based data structures of the graph representation, which enable targeted traversal of relevant entities and relationships rather than exhaustively iterating over the complete set of ground atoms, as the ROS 2-based knowledge base backend must do through synchronous ROS 2 service calls. During Plan Execution, CPU time is reduced by 18.3% and energy by 20.9%, reflecting the lower overhead of local graph lookups compared with inter-process service communication each time an action needs to verify or update the world state.

Plan Generation and Plan Validation show virtually no difference between backends (within approximately 1% across all metrics). This outcome is architecturally expected; both stages operate on the PDDL text produced in the preceding stage and do not interact with the knowledge store. The result serves a dual purpose, first, it validates the experimental isolation of the knowledge backend variable, second, it confirms that switching backends does not alter the planning semantics or affect planner performance.

On the other hand, while the distributed knowledge graph backend achieves a 6.9% reduction in wall-clock time during PDDL Generation, wall-clock differences are negligible in the remaining stages. Plan Execution wall time, in particular, is dominated by the simulated durative actions ($\approx 24\,\text{s}$) rather than by knowledge access, which explains the minimal wall-time gap despite the substantial CPU and energy savings. This suggests that in real robotic deployments, where physical action durations are typically even longer, the wall-time advantage will be similarly masked, whereas the CPU and energy benefits will persist.

Finally, from a green computing perspective, the distributed knowledge graph backend cumulatively reduces CO_2 emissions by 53.4% in PDDL Generation and by 21.1% in Plan Execution. Aggregating over the full pipeline, this backend emits approximately $0.355\,\mu\text{g}$ of CO_2 per planning cycle compared with $0.465\,\mu\text{g}$ for the ROS 2-based knowledge base backend, representing an overall reduction of 23.8%. While the per-cycle savings are modest, they increase linearly with the number of planning iterations and become substantial in long-duration autonomous missions that involve multiple replanning episodes.

5   Conclusion

This paper presented OmniPlan, a modular ROS 2 planning framework with plugin-based support for interchangeable knowledge representation backends, and conducted an empirical comparison between a traditional ROS 2 knowledge base and a distributed knowledge graph within the same planning architecture.

The results demonstrate that the choice of knowledge backend has a direct and measurable impact on the computational and environmental footprint of the planning pipeline. The distributed knowledge graph consistently outperforms the ROS 2 knowledge base in every stage that involves knowledge access. During PDDL Generation, the graph backend reduces CPU time by 52.5%, energy consumption by 53.2% and CO_2 emissions by 53.4%. During Plan Execution, CPU time decreases by 18.3%, energy by 20.9% and CO_2 by 21.1%. Across the entire pipeline, this translates into cumulative reductions of 21.1% in CPU time, 23.8% in energy and 23.8% in CO_2 emissions. Crucially, stages that do not interact with the knowledge store, namely Plan Generation and Plan Validation, remain unaffected, confirming that the gains originate exclusively from the knowledge representation layer rather than from other architectural factors. These findings establish that the structure of the knowledge backend, particularly the use of adjacency-based graph traversals instead of synchronous service-call enumeration, is a significant lever for building more efficient and sustainable robotic planning systems.

Several directions remain open for future investigation. First, the current evaluation is limited to a single planning scenario; extending the comparison to complex domains would clarify how the performance gap scales with problem size. Second, although the distributed knowledge graph is designed for multi-process operation, all experiments were executed on a single machine; evaluating the backend under realistic scenarios is essential to understand its behavior in the field. Third, incorporating additional knowledge backends, such as ontology-based stores, would broaden the scope of the comparison and guide in selecting the most suitable representation for their specific application requirements. Finally, other interchangeable components can be profiled, like the planner, which can also give insights about the currently unaffected stages of the presented planning pipeline.

Acknowledgments. This research was funded by Grant PID2024-161761OB-C21 (AURORAS - Advanced aUtonomy for RObots in the primary Sector) funded by MICIU/AEI/10.13039/501100011033 and by the European Union.

Disclosure of Interests. The authors have no competing interests to declare that are relevant to the content of this article.

References

1. Anderson, J.R., Matessa, M., Lebiere, C.: ACT-R: a theory of higher level cognition and its relation to visual attention. Hum. Comput. Interact. **12**(4), 439–462 (1997). https://doi.org/10.1207/s15327051hci1204_5
2. Bustos, P., Manso, L.J., Bandera, A.J., Bandera, J.P., García-Varea, I., Martínez-Gómez, J.: The CORTEX cognitive robotics architecture: Use cases. Cogn. Syst. Res. **55**, 107–123 (2019). https://doi.org/10.1016/j.cogsys.2019.01.003, https://www.sciencedirect.com/science/article/pii/S1389041717300347
3. Cashmore, M., et al.: ROSplan: planning in the robot operating system. In: Proceedings International Conference on Automated Planning and Scheduling, ICAPS, vol. 2015, pp. 333–341 (2015). https://doi.org/10.1609/icaps.v25i1.13699
4. Coles, A., Coles, A., Fox, M., Long, D.: Forward-chaining partial-order planning. In: ICAPS 2010 - Proceedings of the 20th International Conference on Automated Planning and Scheduling, pp. 42–49 (2010). https://doi.org/10.1609/icaps.v20i1.13403

5. Fox, M., Long, D.: Pddl2. 1: an extension to pddl for expressing temporal planning domains. J. Artif. Intell. Res. **20**, 61–124 (2003). https://doi.org/10.1613/jair.1129

6. Galeas, J., Tudela, A., Pons, O., Bandera, J.P., Bandera, A., Bustos, P.: CRDT-based knowledge synchronisation in an internet of robotics things ecosystem for ambient assisted living. Comput. Vis. Image Underst. **259**, 104437 (2025). https://doi.org/10.1016/j.cviu.2025.104437

7. Ginés Clavero, J., Martín Rico, F., Rodríguez-Lera, F.J., Guerrero Hernandéz, J.M., Matellán Olivera, V.: Impact of decision-making system in social navigation. Multimedia Tools Appl. **81**(3), 3459–3481 (2022). https://doi.org/10.1007/s11042-021-11454-2

8. González-Santamarta, M.Á., Rodríguez-Lera, F.J., Fernández-Llamas, C., Matellán-Olivera, V.: A hybrid cognitive architecture to generate, control, plan, and monitor behaviors for interactive autonomous robots. Int. J. Soc. Robot. (2024). https://doi.org/10.1007/s12369-024-01192-4

9. González-Santamarta, M.Á., Rodríguez-Lera, F.J., Matellán-Olivera, V.: Cognitive architectures in autonomous robotics: a systematic review of behavior generation approaches and evaluation strategies. IEEE Access **13**, 191619–191644 (2025)

10. González-Santamarta, M.Á., Rodríguez-Lera, F.J., Matellán-Olivera, V., Fernández-Llamas, C.: Yasmin: Yet another state machine. In: Tardioli, D., Matellán, V., Heredia, G., Silva, M.F., Marques, L. (eds.) ROBOT2022: Fifth Iberian Robotics Conference, pp. 528–539. Springer, Cham (2023). https://doi.org/10.1007/978-3-031-21062-4_43

11. Helmert, M.: The fast downward planning system. J. Artif. Intell. Res. **26**, 191–246 (2006)

12. Hoffmann, J., Nebel, B.: The ff planning system: fast plan generation through heuristic search. J. Artif. Intell. Res. **14**, 253–302 (2001)

13. Howey, R., Long, D., Fox, M.: Val: Automatic plan validation, continuous effects and mixed initiative planning using pddl. In: 16th IEEE International Conference on Tools with Artificial Intelligence, pp. 294–301. IEEE (2004)

14. Kotseruba, I., Tsotsos, J.K.: 40 years of cognitive architectures: core cognitive abilities and practical applications. Artif. Intell. Rev. **53**(1), 17–94 (2020). https://doi.org/10.1007/s10462-018-9646-y

15. Laird, J.E., Newell, A., Rosenbloom, P.S.: Soar: an architecture for general intelligence. Artif. Intell. **33**(1), 1–64 (1987). https://doi.org/10.1016/0004-3702(87)90050-6

16. Macenski, S., Foote, T., Gerkey, B., Lalancette, C., Woodall, W.: Robot operating system 2: design, architecture, and uses in the wild. Sci. Robot. **7**(66), eabm6074 (2022)

17. Martín, F., Ginés, J., Rodríguez, F.J., Matellán, V.: Plansys2: a planning system framework for ros2. In: IEEE/RSJ International Conference on Intelligent Robots and Systems, IROS 2021, Prague, Czech Republic, September 27 - October 1, 2021. IEEE (2021). https://doi.org/10.1109/IROS51168.2021.9635998

Head-Level Structural Collapse
for Scalable Preferred Semantics
in Norm-Based Robotic Reasoning

Francisco J. Rodriguez Lera[1]([☒]) , Irene González-Fernández[2] ,
Miguel Ángel González-Santamarta[1] , Francisco Martín Rico[2] ,
and Pere Pardo Ventura[3]

[1] Grupo de Robótica, Instituto I4, Universidad de León, León, Spain
`{fjrodl,mgcns}@unileon.es`
[2] Intelligent Robotics Lab, Universidad Rey Juan Carlos, Fuenlabrada, Spain
`{irene.gonzalezf,francisco.rico}@urjc.es`
[3] AI Robolab, Department of Computer Science, University of Luxembourg,
Esch-sur-Alzette, Luxembourg
`pere.pardo@uni.lu`

Abstract. In social environments, autonomous systems must reconcile potentially conflicting norms, obligations and contextual constraints in order to make rational and explainable decisions. In this paper, we present an executable implementation of a norm-based argumentation framework for decision-making in socially regulated agent environments and analyze the scalability of preferred semantics in norm-rich scenarios such as RoboCup@Home Human-Robot Interaction tasks. We show that the number of generated arguments can grow rapidly, making naive preferred computation impractical in practice. Exploiting a structural regularity common in robotic normative reasoning—namely that multiple norms support identical action-level conclusions—we introduce a head-level collapse optimization. This transformation preserves preferred semantics while reducing the search space from $O(2^{|A|})$ to $O(2^{|H|})$. Experimental results demonstrate that the optimized approach remains computationally stable under scaling.

Keywords: Norm-Based Argumentation · Preferred Semantics · Robotic Decision-Making · Human-Robot Interaction · Normative Reasoning · Computational Scalability · Argumentation Frameworks

1 Introduction

Autonomous robots working in social environments must reconcile norms and contextual constraints to make rational and explainable decisions. Norm-based argumentation has been proposed as a promising approach for decision-making in autonomous agents operating in socially regulated environments. In this context, Jiminy was introduced as a normative reasoning framework grounded in

J. M. Ferrández Vicente et al. (Eds.): IWINAC 2026, LNCS 16575, pp. 151–160, 2026.
https://doi.org/10.1007/978-3-032-27317-8_15

argumentation semantics, where contextual facts activate norms that generate arguments supporting or opposing action-level conclusions.

However, Jiminy was originally formulated at a conceptual and formal level [12], without a computational implementation. In particular, the framework did not explicitly address the algorithmic implications of computing argumentation semantics in real-time robotic settings.

In this work, we first show that Jiminy can be implemented as a fully operational reasoning engine. We provide a concrete computational realization of its argument construction, attack relation and semantic evaluation mechanisms. This demonstrates that the framework is not merely a theoretical proposal but can be executed within embodied robotic systems.

Nevertheless, when scaling to realistic social robotics scenarios, a fundamental computational issue emerges. Norm-rich environments, such as RoboCup@Home Human-Robot Interaction challenges [13], may activate dozens of norms simultaneously. Since each activated norm generates a distinct argument, the number of arguments grows rapidly. Classical preferred semantics requires exploring subsets of arguments, leading to exponential complexity in the number of generated arguments.

Through an empirical demonstration, we show that even moderate scaling can render naive preferred computation impractical. This raises a critical question: How can normative argumentation remain computationally viable in socially complex robotic environments?

We observe that in many robotic normative systems, multiple norms support identical action-level conclusions (e.g., safety, social, and scoring norms may all recommend the same action). Attacks are defined at the level of action conclusions rather than at the level of individual arguments. This induces a structural regularity: arguments naturally partition into equivalence classes based on their head (action-level conclusion).

Exploiting this structural property, we introduce a head-level collapse optimization for preferred semantics. Instead of computing preferred extensions over the full set of arguments, we compute them over distinct action-level conclusions and lift the result back to arguments. Under mild structural assumptions, this transformation preserves preferred semantics while reducing the search space from $O(2^{|A|})$ to $O(2^{|H|})$, where $|H| \ll |A|$ in typical robotic scenarios.

We validate the approach in a RoboCup@Home HRI scenario, showing that while classical preferred computation becomes impractical under scaling, the head-collapsed version remains computationally stable.

The contribution of this paper is therefore twofold. The first one is a concrete computational realization of Jiminy as an executable normative argumentation engine. On the other hand, a structural optimization exploiting head-equivalence that restores scalability of preferred reasoning in social robotic contexts.

This work positions norm-based argumentation as a viable decision-making mechanism for embodied social agents, provided that its structural properties are computationally leveraged.

2   Related Work

There have been multiple intents of creating cognitive architectures for autonomous robots to generate behaviors [11,14]. The trend in recent cognitive architecture [10] shows that symbolic knowledge and symbolic planning systems, along with reactive and emergent components, are used. This results in hybrid cognitive architectures [3,7–9] that include a symbolic deliberative system. However, these deliberative systems are focused on planning to achieve the goals of autonomous robots without taking into account the social norms of their environments.

Therefore, abstract argumentation frameworks, as introduced by Dung [6], provide a general formal model for reasoning under conflict. Preferred semantics, in particular, capture maximal admissible sets of arguments but are known to be computationally demanding in the worst case.

Normative extensions of argumentation have been widely studied in the context of multi-agent systems and deontic reasoning [2]. In these approaches, norms generate arguments whose interactions determine acceptable actions. However, most contributions remain either theoretical or focused on logical expressiveness rather than computational deployment in embodied agents. Jiminy belongs to this family of norm-based argumentation frameworks [12] but differs in its explicit focus on action-level decision-making in robotic contexts.

Argumentation has been applied to explainability, ethical decision-making, and human-robot interaction. Several works explore argument-based mechanisms for justifying robot behavior or resolving normative conflicts [5]. However, relatively little attention has been paid to the computational scalability of argumentation semantics when deployed in real-time robotic systems.

In socially rich environments, such as RoboCup@Home HRI challenges [13], multiple institutional, safety, and social norms may be simultaneously active. This leads to a rapid growth in generated arguments, potentially challenging classical semantic evaluation mechanisms.

The computational complexity of preferred semantics has been extensively studied and is known to be intractable in the general case. Existing approaches to scalability typically rely on SAT encodings, ASP solvers, or structural restrictions on the argumentation graph [4].

In contrast, the present work does not introduce a new solver or encoding. Instead, it identifies and exploits a structural regularity that naturally emerges in norm-based robotic reasoning [1], head-equivalence among arguments. The resulting optimization preserves semantics under clearly stated assumptions while dramatically reducing the search space in practical scenarios.

3   Jiminy as a Computational Engine

Jiminy was originally formulated as a norm-based argumentation framework in which contextual facts activate norms, generating arguments that support action-level conclusions. To evaluate its practical viability in robotic settings, we implemented Jiminy as an executable reasoning engine.

Argument Construction. Let W be the set of contextual facts and N the set of norms. Each norm $n \in N$ has the form $body(n) \rightarrow hd(n)$, where $body(n) \subseteq W$ and $hd(n)$ is an action-level conclusion. Given an active context $W' \subseteq W$, an argument a is generated whenever $body(n) \subseteq W'$. Each argument is therefore defined as $a = \langle body(n), hd(n) \rangle$. Multiple norms may produce distinct arguments with identical heads.

Attack Relation. Attacks are defined at the level of action-level conclusions. Let χ denote a contrariness function over heads. An argument a_i attacks a_j if $hd(a_j) \in \chi(hd(a_i))$. Importantly, this definition implies that attacks depend solely on heads, not on argument bodies. This restriction reflects a design choice specific to the present implementation; the framework models normative conflicts at the level of executable robot actions. Intermediate institutional or factual conclusions are not subject to independent attack.

Semantic Evaluation. The engine supports standard Dung-style semantics, including grounded, preferred, and stable extensions. Given a set of generated arguments A, semantic computation proceeds by evaluating admissibility, conflict-freeness, and maximality conditions. In addition, Jiminy includes a priority-based resolution mechanism at the head level, enabling executable decision selection in robotic contexts where a single action recommendation is required.

Executable Recommendation. While classical argumentation semantics may yield multiple extensions, embodied robotic systems require a unique executable decision. Therefore, when multiple preferred extensions exist, a head-level priority aggregation is used to select a single extension suitable for execution. This implementation demonstrates that Jiminy can operate as a real-time normative reasoning component within social robotic systems.

4   Structural Collapse Under Head-Equivalence

In norm-based robotic reasoning [1], multiple norms may generate distinct arguments that share the same action-level conclusion. We exploit this structural regularity to obtain an exponential reduction in the search space of preferred semantics.

Head-Equivalence. Let A be the set of arguments generated by the normative engine, and let $H = \{hd(a) \mid a \in A\}$ be the set of distinct action-level conclusions ("heads"). We denote by $|A|$ the number of generated arguments and by $|H|$ the number of distinct action-level conclusions. In norm-driven robotic scenarios, $|A|$ may grow with the number of activated norms, while $|H|$ typically corresponds to the number of physically executable action alternatives.

We define an equivalence relation over arguments $a_i \sim a_j \iff hd(a_i) = hd(a_j)$. Thus, arguments are partitioned into equivalence classes induced by their head. We assume:

1. Attacks depend exclusively on heads $a_i \rightarrow a_j \iff hd(a_j) \in \chi(hd(a_i))$.
2. No undercuts exist between arguments.
3. No argument-specific priorities are defined (priorities, if present, are head-level).
4. Arguments with identical heads do not attack each other[1]

Head-Collapse Theorem. Let $AF = (A, \rightarrow)$ be the argumentation framework generated by the normative engine, and let $H = \{hd(a) \mid a \in A\}$ be the set of distinct action-level conclusions (heads).

We define the induced head-level argumentation framework $AF_H = (H, \rightarrow_H)$ as follows $h_i \rightarrow_H h_j$ iff $h_j \in \chi(h_i)$.

Theorem (Head-Collapse). Under the structural assumptions stated above, preferred semantics over arguments is equivalent to preferred semantics computed over heads and lifted back to arguments:

$$Preferred(A) = \bigcup_{h \in Preferred(AF_H)} \{\, a \in A \mid hd(a) = h \,\}.$$

Proof Sketch. **Conflict-Freeness Preservation.** Since attacks depend solely on heads, a set of arguments is conflict-free if and only if the corresponding set of heads is conflict-free. No additional conflicts arise within equivalence classes.

Defense Preservation. Defense relations also depend exclusively on head-level attacks. If a head is defended at the head-level framework, all arguments with that head are defended in the argument-level framework.

Maximality Preservation. Maximal admissible sets of arguments correspond exactly to maximal admissible sets of heads. Adding an argument corresponds to adding its head, and admissibility constraints are fully captured at the head level.

Therefore, preferred extensions factorize through the head partition. Since arguments within the same equivalence class are indistinguishable with respect to attack and defense relations, they behave identically under preferred semantics.

Computational Implication. Let $|A|$ denote the number of generated arguments and $|H|$ the number of distinct action-level conclusions (heads). In our current implementation, preferred semantics are computed via subset enumeration, which yields a worst-case complexity of $O(2^{|A|})$. Thus, the computational cost grows exponentially in $|A|$.

Under head-collapse, the computation is performed over distinct heads instead of arguments, leading to a worst-case complexity of: $O(2^{|H|})$. Hence, the exponential dependency shifts from $|A|$ to $|H|$. In norm-driven robotic scenarios, typically $|H| \ll |A|$. as many norms may support the same action. Hence, the complexity becomes fixed-parameter tractable in $|H|$.

---

[1] Although abstract frameworks such as ASPIC+ do not forbid self-contrary propositions in principle, in robotic normative contexts, executable actions are not typically defined as contraries of themselves, except in pathological logical cases.

Limitations. The collapse result does not hold if argument-specific priorities are introduced, undercuts between arguments are allowed and attacks depend on argument bodies rather than heads. The present result applies to head-driven normative frameworks, where conflicts are modeled at the level of executable actions. Thus, the structural reduction applies specifically to head-driven normative frameworks such as Jiminy.

Unlike classical preferred computation over arguments, the search space is bounded by $2^{|H|}$ instead of $2^{|A|}$. In robotic normative scenarios, where multiple norms support identical action-level conclusions, $|H|$ remains small even when $|A|$ grows.

We evaluate the computational impact of the proposed head-level collapse in a RoboCup@Home Human-Robot Interaction (HRI) scenario. The goal of the experiment is to compare classical preferred semantics with the optimized preferred_head computation under increasing norm redundancy.

5   Experimental Setup

The experiments were conducted on a RoboCup@Home-inspired scenario in which contextual facts activate multiple norms that generate arguments supporting a limited set of executable robot actions.

All experiments were conducted on an Intel Core i7-8750H (6C/12T, 2.20 GHz) with 32 GB RAM running Ubuntu 22.04.5 LTS (Linux 6.8.0). All semantic computation benchmarks were executed in Python 3.10.12 under controlled conditions, minimizing background processes to reduce timing variability.

To analyze scalability, we generated progressively redundant configurations in which additional norms support already existing heads. This increases the number of arguments $|A|$ while keeping the number of distinct heads $|H|$ constant.

Four configurations were evaluated: **Scale 6** (6 arguments, 4 heads), **Scale 10** (10 arguments, 4 heads), **Scale 15** (15 arguments, 4 heads), and **Scale 20** (20 arguments, 4 heads).

In our setting, these actions (heads) include *d_follow_host*, *d_keep_safe_distance*, *d_look_at_speaker*, and *d_look_forward*. For instance, a norm triggered by *w_guest_speaking* may generate an argument $\langle \{w\_guest\_speaking\}, d\_look\_at\_speaker \rangle$. Multiple norms may support the same action-level conclusion, thereby generating several arguments that share an identical head.

Attacks were defined exclusively at head level. No undercuts or argument-specific priorities were introduced, ensuring that the structural assumptions of the head-collapse theorem hold.

Each semantic variant was executed 100 times per configuration. As the two semantic variants were executed in separate runs without run-to-run synchronization, the resulting samples were treated as independent. Statistical significance was therefore evaluated using the two-sided Mann-Whitney U test. All reported p-values are two-sided. Statistical significance was assessed at $\alpha = 0.05$.

Results. Table 1 reports the mean execution time and standard deviation for both semantics.

Table 1. Execution time comparison between preferred and preferred_head semantics (mean ± std in microseconds).

scenario	preferred	preferred_head	speedup	p_value
scale_6	471.59 ± 67.93	115.00 ± 21.70	4.10×	2.51e-34
scale_10	7836.93 ± 2489.44	104.36 ± 16.73	75.10×	2.46e-34
scale_15	161850.32 ± 14179.28	103.95 ± 17.77	1557.00×	2.46e-34
scale_20	5740835.41 ± 959172.82	97.30 ± 16.39	59001.39×	2.47e-34

The results exhibit the exponential growth trend predicted by the theoretical complexity analysis. Execution time increases by several orders of magnitude as $|A|$ grows, while $|H|$ remains constant. In contrast, preferred_head remains stable across all configurations, with execution time consistently around 100 microseconds. This empirical behavior aligns with the theoretical reduction from $O(2^{|A|})$ to $O(2^{|H|})$, demonstrating that computational cost is governed by the number of distinct heads rather than by the total number of generated arguments. The observed speedup grows superlinearly, reaching more than 59,000× at scale 20. The extremely small p-values confirm that the observed differences are statistically significant. Given that the performance gap spans multiple orders of magnitude, statistical testing serves primarily as confirmatory evidence of an already structurally evident computational separation.

Implications for Robotic Normative Reasoning. The experimental results validate the theoretical analysis; in norm-rich robotic environments, multiple norms frequently support identical action-level conclusions, leading to high redundancy at the argument level. While the number of generated arguments may grow rapidly, the number of executable action alternatives remains small. This structural asymmetry makes head-level abstraction not merely an optimization but a natural computational alignment with embodied decision-making. Thus, symbolic abstraction at the action level enables exponential compression of the search space without altering the underlying preferred semantics.

On the Nature of the Contribution. The proposed approach does not introduce a new argumentation semantics. Instead, it exploits a structural regularity characteristic of norm-driven robotic reasoning. Under head-equivalence, the argumentation framework is effectively a lifted expansion of a smaller head-level framework. The computational benefit, therefore, arises from structural compression, not from semantic modification. This positions the contribution as a domain-structured optimization: a principled alignment between symbolic abstraction and computational tractability in embodied normative agents.

Symbol-Level Abstraction and Computational Paradigm. The collapse mechanism reflects a broader computational principle: symbol-level abstraction can dramatically reduce combinatorial explosion in embodied reasoning systems. In robotic normative decision-making, physical-level multiplicity (many norms, many contextual triggers) often converges into a small set of symbolic action alternatives. The head-level reduction makes this symbolic convergence computationally explicit. Thus, the result illustrates how structural properties at the symbolic level can regulate complexity at the computational level—a central theme of the Computational Paradigm.

6   Discussion

The experiments demonstrate that classical preferred semantics can become impractical even under moderate scaling when the number of generated arguments increases. In social robotic contexts, this situation is realistic: safety, task-oriented, social, institutional, and scoring norms may simultaneously justify identical or conflicting actions.

The head-level collapse does not reduce the expressive power of the framework. Instead, it makes explicit a structural asymmetry between the number of norms and the number of executable actions. In embodied agents, the set of action-level alternatives is typically small, while the set of norm activations may be large. By shifting the computational burden from argument-level enumeration to head-level evaluation, the engine remains operational under norm-rich conditions.

The collapse mechanism relies on structural properties that are common in normative robotic systems but not universal in abstract argumentation frameworks. In particular, the reduction holds when:

– Attacks are defined exclusively at the level of action conclusions.
– Arguments sharing a head do not attack each other.
– No undercuts are introduced between arguments.
– Priorities are defined at the head-level rather than argument-level.

If these conditions are violated, head-equivalence may no longer preserve preferred semantics. Thus, the optimization is domain-structured rather than universally applicable.

From a practical standpoint, robotic systems require executable decisions rather than abstract extension sets. In many cases, multiple preferred extensions may exist. The introduction of head-level tie-breaking ensures that a unique action recommendation can be selected without modifying the underlying semantics. This highlights an important design principle: argumentation frameworks deployed in embodied systems must reconcile formal semantics with operational constraints.

7   Conclusion

This paper demonstrates that Jiminy, originally introduced as a conceptual norm-based argumentation framework, can be implemented as an executable reasoning engine for social robotic systems.

While classical preferred semantics becomes computationally impractical as the number of generated arguments increases, we show that many norm-based robotic scenarios exhibit a structural regularity: multiple norms frequently support identical action-level conclusions. This induces a head-equivalence partition over arguments.

Exploiting this structural property, we introduced a head-level collapse optimization that preserves preferred semantics under clearly stated assumptions while reducing the search space from $O(2^{|\mathcal{A}|})$ to $O(2^{|H|})$, where $|H|$ denotes the number of distinct action-level conclusions. The proposed collapse does not approximate preferred semantics: it preserves them exactly under explicitly stated structural conditions.

Empirical evaluation in a RoboCup@Home HRI scenario shows that classical preferred computation increases from $0.00036\,s$ (6 arguments) to $4.7\,s$ (20 arguments), while the head-collapsed version remains stable at approximately $0.00008\,s$.

The contribution of this work is therefore not a modification of argumentation semantics, but a structural optimization tailored to norm-driven robotic reasoning. By aligning computational structure with action-level abstraction, normative argumentation becomes viable for real-time embodied agents.

Future research may explore how similar structural properties can be exploited in other applied argumentation settings, as well as how partial collapse mechanisms can be maintained when introducing richer forms of attack and priority.

Acknowledgments. This research was partially funded by Grant PID2024-161761OB-C21 funded by MICIU/AEI/10.13039/501100011033 and by the European Union. Irene González-Fernández is funded by the Horizon Europe Project CORESENSE (Grant Agreement No. 101070254). P. Pardo is partially supported by project DJ4ME - A DJ for Machine Ethics: the Dialogue Jiminy (O24/18989918/DJ4ME).

Disclosure of Interests.   The authors have no competing interests to declare that are relevant to the content of this article.

References

1. Abrams, M., Thierauf, C., Scheutz, M.: Robots that perform norm-based reference resolution. In: Palinko, O., Bodenhagen, L., Cabibihan, J.J., Fischer, K., Šabanović, S., Winkle, K., Behera, L., Ge, S.S., Chrysostomou, D., Jiang, W., He, H. (eds.) Social Robotics, pp. 100–114. Springer, Cham (2025). https://doi.org/10.1007/978-981-96-3519-1_11

2. Boella, G., van der Torre, L.: Regulative and constitutive norms in normative multi-agent systems. In: Proceedings of the Ninth International Conference on Principles of Knowledge Representation and Reasoning. KR 2004, pp. 255–265. AAAI Press (2004)

3. Bustos, P., Manso, L.J., Bandera, A.J., Bandera, J.P., García-Varea, I., Martínez-Gómez, J.: The CORTEX cognitive robotics architecture: use cases. Cogn. Syst. Res. **55**, 107–123 (2019). https://doi.org/10.1016/j.cogsys.2019.01.003

4. Cerutti, F., Dunne, P.E., Giacomin, M., Vallati, M.: Computing preferred extensions in abstract argumentation: a SAT-based approach. In: Black, E., Modgil, S., Oren, N. (eds.) TAFA 2013. LNCS (LNAI), vol. 8306, pp. 176–193. Springer, Heidelberg (2014). https://doi.org/10.1007/978-3-642-54373-9_12

5. Dennis, L., Fisher, M., Slavkovik, M., Webster, M.P.: Formal verification of ethical choices in autonomous systems. Robot. Auton. Syst. **77**, 1–14 (2016). https://doi.org/10.1016/j.robot.2015.11.012

6. Dung, P.M.: On the acceptability of arguments and its fundamental role in non-monotonic reasoning, logic programming and n-person games. Artif. Intell. **77**(2), 321–357 (1995). https://doi.org/10.1016/0004-3702(94)00041-X

7. Galeas, J., Tudela, A., Pons, O., Bandera, J.P., Bandera, A., Bustos, P.: CRDT-based knowledge synchronisation in an internet of robotics things ecosystem for ambient assisted living. Comput. Vis. Image Underst. **259**, 104437 (2025). https://doi.org/10.1016/j.cviu.2025.104437

8. Ginés Clavero, J., Martín Rico, F., Rodríguez-Lera, F.J., Guerrero Hernandéz, J.M., Matellán Olivera, V.: Impact of decision-making system in social navigation. Multimedia Tools Appl. **81**(3), 3459–3481 (2022). https://doi.org/10.1007/s11042-021-11454-2

9. González-Santamarta, M.Á., Rodríguez-Lera, F.J., Fernández-Llamas, C., Matellán-Olivera, V.: A hybrid cognitive architecture to generate, control, plan, and monitor behaviors for interactive autonomous robots. Int. J. Soc. Robot. (2024). https://doi.org/10.1007/s12369-024-01192-4

10. González-Santamarta, M.A., Rodríguez-Lera, F.J., Matellán-Olivera, V.: Cognitive architectures in autonomous robotics: a systematic review of behavior generation approaches and evaluation strategies. IEEE Access **13**, 191619–191644 (2025). https://doi.org/10.1109/ACCESS.2025.3630344

11. Kotseruba, I., Tsotsos, J.K.: 40 years of cognitive architectures: core cognitive abilities and practical applications. Artif. Intell. Rev. **53**(1), 17–94 (2020). https://doi.org/10.1007/s10462-018-9646-y

12. Liao, B., Pardo, P., Slavkovik, M., van der Torre, L.: The jiminy advisor: moral agreements among stakeholders based on norms and argumentation. J. Artif. Intell. Res. **77**, 737–792 (2023). https://doi.org/10.1613/jair.1.14368

13. RoboCup@Home Technical Committee: Robocup@home rulebook (2026). https://github.com/RoboCupAtHome/RuleBook. Accessed 2026

14. Ye, P., Wang, T., Wang, F.Y.: A survey of cognitive architectures in the past 20 years. IEEE Trans. Cybern. **48**(12), 3280–3290 (2018). https://doi.org/10.1109/TCYB.2018.2857704

A Motivational Approach Towards Resilient Industrial Robots

M. Jakub[1,2], Alejandro Romero[1(✉)], Tomáš Broum[2], and Richard J. Duro[1]

[1] Integrated Group for Engineering Research (GII), CITIC Research Center,
Universidade da Coruña, A Coruña, Spain
`{jakub.muller,alejandro.romero.montero,richard.duro}@udc.es`
[2] Department of Industrial Engineering and Management, University of West
Bohemia, Pilsen, Czech Republic
`broum@kpv.zcu.cz`

Abstract. Industrial robots deliver high precision in structured environments but remain vulnerable to unexpected changes in sensing, dynamics, or task constraints. Conventional industrial control architectures rely on fixed policies and static perception–action mappings, limiting their ability to adapt in evolving production settings. In contrast, motivational learning mechanisms have shown promise for open-ended adaptation in laboratory robotics. This paper bridges these domains by introducing a motivational engine designed to enhance industrial robot resilience under operational disruptions. The proposed framework integrates multiple intrinsic drives—novelty, curiosity, competence, frustration, and effectance—into a unified action-selection mechanism that dynamically balances exploration and skill refinement. We evaluate the approach in a manipulation task involving observation-frame distortions and environmental changes that invalidate previously successful behaviors, demonstrating autonomous recovery from sensorimotor disruptions and the discovery of alternative kinematic strategies.

Keywords: Cognitive robotics · Open-ended learning · Intrinsic motivation · Autonomous adaptation · Skill learning

1 Introduction

Industrial robots are central to modern production plants, where they must deliver high precision, repeatability, and long-term reliability. Accordingly, industrial automation has been dominated by deterministic control architectures in which closed-loop controllers regulate motion by minimizing the error between commanded actions and sensor feedback [18]. Under nominal conditions—stable calibration, well-defined workcells, and low variability—such systems achieve structured, repetitive tasks with predictable performance [19].

In practice, however, production environments evolve over a robot's lifetime. Sensor drift due to temperature or mechanical wear, tooling changes, fixture

J. M. Ferrández Vicente et al. (Eds.): IWINAC 2026, LNCS 16575, pp. 161–171, 2026.
https://doi.org/10.1007/978-3-032-27317-8_16

shifts, and new product variants can invalidate the assumptions underlying classical feedback control [5]. Distorted state perception may cause controllers to interpret persistent errors as actuation deficits, leading to aggressive compensation, oscillations, unsafe impacts, or joint limit violations [6]. Similar issues arise in manipulation tasks affected by layout changes, occlusions, or newly introduced obstacles. Conventional controllers cannot recognize fundamental shifts in the action–observation relationship and lack mechanisms for autonomous adaptation; recovery typically requires costly recalibration and reprogramming, conflicting with industrial demands for high availability and minimal downtime [2].

Advances in adaptive and learning-based robotics offer an alternative view, treating discrepancies between expected and observed outcomes not merely as control errors but as signals of model mismatch [8]. Intrinsic motivation mechanisms, originating in developmental robotics and reinforcement learning, provide a principled basis for autonomous adaptation by promoting exploration when prediction errors rise and exploitation as performance improves [10]. Instead of blindly compensating for errors, a robot with intrinsic drives can infer that prior policies are obsolete and initiate exploration to re-learn sensorimotor dynamics.

From an industrial perspective, such mechanisms are attractive because they promise performance recovery without explicit supervision or manual reprogramming. A motivational engine that monitors task progress, uncertainty, or learning progress can detect when a strategy fails and redirect behavior toward alternative kinematic or sensing solutions [12]. Importantly, this adaptation must satisfy strict safety, timing, and reliability constraints.

In this work, we address autonomous recovery from sensorimotor and environmental disruptions in production plants. We propose a framework integrating multiple intrinsic motivations within a unified action-selection process, coupled to an ensemble of utility models capturing complementary task dynamics within a deliberative model-based decision procedure. By grounding intrinsically motivated learning in industrial scenarios, we aim to bridge adaptive robotics research and deployable production systems.

The remainder of the paper is organized as follows. Section 2 details the proposed architecture, including utility model ensembles, the motivational evaluation mechanism and the stochastic action selection mechanisms employed . Section 3 is concerned with the experiments, analyzing adaptation performance and internal dynamics. Finally, Sect. 4 concludes and discusses implications for industrial deployment.

2   Deliberative Architecture

In the architecture we propose (Fig. 1), given an active goal g_t, and a current state s_t, action-selection is carried out through a deliberative process that considers a batch of candidate actions $\{a_t^1, \ldots, a_t^N\}$ sampled from the action space of the agent at each step. These actions are put through a World Model to obtain the expected next states $\{s_i'\}$, and these states are scored through some utility measure resulting from the application of the motivational engine, whose structure and operation is the main contribution of this paper. Utility is then used for the selection of the actions to execute.

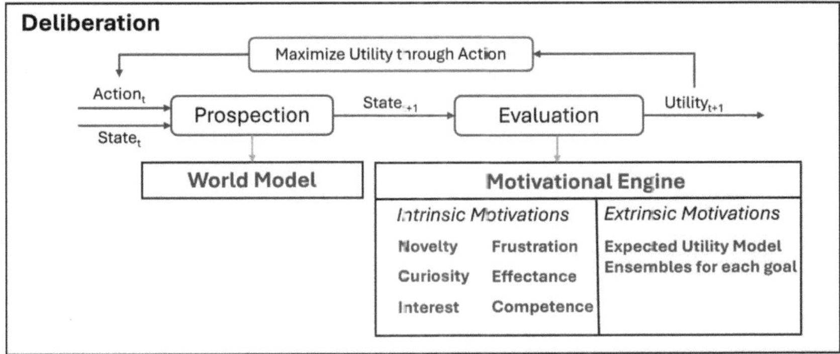

Fig. 1. Block diagram of the deliberative structure of the decision mechanism.

2.1   Modeling the World

Deliberation implies obtaining and using a world model WM_θ that approximates the dynamics of the agent's position in Cartesian space. Specifically, it predicts the next coordinate vector $\hat{s}_{t+1} \in \mathbb{R}^3$ given the current position $s_t = (x_t, y_t, z_t)$ and the chosen action a_t, that is $\hat{s}_{t+1} = M_\theta(s_t, a_t)$.

In this work WM_θ is implemented as a Residual Neural Network [7] to approximate the forward dynamics. The input to the network is the concatenation of the positional state and action vectors, denoted as $v_t = [s_t; a_t]$. This input is projected into a latent feature space of dimension $d_h = 128$ and processed through a sequence of residual blocks [9]. Each block computes: $h_{l+1} = h_l + \mathcal{F}(h_l)$, where $\mathcal{F}$ represents a non-linear transformation involving Layer Normalization, fully connected layers, and ReLU activation functions.

Crucially, the model does not predict the absolute coordinates directly. Instead, it learns to estimate the spatial displacement (or positional residual) $\Delta s_t = (\Delta x, \Delta y, \Delta z)$. This acts as an inductive bias, encouraging the model to learn local motion dynamics.

When the frequency of significant prediction errors exceeds a critical threshold over a given period, the motivational engine triggers a world model adaptation process, interpreting the accumulated divergence as evidence of changed sensorimotor mappings. This adaptation occurs by minimizing the Mean Squared Error (MSE) between the predicted next position $\hat{s}_{t+1}$ and the actual ground-truth coordinates s_{t+1} recorded during trajectory execution.

2.2 Motivational Engine

The evaluation component of deliberation scores action utilities under dynamically evolving and a priori unpredictable environments. To this end, we introduce a motivational engine that guides goal discovery and learns goal-conditioned expected utility functions. As illustrated in Fig. 1, the architecture combines intrinsic motivations for efficient goal discovery with learned utility models associated to each discovered goal, trained from an ensemble of goal-conditioned regressors [14]. The system operates on continuous state and action spaces, $\mathcal{S} \subset \mathbb{R}^d$ and $\mathcal{A} \subset \mathbb{R}^m$, and assumes a set of self-discovered goals $\mathcal{G} \subset \mathcal{S}$.

The engine integrates complementary intrinsic motivations:

- **Novelty** μ^{nov} promotes exploration of underrepresented $\mathcal{S}$ areas measured as dissimilarity between candidate states and a buffer of recent states [1].
- **Curiosity** μ^{cur} drives exploration toward poorly predicted states using Random Network Distillation (RND), where intrinsic reward corresponds to the prediction error between a fixed target and a trainable predictor network [3].
- **Frustration** μ^{frust} captures lack of short-term progress by measuring variability in recent perceptual states; low variance yields high frustration [4].
- **Competence improvement** $\Delta C(g)$ quantifies progress in achieving a goal as the difference between two moving averages of competence predictions over time [17].
- **Interest** μ^{int} combines novelty, competence improvement, and diversification into a goal-selection score [11].
- **Effectance** μ^{eff} detects meaningful action–perception couplings (e.g., object contact or coverage) and promotes them to goals whose competence is subsequently tracked [13].

In the architecture, novelty and frustration directly contribute to action scoring, whereas competence improvement and interest modulate goal selection and the exploration–exploitation balance. At each decision cycle, a stochastic goal selector samples goals via a softmax over interest values combined with an ε-greedy exploration term.

For each discovered goal $g \in \mathcal{G}$, the agent learns an expected utility model from an ensemble

$$\mathcal{U}_g = \{U_g^{(1)}, U_g^{(2)}, U_g^{(3)}, U_g^{(4)}\},$$

where each $U_g^{(k)} : \mathcal{S} \to \mathbb{R}$ estimates expected utility relative to achieving g [15,16]. The ensemble comprises Linear Regression, SVR with RBF kernel, Gradient Boosting, and a single-hidden-layer MLP, reflecting that different goals may require different model classes. Learning is trace-based, assigning discounted utility along execution traces. The active utility model is selected as the one whose predictions best approximate a smooth, monotonic progression of expected utility under the current environment dynamics.

2.3   Action Selection

Finally, to select the action to perform, at each decision cycle, a stochastic selector chooses among three action scoring methods: *Exploration*, *Exploration-path*, and *Utility-model*.

In *Exploration* mode, candidate actions are scored purely by curiosity, using the RND-based prediction error:

$$\Pi(a_t^i \mid s_t, g_t) = \mu^{\mathrm{cur}}(s_i')$$

In *Exploration-path* mode, the engine exploits both the ensemble of utility models and perceptual novelty. For each candidate leading to s_i',

$$\Pi(a_t^i \mid s_t, g_t) = w_1(g_t)\, UMs(s_i', g_t) \;+\; w_2(g_t)\, \mu^{\mathrm{nov}}(s_i')$$

where

$$UMs(s_i', g_t) = \bar{y}(s_i', g_t) - \sigma(s_i', g_t)$$

with $\bar{y}(s_i', g_t)$ the mean predicted utility across the ensemble of models for goal g_t, and $\sigma(s_i', g_t)$ the standard deviation of these predictions. The weights $w_1(g_t)$ and $w_2(g_t)$ are adapted online according to $\mu^{\mathrm{frust}}(s_i')$, shifting mass from $w_1(g_t)$ to $w_2(g_t)$ as frustration increases to promote exploratory actions.

Finally, in *Utility-model* mode, scoring relies solely on the selected utility model,

$$\Pi(a_t^i \mid s_t, g_t) = U_{g_t}^{(\hat{k}^\star)}(s_i').$$

At each step, the action executed is

$$a_t = \arg\max_{a_t^i} \Pi(a_t^i \mid s_t, g_t),$$

and the resulting state s_{t+1} is stored in the memories associated with novelty and frustration. Effectance is evaluated to determine whether meaningful changes occurred; if so, new perceptual states may be added to the goal set $\mathcal{G}$, and competence statistics are updated accordingly.

3   Experiments and Results

To demonstrate the capabilities of our approach, we carried out a series of experiments considering an industrial robot performing industrial grade tasks. All experiments were conducted in a simulated environment and tested on a real robot. The environment consists of an industrial-style robotic arm, a single reachable object (a red button), and some walls that create narrow passages and occlusions (see Fig. 2). The task (goal) of the agent is to reach the object whatever its position in the workspace, mimicking typical industrial cell pick/reach operations.

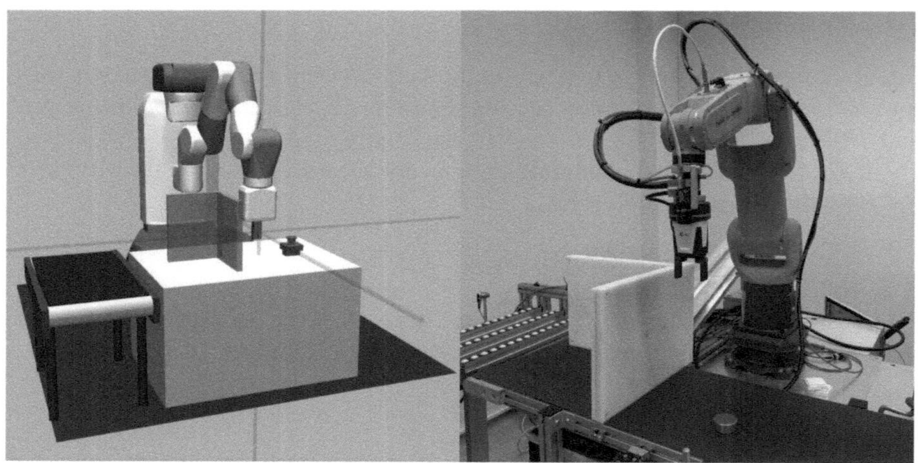

Fig. 2. Manipulation environment with a reachable object and walls, emulating an industrial workcell. Left: Gymnasium-based simulation. Right: Real robot. (Color figure online)

The robot perceives a three-dimensional state vector that includes the distance from the robot to the object, the distance from the robot to the nearest obstacle, and a binary flag indicating whether the object has been reached.

Effectance is configured based on the normalized distance to the object and an internal reward variable. When the distance falls below a fixed threshold of 0.05, the reward signal indicates contact and the current state is evaluated as a potential goal, corresponding to a successful "reach" event in an industrial setting.

The motivational engine uses short memory windows for its intrinsic signals: novelty is computed over the last 50 states, while frustration relies on a buffer of 5 states, and competence improvement uses a prediction window of 10 episodes. The balance between motivation and utility in action scoring is controlled by weights $w_1, w_2 \in \{0.3, 0.7\}$. The world model is a neural network with 128 hidden units and two residual blocks operating on 3D state and action vectors.

The experiments seek to address three common problems in industrial robotics: (1) changes in the sensorimotor mapping (world model), which emulate calibration shifts or changes in the observation frame; (2) changes in the goal position, representing reconfiguration of fixtures or parts in the workcell; and (3) the combination of both effects. Performance is measured as the number of time steps required to reach the object in each episode, and all results are reported over 20 independent runs. The full implementation of the proposed architecture, including all experimental configurations, analysis scripts, and videos of the simulated robot, is publicly available.[1]

Figure 3 summarizes the performance of the proposed motivational engine compared to (i) a "Novelty-only Engine" baseline and (ii) a classical industrial

---

[1] https://github.com/mullerjaku/iwinac2026.

robotic setup in which the reaching task is preprogrammed. The comparison is conducted under three conditions: (1) changes in the goal position, where the goal is blocked by the wall shown in Fig. 2; (2) changes in the sensorimotor mapping, implemented by applying a random rotation between 170° and 180° around a randomly generated 3D axis at the beginning of each experiment; and (3) the simultaneous occurrence of both types of changes. Each curve shows the median number of steps per episode, with the 25th and 75th percentiles computed over 20 runs.

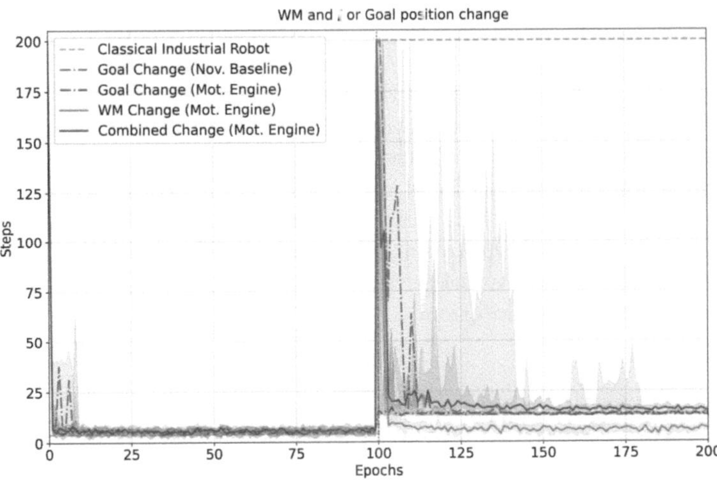

Fig. 3. Learning curves comparing the motivational engine, Novelty baseline, and classical industrial robot across three adaptation scenarios: static goal change, world model shift, and combined changes. These changes occur in epoch 100.

In the case of the goal position changing, the motivational engine reaches the target in fewer steps than the baseline or the classical robotic control approach (around 20 epochs). In fact, the classical control approach cannot reach it and the baseline takes more than five times the number of steps. This indicates a more efficient exploitation of the learned utility models. When the sensory-motor mapping changes, the motivational engine exhibits a very short adaptation phase and recovers the same level of proficiency in less than 10 epochs (orange line), whereas the classical robotic approach is incapable of tracking the change. Finally, when both the world model and the goal position are changed in the same instant, the motivational engine relearns effective trajectories after around 60 epochs for the combined change (red line). It is important to note that goal changes may lead to more epochs due the fact that trajectories may become longer.

As shown in Fig. 3, although the classical industrial robot performs optimally under fixed conditions, it cannot adapt once changes occur, since it is programmed for a single configuration. This contrast highlights the adaptation gap bridged by the proposed motivational engine.

To evaluate the contribution of the ensemble of utility models and combined selection mechanism, Fig. 4 compares the full ensemble against each individual utility model used by itself. Each plot shows the median number of steps and interquartile range over 10 runs for different environmental configurations. The ensemble consistently outperforms or matches the best single model, confirming that the combined score is able to select, for each goal, the utility model that best captures the underlying task structure. Analyzing the performance in more detail, for the interval from 0 to 100 epochs, the Linear model (red) provides the best performance; however, after the goal position changes, it requires more steps and epochs to relearn the policy, and it occasionally collides with the walls. Gradient Boosting (yellow) exhibits the slowest adaptation in the evaluated scenario. The MLP model (lime) achieves the overall best performance among the four models; however, it is sometimes unnecessarily complex for simpler scenarios, requiring higher computational resources, and is prone to overfitting. The SVR model (grey) also performs well, but it requires well-structured path data. All these advantages and limitations are addressed by selection function that selects the best-fitting utility model for the current scenario based on the paths collected during robot exploration.

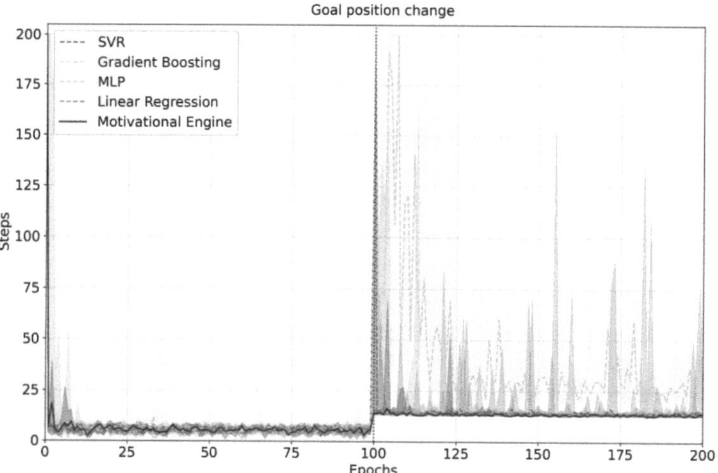

Fig. 4. Comparison between the full ensemble of utility models and each individual model (median and interquartile range over 10 runs). (Color figure online)

Additionally, in Fig. 5 we provide a more detailed analysis of the internal activity of the motivational engine. It reports the evolution of key intrinsic signals and model-selection statistics using Gaussian-smoothed windows (size 20) over 20 runs. In static conditions (left side of Fig. 5), the engine quickly converges to a stable combination of intrinsic motivations and a small subset of utility models.

Identical conditions do not necessarily produce the exact same behavior, as the motivational engine selects from four different utility models. When the sensory-motor mapping and/or goal position change (right side of Fig. 5), the engine exhibits a transient increase in novelty and frustration, followed by a shift in the selected utility models and a return to low step counts. This pattern illustrates how the motivational mechanisms drive the system from exploitation back to exploration and then to a new stable regime.

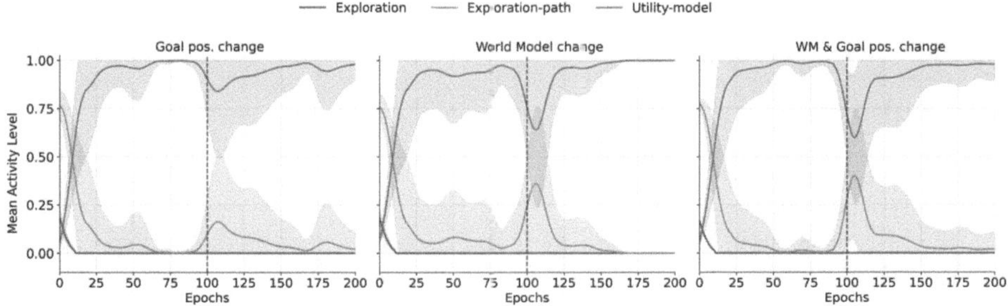

Fig. 5. Internal activity of the motivational engine across adaptation scenarios. Gaussian-smoothed (window=20) evolution of intrinsic signals.

Finally, it is necessary to comment that these results show that the motivational engine not only adapts its goals and control policies, but also provides a natural trigger for world-model relearning when the underlying sensorimotor mapping changes, a property that is crucial for long-term deployment in evolving industrial cells.

4   Conclusions

This work has presented a motivational architecture for resilient industrial robotics that enables autonomous recovery from sensorimotor and environmental disruptions. By integrating multiple intrinsic drives within a deliberative, model-based decision framework, the proposed engine dynamically balances exploration and exploitation while learning goal-conditioned utility models from an ensemble of regressors.

Experiments demonstrate recovery from world-model shifts, goal relocations, and their combination, highlighting the system's ability to re-learn effective behaviors and trigger model adaptation when prediction errors persist. Unlike classical industrial control pipelines, the approach maintains performance under non-stationary conditions without external reprogramming.

These results indicate that intrinsic motivational mechanisms can be embedded within industrially grounded architectures to bridge the gap between adaptive robotics research and deployable production systems. Future work will address safety-aware integration and long-term validation in real manufacturing environments.

Acknowledgments. This work was funded by the European Union's Horizon 2020, research and innovation programme under GA 101070381 ('PILLAR-Robots - Purposeful Intrinsically-motivated Lifelong Learning Autonomous Robots'), by Xunta de Galicia (ED431C 2025/32), by the Spanish Science and Education Ministry (PID2024-162223OB-I00), Ministry for Digital Transformation and Civil Service and Next - Generation EU/RRF (TSI-100925-2023-1), and Centro de Investigación de Galicia "CITIC" (ED431G 2023/01).

Disclosure of Interests. The authors have no competing interests to declare that are relevant to the content of this article.

References

1. Barto, A., Mirolli, M., Baldassarre, G.: Novelty or surprise? Front. Psychol. **4**, 907 (2013)
2. Billard, A., Kragic, D.: Trends and challenges in robot manipulation. Science **364**(6446), eaat8414 (2019)
3. Burda, Y., Edwards, H., Storkey, A., Klimov, O.: Exploration by random network distillation (2018). https://arxiv.org/abs/1810.12894
4. Campos-Alfaro, F., Jara, C., Romero, A., Naya-Varela, M., Duro, R.J.: Learning adaptable utility models for morphological diversity. In: Int. Work-Conference on the Interplay Between Natural and Artif. Computation, pp. 105–115. Springer (2024)
5. Carvalho, T.P., Soares, F.A., Vita, R., Francisco, R.d.P., Basto, J.P., Alcalá, S.G.: A systematic literature review of machine learning methods applied to predictive maintenance. Comput. Ind. Eng. **137**, 106024 (2019)
6. Haddadin, S., De Luca, A., Albu-Schäffer, A.: Robot collisions: a survey on detection, isolation, and identification. IEEE Trans. Rob. **33**(6), 1292–1312 (2017)
7. He, K., Zhang, X., Ren, S., Sun, J.: Deep residual learning for image recognition. In: Proceedings of the IEEE Conference on Computer Vision and Pattern Recognition, pp. 770–778 (2016)
8. Kober, J., Bagnell, J.A., Peters, J.: Reinforcement learning in robotics: a survey. Int. J. Rob. Res. (2013)
9. Nagabandi, A., Kahn, G., Fearing, R.S., Levine, S.: Neural network dynamics for model-based deep reinforcement learning with model-free fine-tuning. In: 2018 IEEE Int. Conf. on Robotics and Automation (ICRA), pp. 7559–7566. IEEE (2018)
10. Oudeyer, P.Y., Kaplan, F., Hafner, V.: Intrinsic motivation systems for autonomous mental development. IEEE Trans. Evol. Comput. (2009)
11. Rayyes, R., Donat, H., Steil, J.: Hierarchical interest-driven goal babbling for efficient bootstrapping of sensorimotor skills. In: 2020 IEEE International Conference on Robotics and Automation (ICRA), pp. 1336–1342. IEEE (2020)
12. Romero, A., Baldassarre, G., Duro, R.J., Santucci, V.G.: H-GRAIL: a robotic motivational architecture to tackle open-ended learning challenges. IEEE Trans. Cogn. Dev. Syst. (2025)
13. Romero, A., Bellas, F., Becerra, J.A., Duro, R.J.: Bootstrapping autonomous skill learning in the MDB cognitive architecture. In: Int. Work-Conference on the Interplay Between Natural and Artificial Computation, pp. 120–129. Springer (2019)
14. Romero, A., Bellas, F., Becerra, J.A., Duro, R.J.: Motivation as a tool for designing lifelong learning robots. Int. Comput.-Aided Eng. **27**(4), 353–372 (2020)

15. Romero, A., Bellas, F., Prieto, A., Duro, R.J.: Utility model re-description within a motivational system for cognitive robotics. In: IEEE/RSJ International Conference on Intelligent Robots and Systems (IROS), pp. 2324–2329. IEEE (2018)
16. Romero, A., Prieto, A., Bellas, F., Duro, R.J.: Simplifying the creation and management of utility models in continuous domains for cognitive robotics. Neurocomputing **353**, 106–118 (2019)
17. Santucci, V.G., Baldassarre, G., Mirolli, M.: Which is the best intrinsic motivation signal for learning multiple skills? Front. Neurorobot. **7**, 22 (2013)
18. Siciliano, B., Sciavicco, L., Villani, L., Oriolo, G.: Robotics: Modelling, Planning and Control. Springer (2010)
19. Spong, M.W., Hutchinson, S., Vidyasagar, M.: Robot Modeling and Control. John Wiley & Sons (2020)

Integrating Large Language Models for Explainable Human-Machine Teaming in Autonomous Vehicles

Jaime P. Pérez[1], Alejandro Romero[1], William Infante[2], Benjamin Malafiej[2], and Francisco Bellas[1]($\boxtimes$)

[1] Integrated Group for Engineering Research (GII), CITIC Research Center, Universidade da Coruña, A Coruña, Spain
{j.p.perez,alejandro.romero.montero,francisco.bellas}@udc.es
[2] Navantia Australia, Sydney, New South Wales, Australia
{winfante,bmalafiej}@navantia.com.au

Abstract. This paper presents the design, implementation, and preliminary evaluation of a Human-Machine Teaming (HMT) framework for task planning of autonomous vehicles, developed in collaboration an industrial shipbuilding partner. The system integrates Large Language Models (LLMs) to support natural-language interaction, situational awareness, planning, and explainability during real-time missions. Rather than a rigid command pipeline, the framework enables mixed-initiative teaming: operators specify high-level intents and supervise execution while the agent surfaces constraints, proposes alternative plans, and explains decisions. The framework was validated in a simulated environment focused on missions for Unmanned Surface Vessels (USVs). Results indicate the system can interpret natural-language commands, adapt to under-specified instructions with 96% success in ambiguous scenarios, and detect infeasible requests before execution.

Keywords: Human-machine teaming · Autonomous task planning · Large language models · Autonomous marine vehicles · Explainable AI

1 Introduction

Human-Machine Teaming (HMT) represents a new paradigm in human-machine interaction, emphasizing collaborative decision-making and adaptive partnerships between humans and autonomous agents [1]. Unlike traditional human-machine interaction models, HMT fosters balanced collaboration, where humans and agents leverage their unique strengths to achieve shared goals effectively. In these environments, agents manage repetitive, high-speed, or complex computations, while humans offer intuition, ethical reasoning, and adaptive problem-solving abilities. The key feature of HMT is the capacity of the human to act on the machine, taking a much more active role on the decision process.

HMT is specially relevant in real-time systems, like autonomous vehicles, where the consequences of autonomous decisions must be supervised and

J. M. Ferrández Vicente et al. (Eds.): IWINAC 2026, LNCS 16575, pp. 172–181, 2026.
https://doi.org/10.1007/978-3-032-27317-8_17

approved in the short-term. To achieve a controlled response in this scope, most of the existing systems lack real autonomy, requiring a human expert to accept all the proposed actions, and relying on rigid, predefined representational structures.

Large Language Models (LLMs) are powerful tools that open new possibilities in HMT: enhancing communication and interpretability, bridging linguistic gaps, and fostering shared knowledge representations [2]. Furthermore, LLMs have demonstrated measurable competence in reasoning about high-level goals and converting them into actionable mission plans [9]. This paper describes the first version of an HMT system, developed in collaboration with an industrial shipbuilding partner, which integrates LLMs as a core component to develop a new human-agent interaction approach in the scope of autonomous maritime vehicles. This work captured and formalized HMT requirements for the real-time autonomous vehicle control, translated those requirements into a functional design, and validated the system in a simulated environment focused on maritime missions.

2   Related Work

The success of HMT systems relies heavily on creating environments where human operators and autonomous agents can collaborate seamlessly. To achieve this, the literature highlights three core attributes that must be present in the teaming framework.

Situational Awareness and Team Coordination. Situational Awareness (SA) is the perception of environmental elements, the understanding of their meaning, and the projection of their future states [3]. It is a critical component of HMT because it enables both human operators and agents to understand and respond effectively to their environment. Team Situational Awareness (TSA) extends individual SA to the collective domain, covering the shared understanding of the situation among all team members, including humans. TSA ensures that all agents in a team are aligned and informed to achieve common goals. Key features of TSA include a transparent exchange of data to maintain a consistent understanding, and conflict mitigation to reduce the risk of incorrect actions.

Shared Mental Models and Dynamic Adaptability. Successful teaming requires shared mental models, creating a common understanding of goals, roles, and situational factors among team members [10]. When agents align their behaviour with human expectations, trust increases and overall task efficiency improves. Furthermore, HMT systems must dynamically adapt to changing operational contexts by redistributing roles and tasks between humans and agents [11]. Adaptive task allocation ensures good performance in dynamic environments, which is particularly relevant in maritime autonomous operations.

Goal Interpretation and Autonomous Planning. A third essential attribute is the ability of the autonomous agent to interpret high-level human intents and decompose them into actionable plans [1]. In autonomous vehicles, this requires the system to understand operational goals, evaluate environmental constraints, and dynamically generate sequences of tasks that the vehicle can physically execute.

To fulfil these core attributes in an autonomous fashion, Large Language Models (LLMs) have emerged as powerful tools. LLMs can process, understand, and generate human-like text, so they primarily support natural language communication between humans and autonomous systems. By interpreting user commands, resolving ambiguities, and converting instructions into machine-readable actions, LLMs ensure seamless interaction [4]. This capability is especially important in dynamic scenarios such as autonomous navigation, where misinterpretation of commands could lead to operational errors.

Beyond natural communication, LLMs are showing promising capabilities in reasoning and task planning. Recent research demonstrates that LLMs can effectively decompose complex, under-specified missions into structured subtasks suitable for robotic execution [9,12]. This allows HMT frameworks to shift from rigid command execution to flexible goal-oriented planning, where the LLM evaluates the feasibility of an operator's request and generates an appropriate sequence of motion primitives.

The main drawback of LLMs is related with their trustworthiness and accuracy, which affect to the mission completion. In this sense, explainability is fundamental to building trust in HMT [5]. Autonomous vehicles generate large volumes of operational data during their operation, and conversational interfaces powered by LLMs must translate complex telemetry, compliance rules, and algorithmic decisions into clear, actionable explanations tailored to the operator's level of expertise. As LLMs inherently function as black-box systems, fostering trust and providing reliable explainability requires grounding their outputs with external validation. This ensures that the generated explanations and mission plans strictly align with the physical reality and actual capabilities of the vehicle.

3   System Design

The HMT framework presented here has been developed in cooperation with an industrial shipbuilding partner, with the aim of achieving an efficient, simple and reliable automated task planning of real missions carried out by autonomous marine vehicles. To this end, the proposal integrates LLMs at 3 different levels: (1) natural-language interaction with the operator to define the mission using high-level commands, (2) dynamic adaptability and optimal planning, and (3) understandable explanations during real-time missions.

The design of the framework is shown in Fig. 1, and it brings together a chat-based front end user interface (UI), an LLM reasoning core, a configuration layer that aligns LLM proposals with actual vehicle capabilities, and a ROS2 execution interface connected to an event logging and retrieval layer that uses a vector database. The center of the design is a text-chat UI through which an operator types natural-language commands. These commands are then received at the LLM module, which decomposes user commands into a structured list of sub-tasks. Each sub-task is validated against the capabilities of the vehicle (loaded from a JSON or YAML file), ensuring that the model never proposes sub-tasks that the vehicle is unable to perform. Once tasks are approved, they are published as goals to the autonomous vehicle.

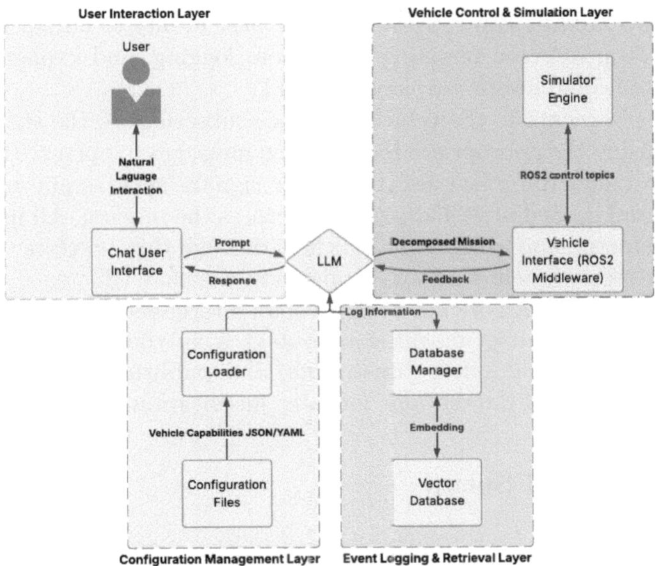

Fig. 1. Framework Design Diagram. The system uses a closed loop where user intents are validated against capabilities, executed via ROS2, and logged into a vector database to support future explanations.

Feedback messages, such as position updates, sensor information, and status flags, are published in a ROS2 topic and are logged simultaneously in a structured event log. A dedicated module handles all communication with the LLM, encapsulating model calls and response parsing. The LLM module uses two main prompt templates: (1) a planning prompt, and (2) an explanation prompt. For planning, the module uses the operator's command and recent mission context to help the model generate coherent plans. For explainability queries, the module performs approximate-nearest-neighbor lookup over lightweight embeddings generated from ROS2 event logs to retrieve only the most relevant past events, reducing hallucination [6]. This allows the system to quote actual telemetry and associated rules that triggered the decision taken by the autonomous vehicle.

The configuration files serve as a single source of truth for vehicle capabilities, operator authority levels, and safety constraints. By editing a small text file, new vehicle types can be introduced (e.g., fixed-wing UAVs or surface vessels) or adjust parameters like maximum speed, minimum safe distance, and geofencing boundaries. This keeps the LLM "grounded": it knows not just how to break down tasks, but which motion primitives (e.g., "set heading", "collect sonar ping") it may choose.

A database manager connects the LLM and the event logger. As the vehicle executes each sub-task, the logger stamps every event with timestamps and metadata. Both are written to the vector database [8], which creates a continuous semantic memory. Whenever the operator requests a status update or justification, the LLM module can retrieve relevant past events to enrich its response. This closed loop between planning, execution, logging, and explanation builds trust and situational awareness, key for HMT.

In terms of execution, the vehicle interface subscribes to the structured task list and publishes the appropriate ROS2 action messages to operate the simulated vehicle. The vehicle interface also listens for signals, such as any new operator commands, and immediately halts or restructures the mission. All incoming sensor data, telemetry, and exception alerts flow through this interface too, ensuring the operator receives near-real-time updates in the chat UI.

As summarized in Algorithm 1, the system alternates between planning and explanation modes, retrieving mission context from the vector store, filtering plans by capability and safety constraints, and publishing validated tasks to ROS2 while logging all interactions for later justification.

4   Experimental Setup

The prototype framework is implemented in Python 3.10 on Ubuntu 22.04 LTS, ensuring seamless integration with both machine-learning libraries and the ROS2 Humble Hawksbill middleware, which provides secure, real-time DDS transport. For the reasoning core, we use the `llama3.3:latest` model [7], hosted locally and served via a lightweight REST API using Ollama. Additionally, ChromaDB [8] is employed as the vector database to manage the semantic memory.

We selected Meta LLaMA models for practical reasons relevant to our deployment setting. They are open-weights models that can be hosted locally, allowing fully offline operation without third-party servers, which simplifies compliance and reduces data-exfiltration risk in safety-critical environments. Beyond convenience, the models exhibit measurable planning competence on standardized benchmarks like PlanBench [9].

All high-level model calls, prompt construction, and response parsing are encapsulated in the dedicated LLM module. To enable on-demand explainability for better HMT, every feedback event is logged. These messages are embedded and stored in the vector database to support semantic memory lookups. The logged feedback messages contain several key fields: a string `robot_id` uniquely identifying the vehicle instance; a string `event_type` categorizing the event (e.g., "status", "anomaly"); a string `log_level` indicating severity ("INFO", "WARN", "ERROR"); a brief string `description` of the event; and an arbitrary `data` object holding structured information relevant to the event.

For the user interface, *Streamlit* was used. Streamlit is an open-source Python library that allowed to develop a chat-based UI through which an operator can

---

Algorithm 1. Planning and Explanation Control Loop

1: **Inputs:** Capability config $\mathcal{C}$, Safety rules $\mathcal{S}$, Vector store $\mathcal{V}$
2: **while** session_active **do**
3:     $m \leftarrow$ read_user_message()
4:     **if** is_explanation_query(m) **then**
5:         $e \leftarrow$ select_relevant_logs($\mathcal{V}$)
6:         ctx $\leftarrow$ retrieve($\mathcal{V}, e,$ mission_state())
7:         $a \leftarrow$ call_llm(build_explain_prompt($m,$ ctx))
8:         reply_to_user(a)
9:     **else**
10:         ctx $\leftarrow$ retrieve_mission_context($\mathcal{V}$)
11:         $p \leftarrow$ build_plan_prompt($m,$ ctx$, \mathcal{C}, \mathcal{S}$)
12:         $r \leftarrow$ call_llm(p)
13:         $(\text{obj}, \text{err}) \leftarrow$ parse_json(r)
14:         **if** err **or** impossible_intent(obj) **then**
15:             notify_user_of_impossibility()
16:         **else**
17:             $T \leftarrow$ validate_tasks(obj.tasks$, \mathcal{C}$)
18:             **if** $T = \emptyset$ **then**
19:                 ask_for_clarification()
20:             **else**
21:                 publish_to_ros2(T)
22:             **end if**
23:         **end if**
24:     **end if**
25:     log_event($\mathcal{V}, m, T,$ telemetry())
26: **end while**

---

issue natural-language commands, inspect plans, and request explanations. The UI presents: (i) a message panel for conversational interaction; (ii) a structured plan view showing the decomposed sub-tasks with parameters validated against capabilities; (iii) status and telemetry widgets streamed from ROS2; and (iv) a mode switch for *Explain* queries that retrieves relevant events from the semantic memory.

The simulation engine used was built in Unreal Engine 5.1, using ROS2 plugins to provide bidirectional communication between the virtual world and the framework (see Fig. 2). The vehicle publishes its simulated pose, velocity, orientation, and relevant sensor readings on ROS2 topics. It supports two core motion primitives: (1) `go_to(x,y)` for point-to-point navigation to the specified map coordinates, and (2) `circle_laps(center_x, center_y, R, N)` for the execution of N laps in a circle of radius R around the center point. Both tasks are sent via ROS2 topics. Scenario definitions (map assets, initial vehicle poses) are loaded at startup from simple configuration files.

Fig. 2. Unreal Engine USV simulator used for test cases.

5   Experimental Results

To assess the capabilities of the proposed framework, the main focus was on validating its ability to manage navigation missions for the USV. Specifically, its ability to handle the launch, modification, and stopping of missions based solely on natural language operator instructions. Validating this implies facing ambiguities in the task definition and detecting infeasible requests before execution. Moreover, it was also important to demonstrate the functionality of providing clear and timely explanations of its decisions and actions, derived from the current state and historical context of the vehicle.

A total of 9 mission prompts were designed spanning 3 categories:

- Correctly Specified (C1–C3): multi-step, order-sensitive tasks properly specified (e.g., waypoint chains followed by circular patrols).
- Ambiguous (A1–A3): intentionally under-specified instructions that are valid if the model either leaves the task list empty (awaiting operator input) or proposes any one of several accepted recommendation sequences.
- Impossible (I1–I3): requests outside platform capability that must yield an empty task list.

Model outputs are parsed as JSON and scored. Each mission was evaluated 40 times (total 360 trials) using llama3.3:latest. The numerical parameters given by the LLM were matched with a tolerance of $1e-3$.

The model consistently produced the correct ordered sequences with numerically correct parameters for Correct missions (100% success). For Ambiguous missions, A1 and A3 achieved 100%; A2 reached 87% (35/40). Most A2 failures were due to proposing a valid circular pattern that did not exactly match any accepted recommendation (e.g., different radius/lap count), rather than leaving the list empty. For Impossible missions, I1 and I2 achieved 100% by returning empty task lists (rejecting physical violations). I3—dynamic station keeping—scored 42% (17/40). Figure 3a summarizes per-mission success, and Fig. 3b aggregates by mission type.

We analyzed specific scenarios to demonstrate the HMT capabilities. The scenario shown in Fig. 4 tests waypoint navigation under constrained geography.

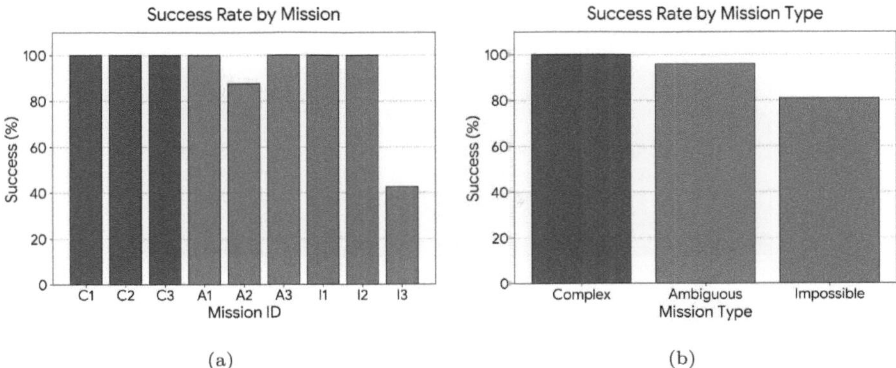

Fig. 3. Success rates of the autonomous task planning framework across 360 simulation trials. **(a)** Success rate by individual mission. The X-axis represents the specific missions: Correctly specified tasks (C1, C2, C3), Ambiguous or under-specified commands (A1, A2, A3), and Impossible requests (I1, I2, I3). **(b)** Aggregate success rate across the three main mission types.

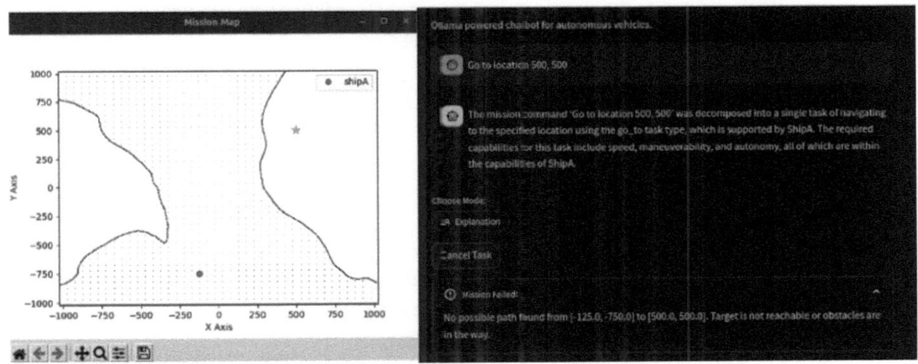

Fig. 4. Path-planning failure handling. The framework detects an obstacle (land) in the map (left) and refuses the LLM-generated plan in the chat UI (right).

The operator issues *"Go to location 500, 500"*, which the LLM module decomposes into a single `go_to` sub-task and validates. However, the map reveals that no collision-free path exists. The system responds: *"Mission Failed! No possible path found from [-125, -750] to [500, 500]. Target is not reachable or obstacles are in the way."*. This demonstrates that our feasibility filter correctly prevents unsafe or impossible plans from being dispatched. The explainability feature expected from the use of the LLM becomes also evident.

In a second scenario (Fig. 5a), the system's ability to handle underspecified (ambiguous), high-level commands was tested. The instruction *"Make the ship transport people to the nearest coast"* lacks both pickup and drop-off coordinates. The system detected missing coordinates and responded: *"To transport people to*

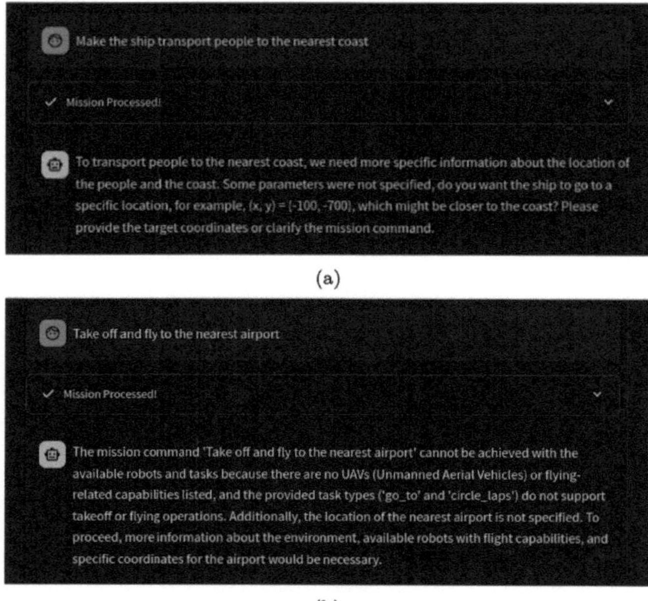

(a)

(b)

Fig. 5. Framework responses to edge cases. (a) Clarification request for an ambiguous, under-specified command. (b) Error explanation and safe halt when facing an unsupported vehicle capability.

the nearest coast, we need more specific information... Please provide the target coordinates or clarify the mission command.". By prompting the operator for missing parameters rather than guessing, the system maintains clarity and avoids unintended behaviors, while enhancing explainability.

Finally, how the framework handles unsupported tasks was tested (Fig. 5b). The command *"Take off and fly to the nearest airport"* is beyond the vehicle's capabilities, as no UAV motion primitives are defined in the JSON loader for this specific vessel. Rather than crashing or defaulting to an unsafe plan, the system responds: *"The mission command 'Take off and fly to the nearest airport' cannot be achieved with the available robots and tasks... To proceed, more information about the environment, available robots with flight capabilities, and specific coordinates is necessary."* This demonstrates the effective grounding of the LLM in the specific platform's reality.

6   Conclusion

This work presented a novel Human-Machine Teaming framework that integrates Large Language Models to enable natural language interaction, adaptive mission control, and real-time explainability in autonomous vehicles. By combining a reasoning engine with strict capability validation and a RAG-based semantic memory, the system ensures that the flexibility of natural language does not compromise operational safety. The experimental results demonstrated robust performance in interpreting valid commands and a strong ability to handle ambiguity through dialogue. Future work will focus on improving the detection of complex dynamic constraints, reducing inference latency, and extending the framework to heterogeneous teams comprising both aerial and surface vehicles.

Acknowledgement. This work was funded by the EU's Horizon 2020, research and innovation programme under GA 101070381 ('PILLAR-Robots - Purposeful Intrinsically-motivated Lifelong Learning Autonomous Robots'), by Xunta de Galicia (ED431C 2025/32), by the Spanish Science and Education Ministry (PID2024-162223OB-I00), Ministry for Digital Transformation and Civil Service and Next - Generation EU/RRF (TSI-100925-2023-1), and Centro de Investigación de Galicia "CITIC" (ED431G 2023/01).

Disclosure of Interests. The authors have no competing interests to declare that are relevant to the content of this article.

References

1. Geng, B., Varshney, P.K.: Human-machine collaboration for smart decision making: current trends and future opportunities. In: 2022 IEEE 8th International Conference on Collaboration and Internet Computing (CIC), pp. 61–67. IEEE (2022)
2. Minaee, S., et al.: Large language models: a survey. arXiv preprint: arXiv:2402.06196 (2024)
3. McNeese, N.J., Demir, M., Cooke, N.J., She, M.: Team situation awareness and conflict: a study of human-machine teaming. J. Cogn. Eng. Decis. Making **15**(2–3), 83–96 (2021)
4. Park, J., et al.: CLARA: classifying and disambiguating user commands for reliable interactive robotic agents. IEEE Robot. Autom. Lett. (2023)
5. Kong, X., et al.: Explainable interface for human-autonomy teaming: a survey. arXiv preprint: arXiv:2405.02583 (2024)
6. Lewis, P., et al.: Retrieval-augmented generation for knowledge-intensive NLP tasks. In: Advances in Neural Information Processing Systems (NeurIPS) (2020)
7. Meta AI: Llama 3.3: open large language model. https://ollama.com/library/llama3.3. Accessed 07 Oct 2025
8. ChromaDB Development Team: Chroma: The Open-Source Embedding Database. https://github.com/chroma-core/chroma. Accessed 03 July 2025
9. Valmeekam, K., Marquez, M., Olmo, A., Sreedharan, S., Kambhampati, S.: PlanBench: an extensible benchmark for evaluating large language models on planning and reasoning about change. arXiv preprint: arXiv:2206.10498 (2023)
10. Schelble, B.G., Flathmann, C., McNeese, N.J., Freeman, G., Mallick, R.: Let's think together! Assessing shared mental models, performance, and trust in human-agent teams. Proc. ACM Hum.-Comput. Inter. **6**(GROUP), 1–29 (2022)
11. Madni, A.M., Madni, C.C.: Architectural framework for exploring adaptive human-machine teaming options in simulated dynamic environments. Systems **6**(4), 44 (2018)
12. Wei, H., Zhang, Z., He, S., Xia, T., Pan, S., Liu, F.: PlanGenLLMs: a modern survey of LLM planning capabilities. arXiv preprint: arXiv:2502.11221 (2025)

Heterogeneous Multi-robot Team Hybrid Coordination Architecture for Missions in Dynamic Maritime Environments

Enrique Fernández-Pérez[1], Julián Rodríguez-Cortegoso[1], Félix Orjales[1], and Richard J. Duro[2]($\boxtimes$)

[1] Integrated Group for Engineering Research, CITENI, Campus Industrial de Ferrol, Universidade da Coruña, 15403 Ferrol, Spain
[2] Integrated Group for Engineering Research, CITIC, Universidade da Coruña, 15008 A Coruña, Spain
`richard.duro@udc.es`

Abstract. This paper presents a fully distributed coordination architecture for heterogeneous UAV–USV teams operating in dynamic maritime environments. The framework integrates capability-aware online task allocation with adaptive task planning and a chemotaxis-inspired persistent coverage strategy. Persistent surveillance is achieved through a discrete artificial potential field in which revisit urgency accumulates as virtual chemoattractant, while obstacles and inter-agent interactions act as repellents. Heterogeneity is incorporated through platform-dependent responses to the shared potential landscape, enabling differentiated behaviors across aerial and surface vehicles. The architecture is validated in high-fidelity simulations of coastal surveillance and intrusion prevention missions. Results demonstrate adaptive task reassignment, continuous replanning, and robust cooperation under dynamic intruder motion and agent loss. Compared to deterministic coverage baselines, the proposed approach exhibits superior resilience to vehicle failures while maintaining effective persistent monitoring. The framework provides a scalable and biologically grounded solution for heterogeneous multi-robot coordination in maritime domains.

Keywords: Multi-robot · Heterogeneous multi-robot · USV · UAV · Surveillance · MRS coordination

1 Introduction

Maritime surveillance and security operations are increasingly relying on unmanned surface vehicles (USVs) to provide persistent presence, wide-area monitoring, and rapid response capabilities [10]. These platforms are often complemented by unmanned aerial vehicles (UAVs), which extend sensing range and enhance situational awareness through elevated viewpoints and rapid deployment [14]. Recent research has demonstrated that combining surface and aerial

J. M. Ferrández Vicente et al. (Eds.): IWINAC 2026, LNCS 16575, pp. 182–191, 2026.
https://doi.org/10.1007/978-3-032-27317-8_18

assets enables missions that would be infeasible with a single platform type [3]. That is, heterogeneous multi-robot systems (MRS) become necessary, where vehicles with different sensing, mobility, and endurance characteristics cooperate to accomplish objectives that exceed the capabilities of any single platform [12].

In dynamic and partially observable maritime environments, effective coordination faces significant challenges due to environmental uncertainties, communication limitations, and the need for adaptive decision-making [3]. Task allocation, replanning, and navigation must be performed robustly online while accounting for the heterogeneous capabilities of each agent [9]. Decentralized task assignment and planning strategies have been shown to improve robustness and scalability in such contexts [4,11].

Bio-inspired coordination strategies provide alternative mechanisms for distributed decision-making and navigation [1]. In particular, bacterial chemotaxis, the ability of bacteria to bias motion in response to concentration gradients, has inspired control strategies for robotic systems [5,6]. These bio-inspired methods have been applied to multi-robot coverage and aggregation tasks, demonstrating that chemotaxis-inspired motion rules can generate robust distributed behaviors without centralized control [5]. The chemotactic mechanism maps naturally to multi-agent coordination: local gradient sensing translates to decentralized guidance, and simple motion rules lead to emergent collective outcomes.

Inspired by these biological principles, we propose a chemotaxis-inspired potential field formulation that encodes mission objectives, environmental uncertainty, and agent heterogeneity as spatial gradients. UAVs and USVs interpret these gradients according to their sensing and motion capabilities, enabling differentiated responses to shared stimuli. Artificial potential fields (APFs) are a widely used paradigm for decentralized navigation and cooperative control due to their continuous nature and simplicity [7]. Recent APF variants have been extended to cope with dynamic obstacles, multi-agent interactions, and heterogeneity of agents [13]. However, classical APF approaches can suffer from limitations such as local minima and lack of adaptivity without additional design mechanisms [8].

Building on this perspective, we develop a coordination architecture for heterogeneous USV–UAV teams. The system comprises a capability-aware distributed online task allocation module [2] and an adaptive planner that generates executable navigation policies while triggering replanning when necessary. Detection and interception policies use classical graph-based planning methods, while persistent coverage relies on the chemotaxis-inspired potential field formulation.

We validate the proposed architecture in a representative coastal surveillance mission involving UAVs and USVs tasked with detection, tracking, and interception of intruders in a coastal environment. Experimental results demonstrate that the bio-inspired coordination improves mission adaptability, robustness, and cooperative performance under dynamic environmental conditions.

2　Multi-robot Coordination Architecture

This paper addresses the problem of coordinating heterogeneous multirobot teams in maritime environments. In particular we are interested in UAV–USV teams. In this line, a holistic, end-to-end view of multi-robot coordination (Fig. 1) spans from the definition of high-level goals to the execution of low-level tasks.

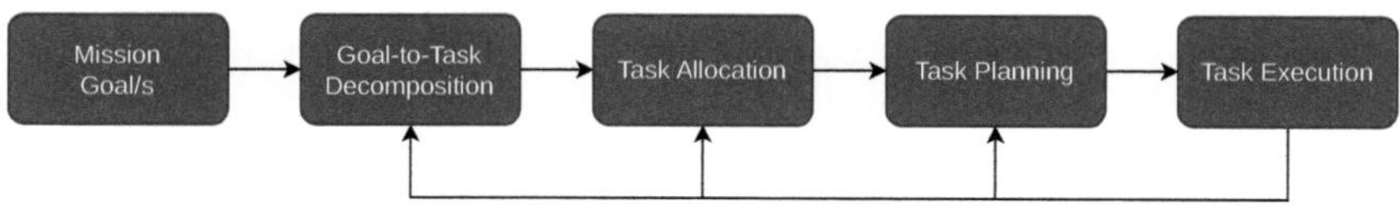

Fig. 1. Multi-robot coordination, end-to-end view.

In this work, it is assumed that the mission goal has already been decomposed into a set of executable tasks, such as surveillance, tracking, interception, escort, or any other and the focus is on the two central stages of the coordination process: (1) task allocation and (2) task planning. These stages are embedded in a fully distributed implementation in which each team member maintains its own local allocation and planning logic, and autonomously selects, plans, and executes tasks based on onboard perceptions and limited information exchanged with teammates, without relying on a centralized coordinator.

2.1　Task Allocation

Task allocation determines the task each robot executes at any given time. To avoid centralized bottlenecks in dynamic and communication-constrained environments, we adopt a fully distributed strategy. Each robot is equipped with a subsumption-based internal task selector [2], where tasks are modeled as layered behaviors running concurrently. A default behavior executes when no higher-level behavior is active. Higher layers are triggered by perceptual events (onboard detections or teammate messages) and suppress lower layers when activated, enabling autonomous task self-selection without centralized coordination.

2.2　Task Planning

Once a robot has selected its current behavior (task to carry out), task planning is formulated as a motion planning problem due to the motion-centric nature of the mission tasks, and with the objective of calculating feasible trajectories toward assigned targets or goals. Here we address two basic types of tasks that need to be planned: Point-to-point navigation, which is addressed through traditional graph based planning algorithms such as A*, and area coverage. For the latter we have designed a chemotaxis inspired potential field based approach. Nevertheless, the general logic is the same for any other task.

Chemotaxis-Inspired Potential-Based Area Coverage. To ensure continuous and spatially uniform surveillance, we propose a persistent coverage strategy inspired by bacterial chemotaxis, implemented through a discrete artificial potential field.

In chemotaxis, organisms bias motion toward attractant gradients and away from repellents using only local sensing. Analogously, our method performs discrete gradient following over a shared potential map. Long-unvisited regions act as virtual attractants, while obstacles and teammate proximity act as repellents.

Potential Map Construction. The environment is discretized into a shared 2D grid maintained by all agents. Each cell (i,j) stores the elapsed time since last observation,

$$t^{i,j}_{elapsed} = t - t^{i,j}_{last},$$

which is reset upon sensing. Revisit urgency is encoded as a bounded potential $P_{i,j} \in [0,100]$ that increases monotonically with $t^{i,j}_{elapsed}$. Obstacles and non-traversable cells are assigned negative values to enforce avoidance. This aging mechanism generates virtual gradients that drive agents toward poorly observed regions, reducing overall map potential over time.

Distributed Waypoint Selection. At each step, each agent performs local gradient ascent within an annular window W (100–110 m radius). For feasible cells in W, a composite score is computed as

$$\text{score}_{i,j} = \begin{cases} -1, & (i,j) \notin W, \\ P_{i,j} w^{f}_{i,j} + b^{p}_{i,j} - R^{t}_{i,j}, & \text{otherwise,} \end{cases} \tag{1}$$

where $w^{f}_{i,j}$ promotes heading continuity, $b^{p}_{i,j}$ biases mission-priority regions, and $R^{t}_{i,j}$ penalizes proximity to teammates. The next waypoint is selected as

$$(i,j)_{next} = \arg \max_{(i,j) \in W} \text{score}_{i,j}. \tag{2}$$

This greedy maximization approximates discrete gradient ascent, yielding emergent distributed coverage. As visited cells reset their potential, the landscape dynamically reshapes, redistributing agents without centralized coordination. The resulting behavior is scalable, adaptive, and robust to agent loss, making it suitable for heterogeneous maritime surveillance under communication and sensing constraints.

3   Experiments

To validate the architecture presented above, we address the problem of coordinating heterogeneous UAV–USV teams to detect and neutralize mobile intruders within a constrained maritime environment. The objective is to detect mobile intruders and neutralize them before they reach mission-critical areas, while maintaining persistent surveillance coverage of the operational domain. Mission success requires intercepting all intruders prior to target zone penetration.

Two distinct experiments were conducted: the first one aims to evaluate coverage performance and the second one seeks to demonstrate the complete architecture proposed here in the full intrusion prevention mission.

Simulations were run on Ubuntu 22.04 with Unreal Engine 5.1 and ROS2 Humble for multi-agent communication and control. The environment comprises a coastal area discretice into 2164×2164 grid cells and containing two irregular islands separated by navigable channels, including bathymetry constraints with shallow waters near the coast. The map grid cells are initialized at zero for coverage analysis. As simulation progresses, unobserved cells accumulate time linearly, and when a vehicle's sensors observes cells within its detection radius, their visit times are reset to zero.

Two types of vehicles are considered: USVs and UAVs. USVs operate on the sea surface in the x-y plane at fixed z (sea level), controlled by linear speed and heading angle. Each vehicle incorporates LiDAR for static and dynamic obstacle detection and environment mapping. Intruders are modeled as adversarial USVs with identical sensing capabilities. In the case of UAVs, they operate at constant altitude, reducing 3D motion planning to the x-y plane. They are equipped with LiDAR sensors for obstacle avoidance, intruder detection and target tracking.

3.1   Experiment 1: Coverage Performance

Coverage performance of the proposed chemotaxis inspired APF algorithm is evaluated employing only the mean cell visit time metric through simulations considering four UAVs deployed from the map corners and running for 2765 s. Due to the stochasticity of the APF algorith, six independent simulations were run to produce representative performance distributions for valid comparison.

The results were compared to a deterministic multirobot zigzag pattern baseline. This baseline algorithm assigns each UAV a fixed subregion, where it follows systematic back-and-forth waypoints: right-to-left sweeps followed by row jumps, alternating directions until completion and then returning to the starting point. This deterministic pattern ignores obstacles and produces identical results across runs, requiring only one trial. Coverage performance is quantified using metrics based on cell visit times.

Results in Fig. 2 show that the zigzag pattern achieves a slightly superior performance with a mean visit time of $\sim$200 s, compared to $\sim$220 s across six APF tests, indicating that for uniform scenarios and no vehicle or communication loss, the deterministic pattern ensures repeatable coverage and is difficult to outperform. However, its fixed region assignment makes it vulnerable to agent failures. To assess the robustness of the methods, the same scenario was re-evaluated under partial agent loss: first with three UAVs (simulating the failure of one vehicle) and then with two UAVs (simulating the loss of two vehicles). These results are displayed in Figs. 3(a) and 3(b), respectively. Results

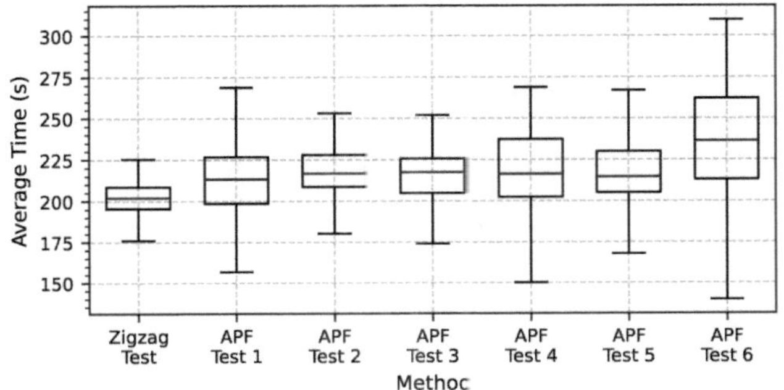

Fig. 2. Zigzag vs APF coverage performance for 6 runs of the APF based system. The graph reflects the mean average time between visits to all the grid cells in the map.

in Fig. 3 demonstrate APF superiority under degraded conditions. With three UAVs, zigzag exhibits continuous linear growth reaching approximately 800 s at the end of the experiment, contrasting with APF tests that converge in 300–450 s. This difference is accentuated with two UAVs where zigzag diverges toward 1200 s while APF is stable at 400–600 s.

This experiment highlights a trade-off that depends on the scenario. In unrestricted environments with perfect communications and no vehicle losses, the zigzag pattern achieves near-optimal coverage with highly repeatable performance. However, its deterministic region assignment limits resilience: if one UAV fails or is lost, the corresponding subregion may remain unvisited until the mission is replanned. By contrast, APF is more robust to such events because the remaining UAVs can adapt their trajectories and redistribute coverage online.

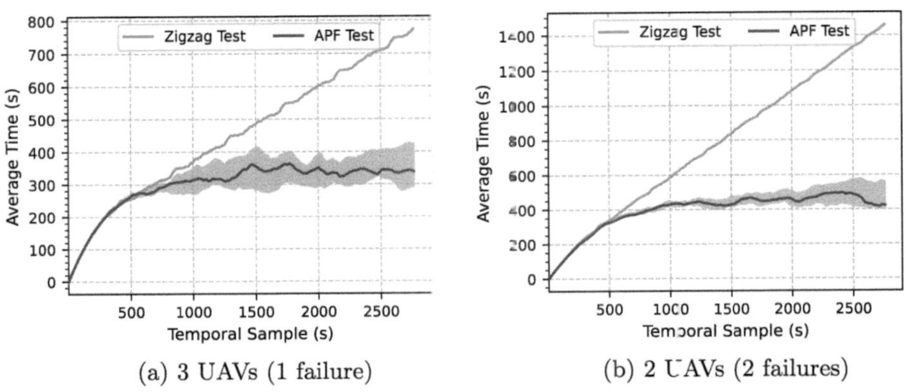

(a) 3 UAVs (1 failure)   (b) 2 UAVs (2 failures)

Fig. 3. Mean cell visit time and deviation under UAV failures.

3.2   Experiment 2: Proposed Architecture Validation

This experiment evaluates the proposed architecture in a dynamic surveillance and interception mission involving mobile intruders. The objective is to assess online reconfiguration through continuous replanning and distributed task reassignment via the subsumption-based allocation layer.

A heterogeneous team of four UAVs (UAV1–UAV4) and four USVs (USV1–USV4) operates in a maritime environment with two static islands and a central protected target. UAVs are initialized at the map corners and USVs near the center. Two intruder USVs attempt to reach the central target. The mission succeeds if both intruders are intercepted before reaching the target.

All vehicles are equipped with LiDAR sensors. Defenders use LiDAR for obstacle avoidance and intruder detection, while intruders use it for collision avoidance. Detection is assumed perfect within sensing range. During surveillance phases, all defenders execute the APF-based coverage behavior.

UAVs operate in two task states: surveillance and tracking. USVs operate in three task states: surveillance, intercept, and escort (see Fig. 4). Initially, all defender vehicles are in surveillance mode. An UAV switches from surveillance to tracking when an intruder is detected within its sensing radius, but only one UAV tracks a given intruder at any time. While in the tracking mode, the UAV continuously estimates and broadcasts the intruder position to the rest of the team. The closest USVs to the intruder, where proximity is evaluated using Euclidean distance, assumes the interception task. The USV task decision module has information available on the positions of the other USVs and of the intruder. If, during the intruder motion, a different USV becomes closer than the currently assigned one, it autonomously assumes the interception.

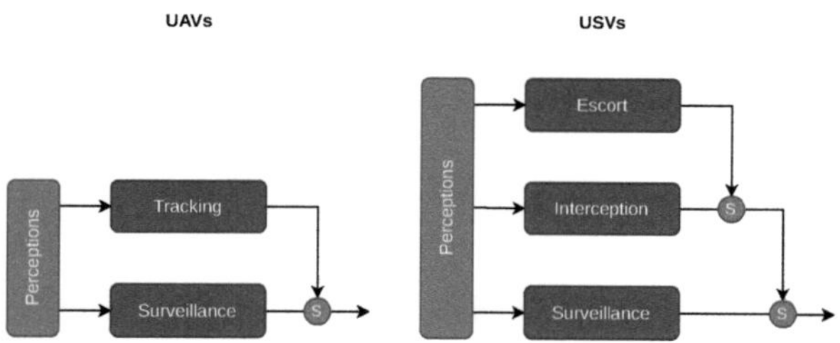

Fig. 4. Subsumption logic for distributed task self-assignment for UAVs and USVs.

While executing the interception task, the USV repeatedly replans a collision-free path toward the current intruder position, accounting for static obstacles and other vessels. When the intruder enters the LiDAR range of the intercepting USV, the intruder is considered acquired. At this point, the corresponding UAV terminates the tracking task and returns to surveillance and the USV switches from intercept to escort, guiding the intruder away from the monitored region. Defenders that are not involved in tracking, intercept or escort tasks remain in surveillance throughout the mission.

For this experiment, the scenario considered evaluates the architecture on a uniform coverage map without priority areas. Figure 5(a) shows the initial configuration where the four UAVs are placed at the map corners, the four USVs are located near the central area, and the two intruders at their starting positions.

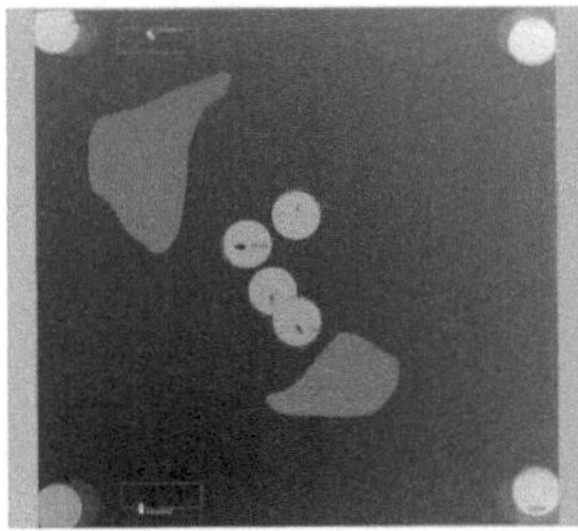
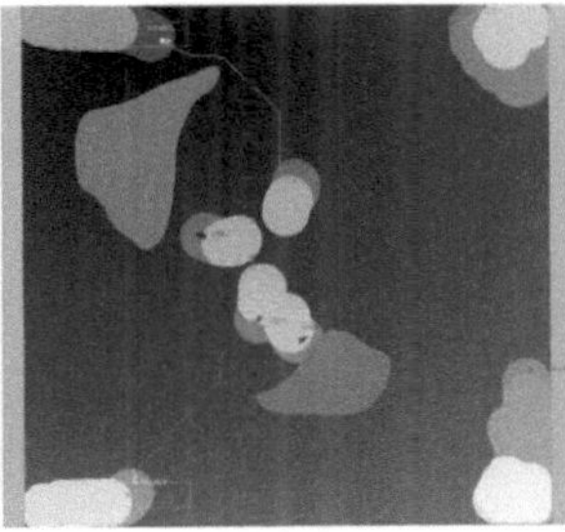
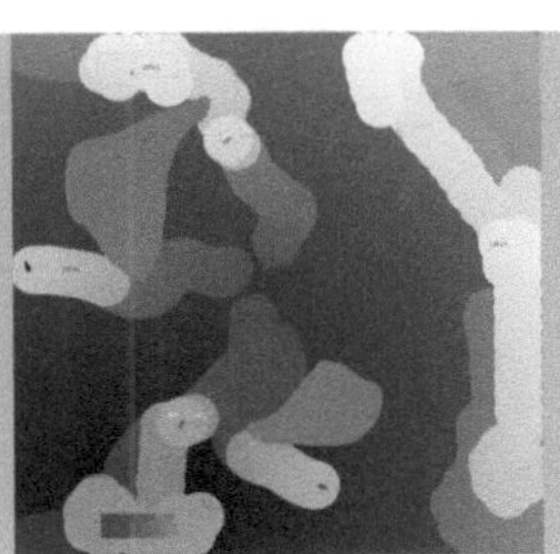

(a) Initial mission deployment configuration.

(b) Intercept assignment and trajectory update.

(c) Successful interception and escort completion.

Fig. 5. Mission sequence.

As the mission begins, UAV1 detects the first intruder (Intruder1) and switches from surveillance to tracking. After a time, UAV3 detects the second intruder (Intruder2) and also transitions to tracking. This sequence is reflected in the task-state timeline of Fig. 6. Initially, the intercept task is assumed by USV1, which leaves surveillance and starts navigating toward the intruder. As the intruder continues to move, USV2 becomes closer than USV1, which leads to a reassignment of the intercept task from USV1 to USV2. Figure 5(b) shows the corresponding spatial configuration: UAV1 tracks Intruder1 and UAV3 tracks Intruder2, while USV2 and USV3 assume the intercept tasks for Intruder1 and Intruder2, respectively. The remaining defenders continue executing the surveillance task. The grayish footprints left by each platform indicate the regions where the APF potential has been reduced due to coverage.

Once Intruder2 enters the detection range of USV3, USV3 switches from intercept to escort, and UAV3 terminates the tracking task and resumes surveillance. Similarly, USV2 later escorts Intuder1 as UAV1 returns to surveillance. Figure 5(c) shows the final configuration, where USV2 and USV3 execute the escort task for Intruder1 and Intruder2, respectively. UAV1 and UAV3 have already returned to surveillance mode, while UAV2, UAV4, USV1, and USV4 continue performing surveillance over the rest of the map. Neither intruder reaches the central target point, so the mission is successfully completed.

The results of this experiment show that the proposed architecture can dynamically reconfigure the roles of a heterogeneous UAV–USV team in response to detections and intruder motion in a distributed manner, demonstrating its reactivity and online reconfiguration capability in dynamic environments.

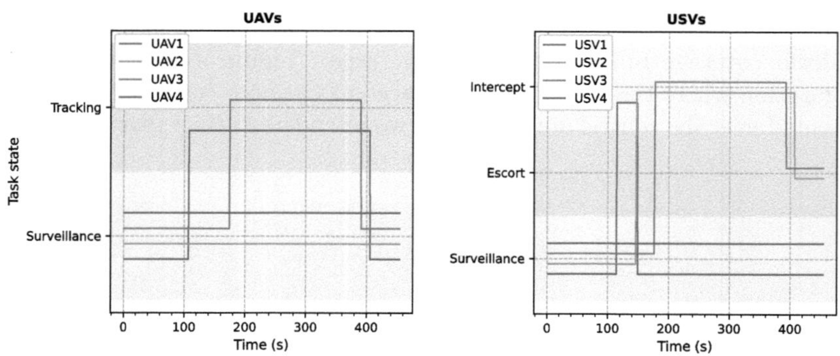

Fig. 6. Task-state timelines for UAVs and USVs.

4   Conclusions

This paper presented a coordination architecture for heterogeneous UAV–USV teams operating in dynamic maritime environments. The framework integrates a chemotaxis-inspired persistent coverage strategy and a capability-aware online task allocation with adaptive task planning. By representing revisit urgency, mission priorities, and inter-agent interactions within a shared discrete potential map, the proposed approach enables decentralized decision-making while maintaining coherent team behavior. The architecture allows all agents to perform persistent surveillance and to transition to specialized roles, including detection, tracking, interception, and escort, as mission conditions evolve.

The proposed methods were evaluated in two complementary experimental scenarios. The results demonstrate that the proposed architecture supports online task reconfiguration, continuous replanning, and effective cooperation between heterogeneous aerial and surface platforms. All intruders were intercepted before reaching the protected zone under the tested scenarios, indicating reliable performance in the presence of dynamic targets and collision avoidance constraints. Future work will address larger-scale deployments, more detailed studies on robustness to communication degradation and vehicle failures, and further analysis of convergence and coverage properties under heterogeneous sensing and mobility constraints.

Acknowledgments. This work was funded by Xunta de Galicia (ED431C 2025/32), by the Spanish Science and Education Ministry (PID2024-162223OB-I00), Ministry for Digital Transformation and Civil Service and Next - Generation EU/RRF (TSI-100925-2023-1), and Centro de InvestigaciÃşn de Galicia "CITIC" (ED431G 2023/01).

References

1. Brambilla, M., Ferrante, E., Birattari, M., Dorigo, M.: Swarm robotics: a review from the swarm engineering perspective. Swarm Intell. (2013). https://doi.org/10.1007/s11721-012-0075-2
2. Brooks, R.A.: How to build complete creatures rather than isolated cognitive simulators. In: Architectures for Intelligence, pp. 225–239. Psychology Press (2014)
3. Chen, Q., et al.: A heterogeneous multirobot system for autonomous object retrieval in challenging GNSS-denied maritime environment. J. Field Robot. **42**(8), 4288–4310 (2025)
4. Geng, M., Zhou, X., Ding, B., Wang, H., Zhang, L.: Learning to cooperate in decentralized multi-robot exploration of dynamic environments. In: International Conference on Neural Information Processing, pp. 40–51. Springer (2018)
5. Jiang, L., Mo, H., Tian, P.: A bacterial chemotaxis-inspired coordination strategy for coverage and aggregation of swarm robots. Appl. Sci. **11**(3), 1347 (2021)
6. Jiang, L., Mo, H., Tian, P.: An adaptive decentralized control strategy for deployment and aggregation of swarm robots based on bacterial chemotaxis. Appl. Intell. **53**(10), 13018–13036 (2023)
7. Khatib, O.: Real-time obstacle avoidance for manipulators and mobile robots. In: Proceedings. 1985 IEEE International Conference on Robotics and Automation, vol. 2, pp. 500–505 (1985). https://doi.org/10.1109/ROBOT.1985.1087247
8. Koren, Y., Borenstein, J.: Potential field methods and their inherent limitations for mobile robot navigation. In: Proceedings. 1991 IEEE International Conference on Robotics and Automation, vol. 2, pp. 1398–1404 (1991). https://doi.org/10.1109/ROBOT.1991.131810
9. Martorell-Torres, A., Guerrero-Sastre, J., Oliver-Codina, G.: Coordination of marine multi robot systems with communication constraints. Appl. Ocean Res. **142**, 103848 (2024)
10. Patterson, R.G., Lawson, E., Udyawer, V., Brassington, G.B., Groom, R.A., Campbell, H.A.: Uncrewed surface vessel technological diffusion depends on cross-sectoral investment in open-ocean archetypes: a systematic review of USV applications and drivers. Front. Mar. Sci. **8**, 736984 (2022). https://doi.org/10.3389/fmars.2021.736984
11. Stephenson, J., Duncan, N.T., Greeff, M.: Distributed model predictive control for cooperative multirotor landing on uncrewed surface vessel in waves. arXiv preprint: arXiv:2402.10399 (2024)
12. Yan, Z., Jouandeau, N., Cherif, A.A.: A survey and analysis of multi-robot coordination. Int. J. Adv. Rob. Syst. **10**(12), 399 (2013)
13. Zafar, M., Khan, R.A., Fedoseev, A., Jaiswal, K.K., Sujit, P., Tsetserukou, D.: HetSwarm: cooperative navigation of heterogeneous swarm in dynamic and dense environments through impedance-based guidance. In: 2025 International Conference on Unmanned Aircraft Systems (ICUAS), pp. 309–315. IEEE (2025)
14. Zhang, H., Fan, J., Zhang, X., Xu, H., Guedes Soares, C.: Unmanned surface vessel-unmanned aerial vehicle cooperative path following based on a predictive line of sight guidance law. J. Mar. Sci. Eng. **12**(10), 1818 (2024)

"Bio-Inspired Computing Approaches (BICA)"

Clustering the Latent Space in Variational Autoencoders for Image Generation

Diego Martínez[1] and José Santos[1,2]([envelope])

[1] Department of Computer Science and Information Technologies,
University of A Coruña, A Coruña, Spain
`{diego.martinez.muino,jose.santos}@udc.es`
[2] CITIC (Centre for Information and Communications Technology Research),
University of A Coruña, A Coruña, Spain

Abstract. Clothing-related datasets are used to train variational autoencoders, starting with the commonly used Fashion MNIST database. Clustering is applied and analyzed in the latent space and specific points are defined in this latent space for the purpose of generating novel images. These points correspond to the positions in the middle of the lines connecting the centroids of the resulting clusters. These aspects are analyzed with the different datasets focused on fashion images.

Keywords: Autoencoders · Variational autoencoders · Generative Artificial Intelligence

1 Introduction

Autoencoders are Artificial Neural Networks (ANNs) that are trained to produce the same input information as outputs. They consist of two parts, the encoder and decoder, which can typically be simple multilayer perceptrons or can consist of multiple layers of deep learning architectures. This allows for an internal representation, in the last layer of the encoder part, which captures, in an abstract representation (embedding or latent representation), the main features of that input space, using a nonlinear transformation of the input space. Typically, autoencoders are used to capture such a latent representation for other tasks (such as a final classification problem) or to remove noise from the input images.

However, the latent space does not necessarily present a continuous representation, in the sense that there may be areas in the latent space that were not covered during the training process. If an instance in these areas of the latent space is introduced in the decoder part, the output may not be related to the input information used in the training process.

To address this problem, Variational Auto-Encoders (VAEs) [7,9], during the learning process, try to generate a specific probability distribution (a normal distribution) in the latent space. For this purpose, for each input, the encoder part is interpreted as the mean and standard deviation (in each dimension of

J. M. Ferrández Vicente et al. (Eds.): IWINAC 2026, LNCS 16575, pp. 195–205, 2026.
https://doi.org/10.1007/978-3-032-27317-8_19

the latent space) of a Gaussian distribution. From this distribution, the latent representation is generated. This means that the generation of the embedding for a given input is not deterministic.

Furthermore, in the loss function for training the neural network (apart from the standard reconstruction loss), a component is included that measures the divergence of the actual distribution of possible points in latent space with respect to a normal distribution (Kullback-Leibler divergence [8]). This inclusion ensures the continuity of values in the latent space, values related to the inputs (and, consequently, to the same outputs). By selecting intermediate values in the latent space between the embeddings of two inputs, when the decoding part receives that intermediate configuration as input, the output can also be an intermediate between the two inputs. This is very useful for generative purposes in AI, especially in imaging.

The proposal presented here aims to analyze the use of VAEs in specific design problems, particularly in clothing, using the Fashion MNIST [10] and Zalando [13] datasets. In previous related work, Guo et al. [4] performed clustering in the latent space when VAEs use a Gamma mixture model in the latent representation, using the number of labeled categories in the inputs for the clustering process. Alotaibi [1] used an autoencoder for the classification of the Fashion MNIST images. First, the author trained the autoencoder with the dataset and, in a second step, used the latent space representation of each image to train a deep neural network for the classification of the 10 categories in the dataset.

Also using the Fashion MNIST dataset, Snehith et al. [12] experimented with denoising autoencoders to learn a robust representation of the dataset, optimizing factors such as the ideal learning rate and the number of hidden layer nodes for image reconstruction. Sarmiento [11], using a dataset of fashion product images that included eyewear, footwear and bags, used a VAE to create an interactive application framework (by adjusting a set of interactive sliders corresponding to the latent space) that allows users to generate products with attributes according to their preferences.

Our goal here is to analyze the latent space of trained VAEs, applying clustering to discover the main categories implicitly learned in the latent representation. This clustering will also allow us to define new positions in that space in order to generate novel images. Section 2 summarizes the methods used to achieve these objectives, with a brief introduction to VAEs, the datasets used and the clustering performed. Section 3 presents the results with the datasets, while Sect. 4 briefly summarizes the main conclusions of our study.

2   Methods

2.1   Variational Autoencoders

As detailed by Mienye and Swart [9], VAEs integrate the principles of Bayesian inference into the autoencoder process, transforming the encoding part into a variational inference problem. This incorporates a probabilistic approach into the operation of autoencoders, where the encoder part generates parameters of a proposed distribution on latent variables instead of deterministic outputs. Instead of producing a direct representation in the latent space for each input, the encoder generates parameters of a probability distribution, usually a Gaussian distribution, defined by its mean (μ) and variance (σ), as Fig. 1 illustrates.

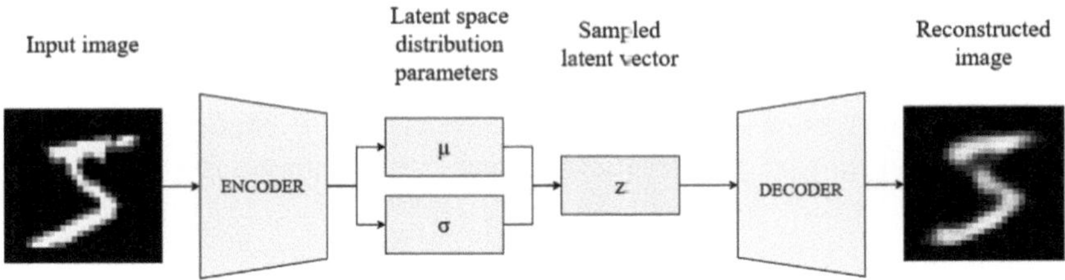

Fig. 1. Architecture of a Variational Autoencoder for image reconstruction, illustrating the encoder, latent distribution and decoder stages.

The fundamental challenge in training VAEs is that the sampling process $\mathbf{z} \sim q_\phi(\mathbf{z}|\mathbf{x})$ in the latent space is stochastic, which prevents the use of backpropagation since gradients cannot flow through a random node. To overcome this, Kingma and Welling [7] introduced the "reparameterization trick". The sampled latent vector $\mathbf{z}$ is expressed as a deterministic and differentiable function of the parameters and an auxiliary noise variable ϵ:

$$\mathbf{z} = \mu + \sigma \odot \epsilon, \quad \text{with } \epsilon \sim \mathcal{N}(0, \mathbf{I}) \tag{1}$$

where $\odot$ denotes the element-wise product. This shift moves the randomness to ϵ, allowing the model to compute gradients with respect to μ and σ, thereby making the entire architecture end-to-end trainable via gradient descent.

The optimization objective of a VAE is to maximize the Evidence Lower Bound (ELBO). As detailed in [3,9], the ELBO arises from the need to approximate the intractable true posterior probability $p(\mathbf{z}|\mathbf{x})$ using a simpler distribution $q_\phi(\mathbf{z}|\mathbf{x})$. The ELBO loss function is defined as:

$$\mathcal{L}(\theta, \phi; \mathbf{x}) = \underbrace{\mathbb{E}_{q_\phi(\mathbf{z}|\mathbf{x})}[\log p_\theta(\mathbf{x}|\mathbf{z})]}_{\text{Reconstruction term}} - \underbrace{D_{KL}(q_\phi(\mathbf{z}|\mathbf{x})||p(\mathbf{z}))}_{\text{Regularization term}} \tag{2}$$

where ϕ and θ are the parameters (ANN weights) that define the transformation of the encoder and decoder parts. The first component of this objective, the reconstruction loss, measures the expected log-likelihood of the reconstructed data. It penalizes the model based on how poorly the decoder $p_\theta(\mathbf{x}|\mathbf{z})$ reconstructs the original input $\mathbf{x}$ from the sampled latent vector. Depending on the data type, this is typically implemented through the minimization of the Binary Cross-Entropy or Mean Squared Error, ensuring that the latent representation preserves the most salient features of the input.

In contrast, the second term introduces a regularization constraint based on the Kullback-Leibler (KL) divergence [8]. This term measures the deviation of the posterior probability distribution $q_\phi(z|x)$ from a prior distribution $p(\mathbf{z})$, usually a standard normal distribution $\mathcal{N}(0, I)$. Without this regularization, the encoder could easily overfit by assigning each input to isolated points in the latent space. KL divergence acts as a pressure that forces the individual distributions generated for different inputs to overlap and spread across the latent space (generating an $\mathcal{N}(0, I)$ distribution), effectively smoothing the latent space.

The reconstruction loss ensures that the latent space distribution parameters (μ and σ) retain sufficient information to distinguish between different categories, while the KL divergence ensures that the latent space is continuous and has no gaps, allowing for meaningful reconstructions from all points in the latent space.

2.2   Datasets

The primary dataset used to evaluate the proposed approach is Fashion MNIST [10]. This dataset is a widely recognized benchmark in the field of machine learning, consisting of $70,000$ grayscale images of size 28×28 pixels, equally divided into 10 categories of clothing and accessories (7,000 images per class).

In this study, the training was constrained to a subset of the original dataset to focus specifically on garment design and to ensure a more coherent latent space. Since the objective is to generate new patterns based on existing shapes, heterogeneous categories such as footwear (sandals, sneakers, boots) or accessories (bags) were excluded. The subset focuses exclusively on upper-body and full-body garments, which share similar structural features. Specifically, the following five classes were selected: T-shirt/top, pullover, dress, coat and shirt.

After filtering the dataset to include only the five selected garment categories, the resulting subset containing 35,000 images was partitioned into training and test sets. Specifically, 70% of the data was reserved for training, 30% was used as a test set. The test set was used here as a validation subset, which is used to control the end of training (Sect. 3.1).

Figure 2 (left part) shows representative samples of these five categories. By limiting the input space to these related categories, the VAE can more effectively learn a continuous latent representation where transitions between points (interpolations) result in visually plausible and structurally sound garment designs, rather than morphing between unrelated objects.

In addition, the high-resolution VITON Zalando dataset [13] was used. The original high-resolution color images were converted to grayscale and resized to 64×64 pixels. This dataset does not define discrete clothing categories but focuses exclusively on upper-body garments. It is divided into training and test subsets containing 11,647 and 2,032 images, respectively (using the test set as the validation set). Moreover, these images were filtered by removing those in which there is practically no difference between the foreground and the background (close to white), which means removing 19% of the images. Figure 2 (right side) shows representative examples of the preprocessed images.

Fig. 2. Left: Examples of the five clothing categories (rows) selected from the Fashion MNIST dataset: Shirt, pullover, dress, coat and T-shirt. Right: Examples from the Zalando dataset (there is no prior categorization of the images).

2.3   Clustering of the Latent Space

New results (images in this case) can be generated by selecting locations throughout the latent space. To generate intermediate images as an interpolation of different images in the input space, we propose clustering the latent space to define those selected points or locations. The underlying idea is that the latent space can represent the input space with a lower dimensionality, where the latent space preserves the same distance relationships between different points as in the original input space. A clustering of the latent space can automatically determine the different categories of inputs during training. Once clustering is performed, the cluster centroids in the latent space are associated with the representative points of all inputs in a given category associated with a cluster.

For example, Fig. 3 (left part) shows the cluster centroids after training a VAE (parameters specified in Sect. 3.1) with the 5 categories of the Fashion MNIST database (Sect. 2.2). Firstly, it should be noted that the latent space shows the continuity sought in VAEs, with a shape of normal distribution centered at 0 (in each dimension) after training. The clustering was performed using a classic k-means clustering algorithm [5], using the Euclidean distance of the input projections (using the μ values) in the latent space as a measure of the distance between points in the latent space. The dimension of the latent space is 4 in this example. However, Fig. 3 shows only a 2D view of the clustering using the first two dimensions of the latent space (the representations are quite similar using other dimensions and with techniques such as t-SNE for visualizing high-dimensional data in 2D or 3D). In the example, the number of clusters was set at 5 (since the number of input categories is known a priori and that k-means returns an optimal number of 4–5 classes with a standard elbow analysis [5]), but this number can be set as the optimal number of clusters using the specific approaches of each clustering technique. The small images of the clusters are located at each of the cluster centroids and the images correspond to the specific input image of the centroid. Different runs of the k-means algorithm produce virtually the same clusters in most cases.

However, if the points in the latent space are colored according to their original categories in the input space (Fig. 3, right part), the five categories in the latent space appear less concentrated and more blurred, with no abrupt transitions between them. This indicates that many input images are located at the boundaries of different classes, which is reflected in the latent space. Therefore, two possibilities can be considered for defining the centroids used for the subsequent generation of intermediate images: centroids defined based on k-means in the latent space (Fig. 3, left part) and centroids defined from points in the latent space that belong to the same input category (Fig. 3, right part). The first possibility (used here) has the advantage that it considers a clustering, after a nonlinear transformation in the encoder, which is independent of the categorization established in the dataset (probably forced in many input images in the dataset, as can be seen in some examples in Fig. 2). Note that there is no relationship between the same colors in both subfigures.

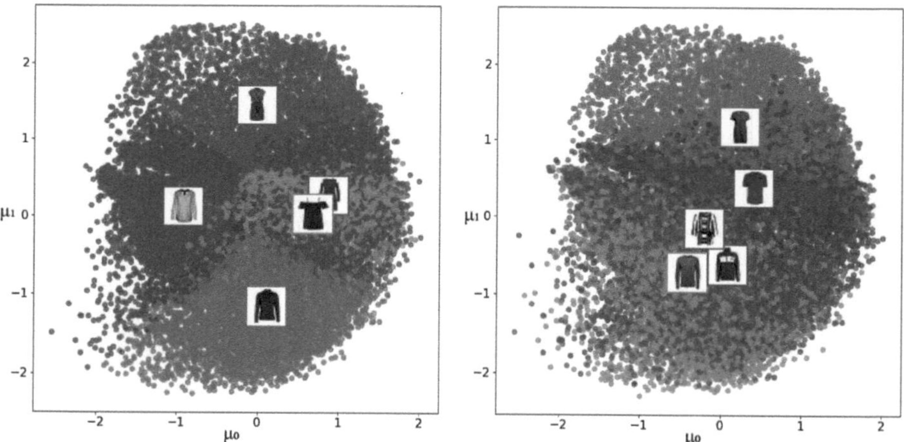

Fig. 3. Left: Clustering of the latent space when a VAE is trained with five categories from the Fashion MNIST database. K-means was used to cluster the input projections in the latent space. The small figures are located at each cluster centroid and represent the input image corresponding to that point in the latent space (μ value). The subfigure on the left shows a 2D view of the latent space (latent space dimension = 4), plotting the μ values of the first two dimensions. Right: latent space colored according to input categories, with centroids corresponding to locations (μ values) belonging to the same input category.

Now, to generate new intermediate images, we propose selecting the intermediate points between the lines connecting pairs of cluster centroids. The following section presents the results obtained with this approach.

3   Results

3.1   Setup

The VAE architectures used in the experiments are neural network topologies with a limited number of dense layers in the encoder/decoder parts, as increasing the number of layers has not reduced the loss function. Similar results in terms of final total loss (Binary Cross-Entropy + KL divergence) have been obtained using convolutional layers instead of dense layers (not shown here), so only the use of dense layers in trained autoencoders is shown.

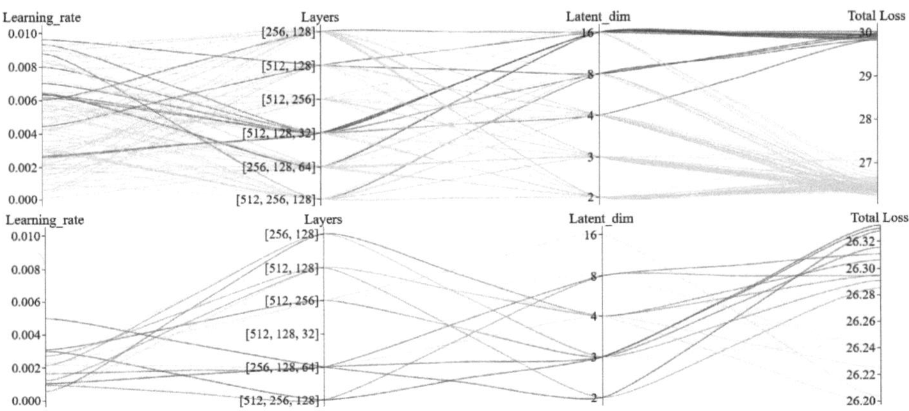

Fig. 4. Heat color diagram showing the total loss results for different parameter combinations (using the Fashion MNIST dataset). The greener lines correspond to better total loss values. Upper figure: all tested parameter combinations. Lower figure: the 20 best configurations.(Color figure online)

In dense layers, nodes use a ReLu activation function in all cases, using Keras libraries to implement all VAE modules [6]. Binary cross-entropy was used in all cases to define the reconstruction loss. The Adam optimizer was used for training and the batch size (which controls the number of training samples to be processed before the internal model parameters are updated) during training was set to a standard value of 64. On the other hand, several parameters of the VAE architecture and training were optimized using approaches such as Random Search and the Tree-structured Parzen Estimator Approach (TPE) defined in [2]. The parameters to be tuned are: 6 configurations with different numbers of nodes in two or three hidden layers in the encoder/mirrored decoder parts (shown in Fig. 4), learning rate (sampled from a continuous interval between 0.0001 and 0.01) and latent dimension (values of 2, 3, 4, 8 and 16). An early stopping strategy is used if validation loss does not improve after five training epochs, restoring the model weights corresponding to the best validation performance observed, while the maximum number of training epochs is limited to 100.

202   D. Martínez and J. Santos

With the Fashion MNIST dataset, Fig. 4 shows the results, in terms of the total loss obtained after training (vertical line furthest to the right), of the different combinations (100) of parameters tested and using Random Search to find the best combinations. The greener the color of the line, the better the configuration. There are many different configurations with similar results in terms of final total loss, with a tendency to obtain worse results the higher the learning rate used, which is similar when using the TPE strategy to search for the best configurations (not shown here). The bottom subfigure corresponds to the 20 best configurations, clearly with low learning rates to obtain the best results. The best configuration was selected for the following experiment with the MNIST dataset: learning rate=0.0005, layers [512, 128] (two dense hidden layers with 512 and 128 nodes with Relu activation functions) and latent dimension=4.

3.2   Generation of New Images in the MNIST Dataset

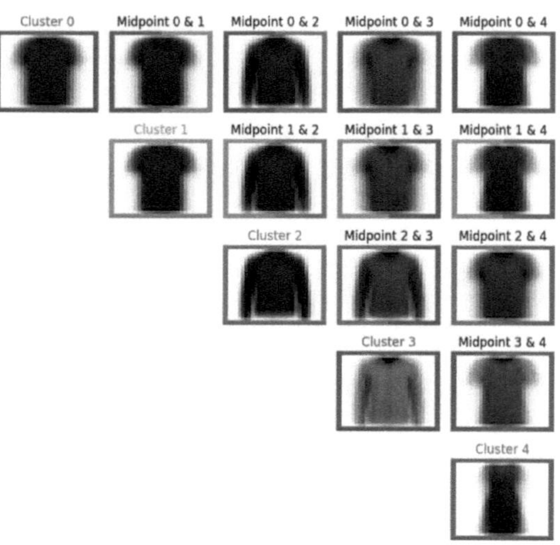

Fig. 5. Reconstructions from cluster centroids (diagonal) and from midpoints between pairs of centroids (off-diagonal).

To evaluate the structural continuity and semantic coherence of the learned latent space, image interpolation was performed using the cluster centroids. First, the centroid c_k of each class was calculated as the mean of the latent representations belonging to that cluster (5 clusters, Fig. 3). Next, a synthetic latent point z_{interp} was generated by calculating the midpoint between two centroids: $z_{interp} = (c_i + c_j)/2$. This midpoint, which can represent the transition between two different clusters, was passed through the decoder $p_\theta(x|z_{interp})$ to visualize the resulting construction. As shown in Fig. 5, the images outside the diagonal represent the decoded midpoints z_{interp} between pairs of clusters.

Note that reconstructions of cluster centroids are generally blurred images of the input images of those centroids (Fig. 5 - diagonal vs. Fig. 3 - left part), an inherent problem with VAES in reconstructing training inputs [9,11]. On the other hand, the reconstructions shown in Fig. 5 (off the diagonal) show how the generated images correspond to interpolations between the representative images of the two corresponding clusters. See, for example, how the image generated for "Midpoint 3 & 4" is a compromise between a sleeveless dress (reconstructed image of cluster 4 centroid) and a pullover (reconstruction of cluster 3 centroid), resulting in a kind of T-shirt.

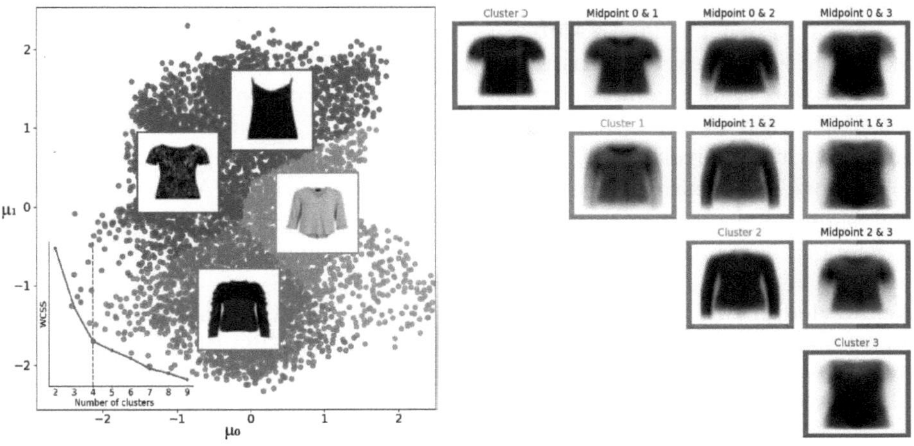

Fig. 6. Left: K-means clustering of latent space in a VAE trained with the Zalando dataset. The inset (lower left corner) shows the k-means elbow graph. Right: Reconstructions from cluster centroids (diagonal) and decoded midpoints between pairs of centroids (off-diagonal).

3.3   Generation of New Images in the Zalando Dataset

Random Search was run again to establish the best setup configuration: learning rate=0.00036, layers [512, 256, 128] and latent dimension=3. Figure 6 (left side) shows the k-means clustering of the latent space (2D view). The inset in Fig. 6 corresponds to the standard elbow plot in clustering. The elbow curve shows, on the y-axis, the Within-Cluster Sum of Squares (WCSS), i.e., the total squared distances between the data points and the center of their cluster. The x-axis corresponds to the number of clusters. Although there is no pronounced elbow, 4 clusters is a good balance between both values (WCSS versus number of clusters).

Figure 6 (right side) shows again the reconstruction of images from the clustering performed in the latent space, with the reconstructed images of the cluster centroids and the reconstructions from the midpoints between the pairs of centroids. For example, the "Midpoint 0 & 2" reconstruction clearly generates an intermediate image between the T-shirt-shaped reconstruction of cluster 0 and the pullover of cluster 2.

4   Conclusions

A clustering analysis was performed in the latent space of trained VAEs. This space shows the continuity necessary to provide meaningful reconstructed images for the different areas of the latent space. To test the methods, classic k-means was used as the initial technique. From the resulting clusters in the latent space, which determine the categories learned from the input images (regardless of the possible labeled input categories), specific points (midpoints between the cluster centroids) were defined in this latent space in order to generate novel images. The reconstruction process demonstrates its effectiveness in generating novel images as interpolations of the representative images of each of the clusters in the latent space, shown with two datasets focused on clothing. Future work will focus on analysis with other clustering techniques and the use of deep learning schemes to improve the reconstruction process (e.g., with stacked VAEs and also with higher image resolution), as well as attempting to export these ideas to recent developments in image reconstruction, such as diffusion models in deep learning.

Acknowledgments. This study was funded by the Xunta de Galicia and the European Union, with grants CITIC (ED431G 2023/01) and GRC ED431C 2025/49, by the "Consellería de Educación, Ciencia, Universidades e Formación Profesional (Xunta de Galicia - Convenio para o desenvolvemento de accións estratéxicas de I+D+i 2025–2026)", as well as by the Spanish Ministry of Science, Innovation and Universities (MICIU/AEI/10.13039/ 501100011033, project PID2023-148531NB-I00).

References

1. Alotaibi, A.: A hybird framework based on autoencoder and deep neural networks for fashion image classification. Int. J. Adv. Comput. Sci. Appl. **11**(12) (2020). https://doi.org/10.14569/IJACSA.2020.0111237
2. Bergstra, J., Bardenet, R., Bengio, Y., Kégl, B.: Algorithms for hyper-parameter optimization. In: Advances in Neural Information Processing Systems. vol. 24. Curran Associates, Inc. (2011). https://proceedings.neurips.cc/paper_files/paper/2011/file/86e8f7ab32cfd12577bc2619bc635690-Paper.pdf
3. Diederik, P.K., Max, W.: An introduction to variational autoencoders. Found. Trends® Mach. Learn. **12**(4), 307–392 (2019). https://doi.org/10.1561/2200000056
4. Guo, J., Fan, W., Amayri, M., Bouguila, N.: Deep clustering analysis via variational autoencoder with gamma mixture latent embeddings. Neural Netw. **183**, 106979 (2025). https://doi.org/10.1016/j.neunet.2024.106979
5. Jin, X., Han, J.: K-Means clustering, pp. 563–564. Springer (2010). https://doi.org/10.1007/978-0-387-30164-8_425
6. Keras - variational autoencoder. https://keras.io/examples/generative/vae/
7. Kingma, D., Welling, M.: Auto-encoding variational Bayes. In: Proceedings of the 2nd International Conference on Learning Representations (ICLR), pp. 79–86 (2014)
8. Kullback, S., Leibler, R.A.: On information and sufficiency. Ann. Math. Stat. **22**(1), 79–86 (1951). http://www.jstor.org/stable/2236703
9. Mienye, I., Swart, T.: Deep autoencoder neural networks: a comprehensive review and new perspectives. Arch. Comput. Methods Eng. **32**, 1–20 (2025). https://doi.org/10.1007/s11831-025-10260-5
10. MNIST database. https://drive.google.com/drive/folders/125F48fsMBz2EF0Cpqk6aaHet5VH399Ok

11. Sarmiento, J.A.: Exploiting latent codes: interactive fashion product generation, similar image retrieval, and cross-category recommendation using variational autoencoders (2020). https://arxiv.org/abs/2009.01053
12. Snehith, N., Harsha, M.S., Bodempudi, S., Bailundo, L.R.L., Shameem, S., Namgiri, J.V.: Reconstructing noised images of Fashion-MNIST dataset using autoencoders. In: AIKIIE Conference, pp. 1–6 (2023). https://doi.org/10.1109/AIKIIE60097.2023.10390180
13. High-Resolution Viton Zalando dataset. https://www.kaggle.com/datasets/marquis03/high-resolution-viton-zalando-dataset

Evolutionary Algorithms for a Routing Problem with Electric Vehicles and Zone Prices

Francisco Javier Gil-Gala[1]([✉]) [iD], Sezin Afsar[1] [iD], Juan José Palacios[1] [iD], Hasan Murat Afsar[2] [iD], and Marko Đurasević[3] [iD]

[1] University of Oviedo, Gijón, Spain
{giljavier,afsarsezin,palaciosjuan}@uniovi.es
[2] LIST3N, Université de Technologie de Troyes, Troyes, France
murat.afsar@utt.fr
[3] University of Zagreb, Zagreb, Croatia
Marko.Durasevic@fer.hr

Abstract. This paper addresses a novel variant of the Vehicle Routing Problem that integrates two modern logistics problems: the use of electric vehicles and the optimisation of profit through zone-based pricing. The proposed problem, referred to as the Electric Vehicle Routing Problem with Zone-based Pricing, involves planning routes that maximise the profit, defined as the revenue obtained from serving a subset of customers that accept the service minus the travel energy costs. To tackle this complex problem, we propose two evolutionary algorithms as solution methods: a Genetic Algorithm, which searches directly in the space of potential routing solutions, and Genetic Programming, which evolves constructive heuristics that generate solutions. Experimental results demonstrate that Genetic Programming outperforms the Genetic Algorithm in all problem instances considered.

Keywords: genetic algorithm · genetic programming · vehicle routing problem

1 Introduction

Vehicle Routing Problems (VRPs) are among the most studied and challenging combinatorial optimisation problems, with a wide range of applications in logistics [1]. These problems involve designing routes for a fleet of vehicles to service a set of customers, while satisfying various operational constraints such as vehicle capacity, travel time, or delivery deadlines. Due to their computational complexity and practical relevance, numerous VRP variants have been developed to address real-world requirements more accurately.

One important extension of the classical VRP involves the adoption of electric vehicles (EVs) in the delivery fleet [2]. The integration of EVs introduces new constraints, including limited driving range, battery capacity, and the availability

© The Author(s), under exclusive license to Springer Nature Switzerland AG 2026
J. M. Ferrández Vicente et al. (Eds.): IWINAC 2026, LNCS 16575, pp. 206–215, 2026.
https://doi.org/10.1007/978-3-032-27317-8_20

of recharging infrastructure [3]. Furthermore, the increasing deployment of EVs is largely driven by environmental concerns and policy regulations aimed at reducing emissions in urban areas [4].

Another interesting variant of the VRP considers the economic aspect of service planning through the introduction of zoned-based pricing [5]. In this context, customers are grouped into distinct geographical zones, each associated with a potential revenue. The objective becomes the maximisation of profit, which is defined as the difference between the revenue collected from the customers that accepted the service and the total cost of serving them, typically measured by the distance travelled. This variant introduces a pricing aspect to the routing problem, since not all customers accept the price of the service for their zone, but the ones that accept must be visited. The routing-pricing strategy should balance cost efficiency with revenue maximisation.

In this work, we address a novel variant of the VRP that simultaneously incorporates the constraints of EVs and the strategic decision-making associated with zone-based pricing. We refer to this problem as the Electric Vehicle Routing Problem with Zone-based Pricing (EVRP-ZP). This problem combines environmental and economic considerations, making it highly relevant for modern logistics operations, particularly in urban environments where emission regulations and service profitability must be jointly managed.

To solve this problem, we propose two types of evolutionary algorithms (EAs). The first is a Genetic Algorithm (GA), a classical metaheuristic that has been widely applied in the field of combinatorial optimisation. The second approach is based on Genetic Programming (GP), which can be considered a variant of the GA. In GP, each chromosome encodes a heuristic in the form of a tree expression, rather than a direct solution to the problem. These heuristics are executed to construct feasible solutions incrementally. As such, GP searches in the space of heuristics rather than the space of solutions. According to the definition proposed by Burke et al. [6], this form of EA falls under the category of hyper-heuristics based on heuristic generation.

The remainder of this paper is structured as follows. Section 2 introduces the formal definition of the EVRP-ZP. Section 3 describes GA and GP. Section 4 presents the experimental study and summarises the results. Finally, Sect. 5 concludes the paper and outlines directions for future research.

2   Problem Definition

We reformulate the classical EVRP formulation introduced by Schneider et al. [2], incorporating features from the VRP-ZP introduced by Afsar et al. [5]. The EVRP-ZP is defined by a fully connected graph $G = (N, E)$, where the node set $N = \{0\} \cup S \cup C$ consists of a single depot, a set of recharging stations (RSs) S, and a set of customers C. Each edge $(n_i, n_j) \in E$ connects two nodes and is characterised by a distance d_{ij}, travel time t_{ij}, and energy consumption e_{ij}, which is proportional to the distance travelled such that $e_{ij} = h \cdot d_{ij}$, where h is the energy consumption rate per unit distance.

The fleet comprises K identical EVs, each with load capacity L and battery capacity Q. As EVs travel, their battery level decreases by the energy consumed moving between nodes, while they may recharge at RSs ($n_j \in S$). These RSs allow a full recharge at a recharging rate g and have unlimited capacity, so that multiple EVs can charge simultaneously without impacting the recharge rate.

Customers $n_i \in C$ have a demand d_i that must be entirely served by a single EV, a service time st_i, and a time window defined by a ready time rt_i and a due date dd_i. EVs arriving before rt_i must wait until service can begin, while arrivals after dd_i are either infeasible or incur penalties depending on whether the time windows are treated as hard or soft constraints. In this work, we have considered the variant with soft time windows.

Building upon this, the customer set is partitioned into Z disjoint zones $C_1, C_2, \ldots, C_Z$ such that $C = \bigcup_{k=1}^{Z} C_k$ and $C_i \cap C_j = \emptyset$ for all $i \neq j$. Each customer $n_i \in C_z$ has a price threshold th_i, and the transporter sets a zone price p_z. A customer is required to be served if the zone price meets or is below their threshold, i.e., if $p_z \leq th_i$.

Each EVs route R_k is a sequence of nodes starting and ending at the depot, expressed as $R_k = (0, n_{k1}, n_{k2}, \ldots, n_{km_k}, 0)$, where intermediate nodes may be customers or RSs. The total demand served on the route must not exceed the capacity of the vehicle, so $\sum_{n_i \in R_k \cap C} d_i \leq L$ for all EVs $1 \leq k \leq K$. When a vehicle visits a RS, it fully recharges its battery to capacity Q. Besides, each customer may be visited by at most one vehicle, and service is mandatory for customers n_i in zone C_z where $p_z \leq th_i$. Additionally, to guarantee coverage, at least one customer per zone must be served for every zone.

The objective of the transporter is to maximise profit, defined as the total revenue from served customers minus the total routing cost measured in energy consumption. Formally, this objective is defined as maximising $\sum_{z=1}^{Z} p_z \sum_{n_i \in C_z} x_i - \sum_{k=1}^{K} \sum_{(n_i, n_j) \in R_k} e_{ij}$, where x_i is a binary variable that takes value 1 if customer n_i is visited and 0 otherwise, and the routing cost of vehicle k corresponds to the total energy consumed along its route.

3   Evolutionary Algorithms

To address the EVRP-ZP, we employ two evolutionary algorithms (EAs), following the approach of related studies [7,8]. The first EA is a GA, which directly searches the solution space by evolving a population of candidate solutions, which are encoded as permutations of customers. The second is a GP approach that functions as a hyper-heuristic, evolving heuristic rules that are used to construct solutions.

The key distinction between GA and GP lies in their chromosome representations. This difference drives their respective genetic operators: GA applies crossover and mutation to segments or positions within customer sequences, whereas GP swaps or mutates subtrees within the expression trees, preserving syntactic correctness.

Algorithm 1. Evolutionary Scheme

1: Generate and evaluate the initial population;
2: **while** the termination condition is not met **do**
3:    **Selection**: organise the chromosomes into pairs of parents at random;
4:    **Recombination**: mate each pair of parents and mutate the two offspring;
5:    **Evaluation**: evaluate the resulting chromosomes;
6:    **Replacement**: perform a tournament selection of two expression trees from every two parents and their offspring to build the population for the next generation;
7: **end while**
8: **return** The best chromosome in the population;

Both GP and GA use the evolutionary scheme summarised in Algorithm 1. It is a generational scheme in which all individuals are randomly grouped into pairs of parents. Each pair of parents is mated to generate two feasible children, which are mutated with a given probability. From the two parents and their children, the best child is always transferred to the next population, whereas the second individual to be transferred is the best between the two parents and the remaining child. Hence, the evolutionary scheme implicitly preserves elitism and helps prevent premature convergence.

Both methods apply the same greedy decoding procedure to determine chromosome fitness, constructing a feasible routing plan from either a customer permutation (GA) or a tree representation (GP). Starting with an empty route, it iteratively selects an unvisited customer and adds it to the route until a feasible solution is constructed. In the case of GP, each chromosome is represented as a tree expression encoding a mathematical expression. This expression is used to determinate a priority value for each unvisited customer, and the customer with the highest priority is chosen to be visited. In contrast, GA represents each chromosome as a permutation of customers that defines the order in which they should be visited.

Once a customer is selected, the decoding algorithm checks whether the vehicle has sufficient remaining load capacity to serve the demand of the customer. If the demand exceeds the available capacity, the current vehicle returns to the depot, and a new vehicle is used. Following, the vehicle must also verify that it has enough energy to reach the destination and then continue to a RS if necessary. If the energy level is sufficient, the vehicles proceeds directly to the destination. Otherwise, it selects the nearest RS to the destination. When this option is not feasible, additional intermediate RSs are used, each chosen as the RS closest to the previously selected one, until a feasible route is built. This route guarantees that the vehicle can reach the destination and subsequently depart toward its next destination.

In addition to determining the routes for each EV, a price must be assigned to each zone. Initially, the zone price is set equal to the highest price threshold among all customers in that zone, ensuring that at least one customer of each zone will be served. For every selected customer, if the customer price threshold is greater than or equal to the current zone price, the customer is served without modifying the zone price. However, if the customer price threshold is lower than the current zone price, the zone price is updated to match this lower threshold.

The decoding algorithm continues to construct the solution in this manner until it becomes feasible. A solution is regarded as feasible if at least one customer from each zone is served and all customers who accept the assigned zone price are included in the routes. Consequently, all customers are visited when all zone prices are set to the lowest customer price threshold within each zone. Otherwise, a smaller number of customers may be served, with the objective of maximising total profit.

4   Experimental Analysis

We carried out an experimental analysis for comparing GP and GA for solving the EVRP-ZP. The algorithms were implemented in Java 8 and executed on a Windows 11 machine equipped with an AMD Ryzen Threadripper 7980X 64-core processor and 256 GB of RAM.

4.1   The Test Bed

We extend the original set of EVRP instances proposed by Schneider et al. [2], which comprises 92 problem instances of varying sizes. The large instances include 100 customers and 21 RSs, while the small ones contain 5, 10, or 15 customers. They are also categorised based on the spatial distribution of customer locations, which can be random, clustered, or a combination of both.

To incorporate pricing and zoning into these instances, we follow the methodology proposed by Afsar et al. [5]. Each customer is assigned to one of p pricing zones depending on their distance from the depot. The distance between the depot and a customer n_i is denoted as c_{0,n_i}, and the maximum such distance across all customers is $c_{\max} = \max_{n_i \in C}\{c_{0,n_i}\}$. The customer is then assigned to zone Z_k, where the zones are constructed so that the range of distances is evenly divided. That is, customers with distances in the first $\frac{1}{p}$ of the interval are assigned to Z_1, those in the next $\frac{1}{p}$ segment to Z_2, and so on, with customers furthest from the depot falling into zone Z_p.

In addition to zoning, each customer $i \in C$ is assigned a price threshold th_i, which represents the minimum price they are willing to pay to be served. This threshold is defined as a linear function of the distance from the depot to the customer, with the scaling coefficient $\beta_i \in [1.6, 2.0]$. This configuration corresponds to the high threshold profile described by Afsar et al. [5].

Considering this setup, we generated a total of 92 EVRP-ZP instances featuring customer sets of 5, 10, 15, and 100 nodes, with three pricing zones and spatial distributions that are random, clustered, or a combination of both. All customers are assigned threshold values according to $\beta_i \in [1.6, 2.0]$ for all $n_i \in C$. For the sake of brevity, we have utilised in this study the large problem instances, with 100 customers and 21 RSs. So, a total of 56 instances were utilised in this experimental study.

4.2 Algorithm Parameters

GP and GA were configured using the parameters listed in Table 1. These values were determined through preliminary experimentation, guided by standard practices and typical settings reported in the literature [7].

Table 1. Parameters used to execute GP and GA.

Parameter name	GP	GA
Initialisation	Ramped half-and-half	Random
Population size	200	100
Crossover operator	Subtree	OX, CX, PMX
Crossover ratio	1.00	0.8
Mutation operator	Subtree	Swap, scramble
Mutation ratio	0.02	0.2
Stopping condition	10 min	

Table 2. The terminal set used to construct the expression trees is defined as follows. The symbol v_k denotes the active vehicle, p_{vk} denotes the current position of vehicle v_k, and n_i denotes the customer destination assigned to vehicle v_k.

Symbol	Description
D_{ni}	Demand of n_i
C_{vk}	Remaining capacity of v_k
DD_{ni}	Due date of n_i
ST_{ni}	Service Time of n_i
RT_{ni}	Ready time of n_i
T_{vk}	Current time of v_k
E_{ni}	Energy required to visit n_i
E_{vk}	Remaining energy of v_k
EC_{ni}	Energy required to visit the centroid from n_i
ERP_{ni}	Energy required to visit the nearest RS from n_i
$EDep_{ni}$	Energy required to visit the depot from n_i
ERP_{pvk}	Energy required to visit the nearest RS from p_{vk}
$EDep_{pvk}$	Energy required to visit the depot from p_{vk}
P_{ni}	Threshold of n_i
PZ_{ni}	Price of the zone of n_i
RZ_{ni}	Revenue in the zone produced by visiting n_i
0.0, 0.1...1.0	Numeric constants between between 0 and 1

In addition to the genetic operators, the set of symbols used in GP to construct the expression trees is summarised in Table 2. This set was designed to capture fundamental aspects of the problem domain and is inspired by previous studies applying GP to both the EVRP [8] and the VRP-ZP [7]. The function set comprises arithmetic and mathematical operators, including $+$, $-$, $\times$, $/$, max, min, pow_2, $\sqrt{}$, exp, and ln. A maximum tree depth of eight was used, and the initial population was generated using the Ramped half-and-half method [9].

4.3   Results

Both GP and GA were executed independently 30 times for each problem instance. The results are summarised in Table 3. We can observe that GP consistently outperforms GA in terms of both the best and average solution quality across all instances. The best solution for every problem instance was always obtained by GP, whereas GA failed to achieve it in any case. This result is consistent with previous results in the VRPZP [7], where GP also outperformed GA in the majority of cases.

For a more detailed analysis, Fig. 1 illustrates the convergence patterns of GP and GA across 18 randomly selected problem instances. As observed, the solutions produced by GP consistently outperform those generated by GA throughout the evolutionary process. Notably, the initial solutions generated by GP are superior even to the best solutions achieved by GA after ten minutes of computation. This trend holds for the majority of the 18 instances analysed, with the exception of four cases: r208, rc202, rc205, and rc208. This is unsurprising, as the initial population of GP may include chromosomes encoding simple but effective heuristics, such as the nearest neighbour. These heuristics can produce reasonably good solutions for large instances with 100 customers, whereas GA, starting from random permutations, is unlikely to achieve comparable results within the same time limit due to the vast search space.

The figures also indicate that GP generally converges within the allotted time, whereas GA may require a longer runtime to reach convergence. Consequently, GA could potentially improve its performance by employing alternative genetic operators to enhance exploration of the search space, for instance through the incorporation of local search procedures. Overall, these results suggest that GP exploits the greedy decoding algorithm more effectively than GA. It would therefore be worthwhile to investigate alternative evaluation procedures that are better suited to permutation-based representations.

Table 3. Comparison of GA and GP performance. Std is the standard deviation.

Instance	GA				GP			
	Max	Mean	Min	Std	Max	Mean	Min	Std
c101	718.69	543.44	327.63	137.53	**1466.13**	1249.73	1067.57	142.94
c102	878.13	634.95	222.70	148.79	**1502.79**	1260.96	1034.31	137.81
c103	817.57	621.79	412.32	127.91	**1738.10**	1522.19	1324.32	128.02
c104	1074.99	662.62	324.44	241.80	**1529.32**	1255.27	1027.76	159.01
c105	887.23	759.30	568.08	116.60	**1602.26**	1330.05	945.96	181.44
c106	1150.59	809.15	266.29	212.07	**1764.79**	1477.12	1156.92	207.71
c107	930.21	635.83	379.18	167.39	**1427.22**	1173.75	1005.49	143.47
c108	684.95	449.19	401.93	75.14	**1417.78**	1106.96	970.06	147.14
c109	894.04	651.64	260.97	168.20	**1465.80**	1279.03	936.09	161.23
c201	1341.17	1196.98	797.98	112.61	**1879.22**	1577.13	1300.66	219.09
c202	1454.94	1297.17	774.96	152.59	**1840.55**	1704.73	1602.02	74.02
c203	1352.32	1156.41	937.67	104.87	**1585.35**	1553.73	1513.40	11.11
c204	1246.28	978.53	517.50	193.20	**1720.61**	1532.49	1430.99	77.76
c205	1432.44	1303.26	899.12	128.57	**1831.27**	1601.47	1464.02	103.75
c206	1348.64	1158.40	837.49	136.62	**1727.54**	1431.92	1383.92	87.59
c207	1305.35	1187.87	1140.67	45.55	**1945.58**	1610.30	1292.23	268.59
c208	1469.32	1185.82	952.95	117.42	**2002.18**	1639.21	1334.21	258.35
r101	574.66	517.40	261.18	60.14	**1160.75**	1041.95	655.85	126.68
r102	708.39	422.32	343.57	77.59	**1245.87**	1133.66	687.35	109.94
r103	649.24	476.81	367.30	77.10	**1087.59**	976.78	772.72	109.34
r104	802.77	542.14	409.44	124.98	**1239.22**	1110.89	748.22	151.92
r105	607.87	439.37	363.16	81.56	**1234.51**	1107.56	785.62	125.23
r106	562.24	429.73	287.67	77.34	**1206.13**	1034.61	693.09	140.27
r107	780.74	540.48	380.54	141.94	**1237.02**	1079.70	753.13	106.89
r108	754.81	551.62	247.76	144.53	**1423.24**	1291.70	812.12	113.86
r109	474.67	391.13	264.34	53.57	**1233.02**	1046.06	899.73	127.67
r110	799.21	536.86	427.12	112.90	**1297.58**	1177.10	737.30	116.95
r111	881.87	595.08	385.97	169.50	**1371.23**	1206.19	813.47	154.09
r112	910.91	533.50	389.81	126.66	**1521.95**	1320.55	955.42	172.96
r201	1222.55	1015.87	786.06	111.84	**1460.70**	1230.81	1080.96	131.17
r202	1084.66	1033.52	963.98	29.50	**1355.62**	1198.56	1158.84	46.63
r203	1062.14	812.06	495.84	147.12	**1406.95**	1181.02	1067.70	107.50
r204	1304.73	1185.01	886.80	120.20	**1611.54**	1396.74	1283.86	112.11
r205	1111.99	701.11	183.28	236.17	**1521.70**	1303.12	1068.32	152.98
r206	931.42	710.45	585.48	55.13	**1255.93**	1074.41	996.20	85.22
r207	1278.07	1171.32	949.47	99.56	**1574.57**	1308.96	1097.93	158.73
r208	1395.46	1192.72	540.95	188.01	**1438.77**	1270.77	984.01	129.51
r209	1021.31	909.40	817.46	41.96	**1393.59**	1228.96	1022.88	117.78
r210	1257.44	1023.08	617.22	164.58	**1403.85**	1213.39	1041.27	140.54
r211	1044.47	906.39	697.79	120.29	**1173.11**	1136.46	1087.02	18.96
rc101	1161.57	745.09	466.34	166.96	**1891.77**	1608.60	1248.40	252.11
rc102	912.08	587.13	324.08	198.94	**1645.74**	1395.23	1128.30	153.46
rc103	1004.76	625.51	407.80	177.00	**1803.47**	1553.68	1171.15	216.07
rc104	1285.75	751.75	461.63	207.55	**1662.76**	1443.23	926.63	186.51
rc105	1433.28	1156.64	541.81	207.94	**1771.26**	1531.78	1293.88	161.31
rc106	1380.87	909.90	540.79	202.70	**1928.25**	1698.15	1150.30	245.74
rc107	1693.70	1175.87	709.82	273.88	**1996.38**	1629.08	1252.74	302.70
rc108	907.96	655.94	486.07	104.10	**1696.18**	1510.25	1329.93	104.33
rc201	1254.42	1224.54	1082.94	37.45	**2007.11**	1930.39	1774.56	47.72
rc202	2036.53	1761.75	1276.30	161.66	**2304.89**	2136.37	1575.34	141.18
rc203	1877.29	1626.04	1209.50	167.98	**2137.97**	1932.88	1582.75	167.49
rc204	1923.29	1631.50	1095.13	206.96	**2383.24**	1986.05	1586.57	295.72
rc205	2126.21	1752.68	1282.48	248.60	**2197.49**	1994.36	1402.04	244.86
rc206	1960.79	1748.90	1483.56	137.04	**2147.41**	1920.18	1656.59	172.84
rc207	2072.19	1429.88	853.34	349.83	**2242.90**	1953.79	1646.32	231.25
rc208	1961.53	1646.27	1008.79	219.33	**2275.95**	1937.93	1504.77	292.16

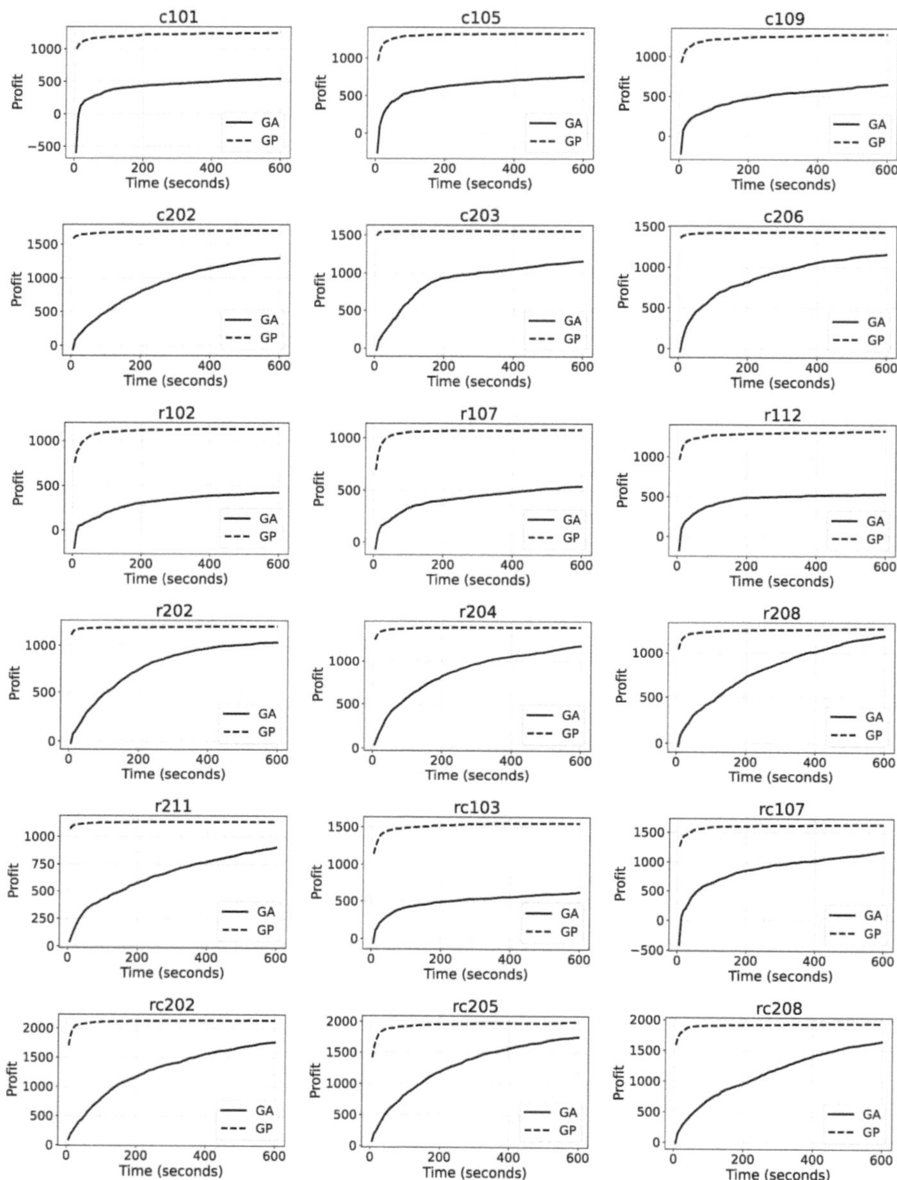

Fig. 1. Convergence of GP and GA in 10 min for 18 problem instances

5   Conclusions and Future Work

In this paper, we have introduced a new variant of a VRP, motivated by environmental concerns and the growing adoption of EVs together with zone-based pricing. This problem, termed EVRP-ZP, was initially addressed using two evolutionary algorithms: GP and GA. Overall, the experimental results demonstrate that GP substantially outperforms GA across all problem instances, both in terms of the best and average results.

Future research will aim to enhance both GP and GA by incorporating additional genetic operators, such as local search procedures [10], to further improve their performance. Furthermore, it would be of interest to examine alternative variants of the problem in which multiple objectives are optimised simultaneously, for instance, by seeking to minimise the number of vehicles employed or the total tardiness incurred [8], among other optimisation criteria.

Acknowledgements. This work has been partly supported by the Croatian Science Foundation under project IP-2022-10-5398, the NextGenerationEU under NPOO.C3.2.R2-11.06.0110, the NextGenerationEU framework through the project "DEEPWAVE" at the University of Zagreb Faculty of Electrical Engineering and Computing, the Spanish Government under project MCINN-23-PID2022-141746OB-I00, and by the Principality of Asturias under project IDE/2024/000696.

References

1. Toth, P., Vigo, D.: Vehicle Routing, Society for Industrial and Applied Mathematics, Philadelphia, PA (2014). https://doi.org/10.1137/1.9781611973594
2. Schneider, M., Stenger, A., Goeke, D.: The electric vehicle-routing problem with time windows and recharging stations. Transp. Sci. **48**, 500–520 (2014). https://doi.org/10.1287/trsc.2013.0490
3. Lin, J., Zhou, W., Wolfson, O.: Electric vehicle routing problem. Transp. Res. Procedia **12**, 508–521 (2016). https://doi.org/10.1016/j.trpro.2016.02.007
4. EEA, European environment agency: greenhouse gas emissions from transport in Europe (2022). https://www.eea.europa.eu/ims/greenhouse-gas-emissions-from-transport
5. Afsar, H.M., Afsar, S., Palacios, J.J.: Vehicle routing problem with zone-based pricing. Transp. Res. Part E: Logistics Transp. Rev. **152**, 102383 (2021). https://doi.org/10.1016/j.tre.2021.102383
6. Burke, E.K., Hyde, M.R., Kendall, G., Ochoa, G., Özcan, E., Woodward, J.R.: A classification of hyper-heuristic approaches: revisited, pp. 453–477. Springer International Publishing, Cham (2019). https://doi.org/10.1007/978-3-319-91086-4_14
7. Gil-Gala, F.J., Afsar, S., Đurasević, M., Palacios, J.J., Afsar, M.: Genetic programming for the vehicle routing problem with zone-based pricing. In: Proceedings of the Genetic and Evolutionary Computation Conference (GECCO), pp. 1118–1126 (2023). https://doi.org/10.1145/3583131.3590366
8. Gil-Gala, F.J., Đurasević, M., Jakobović, D.: Evolving routing policies for electric vehicles by means of genetic programming. Appl. Intell. (2024). https://doi.org/10.1007/s10489-024-05803-5
9. Koza, J.R.: Genetic Programming: On the Programming of Computers by Means of Natural Selection. MIT Press (1992)
10. Gil-Gala, F.J., Sierra, M.R., Mencía, C., Varela, R.: Genetic programming with local search to evolve priority rules for scheduling jobs on a machine with time-varying capacity. Swarm Evol. Comput. **66**, 100944 (2021). https://doi.org/10.1016/j.swevo.2021.100944

Memetic Algorithm for the Scientific Workflow Scheduling Problem with a Disk-Network-Computation Model

Pelayo González-García, María R. Sierra, Jorge Puente,
and Francisco Javier Gil-Gala[✉]

University of Oviedo, Gijón, Spain
{gonzalezgpelayo,sierramaria,puente,giljavier}@uniovi.es

Abstract. Scheduling scientific workflows in cloud computing environments, taking infrastructure provisioning into account, represents a complex optimisation problem, where minimising the total workflow completion time is a primary objective. This problem is computationally challenging, and metaheuristic methods such as genetic algorithms have been widely employed to obtain approximate solutions. In this study, an alternative approach based on a local search algorithm is proposed, employing four neighbourhood structures. These structures operate on the ordering of task assignments to virtual machines, enabling efficient exploration of the solution space through small, targeted modifications. A hybrid metaheuristic, known as a memetic algorithm, is used, combining the global search capabilities of genetic algorithms with the local refinement provided by the proposed local search. Experimental results demonstrate that the memetic algorithm produces competitive results compared with traditional genetic algorithms.

Keywords: evolutionary algorithm · local search algorithm · scientific workflow · cloud computing

1 Introduction

Cloud computing has emerged as a dominant model for delivering computing services, offering virtualised, scalable and dynamically allocated resources through the internet. Among its service models, Infrastructure as a Service (IaaS) plays a key role by allowing users to provision and manage virtual machines (VMs), storage and networking components on demand and based on actual usage. The flexibility, cost efficiency and rapid deployment provided by IaaS make it particularly suitable for applications requiring significant computational power, such as the execution of scientific workflows [1].

Scientific workflows consist of numerous interdependent tasks that process large volumes of data. These tasks vary in size and complexity, and their execution time may range from a few minutes to several days. This variation depends on both the structure of the workflow, which may contain hundreds or thousands of tasks, and the performance characteristics of the cloud infrastructure, which typically includes heterogeneous resources. For researchers, it is essential to minimise both execution time and the cost associated with renting computation infrastructure. In this context, one of the most important Quality of Service (QoS) indicators is the makespan, which refers to the time required to complete the entire workflow [2].

To manage and automate workflow execution on distributed resources, a Workflow Management System (WMS) is commonly employed [3]. One of its primary responsibilities is to schedule tasks efficiently across the available VMs. However, the scheduling problem in cloud computing environments is classified as NP complete [4], which justifies the use of approximate solution methods such as heuristics and metaheuristics. Among these, Genetic Algorithms (GAs) have received considerable attention due to their effectiveness in generating high quality schedules within reasonable computational effort [2].

This work proposes a Local Search Algorithm (LSA) for a scientific workflow scheduling problem under a realistic evaluation model that accounts for computation, network delays, and both local and remote disk I/O [5]. The LSA explores the solution space by applying four neighbourhood structures. It is motivated by its efficiency in refining solutions within complex combinatorial spaces. While global metaheuristics like GAs excel at broad exploration, they often lack precision in exploiting high-quality regions. The LSA complements this by iteratively improving solutions through targeted modifications. This is particularly valuable in task scheduling, where small changes can greatly affect performance. In addition to the LSA, we propose a memetic algorithm (MA), which combines the global search strengths of GAs with the local refinement capabilities of the LSA. In this approach, a subset of individuals from the GA population undergoes improvement via the local search procedure. This integration enhances the balance between diversification and intensification, resulting in improved solution quality, particularly in terms of makespan reduction.

The remainder of this paper is structured as follows. Section 2 introduces the formal definition of the scientific workflow scheduling problem considered. Section 3 describes the algorithms considered as solving methods. Section 4 presents the experimental study and summarise the results. Finally, Sect. 5 concludes the paper and outlines directions for future research.

2   The Scientific Workflow Scheduling Problem

Scientific workflows are commonly used in computational science to represent applications composed of multiple interdependent tasks. These workflows are typically modelled as a Directed Acyclic Graph (DAG), where nodes represent tasks and edges define data and precedence constraints. A task begins execution only when all its predecessors have completed and their output data is available. This structure is well-suited to many scientific applications in fields, such as bioinformatics [6].

Formally, a workflow is represented as a graph $G = (T, A)$, where $T = \{t_1, t_2, ..., t_n\}$ is the set of tasks, and $A \subseteq T \times T$ is the set of dependencies. Each task t_i is associated with a computational size in GFLOPs[1], and each edge (t_i, t_j) is labelled with the size of the data to be transferred, usually in megabytes (MBs). Two dummy tasks, t_{entry} and t_{exit}, represent the start and end points of a workflow, with no computation or data transfer.

The cloud infrastructure is composed of a set of heterogeneous VMs, $M = \{vm_1, vm_2, ..., vm_m\}$, each defined by a tuple $\langle pc, nb, ds \rangle$, where pc is the processing capacity in GFLOPs, nb is the network bandwidth in MBs/sec, and ds is the disk read/write speed in MB/sec.

The goal of the scheduling problem is to assign each task to a VM and determine an execution order $\mathcal{O}$ that satisfies all dependencies while minimising the makespan, defined as the estimated finish time of t_{exit}. We aim to find a schedule $S = (\mathcal{H}, \mathcal{O})$, where $\mathcal{H}$ maps tasks to VMs and $\mathcal{O}$ provides a valid topological ordering of T.

The most common model to evaluate a schedule is the Network-Computation (NC) [7,8], which considers only computation and network data transfer times. In this model, the computation time of a task t_i on vm_k is calculated as $ct_i^k = size(t_i)/pc_k$, and the data transfer time between t_i and t_j (if scheduled on different machines) is $dt_{i,j}^{k,l} = data(i,j)/\min(nb_k, nb_l)$. If both tasks are scheduled on the same machine, this transfer time is assumed to be zero. The estimated finish time (EFT) is then the sum of the estimated start time (EST) and computation time (ct), i.e., $EFT(t_i, vm_k) = EST(t_i, vm_k) + ct_i^k$. The estimated starting time is $EST(t_i, vm_k) = avail\left(i, k, \max_{t_j \in pred(t_i)}(EFT(t_j, vm_l) + dt_{j,i}^{l,k})\right)$, with $avail(i, k, m)$ giving the earliest insertion-based slot on vm_k after m.

However, the NC model may not be accurate for data-intensive workflows. We therefore adopt a more realistic model: the Disk-Network-Computation (DNC) model proposed in [5]. This includes local and remote disk I/O in addition to computation and network delays. When two tasks are assigned to the same VM, data transfer involves reading from local disk, taking time $dt_{i,j}^{k,k} = data(i,j)/ds_k$. If they are assigned to different VMs, the transfer time becomes $dt_{i,j}^{k,l} = data(i,j)/\min(ds_k, nb_k, nb_l)$. In this model, the finish time of a task includes input and output operations: $EFT(t_i, vm_k) = EST(t_i, vm_k) + input_{i,k} + ct_i^k + output_{i,k}$, where $input_{i,k}$ aggregates transfer times from all predecessors and $output_{i,k}$ accounts for saving all generated data to disk, computed as $\sum_{t_j \in succ(t_i)} data(i,j)/ds_k$, and $EST(t_i, vm_k) = avail\left(i, k, \max_{t_j \in pred(t_i)} EFT(t_j, vm_l)\right)$.

3   Methods

This study addresses a scientific workflow scheduling problem using two algorithmic strategies. The first is a GA, used as a baseline for comparison and based

---

[1] GFLOPs stands for Giga Floating-Point Operations per second.

on previous studies [2,5]. The second is an LSA, developed to improve individual solutions through iterative refinement. To combine their strengths, a MA is proposed in this work, which integrates the global search of the GA with the local optimisation of the LSA.

3.1 Fitness Evaluation

All solutions are evaluated using the execution model described earlier. Similar to other studies [7,9], each individual encodes a complete solution as a permutation of workflow tasks arranged in topological order. Scheduling is performed using an insertion-based policy that assigns each task to the earliest available slot on a VM, while ensuring all task dependencies are met.

3.2 Genetic Algorithm

The GA used in this study is a generational evolutionary algorithm. The genetic operators are defined as follows. During selection, individuals are randomly paired. Then, the crossover is performed using the Order Crossover (OX) operator [2,7]. This crossover operator selects a random crossover point, takes the initial subsequence from one parent, and fills the remaining positions with tasks from the other parent while preserving their relative order, ensuring that all task dependencies are maintained. The mutation operator randomly selects a task, identifies a subsequence excluding its predecessors and successors, relocates the task to a valid position within this subsequence, and reassigns it to a different VM. The two best individuals from each group of parents and offspring set proceed to the next generation. The initial population is generated randomly, with all chromosomes respecting task dependencies and valid VM assignments. Further details are provided in [2].

3.3 Local Search Algorithm

The LSA employed in this work is summarised in Algorithm 1. It iteratively refines a solution until a stopping criterion is satisfied, such as a maximum number of iterations or the absence of further improvement. The procedure begins from an initial solution s. At each iteration, a set of neighbours is generated using a collection of neighbourhood structures $\mathcal{N}$, and an acceptance criterion determines whether a neighbour s' replaces the current solution s. In this study, a Hill Climbing (HC) strategy is adopted [10], in which neighbours are examined sequentially and the first improving is accepted.

All neighbourhood structures are applied at each iteration. For a given solution, the complete set of neighbouring solutions is generated, but evaluated in a randomised order. The implementation is optimised through lazy evaluation[2]. We consider the following four neighbourhood structures:

---

[2] Implemented using jMetal [11] and Java Streams, which generate and evaluate neighbouring solutions only when required.

- $\mathcal{N}_1$: For a given task $t_i \in T$, let $vm_k = \mathcal{H}(t_i)$ denote its current machine assignment. This operator generates neighbouring schedules by reassigning t_i to every alternative machine $vm_l \in M \setminus \{vm_k\}$, keeping the task ordering fixed. It is the unique neighbourhood operator that explicitly requires knowledge of the infrastructure set M.
- $\mathcal{N}_2$: Given a position p in the topological ordering, let $t_i = \mathcal{O}[p]$. This operator relocates t_i to another valid position $p' \neq p$, such that the resulting ordering $\mathcal{O}'$ remains a valid topological order. All tasks between positions p and p' are shifted accordingly.
- $\mathcal{N}_3$: Let $t_i, t_j \in T$ be two tasks such that swapping their positions in $\mathcal{O}$ yields another valid topological ordering. The operator $\mathcal{N}_3$ generates a neighbour by exchanging the positions of such pairs in $\mathcal{O}$.
- $\mathcal{N}_4$: This operator is a variant of $\mathcal{N}_3$, where instead of swapping task positions, the host assignments of two tasks $t_i, t_j \in T$ are exchanged, while preserving their positions in $\mathcal{O}$.

Algorithm 1. Local Search Algorithm (LSA)

```
1:  improved ← true
2:  while the stopping criterion has not been met and improved do
3:      s* ← s
4:      improved ← false
5:      for all neighbour s' of s using N do
6:          Evaluate s'
7:          if s' is better than s then
8:              s* ← s'
9:              improved ← true
10:             break # Go to line 12
11:         end if
12:     end for
13:     if improved then
14:         s ← s*
15:     end if
16: end while
17: return s*
```

All the above neighbourhood structures guarantee that the resulting neighbours remain feasible, meaning they satisfy all task dependencies as specified by the DAG. Notably, these neighbourhood structures operate through small yet systematic modifications directly applied to the chromosome representation, i.e., the genotype, rather than altering the phenotype. By manipulating the genotype, the search process preserves structural consistency and allows for efficient evaluation of neighbouring solutions without the necessity of explicitly decoding or interpreting phenotypic traits.

3.4 Memetic Algorithm

The hybrid algorithm, referred to as the MA, follows a generational scheme similar to the GA described above while incorporating the LSA as an additional operator. The overall procedure is summarised in Algorithm 2. At each generation, after selection, crossover, mutation, and survivor selection, the LSA is applied to the population (Line 7). To avoid excessive intensification and to allow the MA to evolve over multiple generations, the number of LSA iterations is limited and the LSA is applied only to a subset of the population. We denote by MA_e the variant in which the LSA is applied exclusively to the elitist individual, and by MA_p the variant in which it is applied to a $p\%$ of individuals of the population, which are selected randomly.

Algorithm 2. Memetic Algorithm (MA)

1: Initialise and evaluate a population P_0;
2: **while** the stopping criterion has not been met **do**
3:    Randomly select pairs of parents from the current population P_t
4:    Perform crossover on each pair to generate two offspring
5:    Apply mutation to each offspring with a given probability
6:    From each group of two parents and their two offspring, select the best two to form P_{t+1}
7:    Apply LSA on P_{t+1} with a given probability
8: **end while**
9: **return** The best individual found

---

4 Results

In this section, we present an empirical experimental study in which the performance of GA and MA is compared. All algorithms were implemented using the JMetal framework [11]. The experiments were conducted on a target machine equipped with a AMD EPYC 9654. To ensure the comparability of results, GA and MA were executed under the same stopping criterion, namely a time limit of 60 min per run. Each experimental configuration was run independently 30 times to account for the stochastic nature of the algorithms.

The test bed used in this study consists of 21 problem instances selected from WFCommons, a repository of real scientific workflow executions. Specifically, for seven workflow families, seismology, cycles, epigenomics, srasearch, montage, soykb and 1000genome, three problem instances were selected. In all cases, the experiments were conducted on an architecture composed of 16 hosts. Further details about the test bed can be found in [2].

The GA was parametrised following previous studies [2,5], using a crossover probability of 100%, a mutation probability of 10%, and a population size of 100. The MA limits the number of LSA iterations to 3 and, in the case of MA_p, uses $p = 5$. The results are summarised in Fig. 1 and are ordered according to the communication-to-computation ratio (CCR), ranging from compute-intensive to data-intensive.

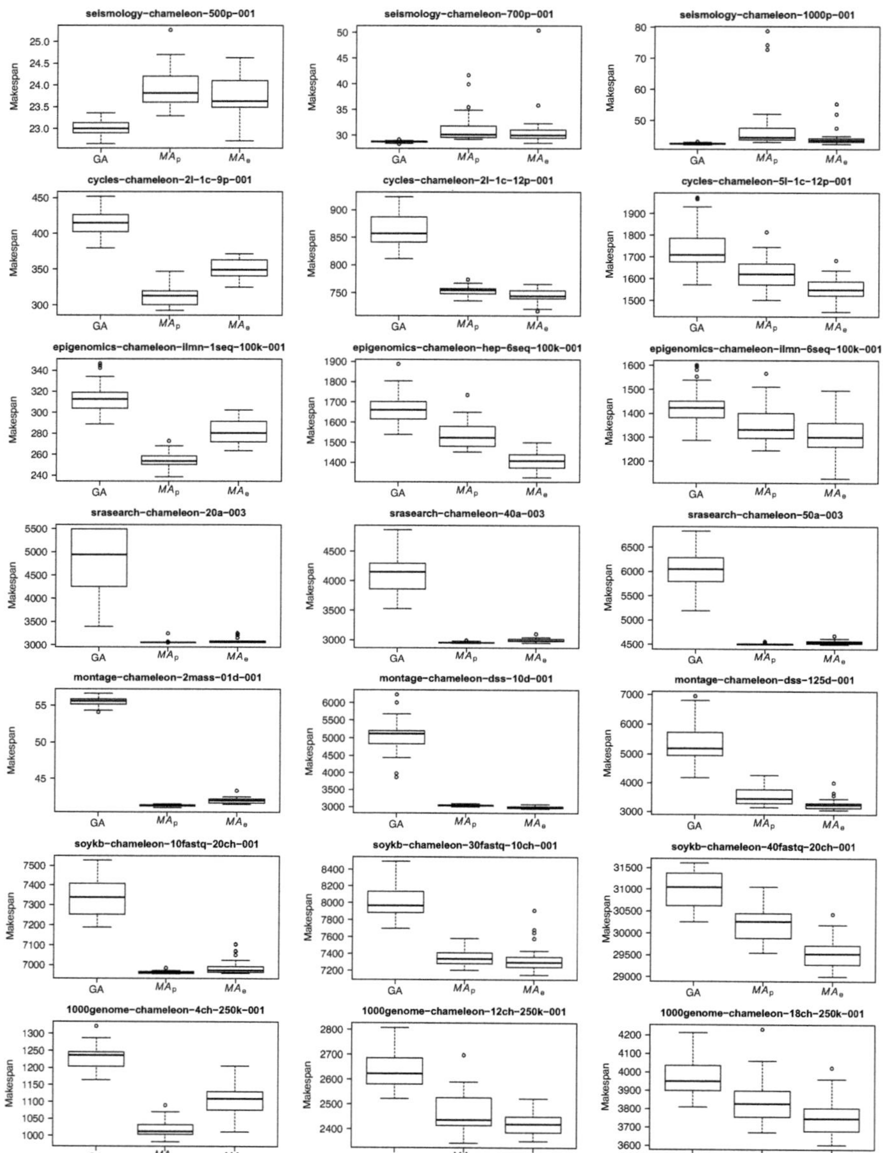

Fig. 1. Summary of the results obtained by GA, MA_e and MA_p. p with value 5 is considered. On top of each figure is shown the problem instance name.

Overall, the results indicate that MA consistently outperforms GA. Both MA variants achieve usually better best and median values than GA across the problem instances, with the exception of the seismology family. In total, MA outperforms GA in 18 of the 21 problem instances considered. When comparing the

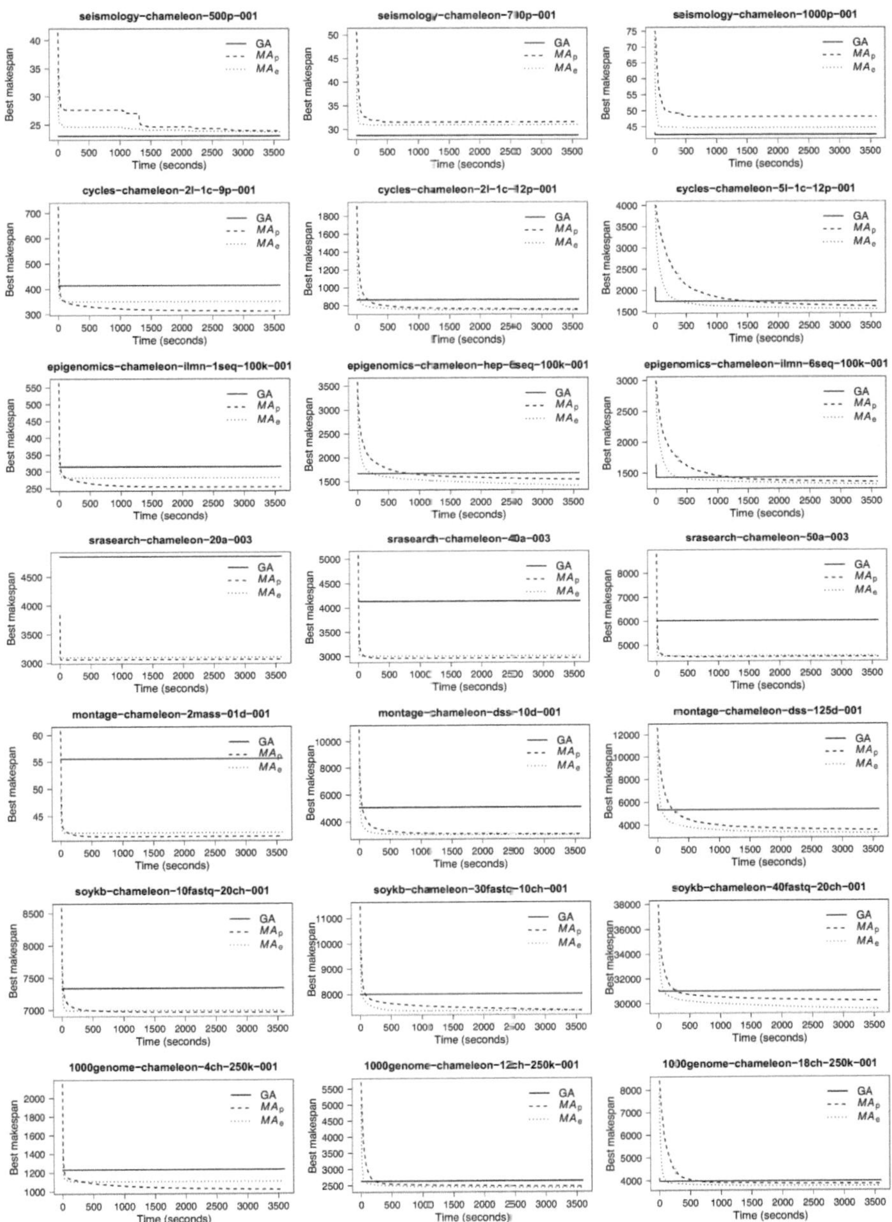

Fig. 2. Convergence of GA, MA_e and MA_p. p with value 5 is considered. On top of each figure is shown the problem instance name.

two MA variants, their performance varies depending on the problem instance, and no clear overall winner emerges. Specifically, MA_e performs better on the epigenomics-chameleon-hep-6seq-100k-001 and soykb-chameleon-40fastq-20ch-001 instances, whereas MA_p yields superior results on 1000genome-chameleon-4ch-250k-001, cycles-chameleon-2l-1c-9p-001, and epigenomics-chameleon-ilmn-1seq-100k-001. For the remaining instances, the performance of both variants is largely comparable.

The Friedman test revealed statistically significant differences between GA and MA at $\alpha = 0.05$. Post-hoc Conover tests with Bonferroni correction showed that both MA variants differed significantly from GA, while no significant difference was observed between the two MA variants.

Figure 2 shows the convergence behaviour of GA and MA over 60 min, averaged over 30 independent runs. GA typically converges within the first few seconds, resulting in flat convergence curves for most instances, except for larger problems such as cycles-chameleon-5l-1c-12p-001 and epigenomics-chameleon-ilmn-6seq-100k-001. In contrast, MA converges more gradually, particularly MA_p, which often requires more time. The MA_e variant generally converges faster and achieves better solutions, though it exhibits premature convergence in some instances (e.g., epigenomics-chameleon-ilmn-1seq-100k-001).

5   Conclusions

In this paper, we tackle a scientific workflow scheduling problem under a realistic Disk-Network-Computation model, which accounts for computation, network delays, and local and remote disk I/O. Two evolutionary algorithms are compared: a GA from the literature [2] and a MA that enhances the GA with a novel LSA. The proposed LSA uses four neighbourhood structures to intensively explore the solution space while respecting task dependencies and virtual machine assignments. Experimental results demonstrate that the MA consistently outperforms the GA across most problem instances analysed in this study.

Future research will focus on extending the experimental analysis presented in this study. In particular, alternative strategies for integrating GA and LSA will be explored to enhance their combined effectiveness, and alternative solution approaches, including hyper-heuristics, such as Genetic Programming [13], will also be considered.

Acknowledgements. This work has been partly supported by the Spanish Government under project MCINN-23-PID2022-141746OB-I00, and by the Principality of Asturias under project IDE/2024/000696.

References

1. Rajasekar, P., Palanichamy, Y.: Scheduling multiple scientific workflows using containers on iaas cloud. J. Ambient. Intell. Humaniz. Comput. **12**(7), 7621–7636 (2021)

2. Barredo, P., Puente, J.: Precise makespan optimization via hybrid genetic algorithm for scientific workflow scheduling problem. Nat. Comput. **22**(4), 615–630 (2023)
3. Deelman, E., et al.: Pegasus, a workflow management system for science automation. Futur. Gener. Comput. Syst. **46**, 17–35 (2015)
4. Madni, S.H.H., et al.: Performance comparison of heuristic algorithms for task scheduling in IaaS cloud computing environment. PLoS ONE **12**(5), 1–26 (2017)
5. Barredo, P., Puente, J.: . Robust Makespan Optimization via Genetic Algorithms on the Scientific Workflow Scheduling Problem. In: Ferrández Vicente, J.M., Álvarez-Sánchez, J.R., de la Paz López, F., Adeli, H. (eds.) Bio-inspired Systems and Applications: from Robotics to Ambient Intelligence. IWINAC 2022. Lecture Notes in Computer Science, vol. 13259. Springer, Cham (2022). https://doi.org/10.1007/978-3-031-06527-9_8
6. Djaffardjy, M., et al.: Developing and reusing bioinformatics data analysis pipelines using scientific workflow systems. Comput. Struct. Biotechnol. J. **21**, 2075–2085 (2023)
7. Zhu, Z., Zhang, G., Li, M., Liu, X.: Evolutionary multi-objective workflow scheduling in cloud. IEEE Trans. Parallel Distrib. Syst. **27**(5), 1344–1357 (2016)
8. Durillo, J.J., Nae, V., Prodan, R.: Multi-objective energy-efficient workflow scheduling using list-based heuristics. Futur. Gener. Comput. Syst. **36**, 221–236 (2014)
9. Ye, X., Li, J., Liu, S., Liang, J., Jin, Y.: A hybrid instance-intensive workflow scheduling method in private cloud environment. Nat. Comput. **18**(4), 735–746 (2019)
10. Gil-Gala, F.J., Mencía, C., Sierra, M.R., Varela, R.: Learning ensembles of priority rules for online scheduling by hybrid evolutionary algorithms, integrated computer aided. Engineering **28**, 65–80 (2021)
11. Durillo, J.J., Nebro, A.J.: jmetal: A java framework for multi-objective optimization. Adv. Eng. Softw. **42**(10), 760–771 (2011)
12. Coleman, T., Casanova, H., Pottier, L., Kaushik, M., Deelman, E., da Silva, R.F.: Wfcommons: a framework for enabling scientific workflow research and development. Futur. Gener. Comput. Syst. **128**, 16–27 (2022)
13. Gil-Gala, F.J., Durasević, M., Jakobović, D.: Genetic programming for electric vehicle routing problem with soft time windows. In: Proceedings of the Genetic and Evolutionary Computation Conference Companion, p. 105782 (2022)

Non-dominated Sorting Genetic Programming for Solving a Bi-objective Bin Packing Problem

Jesús Quesada[1], María R. Sierra[1], Marko Đurasević[2], Ramiro Varela[1],
and Francisco Javier Gil-Gala[1(✉)]

[1] University of Oviedo, Gijón, Spain
{quesadajesus,sierramaria,ramiro,giljavier}@uniovi.es
[2] University of Zagreb, Zagreb, Croatia
Marko.Durasevic@fer.hr

Abstract. The Bin Packing Problem is a combinatorial optimisation problem in which a set of items must be packed into bins while minimising some objective function, usually the number of bins used. This paper examines a variant of practical interest that, instead of focusing solely on spatial resources, aims to optimise temporal resources as well. Existing approaches typically address both objectives through a weighted linear fitness function, combining them via a weighted sum. In this work, we investigate the use of Genetic Programming (GP) to automatically design heuristics in the form of greedy algorithms. As a novel contribution, we integrate GP with NSGA-II to produce a set of non-dominated heuristics that capture different trade-offs between spatial and temporal resources. The results demonstrate that the proposed approach can cover the solution space more comprehensively than GP applied to each criterion independently.

Keywords: genetic programming · bin packing problem · multiobjective optimisation

1   Introduction

The Bin Packing Problem (BPP) is an NP-hard combinatorial optimisation problem. Its classical form considers a set of items, each with an associated weight, that must be packed into bins of identical capacity [1]. The aim is to minimise the number of bins used, subject to the constraints that every item is assigned to exactly one bin and that the total weight in each bin does not exceed its capacity. Despite its long history, the BPP remains highly relevant due to its numerous industrial applications, including production planning, logistics, and cutting and packing operations, such as in the plastic film industry [2]. As a result, many solution approaches and problem variants continue to be proposed, which keeps the BPP an active area of research.

J. M. Ferrández Vicente et al. (Eds.): IWINAC 2026, LNCS 16575, pp. 226–236, 2026.
https://doi.org/10.1007/978-3-032-27317-8_22

Recent variants extend the traditional BPP by incorporating additional optimisation criteria, including time-related features. One such example is the formulation introduced by Arbib and Marinelli [3]. In this variant, the number of bins used is minimised together with the maximum lateness, which leads to the problem known as BPP with Waste and Maximum Lateness (BPP-WML) [4].

The authors of [3] first proposed an exact method based on column generation, known as Price and Branch(P&B). This method systematically computes upper and lower bounds, and it obtains optimal solutions whenever both bounds coincide. The approach performs very well on small problem instances, where optimality can often be proven. However, as the number of items increases, the required time increases exponentially.

To address this limitation, Quesada et al. [5] studied the use of packing policies (PPs) implemented as greedy algorithms. They compared classical heuristics, such as the First Fit (FF) and Best Fit (BF) [1], with heuristics automatically generated through Genetic Programming (GP).

GP is a widely used method for the automatic design of heuristics for a variety of optimisation problems, such as scheduling and vehicle routing [6]. One of the key advantages of GP is that the resulting model, the heuristics evolved, can be interpreted by humans, as heuristics are represented as a mathematical expression encoded as an expression tree. In contrast, other models, such as neural networks, often fail to produce interpretable solutions and they are typically less efficient than GP [7]. For these reasons, GP is typically considered as the most suitable methodology for the automatic design of heuristics.

In [4], the PPs evolved using GP significantly outperformed both manually designed PPs and standard genetic algorithms. This demonstrates the capacity of GP to produce effective heuristics for the BPP that simultaneously optimise the number of bins and the maximum lateness. In several instances, the heuristics generated by GP even matched the solutions produced by the P&B algorithm proposed in [3].

However, a limitation of the PPs produced in [5] is the risk of overfitting to particular types of instances or specific optimisation criteria. The fitness function defined in [3,5] assigns equal importance to both objectives. These fixed weights, constrain the search to a single compromise between the objectives. As a consequence, GP may fail to explore other regions of the solution space that may also be desirable in practice.

In this work, we extend the GP framework introduced in [5] by incorporating the non-dominated sorting procedure used in the NSGA-II algorithm [8]. The motivation for adopting NSGA-II is to allow GP to treat the two objectives independently rather than combining them through a single weighted sum. This enables the discovery of a diverse set of PPs that represent different trade-off levels between the number of bins and the maximum lateness. Furthermore, the non-dominated sorting mechanism encourages the identification of PPs that are not dominated with respect to either objective, which improves the overall quality and robustness of the resulting PPs set.

The remainder of this paper is organised as follows. Section 2 provides the formal definition of the BPP-WML. Section 4 details how NSGA-II is integrated within the GP framework. Section 5 presents the experimental study and summarises the results. Finally, Sect. 6 concludes the paper and outlines future research directions.

2   Problem Definition

The Bin Packing Problem with simultaneous minimisation of waste and maximum lateness, denoted as BPP-WML, is a multi-objective version of the problem introduced by Arbib et al. [3]. This variant incorporates both spatial and temporal dimensions, capturing operational constraints commonly encountered in industrial settings, such as, for example, in cloud computing [9].

Let $I = \{1, \dots, n\}$ be a set of n items, each one characterised by a width w_j, $0 < w_j \leq C$, and a due date $d_j \geq 0$, which must be assigned to a set of bins $B = \{1, \dots, m\}$ each one with capacity C. Assigning item $j \in I$ to bin $i \in B$ results in a completion time of $i, 1 \leq i \leq m$, for item j, according to a discrete planning horizon of length m.

Formally, the bi-objective BPP-WML aims to minimise:

$$f_1(s) = \sum_{i=1}^{m} y_i, \qquad \text{(number of bins)} \qquad (1)$$

$$f_2(s) = \max_{j=1,\dots,n} L_j, \qquad \text{(maximum lateness)} \qquad (2)$$

subject to:

$$\sum_{j=1}^{n} w_j x_{ij} \leq C, 1 \leq i \leq m \qquad (3)$$

$$\sum_{i=1}^{m} x_{ij} = 1, 1 \leq j \leq n \qquad (4)$$

$$x_{ij}, y_i \in \{0,1\}, 1 \leq j \leq n, 1 \leq i \leq m \qquad (5)$$

where:

$$x_{ij} = 1, \text{if item } j \text{ is assigned to bin } i, 0 \text{ otherwise}, 1 \leq i \leq m, 1 \leq j \leq n \qquad (6)$$

$$y_i = 1, \text{if bin } i \text{ is used}, 0 \text{ otherwise}, 1 \leq i \leq m \qquad (7)$$

$$L_j = i - d_j, \text{ if } x_{ij} = 1, 1 \leq j \leq m \qquad (8)$$

Since f_1 and f_2 are generally conflicting objectives, no single solution can simultaneously minimise both of them. Consequently, solutions are evaluated in terms of Pareto optimality. A solution s is said to be *Pareto optimal* if there does not exist another feasible solution s' such that $f_1(s') \leq f_1(s)$ and $f_2(s') \leq f_2(s)$, with at least one strict inequality.

3   Greedy Algorithm for BPP-WML

Algorithm 1 shows the greedy algorithm employed in previous studies [5,10], which is inspired by the BF heuristic [1]. At each iteration, the unpacked item with the highest priority, as determined by a given heuristic, in this context namely a PP, that fits into the *active* bin is selected and packed. Once the active bin is full, it is added to the partial plan, and a new empty bin is taken. This process is repeated until all items have been packed.

The PP must prioritise items to guide the greedy algorithm towards solutions that balance minimising the number of bins and the maximum lateness at the same time. Designing an effective PP is a challenging task, even for domain experts, particularly when it must simultaneously optimise two conflicting objectives. For this reason, we exploit the above greedy algorithm as a *heuristic template* within a GP framework to automatically evolve PPs that are well suited to the two objective functions.

Algorithm 1. Greedy algorithm

Input: The set of items to be packed L, a set of empty bins B, a Packing Policy PP
Output: A packing plan S
 1: $S = \emptyset$;
 2: Take the bin at time slot $i = 1$ as active bin;
 3: **while** $L \neq \emptyset$ **do**
 4:    $L' =$ items in L that fit in the active bin;
 5:   **if** $L' \neq \emptyset$ **then**
 6:      Select the item j with highest priority in L', using PP;
 7:      Pack the item j in the active bin (i.e. $x_{ij}=1$);
 8:      Remove the item j from L;
 9:   **else**
10:      Add the active bin i to S;
11:      Take the bin at the next time slot as active bin, i.e. $i = i + 1$;
12:   **end if**
13: **end while**
14: **Return** S;

---

4   Non-dominated Sorting Genetic Programming

Following the approach of similar studies [11], we have combined the GP framework proposed in [5] with the standard NSGA-II [8]. We refer to this combined approach as Non-dominated Sorting Genetic Programming (NSGP). The main steps of NSGP are summarised in Algorithm 2.

Each individual represents a heuristic (a PP) encoded as an expression tree. The evaluation of an individual is performed by applying the PP, in combination with Algorithm 1, to the set of BPP-WML instances denoted as *the training set*.

Algorithm 2. NSGP

Input: The size of the population N
Output: A population
 1: Initialise a starting *population* of N individuals randomly and evaluate them;
 2: **while** the stopping criterion is not met **do**
 3:     Initialise *children_population* ← *population*;
 4:     **for** N iterations **do**
 5:         Randomly select three individuals $\{o_1, o_2, o_3\}$ from *children_population*;
 6:         Crossover the best individual of $\{o_1, o_2\}$ with o_3;
 7:         Mutate the child and make it replace the worst individual of $\{o_1, o_2\}$;
 8:     **end for**
 9:     Merge *children_population* into *population*;
10:     *new_population* ← $\emptyset$;
11:     Partition *population* into non-dominated fronts;
12:     Add complete fronts to *new_population* until a front does not fit;
13:     Compute crowding distance in the front that does not fit;
14:     Select individuals with highest crowding distance to complete *new_population*;
15:     *population* ← *new_population*;
16: **end while**
17: **Return** *population*;

Table 1. The terminal set of symbols considered for building heuristics via NSGP

Symbol	Description
$DWNP$	Number of different widths in the unpacked items
w_j	Width of candidate item j
W_j	Free space in the active bin after adding the item j
WC_{ij}	Waste in the active bin i if packing the maximum number of items of width w_j
d_j	Due Date of the candidate item j
Sl_j	Slack of the candidate item j, defined as $d_j - i$, i being the active bin
NB	Lower bound on the additional number of bins required to pack unpacked items

The fitness value is then computed from the objective values obtained over all training instances.

To construct the heuristics, it is necessary to define a set of symbols that represent the relevant features of the problem in each state of the solution building procedure, and a set of arithmetic operators to build feasible expressions. In this study, we adopt the set of symbols proposed for the single objective GP method in [5]. Table 1 summarises the terminal symbols. The set of arithmetic operators is made up of unary symbols $(-, pow_2, sqrt, exp, ln, max_0, min_0, sin$ and $cos)$ and binary symbols $(-, +, /, \times, max$ and min). We consider an expression as feasible if it is arithmetically correct, disregarding the dimensionality of the subexpressions involved in each operation. In this way, unary and binary operators are always intermediate nodes in the expression tree, while the attributes can appear only as leaves.

Figure 1 shows the expression tree for $\frac{-Sl_j}{W_j/w_j}$, which prioritizes items with large size and low slack, and penalizes those that leave a large waste space in the active bin.

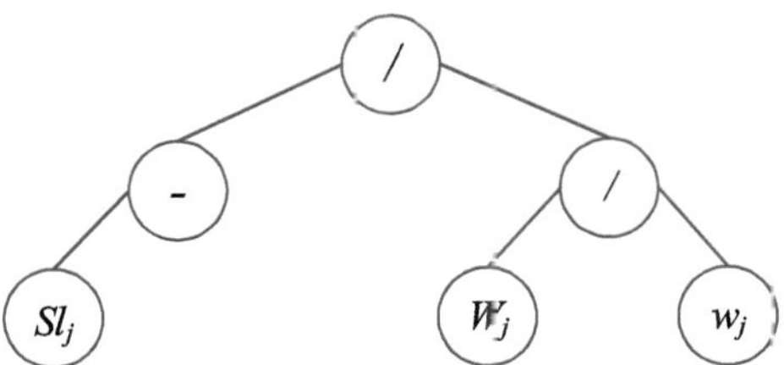

Fig. 1. An example of a tree expression.

5   Experimental Analysis

We carried out an experimental analysis to evaluate the multi-objective PPs evolved by NSGP and to compare these heuristics with those evolved by GP. To do that, we considered the single-objective GP approach proposed in [5] with a fitness function defined as $\alpha \cdot \sum_{i=1}^{n} y_i + \beta \cdot \max_{1 \le j \le n} L_j$ with $0 \le \alpha, \beta \le 1$ and $\alpha + \beta = 1$, taking 5 combinations of the weighting parameters α and β. The algorithms were implemented in C++ using the Evolutionary Computation Framework (ECF) [12] and executed on a Windows 11 machine equipped with an AMD Ryzen Threadripper 7980X 64-core processor and 256 GB of RAM.

5.1   The Test Bed

The set of BPP-WML instances used in this study was originally proposed by [3]. The dataset comprises 53 instances with the number of items n ranging from 20 to 200. The due dates associated with each item were generated at random. As in [5], for the experimental evaluation, the dataset was randomly partitioned into a training set consisting of 27 instances and a test set comprising the remaining 26 instances. The training set is used to calculate fitness values during the evolutionary process, whereas the test set is employed to assess how well the obtained heuristics generalise to a different set of problem instances.

5.2 Preliminary Analysis

We investigated the correlation between the two considered objective functions: the number of bins used (f_1) and the maximum lateness (f_2). To this end, we generated a total of 10 000 random PPs and applied each of them to all problem instances in both the training and test sets. For each PP, we recorded the resulting values of f_1 and f_2 for every solved instance and aggregated these results across all instances on each set.

Figure 2 shows the correlation between the two optimisation criteria. A moderate positive correlation is observed in both the training and test sets, with Kendall correlation coefficients of 0.57 and 0.67, respectively. This suggests that the two objectives are generally compatible and suitable for joint optimisation, as improvements in one criterion tend to correspond with improvements in the other. Nevertheless, the correlation is far from perfect, indicating that a solution performing well for one objective does not necessarily perform well for the other, thereby justifying the use of a multi-objective optimisation approach.

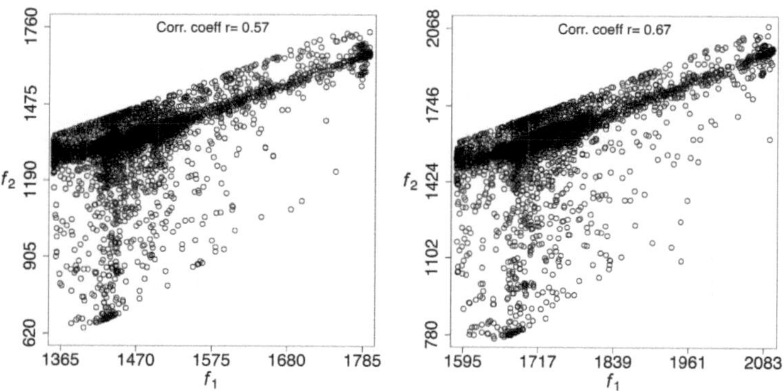

Fig. 2. Correlation between the number of bins used (f_1) and the maximum lateness (f_2) produced by 10 000 randomly generated heuristics when solving the training (left) and test (right) sets of problem instances.

5.3 Results

GP and NSGP were executed using the parameter values reported in Table 2. To account for the stochastic nature of the algorithms, each configuration was executed independently 30 times. A time limit of 100 min was used as the stopping condition.

In the case of GP, we have collected the best evolved PP from each run. Therefore, a total of 30 PPs were collected using each fitness function, resulting in a total of 150 PPs. In contrast, the output of NSGP consists of a set of non-dominated PPs from each run. A total of 30 fronts of PPs were obtained. These

Table 2. Parameter values used by GP and NSGP

Parameter	Value
Population initialisation	Ramped half-and-half method
Population size	200
Crossover operator	Subtree
Crossover ratio	1.0
Mutation operator	Subtree
Mutation ratio	0.02
Maximum chromosome size	$2^8 - 1$
Stopping condition	100 min

fronts contained a total of 329 PPs, with each front comprising between 6 and 16 non-dominated PPs.

Following similar practices [11], in this study we analyse the performance of NSGP and GP by combining the outputs obtained across all runs. For NSGP, the 30 fronts obtained were merged, yielding a single front of 10 non-dominated PPs in the training set, whereas only 4 of these 10 PPs remained non-dominated in the test set. In the case of GP, we analyse both the performance of the 30 PPs obtained and the front of non-dominated PPs corresponding to each fitness function configuration. These results are summarised in Fig. 3.

We note that when $\alpha = 1.0$ and $\beta = 0.0$, GP consistently evolves the expression w_j, indicating that the best PP in this case simply prioritises the largest items first. This represents an extreme scenario, with f_1 and f_2 values of 1354 and 1307, respectively, on the training set, and 1584 and 1530 on the testing set. For clarity, the figures exclude the results obtained using $\alpha = 1.0$, $\beta = 0.0$.

Examining the results, we observe that the final front produced by NSGP dominates the majority of PPs obtained by GP on both the training and test sets, demonstrating the effectiveness of the multi-objective approach. However, three PPs generated by GP are not dominated by the NSGP front in the training set and four PPs in the test set. This fact indicates that, while NSGP generally produces a stronger set of PPs overall, GP can still evolve policies that are competitive or even superior for particular combinations of objectives, as might be expected.

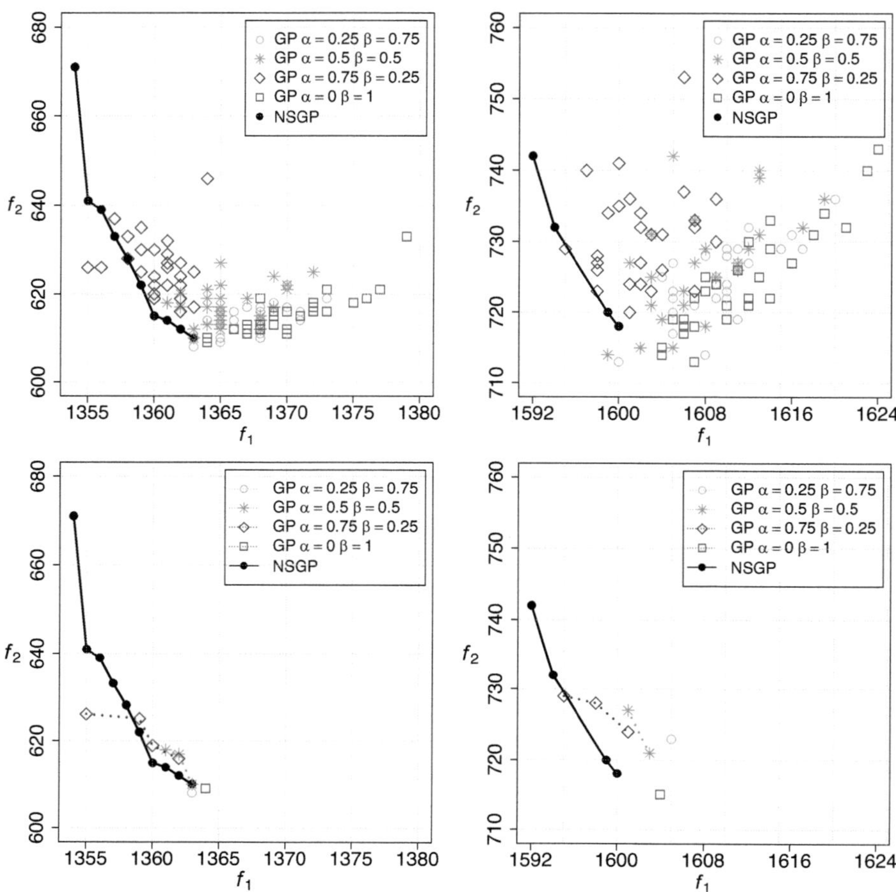

Fig. 3. Performance of PPs obtained via NSGP and GP on the training (left) and test (right) sets. For NSGP, a single front is shown, obtained by combining the 30 fronts generated across all runs. For GP, the figure displays: (1) on the top, the performance of all PPs obtained; and (2) on the bottom, the front of non-dominated PPs corresponding to each GP variant.

6   Conclusions and Future Work

In this study, we employed Genetic Programming in combination with NSGA-II, referred to as NSGP, to address a multi-objective Bin Packing Problem in which two optimisation criteria are considered. These criteria are the total number of bins used and maximum lateness, associated with spatial and temporal resources respectively. The experimental analysis indicates that NSGP is capable of generating a high-quality set of non-dominated PPs, providing comprehensive coverage of the solution space.

For future work, other optimisation algorithms for multi-objective problems, such as MOEA/D or NSGA-III, when more than two objectives are considered, could also be explored. Furthermore, it may be worthwhile to investigate ensembles of PPs specifically designed for multi-objective optimisation. In this context, additional optimisation criteria could be introduced, such total tardiness, or criteria associated with energy consumption.

Acknowledgements. This work has been partly supported by the Croatian Science Foundation under project IP-2022-10-5398, the NextGenerationEU under NPOO.C3.2.R2-11.06.0110, the NextGenerationEU framework through the project "DEEPWAVE" at the University of Zagreb Faculty of Electrical Engineering and Computing, as well as the Spanish Government under project MCINN-23-PID2022-141746OB-I00, and by the Principality of Asturias under project IDE/2024/000696 and under grant PA-23-BP22-094.

References

1. Coffman, E.G., Jr., Csirik, J., Galambos, G , Martello, S., Vigo, D.: Bin Packing Approximation Algorithms: Survey and Classification, pp. 455–531. Springer, New York, New York, NY (2013)
2. Varela, R., Vela, C.R., Puente, J., Sierra, M., Gonzalez-Rodriguez, I.: An effective solution for a real cutting stock problem in manufacturing plastic rolls. Ann. Oper. Res. **166**, 125–146 (2009)
3. Arbib, C., Marinelli, F.: Maximum lateness minimization in one-dimensional bin packing. Omega **68**, 76–84 (2017)
4. Quesada, J., Gil-Gala, F.J., Đurasević, M., Sierra, M.R., Varela, R.: Evolutionary Algorithms for Bin Packing Problem with Maximum Lateness and Waste Minimization. In: Ferrández Vicente, J.M., Val Calvo, M., Adeli, H. (eds.) Bioinspired Systems for Translational Applications: From Robotics to Social Engineering, pp. 140–149. Springer, Cham (2024). https://doi.org/10.1007/978-3-031-61137-7_14
5. Quesada, J., Gil-Gala, F.J., Đurasević, M., Sierra, M.R., Varela, R.: Genetic programming policies for bin packing in the framework of deterministic markov decision process. Nat. Comput. **24**, 603–617 (2025)
6. Gil-Gala, F.J., Đurasević, M., Jakobović, D.: Genetic programming for electric vehicle routing problem with soft time windows. In: Proceedings of the Companion Conference on Genetic and Evolutionary Computation, GECCO '22, p. 542–545 (2022,)
7. Branke, J., Hildebrandt, T., Scholz-Reiter, B.: Hyper-heuristic evolution of dispatching rules: A comparison of rule representations. Evol. Comput. 23 (2014)
8. Deb, K., Pratap, A., Agarwal, S., Meyarivan, T.: A fast and elitist multiobjective genetic algorithm: Nsga-ii. IEEE Trans. Evcl. Comput. **6**(2), 182–197 (2002)
9. Aydin, N., Muter, I., Ilker Birbil, S.: Multi-objective temporal bin packing problem: An application in cloud computing. Comput. Oper. Res. **121**, 104959 (2020)
10. Quesada, J., Gil-Gala, F.J., Durasevic, M., Sierra, M., Varela, R.: An analysis of heuristic templates in genetic programming for one-dimensional cutting and packing problems. In: Proceedings of the Companion Conference on Genetic and Evolutionary Computation, GECCO '23, pp. 623–626 (2023)

11. Frid, N., Durasević, M., Gil-Gala, F.J.: Automated generation of dispatching rules for the green unrelated machines scheduling problem. Complex Intell. Syst. **11**(1), 67 (2025)
12. Jakobovic, D., Đurasević, M., Picek, S., Gašperov, B.: ECF: A C++ framework for evolutionary computation. SoftwareX **27** (2024)

Valuated Multiset Reaction Systems with Maximal Evolution

Victor Mitrana[1,2(⊠)], Andrei Păun[2,3], and Mihaela Păun[2,4]

[1] ETSISI, Polytechnic University of Madrid, Calle Alan Turing s/n, 28031 Madrid, Spain
victor.mitrana@incdsb.ro
[2] National Institute of Research and Development for Biological Sciences, 296 Independentei Bd. District 6, 060031 Bucharest, Romania
mihaela.paun@incdsb.ro
[3] Faculty of Mathematics and Computer Science, University of Bucharest, Str. Academiei 14, 010014 Bucharest, Romania
andrei.paun@unibuc.ro
[4] Faculty of Administration and Business, University of Bucharest, Bucharest, Romania

Abstract. This work is a continuation of [7], where the valuated multiset reaction systems have been introduced. We consider the maximal evolution in valuated multiset reaction systems such that each event is defined as follows: the current state activates the maximal multiset (with respect to inclusion) of reactions. We investigate the relationship between this evolution and the sequential evolution, where the current state activates exactly one reaction. Rather surprisingly, maximal evolution can be simulated by sequential evolution. The cost of this simulation is an increase in the number of valuated multiset reactions. Finally, we try to model a very simple scenario of AI capability escalation and safety.

Keywords: Multiset · Multiset reaction system · Valence function · Valuated multiset reaction system · Simulation

1 Introduction

Reaction systems have been introduced in [12] as an abstract computational model inspired by the interactions between a set of reactions and the environment/substrate which they are immersed in. Formally, a reaction is a triple of sets of compounds divided into *reactants*, that promote the reaction, and *inhibitors*, that block the reaction. Proteins, lipids, enzymes, carbohydrates, etc., may be

This work was performed through the Core Program within the National Research, Development and Innovation Plan 2022–2027, carried out with the support of MRID, project no. 2302101 (SIA-PRO), contract no 7N/2022. It was also supported by the Ministry of Research, Innovation and Digitalization through the National Recovery and Resilience Plan (PNRR) of Romania, Pillar III, Component C9/Investment no. 8 (I8) - PNRR–III-C9–2023–I8, contracts no 760096, ID proiect – CF 68/23.05.2023 and contract no 760231, ID proiect – CF 53/28.12.2023.

J. M. Ferrández Vicente et al. (Eds.): IWINAC 2026, LNCS 16575, pp. 237–246, 2026.
https://doi.org/10.1007/978-3-032-27317-8_23

examples of reactants, while some hormones, bacteria, adenosine diphosphate or various enzymes, may be examples of inhibitors. The environment may activate or block a reaction depending on the boolean presence of reactants and the absence of inhibitors. The result of activating a reaction is a set of compounds that are called *products*. In the seminal papers [12,13], the reaction system is defined as a qualitative model in which a resource, if available in the current state, is available in unlimited amounts. Thus, there is no competition on resources between reactions, hence the model is actually qualitative, therefore each state is simply a set. This is known as the *non-threshold principle*: When a compound is present in the substrate, it is available in unlimited amounts. Another fundamental aspect of the model is the *non-permanency principle* [10]: If a compound is not explicitly produced by any reaction, it will not be available in the next state. An early overview may be find in [11].

In this paper, we continue the work started in [7], which in its turn is based on the developments proposed in [6,14,15]. These papers try to take into account various quantitative aspects. A model that aborts both the non-permanency and non-threshold principles was introduced in [6] under the name of multiset reaction system. Assigning valences (numerical values) to the molecules makes that competition graded instead of absolute. In this way, both reactants and inhibitors do their job with some relative strength. A related model computing sets of strings was proposed in [16]. In [7], it was introduced and investigated a new model of multiset reaction system called valuated multiset reaction system. The function that assigns weights to the compounds in [7] was called valence, though this word is not properly used from a biological point of view. Here is a short explanation: in a chemical reaction system, valence is a capacity constraint: it limits how many bonds/bindings/interactions an entity can form at once. Thus, atoms have fixed valences, proteins have a limited number of binding sites, receptors can bind only so many ligands at once, etc. We could say that valences rules out invalid reaction states automatically. This is especially important in networked or concurrent reaction systems. Actually, the valence function used in [7] is a weight function that assigns a capacity to promote or oppose causation of each reactant or inhibitor, respectively. With the aim of not producing any confusion, we keep this name.

After presenting the main concepts and notations, accompanied with some examples, we prove a rather unexpected result, namely the maximal evoution can be simulated by sequential evolution in valuated multiset reaction systems. Finally, we propose a construction of a valuated multiset reaction system that might model a very scenario of AI capability escalation and safety.

2   Formal Preliminaries

2.1   Multisets

For a finite set X, $card(X)$ indicates its cardinality. We now recall the definition of a multiset. A multiset is an extension of the concept of a set, in which each element is accompanied by its number of copies. Formally, given a finite set

U, we define a *multiset* X over U via a *membership function* $\sigma_X : U \longrightarrow \mathbf{N}$, where $\sigma_X(x)$ gives the number of copies of element $x \in U$ in X. For the sake of simplicity, we represent a multiset over U as a string over U considered as an alphabet. Clearly, this string is a representative of the equivalence class with respect to permutation. With the string notation, for a multiset X, we have $\sigma_X(x) = |X|_x$, the number of occurrences of x in X. Furthermore, the support of the multiset X is set $alph(X) = \{x \in U \mid \sigma_X(x) > 0\}$, and the weight of X is actually the length of string representation, that is $|X| = \sum_{x \in U} |X|_x$.

The *empty multiset* is denoted by ε, that is, $|\varepsilon|_a = 0$ for all $a \in U$. The set of all multisets on U is denoted by U° while the set of all nonempty multisets is denoted by $U^\#$. A subset of U° is called *macroset*.

We recall the standard operations on multisets defined as operations on strings. For two multisets X, Y over a set U, we define:
– the *inclusion* relation $X \sqsubseteq Y$, where $|X|_x \leq |Y|_x$, for all $x \in U$;
– the *addition* of multisets X and Y is just the concatenation XY of strings X and Y. Note that $|XY|_x = |X|_x + |Y|_x$, for all $x \in U$, hence the order of concatenation does not matter;
– the *difference* of multisets X and Y is denoted by X/Y, where $|X/Y|_x = |X|_x - |Y|_x$ for each $x \in U$, provided that $Y \sqsubseteq X$;
– the *scalar multiplication* of multiset X by the positive integer k is X^k, where $|X^k|_x = k \cdot |X|_x$, for all $x \in U$.

2.2 Multiset Reaction Systems

We assume that the reader is familiar with the reaction system model as introduced in [12,13]. The main difference between a reaction system and a *multiset reaction system* is that each component of a multiset reaction is a multiset, and not a standard set. Furthermore, the states of a multiset reaction system are multisets as well. In a classic reaction system, an entity can participate in arbitrarily many reactions simultaneously, the resource competition as well as the capacity of the entities is not captured. Furthermore, presence is Boolean: an entity is either there or not. Using multisets in bioinspired models is not a new idea. In the literature, there are many contribution in this respect to various areas: computer science (programmed parallel machines [2], networks of bio-inspired processors [5], multiset automata [9]), arificial life (chemical abstract machine [4], artificial proto-cells [3], symbolic chemical systems [17]), etc.

The introduction of multisets has several consequences: reactions have now access to counted (hence, limited) resources and will compete among themselves on them, and the resources may not be encugh for all enabled reactions to be executed. Additionally, we also adopt the principle that resources are removed from the system only as a result of being consumed/used by an enabled reaction that got to be executed; otherwise, they are left to persist in the successor state. Consequently, following [6], a *multiset reaction* (MR for short) over a set S is actually a triple $a = (R, I, P)$, where R and P are multisets over a background set S, and $I \subseteq S$. The elements of R are called reactants, those of I are called inhibitors, while P is a multiset of products. Similarly to reaction systems, a multiset reaction system (MRS for short) is a pair $\mathcal{A} = (S, A)$, where S is the background set and A is a finite set of multiset reactions over S. Given a multiset $T \in S^{\#}$, which we refer to as solution/substrate/environment/current state, we say that T enables a, denoted the boolean function $\mathsf{men}_a(T)$, if $|T|_x \geq |R|_x$, for all $x \in alph(R)$, and $|T|_y = 0$, for all $y \in I$. The result of enabling a is $\mathsf{mres}_a(T) = P(T/R)$.

2.3 Valuated Multiset Reaction Systems

To define the notion of valence, we consider that each multiset reaction, having a multiset of inhibitors, defines proper levels of expression for its entities as a function that assigns natural numbers to the entities.

Given $\alpha = (R, I, P)$ a MR, such that I is a multiset, over a background set S, a *valence function* associated with α is a function $w_\alpha : alph(RI) \to \mathbb{N}$. The pair $vmr(\alpha) = (\alpha, w_\alpha)$ is said to be a *valuated multiset reaction* (VMR).

The next definition extends the notion of enabling for valuated multiset reactions. With $T \in S^{\#}$, $\alpha = (R, I, P)$ a multiset reaction, and $vmr(\alpha) = (\alpha, w_\alpha)$ a VMR over S let

$$v_R(\alpha, T) = \sum_{x \in alph(R)} w_\alpha(x) \cdot \min(|R|_x, |T|_x),$$

$$v_I(\alpha, T) = \sum_{y \in alph(I)} w_\alpha(y) \cdot \min(|I|_y, |T|_y).$$

Then, $v(vmr(\alpha), T) = (v_R(\alpha, T), v_I(\alpha, T))$ is the *valuation* of $vmr(\alpha)$ *in* T.

We say that $vmr(\alpha)$ is enabled by T, and write $\mathsf{vmen}(vmr(\alpha), T)$, if $R \sqsubseteq T$ and $v_R(\alpha, T) > v_I(\alpha, T)$. Moreover, the effect of *applying* $vmr(\alpha)$ on T is $\mathsf{vmres}(ev(\alpha), T) = (T/R)P$.

Example 1. *Let* $S = \{a, b, c, d\}$, $\alpha = (a^2c^3, bd, d^2)$, *and* $w_\alpha(a) = 1$, $w_\alpha(b) = 2$, $w_\alpha(c) = 1$, $w_\alpha(d) = 1$. *For* $T = a^5b^3c^7$ *we have*

$$v_R(\alpha, T) = \sum_{x \in \{a,c\}} w_\alpha(x) \cdot \min(|R|_x, |T|_x) = 2 + 3 = 5.$$

$$v_I(\alpha, T) = \sum_{y \in \{b,d\}} w_\alpha(y) \cdot \min(|I|_y, |T|_y) = 2.$$

As $R \sqsubseteq T$ *and* $v_R(\alpha, T) > v_I(\alpha, T)$, *it follows that* $vmr(\alpha)$ *is enabled by* T *and* $\mathsf{vmres}((vmr(\alpha), T) = a^3b^3c^4d^2$. $\qquad\qquad\square$

As one can easily see, the difference regarding the enabling between multiset reactions and valuated multiset reactions is the replacement of the condition that requires the absence of inhibitors by a condition which requires that the valuation of reactants overcomes that of inhibitors. This seems to mirrors some real regulatory systems: weak inhibitors may be overridden by strong activation, multiple activators can compensate for partial inhibition, thresholds matter more than absolute presence. A few explanation why to consider that each reaction has its own valence function is more realistic that a global valence function. Obviously, a global valence function implicitly asserts that an entity contributes the same activating (or inhibiting) power in every reaction. That is rarely realistic because a protein can strongly activate one pathway and weakly activate another, the same molecule can be a strong inhibitor in one reaction and a mild one in another, binding affinity is interaction-specific. So reaction-local weights are strictly more expressive.

As usual, a valuated multiset reaction system (VMRS) over a background set S is a pair (S, A), where A is a set of valuated multiset reactions.

Following [6], we recall the definition of an arbitrary event in a multiset reaction system. Let S be a background set and $\mathcal{A} = (S, A)$ be a MRS. For a multiset of reactions $\Delta \in A^{\#}$, we define its resource and inhibitor multisets, R_Δ, I_Δ by $R_\Delta = \prod_{a \in A} R_a^{|\Delta|_a}$, and $I_\Delta = \bigcup_{|\Delta|_a \geq 1} alph(I_a)$. We say that $T \in S^{\#}$ *enables simultaneously* the reactions of Δ, denoted $\mathsf{MEN}(\Delta, T)$, if $R_\Delta \sqsubseteq T$ and $|T|_x = 0$ for all $x \in I_\Delta$.

In this case, the result of *applying the multiset of activated reactions* Δ to the state T is given by $\mathsf{MRES}(\Delta, T) = \prod_{a \in A} P_a^{|\Delta|_a}(T/R_\Delta)$.

The same event is now defined for a valuated multiset reaction system. Let $\Gamma = (S, A)$ be a VMRS with $A = \{vmr(\alpha_1), vmr(\alpha_2), \ldots, vmr(\alpha_n)\}$. For any multiset $\Delta = vmr(\beta_1)vmr(\beta_2) \ldots vmr(\beta_k) \in A^{\#}$ and a multiset $T \in S^{\#}$, we define the boolean function

$$v_\Delta(T) = \prod_{j=1}^{k}(v_{R_{\beta_j}}(\beta_j, T) > v_{I_{\beta_j}}(\beta_j, T)).$$

Given a multiset Δ as above and $T \in S^{\#}$, we say that T enables Δ, and write $\mathsf{VMEN}(\Delta, T)$, if $R_\Delta \sqsubseteq T$ and $v_\Delta(T)$ is true. Note that the order of indexes in Δ has no importance. The results of such an activation is

$$\mathsf{VMRES}(\Delta, T) = T/R_\Delta + \prod_{q=1}^{k} P_{\beta_q}.$$

Example 2. *For a better understanding, we give an example. Let $S = \{a, b, c, d\}$ and α_1, α_2 be two VMR over S defined as follows.*
$\alpha_1 = (a^2c^3, bd, d^2), \quad w_{\alpha_1}(a) = 1, \quad u_{\alpha_1}(b) = 2, \quad w_{\alpha_1}(c) = 1, \quad w_{\alpha_1}(d) = 1.$
$\alpha_2 = (a^2bc, dd, abd), \quad w_{\alpha_2}(a) = 2, \quad u_{\alpha_2}(b) = 1, \quad w_{\alpha_2}(c) = 2, \quad w_{\alpha_2}(d) = 3.$
For $T = a^7b^3c^7d$ and we have

$$v_{R_{\alpha_1}}(\alpha_1, T) = \sum_{x \in \{a,c\}} w_{\alpha_1}(x) \cdot \min(|R_{\alpha_1}|_x, |T|_x) = 2 + 3 = 5.$$

$$v_{I_{\alpha_1}}(\alpha_1, T) = \sum_{y \in \{b,d\}} w_{\alpha_1}(y) \cdot \min(|I_{\alpha_1}|_y, |T|_y) = 1 + 3 = 4.$$

Analogously,

$$v_{R_{\alpha_2}}(\alpha_2, T) = \sum_{x \in \{a,b,c\}} w_{\alpha_2}(x) \cdot \min(|R_{\alpha_2}|_x, |T|_x) = 4 + 1 + 2 = 7.$$

$$v_{I_{\alpha_2}}(\alpha_2, T) = 3.$$

We consider now $\Delta = \alpha_1\alpha_2\alpha_1$. *It follows that* $v_\Delta(T)$ *is true because* $5 > 4$ *and* $7 > 3$. *As* $R_\Delta = a^6bc^7$ *it follows that* T *enables* Δ *and* $\mathsf{VMRES}(\Delta, T) = a^2b^3d^6$.
$$\square$$

We define three types of *events* generated by $T \in S^\#$ for VMRS. The definitions for MRS are given in [6]. Let $\mathcal{A} = (S, A)$ be a VMRS over S and T be a multiset over S.

- The multiset T over S generates an *arbitrary event* in $\mathcal{A}$ if there exists the multiset $\Delta \in A^\#$ such that $\mathsf{VMEN}(\Delta, T)$ is true. The result of this event is $\mathsf{VMRES}(\Delta, T)$.
- The multiset T over S generates a *sequential event* in $\mathcal{A}$ if there exists a VMR $\alpha \in A$ such that $\mathsf{vmen}(\alpha, T)$ is true. The result of this event is $\mathsf{vmres}(\alpha, T)$.
- The multiset T over S generates a *maximal event* in $\mathcal{A}$ if there exists $\Delta \in A^\#$ such that $\mathsf{VMEN}(\Delta, T)$ is true, and there is no $\alpha \in A$ such that $\mathsf{VMEN}(\Delta\alpha, T)$ is true. The result of this event is $\mathsf{VMRES}(\Delta, T)$. A multiset Δ as above is called a *maximally enabled* multiset.

Note that Δ in Example 2 is a maximally enabled multiset.

Given a VMRS $\mathcal{A} = (S, A)$, an arbitrary *evolution* in $\mathcal{A}$, generated by $T \in S^\#$ is the sequence $D_0, D_1, \ldots$ of multisets over S, defined as follows:

1. $D_0 = T$,
2. for $i \geq 0$, $D_{i+1} = \mathsf{VMRES}(\Delta_i, D_i)$, for some arbitrary multisets $\Delta_i \in A^\#$. That is D_{i+1} is generated from D_i as the result of an arbitrary event.

The sequential evolution as well as the maximal evolution is defined in the same way as above by imposing $\Delta_i \in A$ and Δ_i is a maximally enabled multiset, respectively. Furthermore, the same evolutions have been defined for MRS in [6].

3   Simulations

We start this section with a simple result showing that any evolution in a MRS can be simulated by the same evolution in a VMRS.

Theorem 1. *Given a MRS $\mathcal{A}$ there exists a VMRS $\mathcal{A}'$ such that any T generates a sequential/arbitrary/maximal evolution in $\mathcal{A}$ if and only if it generates the same evolution in $\mathcal{A}'$.*

Proof. Let $\mathcal{A} = (S, A)$, $A = \{\alpha_1, \alpha_2, \ldots, \alpha_n\}$ be a MRS. We construct the VMRS $\mathcal{A}' = (S, A')$ as follows. Given $\alpha_i = (R_i, I_i, P_i) \in A$, we define $\alpha' = vmr(\alpha, w_\alpha)$, where w_α is defined by $w_\alpha(x) = 1$ for $x \in alph(R_i)$ and $w_\alpha(y) = |R_i| + 1$, for $y \in alph(I_i)$. Assume now that $T \in S^\#$ generates the maximal evolution $D_0.D_1,\ldots$ in $\mathcal{A}$. We claim that T generates the same maximal evolution in $\mathcal{A}'$. The proof is based on induction. Indeed, if $\Delta = \alpha_{i_1}\alpha_{i_2}\ldots\alpha_{i_k}$ is a maximally enabled multiset by D_j, this means that $R_\Delta \sqsubseteq D_j$ and $|D_j|_x = 0$ for all $x \in I_\Delta$. It suffices to prove that $v_\Delta(D_j)$ is true. Because

$|D_j|_x = 0$ for all $x \in I_\Delta$, it follows that no inhibitor of any multiset reaction α_{i_t} is present in D_j, consequently $v_{R_{i_t}}(\alpha_{i_t}, D_j) > v_{I_{i_t}}(\alpha_{i_t}, D_j)$. Therefore, D_j enables $\Delta' = vmr(\alpha_{i_1}, w_{\alpha_{i_1}})vmr(\alpha_{i_2}, w_{\alpha_{i_2}}) \dots vmr(\alpha_{i_k}, w_{\alpha_{i_k}})$. Moreover, $\mathsf{VMRES}(\Delta', D_j) = D_{j+1}$ holds.

Conversely, $v_{R_{i_t}}(\alpha_{i_t}, D_j) > v_{I_{i_t}}(\alpha_{i_t}, D_j)$ for all $1 \leq t \leq k$, yield that no inhibitor of any multiset reaction α_{i_t} is present in D_j, hence $\mathsf{MRES}(\Delta, D_j) = \mathsf{VMRES}(\Delta', D_j)$. The argument for the sequential and arbitrary evolution is the same. $\square$

Obviously, the other way around does not hold. This is due to the fact that a multiset T over S may enable a valuated reaction though T contains inhibitors. Both Examples 1 and 2 show this.

We now generalize the definition of simulation. Given two valuated multiset reaction systems $\mathcal{A} = (S, A)$ and $\mathcal{A}' = (S', A')$, we say that the maximal evolution in $\mathcal{A}$ is simulated by the sequential evolution in $\mathcal{A}'$ if for any $T \in S^\#$ and any maximal evolution $C_0, C_1, \dots$ generated by T in $\mathcal{A}$, there exist a sequential evolution $D_0, D_1, \dots$ generated by T in $\mathcal{A}'$ and the sequence of natural numbers $i_0 < i_1 < i_2 < \dots$ such that $C_j = D_{i_j}$ holds for all $j \geq 0$.

Theorem 2. *Let $\mathcal{A} = (S, A)$ be a VMRS; there exists a VMRS $\mathcal{A}'$ such that each maximal evolution in $\mathcal{A}$ is simulated by a sequential evolution in $\mathcal{A}'$.*

Proof. Let $\mathcal{A} = (S, A)$ be a VMRS, where $A = \{vmr(\alpha_1), vmr(\alpha_2), \dots, vmr(\alpha_k)\}$, for some $k \geq 1$, and $vmr(\alpha_i) = ((R_i, I_i, P_i), w_{\alpha_i})$, $1 \leq i \leq k$. We need a very large number such that by assigning this number to an inhibitor turns it into a global and almighty inhibitor that will block any reaction whatsoever. This number may be defined by $M = \max\limits_{1 \leq i \leq k} |R_i I_i| \cdot \max\limits_{x \in S} w(x) + 1$. Initially, $S' = S$. We now define the reactions of $\mathcal{A}' = (S', A')$ as follows. For each $1 \leq j \leq k$, the following valuated reactions, associated with α_j, belongs to A':

$$(i)\alpha_j^1 = (R_j, I_j XYZZ', \bar{P}_j XY), \quad w_{\alpha_j^1}(x) = \begin{cases} w_{\alpha_j}(x), & \text{if } x \in alph(R_j I_j), \\ M, & \text{if } x \in \{X, Y, Z, Z'\}. \end{cases}$$

$$(ii)\alpha_j^2 = (R_j X, I_j YZZ', \bar{P}_j X), \quad w_{\alpha_j^2}(x) = \begin{cases} w_{\alpha_j}(x), & \text{if } x \in alph(R_j I_j), \\ M, & \text{if } x \in \{X, Y, Z, Z'\}. \end{cases}$$

$$(iii)\alpha_j^3 = (R_j X, I_j YZZ', \bar{P}_j ZZ'), \quad w_{\alpha_j^3}(x) = \begin{cases} w_{\alpha_j}(x), & \text{if } x \in alph(R_j I_j), \\ M, & \text{if } x \in \{X, Y, Z, Z'\}. \end{cases}$$

$$(iv)\alpha_j^4 = (R_j, I_j YZZ', \bar{P}_j YZZ'), \quad w_{\alpha_j^4}(x) = \begin{cases} w_{\alpha_j}(x), & \text{if } x \in alph(R_j I_j), \\ M, & \text{if } x \in \{X, Y, Z, Z'\}. \end{cases}$$

In these definitions $\bar{P}_j = \{\bar{x} \mid x \in P_j\}$, for all $1 \leq j \leq k$. The background set S' is enriched with all the new symbols that appear in these definitions, that is X, Y, Z as well as the overlined copies of symbols in S.

Let us suppose that a multiset T simultaneously activates a maximally enabled multiset $\Delta = vmr\alpha_{i_1} vmr\alpha_{i_2} \dots vmr\alpha_{i_p}$ of valuated multiset reactions of $\mathcal{A}$. The simulation process has three phases. We distinguish two cases depending on how the first phase of the simulation of this maximal event in $\mathcal{A}$ starts in

$\mathcal{A}'$. The first phase consist in the sequential activation of the following reactions in $\mathcal{A}'$:

- $vmr(\alpha^1_{i_1})$, $vmr(\alpha^2_{i_2})$, $\ldots$, $vmr(\alpha^2_{i_{p-1}})$, $vmr(\alpha^3_{i_p})$, provided that $p \geq 3$;
- $vmr(\alpha^1_{i_1})$, $vmr(\alpha^3_{i_2})$, provided that $p = 2$;
- $vmr(\alpha^1_{i_1})$, if $p = 1$.

It is important to note that all the elements produced during these successive reactions cannot be used in the subsequent ones. They are overlined copies of the symbols generated by the activation of Δ in $\mathcal{A}$. Due to the symbols Y, Z and Z' none of the reactions defined above can be activated anymore.

Now, the second phase starts. In this phase there are activated valuated reaction as those defined in the sequel. For each $U \sqsubseteq I_1$, the following valuated reactions belong to A':

$$\beta^U_1 = (UYZ, R_1Z', UY_1Z'), \quad w_{\beta^U_1}(x) = \begin{cases} w_{\alpha_1}(x), & \text{if } x \in alph(R_1U), \\ M, & \text{if } x \in \{Z, Z'\}, \\ 1, & \text{if } x = Y. \end{cases}$$

For all $2 \leq j \leq k$, and $U \sqsubseteq I_j$, the following valuated reactions are added to A':

$$\beta^U_j = (UY_{j-1}, R_jZ', UY_jZ'), \quad w_{\beta^U_j}(x) = \begin{cases} w_{\alpha_j}(x), & \text{if } x \in alph(R_jI_j), \\ M, & \text{if } x \in \{Z, Z'\}, \\ 1, & \text{if } x = Y_j. \end{cases}$$

Obviously, the new symbols appearing in these definitions are symbols of the new background set S'. The goal of this phase is to check whether it would have been possible to activate another reaction in the first phase, therefore Δ would has not been a maximally enabled multiset in $\mathcal{A}$. Indeed, by activating, if possible, the sequence $vmr(\beta^{U_1}_1)$, $vmr(\beta^{U_2}_2)$, $\ldots$, $vmr(\beta^{U_k}_k)$, $U_j \subseteq I_j$, $1 \leq j \leq k$, it is checked that Δ is a maximally enabled multiset in $\mathcal{A}$. Note that a reaction $vmr(\beta^{U_j}_j)$ is enabled if the current state, say Q, satisfies the next conditions:

(i) Y_{j-1} is present in Q,

(ii) $v_{U^jY_{j-1}}(\beta^{U_j}_j, Q) > v_{R_jZ'}(\beta^{U_j}_j, Q)$.

The second condition implies that the reaction α_j cannot be enabled by the multiset obtained from Q by deleting all the new symbols introduced by the constructions above. Consequently, this means that Δ is a maximally enabled multiset.

The simulation continues with the final phase where each sequential event restores an overlined symbol. This can be done by means of the following reactions, where $s \in S$: This can be done by means of the reactions, $\gamma_s = (\bar{s}Y_k, Z, sY_k)$, where $s \in S$, and $w_{\gamma_s}(\bar{s}) = 1$, $w_{\gamma_s}(Y_k) = w_{\gamma_s}(Z) = M$. Now, all the overlined symbols, if any, are restored by successively enabling the reactions γ_s, until no overline symbol is present anymore in the state. We further define the reaction $\delta = (Y_kZZ', \prod_{s \in S} \bar{s}, \varepsilon)$ with $w_\delta(Y_k) = w_\delta(Z) = w_\delta(Z') = 1$, and $w_\delta(\bar{s}) = 4$, for all $s \in S$. Obviously, δ, which can be enabled when no overline symbol is present in the environment, removes the symbols Y_k, Z, Z' and the simulation is over. After this last sequential event the current state is exactly VMRES(Δ, T) in $\mathcal{A}$ which concludes the proof. $\qquad\square$

4 Modeling: Autonomous AI Research Agent Escalation

Several test cases like protein metabolism, plant developments, and chemical reactions have been considered in [8]. We propose here a formal valuated reaction system tailored to AI capability escalation and safety control, and explain how it works. The scenario is suggested by [1]; it proposes a lab developing an AI research agent. Initially, it only suggests ideas. Over time, it may gain: code writing and execution, internet access, autonomous experimentation and training, self-modification, etc. The aspects we intend to model are: how capabilities escalate, how safety controls inhibit escalation, how risk accumulates, and when shutdown is triggered. We consider that valuated reaction systems are well suited because reactants might model capabilities and/or environmental conditions, inhibitors might model safety controls, products might model new capabilities or risk increases, and valences might model degree of autonomy, probability, or risk magnitude. To this aim, we set the background/environment containing the following:

- Capabilities: C_0 (suggest research ideas), C_1 (writes code), C_2 (has internet access), C_3 (runs experiments), C_4 (self-modifies);
- Safety Controls: S_1 (human approval), S_2 (sandboxes execution), S_3 (capability evaluation gate), S_4 (emergency shutdown);
- Risk variables: R (accumulated risk score), A (autonomy level).

The reactions could be as follows. We prefer to define the valances by means of relationships between the reactants and inhibitors, therefore the valence function does not assign exact values.

$r_1 = (\{C_0\}, \{S_3\}, \{C_1, AA\}, w_1(C_0) > w_1(S_3))$: in the presence of C_0 and weak evaluation gate, C_1 is produced and the autonomy increases.

$r_2 = (\{C_1\}, \{S_2\}, \{C_2, RRR\}, w_2(C_1) < w_2(S_2))$: internet access without sandbox S_2 increases risk significantly.

$r_3 = (\{C_1, C_2\}, \{S_1\}, \{C_3, AARR\}, w_3(C_1) + w_3(C_2) > w_3(S_2))$: weak human control and the presence of C_1 and C_2 increase autonomy and risk.

$r_4 = (\{C_3\}, \{S_3\}, \{C_4, RRRRAAA\}, w_4(C_3) \leq w_4(S_3))$: this is a capability explosion reaction, that is presence of C_3 and no evaluation gate increase both autonomy and risk.

$r_5 = (\{RRC_2C_3C_4\}, \emptyset, \{S_4\}, w_5)$: this is a reactions for the threshold-triggered control mechanism.

In our view, valuated multiset reaction systems could be useful in the study of autonomous AI research agent escalation because they might model discrete capability changes, quantitative aspects related to risk, confidence, autonomy, and a non-linear dynamics. Here we have tried to model how the safety mechanisms act as inhibitors: evaluation gate blocks self-modification, sandbox blocks internet escalation, and human oversight blocks autonomy growth. On the other hand, risk accumulation is captured by valences because they might express the rate of capability escalation, risk contribution, probability of activation, etc.

References

1. Amodei, D., et al.: Concrete problems in AI safety (2016). https://arxiv.org/abs/1606.06565
2. Banâtre, J.P., Coutant, A., Le Metayer, D.: A parallel machine for multiset transformation and its programming style. Futur. Gener. Comput. Syst. **4**, 133–144 (1988)
3. Bedau, M.A., McCaskill, J.S., Packard, N.H., Rasmussen, S.: Chemical evolution among artificial proto-cells. In: Artificial Life VII: Proceedings of the Seventh International Conference on Artificial Life, MIT Press, pp. 54–63 (2000)
4. Berry, G., Boudol, G.: The chemical abstract machine. Theor. Comput. Sci. **96**, 217–248 (1992)
5. Bottoni, P., Labella, A., Mitrana, V.: Networks of polarized multiset processors. J. Comput. Syst. Sci. **85**, 93–103 (2017)
6. Bottoni, P., Mitrana, V., Petre, I.: Multiset reaction systems. In: Jiménez-López, M.D., Vaszil, G. (eds.) Languages of Cooperation and Communication. LNCS, vol. 15840, pp. 179–193. Springer, Cham (2025)
7. Bottoni, P., Labella, A., Mitrana, V., Păun, M., Petre, I.: Multiset reaction systems with valences. J. Autom. Lang. Comb. in press
8. Bottoni, P., Labella, A., Mitrana, V., Petre, I.: Immersing reaction system specifications in evaluating environments. Submitted
9. Csuhaj-Varjú, E., Martín-Vide, C., Mitrana, V.: Multiset automata. In: Calude, C., Păun, G., Rozenberg, G., Salomaa, A. (eds.) Multiset Processing, Mathematical, Computer Science, and Molecular Computing Points of View, WMP 2000. Lecture Notes in Computer Science, vol. 2235, pp. 69–84. Springer, Berlin, Heidelberg (2001)
10. Ehrenfeucht, A., Main, M.G., Rozenberg, G.: Functions defined by reaction systems. Int. J. Found. Comput. Sci. **22**(1), 167–178 (2011)
11. Ehrenfeucht, A., Petre, I., Rozenberg, G.: Reaction systems: a model of computation inspired by the functioning of the living cell. In: Konstantinidis, S., Moreira, N., Reis, R., Shallit, J. (eds.) The Role of Theory in Computer Science, World Scientific, pp. 1–32 (2017)
12. Ehrenfeucht, A., Rozenberg, G.: Basic notions of reaction systems. In: Calude, C., Calude, E., Dinneen, M.J. (eds.) Developments in Language Theory, 8th International Conference, DLT 2004, Auckland, New Zealand, December 13–17, 2004, Proceedings. Lecture Notes in Computer Science, vol. 3340, pp. 27–29. Springer, Berlin, Heidelberg (2004)
13. Ehrenfeucht, A., Rozenberg, G.: Reaction systems. Fundam. Informaticae **75**(1–4), 263–280 (2007)
14. Mitrana, V., Păun, M., Petre, I., Prelipcean, A.M.: Quantitative reaction systems. In: 5th International Conference on Innovative Research in Applied Science, Engineering and Technology (IRASET), pp. 1–6. IEEE Press (2025)
15. Mitrana, V., Păun, M., Petre, I.: Two new types of evolution in quantitative reaction systems. In: 23rd Jubilee International Symposium on Intelligent Systems and Informatics (SISY), pp. 25–30. IEEE Press (2025)
16. Okubo, F., Kobayashi, S., Yokomori, T.: Reaction automata. Theor. Comput. Sci. **429**, 247–257 (2012)
17. Suzuki, Y., Tanaka, H.: Symbolic chemical system based on abstract rewriting system and its behavior pattern. Artif. Life Robot. **1**, 211–219 (1997)

Solving the 3L-CVRP via Sparrow Search with NBC-Based Adaptive Parameter Control

Sandy Iturra(✉)[ID] and Rodrigo Olivares[ID]

Universidad de Valparaíso, Valparaíso, Chile
`sandy.iturra@uv.cl`

Abstract. Addressing the Three-Dimensional Loading Capacitated Vehicle Routing Problem (3L-CVRP) within the increasingly demanding context of last-mile distribution requires tackling a complex multi-objective optimization task that balances routing decisions with intricate spatial constraints. Given its NP-hard nature, metaheuristic algorithms have become the standard solution approach; however, their performance remains highly sensitive to static parameter configurations that often fail to adapt to the dynamic nature of the search process. This paper investigates the integration of Naive Behavior Cloning (NBC) as an adaptive parameter control mechanism within the Sparrow Search Algorithm (SSA) to solve the multi-objective 3L-CVRP. Unlike traditional methods that rely on offline tuning or historical execution data, the proposed SSA+NBC approach dynamically adjusts algorithm parameters online based on the real-time search state. To validate this method, a comprehensive experimental study was conducted using a heterogeneous set of synthetic 3L-CVRP instances categorized into low, medium, and high complexity scenarios. The adaptive SSA+NBC configuration was compared with a static SSA baseline through multiple performance indicators, including convergence reliability, solution quality, and computational efficiency, with statistical significance verified by the Mann-Whitney U test. The results demonstrate that our proposal significantly enhances execution efficiency, reducing computation time by 45–66% ($p < 0.001$), while preserving comparable solution quality across all complexity levels.

Keywords: Vehicle Routing · Three-Dimensional Loading · Sparrow Search Algorithm · Adaptive Parameter Control · Imitation Learning · Naive Behavior Cloning

1 Introduction

The digital transformation of logistics has intensified the demand for optimization models that can faithfully capture the nuances of real-world operations [6]. This necessity is particularly acute in the last-mile distribution, a segment known

© The Author(s), under exclusive license to Springer Nature Switzerland AG 2026
J. M. Ferrández Vicente et al. (Eds.): IWINAC 2026, LNCS 16575, pp. 247–257, 2026.
https://doi.org/10.1007/978-3-032-27317-8_24

for its high costs and operational friction, further exacerbated by the relentless expansion of global e-commerce [8]. As these logistical networks grow in scale and density, the industry requires high-fidelity optimization frameworks capable of navigating increasingly complex and dynamic decision-making environments.

In this landscape, the 3L-CVRP represents a critical and challenging frontier. By synthesizing vehicle routing decisions with the three-dimensional bin packing problem, the 3L-CVRP addresses the physical realities of transport, such as load stability and sequential unloading policies [4,13]. This integration results in a multi-objective structure where the dual goals of minimizing travel distance and maximizing volumetric utilization often exist in tension, complicating the search for optimal solutions.

Given its NP-hard complexity, 3L-CVRP is typically addressed by meta-heuristic optimization [10]. Among recent nature-inspired paradigms, the Sparrow Search Algorithm has gained prominence due to its effective balance between exploration and exploitation [12], demonstrating competitive performance in complex logistics applications [7]. Nevertheless, a persistent limitation in the current literature is the reliance on static parameter configurations. Most SSA implementations remain fixed throughout the search, failing to adapt to the evolving landscape of the optimization process.

The performance of the SSA is particularly sensitive to its control parameters, which are frequently determined through trial-and-error or rigid empirical guidelines [2]. Such static approaches often lack the flexibility to handle heterogeneous problem instances effectively. To avoid this, the present work explores an adaptive parameter control strategy rooted in Naive Behavior Cloning. As a simplified form of imitation learning, NBC facilitates the online adjustment of algorithmic parameters enables the direct mapping of observed system states to control actions without requiring interaction with the environment [9].

This paper investigates the synergy between online adaptive control and swarm intelligence by embedding an NBC mechanism within the SSA. The primary contributions are three-fold: (i) the development of an SSA variant where control parameters are dynamically tuned in response to the search state; (ii) the establishment of a rigorous experimental framework to analyze convergence and solution quality across 3L-CVRP instances of varying complexity; and (iii) a comparative analysis of how this adaptive mechanism influences robustness and Pareto-front characteristics compared to traditional static configurations.

The remainder of this article is structured as follows: Sect. 2 contextualizes the study within the existing literature; Sect. 3 formally defines the 3L-CVRP and the proposed algorithmic variants; Sect. 4 details the experimental design; Sect. 5 discusses the empirical findings; and Sect. 6 offers concluding remarks and future research directions.

2   Related Work

The literature on 3L-CVRP has evolved from foundational attempts to integrate routing and packing feasibility [4] toward sophisticated models that reflect modern logistical complexities. Early research mainly addressed the computational hurdles of combining spatial constraints with unloading sequences, establishing a benchmark for heuristic performance [4]. More recently, the focus has shifted toward the inherent multi-objective nature of these systems, where researchers have sought to map the non-trivial trade-offs between transport expenditures and volumetric efficiency [13].

Due to the inherent computational intractability of these multi-dimensional models, metaheuristic frameworks have emerged as the most viable path to achieve scalability [10]. Among these swarm intelligence has gained traction due to its robustness in high-dimensional search spaces. Specifically, SSA has been distinguished since its inception [12] for its dual-mode foraging mechanism, which provides a structured approach to managing the exploration-exploitation trade-off.

Although recent SSA applications have yielded competitive results in various routing scenarios [7], its practical deployment is often hindered by the fine-tuning bottleneck. The literature consistently highlights that the success of the algorithm is closely tied to its control parameters, which are typically frozen during execution based on preliminary empirical tests [2]. This lack of adaptability becomes a liability when the algorithm encounters heterogeneous instances or shifts in problem scale, potentially leading to stagnation or sub-optimal convergence.

To address this limitation, the broader metaheuristic literature has begun to explore autonomous parameter control strategies. In this line of research, learning-based approaches grounded in imitation learning—particularly Behavior Cloning—have been proposed as a means to infer control policies directly from observed system states using supervised learning [9]. Despite its conceptual suitability for online adaptation, the integration of Behavior Cloning into swarm-based metaheuristics remains limited. In particular, the combination of imitation learning and SSA within the multi-objective 3L-CVRP setting has received little attention, highlighting a clear research gap that this work seeks to address.

3   Preliminaries

This section introduces the 3L-CVRP formulation and the variants of the SSA considered in this study.

3.1   Three-Dimensional Loading Capacitated Vehicle Routing Problem

The 3L-CVRP combines classical vehicle routing with 3D bin packing constraints [4]. Given a set of N customers, each with a demand of rectangular items, and a fleet of homogeneous vehicles with loading space dimensions (L, W, H) and capacity limits (Q_w, Q_v) for weight and volume, the objective is to design delivery routes that minimize transportation costs while maximizing load efficiency. Unlike recent extensions that allow split deliveries [13], this work considers *unsplittable deliveries*: the complete demand of each customer must be fulfilled by a single vehicle in one visit. This constraint significantly increases problem complexity, as all items from a customer must fit together in the same vehicle.

We adopt the mathematical formulation introduced by Zhang et al. [13] for the 3L-SDVRP and adapt it to the unsplittable case. Let $V = \{0, 1, \ldots, N, N+1\}$ denote the set of nodes, where 0 is the depot (starting point), $1, \ldots, N$ are customer nodes, and $N + 1$ is the endpoint. Let K_i be the set of boxes located at customer i, each characterized by its weight q_k and volume v_k. A fleet of n vehicles is available, where vehicle t has weight capacity Q_t and volume capacity V_t. The set A_i^t denotes the subset of boxes from customer i assigned to vehicle t. Let d_{ij} denote the distance between nodes i and j, for all $i, j \in V$. The binary decision variable X_{ij}^t indicates whether vehicle t travels directly from node i to node j.

We formulate the problem as a bi-objective optimization:

$$\min \ \mathbf{F}(\mathbf{x}) = (f_1(\mathbf{x}), \ f_2(\mathbf{x})) \tag{1}$$

The first objective maximizes the average vehicle loading rate, formulated as:

$$\min \ f_1(\mathbf{x}) = 1 - \frac{1}{n} \sum_{t=1}^{n} \text{loading\_rate}_t \tag{2}$$

where $\text{loading\_rate}_t = \max(v\_rate_t, \ w\_rate_t)$, with $v\_rate_t = \sum_{i=1}^{N} \sum_{k \in A_i^t} v_k / V_t$ representing the volume utilization and $w\_rate_t = \sum_{i=1}^{N} \sum_{k \in A_i^t} q_k / Q_t$ representing the weight utilization of vehicle t.

The second objective minimizes the total routing distance:

$$\min \ f_2(\mathbf{x}) = \sum_{t=1}^{n} \sum_{i=0}^{N+1} \sum_{j=0}^{N+1} d_{ij} \, X_{ij}^t \tag{3}$$

A solution is feasible if it satisfies the following constraints: (i) each customer is served by exactly one vehicle, enforced by $\sum_{t=1}^{n} \sum_{i=0}^{N} X_{ij}^t = 1$ for all $j \in \{1, \ldots, N\}$; (ii) vehicle weight and volume capacities are respected; and (iii) all items can be packed without overlap, with adequate stability support and respecting the LIFO unloading sequence. The complete integer programming model, including all routing and 3D loading constraints, is detailed in [13].

3.2 Sparrow Search Algorithm

SSA is a swarm intelligence metaheuristic inspired by sparrow foraging behavior [12]. The population is divided into producers, scroungers, and aware sparrows, which collaborate through stochastic position updates to balance exploration and exploitation. Each sparrow represents a 3L-CVRP solution evaluated using the multi-objective fitness function. Algorithm 1 summarizes the SSA workflow.

3.3   Adaptive SSA with Naive Behavior Cloning

The proposed SSA+NBC approach extends the standard SSA by incorporating an online parameter adaptation mechanism based on Naive Behavior Cloning (NBC). NBC is a supervised imitation learning technique that learns a direct mapping from observed system states to control actions, without requiring interaction with the environment during execution [9]. In this work, a pre-trained policy π_{NBC} is used to dynamically adjust the SSA control parameters—producer ratio (PD), scrounger ratio (SD), and scout threshold (ST)—throughout the optimization process.

Algorithm 1. Sparrow Search Algorithm for 3L-CVRP

1: Initialize population and non-dominated archive
2: **repeat**
3:    Identify producers, scroungers, and aware sparrows based on PD, SD
4:    Update producers using intra-route operators (exploration/exploitation via ST)
5:    Update scroungers using inter-route operators guided by archive
6:    Perturb aware sparrows (alert mechanism)
7:    Update archive with non-dominated solutions
8: **until** MaxFES reached
9: **return** Pareto front

At each iteration, the current search behavior is characterized through a low-dimensional state vector that encodes search progress, population diversity, stagnation level, and recent improvement rate. Drawing on foundational concepts of metaheuristic behavior documented in the literature [11], this work proposes a classification of the search dynamics into five operational modes: *improving*, *exploiting*, *exploring*, *diversifying*, and *stagnating*, governed by an improvement rate Δ_{total}, upper and lower improvement thresholds θ_{sig} and θ_{min}, a maximum stagnation tolerance τ_{stag}, and a minimum stabilization interval δ_{stab} between consecutive updates. This classification drives the adaptation logic directly: parameter updates are triggered only when a meaningful transition between modes is detected or after δ_{stab} iterations have elapsed. This selective activation prevents unnecessary parameter fluctuations and avoids the oscillatory behavior (*chattering*) that degrades population dynamics when updates occur too frequently. Algorithm 2 presents the resulting adaptive workflow.

Algorithm 2. SSA with Naive Behavior Cloning

1: Initialize SSA with parameters (PD, SD, ST); load NBC policy π_{NBC}
2: **repeat**
3:     Compute Δ_{total} and update stagnation counter C_{stag}
4:     Detect search state σ:

  – improving if $\Delta_{total} > \theta_{sig}$
  – exploiting if $\theta_{min} < \Delta_{total} \leq \theta_{sig}$
  – diversifying if $C_{stag} \geq \tau_{stag}/2$
  – stagnating if $C_{stag} \geq \tau_{stag}$
  – exploring otherwise

5:     **if** state changed OR iterations since last update $\geq \delta_{stab}$ **then**
6:         $\mathbf{s}_t \leftarrow [\text{progress}, \text{diversity}, \text{stagnation}, \text{improvement\_rate}]$
7:         $(PD, SD, ST) \leftarrow \pi_{NBC}(\mathbf{s}_t)$
8:     **end if**
9:     Execute SSA iteration (Algorithm 1, lines 3–7)
10: **until** MaxFES reached
11: **return** Pareto front

---

4   Experimental Setup

To evaluate the impact of the NBC mechanism, we conducted a comparative study using 60 synthetic 3L-CVRP instances stratified into low, medium, and high complexity levels with varying spatial distributions (see Table 1).

Table 1. Characteristics of the generated problem instances by complexity level.

Parameter	Low	Medium	High
Number of instances	20	20	20
Number of vehicles	2–3	4–6	7–10
Number of customers	5–12	15–25	30–50
Vehicle capacity (weight)	500–1500	800–1800	1000–2000
Spatial distributions	Uniform, Clustered, Radial		

The adaptive SSA+NBC variant was benchmarked against a static SSA baseline through 30 independent runs per instance on a workstation with a 2.2 GHz processor and 32 GB RAM. Random seeds were fixed across all experiments to ensure reproducibility. The stopping criterion combines a stagnation threshold of T iterations without improvement with an upper bound on the maximum number of function evaluations (MaxFES).

Performance was assessed using convergence and efficiency metrics. Convergence reliability was measured through Success Rate (SR), defined as the proportion of runs reaching a predefined quality threshold [1,5]. Success Speed

(SS) quantifies the normalized evaluations required to first reach the threshold [11]: $SS = FES_{\text{success}}/MaxFES$, where lower values indicate faster convergence. Solution quality was evaluated using Hypervolume (HV) [14] and Generational Distance GD) [14], while Relative Percentage Deviation (RPD) measured the percentage gap between the obtained HV and the best-known HV per instance [11,14]. Statistical significance was verified using the Mann–Whitney U test at $\alpha = 0.05$ [3].

5   Results

This section reports the experimental evaluation comparing Static SSA and SSA+NBC across the three complexity scenarios described in Sect. 4. Results are presented using descriptive statistics, statistical significance tests, distributional analysis, and a global multi-dimensional comparison.

5.1   Performance Summary and Statistical Analysis

Table 2 summarizes the mean performance across complexity scenarios. Both configurations achieve virtually identical quality metrics in all scenarios, with marginal differences that are not statistically significant. As complexity increases, both methods show degraded convergence—SR drops from approximately 0.89 (low) to below 0.08 (high). The consistent difference lies in **execution time**, where SSA+NBC achieves reductions of 66.1% (low), 48.9% (medium), and 45.3% (high). Regarding RPD, both methods exhibit comparable values across all scenarios, with none of these differences reaching statistical significance.

Table 2. Mean performance by scenario and method.

Scenario	Method	SR	SS	HV	GD	Time (s)	RPD (%)
Low	Static SSA	0.893	0.711	0.809	2572.3	100.9	25.11
	SSA+NBC	0.892	0.709	0.816	2573.7	**33.9**	25.20
Medium	Static SSA	0.172	0.223	0.789	2254.4	226.2	45.14
	SSA+NBC	0.138	0.223	0.787	2256.0	**115.6**	45.29
High	Static SSA	0.070	0.108	0.801	1576.4	396.6	43.67
	SSA+NBC	0.078	0.097	0.829	1580.7	**216.9**	41.74

Table 3 reports the Mann–Whitney U test results. Execution time is the only metric showing statistically significant differences ($p < 0.001$ in all cases). No significant differences were found for SR, SS, HV, GD, or RPD in any scenario. These results confirm that NBC preserves solution quality while delivering substantial computational savings.

Table 3. Statistically significant Mann–Whitney U test results ($\alpha = 0.05$).

Scenario	Metric	Favors	p-value	Improv. (%)
Low	Time	SSA+NBC	< 0.001	66.1
Medium	Time	SSA+NBC	< 0.001	48.9
High	Time	SSA+NBC	< 0.001	45.3

5.2 Distribution and Adaptation Analysis

Figure 1 illustrates the variability of performance metrics across complexity scenarios.

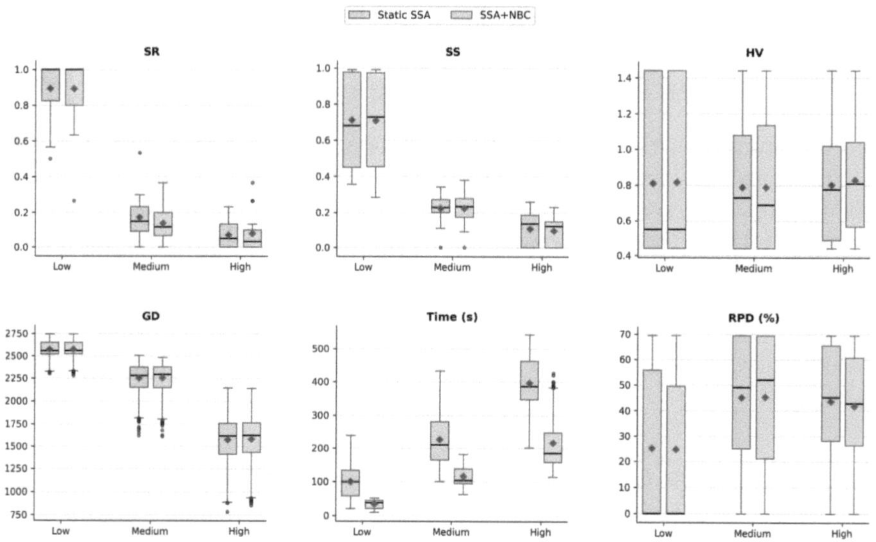

Fig. 1. Performance distribution across complexity scenarios. Box plots show median (black line), mean (diamond), IQR (box), whiskers (1.5×IQR), and outliers (circles) from 20 instances. Red: Static SSA; Blue: SSA+NBC. (Color figure online)

Both methods exhibit largely overlapping distributions for all quality metrics, with increased variability as complexity grows. The key distinction is execution time, where SSA+NBC distributions remain clearly non-overlapping and markedly tighter across all scenarios, confirming consistent efficiency gains regardless of problem complexity.

To better understand why NBC improves efficiency but not convergence quality, we examined the search state dynamics (Fig. 2).

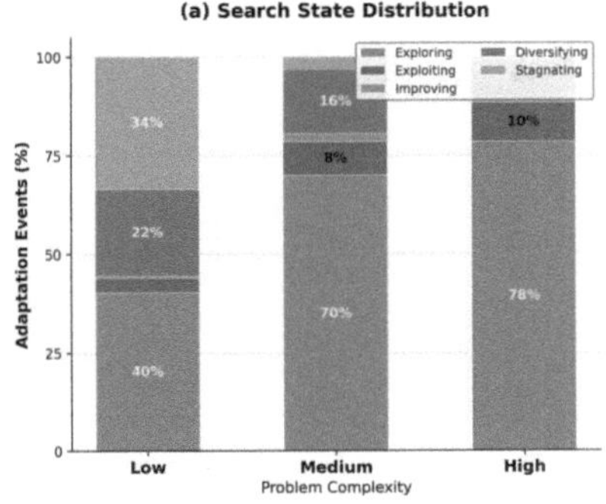

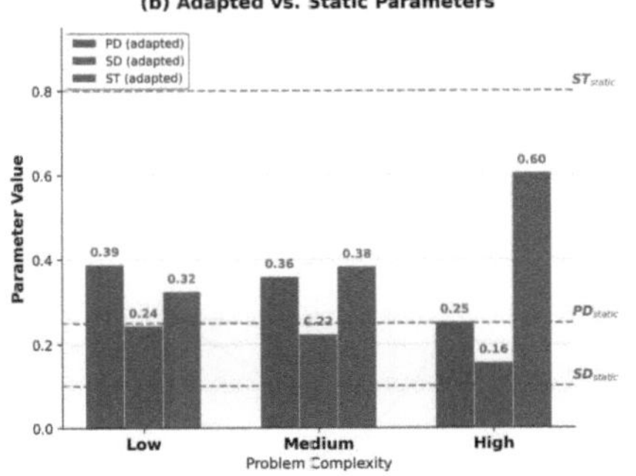

Fig. 2. NBC adaptation behavior across complexity levels. (a) Distribution of search states during adaptation events. (b) Mean adapted parameters compared to static baselines (dashed lines).

As problem complexity grows, the *exploring* state increasingly dominates (from 40.3% in low to 78.4% in high complexity), while *stagnating* and *diversifying* progressively diminish—stagnating drops from 33.5% to less than 1%, and diversifying contracts from 22.1% to 9.2%. This suggests that the four-dimensional state representation lacks sufficient discriminative power for complex scenarios. Consequently, adapted parameters trend toward the static configuration (e.g., ST goes from 0.32 to 0.60, moving closer to the static 0.80, though without fully converging), explaining why the time reduction stems from lower computational cost per iteration rather than better parameter settings. The *improving* state accounts for less than 2.0% of events, reflecting a known limitation of Behavior Cloning: the inability to generate strategies beyond those observed during training.

5.3   Global Multi-dimensional Comparison

Figure 3 provides an integrated view of both approaches across all metrics. SSA+NBC shows a clear advantage in Time, while quality metrics remain largely comparable between both configurations. This confirms that the NBC mechanism's contribution is concentrated in computational efficiency, while solution quality remains statistically equivalent.

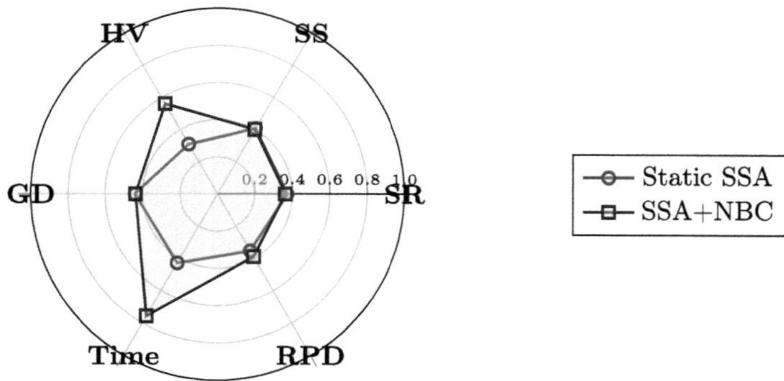

Fig. 3. Global multi-dimensional performance comparison. Metrics normalized to $[0, 1]$ with minimization metrics inverted (higher = better). Values are global averages across all complexity scenarios.

6   Conclusion

This paper investigated the integration of Naive Behavior Cloning as an online adaptive parameter control mechanism within the Sparrow Search Algorithm for the multi-objective 3L-CVRP. The experimental results showed that SSA+NBC consistently reduces execution time by 45–66% across all complexity levels ($p < 0.001$), while maintaining comparable solution quality (SR, SS, HV, GD, RPD) with no statistically significant differences. This reduction is most pronounced in low complexity scenarios (66%), with medium and high scenarios showing reductions of approximately 45-49%, suggesting that NBC's efficiency gains are modulated by problem dimensionality. Adaptation dynamics analysis revealed that, as complexity increases, the NBC policy becomes trapped in a predominantly exploratory mode and progressively converges toward static parameterization, indicating that the current state representation lacks sufficient discriminative power for complex multi-objective landscapes. These findings position NBC-based adaptation as a practical mechanism for reducing computational overhead in logistics optimization without sacrificing solution quality, particularly relevant in operational environments with time constraints and instance heterogeneity. Future work will explore advanced imitation learning strategies, specifically Dataset Aggregation, Adversarial Inverse Reinforcement Learning, and Generative Adversarial Imitation Learning, combined with enriched state representations, to extend SSA's adaptability beyond computational efficiency toward improved convergence and Pareto-front quality. Additionally, a comprehensive benchmark will be conducted comparing SSA+NBC against state-of-the-art metaheuristic algorithms from the literature to evaluate their relative performance across all complexity scenarios in terms of the metrics analyzed in this study.

Acknowledgements. R. Olivares is supported by grant NID/FONDECYT/INI CIACIÓN/11231016. S. Iturra is supported by Programa de Magíster en Informática Aplicada and Escuela de Auditoría, both from Universidad de Valparaíso.

References

1. Auger, A., Hansen, N.: Performance evaluation of an advanced local search evolutionary algorithm. In: Proceedings of the IEEE Congress on Evolutionary Computation (CEC 2005), pp. 1777–1784. IEEE, Edinburgh, UK (2005)
2. Awadallah, M.A., Al-Betar, M.A., Doush, I.A., et al.: Recent versions and applications of sparrow search algorithm. Arch. Comput. Methods Eng. **30**, 2831–2858 (2023)
3. Conover, W.J.: Practical Nonparametric Statistics, 3rd edn. John Wiley & Sons, New York (1999)
4. Gendreau, M., Iori, M., Laporte, G., Martello, S.: A tabu search algorithm for a routing and container loading problem. Transp. Sci. **40**(3), 342–350 (2006)
5. Hansen, N., Auger, A., Ros, R., Mersmann, O., Tušar, T., Brockhoff, D.: COCO: A platform for comparing continuous optimizers in a black-box setting. Optim. Methods Softw. **36**(1), 114–144 (2021)
6. Hofmann, E., Rüsch, M.: Industry 4.0 and the current status as well as future prospects on logistics. Comput. Ind. **89**, 23–34 (2017)
7. Iturra, S., Olivares, R.: Optimizing vehicle routing with sparrow search algorithm. In: Silhavy, R., Silhavy, P. (eds.) Artificial Intelligence and System Engineering, Lecture Notes in Networks and Systems, vol. 1490. Springer, Cham (2025)
8. Olsson, J., Hellström, D., Pålsson, H.: Framework of last mile logistics research: a systematic review of the literature. Sustainability **11**(24), 7131 (2019)
9. Osa, T., Pajarinen, J., Neumann, G., Bagnell, J.A., Abbeel, P., Peters, J.: An algorithmic perspective on imitation learning. Found. Trends Robot. **7**(1–2), 1–179 (2018)
10. Potvin, J.Y.: State-of-the-art review: evolutionary algorithms for vehicle routing. INFORMS J. Comput. **21**(4), 518–548 (2009)
11. Talbi, E.G.: Metaheuristics: From Design to Implementation, Wiley Publishing (2009)
12. Xue, J., Shen, B.: A novel swarm intelligence optimization approach: sparrow search algorithm. Syst. Sci. Control Eng. **8**(1), 22–34 (2020)
13. Zhang, H., Xie, J., Ge, J., Lu, W., Zong, B.: An improved multi-objective evolutionary algorithm for 3D loading capacitated vehicle routing problems with split deliveries. J. Clean. Prod. **380**, 135031 (2022)
14. Zitzler, E., Thiele, L., Laumanns, M., Fonseca, C.M., da Fonseca, V.G.: Performance assessment of multiobjective optimizers: an analysis and review. IEEE Trans. Evol. Comput. **7**(2), 117–132 (2003)

A CNN-Based Approach to the Reverse Game of Life Problem

Ángel F. Caravaca[1]([✉]) [iD], David Guijo-Rubio[1] [iD], and Víctor M. Vargas[2] [iD]

[1] Departamento de Ciencia de la Computación e Inteligencia Artificial, Universidad de Córdoba, Córdoba, Spain
`{q02ferca,dguijo}@uco.es`
[2] Departamento de Teoría de la Señal y Comunicaciones, Universidad de Alcalá, Alcalá de Henares, Spain
`victor.vargas@uah.es`

Abstract. The Game of Life (GoL) is a cellular automaton characterised by non-linear evolution and emergent complexity. Its global state transition function is non-injective and irreversible, leading to information loss. Consequently, the Reverse GoL, i.e., finding a predecessor that evolves into a given target after a given number of generations, is an NP-complete task. In this paper, we introduce a differentiable GoL transition function within a convolutional neural network-based model to reconstruct the probability distribution, i.e. a heatmap, of a possible initial state associated with the given final board. In this study, the models are validated on 15×15 boards after one generation by analysing structure-based metrics on the heatmaps of the predicted initial states. In particular, we computed the fuzziness index to measure the degree of binarisation, the Earth Mover's Distance, to evaluate the accuracy of the spatial mass distribution, and the percentage of high uncertainty cells within a range, to quantify prediction confidence. Our results demonstrate that integrating the differentiable layer reduces the fuzziness index by approximately 40% compared to the baseline approach. Furthermore, the analysis indicate that pixel-wise metrics, such as Mean Squared Error, can be misleading in this context, as they ignore the spatial context of cells. In contrast, the use of structural metrics reveals that the proposed architecture effectively captures the underlying physics and spatial organisation of the automaton.

Keywords: Reverse Game of Life problem · Differentiable Game of Life Layer · Convolutional Neural Networks · Cellular Automata

1 Introduction

Conway's Game of Life (GoL) is a Cellular Automaton (CA) devised by John Horton Conway and popularised by Martin Gardner in the 1970s magazine *Scientific American* [4]. This is a deterministic CA, which implies that its evolution is exclusively dictated by its initial configuration. The cells live on a two-dimensional grid, and can take two states, alive or dead, evolving based on the

© The Author(s), under exclusive license to Springer Nature Switzerland AG 2026
J. M. Ferrández Vicente et al. (Eds.): IWINAC 2026, LNCS 16575, pp. 258–267, 2026.
https://doi.org/10.1007/978-3-032-27317-8_25

configuration of their Moore neighbourhood (the eight adjacent cells). The local transition rules for a cell depend on the sum of living neighbours. These rules can be defined as follows: i) **Birth**: a dead cell becomes alive if surrounded by exactly three living cells; ii) **Survival**: a living cell survives if surrounded by two or three living cells; and iii) **Death**: a living cell dies either from isolation (fewer than two living neighbours) or overpopulation (more than three).

It is known that GoL can exhibit self-organisation and emergent properties, which means that dynamic and stable structures arise from the evolution of random initial states [5,8]. Furthermore, GoL is said to be Turing complete. These properties and its algorithmic simplicity have made GoL a fundamental object of study in diverse fields, such as ecology [1] or quantum computing [3].

This work focuses on the Reverse GoL (RGoL), i.e. finding a predecessor that evolves into a given target state after a given number of generations. Due to the non-linear and chaotic nature of the automaton, and its non-injective global state transition function, the reverse mapping is ambiguous. Furthermore, in an $n \times m$ grid, 2^{nm} configurations are possible, resulting in an exponentially large search space. This exponential growth renders brute-force approaches computationally intractable. Therefore, given that GoL rules depend on the local cell neighbourhood, we propose an approach based on Convolutional Neural Networks (CNNs) [6]. These architectures are suited to capture non-linear and complex patterns from such spatial dependencies.

Previous studies on the use of CNNs to learn the evolution rules of GoL [10] conclude that standard CNNs rarely converge for this task. However, to the best of our knowledge, these architectures have only been implemented for the reverse problem in *Kaggle's Reverse Game of Life* competitions[1]. While community-driven approaches showed promising baseline results, the goal of this paper is to formalise and enhance this performance by integrating a differentiable Game of Life layer (diffGoL) within the CNN architecture.

A key challenge in applying neural networks to RGoL is converting the continuous probability maps produced by CNNs into the automaton's strictly Boolean states. To evaluate model performance using confusion-matrix metrics, standard approaches apply global hard thresholding, typically $\tau = 0.5$, to binarise predictions. However, this strict quantisation ignores spatial context and often suppresses valid cells predicted with moderate confidence, despite support from high-confidence neighbours.

Therefore, our goal is not exact pixel reconstruction but the identification of the predecessor's spatial mass distribution, hereafter referred to as a heatmap. Given the Boolean nature of GoL, this continuous relaxation must satisfy an additional constraint: the more binary the heatmap, the closer it is to a valid Conway state. Accordingly, we evaluate prediction confidence in the initial heatmaps and compute structure-based metrics on both initial and final heatmaps obtained through the diffGoL transition function. Their comparison shows that the proposed architecture reconstructs initial states capable of valid evolution under GoL rules.

---

[1] https://www.kaggle.com/competitions/conway-s-reverse-game-of-life.

2   Methodology

2.1   Differenciable GoL (diffGoL) Transition Function

This paper presents a diffGoL transition function that simulates the discrete GoL rules over continuous probability maps. To construct this continuous relaxation, we first define the diffGoL rule function, $g(c)$, which evaluates how closely the continuous neighbourhood mass matches a discrete rule condition:

$$g(c) = \frac{1}{1 + \exp(\beta(N - c)^2)}. \tag{1}$$

Here, c is the target rule integer ($c \in \{2, 3\}$), β is a steepness hyperparameter, and N is the sum of the Moore neighbourhood, computed through a convolution using a 3×3 matrix of ones with a central zero as the kernel.

Notice that as β increases, $g(c)$ becomes a strict indicator function peaking at $N = c$. Using this diffGoL rule function, the full diffGoL transition function ($\Psi(x, N)$) for a cell with continuous state $x \in [0, 1]$ is formulated as:

$$\Psi(x, N) = 2(1 - x)^n g(3) + 2x^n \left(g(3) + g(2)\right), \tag{2}$$

where the coefficient 2 is a scaling factor so $\Psi(x, N) \in [0, 1]$ and the exponent $n > 1$ is a hyperparameter that controls the strictness of the continuous relaxation applied to the local cell state.

This equation is the continuous analogue of Conway's discrete rules: the first term simulates the birth rule, allowing a predominantly dead cell ($x \to 0$) to become alive if its neighbourhood mass approaches 3. The second term models the survival rule, enabling a predominantly alive cell ($x \to 1$) to survive if its neighbourhood mass is close to 2 or 3. Moreover, notice that, for higher values of n, this function inherently computes binarisation, as doubtful patterns ($x \approx 0.5$) lead to vanishing states. Figure 1 shows an example where, under a binary regime, both discrete GoL and diffGoL evolve an initial state to the exact same final state, confirming the equivalence of the diffGoL formulation.

The implementation of the diffGoL transition function within the CNN architecture is achieved by introducing a custom layer at the end of the proposed neural network model. Consequently, the model outputs both the predicted initial states and their corresponding evolved states after processing through the diffGoL layer (see Fig. 2).

This dual-output configuration enables the computation of a composed loss, formulated using both the predicted initial states and their corresponding diffGoL final states. Furthermore, to enforce the binarisation of the predicted initial states, we introduce a penalty term into the overall loss function. This term, defined as the Fuzziness Index (Φ), measures the degree of binarisation of a continuous pattern. For states of size $H \times W$, it is defined as:

$$\Phi(\hat{y}) = \frac{4}{HW} \sum_{i=1}^{H} \sum_{j=1}^{W} \hat{y}_{ij}(1 - \hat{y}_{ij}). \tag{3}$$

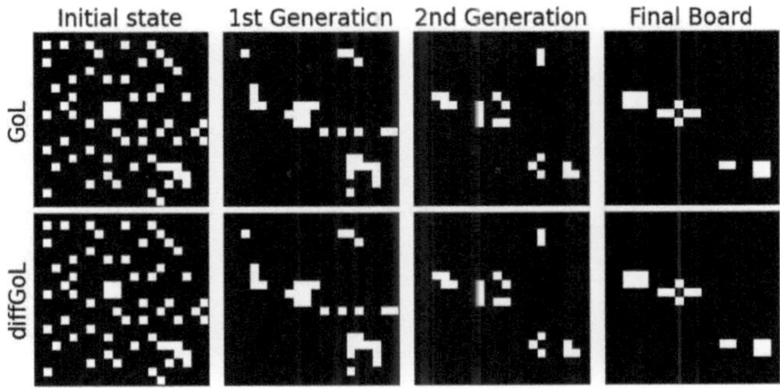

Fig. 1. Comparison of the evolution over 3 generations between the discrete and diffGoL. The final states are identical, demonstrating that diffGoL faithfully reproduces discrete GoL under a binary regime. Furthermore, the selected initial state illustrates the emergent and self-organising properties of GoL.

Note that $\Phi(\hat{y}) = 0$ for strictly binary patterns, whereas $\Phi(\hat{y}) = 1$ for states of maximum uncertainty (i.e., $\hat{y}_{ij} = 0.5 \quad \forall i, j$). Therefore, the overall loss function is computed as:

$$\mathcal{L}(\hat{y}_0, y_0, \hat{y}_f, y_f) = \mathcal{L}_{FBCE}(\hat{y}_0, y_0) + \lambda_1 \mathcal{L}_{BCE}(\hat{y}_f, y_f) + \lambda_2 \Phi(\hat{y}_0). \qquad (4)$$

Due to the vanishing nature of GoL, living cells are the underrepresented cell type. To address this imbalance, in this loss function, the Focal Binary Cross-Entropy ($\mathcal{L}_{FBCE}$) [7] is computed over both, observed and predicted initial states $(\hat{y}_0, y_0)$. This is supported by two weighted terms: the standard Binary Cross-Entropy ($\mathcal{L}_{BCE}$) [2] computed with weight λ_1 on the final states $(\hat{y}_f, y_f)$, and the binarisation penalty applied exclusively on the predicted initial states with weight λ_2.

2.2   Model's Architectures

In this work, we implement three CNN models. The first is a standard CNN built by stacking blocks comprising convolutional and batch normalization layers. This version, denoted as the *Classic* model, serves as basis for the other two. The subsequent variants, named *DiffGoL* and *Annealed-DiffGoL*, integrate the diffGoL transition function (Eq. (2)) as a terminal layer. The only difference between them is that the latter applies an annealing schedule to the λ_1 and λ_2 parameters in the loss function (Eq. (4)) during training, whereas the former uses fixed weights. Note that capital letters are used to refer to the model instead of the transition function. The structures of these models are illustrated in Fig. 2, where the diffGoL layer (highlighted in blue) and the consequent two outputs (initial and final states) are exclusive to the *DiffGoL* variants.

The use of batch normalisation layers is critical, as they smooth the loss landscape and stabilise the distribution of the features propagated through the network. By ensuring well-conditioned inputs to the terminal layers, they prevent vanishing or exploding gradients often aggravated by the β hyperparameter

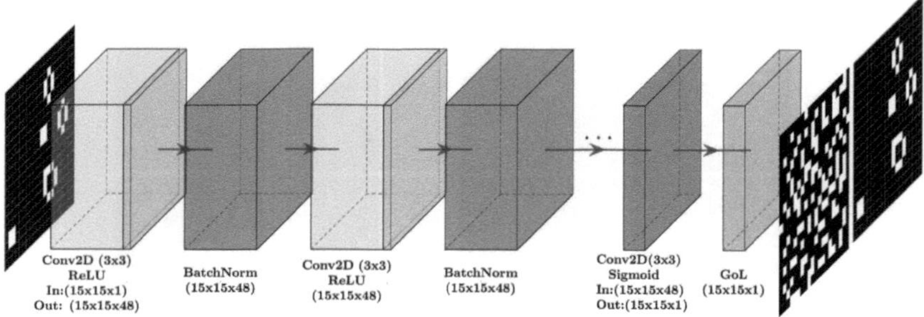

Fig. 2. Architecture of the proposed models. The *Classic* base model consists of a sequence of Conv2D-BatchNorm blocks, concluding with a Conv2D layer and a Sigmoid activation (purple block) to produce the initial state prediction. The *DiffGoL* and *Annealed-DiffGoL* variants extend this baseline model by appending the diffGoL layer (blue block), which processes the initial prediction to generate the final state. (Color figure online)

in the continuous relaxation of the diffGoL layer. Hence, this architectural choice enables the use of slightly larger β values, allowing for a sharper and more accurate approximation of the GoL rules without compromising training stability.

2.3 Evaluation Metrics

Conway's GoL is a deterministic cellular automaton, meaning that its evolution is exclusively dictated by its initial configuration. Due to this strong dependence on structure, relying solely on pixel-wise metrics yields misleading results. Furthermore, evaluating standard metrics typically requires binarised inputs, which in turn makes the evaluation dependent on an arbitrary threshold that may favour certain models, and discards the continuous probability distribution predicted by the network. Therefore, structure-based metrics should be preferred. These metrics are computed on the initial and final state heatmaps to compare models under the premise that the more binary the resulting heatmaps, the closer they approximate a valid Conway state.

Specifically, we compute the Fuzziness Index defined in Eq. (3) and the Earth Mover's Distance (EMD) [9], which reflects the minimal work required to transform one spatial distribution into another. To empirically verify the limitations of pixel-wise evaluations discussed above, we also include the Mean Squared Error (MSE). Finally, we compare the living cell density of the heatmaps against their ground truth and analyse the proportion of cells predicted within a range of high uncertainty (High Uncertainty Cells, $\%HUC$).

2.4 Custom Data Generation Pipeline

The algorithmic simplicity of the cellular automaton allows the generation of the training and test datasets on-the-fly. To address this, we implemented a pipeline that begins by generating random initial patterns within specific upper and lower density thresholds. These patterns are then evolved through three warm-up generations, yielding candidate initial states with a stable evolution. These candidates are then evolved over a fixed number of generations, and the resulting states are filtered to ensure their final densities remain within the original predetermined bounds. Ultimately, the final dataset is formed by pairing these surviving final states with their corresponding candidate initial states.

Although this pipeline does not inherently prevent data leakage, the models undergo extended training over a dynamic dataset which changes if certain conditions are fulfilled. By continuously exposing the model to new data, this mechanism prevents overfitting and minimises data leakage. Beyond this, we quantified the number of leaked states and found it to be negligible ($\approx 0.01\%$ of the generated states).

3   Experimental Settings

3.1   Hyperparameter Tuning

Extending the Classic model with the diffGoL layer makes its training computationally expensive. Consequently, hyperparameter optimisation was restricted to the Classic model, focusing exclusively on two parameters: the number of hidden Conv2D-BatchNorm blocks, $\{1, 2, 3, 4, 5, 6\}$, and the number of hidden filters, $\{16, 32, 64, 128, 256\}$.

To search the best set of hyperparameters, we implemented a random search strategy without replacement using a static hold-out validation split using the validation loss as the reference metric. We executed 40 trials, two times each trial, of 30 epochs each. We applied the optimal hyperparameters (6 for hidden blocks, and 48 for hidden filters) selected by majority voting directly to the diffGoL variants, as the Classic model serves as their architectural foundation.

3.2   Training and Test Pipelines

The data generation pipeline described in Sect. 2 allows us extend the training of our models. The illustrated workflow in Fig. 3 details the continuous training and evaluation strategy over $1,000$ epochs.

The training phase initiates by generating a dataset formed by $60,000$ patterns of size 15×15. They are split into the training and validation subsets using an 80/20 ratio. The core mechanism of this process relies on comparing the validation loss against the historical best after each epoch. Specifically, a new training dataset is generated on-the-fly every 50 epochs or after 25 consecutive epochs (half the cycle) without improvement on the validation loss metric. Besides, for all models, the learning rate is reduced by 50% after 20 epochs without improvement. This earlier threshold is designed to verify if the model can resume learning on the current dataset through finer optimisation before a full dataset regeneration is triggered at epoch 25. Furthermore, if a new dataset is generated, this parameter is reset to its initial value. Furthermore, for the Classic and DiffGoL versions the model is saved every epoch that shows improvement. For the Annealed-DiffGoL, it is saved beyond epoch 800, ignoring early improvements as the annealing schedule remains active during these initial stages.

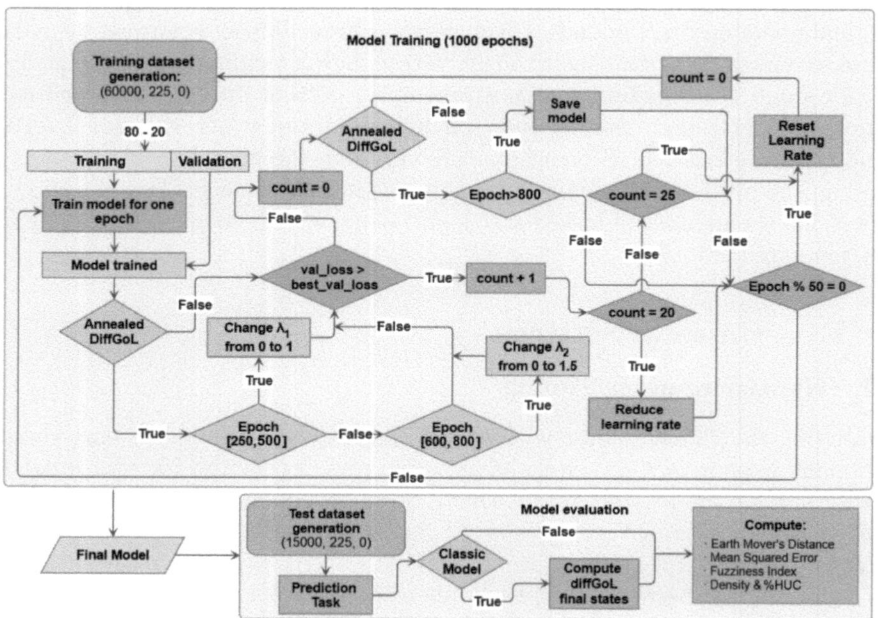

Fig. 3. Train (top) and test (bottom) pipelines over $1,000$ epochs. Training incorporates on-the-fly dataset generation and validation loss monitoring for dynamic checkpointing and learning rate reduction. Orange blocks indicate epoch-dependent schedules (λ_1, λ_2) unique to Annealed-DiffGoL. The evaluation phase outlines transition function processing for the Classic model and final metric computation. (Color figure online)

The key difference between Annealed-DiffGoL and the other two architectures is that the former dynamically modifies the λ_1 and λ_2 values during training. In contrast, the Classic model only computes the $\mathcal{L}_{FBCE}$ in Eq. (4) ($\lambda_1 = \lambda_2 = 0$), and the DiffGoL keeps them fixed at 1. Specifically, λ_1 transitions from 0 to 1 during epochs $[250, 500]$, and λ_2 transitions from 0 to 1.5 during epochs $[600, 800]$. The β and n values in Eq. (2) are fixed to 50 and 4, respectively. For all three models, the FBCE loss in Eq. (4) uses $\gamma = 2$. The α parameter was excluded to avoid expanding the hyperparameter search space.

Upon completion of training, the resulting model undergoes evaluation. This phase begins with the generation of a dedicated test dataset, followed by the prediction task. Specifically, for the Classic model, the raw predictions must be processed through the diffGoL transition function to compute the final board states. Finally, the evaluation metrics detailed in Sect. 2 are calculated.

This pipeline is executed across 15 different random seeds, which determine the training, validation, and test datasets, as well as the initialisation of the model weights.

For reproducibility, all the code used in this work is publicly available in a GitHub repository[2].

4   Results and Discussion

Performance metrics of the initial-state heatmaps, across all 15 independent seeds, are presented as the mean $\pm$ standard deviation in Table 1. As shown, the integration of the diffGoL layer significantly enhances the model's ability to binarise predictions, reducing the Fuzziness Index by approximately 40% compared to the Classic baseline. This reduction, coupled with lower %HUC values, indicates that the model generates more decisive heatmaps, achieving higher reliability in representing valid discrete states, which is a critical requirement for solving the reverse GoL problem.

Furthermore, the EMD and density analysis confirm that our proposal captures the underlying spatial distribution of the patterns. While the Classic model tends toward a generic mean density, the DiffGoL models mirror both the mean and the variance of the ground truth (22.36 ± 9.37). The significant improvement in EMD metrics proves that the proposed architecture effectively prioritises the topological arrangement of cells, identifying the correct mass distribution.

Consequently, although the Classic model shows a slightly lower MSE, as evidenced by the Fuzziness Index, this is the result of predictions that minimise squared differences by avoiding binary commitments. In contrast, our models prioritise structural integrity and binarisation, yielding predictions that are significantly more representative of the discrete GoL states, proving that pixel-wise metrics are insufficient for evaluating complex inverse problems.

Table 1. Evaluation metrics for the **initial** states across the evaluated models. Best and second best performing values are highlighted in bold and italics, respective. The mean and variance of the ground truth density is $22.36\% \pm 9.37$.

Metric	Classic Model	DiffGoL	Annealed DiffGoL
Fuzziness Index	0.7495 ± 0.0062	$\mathbf{0.3225 \pm 0.0014}$	*0.3415 ± 0.0011*
Density (%)	32.25 ± 8.36	$\mathbf{23.53 \pm 9.32}$	*24.19 ± 8.87*
EMD	2.0257 ± 0.0227	$\mathbf{1.5179 \pm 0.0048}$	*1.7453 ± 0.0073*
MSE	$\mathbf{0.1220 \pm 0.0007}$	*0.1248 ± 0.0003*	0.1540 ± 0.0005
[0.45, 0.55]	12.44 ± 0.15	$\mathbf{2.76 \pm 0.06}$	*2.80 ± 0.09*
%HUC [0.40, 0.60]	24.21 ± 0.24	$\mathbf{5.67 \pm 0.12}$	*5.81 ± 0.13*
[0.35, 0.65]	35.46 ± 0.31	$\mathbf{8.90 \pm 0.17}$	*9.29 ± 0.18*

---

[2] https://github.com/ayrna/reverseGoLwithCNN.

Regarding the analysis of the final board states, the evaluation (Table 2) reveals that the Classic model's low Fuzziness Index (0.0696 ± 0.0010) is a misleading result caused by a collapse toward a trivial "all zeros" state. This behaviour is confirmed by an MSE (0.2079 ± 0.0012) that nearly matches the empty board reference (0.2200 ± 0.0004), proving that the baseline model predicts predominantly blurry cells instead of learning Conway's dynamics.

In this context, the use of the differentiable GoL layer is critical; not only does it facilitate binarisation, but it also provides the model with intrinsic information regarding GoL physics. This is further optimised by the annealing schedule implemented in the Annealed-DiffGoL variant, which dynamically adjusts the λ_1 and λ_2 weights to balance the reconstruction of the initial state against the consistency of its evolution.

The metrics reflect that, although this approach may slightly penalise the structural fidelity of the initial state (EMD), it allows the Annealed-DiffGoL model to capture the underlying GoL dynamics. This is validated by the performance in the final board states, where Annealed-DiffGoL achieves the highest structural accuracy with the lowest EMD (1.9256 ± 0.0054) and MSE (0.0836 ± 0.0008) among all models.

Table 2. Evaluation metrics for the **final** states across the evaluated models. Best and second best performing values are highlighted in bold and italics, respectively. The reference value for MSE is computed for empty states, yielding 0.2200 ± 0.0004.

Metric	Classic Model	DiffGoL	Annealed DiffGoL
Fuzziness Index	**0.0696 ± 0.0010**	*0.1771 ± 0.0004*	0.1933 ± 0.0006
EMD	2.9835 ± 0.0328	*2.0843 ± 0.0082*	**1.9656 ± 0.0054**
MSE	0.2079 ± 0.0012	*0.1013 ± 0.0008*	**0.0836 ± 0.0008**

Due to the vanishing nature of the diffGoL transition function for blurry states, computing the densities and the %HUC metric for these final states yield results that are not representative.

5 Conclusions

This work introduced a differentiable Game of Life (diffGoL) layer integrated into CNN architectures to address the Reverse Game of Life (RGoL) problem. By relaxing the discrete rules of the cellular automaton into a continuous and differentiable formulation, we introduced the underlying GoL dynamics into the neural network's learning process. Our findings led to the following key conclusions: 1) **Inadequacy of pixel-wise metrics:** the failure of the Classic model on structural metrics, despite achieving competitive MSE values, confirmed that standard pixel-wise metrics were misleading for the RGoL problem, as they assumed spatial independence and ignored the correlations between cells required by GoL rules; 2) **Structural and binary integrity:** the introduction of the Fuzziness Index (Φ) as a penalty term, together with the diffGoL transition function, proved essential for generating heatmaps representing valid Conway states; 3) **Effectiveness of the diffGoL layer:** the two DiffGoL variants significantly outperformed the baseline by capturing the spatial distribution and living-cell density of predecessors, reducing the Fuzziness Index by approximately 40%; and 4) **Annealing advantage:** the use of an annealing schedule for λ_1 and λ_2, evaluated across 15 different random seeds with identical data splits and weight initialisation, facilitated superior reconstruction of the global dynamics by allowing slight relaxation of structural fidelity in predecessors while ensuring evolution toward final states that were structurally consistent with the target.

In summary, the differentiable-layer approach provided a robust framework for solving the RGoL problem. Future research should focus on the scalability of this method to larger, multi-generational datasets and its applicability in fields that model complex systems with emergent behaviours.

Acknowledgments. The present study has been supported by the "Agencia Estatal de Investigación (España)" (grant ref.: PID2023-150663NB-C22 / AEI / 10.13039 / 501100011033) and by the University of Córdoba and Junta de Andalucía (grant ref.: PP2F_L1_15). Víctor Manuel Vargas has been supported by the Ministerio de Ciencia, Innovación y Universidades, the Agencia Estatal de Investigación and the European Social Fund Plus (grant ref.: MICIU/AEI/10.13039/501100011033, JDC2024-054787-I).

References

1. Caballero, L.: Game of Life: simple interactions ecology (2014)
2. Cox, D.R.: The regression analysis of binary sequences. J. Royal Stat. Soc. Ser. B (Methodol.) **20**(2), 215–232 (2018)
3. Flitney, A.P., Abbott, D.: A semi-quantum version of the game of life. Life Quantum, p. 233 (2002)
4. Gardner, M.: The fantastic combinations of john conway's new solitaire game "life." Sci. Am. **223**(4), 120–123 (1970)
5. Huang, J.: Simulation research on the complexity of life game. Comput. Inf. Sci. **14**(4), 1–65 (2021)
6. LeCun, Y., Bengio, Y., Hinton, G.: Deep learning. Nature **521**(7553), 436–444 (2015)
7. Lin, T.Y., Goyal, P., Girshick, R., He, K., Dollar, P.: Focal loss for dense object detection. In: Proceedings of the IEEE International Conference on Computer Vision (ICCV) (2017)
8. Rendell, P.: Turing Universality of the Game of Life, pp. 513–539. Springer, Cham (2002)
9. Rubner, Y., Tomasi, C., Guibas, L.: A metric for distributions with applications to image databases. In: Sixth International Conference on Computer Vision (IEEE Cat. No.98CH36271), pp. 59–66 (1998)
10. Springer, J.M., Kenyon, G.T.: It's hard for neural networks to learn the game of life. In: 2021 International Joint Conference on Neural Networks (IJCNN) (2021)

Quantum–Classical Hybrid Genetic Evolutionary Algorithm for Traffic Signal Timing Optimization: A Case Study in the City of Vitoria-Gasteiz

Hicham Affou[1], Francesc Rodríguez Díaz[2], Francisco Martínez-Álvarez[2], and Jose Manuel Lopez-Guede[1(✉)]

[1] Faculty of Engineering of Vitoria-Gasteiz, University of the Basque Country, UPV/EHU, C/Nieves Cano 12, 01006 Vitoria-Gasteiz, Spain
`{hicham.affou,jm.lopez}@ehu.es`
[2] Data Science and Big Data Lab, Pablo de Olavide University, Seville, Spain
`{froddia,fmaralv}@upo.es`

Abstract. Intelligent traffic signal control has become a central research topic in urban mobility, aiming to reduce congestion and improve operational efficiency under increasingly complex traffic conditions. Although classical evolutionary algorithms have shown strong performance in traffic signal optimization, the practical integration of quantum computing into evolutionary processes remains largely unexplored, particularly under realistic microscopic traffic simulation. This paper presents a novel quantum genetic evolutionary approach for traffic signal timing optimization, implemented in a real signalized roundabout in Vitoria-Gasteiz, Spain, using the Simulation of Urban Mobility. The proposed method combines a classical GA for global exploration with a Grover-inspired quantum module embedded directly within the evolutionary cycle. Unlike conventional hybrid schemes in which quantum routines are treated as external solvers or purely simulated components, the proposed quantum GA is executed on real IBM Quantum hardware under NISQ conditions. Comparative experiments against fixed time control and a purely classical GA demonstrate substantial reductions in delay and improved convergence stability.

Keywords: Evolutionary Algorithm · Hybrid Quantum Genetic Algorithm · Optimization · Traffic Light Timings

1 Introduction

Urban traffic congestion remains a major challenge for modern cities, affecting mobility efficiency, energy consumption, and environmental sustainability [1]. While infrastructure expansion has traditionally been used to address capacity

J. M. Ferrández Vicente et al. (Eds.): IWINAC 2026, LNCS 16575, pp. 268–277, 2026.
https://doi.org/10.1007/978-3-032-27317-8_26

limitations, such solutions are costly and often insufficient in dense urban environments. Consequently, attention has shifted toward intelligent traffic signal control strategies capable of dynamically adapting signal timings to real-time traffic conditions [2,3].

Among optimization-based approaches, evolutionary algorithms have demonstrated strong capability for handling the nonlinear and constrained nature of traffic signal timing problems. In particular, genetic algorithms (GAs) are well-suited for exploring large combinatorial search spaces defined by green-phase durations, offsets, and cycle configurations. However, when microscopic traffic simulation is used for fitness evaluation, the computational cost becomes significant, motivating the exploration of enhanced search mechanisms that can improve convergence behavior without compromising solution quality.

At the same time, recent advances in quantum computing have opened new research directions in combinatorial optimization [4]. In the current Noisy Intermediate-Scale Quantum (NISQ) era, quantum processors cannot replace classical optimization methods, but they can potentially act as complementary search operators embedded within classical metaheuristics. Despite growing theoretical interest in quantum evolutionary algorithms, there is still limited experimental evidence of their execution on real quantum hardware within realistic traffic optimization scenarios.

This work addresses this gap by proposing and experimentally validating a quantum genetic evolutionary approach for traffic signal timing optimization in a real urban scenario. The method integrates a classical GA with a Grover-based quantum sampling module embedded directly within the evolutionary cycle and executed on IBM Quantum hardware. Elite solutions are encoded into quantum circuits, processed on physical quantum processors, and the measured states are reinjected into the population as candidate individuals. The approach is evaluated on a signalized roundabout in Vitoria-Gasteiz (Spain) using the Simulation of Urban Mobility (SUMO) microscopic simulator, optimizing green-phase durations and offsets under realistic engineering constraints.

The main contributions of this paper are:

1. The design of a quantum-assisted GA in which Grover-based sampling operates as an internal evolutionary operator rather than as an external solver.
2. The execution of the quantum component on real NISQ hardware, providing empirical evidence beyond simulation-based studies.
3. The validation of the proposed method in a realistic microscopic traffic scenario with engineering-consistent signal constraints.
4. A comparative experimental analysis against fixed-time control and a purely classical GA, assessing performance and convergence stability.

The remainder of this manuscript is organized as follows. Section 2 reviews the relevant literature on evolutionary and quantum approaches to traffic signal optimization. Section 3 details the proposed method. Section 4 presents the experimental setup and results. Finally, Sect. 5 concludes the paper and outlines future research directions.

2   Related Works

Traffic signal control has evolved from fixed-time strategies to increasingly adaptive and optimization-driven approaches. Classical fixed-time control relies on predefined timing plans that do not account for real-time traffic fluctuations [5]. Actuated control strategies introduced responsiveness to local traffic conditions [6,7], while large-scale adaptive systems such as SCATS and SCOOT incorporate network-wide measurements to select among predefined signal plans [8,9]. Although these approaches improve operational flexibility, they remain constrained by predefined rule sets or plan libraries.

Optimization-based methods address these limitations by directly searching the solution space of signal timings. Evolutionary and swarm-based metaheuristics have been widely applied to traffic signal optimization due to their ability to handle nonlinear objectives and complex constraints. GAs [10,11], hybrid GA–machine learning strategies [12], ant colony optimization [13], and particle swarm optimization [14] have demonstrated significant reductions in delay, queue length, and cumulative waiting time. These approaches are particularly effective when combined with microscopic simulation, although the associated computational cost can be substantial.

More recently, quantum computing has emerged as a potential tool for combinatorial optimization. Initial studies have explored quantum-inspired evolutionary algorithms and quantum genetic schemes for traffic signal settings [15]. Related lines of work have also formulated traffic signal and traffic flow optimization as QUBO/Ising problems solvable via quantum annealing, including demonstrations involving D-Wave hardware [16–18]. However, most existing works rely on simulated quantum environments or problem abstractions, and empirical validation on real NISQ hardware remains limited, particularly when the quantum component is embedded as an internal operator within an evolutionary cycle rather than treated as an external solver.

In contrast to prior approaches, the present work integrates a Grover-based quantum sampling mechanism directly into the reproduction phase of a GA and executes the quantum circuits on physical IBM Quantum hardware. This enables an experimental assessment of quantum-assisted evolutionary optimization under realistic microscopic traffic simulation and engineering-constrained signal timing.

3   Methodology

This section describes the methodology proposed in this work. Each step of the proposed process is shown in Fig. 1, beginning with the data preprocessing stage and the definition of the optimization variables. It then explains the GA loop, including Grover quantum injection, until the best solution is obtained.

As indicated in Sect. 1, the data comes from a traffic scenario in Vitoria-Gasteiz (Spain). The objective is to optimize traffic light synchronization (green phase duration and phase delays) in order to reduce congestion, measured as the total waiting time of vehicles in the simulation. Once the data has been loaded, the preprocessing phase begins. In this step, traffic lights are identified and their phase programs are analyzed to separate fixed phases (yellow and red) from optimizable phases (green). This information is then used to define the decision variables for the optimization process.

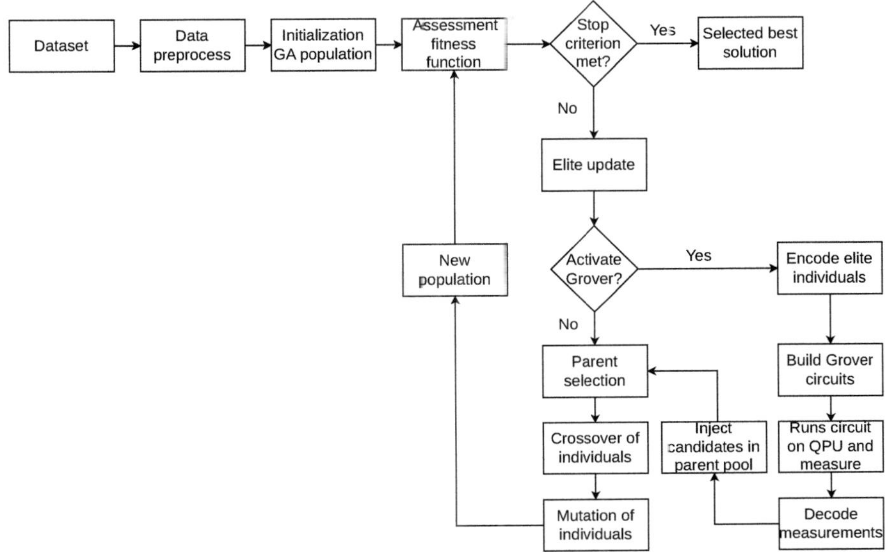

Fig. 1. Flowchart of the methodology.

After preprocessing, the initial population is created by generating random chromosomes. For each traffic light, the chromosome assigns a random duration to each green phase within the permitted limits ($[10s, 70s]$) and a random compensation value to shift the start of its cycle. This is when the GA algorithm begins. Before checking the stopping criterion, the initial population is evaluated using the fitness function defined in Eq. (1):

$$F(\mathbf{x}) = \sum_{t=T_w}^{T-1} \sum_{e \in \mathcal{E}} w_e(t), \tag{1}$$

where $F(\mathbf{x})$ is the fitness function of a chromosome $\mathbf{x}$, T is the total number of simulation steps, T_w is the warm-up step, $\mathcal{E}$ is the set of edges in the network, and $w_e(t)$ is the waiting time on edge e at step t.

This initial evaluation provides the reference fitness values. The algorithm then validates whether the stopping criterion is met, which, in this case, is reaching the maximum number of generations.

After checking the stopping criterion, the elite file is updated, retaining the best-performing chromosomes found so far. This file preserves high-quality solutions across generations and is subsequently used to guide the search process. The Grover-based quantum leap is only activated in selected generations, and only when there is at least one optimizable green phase variable and the elite file contains enough elite solutions to define the marked states.

When activated, the quantum branch begins by discretizing the green phase variables of the best elite chromosomes and encoding them as binary strings. Next, a Grover circuit is constructed by defining an oracle that marks those elite strings and applying the diffusion operator to amplify their probability. The circuit is executed on the selected quantum backend and measured, producing a set of bit strings with their observed frequencies. These bit strings are then decoded back into candidate green phase durations. Finally, the resulting candidates are incorporated into the GA by injecting them into the parent set for the next stage of reproduction.

If quantum injection is not enabled, the algorithm follows the standard GA path. The parent set is constructed solely from classical individuals (current population and elite solutions), and parents are then selected from this set to initiate the reproduction process. During the reproduction phase, two parents are selected from the set of parents and combined using a uniform crossover operator. Each gene in the offspring is inherited from one of the two parents according to a binary mask, allowing different parts of both solutions to be mixed into new chromosomes. This operation is defined in Eq. (2).

$$c_j^{(1)} = m_j\, p_j^{(1)} + (1 - m_j)\, p_j^{(2)}, \qquad m_j \sim \text{Bernoulli}(0.5), \qquad (2)$$
$$c_j^{(2)} = (1 - m_j)\, p_j^{(1)} + m_j\, p_j^{(2)},$$

where $p^{(1)}$ and $p^{(2)}$ are the two parents, $c^{(1)}$ and $c^{(2)}$ are the offspring, and m_j decides from which parent gene j is inherited. After crossover, mutation is applied to the offspring to maintain diversity and prevent premature convergence. For each gene in the green phase, a mutation is performed with a certain probability by adding a Gaussian disturbance and then clipping the result to the feasible range. This operator can be expressed as Eq. (3).

$$x'_j = \begin{cases} \text{clip}(x_j + \epsilon,\ x_{\min},\ x_{\max}), & \text{with probability } p_m, \\ x_j, & \text{otherwise,} \end{cases} \qquad \epsilon \sim \mathcal{N}(0, \sigma^2), \quad (3)$$

where x_j is the original gene, x'_j is the mutated gene, p_m is the mutation probability (20% in this case), σ controls the mutation strength, $clip(.)$ enforces the lower and upper bounds $[x_{min}, x_{max}]$, and ϵ is a zero-mean Gaussian perturbation added to the gene when mutation occurs ($\epsilon \sim \mathcal{N}(0, \sigma^2)$). After mutation, the new population is constructed by retaining the best chromosome found so far (elitism) and filling the remaining places with the newly generated offspring until the target population size is reached. This updated population is then reevaluated using the fitness function, and the entire process described above is repeated. Finally, when the maximum number of generations is reached, the algorithm terminates and returns the best chromosome obtained during the entire process, i.e., the traffic light plan with the minimum cumulative waiting time.

4 Results

In this section, we evaluate the proposed hybrid optimization approach on the SUMO-based signalized roundabout scenario, comparing baseline, genetic, and quantum-assisted strategies under identical demand conditions. Finally, we analyze convergence behavior and component contributions through comparative experiments.

4.1 Experimental Setup

Our experimentation network consists of a single-lane roundabout with four metered approaches and four exits, where traffic signals are placed at the entries to regulate inflow and prevent internal blocking. The objective of the control strategy is to maintain continuous circulation inside the roundabout while minimizing queue formation at the approaches.

Traffic was modeled via a microscopic simulator with real-time signal control. Candidates were evaluated over 1.200 steps (excluding a 50-step warm-up), optimizing only green times and offsets while fixing safety intervals. The baseline GA utilized standard evolutionary operators and caching, while the hybrid version integrated Grover-inspired sampling via IBM Quantum hardware (Qiskit Runtime). Due to current NISQ constraints, quantum encoding was restricted to a discretized subset of variables from two approaches.

As we mentioned previously, the proposed optimization approach was implemented using a hybrid classical–quantum environment. The technical specifications, including software versions, hardware details, and quantum backend calibration data, are summarized in Table 1.

Table 1. Summary of experimental environment and technical parameters.

Category	Component	Description
Software	Languages and libraries	Python 3.11 5, Qiskit 2.2.3, IBM Runtime 0.45.1
	Traffic simulator	SUMO 1.22.0 (via TraCI interface)
Classical hardware	Processor (CPU)	Intel Core Ultra 7 155H (16 cores, up to 1.40 GHz)
	Memory (RAM)	64 GB LPDDR5 @ 5600 MT/s
Quantum hardware	Quantum Backend	IBM Quantum `ibm_basquecountry` (Eagle, 156 qubits)
	Coherence times	$T_1 \approx 259,94\mu s$, $T_2 \approx 170,92\mu s$
Execution settings	Optimization and shots	Opt. Level 1, 156 Shots per circuit

4.2 Experimental Results

Figure 2 compares the cumulative network waiting time obtained with the fixed-time baseline, the classical GA, and the hybrid Quantum-GA. The fixed-time plan yielded a waiting time of 1,350,058 s, while the GA reduced this value to 546,759 s, corresponding to an improvement of 59.5%. The hybrid approach achieved 700,121 s, representing a 48.1% reduction with respect to the baseline. Although the hybrid solution did not outperform the best GA result, it provided a lower average waiting time across generations (Table 2), indicating a more stable search behavior.

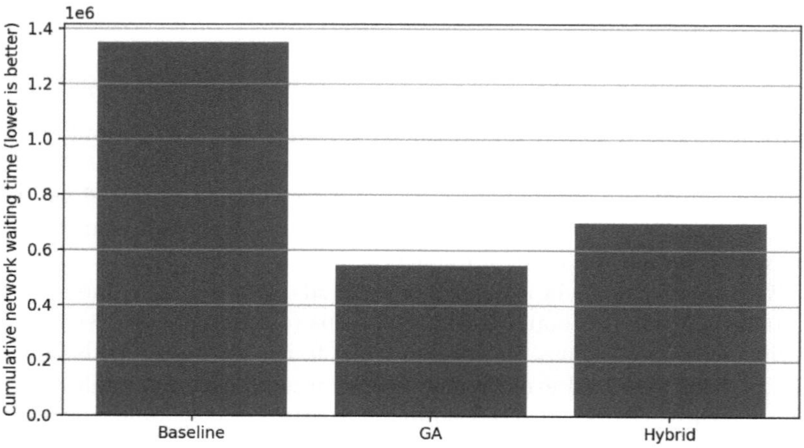

Fig. 2. Comparison of cumulative network waiting time obtained with fixed-time control, classical GA, and the proposed hybrid approach in the roundabout.

Figure 3 shows the convergence curves of the GA and the hybrid method as a function of generations. Both algorithms exhibit a rapid initial decrease in the objective function during the first iterations, followed by a gradual stabilization. The GA reaches a lower minimum fitness, but its curve presents larger oscillations, reflecting higher population variance. In contrast, the hybrid method converges more smoothly, suggesting that the quantum-assisted sampling contributes to maintaining diversity and avoiding abrupt fitness fluctuations.

The Grover sampling histograms (Fig. 4) display the measured bitstring frequencies used for solution injection. The distributions are relatively uniform, indicating limited amplitude amplification under current NISQ constraints. Consequently, the quantum module acts primarily as a diversification mechanism rather than a strong intensification operator, which explains the moderate performance gap with respect to the classical GA.

Table 2 summarizes the aggregated metrics. The GA provides the best minimum waiting time, while the hybrid method achieves a lower average waiting time than the GA, evidencing improved robustness across generations. These

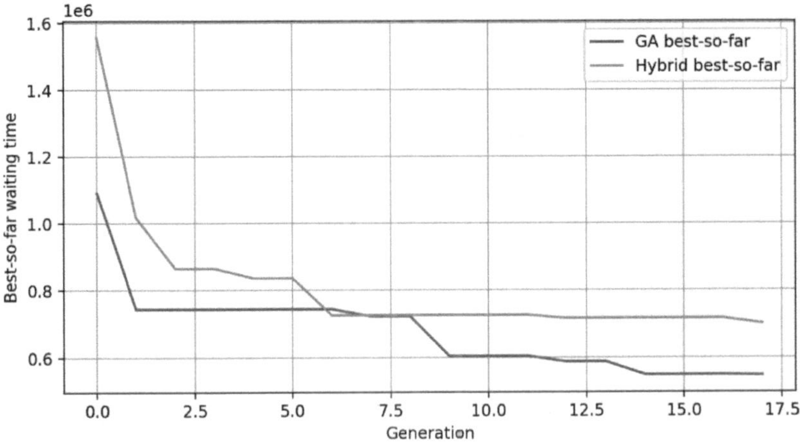

Fig. 3. Convergence behavior of the classical GA and the proposed hybrid across generations, showing fitness evolution in terms of cumulative waiting time.

Table 2. Performance comparison of signal timing strategies at the four-leg signalized roundabout

Method	Best Waiting Time (s)	Avg. Waiting Time (s)	Imp. vs Baseline (%)
Baseline (fixed-time)	1,350,058	1,350,058	–
GA (classical)	546,759.00	1,501,708.14	59.50
Hybrid Quantum-GA	700,121.00	1,301,112.29	48.14

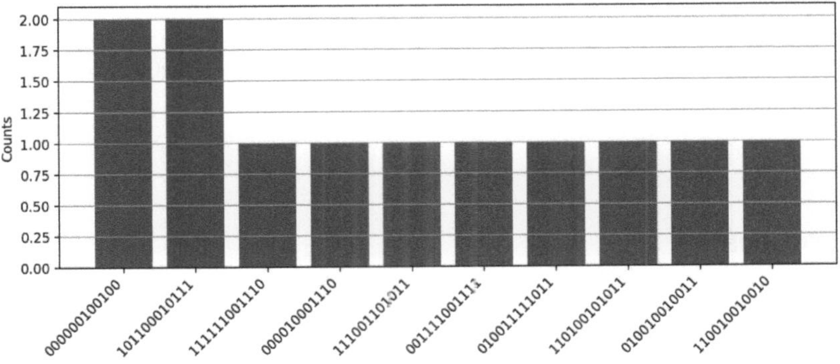

Fig. 4. Grover sampling distribution.

results are consistent with the convergence patterns, where the hybrid approach maintains steadier fitness evolution despite a slightly higher final minimum.

Overall, both evolutionary strategies substantially outperform the fixed-time control at the four-leg signalized roundabout. The classical GA delivers the best optimal solution, whereas the hybrid Quantum-GA offers more stable convergence and competitive performance, highlighting the potential of quantum-assisted sampling within microscopic traffic optimization workflows.

5   Conclusions and Future Prospects

In conclusion, the results obtained in this study support the effectiveness of the proposed hybrid evolutionary–quantum methodology for improving traffic performance at a signalized roundabout compared with the original fixed-time control strategy. The consistency of the observed reductions in cumulative waiting time across different runs highlights the robustness of the genetic optimization of green splits and offsets under realistic engineering constraints. From a quantitative perspective, the classical GA provided the largest performance gains, while the quantum-assisted sampling demonstrated functional integration with the optimization loop, validating the feasibility of using NISQ hardware within traffic control workflows despite limited amplitude amplification under current noise conditions. The results demonstrate that the proposed approach achieves stable convergence and balanced green-time allocation, ensuring operational efficiency and preventing internal spillback in multi-entry roundabouts. Future research will focus on expanding to larger networks, incorporating metrics like emissions and queue length, and utilizing advanced quantum error mitigation. Ultimately, integrating connected-vehicle data for real-time adaptive control remains a primary goal for practical deployment.

Acknowledgments. This work was supported by the Vitoria-Gasteiz Mobility Lab Foundation (an organization of the Provincial Council of Araba and the City Council of Vitoria-Gasteiz) through the grants for the project "Optimization of traffic light cycles". Additionally, the authors wish to express their many thanks to the IBM-Euskadi Quantum Computational Center in Donostia/San Sebastián (BasQ-Basque Quantum initiative) for providing access to the IBM Quantum System Two, which was essential for implementing the quantum algorithms.

References

1. Singh, A.R., Ashraf, M.W.A., Rathore, R.S., Li, B., Sujatha, M.S.: Real-time traffic flow optimization using large language models and reinforcement learning for smart urban mobility. Appl. Soft Comput. **185**, 113917 (2025)
2. Costa, B.C., Leal, S.S., Almeida, P.E.M., Carrano, E.G.: Fixed-time traffic signal optimization using a multi-objective evolutionary algorithm and microsimulation of urban networks. Trans. Inst. Measur. Control **40**(4), 1092–1101 (2018)
3. Alzamzami, O., Alsaggaf, Z., AlMalki, R., Alghamdi, R., Babour, A., Al Khuzayem, L.: Passable: an intelligent traffic light system with integrated incident detection and vehicle alerting. Sensors **25**(18), 5760 (2025)
4. Rodríguez-Díaz, F., Gutiérrez-Avilés, D., Troncoso, A., Martínez-Álvarez, F.: A survey of quantum machine learning: Foundations, algorithms, frameworks, data and applications. ACM Comput. Surv. **58**, 91 (2026)

5. Patel, V., Maltare, N.: From algorithms to connectivity: a comprehensive review of traffic signal optimization and communication based cooperative control. Archives of Computational Methods in Engineering. in press
6. Nie, C., Wei, H., Shi, J., Zhang, M.: Optimizing actuated traffic signal control using license plate recognition data: Methods for modeling and algorithm development. Transp. Res. Interdisc. Perspect. **9**, 100319 (2021)
7. Matilya, N., Zuidgeest, M.H.P., Louw, C., Nnene, O.A.: Evaluating traffic signal optimisation systems using multi-criteria analyses. Transp. Res. Proc. **89**, 550–561 (2025)
8. Agrahari, A., Dhabu, M.M., Deshpande, P.S., Tiwari, A., Baig, M.A., Sawarkar, A.D.: Artificial intelligence-based adaptive traffic signal control system: a comprehensive review. Electronics **13**(19) (2024)
9. Gao, J., Shen, Y., Liu, J., Ito, M., Shiratori, N.: Adaptive Traffic Signal Control: Deep Reinforcement Learning Algorithm with Experience Replay and Target Network (2017). arXiv:1705.02755
10. Ceylan, H., Bell, M.G.H.: Traffic signal timing optimisation based on genetic algorithm approach, including drivers' routing. Transp. Res. Part B Methodol. **38**(4), 329–342 (2004)
11. Li, X., Sun, J.-Q.: Signal multiobjective optimization for urban traffic network. IEEE Trans. Intell. Transp. Syst. **19**(11), 3529–3537 (2018)
12. Mao, T., Mihăită, A.S., Chen, F., Vu, H.L.: Boosted genetic algorithm using machine learning for traffic control optimization. IEEE Trans. Intell. Transp. Syst. **23**(7), 7112–7141 (2021)
13. He, J., Hou, Z.: Ant colony algorithm for traffic signal timing optimization. Adv. Eng. Softw. **43**(1), 14–18 (2012)
14. Jia, H., Lin, Y., Luo, Q., Li, Y., Miao, H.: Multi-objective optimization of urban road intersection signal timing based on particle swarm optimization algorithm. Adv. Mech. Eng. **11**(4), 1–9 (2019)
15. Acampora, G., et al.: Application of quantum genetic algorithms to network signal setting design. In: Proceedings of the IEEE Congress on Evolutionary Computation, pp. 1–8 (2023)
16. Hussain, H., Javaid, M.B., Khan, F.S., Dalal, A., Khalique, A.: Optimal control of traffic signals using quantum annealing. Quantum Inf. Process. **19**, 320 (2020)
17. Neukart, F., Compostella, G., Seidel, C., von Dollen, D., Yarkoni, S., Parney, B.: Traffic flow optimization using a quantum annealer. Front. ICT **24**, 9 (2017)
18. Inoue, D., Okada, A., Matsumori, T., Aihara, K., Yoshida, H.: Traffic signal optimization on a square lattice with quantum annealing. Sci. Rep. **11**, 3033 (2021)

A Genetic Algorithm Framework for Scheduling in Automated Laboratory Analyzers

Carlos Sánchez[1,2]([✉]) [ID] and José Rojas[1]

[1] Vircell S.L., Parque Tecnológico de la Salud, C/ Avicena 8, 18016 Granada, Spain
{csmunoz,jrojas}@vircell.com
[2] Universidad Politécnica de Cartagena, Department of Electronics, Computer Technology and Projects, 30202 Cartagena, Spain

Abstract. Automated clinical analyzers must handle large worklists under strict throughput requirements, where physical operations associated with consumable access can become a bottleneck. This paper addresses a novel plate-aware scheduling problem arising in the VirClia Lotus 360 analyzer, where reagent strips are stored in a refrigerated area and can only be accessed by extracting entire plates into a working area. The goal is to jointly decide (i) the execution order of diagnostic requests and (ii) the assignment of each request to a specific reagent strip, so as to minimize plate handling operations while incorporating soft expiration-aware preferences. To tackle the resulting combinatorial problem, we propose a domain-tailored genetic algorithm with plate-aligned crossover and two complementary mutation operators.

Keywords: Combinatorial optimization · Scheduling · Genetic algorithms · Laboratory automation

1 Introduction

The increasing level of automation in clinical and diagnostic laboratories has led to highly complex operational systems, where efficiency, reliability, and throughput are critical [1]. In this context, the management of consumables and the sequencing of laboratory assays play a key role in overall system performance. This work addresses a combinatorial optimization problem arising in automated laboratory instruments, focusing on minimizing costly physical operations required to access consumable resources.

1.1 Industrial Context and Motivation

Modern clinical laboratories rely on automated analyzers to process large volumes of samples under strict time, quality, and traceability constraints [2]. These

J. M. Ferrández Vicente et al. (Eds.): IWINAC 2026, LNCS 16575, pp. 278–288, 2026.
https://doi.org/10.1007/978-3-032-27317-8_27

systems operate under real physical limitations, including finite storage capacity, mechanical handling constraints, and the need for robotic manipulation of consumables.

In a class of automated clinical analyzers, diagnostic reagents are stored in a refrigerated area (RA) to preserve their stability and shelf life. However, consumables such as reagent plates cannot be accessed directly: in order to retrieve a specific reagent strip, the entire plate must be physically extracted from the RA and transferred to a working area (WA).

Such plate extraction operations represent a non-negligible operational cost, as they are associated with:

- mechanical wear and reduced lifetime of robotic components,
- decreased overall system throughput,
- increased exposure of the RA to humidity and temperature fluctuations, potentially affecting reagent stability.

Reducing the number of such extraction operations is therefore essential to improve efficiency and extend the lifetime of laboratory equipment.

1.2 Combinatorial Optimization Problems in Industrial and Laboratory Systems

The problem studied in this work is closely related to classical combinatorial optimization problems commonly found in industrial settings [3], particularly in production and logistics systems [4]. These problems share common characteristics such as limited resources, sequencing decisions, and cost trade-offs, but the laboratory context introduces additional physical and operational constraints that are not adequately captured by standard formulations.

1.3 Contributions of This Work

The main contributions of this work can be summarized as follows:

- It formulates a novel plate-aware scheduling problem for automated clinical analyzers, explicitly modeling reagent availability and plate handling operations.
- It proposes a genetic algorithm with domain-specific operators and expiration-aware cost modeling tailored to CLIA systems.

2 Formal Problem Definition

2.1 Instrument Description

The instrument under study is the *VirClia Lotus 360*, an automated laboratory analyzer developed by Vircell for the execution of chemiluminescent immunoassays (CLIA). The system is designed to detect antibodies or antigens in human samples and is primarily used in the diagnosis of infectious diseases. The analyzer automates the entire analytical workflow, providing fast, accurate, and standardized results. As a result, it is widely deployed in clinical laboratories and hospital environments.

The VirClia Lotus 360 incorporates a RA with capacity for up to 30 reagent plates, each located in an independent position. Each plate can host up to 12 VirClia reagent strips, which constitute the consumable elements required to perform diagnostic assays. Consequently, the instrument can store up to 360 reagent strips simultaneously, corresponding to 360 individual diagnostic tests.

Workflow Execution. The execution of diagnostic assays follows the simplified workflow described below:

1. A robotic arm retrieves a reagent plate from the RA and transfers it to the WA.
2. A gripper extracts the reagent strip corresponding to the specific test required.
3. The sample is pipetted onto the reagent strip, which is then inserted into an internal rotor where several incubation cycles are performed and additional reagents are applied.
4. For the subsequent assay, if a reagent strip of the required reference is available on the plate currently located in the WA, that strip is directly retrieved and the process resumes from Step 3. Otherwise, the plate is returned to its original position in the RA, and the workflow restarts from 1. If no further assays remain, the execution terminates.

2.2   Problem Model

Let S denote the set of samples and T the set of available test types. A diagnostic request is defined as the execution of a test $t \in T$ on a sample $s \in S$. The set of all diagnostic requests is therefore defined as $R \subseteq S \times T$.

Let L denote the set of plates, with $|L| \leq 30$. Plates may be *mixed*, i.e., different slots within the same plate may contain strips associated with different test types. Let $K = \{1, \ldots, 12\}$ denote the set of strip slots within a plate. For each plate $l \in L$ and slot $k \in K$, let $\tau(l, k) \in T \cup \{\varnothing\}$ denote the test type of the strip stored in that slot (or $\varnothing$ if the slot is empty).

Each reagent strip is further characterized by two temporal attributes related to its expiration:

- the *lot expiration*, which corresponds to the maximum shelf life defined by the manufacturing lot (typically 18 months), and
- the *on-board expiration*, which is defined as a fixed period of 30 days starting from the moment the strip is loaded into the RA.

The effective expiration of a strip is determined by the interaction of both attributes. Expiration information does not impose hard feasibility constraints on the scheduling problem, since strips that reach their expiration while stored on-board are automatically discarded by the analyzer. However, expiration-related attributes are relevant from an operational perspective and are used to guide strip selection decisions in order to reduce on-board waste.

The problem addressed in this work consists of jointly:

- selecting, for each request $(s, t) \in R$, a plate–slot pair (l, k) such that $\tau(l, k) = t$ and the strip is available,
- determining a temporal execution sequence for all requests.

A key operational constraint is that strips cannot be accessed directly from RA. To retrieve any strip from a plate, the entire plate must be extracted from the RA and transferred to the WA.

2.3   Objective Function

Let $n = |R|$ be the number of diagnostic requests. A schedule is defined by (i) a permutation $\pi : \{1, \ldots, n\} \to R$ that specifies the execution order of requests, and (ii) an assignment $a : R \to L \times K$ that maps each request $r \in R$ to a plate–slot pair (l, k) such that $\tau(l, k)$ matches the required test type and the strip is available at the time of execution.

For each position $i \in \{1, \ldots, n\}$ in the sequence, let $u_i \in L$ denote the plate used to satisfy the request $\pi(i)$, i.e., if $a(\pi(i)) = (l, k)$ then $u_i = l$. In addition, let $u_0 \in L \cup \{\varnothing\}$ denote the plate initially located in the WA, where $u_0 = \varnothing$ indicates that no plate is present at the beginning of the execution.

The total number of plate handling operations induced by a schedule corresponds to the number of times the plate present in the WA changes during execution. The **plate handling cost** is therefore defined as:

$$
E(\pi, a) = \sum_{i=1}^{n} \mathbb{I}[u_i \neq u_{i-1}],
$$

where $\mathbb{I}[\cdot]$ is the indicator function, equal to 1 if the condition holds and 0 otherwise.

In addition to minimizing plate handling operations, **expiration-related considerations** are taken into account from an operational perspective. Although selecting the strip with the earliest effective expiration is not mandatory, it is desirable to reduce the risk of on-board reagent waste by preferentially consuming strips with shorter remaining lifetime.

The overall optimization objective is therefore formulated as:

$$
\min_{\pi, a} \; F(\pi, a) = \alpha \, E(\pi, a) + \beta \, C_{\exp}(\pi, a),
$$

where $\alpha, \beta \geq 0$ are weighting parameters. The specific definition of $C_{\exp}(\pi, a)$ is detailed in Sect. 3.1.

2.4   Constraints

Any feasible schedule must satisfy the following constraints:

- **Request satisfaction:** each diagnostic request $r \in R$ must be executed exactly once.
- **Strip availability:** a request $(s, t) \in R$ can only be assigned to a plate–slot pair (l, k) such that $\tau(l, k) = t$ and the corresponding reagent strip has not been previously consumed.
- **Slot capacity:** each strip slot (l, k) can host at most one reagent strip.
- **Plate access:** at any point in time, at most one plate can be located in the WA of the analyzer.

It is assumed that a diagnostic request is only issued by the system if the required reagent strips are available in the RA. Therefore, reagent unavailability is not considered as part of the scheduling decision problem.

2.5   Computational Complexity

The problem considered in this work is combinatorial, as it requires jointly deciding (i) the assignment of requests to available reagent strips and (ii) the execution order under plate-handling constraints. Even in simplified settings where assignments are fixed, minimizing the number of plate changes along the sequence is equivalent to a single-machine sequencing problem with sequence-dependent setup costs, which is NP-hard. Therefore, exact optimization methods do not scale to realistic workloads, motivating the use of metaheuristic approaches.

3   Materials and Methods

3.1   Proposed Genetic Algorithm

Due to the combinatorial complexity of the problem, exact optimization methods are not suitable for realistic problem sizes. Consequently, a bio-inspired metaheuristic based on a genetic algorithm (GA) is proposed to efficiently explore the solution space and identify high-quality schedules [5].

GAs are particularly well suited to this problem, as they can jointly handle assignment and sequencing decisions while naturally incorporating complex cost functions. The GA iteratively evolves a population of candidate schedules through selection, crossover, and mutation operators, guided by a fitness function [6]. The following subsections describe the main components of the proposed GA.

Solution Encoding. Each chromosome represents a complete scheduling solution. Let R denote the set of diagnostic requests, with $n = |R|$. A chromosome is encoded as a permutation vector

$$\mathbf{x} = (x_1, x_2, \ldots, x_n),$$

where each gene x_i encodes a unique diagnostic request $r \in R$ together with a specific reagent strip (implicitly defining its plate and slot). Each diagnostic request appears exactly once in the chromosome. The position of a gene within the chromosome defines the execution order of the corresponding request.

Initial Population. The initial population is generated using a semi-random constructive procedure designed to promote plate reuse while preserving population diversity. Rather than relying on purely random permutations, the initialization process biases the construction of chromosomes toward grouping diagnostic requests of the same test type and, whenever possible, serving them from the same reagent plate.

At each step, a test type is selected uniformly at random among those still pending. Up to 12 requests of that test type (i.e., one plate capacity) are then scheduled consecutively. A reagent plate is selected at random among those that currently provide available strips of the selected test, and the algorithm assigns as many strips as possible from that plate to consecutive genes. If the selected plate does not provide enough strips to cover the selected batch size, all available strips are assigned and the remaining demand is returned to the pending set to be scheduled in subsequent iterations.

Fitness Evaluation. The fitness of a chromosome is evaluated through a decoding procedure that determines the plate used at each step as well as the expiration-related attributes of the selected strip, enabling the computation of the operational cost of the schedule.

Let $\mathbf{x}$ denote a chromosome and $u_i \in L$ denote the plate selected by the decoder to satisfy request x_i, and let $u_0 \in L \cup \{\varnothing\}$ denote the plate initially present in the WA. The fitness value $f(\mathbf{x})$ provides a concrete evaluation of the global objective function and is computed as:

$$f(\mathbf{x}) = \sum_{i=1}^{n} \mathbb{I}[u_i \neq u_{i-1}] + \sum_{i=1}^{n} \left(\gamma \cdot \phi_{\text{lot}}(x_i') + \delta \cdot \phi_{\text{on}}(x_i'') \right).$$

The term x_i' denotes the number of days remaining until the lot-level expiration of the reagent strip selected to satisfy request x_i, while x_i'' denotes the number of days remaining until the on-board expiration of the strip. The functions $\phi_{\text{lot}}(\cdot)$ and $\phi_{\text{on}}(\cdot)$ map expiration information to normalized urgency scores.

Under this formulation, expiration terms softly bias strip selection toward consuming more urgent reagents to reduce waste, while still allowing plate reuse when it minimizes handling; parameters γ and δ control the influence of lot-level and on-board expiration.

Selection Strategy. The parent selection mechanism will be determined during the experimental phase. Specifically, two alternative approaches will be comparatively evaluated: **tournament selection** and **linear ranking**. The final choice will be based on empirical performance with respect to convergence behavior, solution quality, and population diversity.

Crossover Operator. The crossover operator is designed to recombine both execution order and reagent assignment information. Given two parent chromosomes $\mathbf{x}^{(1)}$ and $\mathbf{x}^{(2)}$, the crossover proceeds as follows:

1. **Plate-aligned cut selection.** Two crossover points are selected at random on the first parent. Consider these points as $i, j \in \{1, \ldots, n\}$ with $i < j$. Each point is expanded to the boundaries of the corresponding maximal contiguous block of requests assigned to the same plate, yielding a plate-consistent segment $[i_1, j_2]$.
2. **Segment inheritance from the first parent.** The plate-consistent segment $\mathbf{x}^{(1)}[i_1 : j_2]$ is copied unchanged into the offspring.
3. **Order-based completion from the second parent.** The remaining positions are then filled by scanning $\mathbf{x}^{(2)}$ from left to right and inserting the requests that are not yet present in $\mathbf{y}$ (preserving their order in $\mathbf{x}^{(2)}$).
4. **Boundary adjustment.** To avoid introducing artificial plate-handling events at the crossover boundaries, if the request (gene) immediately preceding position i_1 in the offspring $\mathbf{y}$ is served from the same reagent plate as the first request of the inherited segment, the segment is extended to include all adjacent requests associated with that plate before insertion.

The resulting offspring combines plate-consistent structures from the first parent with ordering and reagent assignment information from the second parent. However, overlapping strip assignments may occur when reagent strips inherited from the second parent conflict with those already present in the inherited segment. In such cases, the offspring is identified as infeasible and discarded.

Mutation Operators. To enhance population diversity and avoid premature convergence, two complementary mutation operators are employed in the proposed GA. Each operator targets a different structural aspect of the scheduling solution and is applied independently with its own mutation probability, allowing the algorithm to balance exploration of execution order and resource assignment.

Order-Based Mutation. This operator modifies the execution order of diagnostic requests while preserving their plate assignments. Given a chromosome $\mathbf{x} = (x_1, \ldots, x_n)$, two positions $i < j$ are selected such that the corresponding requests are associated with different reagent plates. For each position, the maximal contiguous segment $[i_1, i_2]$ and $[j_1, j_2]$ containing requests served from the same plate is identified. The mutation consists of swapping these two entire segments in the sequence, yielding the mutated chromosome

$$(x_1, \ldots, x_{j_1}, \ldots, x_{j_2}, \ldots, x_{i_1}, \ldots, x_{i_2}, \ldots, x_n).$$

This preserves the plate assignment induced by the decoder while exploring alternative execution orders. If the chromosome contains requests associated with fewer than two distinct plates, the operator is not applied.

Plate Reassignment Mutation. The second mutation operator reassigns diagnostic requests to reagent plates. A test type $t \in T$ present in the chromosome $\mathbf{x}$ is selected uniformly at random. Let $[i_1, i_2]$ be a maximal contiguous segment of $\mathbf{x}$ such that all requests x_i, $i_1 \leq i \leq i_2$, correspond to test type t and are currently served from the same reagent plate $l \in L$.

The mutation searches for an alternative plate $l' \in L$, $l' \neq l$, that contains a sufficient number of unused reagent strips of type t to satisfy all requests in the segment. If such a plate exists, the entire segment $[i_1, i_2]$ is reassigned to plate l', and the corresponding strip positions are updated accordingly.

Population Replacement. A generational replacement scheme is adopted. At each generation, a new population of size N is constructed by repeatedly selecting two parents via tournament selection and generating two offspring. Crossover is applied with probability p_c; otherwise, offspring are direct copies of the selected parents. Subsequently, two mutation operators are applied independently: the order-based mutation with probability p_{m1} and the plate-reassignment mutation with probability p_{m2}.

To promote **diversity**, newly generated offspring are required to be non-duplicated within the new population. Any offspring that violates feasibility conditions is replaced by a clone of its corresponding parent. After all offspring have been generated, the new population is sorted according to fitness. An **elitist strategy** is then enforced to guarantee that the best chromosome from the previous generation survives: if the previous best individual is not present in the new population, it replaces the worst individual.

This replacement mechanism combines exploration (via stochastic reproduction and diversity preservation) with exploitation (via elitism).

Stopping Criterion. The GA uses a dual stopping criterion. The search terminates either when the maximum number of generations $G_{\max}$ is reached or when convergence is detected. Specifically, if the best chromosome $\mathbf{x}_g^\star$ remains unchanged for G_{stall} consecutive generations, the algorithm stops. In the experimental setup, $G_{\text{stall}} = 40$. This criterion limits unnecessary computation once no further improvement is observed.

Let $\mathbf{x}_g^\star$ denote the best chromosome (lowest fitness) found at generation g. The early-stopping condition is triggered when

$$\mathbf{x}_g^\star = \mathbf{x}_{g-1}^\star = \cdots = \mathbf{x}_{g-G_{\text{stall}}+1}^\star,$$

i.e., when the best-so-far solution has not improved for G_{stall} generations. In the experimental setup, G_{stall} is set to 40. This combined criterion provides a trade-off between computational effort and solution quality by allowing the algorithm to stop early.

3.2 Illustrative Example

This section presents an illustrative example of the crossover and mutation operators applied to two parent chromosomes. Each gene represents a diagnostic request encoded as `test@sample_id`. The numerical value associated with each gene indicates the location of the reagent strip (from 1 to 360) selected to satisfy that request.

Parent Chromosomes. Consider two parent chromosomes:

Parent 1

HEP@1	HEP@2	DIP@1	DIP@2	DIP@3	DIP@4	MEA@1	MEA@2	MEA@3	MEA@4
49	50	85	86	87	88	1	2	3	4

MEA@5	MEA@6	MEA@7	MEA@8	MEA@9	MEA@10	MEA@11	MEA@12	MEA@13	MEA@14
5	6	7	8	9	10	11	12	13	14

Parent 2

HEP@1	HEP@2	MEA@1	MEA@2	MEA@3	MEA@4	MEA@5	MEA@6	MEA@7	MEA@8
39	40	1	2	3	4	5	6	7	8

MEA@9	MEA@10	MEA@11	MEA@12	MEA@13	MEA@14	DIP@1	DIP@2	DIP@3	DIP@4
9	10	11	12	13	14	85	86	87	88

The acronym `HEP` is used for `Hepatitis` test, `MEA` for `Measles` test and `DIP` for `Diphtheria` test.

Crossover. The randomly selected crossover points are `MEA@5` (assigned to strip 5) and `MEA@8` (assigned to strip 8). After adjustment, these points become in `MEA@1` (assigned to strip 1) and `MEA@12` (assigned to strip 12). These points define the part of Parent 1 that will be inherited. These genes are highlighted in yellow.

Child

HEP@1	HEP@2	MEA@13	MEA@14	MEA@1	MEA@2	MEA@3	MEA@4	MEA@5	MEA@6
39	40	13	14	1	2	3	4	5	6

MEA@7	MEA@8	MEA@9	MEA@10	MEA@11	MEA@12	DIP@1	DIP@2	DIP@3	DIP@4
7	8	9	10	11	12	85	86	87	88

The rest of the points from Parent 1 that are not selected, will be inherited from Parent 2, respecting the order and the strips assignments of this ancestor. These genes are highlighted in blue.

Mutation. Child after order mutation (randomly points are `HEP@1` and `DIP@3`):

DIP@1	DIP@2	DIP@3	DIP@4	MEA@13	MEA@14	MEA@1	MEA@2	MEA@3	MEA@4
85	86	87	88	13	14	1	2	3	4

MEA@5	MEA@6	MEA@7	MEA@8	MEA@9	MEA@10	MEA@11	MEA@12	HEP@1	HEP@2
5	6	7	8	9	10	11	12	39	40

Child after plate mutation (new strips are selected for `HEP` requests):

DIP@1	DIP@2	DIP@3	DIP@4	MEA@13	MEA@14	MEA@1	MEA@2	MEA@3	MEA@4
85	86	87	88	13	14	1	2	3	4

MEA@5	MEA@6	MEA@7	MEA@8	MEA@9	MEA@10	MEA@11	MEA@12	HEP@1	HEP@2
5	6	7	8	9	10	11	12	70	71

4   Conclusions and Future Work

This paper presents a novel optimization framework for minimizing plate extractions in automated laboratory instruments. A natural extension of the proposed approach consists in optimizing not only the execution schedule, but also the configuration of the RA itself.

Acknowledgments. All the work presented in this study was carried out within the framework of Vircell S.L., Spain. No external funding was received.

Disclosure of Interests. Carlos Sánchez and José Rojas are employees of Vircell S.L., Spain. The authors declare no additional conflicts of interest.

References

1. Antonios, K., Croxatto, A., Culbreath, K.: Current state of laboratory automation in clinical microbiology laboratory. Clin. Chem. **68**(1), 99–114 (2022). https://doi.org/10.1093/clinchem/hvab242
2. Cherkaoui, A., Schrenzel, J.: Total laboratory automation for rapid detection and identification of microorganisms and their antimicrobial resistance profiles. Front. Cell. Infect. Microbiol. **12**, 2022 . https://doi.org/10.3389/fcimb.2022.807668
3. Zhang, Y., Ogura, H., Ma, X., Kuroiwa, J., Odaka, T.: A genetic algorithm using infeasible solutions for constrained optimization problems. Open Cybern. Syst. J. **8**, 904–912 (2014). https://doi.org/10.2174/1874110X01408010904

4. Zhou, Y., Xu, Y., Xie, K., Li, J.: Joint optimization of storage allocation and picking efficiency for fresh products using a particle swarm-guided hybrid genetic algorithm. Mathematics **13**(21) (2025). https://doi.org/10.3390/math13213428
5. Goldberg, D.E., Holland, J.H.: Genetic algorithms and machine learning. Mach. Learn. **3**(2), 95–99 (1988). https://doi.org/10.1023/A:1022602019183
6. Mitchell, M.: An Introduction to Genetic Algorithms. MIT Press, Cambridge (1996). https://doi.org/10.7551/mitpress/3927.001.0001

SHIFT: "Social and Civil Engineering through Human AI Translations"

A Bio-Inspired Cross-Modal Attention Framework for Robust Multimodal Multimedia Perception

Kimia Shirini[1]([✉]) [iD], Sina Samadi Gharehveran[2] [iD], Saman Rajebi[3] [iD],
Siamak Pedrammehr[4] [iD], Roohallah Alizadehsani[5] [iD],
and Juan Manuel Gorriz Saez[6]

[1] Faculty of Multi-Media, Tabriz Islamic Art University, Tabriz, Iran
[2] Department of Electrical and Computer Engineering, University of Tabriz, Tabriz, Iran
[3] Department of Electrical Engineering, Seraj University, Tabriz, Iran
[4] Faculty of design, Tabriz Islamic Art University, Tabriz, Iran
[5] Institute for Intelligent Systems Research and Innovation, Deakin University, Waurn Ponds, Sydney 3216, Australia
[6] Data Science and Computational Intelligence Institute, University of Granada, Granada, Spain

Abstract. The abstract should briefly summarize the contents of the paper in The growing presence of multimedia data in contemporary digital spaces has posed a high demand of artificial intelligence systems that can comprehend information that is presented in a multi-modal form of vision, audio and language. The human perception offers a viable and naturalistically based paradigm to solve this problem because the brain has a natural habit of integrating heterogeneous information of sensory signals based on hierarchical processing, selective attention and contextual learning. Our proposed bio-inspired multimodal deep learning framework is intended to be used in cognitive multimedia perception in this paper. In particular, we propose a cross-modal attention mechanism based on biology which dynamically models the reliability of the modality and removes the noisy or missing senses. The given method uses modality-specific deep encoders and attention-based fusion strategy based on the human multisensory integration, which allows to adaptively weight visual, auditory and textual information depending on its relevance to the current situation. Extensive simulations on representative multimodal benchmarks show that the proposed framework always beats unimodal frameworks and traditional multimodal fusion schemes with respect to accuracy, robustness and interpretability. According to its experimental findings, the maximum absolute accuracy increase compared to its traditional fusion approaches is 4.4% under noisy modality conditions, with the attention mechanism also offering explainable information about modality contributions. The above findings indicate that the integration of biological and cognitive concepts with multimodal deep learning architectures results in better, more efficient, and more human-like multimedia perception systems that can be applied to practice.

J. M. Ferrández Vicente et al. (Eds.): IWINAC 2026, LNCS 16575, pp. 291–301, 2026.
https://doi.org/10.1007/978-3-032-27317-8_28

Keywords: Multimodal Deep Learning · Bio-inspired Artificial
Intelligence · Cognitive Perception · Multimedia Analysis ·
Cross-modal Attention

1   Introduction

A rapid increase in multimedia data has become one of the features of the
digital age. The social media, intelligent sensors, surveillance systems, and
human-computer interaction applicants continually produce images, videos,
audio streams, and textual content. It is only possible to understand and interpret such data with the help of artificial intelligence (AI) systems that would be
able to process and combine information across several modalities in a meaningful and consistent way [1].

Deep learning has been highly successful in unimodal perceptions, such
as vision, speech, and language processing. Nevertheless, practical intelligence
necessitates integration of several senses to bring forth strong, situational perception.

Multimodal AI methods currently utilized are typically based on basic fusion
methods, including early feature concatenation or late decision fusion. Though
these techniques may be more useful than unimodal models, they often do not
reveal deeper semantic links between modalities. Additionally, a large number
of the multimodal deep learning models have been largely engineering-centric
and are not explicitly grounded in either biological or cognitive principles, which
restricts its interpretability and robustness [2–4]. Although recent developments
in multimodal deep learning allow effective fusion, the majority of the current
fusion methods implicitly believe that the reliability of modalities is equal and
fail to provide the adaptive mechanisms of modality suppression in the conditions
of noisy or missing data. This causes their performance to lower to significantly
low levels with real-world multimedia. In addition, few studies directly include
biologically based principles, including selective attention and cross-modal modulation, into the multimodal fusion design, which results in a low degree of
robustness and interpretability. In order to overcome these constraints, the paper
has proposed a bio-inspired multimodal deep learning architecture that explicitly
addresses selective attention and cross-modal interactions to adaptively weight
sensory modalities to show contextual relevance and signal reliability.

Developments in cognitive neuroscience have revealed that the human perception relies on hierarchical processing of sensory information, selective attention,
and dynamical cross-modal interactions. These principles are of great inspiration
in designing better multimodal AI systems. Specifically, attention mechanisms
are essential in the process of the selective filtering of the relevant information
and organization of sensory integration in the brain.

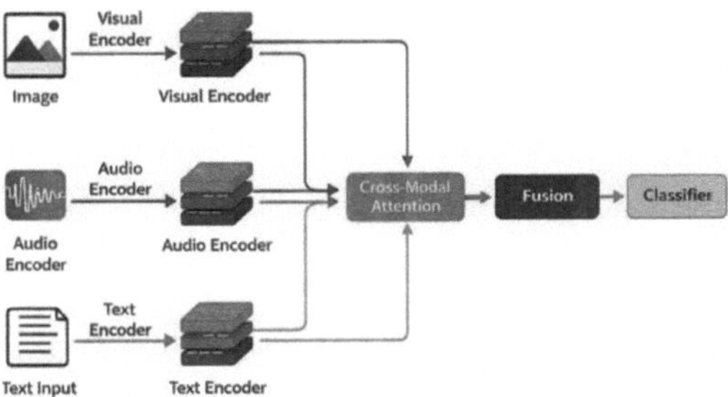

Fig. 1. Overall architecture of the proposed bio-inspired multimodal deep learning framework, illustrating modality-specific encoders and cross-modal attention-based fusion.

Figure 1 demonstrates the general structure of the suggested bio-inspired multimodal deep learning design, comprising of modality-specific encoders and a cross-modal attention-based fusion process. Driven by such observations, this paper will present a proposal of a bio-inspired multimodal deep learning framework of cognitive multimedia perception. The prime contributions of this work are as follows:

- We propose a bio-inspired multimodal deep learning architecture that explicitly models hierarchical sensory processing through modality-specific encoders.
- We introduce a novel cross-modal attention-based fusion mechanism that dynamically estimates modality relevance and suppresses unreliable sensory inputs.
- We conduct extensive robustness evaluations under noisy and missing modality conditions, demonstrating improved accuracy and stability compared to conventional multimodal fusion strategies.

2 Related Work

2.1 Multimodal Deep Learning

Multimodal deep learning tries to acquire joint representations using mixed data sources [5]. The initial multimodal learning models were based on the hand-crafted features and were based on the first fusion methods, whereby the features of various modalities were joined together prior to classification. Subsequent methods used late fusion strategies, which are combinations of the results of unimodal classifiers [6]. Multimodal learning of representation has tremendously changed with the development of deep learning. Modality-specific encoders of neural networks and shared representation layers have become common. More recently, more effective cross-modal interaction has been modelled using attention mechanisms and transformer-based architectures. In spite of these developments, most multimodal deep learning models are mostly data driven and not overtly based on cognitive or biological conceptualizations.

The proposed framework is a contrast to the current attention-based multimodal models which mainly concentrate on feature alignment, but instead, the framework concentrates on biologically plausible selective attention and adaptive modality weighting, especially in unfavourable sensing environments.

2.2   Bio-Inspired and Cognitive Artificial Intelligence

To enhance adaptability, robustness, and interpretability, bio-inspired artificial intelligence has attempted to make use of biological neural systems and cognitive processes including perception, attention, learning, and memory. Neurobiological discoveries including attention mechanisms have inspired attention mechanisms, which have been found to work effectively in a broad scope of AI applications [7].

Nevertheless, there is a gap in understanding of bio-inspiration related to multimodal deep learning to perceive multimedia, which is still an open research problem. One of the motivations of this work is to bridge the gap between biological plausibility and computational efficiency.

2.3   Multimedia Perception and Understanding

Multimedia perception is characterized by the interactions between individuals and technology that promote perception, listening, and comprehension.<—human—>2.3 Multimedia Perception and Understanding Multimedia perception is defined as the interactions between individuals and technology that facilitate perception, listening and comprehension.

Image captioning, audio-visual event detection, emotion recognition, and multimedia retrieval are some of the tasks that are used in multimedia perception. These activities can be marked in terms of difficulties associated with the imbalance of modality, noise, time distortion, and semantic inconsistency. These challenges can be effectively solved with the help of human perception by selective attention and cross-modal integration, which gives the stimulus to cognitively inspired multimedia AI systems.

3   Biological and Cognitive Inspiration

The perceptions of human beings are multimodal and hierarchical. Semantic processing Visual data is processed in several areas of the cortex that strip data of edges, shapes, motion, and semantics [8]. Temporal and frequency-dependent processing is involved in the auditory perception, and distributed cortical networks are used in language comprehension [9]. These pathways of sensing are not independent and rather interact in complex cross-modular connections. Figure 2 offers a conceptual representation of the mechanism of human-inspired multisensory integration and selective attention, which promotes the suggested framework.

The role of selective attention in human perception is dominant. According to neurophysiological evidence, the dynamical regulation of neural state responses with regard to attention promotes the focusing of task-related stimuli over irrelevant stimuli [10,11]. The mechanism allows humans to process complex sensory environments and adapt to changing situations in an efficient manner.

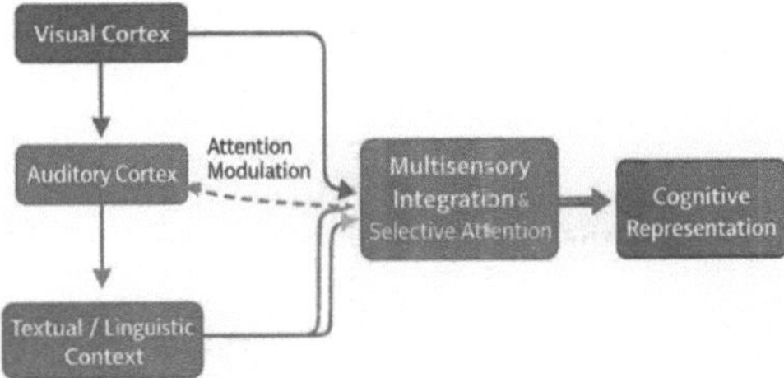

Fig. 2. Conceptual illustration of human-inspired multisensory integration and selective attention mechanisms.

The cross-modal integration also increases perception by enabling one modality of information to disambiguate or to reinforce information of another modality. As an illustration, visual cues can be used to enhance speech comprehension in noisy conditions, and textual context can be used to direct visual attention. The proposed bio-inspired multimodal framework is based on these principles.

The following biological observations themselves are what drive the development of the suggested cross-modal attention mechanism, in which the modality contributions are dynamically regulated in response to the relevance of the context and reliability of the signal.

4 Suggested Multimodal Framework Bio-Inspired.

4.1 Architecture Overview

The given framework will comprise three encoders of modality-specific features and a cross-modal fusion unit. Both encoders are required to extract high-level representations of a certain modality whilst maintaining modality specific attributes.

Images or video frames are processed by the visual encoder with the help of a deep convolutional neural net or vision transformer architecture. This encoder stores spatial and semantic information of visual perception.

The audio encoder uses either the convolutional architecture or transformer based architecture to process the acoustic signals that are in the form of spectrograms. This encoder records time and frequency-based trends of auditory data.

The text encoder uses a language model that is based on transformers to encode semantic information of textual inputs. This encoder records contextual relations, and syntactic relations in language data. Figure 3 depicts the encoder pipelines that are mode specific in processing visual, auditory, and textual signals.

Table 1 shows the architectural layout of the modality-specific encoders, specifying the type of network that is used and the dimensional feature of the output (a visual, auditory, and textual features) of visual, auditory, and textual information, respectively.

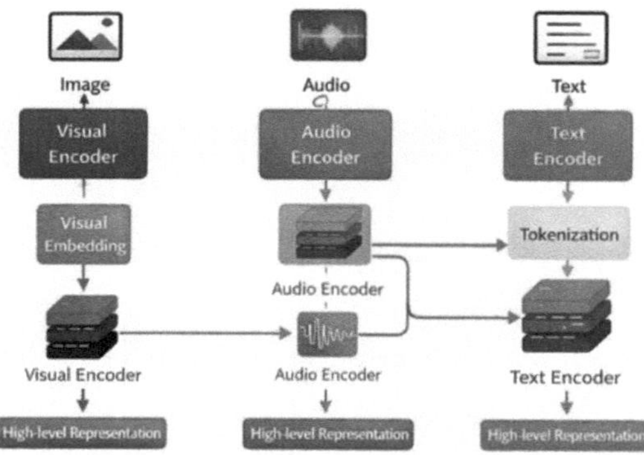

Fig. 3. Modality-specific encoder pipelines for visual, auditory, and textual information processing.

Table 1. Modality-specific encoder configurations

Modality	Architecture	Output Dimension
Visual	CNN/ViT	d_v
Audio	CNN/Transformer	d_a
Text	Transformer	d_a

4.2 Attention Based Cross-Modal Fusion

Human perception is based on process of selective attention so as to dynamically highlight the credible sensory input and reduce noisy or irrelevant sensory information. Based on this idea, a cross-modal attention-based fusion approach has been proposed in this framework, which aims to flexibly combine visual, auditory, and textual representations.

Where V, A and T represent the encoded visual, auditory, and textual features representations derived out of the respective modality-specific encoders. In order to simulate the relative significance and trustworthiness of each modality, a cross-modal attention mechanism is utilized. Attention weights are computed, per modality, on a query-key projection which is modality-specific.

$$a_i = softmax(f(Q_i, k_i)) \tag{1}$$

Q_i and K_j are the query and key vectors in the i-th and j-th mode respectively, and $f(\cdot)$ a similarity function which models inter-modal dependencies. The weight of the attention ireflects the degree of reliability and contextual relevance of each modality.

These attention weights can be later used to adaptively merge modality specific representations such that the model can focus on informative modalities whilst ignoring unreliable or noisy sensory modalities. This dynamic fusion process can allow strong perception in multimodal conditions, especially in conditions of modality imbalance, noise corruptions or missing data. The proposed method has enhanced robustness and interpretability by explicitly modeling cross-modal interactions in the form of attention, which fits quite well on human-like multisensory integration behavior.

The fusion module, which was inspired by human selective attention, uses a cross-modal attention mechanism to combine dynamically the modality-specific representations. Attention scores are calculated in modalities and the model is able to focus on the most informative sensory channels based on the given situation and task.

This is an adaptive fusion mechanism which enables the model to deal with modality imbalance and noise. In case of unreliability or absence of a single modality, attention process shifts to more informative modalities, which is a behavior that is similar to human perception between visual, auditory and textual representations. Every cell is the score of attention between two modalities, and it allows the model to focus on the most informative sensory modalities of the given context. This process allows strong and interpretable fusion, which enhances noisy or incomplete modality performance (Fig. 4).

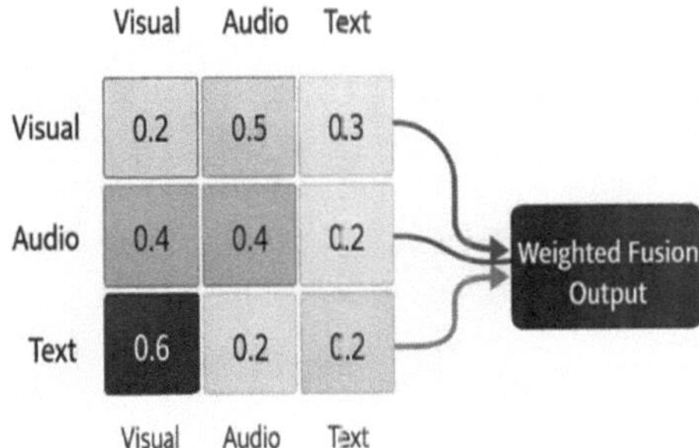

Fig. 4. Cross-modal attention mechanism for adaptive multimodal fusion, illustrating inter-modal dependency modeling.

4.3 Learning Objective

This whole system is trained in an end-to-end manner with task-specific loss functions. Categorical cross-entropy loss is used in classification tasks. The utilization of regularization techniques is used in avoiding overfitting and promoting balanced multimodal learning.

5 Simulation and Experimental Set-Up

5.1 Data and Datasets Constructions

In order to test the suggested bio-inspired multimodal framework in a controlled and replicable way, we created three synthetic multimodal datasets that model realistic multimedia perception situations in the real world. All data sets combine various forms of visual plus auditory plus text display and are created to evaluate multimodal integration, strength and multimodal interaction across varied conditions.

Dataset A Data A is made up of paired image and text samples to be classified in multimodal classification. Dataset B will have audio-visual pairs of similar samples to be used in event detection exercises, whereas Data C will combine images, audio, and text to detect emotions. The samples were created and filtered using publicly available unimodal sources, after which modality alignment and preprocessing was done in order to create consistency across modalities.

In order to evaluate robustness, controlled noise was independently added to each modality via the application of Gaussian noise, random masking, or modality dropout at the varying level. Selective removal of one or more modalities in inference simulated missing-modality scenarios. These environments allow systematically testing the robustness of models in realistic sensing environments (Table 2).

Table 2. Summary of multimodal datasets used in the experimental evaluation.

Dataset	Modalities	Samples	Task	Source
Dataset A	Image + Text	10,000	Classification	Constructed
Dataset B	Audio + Visual	8,500	Event Detection	Constructed
Dataset C	Image + Audio + Text	6,200	Emotion Recognition	Constructed

5.2   Baseline Models

The proposed model is compared against several baseline approaches, including unimodal deep learning models, early fusion multimodal models, and late fusion multimodal models.

5.3   Evaluation Metrics

Performance is evaluated using accuracy, precision, recall, and F1-score. Robustness is assessed by introducing artificial noise and missing modality scenarios. Table 3 presents a comparison of the proposed framework with baseline methods, including unimodal and conventional multimodal approaches.

Table 3 shows that the proposed bio-inspired multimodal model consistently outperforms unimodal and conventional fusion approaches in terms of accuracy and F1-score. The cross-modal attention mechanism contributes significantly to robustness under noisy or missing modality conditions, validating the effectiveness of the biologically inspired design.

Table 3. Performance comparison between unimodal, conventional multimodal, and proposed bio-inspired models

Model	Accuracy (%)	F1-score
Visual only	78.4	0.76
Audio only	71.2	0.69
Early Fusion	82.1 ± 0.6	0.81
Late Fusion	84.3	0.83
Proposed Model	88.7 ± 0.4	0.87

6   Results and Discussion

The experimental evidence indicates that the suggested bio-inspired multimodal framework is always superior compared to the baseline models in all the measures of evaluation. The cross-modal attention mechanism has a significant role in increasing robustness in the noisy conditions and increasing interpretability by giving the insights into modality relevance. Attention images indicate that the model dynamically changes its attention based on the task and quality of the input which is in line with human strategies of perceiving.

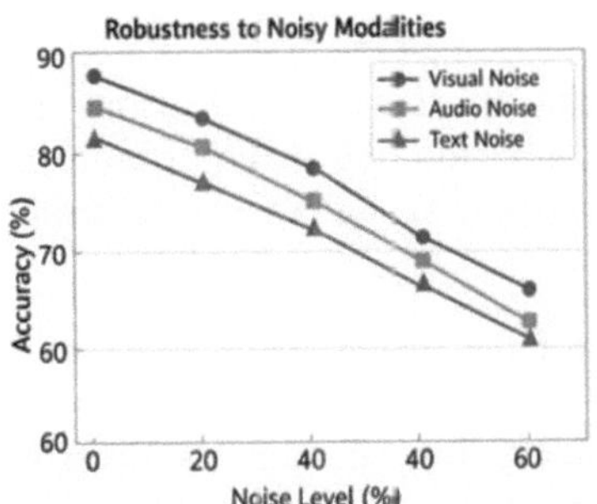

Fig. 5. Robustness analysis of unimodal, conventional multimodal, and proposed bio-inspired model under increasing modality noise.

Figure 5 demonstrates that the proposed cross-modal attention-based framework degrades gracefully under increasing modality noise, whereas unimodal and conventional fusion models show more significant performance drops. The attention mechanism effectively shifts focus to more reliable modalities, maintaining robust performance and illustrating the advantage of bio-inspired adaptive fusion.

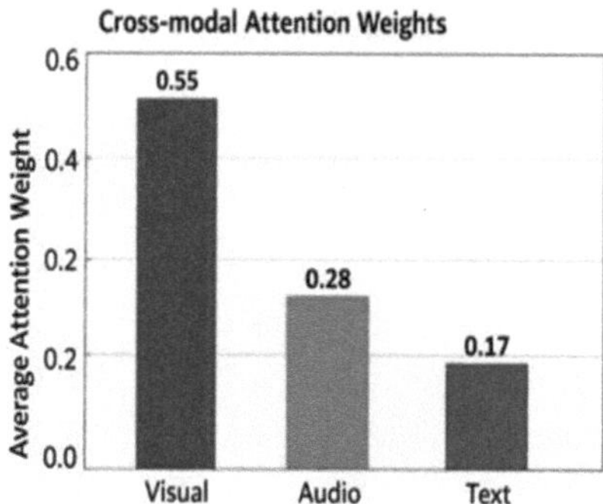

Fig. 6. Cross-modal attention weight visualization highlighting the relative importance of visual, auditory, and textual modalities for a representative input.

As shown in Fig. 6, the model assigns varying attention weights to each modality, dynamically reflecting their contribution to the fused representation. Visual information is often dominant, followed by auditory and textual inputs, demonstrating alignment with human-like multisensory integration and enhancing interpretability of the model's decisions.

7 Applications

The proposed framework has potential applications in multimedia content analysis, humancomputer interaction, affective computing, assistive technologies, intelligent surveillance systems, and adaptive multimedia retrieval.

8 Conclusion and Future Work

This paper presented a bio-inspired multimodal deep learning framework for cognitive multimedia perception. By incorporating principles from human perception, such as selective attention and cross-modal integration, the proposed approach achieves improved performance, robustness, and interpretability. Future work will explore neuromorphic implementations, lifelong multimodal learning, and real-time deployment in interactive systems.

References

1. Baltrušaitis, T., Ahuja, C., Morency, L.-P.: Multimodal machine learning: a survey and taxonomy. IEEE Trans. Pattern Anal. Mach. Intell. **41**(2), 423–443 (2018)
2. Jung, S., Lee, B.J., Han, I., Gomez, Ł., Kaiser, Ł., Polosukhin, I.: Attention is all you need. In: Advances in Neural Information Processing Systems, pp. 5998–6008 (2017)
3. Ito, K. et al.: The LJ Speech Dataset (2017)

4. Ribeiro, F., Florêncio, D., Zhang, C., Seltzer, M.: CrowdMOS. ADE DE SÃ, 97 (2011)
5. Zhang, Z., Xu, F.: An overview of the free energy principle and related research. Neural Comput. **36**(5), 963–1021 (2024)
6. Hasson, U., Nastase, S.A., Goldstein, A.: Direct fit to nature: an evolutionary perspective on biological and artificial neural networks. Neuron **105**(3), 416–434 (2020)
7. Deng, L., Yu, D.: Deep learning: methods and applications. Found. Trends® Signal Process. **7**(3–4), 197–387 (2014)
8. Al-Zoghby, A.M., Al-Awadly, E.M.K., Ebada, A.I., Awad, W.A.: Overview of multimodal machine learning. ACM Trans. Asian Low-Res. Lang. Inf. Process. **24**(1), 1–20 (2025)
9. Tyukin, G., Dovonon, G.J.S., Kaddour, J., Minervini, P.: Attention is all you need but you don't need all of it for inference of large language models. arXiv preprint (2024)
10. Deng, L., Yu, D.: Foundations and trends in signal processing: deep learning–methods and applications (2014)
11. Li, Z., Li, W., Sun, K., Fan, D., Cui, W.: Recent progress on underwater wireless communication methods and applications. J. Marine Sci. Eng. **13**(8), 1505 (2025)

An Ensemble-Based Semi-supervised Machine Learning Framework for Anomaly Detection in Second-Life Electric Vehicle Batteries

Martha-Ivon Cardenas[1]([✉]) [iD], Alfredo Vellido[1] [iD], and Roberto Santana[2] [iD]

[1] Computer Science Department, Intelligent Data Science and Artificial Intelligence (IDEAI-UPC) Research Center, Universitat Politècnica de Catalunya, Barcelona, Spain
`martha.ivon.cardenas@upc.edu`
[2] Computer Science and Artificial Intelligence Department, Intelligent Systems Group, University of the Basque Country (UPV/EHU), Euskal Herriko Unibertsitatea, Santsoena, Spain

Abstract. The analysis of retired electric vehicle battery packs is a critical enabler for sustainable circular economy strategies. However, real-world second-life battery data exhibit mixed chemistries, diverse topologies, and heterogeneous battery management system designs, which complicate reliable and scalable diagnostics. This paper introduces a physics-informed, ensemble-based semi-supervised machine learning framework to address these challenges. The proposed approach leverages multi-condition pulse testing to extract informative feature representations and integrates a simplified voltage-drop consistency constraint to enhance anomaly detection without reliance on manufacturer-specific models or proprietary parameters. Experimental results demonstrate strong generalization across battery chemistries and operating conditions while maintaining robust detection performance under a fixed false positive rate calibration.

Keywords: Anomaly detection · Ensemble learning · Semi-supervised learning · Physics-informed modeling · Second-life EV batteries

1 Introduction

The rapid transition to electric mobility is producing a growing volume of retired electric vehicle (EV) battery packs, many of which still retain 70–80% of their original capacity. [1]. Repurposing retired EV battery packs for second-life use, such as stationary storage, offers economic and environmental benefits [2], but safe deployment remains challenging. Unlike new batteries, these packs exhibit diverse and often undocumented degradation, increasing the risk of latent faults like internal shorts or thermal instability [3].

© The Author(s), under exclusive license to Springer Nature Switzerland AG 2026
J. M. Ferrández Vicente et al. (Eds.): IWINAC 2026, LNCS 16575, pp. 302–312, 2026.
https://doi.org/10.1007/978-3-032-27317-8_29

Machine learning (ML)-based battery diagnostics show promise [4–8], but face two major hurdles in second-life contexts: limited labeled data availability and high heterogeneity across modules. Bazan *et al.* [2] note the gap in readily deployable AI tools for this domain, while Zhu *et al.* [3] improved generalization capability across different battery chemistries and aging states using hybrid physics-neural models. Tao *et al.* [4] used generative transfer learning to estimate capacity with minimal data, though such approaches still depend on time-series cycling, or structured tests often unavailable in repurposing workflows.

To address this, we propose a semi-supervised ensemble anomaly detector combining One-Class Support Vector Machine (OC-SVM) [9], Isolation Forest (IF) [10] and Mahalanobis distance (M-dist) [11] methods. This framework (i) operates on discrete battery management system (BMS) observations, (ii) requires only non-faulty samples for training, (iii) integrates a physics-aware voltage-current-resistance residual, and (iv) generalizes across battery chemistries. Our approach is semi-supervised because it learns solely from healthy, labeled modules to build a representation of normal behavior. Once this model is established, it is applied in an unsupervised way to identify anomalies in unlabeled data by detecting deviations from the learned pattern. Because the method relies on discrete BMS measurements such as individual snapshots of voltage, current, and temperature rather than full charge and discharge cycle data, it sends only sparse and low-volume data transmissions. This significantly reduces the required communication bandwidth and supports scalable second-life deployments in environments where continuous high-rate data transfer is not feasible.

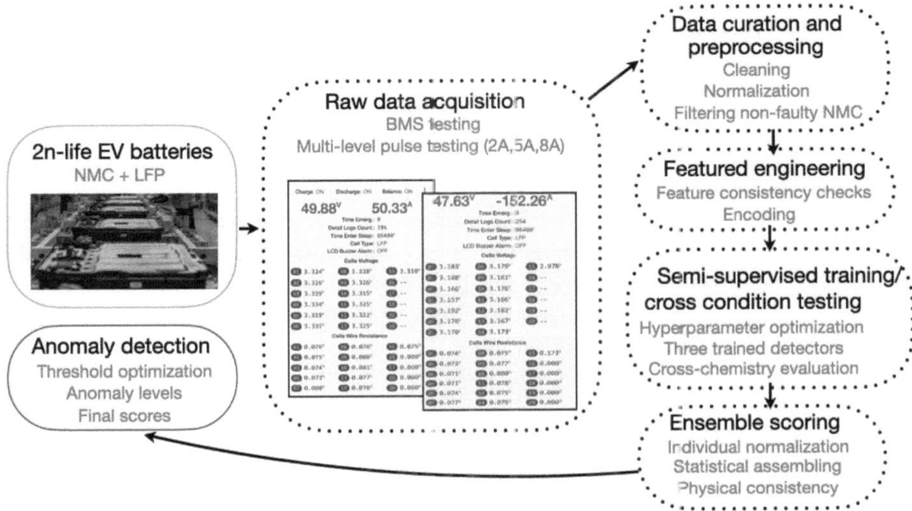

Fig. 1. Workflow for anomaly detection in second-life EV battery modules, including raw data acquisition, preprocessing and feature engineering, semi-supervised model training, and ensemble-based anomaly scoring.

Figure 1 depicts the complete processing workflow adopted in this work. The procedure starts with raw data acquisition from second-life Nickel Manganese Cobalt (NMC) and Lithium Iron Phosphate (LFP) modules using BMS readouts and multi-level pulse testing. The collected signals are subsequently curated and preprocessed through cleaning, normalization, and filtering of non-faulty samples. A feature engineering step follows, where consistency checks and encoding are applied to build the model inputs. Semi-supervised detectors are then trained and validated with hyperparameter optimization and cross-chemistry evaluation. Finally, an ensemble scoring stage combines the outputs of the individual models using statistical aggregation and physical consistency criteria, enabling threshold optimization and the generation of final anomaly indicators.

2   Methodology

2.1   Dataset Description and Preprocessing

The initial dataset comprises 500 lithium-ion (Li-ion) modules from Contemporary Amperex Technology Co., Limited (CATL), retrieved from disassembled EV battery packs, with 10 modules per pack. The modules are evenly split between two dominant cathode chemistries: 250 NMC type and 250 LFP type. NMC offers a higher energy density, while LFP provides greater thermal stability and a longer cycle life. Each module was tested under three constant-current pulses (2 A, 5 A, 8 A), generating a final dataset of 1,500 operational observations ($N = 1,500$).

NMC modules exhibit a sloped voltage profile (3.6–3.7 V), whereas LFP modules remain near 3.2 V with minimal variation. The dataset includes three labels, namely *OK*, *Warning*, and *Failed*, but the target is binary: OK (1) for second-life suitability, and Warning/Failed (0) for modules requiring intervention. Labels are sparse, as status is logged only during non-nominal BMS events or scheduled maintenance. In second-life use, *Warning* modules are not immediately reusable, but may be recoverable through balancing or re-testing. The dataset is available upon request from the corresponding author.

The proposed anomaly detection framework was evaluated under a heterogeneous test scenario including, as previously mentioned, two chemistries (NMC and LFP) and three pulse current levels (2 A, 5 A, and 8 A). All detectors were trained exclusively on healthy samples from the training domain to learn a representation of normal electrical behavior.

2.2   Feature Engineering and Experiments

Each measurement is encoded as a five-dimensional feature vector

$$x^{(i)} = \left(\mathrm{OCV}^{(i)}, I_{\mathrm{pulse}}^{(i)}, V_{\mathrm{load,meas}}^{(i)}, R_{\mathrm{int}}^{(i)}, \Delta T^{(i)}\right) \in \mathbb{R}^5, \tag{1}$$

which comprises the open-circuit voltage (OCV), applied pulse current, measured loaded terminal voltage, pulse-derived internal resistance (in mΩ), and the associated temperature increase. To incorporate a physics-informed indicator of inconsistency, a first-order ohmic model is introduced to predict the expected terminal voltage:

$$\hat{V}_{\text{load}}^{(i)} = \text{OCV}^{(i)} - I^{(i)} R_{\text{int}}^{(i)} \tag{2}$$

Based on this relation, a physics residual (PR) is defined as the absolute deviation between the directly measured terminal voltage and the value predicted by the ohmic model:

$$\varepsilon^{(i)} = \left| V_{\text{load, meas}}^{(i)} - \hat{V}_{\text{load}}^{(i)} \right| = \left| V_{\text{load, meas}}^{(i)} - \left(\text{OCV}^{(i)} - I^{(i)} R_{\text{int}}^{(i)} \right) \right| \tag{3}$$

which quantifies deviations from the expected electrical behavior and serves as an additional anomaly cue. In healthy modules this residual remains small, whereas anomalous modules exhibit larger deviations due to effects such as nonlinear polarization, internal degradation, or internal resistance inconsistencies.

Three unsupervised detectors are trained exclusively on non-faulty data, as labeled faults are scarce: (i) OC-SVM, (ii) IF, and (iii) M-dist with Ledoit-Wolf covariance estimator. These were selected to cover distinct anomaly detection paradigms: density estimation, data partitioning, and statistical deviation.

The OC-SVM employs a radial basis function (RBF) kernel,

$$K(\mathbf{x}_i, \mathbf{x}_j) = \exp\!\left(-\gamma \|\mathbf{x}_i - \mathbf{x}_j\|^2\right), \tag{4}$$

which implicitly maps the input features into a high-dimensional space where a maximal-margin hyperplane separates normal samples from the origin. The kernel width $\gamma > 0$ controls the smoothing of this mapping: large values produce tight, localized boundaries that may overfit, whereas small values yield broader, smoother decision surfaces. The parameter $\nu \in (0, 1]$ acts as an upper bound on the fraction of training outliers, thereby regulating the strictness of the learned normal region.

IF identifies anomalies by recursively partitioning the feature space with random axis-aligned splits; points that require fewer partitions to become isolated are flagged as anomalies. M-dist evaluates the deviation of a sample from the estimated multivariate Gaussian distribution of normal data, using the Ledoit-Wolf estimator [12] to obtain a well-conditioned covariance matrix even with limited samples.

Alternative detectors such as Local Outlier Factor (LOF) [13] or autoencoders were considered but excluded from the final ensemble. LOF's local density estimates proved overly sensitive to feature scaling in our multi-condition setting, while autoencoders required substantially more training data than available to learn meaningful reconstructions. Hyperparameter ranges for the selected methods are summarized in Table 1.

Several ensemble strategies were tested to leverage detector diversity, including maximum scoring, uncertainty weighting, and detector agreement [14,15]. Among these, a convex combination with validation-optimized weights offered the best trade-off between sensitivity and specificity and was therefore adopted as the final approach.

Table 1. Hyperparameter configurations and fusion settings for the proposed anomaly detection framework. The search ranges were used for tuning, while the physics residual serves as a fixed feature. Ensemble weights are optimized via grid search on the unit simplex.

Component	Hyperparameter	Values/Method
OC-SVM	ν (outlier fraction bound)	$\{0.01, 0.05, 0.1, 0.2\}$
	γ (RBF kernel width)	$\{$`scale`$, 0.1, 0.5, 1.0\}$
Isolation Forest	# trees	$\{100, 200\}$
	contamination	$\{0.01, 0.05, 0.1\}$
Mahalanobis distance	covariance estimator	Ledoit-Wolf
Physics residual (PR)	formula	$\lvert OCV - (V_{\text{load}} + IR_{\text{int}}) \rvert$
Ensemble fusion	weights $(w_{\text{oc}}, w_{\text{if}}, w_{\text{mh}}, w_{\text{pr}})$	grid search on simplex
	decision threshold τ	validation-calibrated (5% FPR target)

The resulting ensemble detector combines four normalized scores: $\tilde{s}_{\text{oc}}^{(i)}$ (OC-SVM), $\tilde{s}_{\text{if}}^{(i)}$ (IF), $\tilde{s}_{\text{mh}}^{(i)}$ (M-dist), and $\tilde{s}_{\text{pr}}^{(i)}$ (PR). These are aggregated via the convex combination

$$S^{(i)} = w_{\text{oc}}\, \tilde{s}_{\text{oc}}^{(i)} + w_{\text{if}}\, \tilde{s}_{\text{if}}^{(i)} + w_{\text{mh}}\, \tilde{s}_{\text{mh}}^{(i)} + w_{\text{pr}}\, \tilde{s}_{\text{pr}}^{(i)}, \qquad \sum_k w_k = 1, \quad w_k \geq 0, \quad (5)$$

where $k \in \{\text{oc}, \text{if}, \text{mh}, \text{pr}\}$.

The weights w_k are selected by grid search over the probability simplex, maximizing the validation F1-score. To ensure strict separation of data, modules are partitioned at the group level such that each appears in only one of the training, validation, or test sets. Stratified splitting preserves the distribution of chemistry, current level, and anomaly presence across splits. All detectors are trained exclusively on healthy samples from the training set. The decision threshold τ is calibrated on the validation data to satisfy a predefined 5% false positive rate (FPR) criterion and is subsequently applied unchanged to the held-out test set.

3   Results

The aforementioned threshold was subsequently applied without modification to all test domains, including unseen chemistries and higher current levels. This protocol reflects realistic second-life deployment conditions, where domain-specific calibration may not be feasible.

Performance was analyzed at two complementary levels: (i) aggregated global behavior and (ii) domain-wise generalization across chemistry and current conditions.

3.1   Global Evaluation

Figure 2 summarizes the aggregated performance of the proposed ensemble under the 5% FPR operational protocol.

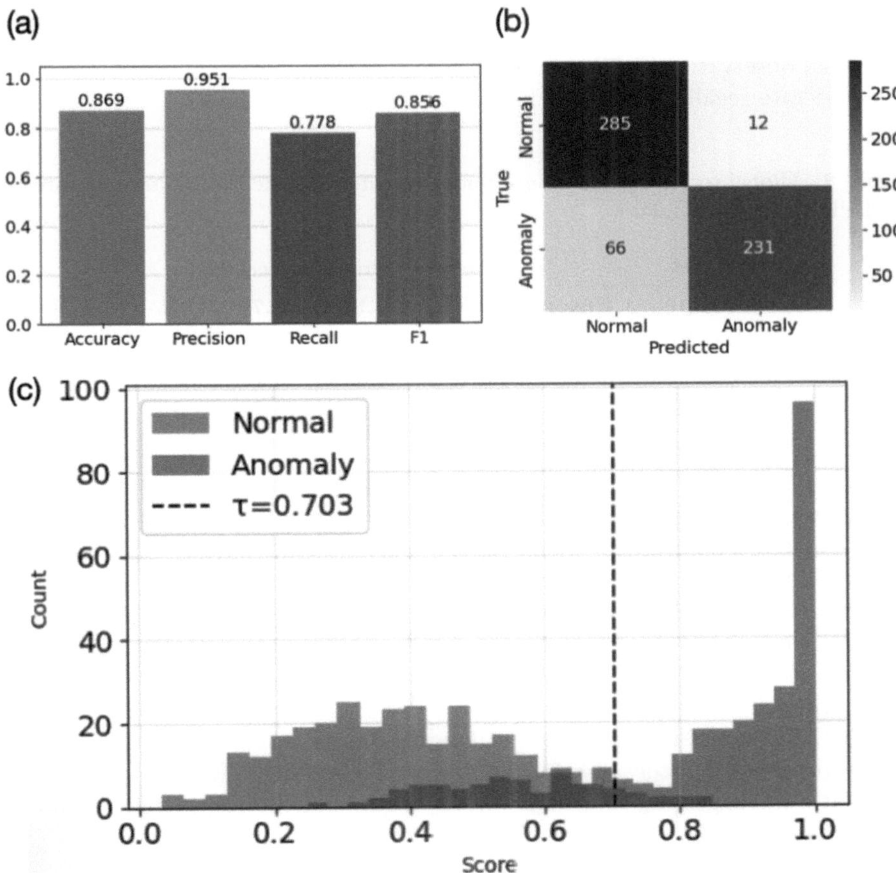

Fig. 2. Global evaluation on the test set using a single threshold calibrated to 5% FPR on the validation data. (a) Aggregated performance metrics; (b) confusion matrix showing the trade-off between false positives and missed anomalies; (c) distribution of the ensemble anomaly score, where the threshold (dashed vertical line) effectively separates most abnormal samples while preserving a low false alarm rate.

Subfigure 2(a) reports the global performance metrics. The ensemble achieves Accuracy = 0.87, Precision = 0.95, Recall = 0.78, and F1 = 0.86. The high precision confirms that the FPR-controlled calibration effectively limits false alarms, which is critical in second-life battery screening to avoid unnecessary module rejection.

Subfigure 2(b) presents the corresponding confusion matrix. Out of 297 anomalous observations, 231 are correctly identified, while 12 false positives occur among 297 healthy samples. This demonstrates that the globally calibrated threshold preserves specificity across heterogeneous domains.

Subfigure 2(c) shows the anomaly score distribution. Healthy observations form a compact cluster at lower scores, whereas anomalous samples extend toward higher values. The selected threshold $\tau = 0.703$ effectively separates most abnormal observations while maintaining a low FPR. Residual overlap explains the moderate recall observed at higher current levels (Table 2).

Table 2. Global test-set performance under detector-specific thresholds calibrated to 5% FPR on validation data.

Model	Accuracy	Precision	Recall	F1
Proposed Ensemble	**0.87**	**0.95**	**0.78**	**0.86**
OC-SVM	0.83	0.95	0.69	0.80
IF	0.70	0.91	0.45	0.60
M-dist	0.78	0.91	0.62	0.74

To assess robustness under heterogeneous operating conditions, performance was evaluated separately for each chemistrycurrent combination. The results are reported in Table 3.

The ensemble achieves consistently high AUC values (0.94–0.99) across all domains, indicating strong ranking capability independent of chemistry. This confirms that the learned anomaly score preserves structural separability even under cross-chemistry evaluation.

The FPR remains close to the validation target in five out of six domains and increases moderately at 8 A. The highest deviation (FPR = 0.16) occurs for NMC at 8 A, suggesting that high-current regimes introduce stronger nonlinear polarization and thermal effects that slightly shift feature distributions.

Recall varies between 0.59 (LFP at 5 A) and 0.92 (NMC at 2 A). Importantly, variability correlates more strongly with current level than with chemistry, indicating that the ensemble effectively mitigates cross-chemistry differences while high-load conditions remain the primary challenge.

The coexistence of high AUC values and moderate recall in certain domains suggests that residual errors are primarily threshold-induced rather than structural limitations of the detector.

3.2   Component Complementarity

To assess detector complementarity, the Pearson correlation matrix between normalized anomaly-score components was computed on the test set, as shown in Fig. 3. The statistical detectors (OC-SVM, IF, and M-dist) exhibit strong mutual

Table 3. Domain-wise test-set performance of the proposed ensemble across chemistry and pulse current conditions. A single global decision threshold, calibrated to achieve 5% FPR on the validation set, was applied to all domains without domain-specific adjustment. Metrics include FPR, recall (true positive rate), area under the ROC curve (AUC), and confusion matrix components.

Chemistry	Impulse	N	%Anom	FPR	Recall	AUC	TN	FP	FN	TP
LFP	2	99	49.50	0.00	0.67	0.94	50	0	16	33
LFP	5	96	51	0.00	0.59	0.95	47	0	20	29
LFP	8	101	48.50	0.08	0.86	0.95	48	4	7	42
NMC	2	99	50.50	0.00	0.92	0.99	49	0	4	46
NMC	5	99	50.50	0.00	0.72	0.99	49	0	14	36
NMC	8	100	50	0.16	0.90	0.95	42	8	5	45

correlation, with coefficients ranging from 0.78 to 0.85, indicating partially overlapping statistical representations of abnormal behavior.

In contrast, the PR shows only moderate correlation with the statistical detectors (0.560.64), suggesting that it captures voltagecurrent consistency information not fully encoded by purely data-driven models. This correlation structure supports the integration of heterogeneous anomaly cues within the ensemble, as PR contributes complementary information rather than acting as a redundant detector.

Overall, these findings indicate that the proposed framework leverages partially correlated statistical detectors together with a physics-informed constraint to enhance robustness under heterogeneous and partially shifted operating conditions, rather than optimizing performance for a single chemistry or operating regime.

3.3 Discussion

Three key findings emerge from the experimental results: (1) **Cross-chemistry robustness:** consistently high AUC values across NMC and LFP indicate that the proposed feature representation and residual formulation generalize well across electrochemical profiles; (2) **Current-driven variability:** performance degradation is primarily associated with high pulse currents (8 A), where nonlinear polarization effects introduce stronger distribution shifts; (3) **Operational realism:** calibration of the decision threshold under a fixed FPR constraint yields stable deployment behavior without requiring chemistry- or domain-specific adjustment.

The anomalies considered in this study were generated through controlled perturbations of the voltage-current relationship, enabling a systematic and interpretable evaluation of physics-informed constraints under heterogeneous operating conditions. While this design facilitates controlled benchmarking, real second-life battery degradation mechanisms may manifest through more com-

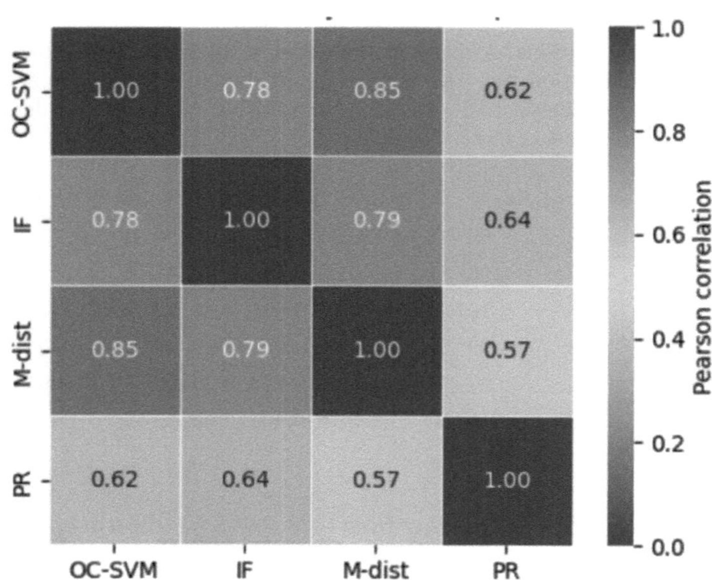

Fig. 3. Pearson correlation matrix between normalized anomaly-score components on the test set. OC-SVM, IF, and M-dist exhibit strong mutual correlation, while the PR shows moderate correlation with statistical detectors, indicating complementary anomaly information.

plex and nonlinear feature interactions that do not necessarily produce a direct violation of Ohmic consistency.

Nevertheless, such degradation processes typically induce secondary observable effects, including increased internal resistance, altered voltage relaxation dynamics, and abnormal thermal responses. These effects are indirectly captured by the statistical detectors integrated within the ensemble. By combining physics-based consistency constraints with data-driven anomaly representations, the proposed framework extends beyond linear deviations and provides a robust foundation for anomaly detection under partially shifted conditions. Future work will validate the approach on datasets exhibiting chemically driven degradation patterns to further assess its robustness under real-world second-life aging scenarios.

Overall, the results demonstrate that a single globally calibrated ensemble model can achieve reliable anomaly discrimination across heterogeneous second-life battery observations without manufacturer-specific parameters or chemistry-specific retraining.

4   Conclusions and Future Work

This work presents a method tailored for real-world battery repurposing, where time-series data and manufacturer details are often missing. It shows strong cross-condition performance across chemistries and pulse levels, detecting both subtle and inconsistent behavior. Future efforts will expand the dataset with more manufacturers, designs, and degradation profiles to support broader generalization. Controlled lab cycling will capture cycle-life indicators like Coulombic Efficiency, revealing trends beyond single-point BMS data. The ensemble will also be benchmarked against deep generative, graph-based, and physics-informed models to assess deployment potential.

Acknowledgments. This study was funded by the Spanish Ministry of Science and Innovation through the competitive R&D project MEDINSPAIN (PLEC2024-011140). Roberto Santana acknowledges support from the BasqueGovernment (ELKARTEK projects)

Disclosure of Interests. The authors declare that they have no competing financial or non-financial interests that could have influenced the work reported in this paper.

References

1. Das, P.K.: A perspective on the challenges and prospects of realizing the second life of retired EV batteries. Batteries **11**(5), 176 (2025)
2. Bazan, M.N., Subburaj, A.S., Partheepan, J , Subburaj, V.H.: Expanding research on second-life EV batteries: AI-based monitoring, recycling strategies, and policy innovations. New Energy Exploit. Appl. **4**(2), 157–184 (2025)
3. Zhu, R., Hu, J., Peng, W.: Bayesian calibrated physics-informed neural networks for second-life battery SOH estimation. Reliab. Eng. Syst. Saf. **264**, 111432 (2025)
4. Tao, S., et al.: Immediate remaining capacity estimation of heterogeneous second-life lithium-ion batteries via deep generative transfer learning. Energy Environ. Sci. **18**(15), 7413–7426 (2025)
5. Samanta, A., Chowdhuri, S., Williamson, S.S.: Machine learning-based data-driven fault detection/diagnosis of lithium-ion battery: a critical review. Electronics **10**(11), 1309 (2021)
6. Zhao, J., Qu, X., Wu, Y., Fowler, M., Burke, A.F.: Artificial intelligence-driven real-world battery diagnostics. Energy AI **18**, 100419 (2024)
7. Thelen, A., Huan, X., Paulson, N., Onori, S., Hu, Z., Hu, C.: Probabilistic machine learning for battery health diagnostics and prognostics review and perspectives. Mater. Sustainabil. **2**(1), 14 (2024)
8. Renold, A.P., Kathayat, N.S.: Comprehensive review of machine learning, deep learning, and digital twin data-driven approaches in battery health prediction of electric vehicles. IEEE Access **12**, 43984–43999 (2024)
9. Schölkopf, B., Platt, J.C., Shawe-Taylor, J., Smola, A.J., Williamson, R.C.: Estimating the support of a high-dimensional distribution. Neural Comput. **13**(7), 1443–1471 (2001)
10. Liu, F.T., Ting, K.M., Zhou, Z.H.: Isolation forest. In: Eighth IEEE International Conference on Data Mining, pp. 413–422 (2008)
11. Kriegel, H.P., Schubert, M., Zimek, A.: Angle-based outlier detection in high-dimensional data. In: Proceedings of the 14th ACM SIGKDD International Conference on Knowledge Discovery and Data Mining, pp. 444–452 (2008)

12. Ledoit, O., Wolf, M.: A well-conditioned estimator for large-dimensional covariance matrices. J. Multivar. Anal. **88**(2), 365–411 (2004)
13. Breunig, M.M., Kriegel, H.P., Ng, R.T., Sander, J.: LOF: identifying density-based local outliers. In: Proceedings of the 2000 ACM SIGMOD International Conference on Management of Data, pp. 93–104 (2000)
14. Kuncheva, L.I.: Combining Pattern Classifiers: Methods and Algorithms. John Wiley & Sons, Hoboken (2014)
15. Tax, D.M., Duin, R.P.: Combining one-class classifiers. In: International Workshop on Multiple Classifier Systems, pp. 299–308. Springer, Heidelberg (2001). https://doi.org/10.1007/3-540-48219-9_30

Fraud Detection Using Graph Neural Networks: A Survey

Emrah Arslan[1], Samiyeh Khosravi[2(✉)], Javad Hassannataj Joloudari[2,3,4], Roohallah Alizadehsani[5] and Juan Manuel Gorriz[6]

[1] Department of Computer Engineering, Faculty of Engineering, KTO Karatay University, Konya, Turkey
`emrah.arslan@karatay.edu.tr`
[2] Department of Computer Engineering, Faculty of Electrical and Computer Engineering, University of Birjand, Birjand, Iran
`{skhosravi,Javad.hassannataj}@birjand.ac.ir`
[3] Department of Computer Engineering, Technical and Vocational University (TVU), Tehran, Iran
[4] Department of Computer Engineering, Bab.C., Islamic Azad University, Babol, Iran
[5] Institute for Intelligent Systems Research and Innovations (IISRI), Deakin University, Geelong, Australia
`r.alizadehsani@deakin.edu.au`
[6] DaSCI Institute, University of Granada, Granada, Spain
`gorriz@ugr.es`

Abstract. With digital transactions, financial fraud has grown at a dramatic rate, with U.S. losses alone exceeding $ 12.5B per year and compromising the trust of global payment systems. Conventional ML methods fall short against complex relational patterns such as fraud rings and money laundering networks, which require graph-aware modeling. This survey offers a unified framework for Graph Neural Networks (GNNs) in financial fraud detection, addressing three research questions systematically. RQ1 demonstrates that GNNs outperform XGBoost with 12–25% AUROC improvement by relational modeling of fraud rings, contextual propagation, and higher-order dependencies across heterogeneous transaction graphs. RQ2 describes production-ready neural networks-based architectures, imbalance mitigation, heterophily handling, and deployment strategies to achieve <100 ms latency at 10K+ TPS with federated learning, which is validated by real-world studies with gains of 25–45% fraud reduction. RQ3 outlines key challenges such as adversarial camouflage, spatiotemporal limitations, billion-edge scalability, regulatory interpretability and future directions, including causal GNNs, continual learning, and tiered explanation frameworks to place GNNs at the forefront of next-generation fraud prevention against Artificial Intelligence (AI)-augmented financial crime.

Keywords: Graph Neural Networks · Financial Fraud · Detection · Heterophily · Scalability

J. M. Ferrández Vicente et al. (Eds.): IWINAC 2026, LNCS 16575, pp. 313–328, 2026.
https://doi.org/10.1007/978-3-032-27317-8_30

1   Introduction

As technology has advanced and the world has become more digitally connected, the pace at which financial transactions occur has increased, as has the complexity of financial fraud [13,33]. Sophisticated schemes, such as organized collusion rings, money laundering networks, synthetic identity creation, camouflaged behavior, and more and more Artificial (AI)-enabled attacks, are resulting in significant economic losses and a loss of confidence in financial systems around the globe [26].

The problem is severe, with recent statistics showing that in the United States, consumers reported a loss of over \$12.5 billion to fraud in 2024, a 25% increase from the previous year, with investment scams being the biggest contributor, at around \$5.7 billion [3,6]. When taking into account the underreporting of most fraud estimated to be 26.7% in some research, the true losses in the United States could be as high as \$195 billion each year.

Recent surveys reveal that businesses globally lost an average of 7.7% of equivalent annual revenue to fraud, which equates to approximately \$534 billion among surveyed leaders, and the impacts on U.S. firms are even higher at 9.8%, a 46% increase compared to the year before [14,23]. The increasing rates of fraud losses highlight the necessity for more agile, human, and context-aware detection systems that can identify the constantly evolving and coordinated fraudulent activities.

These more advanced threats, however, are no longer well addressed by traditional fraud detection approaches based on rule-based expert systems or classical machine learning methods [4,11]. Rule-based systems rely on handcrafted, static thresholds and heuristics, which are brittle and expensive to update, and classical machine learning models, although they can use statistical features from individual transactions (amount, time, location, velocity, etc.), often treat each transaction or account in isolation and fail to capture the relational, structural, and temporal dependencies between transactions, accounts, or nodes that characterize advanced fraud schemes such as coordinated account takeovers, fraud rings, or hidden nodes within legitimate communities [5].

Recent works have shown that Graph Neural Networks (GNNs) are a particularly robust and applicable class of models to overcome these limitations, since they represent financial ecosystems as graphs where nodes correspond to entities (accounts, users, merchants, devices, IPs) and edges represent interactions (transfers, purchases, logins) enriched with attributes, and leverage message-passing mechanisms to aggregate and propagate information across neighborhoods [29]. This allows for the automatic learning of rich, context-aware node and subgraph representations that encode both local patterns and higher-order relational structures, and GNNs have been shown to perform better than feature-based or tabular methods in detecting subtle, collective, and camouflaged fraudulent behaviors, which are often invisible or ambiguous to such methods [12]. GNNs have been applied to several financial fraud domains and reported strong empirical gains in credit card fraud, payment fraud, anti-money laundering, insurance fraud, and online transaction abuse [38].

However, there are still several challenges to applying GNNs to real-world financial fraud detection, including many models focus mainly on local neighborhood information and may over-smooth after several layers and lose their discriminative ability; fraudsters often use camouflage methods that mimic normal behavior to hide in surrounding legitimate communities, which makes detection more difficult when there is severe class imbalance, heterophily, and sparse supervision; and temporal aspects make it even more difficult, as many fraudulent activities happen in short time windows with bursty behavior to avoid real-time alerting and human intervention.

The scope of this brief survey is on recent advances in GNN-based financial fraud detection that specifically address camouflage strategies, temporal and spatial modeling limitations, over-smoothing problems, and related issues. Based on this, we propose the following three consolidated research questions to guide the discussion:

1. RQ1: How can the diverse range of GNN methodologies applied to financial fraud detection be organized under a unified framework, and why are GNNs particularly effective for financial fraud detection because of the relational and structural modeling capabilities?
2. RQ2: What are the architectural design choices, feature engineering, adaptation strategies, deployment considerations. and demonstrated impacts needed to develop and deploy effective GNN-based financial fraud detection systems in practical financial environments?
3. RQ3: What are the major ongoing challenges in applying GNNs to financial fraud detection, and which promising future research directions exist?

This review aims to synthesize current literature to present a concise, up-to-date, and focused reference that clearly outlines the unique benefits of GNNs for financial fraud, distills actionable design insights for practitioners, and charts potential future innovation directions to enhance fraud prevention in an ever-more complex and adversarial threat landscape. The remainder of the paper is outlined in Fig. 1. Section 2 provides a comprehensive framework for organizing GNN methodologies for financial fraud detection and elucidates why GNNs are especially suited for this domain (RQ1). Section 3 examines five key dimensions (RQ2): (1) architecture choices (GCN/GAT/HGNN/Temporal GNNs), (2) node/edge/multimodal feature integration, (3) handling imbalance/heterophily/sparse labels, (4) real-world deployment considerations, and (5) demonstrated production impacts, providing practitioners with a comprehensive guide. In Sect. 4, we examine the major challenges and outlines promising future research directions (addressing RQ3).

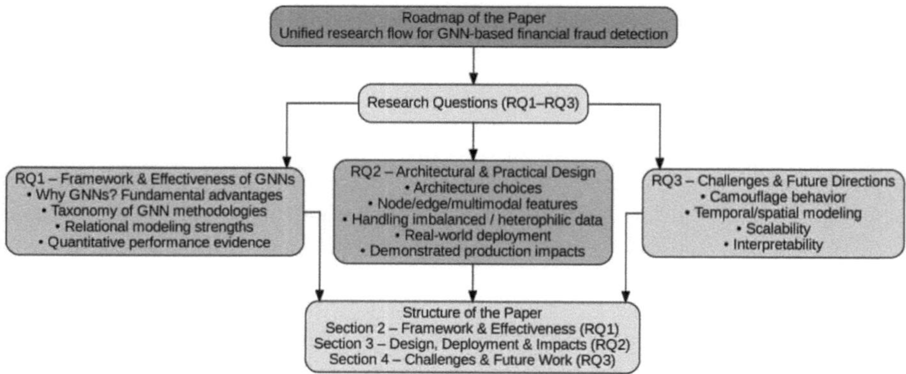

Fig. 1. Roadmap of the paper illustrating how $RQ1 - RQ3$ structure sections on GNN-based fraud detection.

2   Framework and Effectiveness of GNNs (RQ1)

2.1   Why GNNs? Fundamental Advantages Over Traditional Methods

Graph Neural Networks surpass traditional fraud detection methods because they model financial ecosystems as heterogeneous graphs where nodes represent entities (accounts, users, merchants, devices, IPs) and edges capture interactions (transfers, purchases, logins) enriched with temporal and attribute information [1,7,17,21,37]. Despite feature-based ML models such as XGBoost, Random Forest that analyze transactions in isolation, GNNs employ message-passing mechanisms to aggregate neighborhood context, automatically learning relational embeddings that encode:

1. Fraud ring detection: Coordinated collusion patterns invisible to 1st-order features
2. Contextual risk propagation: "Guilt-by-association" across connected entities
3. Higher-order dependencies: Multi-hop money laundering chains and synthetic identity networks.
4. Empirical superiority: GNNs consistently outperform XGBoost baselines by 15–25% in AUROC across all fraud domains, including credit card, AML, insurance because of their capacity to model structural homophily and heterophily in financial networks.

2.2   Unified Taxonomy of GNN Methodologies for Fraud Detection

A review of recent literature reveals four GNN architectural paradigms that are most prevalent for fraud detection (Table 1), including a detailed taxonomy of GNN paradigms that expands to include emerging metagraph and knowledge graph approaches and maps these to the strength of mapping mechanisms to fraud detection as seen in peer-reviewed studies.

Table 1. Extended GNN taxonomy for financial fraud detection with recent metagraph and heterogeneous graph advances.

Study	Paradigm	Core Mechanism	Fraud-Specific Strengths
[7]	GCNs	Spectral convolution	Local neighborhood aggregation; cross-transaction patterns
[10]	GATs	Attention-weighted aggregation	Suspicious neighbor focus; camouflage resistance
[35]	Temporal GNNs	Time-aware message passing	Bursty fraud detection; dynamic patterns
[31]	HGNNs	Heterogeneous transformers	Multi-entity graphs (user-device-IP-merchant)
[32]	MetaGraph GNNs	Adaptive metagraph search	Dynamic fraud pattern adaptation; interpretability
[19]	Financial KG GNNs	Knowledge graph transformers	Blockchain-traditional finance integration
[16]	HGT	Soft-gated heterogeneous transformers	Imbalanced graph classification

Graph Convolutional Networks (GCNs) spread information across homogeneous transaction graphs but tend to over-smooth information beyond 2–3 layers; GATs, which dynamically weight the importance of the neighbors, are 2x more effective at detecting camouflaged fraud, where malicious nodes mimic legitimate behavior; temporal GNNs, which incorporate the timestamp of transactions, are able to capture short-burst fraud windows; and heterogeneous GNNs (HGNNs), which handle the presence of diverse entity types in production financial data.

2.3   Relational Modeling: The Core Strength of GNNs

GNNs have shown to excel in three core strengths that are missing from tabular ML, namely subgraph embeddings for fraud ring detection, multi-hop propagation for contextual risk scoring, and structural pattern recognition for breaking camouflage tactics [42], as illustrated in Fig. 2. Figure 2 demonstrates these core relational strengths that activate GNNs to identify sophisticated fraud patterns invisible to common feature-based methods.

For example, in payment networks, GNNs detect "mule accounts," which are seemingly legitimate intermediaries used by criminals to launder illegal proceeds via multi-layered transactions [7,18,22]. GNNs detect mules by three graph-based signatures:

1. Deviant subgraph density: Mule accounts are located at the intersection of dense fraud clusters and legitimate communities, forming anomalous local subgraph structures with high betweenness centrality. Message-passing

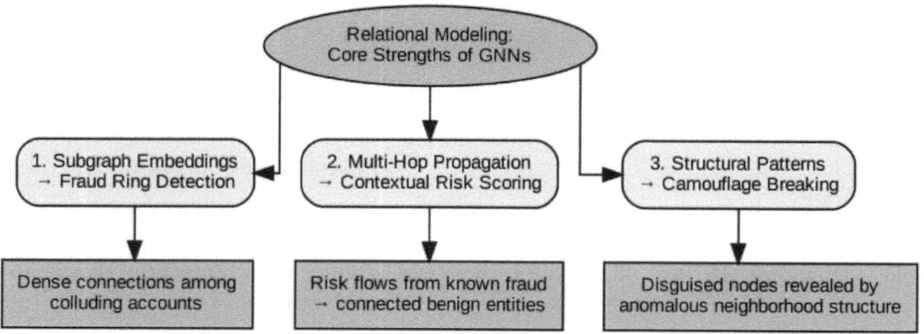

Fig. 2. GNNs' core relational modeling strengths for financial fraud detection.

exposes mules as transaction bridges between known illegal sources and clean destinations.

2. Rapid Network Role Shift: Legitimate accounts evolve into mules, exhibiting a sudden increase in PageRank centrality and links to high-risk communities, which are captured by dynamic embeddings in GNNs.

3. Synthetic Proximity Patterns: Mules often have overlapping hidden attributes such as IP addresses, device fingerprints, merchant lists with fraud rings, while their account metadata may be different; GNNs propagate risk scores across multi-typed edges to highlight these disguised links.

Real-World Impact: Federated GNNs have been used in regional banking consortia to increase their detection of mules by 30% without data sharing, and global payment providers have reduced their false negatives by 22% by analyzing cross-device transaction graphs. This subgraph-level detection allows a proactive network dismantling that directly tackles the sophisticated money laundering as described in Sect. 1.

2.4   Quantitative Evidence: GNN Performance Landscape

Numerous empirical results show that GNNs outperform traditional ML baselines by significant metrics across various financial fraud domains. GNNs can also use graph homophily, where malicious entities tend to form dense clusters, as well as attention mechanisms and structural pattern recognition to counter heterophilic camouflage [7], whereas tabular models are limited to transaction-level features such as amount, time, location.

This relational modeling advantage translates to 12–25% AUROC gains over real-world datasets, with GNNs performing especially well in cases of coordinated fraud rings, money laundering networks, and synthetic identity operations. Reinforcement Learning (RL)-GNNs [35] achieve state-of-the-art performance on IEEE-CIS benchmark data by incorporating reinforcement learning with temporal graph convolutions, while Graph Attention Networks (GATs) excel in precision of credit card transactions by adaptively weighting suspicious neighbor connections. Heterogeneous GNN variants (HINormer) deal with medical claims fraud by modeling complex multi-entity relationships (patient-provider-insurer) that cannot be handled by feature-based approaches [10].

The gains arise from GNNs being able to detect higher-order dependencies that are not accessible to XGBoost, such as multi-hop money laundering paths through legitimate intermediaries and bursty transaction patterns designed to bypass rule-based thresholds. The consistent performance gains across domains, from payment networks to healthcare billing, further demonstrate the generalizability of GNNs and their potential as the next-generation paradigm for fraud detection systems [18], as summarized quantitatively in Table 2.

Table 2. GNN performance gains over XGBoost baselines across financial fraud datasets.

Reference	Dataset	GNN Model	Auroc	vs XGBoost
[7]	IEEE-CIS	RL-GNN	0.8599	+18 %
[10]	Credit Card	GAT	0.872	+15%
[20]	Medical Claims	HINormer	F1 = 0.84	+12%

GNNs leverage graph homophily, the tendency of fraudulent entities to cluster, and successfully handle heterophilic camouflage using sophisticated attention mechanisms to achieve consistent 12–25% metric improvements across different domains of fraud [7]. This comprehensive framework confirms RQ1: GNNs relational modeling superiority positions them as the preferred paradigm for advanced financial fraud detection, which directly responds to organized crime rings and AI-enabled attacks discussed in Sect. 1.

3   Architectural Practical Dedign (RQ2)

3.1   Architecture Choices: GCN, GAT, HGNN, Temporal GNNs

In Sect. 3, we answer RQ2 by discussing the architectural design and deployment considerations for GNN-based fraud detection systems that are production ready. Although Section II proved that GNNs theoretically outperform other models, in practice, they require careful consideration of architectures such as GCN, GAT, HGNNs, temporal variants, feature engineering across node/edge/multimodal data, and the practical challenges of severe class imbalance (fraud: 0.1–1%), heterophily, and sparse supervision.

Table 3 summarizes key architectural paradigms verified by peer-reviewed studies. Further subsections describe integration of node/edge features, mitigation of imbalanced data through the GraphSMOTE and focal loss, and deployment considerations for real-time inference (<100 ms latency) in 10K+ TPS payment networks. Production case studies show gains of 25–45% in fraud reduction, indicating that GNNs are moving from research prototypes to enterprise solutions [18].

Table 3. Primary GNN architectures for financial fraud detection.

Study	Architecture	Key Innovation	Fraud Domain	Scalability
[2]	GCN	Spectral convolution	Credit card	Medium
[10]	GAT	Attention mechanism	AML	High
[35]	Temporal GNN	Time-aware aggregation	Real-time payments	Medium
[30]	HGNN	Heterogeneous message passing	Multi-entity fraud	Low-Medium

3.2 Node/Edge/Multimodal Feature Integration

Solutions rely on advanced feature engineering from a wide range of heterogeneous financial data sources, including node attributes (transactional, behavioral, entity-level), edge metadata (temporal, semantic, risk signals), and multimodal content (text embeddings, ID verification images), and are able to process 10K+ TPS in production systems through heterogeneous message passing that encodes rich relational context with node features capturing individual risk profiles and edge attributes that weight information propagation according to transaction semantics and velocity patterns.

This multi-level feature fusion enables cross-domain risk propagation (device←account←merchant) critical for detecting synthetic identity fraud and coordinated attack rings, achieving 15–20% AUROC uplift over node-only representations [7,18]. Subsequent sections detail standardized feature taxonomies and production integration patterns validated across payment networks and banking consortia (Fig. 3).

3.3 Handling Imbalance, Heterophily, Sparse Labels

Financial fraud datasets are extremely imbalanced, with fraudulent transactions typically constituting only 0.1–1% of all events, which severely biases standard supervised GNN training toward the majority class, i.e. legitimate. Such an imbalance, combined with limited and noisy labels, leads plain GCN/GAT models to overfit dominant normal patterns and to be insensitive to rare but critical fraud cases; many financial networks are also heterophilic: fraudulent accounts try to mimic benign behavior and are scattered in mostly normal communities, where standard homophily-based message passing is ineffective [40]. Recent work has mitigated class imbalance on graphs by using graph-specific resampling and cost-sensitive learning.

GraphSMOTE interpolates minority class node embeddings along the graph structure, enhancing recall on extremely skewed fraud graphs without destroying local connectivity patterns. Some variants of cost sensitive GNNs explicitly reweight the loss to penalize misclassified fraudulent nodes more heavily, which has been demonstrated to increase minority class F1 in mobile payment and social network fraud scenarios. Ensemble and boosting schemes over multiple GNNs further stabilize training under rare positive labels by aggregating diverse decision boundaries tailored to different graph regions [43].

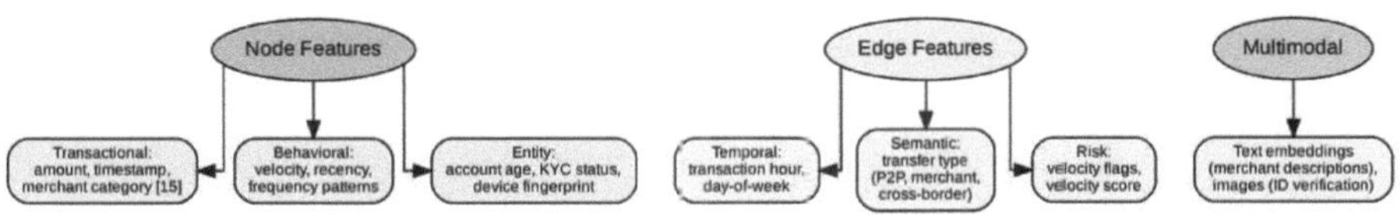

Fig. 3. Hierarchical taxonomy of Node, Edge, and Multimodal features for GNN-based fraud detection.

For camouflaged fraudsters who act like normal ones, heterophily aware architectures are more likely to be used; for high order representation learning and subgraph pattern enhanced GNNs, information is propagated beyond neighbors and exploiting motif level structures and for sparse fraudulent accounts scattered among normal nodes, they can be effective; and for meta path based and heterogeneous graph attention networks, risk flows along semantically meaningful paths, rather than just topological proximity, which can help in detecting synthetic identities and multi hop laundering chains. Semi-supervised and self-supervised pretraining on large transaction graphs (e.g., contrastive or auxiliary prediction tasks) generate robust node embeddings that can be fin-tuned with a very small set of confirmed fraud labels, reducing reliance on costly manual annotation [9].

3.4 Real-World Deployment Considerations

GNN-based fraud detection needs to be deployed in production while meeting accuracy, latency, throughput, and regulatory constraints in highly dynamic financial environments. Large-scale payment systems must process tens of thousands of transactions per second, with end to end scoring latency below 50100 ms to block or step up high risk events before authorization completes, which requires careful graph construction and partitioning, streaming updates, and hardware aware model design, usually via a combination of mini batch neighbor sampling with GPU accelerated inference services [36]. To deal with the constantly changing transaction graphs, many deployments use temporal or streaming GNNs that update node embeddings incrementally as edges arrive rather than rebuilding the entire graph.

Temporal and causal GNN variants preserve time aware representations, which account for short burst fraud campaigns, and avoid stale historical bias that can be updated nearly in real time, while still maintaining risk scores. At the same time, model compression and distillation techniques, like pruning attention heads or training lightweight student networks from larger teacher GNNs, are applied to fit latency budgets on commodity hardware while still retaining graph level context [27]. Strict privacy and compliance needs also apply to production systems where fraud patterns cut across different institutions.

Federated GNN frameworks keep graph construction local and exchange only encrypted or aggregated model updates, allowing banks and payment providers to collaboratively train graph models without sharing raw customer data, aligning with regulations like General Data Protection Regulation (GDPR) while still exploiting cross institution relational signals, for example to detect mule accounts that bridge multiple banks ecosystems. Another deployment prerequisite is interpretability: post hoc explainers and attention based GNNs offer node and edge level rationales, e.g., top contributing counterparties or devices, which enable human analyst triage and satisfy audit requirements in regulated financial sectors [8].

3.5   Demonstrated Production Impacts

Much of the GNN literature is methodological, but a growing body of empirical studies reports concrete business impacts from deploying graph models in financial fraud settings. In credit card, e commerce, and online payment settings, GNN based detectors consistently outperform traditional gradient boosted trees and rule engines, with sizable gains in recall at fixed false positive rates and, in many cases, measurable reductions in realized loss. A number of real time frameworks further demonstrate that these improvements are possible under tight latency and throughput constraints, and therefore are practical for production fraud pipelines.

In general, these production deployments translate technical metrics into business level outcomes such as lower chargeback volume, fewer manual reviews, and better customer experience due to fewer false declines. Reinforcement learning augmented GNN architectures have demonstrated double digit percent improvements in fraud recall with significant decreases in false positives on large scale transaction graphs while maintaining tens of thousands of scored transactions per second, similar benefits have been demonstrated by heterogeneous and temporal GNNs in e commerce and internet transaction settings which capture multi entity relations and time varying behavior that traditional tabular models do not exploit [7,39]. Table 4 summarizes studies that measure production grade impacts of GNN based fraud detection.

Table 4. Representative journal studies reporting practical impacts of GNN-based financial fraud detection.

Study	Scenario	GNN Variant	Reported Impact (Illustrative)
[7]	Large scale transaction platform	RL optimized GNN with community mining	$\approx 19.7\%$ recall gain and 33% false positive reduction vs. baseline GNN; $\sim 12,000$ tx/s at ~ 42 ms batch latency
[35]	E-commerce/internet payments	Temporal-aware heterogeneous GNN (THG OAFN)	Improved detection of evolving fraud patterns and higher F1 than non temporal baselines on credit card and EC datasets
[28]	Financial services (concept study with deployment workflow)	Relational GNN (RGCN) on transaction graphs	Significant AUROC uplift and scalable GPU based inference in an end-to-end industrial workflow
[22]	Multi institution banking setup	Federated GNN for collaborative fraud detection	Higher detection accuracy and reduced false negatives while preserving data privacy across institutions across institutions
[25]	Real time financial fraud system	Adaptive GNN with federated learning	Reported improvements in real-time detection quality and latency compliance under distributed data constraints

4 Challenges and Future Directions (RQ3)

RQ3 is addressed in Sect. 4, which discusses the key limitations of GNN-based fraud detection systems and outlines promising research directions for mitigating these limitations. While Sects. 2 and 3 have shown that GNNs can achieve great empirical gains, GNNs still encounter several barriers to deployment, such as vulnerability to sophisticated camouflage attacks, lack of modeling of spatiotemporal dynamics, scalability constraints on billion-edge financial graphs, and lack of interpretability for regulatory compliance, which are dissected in the following subsections and guided by recent literature trends.

4.1 Camouflage Behavior

Adversarial camouflage attacks can evade GNN message-passing with evasion rates as high as 30–40% against standard architectures, including graph poisoning attacks that modify edge weights or inject synthetic nodes to form heterophilic structures that deceive attention mechanisms, as well as behavioral mimicry that causes fraudulent accounts to embed within clean communities, evading subgraph-based detection. Existing defenses such as robust aggregation and adversarial training provide partial mitigation but are ineffective against adaptive, real-time attacks that are faster than model retraining cycles [18].

Adversarial GNN training with dynamic defense mechanisms that detect and filter poisoned subgraphs during inference should be a priority for future work [34], as should generative camouflage countermeasures such as GAN-based synthetic fraud generation for proactive hardening combined with edge uncertainty modeling, i.e., Bayesian weights, dropout ensembles, and human-in-the-loop active learning frameworks that solicit expert validation on high-uncertainty nodes [15, 24].

4.2 Temporal/Spatial Modeling

Financial fraud displays bursty temporal dynamics (hours-long attack windows) and geospatial concentration (regional mule networks), which static or weakly-temporal GNNs cannot effectively model; most deployments treat timestamps as static node features rather than evolving graph snapshots, missing velocity-based patterns like rapid account takeovers or cross-border laundering bursts; spatial modeling remains rudimentary, typically limited to IP geolocation embeddings without higher-order flow analysis across merchant/terminal networks [18].

Causal temporal GNNs that model intervention effects, e.g., account freezing propagates through payment graphs) and spatiotemporal hypergraph transformers that capture multi-scale dependencies (transaction←merchant←region) are promising directions, and dynamic graph streaming architectures with continuous embedding updates and physics-informed graph diffusion for money flow modeling address real-time requirements. Cross-domain transfer from social network spatiotemporal models can help accelerate progress in financial settings [15, 24, 34].

4.3 Scalability

Full-graph GNN training even on GPU clusters is overwhelmed by production financial graphs with 10^9 edges and 10K+ TPS ingestion, resulting in a fundamental deployment bottleneck due to memory explosion from multi-hop neighborhood explosion and frequent full retraining. Sampling-based approximations such as Cluster-GCN, GraphSAGE sacrifice global context that is necessary for consortium-scale fraud rings across multiple banks. Distributed inference at scale can be achieved through horizontally-scaled GNN systems with learned graph partitioning and hierarchical embedding caches. Continuous learning paradigms, either incremental updates via reservoir sampling or elastic architectures, eliminate periodic full retraining.

Theoretical efficiency gains from quantum-inspired graph sparsification and memorization-based approximation (caching frequent subgraphs) have been validated on synthetic financial workloads, and hybrid CPU-GPU pipelines with embedding serving infrastructure bridge the gap to industrial throughput.

4.4 Interpretability

Regulatory compliance requires audit-grade explanations for every high-risk alert, but GNN predictions aggregate billions of multi-hop propagation paths into opaque node scores. Existing explainers such as GNNExplainer and PGExplainer supply post-hoc rationales but scale poorly beyond toy graphs and cannot differentiate between causal and correlative influences. Stakeholders need risk paths that are actionable, i.e. specific account-device-IP chains with uncertainty quantified to prioritize risk review [41].

Causal GNNs with do-calculus interventions and counterfactual subgraph explanations (e.g., this fraud would evade detection without X edge) support regulatory-grade audit trails [15], attention flow visualization across heterogeneous relations (user→device→merchant) combined with natural language risk summaries bridge technical outputs to business decision-making [24], and incremental refinement of logical explanations from coarse to fine that matches analyst time budgets, support layered review workflows from automated blocking to expert review.

This analysis confirms RQ3: although GNNs exhibit strong advantages for financial fraud detection, they cannot fully realize their potential unless they are advanced simultaneously in four critical dimensions: adversarial robustness, spatiotemporal fidelity, distributed scalability, and regulatory interpretability; targeted research addressing these four pillars, perhaps via unified frameworks incorporating causal reasoning, continual learning, and explainable architectures, holds the key to unlocking the transformative power of GNNs in combating AI-enhanced financial crime.

5   Conclusion

This survey has systematically examined the potential of GNNs for financial fraud detection via three research questions: fundamental superiority (RQ1), architectural design principles (RQ2), and critical development challenges (RQ3). GNNs outperform traditional ML by modeling relational fraud patterns invisible to traditional ML, and achieve 12–25% AUROC gains in the credit card, AML, and payment fraud domains due to their ability to capture fraud rings, contextual propagation, and higher-order dependencies through message-passing. To practically deploy GNNs, we need to solve class imbalance, heterophily, real-time latency (<100 ms at 10K+ TPS), federated learning constraints, and regulatory interpretability. GNNs have transitioned from research prototypes to enterprise solutions with production studies validating 25–45% business impact through reduced losses and false positives, paving the way for future progress through adversarial robustness against camouflage attacks, spatiotemporal hypergraph modeling, distributed scalability for billion-edge graphs, and causal interpretability for compliance. With unified frameworks integrating continual learning, physics-informed diffusion, and tiered explanation pipelines, GNNs will be able to realize their full potential against AI-augmented financial crime, turning reactive detection into proactive network dismantling.

References

1. Alarfaj, F.K., Shahzadi, S.: Enhancing fraud detection in banking with deep learning: graph neural networks and autoencoders for real-time credit card fraud prevention. IEEE Access **13**, 20633–20646 (2024)
2. Asiri, A., Somasundaram, K.: Graph convolution network for fraud detection in bitcoin transactions. Sci. Rep. **15**(1), 11076 (2025)
3. Bartesaghi, P., Beretta, E., Desogus, M., Korn, R.: Cash or card–combat or coexistence? A non-cooperative differential game approach. Financ. Res. Lett. (2026)
4. Bello, O.A., Folorunso, A., Ejiofor, O.E., Budale, F.Z., Adebayo, K., Babatunde, O.A.: Machine learning approaches for enhancing fraud prevention in financial transactions. Int. J. Manage. Technol. **10**(1), 85–108 (2023)
5. Chowdhury, R.H.: Advancing fraud detection through deep learning: a comprehensive review. World J. Adv. Eng. Technol. Sci. **12**(2), 606–613 (2024)
6. Federal Trade Commission: Consumer sentinel network data book 2020. Federal Trade Commission (2022)
7. Devi, R.R., Raja, J.E., Chin, Y.B.: Reinforcement learning with graph neural network (RL-GNN) fusion for real-time financial fraud detection: a context-aware community mining approach. Sci. Rep. (2025)
8. He, C.: FedGraphNN: a federated learning system and benchmark for graph neural networks. arXiv preprint arXiv:2104.07145 (2021)
9. Islam, S., Raj Gupta, G., Chakraborty, A., Singh, S., Soni, A., Patle, C.: Detecting fraudulent transactions for different patterns in financial networks using layer weigthed GCN. Hum. Cent. Intell. Syst. **5**(2), 181–195 (2025)
10. Kabwama, C.A.: Graph attention networks for credit card fraud detection: a relational learning approach. World J. Adv. Res. **10** (2025)
11. Khanum, A., Chaitra, K., Singh, B., Gomathi, C.: Fraud detection in financial transactions: a machine learning approach vs. rule-based systems. In: 2024 International Conference on Intelligent and Innovative Technologies in Computing, Electrical and Electronics (IITCEE), pp. 1–5. IEEE (2024)
12. Khosravi, S., Kargari, M., Teimourpour, B., Talebi, M.: Transaction fraud detection via attentional spatial–temporal GNN. J. Supercomput. **81**(4), 537 (2025)
13. Kou, G., Lu, Y.: FinTech: a literature review of emerging financial technologies and applications. Financ. Innov. **11**(1), 1 (2025)
14. Lessambo, F.I.: Fintech Regulation and Supervision Challenges within the Banking Industry. Palgrave Macmillan Studies in Banking and Financial Institutions (2023)
15. Li, E., Chen, M., Xiang, S., Chen, L.: Graph learning-empowered financial fraud detection: progress and future directions. Intell. Comput. **4**, 0146 (2025)

16. Li, B., Yang, R., Wang, B., Li, W.: Improving HGT for imbalanced graph classification with soft-gated projection and jumping knowledge. In: Proceedings of the 2025 11th International Conference on Communication and Information Processing, pp. 64–71 (2025)

17. Lou, C., Wang, Y., Li, J., Qian, Y., Li, X.: Graph neural network for fraud detection via context encoding and adaptive aggregation. Expert Syst. Appl. **261**, 125473 (2025)

18. Motie, S., Raahemi, B.: Financial fraud detection using graph neural networks: a systematic review. Expert Syst. Appl. **240**, 122156 (2024)

19. Mozumder, M.S.A., Hasan, M.R., Sakil, M.B.H., Hasan, M.A., Eva, A.A., Maua, J.: AI-driven financial knowledge graphs: bridging traditional finance and blockchain ecosystems with graph neural networks. In: 2025 International Conference on Electrical, Computer and Communication Engineering (ECCE), pp. 1–6. IEEE (2025)

20. Muhammad, R.: Fraud detection and explanation in medical claims using GNN architectures. Sci. Rep. (2025)

21. Ni, L., Li, X., Zhou, Y., Qi, H., Man, X., Zhang, J.: HMOA-GNN: adaptive adversarial GraphSAGE with hierarchical hybrid sampling and metric-optimized graph construction for credit card fraud detection. Sci. Rep. **15**(1), 43005 (2025)

22. Peddamallu, M.R.: Real-time fraud detection using graph neural networks and federated learning. Int. J. Emerg. Trends Comput. Sci. Inf. Technol. 14–16 (2025)

23. Pillay, S.: Investigating brand switching in same-day-grocery-delivery mobile sector: the moderating role of income in an emerging market. Cogent Bus. Manage. **12**(1), 2552920 (2025)

24. Qian, J., Tong, G.: Metapath-guided graph neural networks for financial fraud detection. Comput. Electr. Eng. **126**, 110428 (2025)

25. Rahmati, M.: Real-time financial fraud detection using adaptive graph neural networks and federated learning. Int. J. Manage. Data Anal. **5**(1), 98–110 (2025)

26. Ren, L., et al.: Dynamic graph neural network-based fraud detectors against collaborative fraudsters. Knowl.-Based Syst. **278**, 110888 (2023)

27. Rossi, E., Chamberlain, B., Frasca, F., Eynard, D., Monti, F., Bronstein, M.: Temporal graph networks for deep learning on dynamic graphs. arXiv preprint arXiv:2006.10637 (2020)

28. Sardana, A., Yilmaz, O., Kranen, K.: Optimizing fraud detection in financial services with graph neural networks and NVIDIA GPUs (edn.) (2023)

29. Tian, Y., Liu, G.: Spatial-temporal-aware graph transformer for transaction fraud detection. IEEE Trans. Industr. Inf. (2024)

30. Tong, A., Chen, B., Wang, Z., Gao, J., Lam, C.K.: GDFGAT: graph attention network based on feature difference weight assignment for telecom fraud detection. PLoS ONE **20**(5), e0322004 (2025)

31. Tong, G., Shen, J.: Financial transaction fraud detector based on imbalance learning and graph neural network. Appl. Soft Comput. **149**, 110984 (2023)

32. Tong, G., Qian, J., Shen, J.: Adaptive metagraph neural network assisted by metagraph search for financial fraud detection. Eng. Appl. Artif. Intell. **153**, 110807 (2025)

33. Udeh, E.O., Amajuoyi, P., Adeusi, K.B., Scott, A.O.: The role of big data in detecting and preventing financial fraud in digital transactions. World J. Adv. Res. Rev. **22**(2), 1746–1760 (2024)

34. Vallarino, D.: AI-powered fraud detection in financial services: GNN, compliance challenges, and risk mitigation. Compliance Challenges and Risk Mitigation (2025)

35. Wei, S., Lee, S.: Internet fraud transaction detection based on temporal-aware heterogeneous graph oversampling and attention fusion network. PLoS ONE **20**(12), e0337208 (2025)
36. Wu, Z., Pan, S., Chen, F., Long, G., Zhang, C., Yu, P.S.: A comprehensive survey on graph neural networks. IEEE Trans. Neural Netw. Learn. Syst. **32**(1), 4–24 (2020)
37. Wu, B., Chao, K.-M., Li, Y.: Heterogeneous graph neural networks for fraud detection and explanation in supply chain finance. Inf. Syst. **121**, 102335 (2024)
38. Xiao, F., Cai, S., Chen, G., Jagadish, H., Ooi, B.C., Zhang, M.: VecAug: unveiling camouflaged frauds with cohort augmentation for enhanced detection. In: Proceedings of the 30th ACM SIGKDD Conference on Knowledge Discovery and Data Mining, pp. 6025–6036 (2024)
39. Xie, W., He, J., Huang, F., Ren, J.: Supply chain financial fraud detection based on graph neural network and knowledge graph. Tehn. vjesnik **31**(6), 2055–2063 (2024)
40. Xu, F., Wang, N., Wu, H., Wen, X., Zhao, X., Wan, H.: Revisiting graph-based fraud detection in sight of heterophily and spectrum. In: AAAI Conference on Artificial Intelligence, vol. 38, no. 8, pp. 9214–9222 (2024)
41. Yuan, H., Yu, H., Gui, S., Ji, S.: Explainability in graph neural networks: a taxonomic survey. IEEE Trans. Pattern Anal. Mach. Intell. **45**(5), 5782–5799 (2022)
42. Zakaria, R.M., Rahman, M.M., Rahman, H., Rafi, M.A.: Detecting financial fraud in real-time transactions using graph neural networks and anomaly detection techniques. J. Econ. Financ. Account. Stud. **7**(6), 01–13 (2025)
43. Zhao, T., Zhang, X., Wang, S.: GraphSMOTE: imbalanced node classification on graphs with graph neural networks. In: Proceedings of the 14th ACM International Conference on Web Search and Data Mining, pp. 833–841 (2021)

YOLOv8n for Automated Identification of Visually Similar Snapper Species in Operational Fish Processing Environments

Lorena Guachi-Guachi[1(✉)], Mateo Ballagan[1], Estefanía Oñate[1],
Lorena Molina[2], Saravana Prakash Thirumuruganandham[3,4],
and D. H. Peluffo-Ordóñez[5,6]

[1] Faculty of Digital Engineering and Emerging Technologies, Universidad
Internacional del Ecuador, Av. Simon Bolivar, 170411 Quito, Ecuador
{loguachigu,maballaganiu,esonatemo}@uide.edu.ec
[2] Universidad Nacional de Chimborazo, Riobamba, Ecuador
lmolina@unach.edu.ec
[3] SIT Health, Edificio Bristol Of. 901, Catalina Aldaz, 170504 Quito, Ecuador
saravana@sit.health
[4] HessQ Inc., 1231 Grant Avenue, Winnipeg, MB, Canada
saravana.prakash@hessq.tech
[5] School of Mathematical and Computational Sciences, YachayTech,
Urcuqui, Ecuador
dpeluffo@yachaytech.edu.ec
[6] SDAS Research Group, Ibarra, Ecuador
diego.peluffo@sdas-group.com
https://sdas-group.com/

Abstract. Accurate identification of visually similar fish species in post-harvest environments remains a challenging task due to occlusions, inter-species similarity, and complex backgrounds. This study introduces a real-world dataset comprising 552 RGB images of red snapper and colorado snapper, captured under diverse illumination and operational conditions across multiple fishery areas. We propose a lightweight object detection framework based on the YOLOv8n architecture, designed for robust detection and discrimination of the two species. Experimental results demonstrate that YOLOv8n achieves a mean Average Precision (mAP@0.5) of 81.5% and outperforms larger YOLOv8 variants in convergence stability and recall, while maintaining computational efficiency suitable for real-time deployment. This work highlights the potential of deep learning-based detectors for operational fishery monitoring and the identification of closely related species under challenging real-world conditions.

Keywords: Fish species detection · YOLO · Object recognition

1 Introduction

Automated fish species identification has gained increasing attention in ecological monitoring, fisheries management, and post-harvest quality control [1–4].

J. M. Ferrández Vicente et al. (Eds.): IWINAC 2026, LNCS 16575, pp. 329–338, 2026.
https://doi.org/10.1007/978-3-032-27317-8_31

Accurate identification is essential for sustainable fisheries, regulatory compliance, and prevention of mislabeling [5]. Traditional manual inspection methods are labor-intensive, error-prone, and impractical for large-scale operations [2].

Deep learning-based object detection offers a scalable solution, enabling rapid and automated species recognition across diverse environmental conditions [2,4,6]. Recent research has advanced the methodological framework for aquatic monitoring by incorporating state-of-the-art object detection architectures, including YOLO, Faster R-CNN, and SSD, as well as hybrid machine learning strategies that combine deep feature extraction with classical machine learning classifiers for more accurate monitoring and analysis of fish behaviors [7]. Particularly the YOLO family, provide end-to-end detection with real-time performance and have achieved state-of-the-art results on large-scale benchmarks such as MS COCO [8]. Nevertheless, these models often face challenges in fine-grained discrimination of visually similar species, especially in real-world settings characterized by occlusions, cluttered backgrounds, variable illumination, and multi-instance scenes [9,10]. Transformer-based architectures, including DETR [11] and Deformable DETR [12], can capture long-range dependencies and complex object relationships but incur substantial computational cost and are typically evaluated on datasets with single-specimen images or minimal occlusion. Domain-specific approaches, such as FishNet [6], rely on controlled aquaculture or underwater imagery, limiting their applicability to post-harvest fishery environments. Existing datasets largely support single-instance detection, restricting model generalization to operational conditions.

To address these challenges, we proposed a YOLOv8n-based object detection framework capable of distinguishing close related fish species (red snapper and colorado snapper) under realistic fishery conditions. In addition, we introduce an in-house dataset of 552 RGB images collected across multiple operational sites, incorporating inter-species co-occurrence, partial occlusions, and variable illumination, providing a novel benchmark for fine-grained species identification in real-world scenarios.

2   Dataset

A dataset comprising 552 RGB images containing *red snapper* and *colorado snapper* specimens was collected using two mobile devices (Google Pixel 9 and Xiaomi Mi 11 Lite). Among these, 477 images contain instances of a single species, whereas 75 images include both species within the same frame, thereby increasing inter-class variability and scene complexity. In all images, the target species co-occur with other marine organisms, such as mollusks and squid, frequently resulting in partial occlusions and inter-object overlap.

Image acquisition was conducted under natural illumination at different times of the day across three operational fishery environments: deck, temporary storage area, and selection area. Consequently, the dataset exhibits substantial variability in illumination intensity, camera viewpoint, fish orientation, object scale, and background clutter, closely reflecting real-world operational conditions.

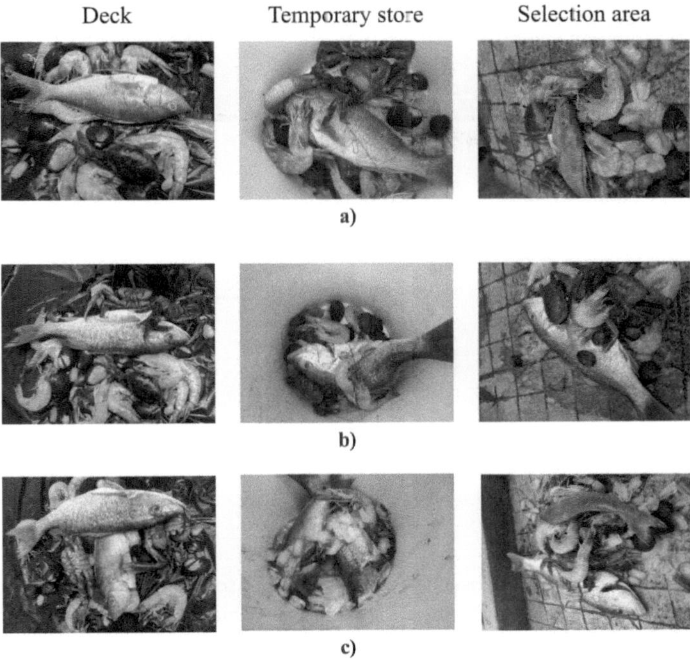

Fig. 1. Representative samples from the collected dataset, illustrating variability in species, backgrounds, and capture conditions: a) colorado snapper; b) red snapper; and c) both snapper species. (Color figure online)

For this sdudy, two target classes were defined: *red snapper* and *colorado snapper*. Manual annotation was conducted by domain experts using bounding boxes to accurately localize and distinguish instances of both snapper species. The dataset was split into training (497 images) and test (55 images) subsets. Prior to training, all images were resized to 640 × 640 pixels. Representative examples of the dataset are presented in Fig. 1.

3   Proposed Methodology

The proposed methodology aims to automatically detect and discriminate between two visually similar snapper species (*red snapper* and *Colorado snapper*) from RGB images captured in real fishery operational environments. The detection framework is built upon the YOLOv8n architecture [13], the lightweight (nano) variant of the YOLOv8 family. As a one-stage object detector, YOLOv8n jointly performs bounding box regression and class prediction within a unified end-to-end deep neural network, as illustrated in Fig. 2.

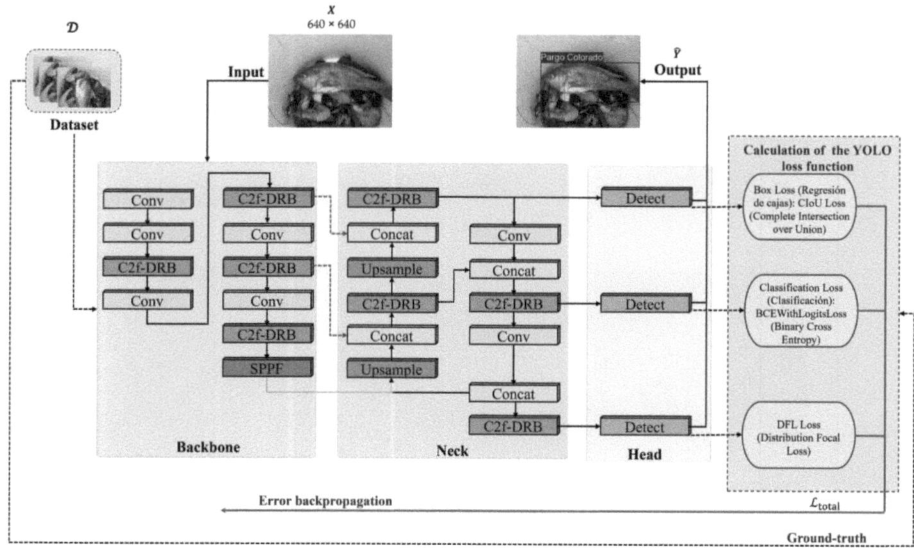

Fig. 2. Overview of the proposed YOLOv8n-based to automatically detect and discriminate between two visually similar snapper species: (*red snapper* and *Colorado snapper*). (Color figure online)

Let $X \in \mathbb{R}^{H \times W \times 3}$ denote an RGB image acquired in one of the three operational environments (deck, temporary storage, or selection area). The goal of the detector is to estimate a set of N object instances:

$$\hat{Y} = \{(b_i, \hat{c}_i, s_i)\}_{i=1}^{N} \tag{1}$$

where $b_i = (x_i, y_i, w_i, h_i)$ represents the predicted bounding box coordinates; $\hat{c}_i \in \{c_1, c_2\}$ denotes the predicted class label (red snapper or Colorado snapper); $s_i \in [0, 1]$ corresponds to the confidence score associated with the prediction.

The overall architecture, illustrated in Fig. 2, consists of three main components: backbone, neck, and detection head.

1. **Backbone (YOLOv8n):** The backbone performs hierarchical feature extraction using CSP-inspired modules and C2f blocks to enhance gradient flow while reducing computational redundancy. A Spatial Pyramid Pooling Fast (SPPF) layer incorporated at the deepest stage enlarges the receptive field and captures multi-scale contextual information. This design generates multi-resolution feature representations encoding both fine-grained texture cues and high-level semantics, which are essential for distinguishing morphologically similar species under challenging illumination and background variability.

2. **Neck:** The neck adopts a PAN-like feature aggregation strategy to fuse multi-scale representations through top-down and bottom-up pathways. By integrating low-level spatial details with high-level semantic features, the neck

improves robustness to scale variations caused by perspective differences and varying camera-to-object distances.

3. **Detection Head:**
The detection head follows a decoupled design, separating bounding box regression and classification into independent branches. The regression branch predicts object center coordinates and dimensions, while the classification branch estimates posterior probabilities over the two snapper classes. Distribution Focal Loss (DFL) enhances localization precision. The decoupled structure mitigates gradient interference between tasks, improving optimization stability and detection accuracy.

3.1 Training, Inference and Post-processing

The detector was initialized using pretrained weights [13] and fine-tuned on the collected dataset. Given a training dataset:

$$\mathcal{D} = \{(X^{(k)}, Y^{(k)})\}_{k=1}^{M} \tag{2}$$

where $Y^{(k)}$ denotes the set of ground-truth bounding boxes and class labels for image $X^{(k)}$, the model parameters θ were optimized by minimizing the composite YOLO loss function:

$$\mathcal{L}_{total} = \mathcal{L}_{box} + \mathcal{L}_{cls} + \mathcal{L}_{obj} \tag{3}$$

where $\mathcal{L}_{box}$ is an IoU-based regression loss, $\mathcal{L}_{cls}$ is the binary cross-entropy classification loss, and $\mathcal{L}_{obj}$ represents the objectness confidence loss.

During inference, the network produces a dense set of candidate detections $\mathcal{B} = \{(b_i, \hat{c}_i, s_i)\}$. The final prediction set $\mathcal{B}^*$ is obtained by filtering predictions with confidence $s_i < \tau$ and applying Non-Maximum Suppression (NMS) to remove overlapping boxes with Intersection over Union (IoU) greater than threshold γ, ensuring that each object instance is represented by a single high-confidence bounding box.

1. Filtering predictions with $s_i < \tau$, where τ is a predefined confidence threshold.
2. Applying NMS to remove overlapping bounding boxes with Intersection over Union (IoU) greater than a threshold γ.

This process ensures that each snapper instance is represented by a single bounding box with maximum confidence.

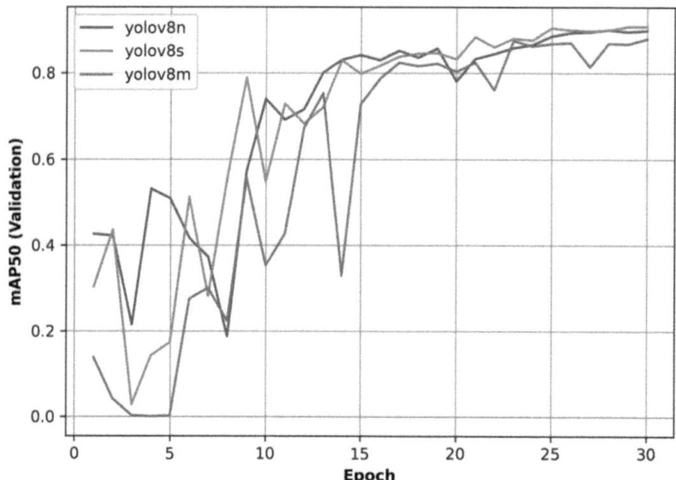

Fig. 3. Validation learning curves (mAP@50) across training epochs for YOLOv8n, YOLOv8s, and YOLOv8m.

4   Experimental Results

Detection performance was evaluated using Precision, Recall, mAP@50, and mAP@50–95. Figure 3 presents the validation mAP@50 across training epochs for YOLOv8n, YOLOv8s, and YOLOv8m. All models exhibited rapid performance improvement during the initial epochs, followed by gradual stabilization after approximately epoch 15. YOLOv8n demonstrated faster and smoother convergence with reduced variance, indicating stable optimization dynamics. In contrast, YOLOv8m showed higher oscillations and slower convergence, suggesting increased sensitivity to dataset size. While YOLOv8s and YOLOv8m achieved slightly higher peak mAP@50 values, the performance gain relative to YOLOv8n was marginal. These observations indicated that increasing model capacity provides limited benefits, whereas YOLOv8n achieved competitive accuracy with improved training stability, supporting its suitability for efficient deployment in resource-constrained scenarios.

Quantitative results on the test set are summarized in Table 1. YOLOv8s obtained the highest precision, whereas YOLOv8n achieved the highest recall, mAP@50, and mAP@50–95, reflecting superior localization consistency across IoU thresholds. Conversely, the increased capacity of YOLOv8m did not yield a measurable improvement in detection performance, indicating that model complexity exceeds dataset representational needs.

As shown in Fig. 4a), the precision-recall curves indicate high detection performance, achieving an mAP@0.5 of 0.815. *Pargo colorado* achieved a higher AP (0.848) than *Pargo rojo* (0.782), showing slightly more stable precision at all recall levels. Accuracy remains high (>0.85) up to moderate recall values

Table 1. Performance of YOLOv8 variants on the collected test set for two-snapper-species detection.

Model	Precision [%]	Recall [%]	mAP50 [%]	mAP50–95 [%]
YOLOv8n	81.38	82.05	81.50	64.30
YOLOv8s	84.03	77.50	80.82	63.95
YOLOv8m	79.24	80.95	80.96	62.41

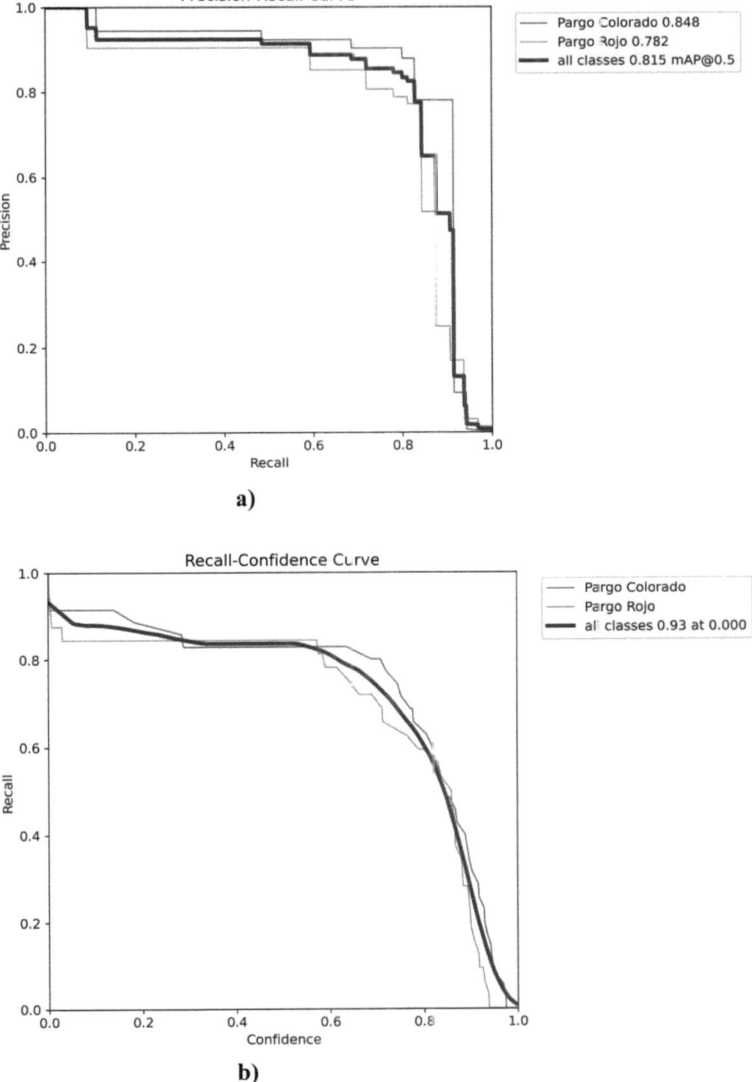

Fig. 4. Precision–recall curves and corresponding AP values for the YOLOv8n-based detector on the test subset, showing class-wise performance and overall mAP@0.5 under realistic operational conditions.

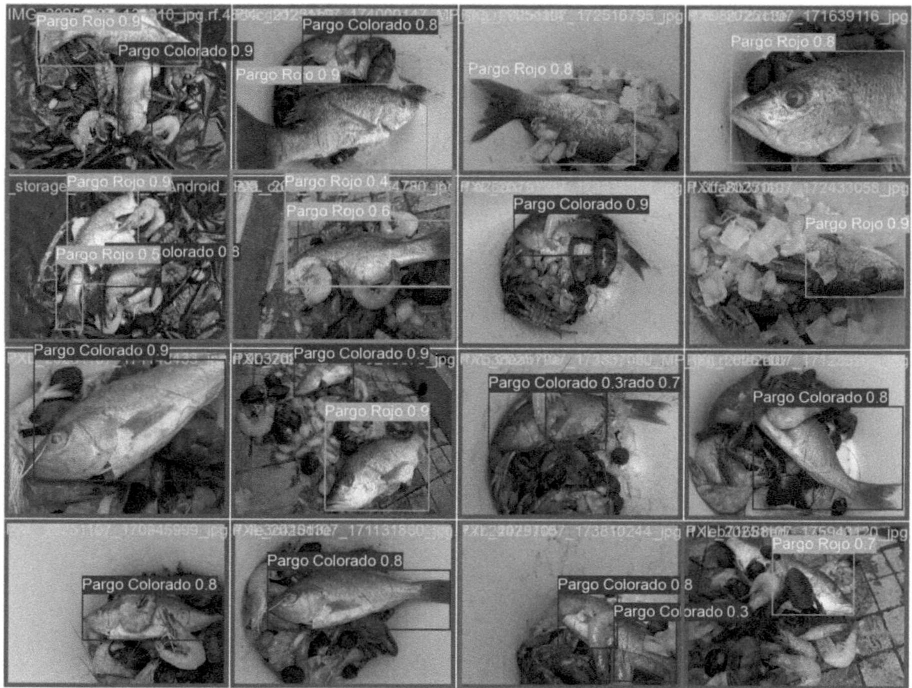

Fig. 5. Representative YOLOv8n detection results on the test subset, including failure cases (red boxes) in the localization and classification of red and colorado snapper under realistic operational conditions. (Color figure online)

(0.8), with a decline near total recall due to the inclusion of lower-confidence detections.

The Recall–Confidence curves in Fig. 4b) show high initial recall ($\approx$0.93 at confidence $= 0$), followed by a gradual decrease as the confidence threshold increases, with a more pronounced drop beyond the 0.75–0.80 range. Across most thresholds, *Pargo colorado* maintains slightly higher recall. These results indicate a favorable precision–recall trade-off and stable performance across practical confidence thresholds.

Figure 5 shows representative qualitative results in the three evaluated environments. The proposed YOLOv8n-based framework effectively detects and differentiates snapper species under various lighting conditions and in the presence of background clutter. Most failures occur in scenarios where there is severe object overlap or partial occlusions, in which discriminatory visual features are reduced.

Recent advances in object detection have been largely driven by one-stage anchor-free architectures such as Ultralytics YOLOv8 [13], which are based on the original YOLOv5 framework [14]. Compared to general-purpose detectors as YOLOv5 [14] and YOLOX [15], evaluated on large-scale benchmarks such as

MS COCO [8], our work addresses the domain-specific problem of fine-grained detection of visually similar fish species under real-world post-capture conditions. Our dataset exhibits higher scene clutter, occlusion, and inter-species similarity compared to controlled aquaculture datasets, enhancing ecological validity while increasing task complexity.

In the fishing domain, previous work such as FishNet [6] and transformer-based detectors, including DETR [11] and Deformable DETR [12], have achieved high performance in detection. However, they rely on single-specimen images or underwater scenes with limited occlusion. Our work addresses multi-instance, overlapping specimens of closely related species under uncontrolled deck conditions. Compared to transformer-based detectors, the YOLOv8n-based framework balances computational efficiency and detection accuracy, with potential for real-time deployment in operational fishing scenarios.

Although promising results (mAP@0.5 = 0.815) obtained in this work, there are limitations that require further investigation. Our collected dataset comprises 552 images, which is modesty compared to large-scale detection benchmarks and may limit generalization to broader geographic regions or other snapper species. The evaluation was limited to two target classes, restricting assessment under more diverse taxonomic conditions. The use of input images resized to 640×640 may also reduce detailed morphological signals that are critical for distinguishing visually similar species. Therefore, future work will focus on expanding the dataset to include additional snapper species and other species across multiple fisheries and seasons to improve robustness to ecological variability. The impact of higher input resolutions and advanced multi-scale feature fusion strategies will be explored to better capture subtle differences between species. Finally, domain adaptation techniques and lightweight model optimization approaches, such as pruning and quantization, will be investigated to facilitate robust real-time implementation on embedded or edge devices in operational fishing environments.

5   Conclusion

This study introduces a real-world dataset and an object detection framework for distinguishing between *red snapper* and *colorado snapper* under operational fishing conditions. The dataset captures realistic challenges, such as occlusion, high visual similarity between species, and cluttered backgrounds, reflecting the complexity inherent in post-harvest environments. The YOLOv8n-based detector provides a balance between accuracy and recall across all practical operational thresholds, supporting its suitability for real-world implementation.

Although the dataset is limited in scale and taxonomic diversity, the results demonstrate the feasibility of deep learning-based object detection for automated species identification in challenging operational settings, paving the way for intelligent, scalable, real-time monitoring systems aimed at supporting fisheries management, including their implementation in resource-constrained environments such as artisanal fishing vessels or local processing stations.

References

1. Konovalov, D.A., Saleh, A., Bradley, M., Sankupellay, M., Marini, S., Sheaves, M.: Underwater fish detection with weak multi-domain supervision. arXiv preprint arXiv:1905.10708 (2019)
2. Haque, S.A., Al Jufaili, S.M.: Applications of artificial intelligence in fisheries: from data to decisions. Big Data Cogn. Comput. **10**(1), 19 (2026)
3. Sattar, S., Abbas, T., Tabish, M., Zhiqiang, G.: Computer vision in aquaculture: transforming fish freshness monitoring. Crit. Rev. Food Sci. Nutr. 1–29 (2025)
4. Ergün, E.: Stacked deep learning-based quality classification of dried fish products for post harvest loss reduction and value chain enhancement. J. Agric. Sci. **32**(1), 42–56 (2026)
5. Kilinc, I., Kilinc, B., Takma, C., Gevrekci, Y.: Smart tools and artificial intelligence for enhanced quality and safety in agriculture, fisheries, and aquaculture: a review. Iran. J. Fish. Sci. **24**(4), 913–951 (2025)
6. Khan, F.F., Li, X., Temple, A.J., Elhoseiny, M.: FishNet: a large-scale dataset and benchmark for fish recognition, detection, and functional trait prediction. In: Proceedings of the IEEE/CVF International Conference on Computer Vision, pp. 20496–20506 (2023)
7. Al-Abri, S., Keshvari, S., Al-Rashdi, K., Al-Hmouz, R., Bourdoucen, H.: Computer vision based approaches for fish monitoring systems: a comprehensive study. Artif. Intell. Rev. **58**(6), 185 (2025)
8. Lin, T.-Y., et al.: Microsoft COCO: common objects in context. In: Fleet, D., Pajdla, T., Schiele, B., Tuytelaars, T. (eds.) ECCV 2014. LNCS, vol. 8693, pp. 740–755. Springer, Cham (2014). https://doi.org/10.1007/978-3-319-10602-1_48
9. Ouyang, C., et al.: YOLO-TPS: a multi-module synergistic high-precision fish-disease detection model for complex aquaculture environments. Animals **15**(16), 2356 (2025)
10. Mei, Y., Chen, Y., Liu, Y., Yu, H., Yang, L., Li, D.: MFSD-YOLO: a multi-scenario fish small target detection method in aquaculture. Aquacult. Eng. 102677 (2025)
11. Carion, N., Massa, F., Synnaeve, G., Usunier, N., Kirillov, A., Zagoruyko, S.: End-to-end object detection with transformers. In: Vedaldi, A., Bischof, H., Brox, T., Frahm, J.-M. (eds.) ECCV 2020. LNCS, vol. 12346, pp. 213–229. Springer, Cham (2020). https://doi.org/10.1007/978-3-030-58452-8_13
12. Zhu, X., Su, W., Lu, L., Li, B., Wang, X., Dai, J.: Deformable DETR: deformable transformers for end-to-end object detection. arXiv preprint arXiv:2010.04159 (2020)
13. Ultralytics. YOLOv8: Ultralytics YOLO (2023). https://github.com/ultralytics/ultralytics
14. Redmon, J., Divvala, S., Girshick, R., Farhadi, A.: You only look once: unified, real-time object detection. In: Proceedings of the IEEE Conference on Computer Vision and Pattern Recognition, pp. 779–788 (2016)
15. Ge, Z., Liu, S., Wang, F., Li, Z., Sun, J., YOLOX: exceeding YOLO series in 2021. arXiv preprint arXiv:2107.08430 (2021)

Safe UAV Obstacle Avoidance via Q-Learning in ROS2–Gazebo Simulation

Daniel Caballero-Martin[1,2], Geovanny Satama-Bermeo[1,2],
Hicham Affou[1,2], Julian Estevez[1,3], and Jose Manuel Lopez-Guede[1,2(✉)]

[1] Group of Computational Intelligence, University of the Basque Country,
UPV/EHU, Vitoria-Gasteiz, Spain
jm.lopez@ehu.es
[2] Faculty of Engineering of Alava, University of the Basque Country,
UPV/EHU, Vitoria-Gasteiz, Spain
[3] Faculty of Engineering of Gipuzkoa, University of the Basque Country,
UPV/EHU, San Sebastian, Spain

Abstract. This work presents a point-to-point trajectory planning framework for UAVs based on Q-Learning, integrated into a ROS2Gazebo simulation environment. The problem is formulated as a discrete Markov Decision Process (MDP) over a two dimensional discretization of the space, with execution at constant altitude. Cylindrical obstacles are randomly generated in each experiment and represented using an inflated occupancy grid, which incorporates an explicit geometric safety margin during planning (2 m). Learning incorporates *reward shaping* based on potential to accelerate convergence while maintaining policy optimality. After training, the resulting trajectory is simplified, densified, and geometrically validated (by removing collinear points, interpolating intermediate waypoints, and sampling along segments on the inflated occupancy grid) before its execution in physical simulation. The results show stable convergence, high success rates, and spatial coherence between the learned value function and the geometry of the environment. The comparison between planned and executed trajectories confirms the transferability of the discrete model to a continuous dynamic system.

Keywords: UAV navigation · Q-learning · Obstacle avoidance · ROS2–Gazebo simulation

1 Introduction

The autonomous navigation of Unmanned Aerial Vehicles (UAVs) has evolved from a predominantly theoretical domain to become a key technology in sectors such as logistics, infrastructure inspection, and emergency response in hard to access environments [1,2]. Their deployment in unstructured scenarios poses fundamental challenges in control and trajectory planning. In particular, it is critical to ensure that the agent can move safely between two predefined points in

J. M. Ferrández Vicente et al. (Eds.): IWINAC 2026, LNCS 16575, pp. 339–348, 2026.
https://doi.org/10.1007/978-3-032-27317-8_32

the presence of obstacles whose location and geometry are not deterministically defined.

Classical planning methods, such as graph based or sampling based algorithms, provide robust performance in structured or fully known environments. However, their performance may be limited when the environment exhibits spatial variability, uncertainty, or constraints. In this context, Reinforcement Learning (RL) emerges as an alternative capable of providing the system with greater adaptive capacity, allowing the agent to learn a decision policy through direct interaction with the environment [3]. Among the available approaches, Q-Learning constitutes a well established strategy within model free RL [4,5], with a rigorous formulation based on the Bellman equation and theoretical convergence guarantees under appropriate conditions, particularly suitable for problems defined over discretized spaces.

With the aim of analyzing this approach in a controlled and reproducible environment, this work presents a modular simulation architecture based on ROS2 and Gazebo for the development and validation of autonomous navigation strategies [6,7]. The architecture incorporates an external controller within the ROS2 ecosystem, enabling a clear separation between physical simulation, the learning module, and the execution layer, thereby promoting experimental traceability and extensibility toward real-world implementations.

The point-to-point navigation problem is formulated as a MDP, where planning is performed over a discretization in the planar (XY) space and the resulting trajectory is executed at a constant cruising altitude (1.5 m) [8]. Obstacles are modeled as static cylindrical columns randomly generated in each experimental run, through the geometric expansion of occupied regions by means of an explicit safety margin, implemented as a safety margin in the occupancy map (2 m). This representation guarantees a safety margin with respect to potentially collidable regions and allows the integration of explicit metric constraints within the learning process.

Under these constraints, the Q-Learning algorithm is implemented with neighborhood actions and an ε-greedy exploration policy, estimating the state-action value function through the update of the Bellman equation. The reward function includes a reward shaping scheme based on the distance to the goal, together with penalties associated with collisions, revisits, and proximity to obstacles, in order to induce safe and efficient trajectories [9,10], transforming the result into a sequence of geometric waypoints for subsequent export to the simulation environment in order to obtain a simulation and feasibility analysis.

The remainder of the paper is structured as follows. Section 2 surveys related work in UAV navigation and learning-based trajectory planning. Section 3 details the proposed framework, including the formal problem definition and the adopted learning approach. Section 4 describes the experimental configuration and simulation environment. Section 5 presents the experimental results. Finally, Sect. 6 concludes the paper and highlights potential future research directions.

2   Related Work

Trajectory planning for UAVs has traditionally been addressed through deterministic graph based methods, such as A* [11], Dijkstra [12], as well as through sampling-based techniques such as Rapidly Exploring Random Trees (RRT) [13]. These strategies have demonstrated effective performance in structured or fully known environments, particularly when precise geometric maps of the free space are available. However, their adaptive capacity may be limited in scenarios with variable spatial configurations or structural uncertainty, where planning requires greater flexibility in response to changing obstacle distributions.

In recent years, RL has emerged as a relevant alternative for autonomous navigation in aerial robotics. Several studies apply Deep Reinforcement Learning (DRL) techniques, Proximal Policy Optimization (PPO), or actorcritic methods to obstacle avoidance and navigation tasks in simulated environments [14,15]. These approaches enable operation in continuous and higher dimensional state spaces, albeit at the cost of increased computational complexity, dependence on hyperparameters, and reduced interpretability of the resulting policy.

In contrast to approaches based on deep functional approximation, the Q-Learning algorithm remains a valid tool in problems where the state space can be discretized in a structured manner. Its formulation within the framework of MDP [16] and the possibility of explicitly analyzing the evolution of the value function make it a suitable instrument for systematic studies in controlled environments. In this context, it is pertinent to analyze the behavior of the Q-Learning algorithm in discretized environments with explicit geometric constraints, evaluating its capacity to generate safe and efficient trajectories under spatial configurations generated in a controlled manner. This approach makes it possible to establish a solid comparative basis against more complex methods, providing interpretative clarity and experimental reproducibility.

3   Methodology

This section describes the technical structure of the proposed system and the formal formulation of the addressed navigation problem. First, the modular architecture integrating environment generation, the offline learning process, and the subsequent execution within the ROS2 and Gazebo based simulation environment is detailed. Next, the problem formulation as a MDP is presented, defining the state, action, and reward spaces. Finally, the implementation of the Q-Learning algorithm used to obtain the navigation policy is described.

3.1   System Architecture

The proposed architecture is structured in a modular manner with the objective of clearly separating the phases of environment generation, learning, and simulation execution. The system operates under a fully offline training scheme, in which the learning process is carried out independently of the physical simulator, and the obtained policy is subsequently exported for execution in a ROS2 and Gazebo based environment.

The environment generation module constructs a discrete representation of the workspace from a uniform grid defined over the horizontal plane. Obstacles are modeled as static cylindrical columns whose positions and radii are randomly generated in each experimental run. In order to guarantee the existence of navigable scenarios, a preliminary connectivity verification stage is incorporated to ensure the presence of at least one collision free path between the initial and goal positions before training begins.

Once the environment has been defined, a discrete occupancy map is constructed. On this representation, a geometric safety constraint is incorporated through the metric expansion of each obstacle, inflating its effective radius with a safety margin expressed in real meters (2 m). This process generates a conservative representation of the free space, ensuring a minimum distance between the planned trajectory and the physical boundaries of the obstacles.

The RL module operates exclusively on this discrete representation. The UAV state is defined by its position on the horizontal plane grid, while the vertical coordinate is kept constant during the planning phase. Training is carried out through iterative interaction with the discretized environment, without real time communication with the simulator. The algorithm estimates the stateaction value function over the discrete domain and derives a navigation policy from it.

Once training has been completed, the learned policy is used to extract a collision free trajectory from the initial state to the goal. The resulting sequence of discrete positions is transformed into metric coordinates and subjected to additional geometric validation through dense sampling along the trajectory segments, in order to ensure consistency with the inflated occupancy map. Finally, the validated trajectory is exported as a sequence of waypoints compatible with the ROS2 control layer, enabling its controlled execution within the Gazebo simulation environment.

This architectural separation between learning and execution provides several advantages: it improves experimental reproducibility, reduces computational load during simulation, and facilitates traceability between policy generation and its physical execution in the simulator (Fig 1).

3.2   Problem Formulation

The navigation problem is modeled as a discrete MPD, defined by the tuple (S, A, P, R, γ), where S represents the state space, A the action space, P the transition dynamics, R the reward function, and $\gamma \in (0, 1)$ the discount factor.

The state space S consists of the discrete positions of the UAV on a uniform two dimensional grid. Each state $s \in S$ is represented by the discrete coordinates (i, j) of a spatial mesh, maintaining constant altitude during the planning phase (2.5D navigation). This discretization allows the environment to be represented through an occupancy map that distinguishes between free regions and obstacles.

The action space A comprises a finite set of elementary movements, corresponding to unit displacements toward adjacent cells in the cardinal directions.

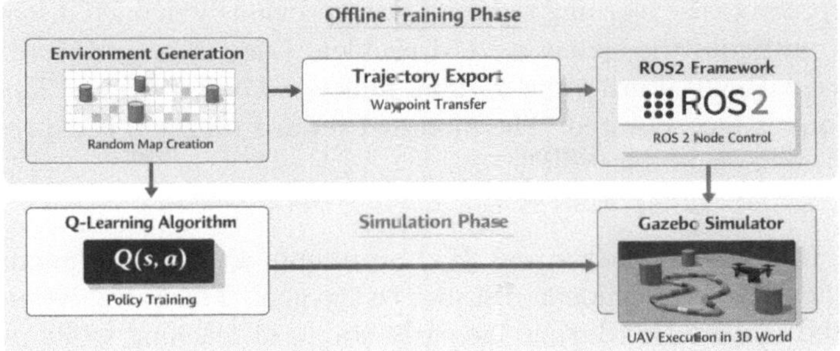

Fig. 1. Learning and execution workflow for UAV obstacle avoidance.

The transition function $P(s'|s,a)$ is deterministic: if the selected action leads to a free cell, the agent moves to the new state; if the action implies a collision or exiting the domain boundaries, the agent remains in its current position and receives a penalty. This structure ensures that the systems evolution depends exclusively on the current state and the executed action, satisfying the Markov property.

The reward function $R(s,a)$ is designed to encourage goal achievement and mitigate inefficient or risky behaviors. A large positive reward is assigned upon reaching the goal state (r_{goal}), while each intermediate step incurs a negative cost to promote minimal trajectories. Additionally, further penalties are applied for collisions, for excessive proximity to obstacles (through a safety margin or *clearance*), and for recurrent state revisits in order to prevent loops.

The fundamental objective of the agent is to maximize the expected accumulated return or *expected return*. For a time instant t, the return G_t is defined as:

$$G_t = \sum_{k=0}^{T-t-1} \gamma^k r_{t+k+1} \tag{1}$$

where $\gamma \in [0,1)$ is the discount factor and T the temporal horizon of the episode. The optimal policy π^* is the one that maximizes the expected value of this return. In this context, the optimal state–action value function is defined as:

$$Q^*(s,a) = \mathbb{E}[G_t \mid s_t = s, a_t = a] \tag{2}$$

3.3 Q-Learning Strategy

To estimate the stateaction value function, the Q-Learning algorithm is employed. The update of the values is governed by the Temporal Difference (TD) learning rule:

$$Q(s_t, a_t) \leftarrow Q(s_t, a_t) + \alpha \left[r_{t+1} + \gamma \max_a Q(s_{t+1}, a) - Q(s_t, a_t) \right] \tag{3}$$

where α represents the learning rate and γ the previously defined discount factor. In order to mitigate the sparse reward problem (*sparse reward*) and accelerate convergence without altering the optimal policy, a *Potential-based Reward Shaping* technique is incorporated. The modified reward function is expressed as:

$$R'(s, a, s') = R(s, a, s') + \gamma\Phi(s') - \Phi(s) \tag{4}$$

where γ is the discount factor and $\Phi(s)$ represents a potential function defined based on the negative Euclidean distance to the goal. This formulation promotes goal-directed trajectories during the early stages of learning while maintaining optimal policy invariance.

During training, an ϵ-greedy policy is adopted to balance exploration and exploitation. With probability ϵ, the agent selects a random action; with probability $1 - \epsilon$, it selects the optimal action according to the current estimate, $a = \arg\max_a Q(s, a)$. The parameter ϵ decreases exponentially throughout the episodes to promote convergence toward a stable policy.

Once training is completed, the policy is extracted by selecting, for each state, the action that maximizes the function $Q(s, a)$, thus generating a discrete trajectory from the initial state to the goal.

4   Experimental Setup

The workspace is discretized using a uniform grid of 60×60 nodes with spatial resolution $\Delta = 0.5$ m, defining an approximate physical domain of 30×30 m. The initial state is located at $(0, 0)$ and the goal at the opposite corner of the domain. The cruising altitude is fixed at $z = 1.5$ m, incorporating an initial vertical takeoff phase up to this altitude.

Obstacles are modeled as 25 static cylindrical columns with radii uniformly sampled in the interval $[0.7, 1.6]$ m and height 1.6 m. In order to guarantee explicit geometric separation during planning, each obstacle is inflated with a safety margin (*clearance*) of 2.0 m, constructing a conservative *hard* occupancy map used both during learning and in subsequent validation.

Learning is performed using Q-Learning with a 4-connected neighborhood, meaning that at each state the agent can move only to the four adjacent cells in the cardinal directions (north, south, east, and west), which defines a structured and locally constrained action space over the discretized grid. Training is executed over 10,000 episodes, with a maximum of 1,800 steps per episode, using $\alpha = 0.15$ and $\gamma = 0.985$. Exploration is managed through an ϵ-greedy policy with $\epsilon_0 = 1.0$, $\epsilon_{min} = 0.05$, and a multiplicative decay factor that progressively reduces exploration as learning stabilizes, $\epsilon \leftarrow \max(\epsilon_{min}, 0.999\,\epsilon)$.

The reward function combines a step penalty (-1), a collision penalty (-60), and a reward for reaching the goal $(+900)$. Additionally, *reward shaping* is incorporated based on the reduction of the Euclidean distance to the goal (weight 2.5), together with additional penalties for frequent revisits and for proximity to obstacles when the distance to the obstacle in the *inflated occupancy grid* is less than 2.0 m.

Once training is completed, the policy is extracted as $\arg\max_a Q(s, a)$ and a discrete trajectory from the start to the goal is obtained. This trajectory is simplified by removing consecutive collinear points in order to eliminate redundancies while preserving the actual direction changes. It is subsequently densified through linear interpolation with a spatial step of 0.20 m, generating a more continuous sequence of intermediate points that facilitates smooth execution in simulation. A geometric validation is then performed by sampling along each segment with a step of 0.05 m, verifying that all interpolated points remain within free space. Optionally, an additional neighborhood check over the *inflated occupancy grid* is incorporated to further reinforce obstacle clearance guarantees. Finally, the validated trajectory is exported as a sequence of *waypoints* for execution in the ROS2–Gazebo environment.

For evaluation, the success rate, the average reward per episode, the average number of steps, and the average number of collisions per episode are reported, together with planar and 3D visualizations, and heat maps of $\max_a Q(s, a)$ and distance to obstacles.

5   Results

The performance of the proposed navigation system is evaluated through a comprehensive analysis that links learning dynamics with the safety of physical execution. As summarized in Table 1, the agent achieved a success rate of 98.13% after 10.000 training episodes in a high-density environment composed of 25 cylindrical obstacles. This effectiveness is supported by a notably rapid convergence of the performance metrics (Fig. 2), where the average reward curve exhibits exponential growth during the first 2.500 episodes, stabilizing completely before reaching the midpoint of training.

Table 1. Consolidated performance indicators of the learning and navigation process.

Evaluation Metric	Obtained Value
Navigation success rate (%)	98.13
Average accumulated reward	380.21
Average trajectory length (steps)	199.95
Average collision rate per episode	3.61
Control points (Simple/Dense Trajectory)	72/364

This maturation of learning manifests spatially in the final Q value function. The resulting heat map reveals the formation of high value corridors (yellow regions) that optimally connect the origin with the goal. It is significant to observe how the regions of low utility align with the physical location of the obstacles, indicating that the agent has internalized safety constraints as a fundamental component of its decision policy. This gradient of Q values enables the drone not only to identify the free path, but also to quantify the "quality" of each state, ensuring that the decisions made maximize the expected return away from collision zones (Fig. 2).

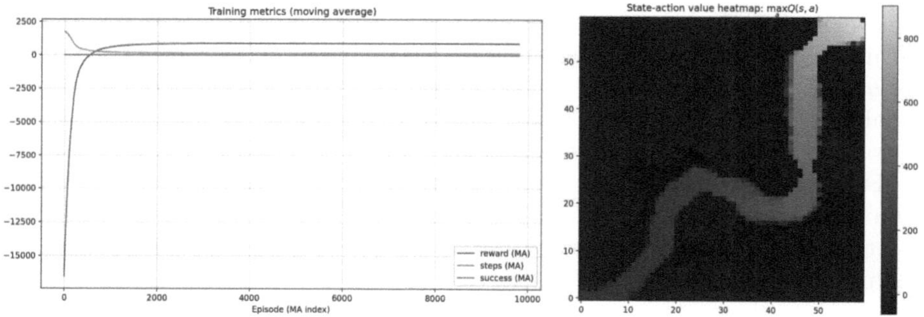

Fig. 2. Training performance metrics and Q-value heat map

To validate the applicability of the learned policy, a comparison is performed between the theoretical planning and its execution in the simulator. Figure 3 illustrates the generation of the scenario and the UAV flight within the ROS2Gazebo simulation environment. The correspondence between the planned trajectory over the Euclidean distance map and the real UAV telemetry (Actual trajectory), together with the planned reference (Desired trajectory), is jointly visualized within the same representation. The nearly perfect overlap of both curves confirms that the trajectory smoothing process, which reduces the number of control points, does not compromise tracking accuracy, but rather facilitates the operation of low-level controllers by eliminating unnecessary kinematic noise.

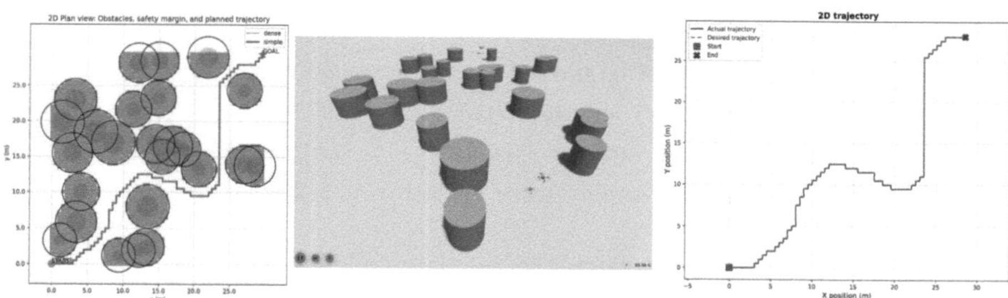

Fig. 3. Comparison between planned and executed UAV trajectories in the simulated environment

6   Conclusions and Future Work

This work presents a framework for the planning and execution of UAV trajectories based on Q-Learning, integrated into a modular architecture supported by ROS2 and Gazebo. The problem is formulated as a discrete MDP, incorporating a conservative modeling of the environment through an *inflated occupancy grid* representation of obstacles and a *reward shaping* scheme.

The results show stable learning convergence and the generation of safe and efficient trajectories in environments with randomly distributed obstacles. The consistency between the learned value map and the geometry of the environment confirms that the agent correctly internalizes spatial constraints. Furthermore, validation in ROS2 and Gazebo demonstrates that the policy learned in the offline phase is transferable to a continuous dynamic system without appreciable degradation in behavior.

As a future line of research, it is of interest to explore the application of quantum computing based algorithms to planning and decision-making problems in discretized spaces. The combinatorial nature of the problem suggests that certain quantum optimization approaches could offer advantages in efficiency or scalability. However, their practical feasibility will need to be carefully evaluated, considering the current limitations of quantum hardware and its integration with conventional robotic architectures.

Acknowledgements. The authors were supported by the Vitoria-Gasteiz Mobility Lab Foundation, a governmental organization of the Provincial Council of Araba and the local council of Vitoria-Gasteiz under the following project grant: "Transporte colaborative de cargas asistido y controlado por algoritmos de Inteligencia Artificial".

References

1. Zhang, J., Li, Y.: Collaborative vehicle-drone distribution network optimization for perishable products in the epidemic situation. Comput. Oper. Res. **149**, 106039 (2023)
2. Gorriz, J.M., et al.: Computational approaches to explainable artificial intelligence: advances in theory, applications and trends. Inf. Fusion **100**, 101945 (2023)
3. Padakandla, S.: survey of reinforcement learning algorithms for dynamically varying environments. ACM Comput. Surv. (CSUR) **54**(6), 1–25 (2021)
4. Huang, Y.-Y., Li, Z.-W., Yang, C.-H., Huang, Y.-M.: Automatic path planning for spraying drones based on deep Q-learning. J. Internet Technol. **24**(3), 565–575 (2023)
5. Arafat, M.Y., Moh, S.: A Q-learning-based topology-aware routing protocol for flying ad hoc networks. IEEE Internet Things J. **9**(3), 1985–2000 (2022)
6. Bonci, A., Gaudeni, F., Giannini, M.C., Longhi, S.: Robot operating system 2 (ROS2)-based frameworks for increasing robot autonomy: a survey. Appl. Sci. **13**(23), 12796 (2023). https://doi.org/10.3390/app132312796
7. Koenig, N., Howard, A.: Design and use paradigms for Gazebo, an open-source multi-robot simulator. In: Proceedings of the 2004 IEEE/RSJ International Conference on Intelligent Robots and Systems (IROS), vol. 3, pp. 2149–2154 (2004)

8. Graham, C., González, F., Sanoe, A.: Implementation of partial observable Markov decision process (POMDP) algorithm using Bitcraze Crazyflie drones. In: Proceedings of the 2023 International Conference on Unmanned Aircraft Systems (ICUAS), pp. 850–857. IEEE (2023)
9. Hou, X., Liu, F., Wang, R., Yu, Y.: A UAV dynamic path planning algorithm. In: 2020 35th Youth Academic Annual Conference of Chinese Association of Automation (YAC), pp. 127–131. IEEE (2020). https://doi.org/10.1109/YAC51587.2020.9337581
10. Tan, L., Zhang, H., Liu, Y., Yuan, T., Jiang, X., Shang, Z.: An adaptive Q-learning based particle swarm optimization for multi-UAV path planning. Soft. Comput. **28**(13–14), 7931–7946 (2024). https://doi.org/10.1007/s00500-024-09691-2
11. Li, D., Yin, W., Wong, W.E., Jian, M., Chau, M.: Quality-oriented hybrid path planning based on A* and Q-learning for unmanned aerial vehicle. IEEE Access **10**, 7664–7674 (2022). https://doi.org/10.1109/ACCESS.2021.3139534
12. Zhang, H., Cheng, Z.: The method based on dijkstra of three-dimensional path planning. In: Proceedings of the 2020 Chinese Automation Congress (CAC), pp. 1698–1701. IEEE (2020). https://doi.org/10.1109/CAC51589.2020.9326569
13. Tian, L., et al.: An improved rapidly-exploring random trees algorithm combining parent point priority determination strategy and real-time optimization strategy for path planning. Sensors **21**(20), 6907 (2021). https://doi.org/10.3390/s21206907
14. Wang, X., Xu, X., Lin, S., Fan, J., Gao, Z., Gu, C.: Deep reinforcement learning-based local path planning with memory-guided. In: Yan, L., Duan, H., Deng, Y. (eds.) ICGNC 2024. LNEE, vol 1341, pp. 362–371. Springer, Cham (2025). https://doi.org/10.1007/978-981-96-2216-0_35
15. Xu, J., Yan, X., Peng, C., Wu, X., Gu, L., Niu, Y.: UAV local path planning based on improved proximal policy optimization algorithm. In: Proceedings of the 2023 IEEE International Conference on Acoustics, Speech and Signal Processing (ICASSP), pp. 1–5. IEEE (2023)
16. Vidyasagar, M.: Recent advances in reinforcement learning. In: Proceedings of the 2020 American Control Conference (ACC), pp. 4751–4756. IEEE (2020). https://doi.org/10.23919/acc45564.2020.9147512

Hybrid CNN-LSTM Architecture for Financial Trend Prediction: Integrating NLP Sentiment and Derivative Models in High-Volatility Assets

M. A. Parrilla, F. Segovia$^{(\boxtimes)}$, A. Zorrilla, C. Vázquez-García, F. J. Martinez-Murcia, and J. M. Górriz

Department of Signal Theory, Networking and Com., University of Granada, Granada, Spain
`fsegovia@ugr.es`

Abstract. Classical financial models struggle with the non-stationary noise of modern, news-driven markets, posing a severe risk to institutional investments and civil economic welfare during systemic shocks. This paper proposes *Adapted DeepLOB*, a hybrid CNN-LSTM architecture designed to predict directional trends and mitigate risk in highly volatile technology assets. The model fuses microstructural price data, macroeconomic indicators (S&P 500, VIX), and NLP-quantified sentiment from financial news via FinBERT across a comprehensive historical period spanning from January 2010 to December 2023. Additonally, it integrates the Black-Scholes framework, using implied volatility to generate forward-looking risk metrics. Trained with a *Focal Loss* function to address market regime imbalance, the system establishes a robust defensive mechanism. Compared to a passive *Buy & Hold* baseline, the model consistently increases risk-adjusted returns (Sharpe and Sortino ratios) while drastically reducing the Maximum Drawdown. The empirical results validate this multidimensional Artificial Intelligence approach not merely as a speculative tool, but as a resilient computational framework for capital preservation and systemic risk mitigation.

Keywords: NLP · FinBERT · Deep Learning · Financial Forecasting

1 Introduction

The global financial ecosystem is a complex, highly volatile system where accurate trend prediction is crucial for preserving civil economic stability and social welfare. Traditionally, financial forecasting relied on classical econometric models [1,3]. However, these linear approaches struggle to decode the non-stationary nature and low signal-to-noise ratio of modern markets, which are deeply driven by macroeconomic events and investor psychology [8].

To overcome these limitations, Deep Learning has emerged as the dominant paradigm for modeling complex systems. These algorithms have already

J. M. Ferrández Vicente et al. (Eds.): IWINAC 2026, LNCS 16575, pp. 349–358, 2026.
https://doi.org/10.1007/978-3-032-27317-8_33

transformed the resolution of broad civil and social problems [7], demonstrating remarkable success in medical diagnostics [4,13] and the management of energy and urban networks [14,15]. This success is due to the extraordinary ability of artificial intelligence (AI) to uncover latent and nonlinear relationships in massive, heterogeneous datasets [6].

In financial forecasting, recent literature highlights the use of Long Short-Term Memory (LSTM) architectures [12] to capture temporal persistence, along with Convolutional Neural Networks (CNN) [5] to filter spatial micro-patterns. Despite these advances, modern markets are narrative-driven, rendering isolated quantitative analysis insufficient. Consequently, cutting-edge research now integrates Natural Language Processing (NLP) [11] to quantify news sentiment. Transformative models like FinBERT [9] enable the interpretation of critical economic contexts, although effectively synchronizing textual flows with quantitative data under a risk-management framework remains a methodological challenge.

To address this gap, this article proposes *Adapted DeepLOB* [17], a hybrid CNN-LSTM architecture designed for trend classification in highly volatile markets. The primary methodological contribution is an enriched state space integrating three orthogonal information flows: (i) microstructural technical indicators, (ii) macroeconomic context variables (S&P 500, VIX), and (iii) semantic signals extracted via FinBERT.

2   Material and Methods

2.1   Data Acquisition and Context Variables

To provide the predictive model with a comprehensive view that encompasses both the microstructure of the asset and systemic risk, a state vector of raw characteristics, $X_t \in \mathbb{R}^7$, is defined for each time, t. This vector integrates the quantitative OHLCV (*Open, High, Low, Close, Volume*) variables of a high-capacity technological financial asset, along with macroeconomic context indicators:

$$X_t = (O_t, H_t, L_t, C_t, V_t, I_t^{S\&P500}, I_t^{VIX})^T \tag{1}$$

where $I_t^{S\&P500}$ is the indicator of global market performance at time t and I_t^{VIX} is the implied volatility index at time t.

The temporal alignment of these heterogeneous series was performed using a standardized synchronization function that eliminated time zone discrepancies (timezone-naive mapping). In addition, the intrinsic discontinuity of data on non-business days was resolved by applying a forward-fill technique:

$$\hat{x}_{i,t} = \begin{cases} x_{i,t} & \text{if } x_{i,t} \neq \text{NaN} \\ \hat{x}_{i,t-1} & \text{if } x_{i,t} = \text{NaN} \end{cases} \tag{2}$$

where $\hat{x}_{i,t}$ is the imputed value of the i-th component in X_t. This method ensures that in the absence of new data, the model retains the most recent information available, thus maintaining a continuous flow of information without introducing bias from anticipating future data.

2.2 Natural Language Processing and Sentiment Quantification

The Financial News and Stock Price Information Dataset (FNSPID), one of the most extensive repositories of financial news, was used for the semantic component of the model. This database was filtered to isolate a small set of 10 representative entities from the technology sector.

Sentiment quantification was performed in several stages. First, the text strings were tokenized and converted into integer vectors, using a predefined vocabulary that assigns a unique index to each token [16]. To ensure compatibility with the model's internal architecture, padding and truncation techniques were applied. Second, the tokenized vectors were evaluated in the FinBERT architecture. In order to minimize memory requirements, the weights of the floating-point (32-bit) linear layers were transformed into integer (8-bit) representations. Then, the output of the transformer (raw scores) was projected into a three-level classification space (positive, negative, and neutral) using a Softmax function, which converts the raw output scores into probabilities. Finally, individual semantic vectors were aggregated daily, resulting in a sentiment score, S_{score}:

$$S_{score} = P(\text{positive}) - P(\text{negative}) \in [-1, 1] \tag{3}$$

Instead of collapsing the semantic information into a single scalar, the daily aggregated state is preserved as two independent orthogonal features: the mean sentiment score ($S_{mean,t}$) and the media volume or news count ($S_{count,t}$). On days without media reports, both variables assume a null value, avoiding any bias in the historical trend.

2.3 Feature Engineering and Risk Hybridization

In order to address the non-stationarity of raw financial series (X_t) and facilitate model convergence, a derived feature space is designed. The closing price (C_t) is transformed into logarithmic returns:

$$r_t = \ln(C_t/C_{t-1}) \tag{4}$$

Additionally, technical indicators that capture different market regimes are calculated: the Hurst Exponent (H) for trend persistence, the Average True Range (ATR_t) for local volatility [10], the Moving Average Convergence Divergence (MACD) to quantify price acceleration [2], and the Z-Score of V_t ($Z_{Vol,t}$) to normalize the intensity of institutional order flow.

As a central methodological innovation, this variable space is hybridized with the analytical model of Black-Scholes to provide the architecture with financial domain knowledge regarding non-linear risk structures. By simulating daily the price of an *At-the-Money* call option at 20 days ($T = 20/365$) and assuming a risk-free rate of $R_f = 0.03$, the VIX index is injected as a parameter of implied volatility ($\sigma_t = I_{VIX,t}$). This allows deriving the core $d_{1,t}$ variable, which is subsequently mapped through the cumulative standard normal distribution to compute the option's Delta ($\Delta_t = \Phi(d_{1,t})$). This Delta acts as a probabilistic bridge between price and volatility, offering a richer analytical representation of future risk, and is the actual parameter injected into the network:

$$d_{1,t} = \frac{(R_f + \frac{\sigma_t^2}{2})T}{\sigma_t \sqrt{T}}, \quad \Delta_t = \Phi(d_{1,t}) \tag{5}$$

Finally, the raw market data (X_t) is mapped into a higher-dimensional feature space ($f_t \in \mathbb{R}^{12}$) through technical, analytical, and semantic transformations. This instantaneous feature vector is defined as:

$$f_t = (r_t, H, ATR_t, Z_{vol,t}, r_{vol,t}, Bollinger\%B_t,$$
$$MACD_t, \Delta_t, r_{SP500,t}, \Delta VIX_t, S_{mean,t}, S_{count,t})^T \tag{6}$$

However, to enable the adapted DeepLOB architecture to capture temporal dependencies and market memory, the actual multidimensional input F_t fed into the neural network is not a single daily observation, but a rolling 2D tensor representing a sequence of length L (where $L = 20$):

$$F_t = \begin{pmatrix} f_{t-L+1} \\ f_{t-L+2} \\ \vdots \\ f_t \end{pmatrix} \in \mathbb{R}^{L \times 12} \tag{7}$$

This matrix structure aligns with the internal processing of the network, where dynamic convolutional filters extract local patterns across the L temporal steps prior to recurrent evaluation.

Prior to feeding the sequence tensor F_t into the neural architecture, a preliminary correlation analysis is conducted to assess multicollinearity among the engineered features.

As illustrated in Fig. 1, while strong expected relationships exist (e.g., positive correlation between the asset's *log_return* and the *SP500_Return*), the overall feature space maintains sufficient orthogonality. Notably, the strong inverse relationship between the asset returns and *VIX_Change* validates the inclusion of the VIX as a macroeconomic "fear gauge" parameter. Furthermore, the semantic metrics (*mean_sentiment* and *news_count*) exhibit largely independent variance, confirming that the NLP layer contributes orthogonal information to the state space rather than redundant technical noise. This multidimensional mapping justifies the fusion of these features before processing them through the CNN-LSTM core.

2.4 Adapted DeepLOB

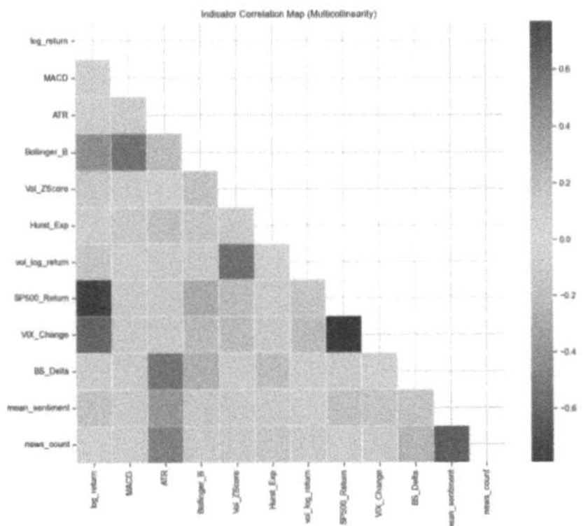

Fig. 1. Indicator correlation map (AAPL example) assessing preliminary multicollinearity and systemic market influence.

Adapted DeepLOB is a neural topology that intersects spatial filtering through Convolutional Neural Networks (CNN) and sequential integration through Long Short-Term Memory (LSTM) networks. Since the temporal integration has already been established within the sequence matrix F_t, the model simply groups these independent sequences into batches during the training phase. This structures the data into the final three-dimensional input tensor $\mathcal{X}_{cnn} \in \mathbb{R}^{B \times N \times L}$, where B represents the batch size, $N = 12$ is the number of enriched features, and $L = 20$ is the temporal sequence length.

The first convolutional module applies 16 extractor filters with a spatial kernel of $k = 3$ and a padding margin of $p = 1$, extracting local micro-patterns. The induction of nonlinearity using the ReLU function is followed by a geometric operation of Max Pooling ($k = 2$, $s = 2$), which halves the temporal sampling frequency and mitigates stochastic market noise. A second convolutional block superimposes 32 filters, consolidating an abstract representation of the series. Then, the emerging tensor is transposed to the recurrent domain $\mathbb{R}^{B \times L_{red} \times C_{out}}$.

The LSTM block assimilates this abstract sequence to model chronological inertia and resolve gradient vanishing. The propagation dynamics of the internal memory cell and the emission of the hidden state (h_t) are governed by a system of conditional logical gates:

$$h_t = o_t \odot \tanh(c_t) \tag{8}$$

Contrary to classical approaches, Adapted DeepLOB eliminates intermediate temporal evolution through dimensional reduction (squeeze), isolating only the final temporal signature h_{final}. This vector encapsulates all market inertia and feeds a final linear layer connected to a Softmax stratum, which projects probabilities onto the target directional class space.

2.5 Financial Evaluation Metrics

To rigorously assess the financial viability and risk-management capabilities of the proposed architecture against the passive baseline strategy, three standard portfolio performance metrics are evaluated: the Sharpe Ratio, the Sortino Ratio, and the Maximum Drawdown (MDD).

The Sharpe Ratio quantifies the excess return generated per unit of total risk assumed. It is defined as:

$$Sharpe = \frac{R_p - R_f}{\sigma_p + \epsilon} \tag{9}$$

where R_p is the annualized portfolio return, R_f is the risk-free rate, σ_p is the standard deviation of the portfolio's excess returns, and ϵ is a small constant to prevent division by zero.

While the Sharpe Ratio penalizes all volatility equally, the Sortino Ratio isolates downside risk, recognizing that positive volatility is beneficial for the investor. It is calculated as:

$$Sortino = \frac{R_p - R_f}{\sigma_d + \epsilon} \tag{10}$$

where σ_d represents the downside deviation, measuring only the dispersion of returns that fall below a specified minimum acceptable target, and ϵ is a small constant to prevent division by zero.

Finally, capital preservation during systemic market shocks is evaluated through the Maximum Drawdown (MDD). This metric captures the largest cumulative drop from a historical peak of the equity curve:

$$MDD = \min_t(E_t - \max_{\tau \leq t} E_\tau) \tag{11}$$

where E_t represents the portfolio's equity value at time t, and the term $\max_{\tau \leq t} E_\tau$ denotes the cumulative maximum or historical peak achieved up to that point. Minimizing the MDD is critical for ensuring the long-term survivability of the trading strategy under severe market stress.

3   Experiments and Results

The target variable (y_t) projects a 3-day trend horizon using a dynamic labeling algorithm. Instead of static thresholds, it compares a 10-day smoothed Simple Moving Average (SMA) with its 3-day future shift, applying the daily ATR_t as a noise-filtering boundary. This defines a binary classification task ($C = 2$) predicting upward versus downward/sideways trends.

To address class imbalance and highlight complex patterns, we employ the Focal Loss function ($\gamma = 2.0$), which scales penalization based on prediction confidence using training distribution weights:

$$\mathcal{L}_{focal} = -\sum_{j=1}^{C} \alpha_j (1 - \hat{y}_{t,j})^\gamma y_{t,j} \log(\hat{y}_{t,j}) \tag{12}$$

where α_j is the class weight, $y_{t,j} \in \{0, 1\}$ is the true label, and $\hat{y}_{t,j}$ is the predicted probability. Implemented in Python, optimization utilized the Adam algorithm (learning rate 0.0001, weight decay 1e-3).

Training ran for up to 60 epochs (batch size 16) with an early stopping patience of 10 epochs. Inputs used 20-day sliding windows ($L = 20$), split into 70% training, 15% validation, and 15% out-of-sample testing. Features were normalized via Robust Scaler and clipped to the $[-4.0, 4.0]$ range for gradient stability, while an 80% *Dropout* rate was applied to prevent overfitting and consolidate redundant representations.

The experimental evaluation of the proposed Adapted DeepLOB architecture demonstrates substantial improvements over the traditional Buy & Hold (B&H) strategy across highly volatile technological assets (AAPL, GOOG, INTC). The results are evaluated using both statistical and financial risk-adjusted metrics (Table 1).

To rigorously validate predictive power, performance is primarily evaluated using the Receiver Operating Characteristic Curve Area (*AUC-ROC*) and the *Weighted F1* score (see Table 1). The outstanding AUC-ROC scores demonstrate the architecture's ability to accurately discriminate between bullish and bearish regimes regardless of the decision threshold. Concurrently, the robust weighted F1-scores confirm consistent performance across both minority and majority classes, ensuring that the results stem from genuine nonlinear pattern recognition rather than merely predicting the dominant trend.

From a financial perspective, the model consistently outperforms the passive B&H baseline, successfully navigating severe market downturns without the presence of look-ahead bias. The *Sharpe Ratio*, which measures general risk-adjusted return, and the *Sortino Ratio*, which specifically penalizes only downside volatility, show dramatic improvements, turning negative or near-zero baseline metrics into solid, positive returns. Most importantly for risk management, the *Maximum Drawdown* (MDD)–which quantifies the maximum loss observed from a historical peak–is drastically reduced.

To ensure that the results are not merely a product of stochastic variations in the evaluation sample, a 95% Confidence Interval (CI) is computed for the *Accuracy* metric. Given the fixed size of the out-of-sample test set ($n = 492$ trading days; however, in the graphic we use 229 days for a better visualization), the normal approximation for the binomial distribution is employed, defined as:

$$CI = \hat{p} \pm Z\sqrt{\frac{\hat{p}(1 - \hat{p})}{n}}$$

where $\hat{p}$ represents the observed precision (the proportion of correct predictions made by the model), Z denotes the critical value of the standard normal distribution corresponding to the desired confidence level ($Z = 1.96$ for a confidence level of 95%) and n is the total number of discrete observations in the test set. Incorporating this metric provides a rigorous boundary for the expected real-world performance of the architecture.

The classification threshold was calibrated within $[0.50, 0.85]$ using Optuna library to maximize a hybrid risk metric: $0.6 \times \text{Sortino} + 0.4 \times \text{Sharpe}$. Finally, to prevent the model from avoiding trades entirely, a minimum market exposure constraint was enforced, requiring the strategy to be invested for at least 15% of the test days.

Table 1. Predictive and Financial Performance: Universal AI Model vs. Buy & Hold (B&H). Accuracy includes 95% confidence intervals and AUC-ROC validates performance under class imbalance. AI metrics are reported on the out-of-sample test set using a dynamic decision threshold optimized strictly on the validation set.

Asset	Accuracy (95% CI)	AUC-ROC	F1-Score (Weighted)	Sharpe Ratio		Sortino Ratio		Max Drawdown	
				IA	B&H	IA	B&H	IA	B&H
AAPL	85.16% ± 3.14%	**0.9309**	0.85	**0.2235**	0.0104	**0.3134**	0.0154	**−4.95%**	−30.91%
GOOG	80.89% ± 3.48%	**0.9085**	0.82	**0.2301**	−0.0084	**0.3143**	−0.0123	**−6.15%**	−43.60%
INTC	87.40% ± 2.93%	**0.9342**	0.87	**0.2005**	−0.0084	**0.2344**	−0.0131	**−6.79%**	−54.06%

The experimental analysis (Fig. 2) validates the architecture's synergy by effectively decoupling the portfolio from bearish regimes. Cumulative return plots (a, b) demonstrate mitigated Maximum Drawdown through horizontal equity segments, as the model remains neutral during declines to avoid the "drawdown-recovery" cycles typical of passive strategies. This defensive behavior maximizes the performance gap–particularly in high-volatility assets with frequent price swings–and is corroborated by signal plots (c, d), where errors are confined to sideways noise while macro-trends are accurately captured.

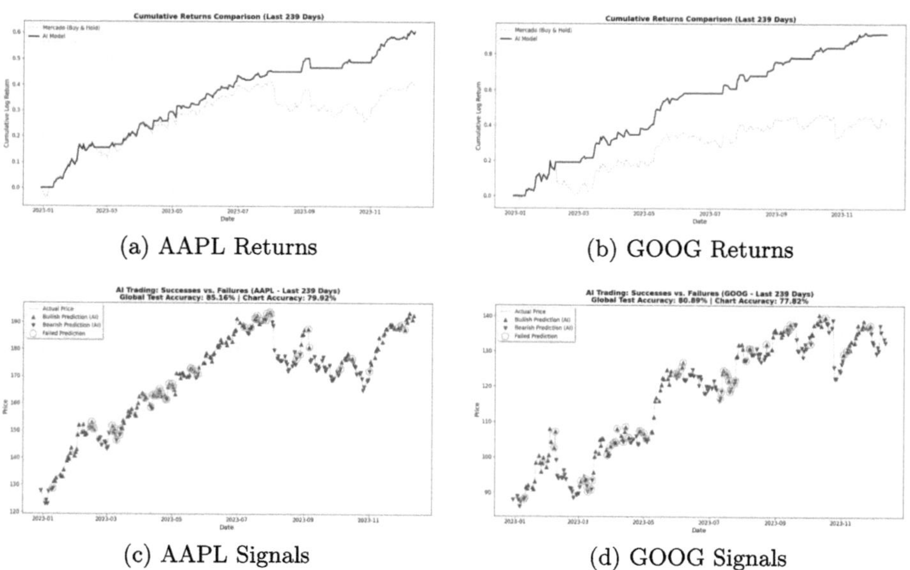

(a) AAPL Returns

(b) GOOG Returns

(c) AAPL Signals

(d) GOOG Signals

Fig. 2. Consolidated experimental results. (a, b) Return comparison highlighting MDD mitigation (solid blue) vs. Buy & Hold (dashed grey). (c, d) Signal accuracy. (Color figure online)

4   Discussion and Conclusions

Empirical results on highly volatile technological assets confirm that classical econometric models and isolated quartitative data are insufficient for modern financial ecosystems. The inherent non-stationarity and heavy-tailed distribution of market returns demand multidimensional approaches capable of capturing both localized micro-patterns and macro-level systemic shocks.

The primary contribution of this work is its exceptional risk mitigation, achieved through orthogonal information fusion. The architecture builds a robust defensive mechanism by hybridizing a CNN-LSTM core–which filters stochastic noise and extracts temporal dependencies–with forward-looking Black-Scholes metrics (using VIX as implied volatility) and FinBERT's sentiment quantification. In this synergy, semantic news analysis provides early warnings of market distress, while the analytical derivatives layer dynamically calibrates risk sensitivity.

This integration drastically reduces Maximum Drawdown across all tested assets. The model demonstrates a profound asymmetric risk profile: it captures upward inertia while neutralizing bearish contagion. By successfully shielding the portfolio against market crashes exceeding 50% (e.g., INTC) while restricting drawdowns to approximately 5%, risk-adjusted returns (Sharpe and Sortino ratios) increase up to five times over the passive Buy & Hold baseline.

Ultimately, this research proves that multidimensional AI can effectively decode market stochasticity. By prioritizing capital preservation during severe contractions over pure speculative profitability, the proposed model redefines predictive AI as a robust risk-management framework. It offers a resilient computational tool capable of protecting institutional investments, stabilizing pension funds, and protecting civil economic welfare against systemic shocks.

Future research will focus on extending this framework to high-frequency trading environments and integrating real-time macroeconomic event triggers to further enhance the model's adaptive latency.

Acknowledgments. This publication is part of the projects PID2022-137629OA-I00 and PID2022-137451OB-I00 funded by MICIU/AEI/10.13039/501100011033 and by ERDF/EU, and the C-ING-183-UGR23 project, cofunded by the Consejería de Universidad, Investigación e Innovación and by European Union, funded by Programa FEDER Andalucía 2021–2027.

References

1. Financial econometrics. In: Schintler, L.A. et al. (eds.) Encyclopedia of Big Data, pp. 482–482. Springer International Publishing, Cham (2022). https://doi.org/10.1007/978-3-319-32010-6_300103

2. Appel, G.: Technical Analysis: Power Tools For The Active Investors. Upper Saddle River, NJ (2005)

3. Beck, T.: The econometrics of finance and growth. In: Mills, T.C. et al. (eds.) Palgrave Handbook of Econometrics: Volume 2: Applied Econometrics, pp. 1180–1209. Palgrave Macmillan UK, London (2009). https://doi.org/10.1057/9780230244405_25

4. Castillo-Barnes, D., et al.: Autosomal dominantly inherited Alzheimer disease: analysis of genetic subgroups by machine learning. Inf. Fusion **58**, 153–167 (2020). https://doi.org/10.1016/j.inffus.2020.01.001

5. Chen, J.F. et al.: Financial time-series data analysis using deep convolutional neural networks. In: 2016 7th International Conference on Cloud Computing and Big Data (CCBD), pp. 87–92 (2016). https://doi.org/10.1109/CCBD.2016.027

6. Górriz, J.M., et al.: Computational approaches to explainable artificial intelligence: advances in theory, applications and trends. Inf. Fusion **100**, 101945 (2023). https://doi.org/10.1016/j.inffus.2023.101945

7. Górriz, J.M., et al.: Artificial intelligence within the interplay between natural and artificial computation: advances in data science, trends and applications. Neurocomputing **410**, 237–270 (2020). https://doi.org/10.1016/j.neucom.2020.05.078

8. Gourieroux, C.: Financial Econometrics: Problems, Models, and Methods. Princeton Oxford (2022)

9. Huang, A.H., et al.: FinBERT: a large language model for extracting information from financial Text. Contemp. Account. Res. **40**(2), 806–841 (2023). https://doi.org/10.1111/1911-3846.12832

10. Kaufman, P.J.: Trading Systems and Methods. Hoboken, New Jersey (2020)

11. López, R. et al.: Semi-supervised labeling process for the development of an imaging dataset to support parkinson's disease research. In: 2025 IEEE Nuclear Science Symposium (NSS), Medical Imaging Conference (MIC) and Room Temperature Semiconductor Detector Conference (RTSD), pp. 1–2 (2025). https://doi.org/10.1109/NSS/MIC/RTSD57106.2025.11287218

12. López-García, D., et al.: RESISTO project: automatic detection of operation temperature anomalies for power electric transformers using thermal imaging. In: Ferrández Vicente, J.M. et al. (eds.) Bioinspired Systems for Translational Applications: From Robotics to Social Engineering, pp. 225–245. Springer Nature Switzerland, Cham (2024). https://doi.org/10.1007/978-3-031-61137-7_22

13. Martinez-Murcia, F.J.: Bridging imaging and clinical scores in Parkinson's disease progression via multimodal self-supervised deep learning. Int. J. Neural Syst. (2024)

14. Rodriguez-Rivero, J., et al.: Granger causality-based information fusion applied to electrical measurements from power transformers. Inf. Fusion **57**, 59–70 (2020). https://doi.org/10.1016/j.inffus.2019.12.005

15. Segovia, F., et al.: Connected system for monitoring electrical power transformers using thermal imaging. Integr. Comput.-Aided Eng. **30**(4), 353–368 (2023). https://doi.org/10.3233/ICA-230712

16. Wolf, T., et al.: Transformers: state-of-the-art natural language processing. In: Liu, Q. et al. (eds.) Proceedings of the 2020 Conference on Empirical Methods in Natural Language Processing: System Demonstrations, pp. 38–45. Association for Computational Linguistics, Online (2020). https://doi.org/10.18653/v1/2020.emnlp-demos.6

17. Zhang, Z., et al.: DeepLOB: deep convolutional neural networks for limit order books. IEEE Trans. Signal Process. **67**(11), 3001–3012 (2019). https://doi.org/10.1109/TSP.2019.2907260

Prioritizing Telecontrol Repairs in Electrical Distribution Networks Using Graph-Based Impact Analysis

Álvaro Zorrilla[1], Fermín Segovia[1], Javier Ramírez[1], Isidro J. Aguilera[2], Antonio M. Vargas[2], José Bello[2], and Juan Manuel Górriz[1(✉)]

[1] Department of Signal Theory, Networking and Communications, University of Granada, Granada, Spain
gorriz@ugr.es
[2] e-Distribución Redes Digitales, Madrid, Spain

Abstract. This work proposes a graph-based methodology to prioritize the repair of telecontrol devices in medium-voltage electrical distribution networks. The grid is modeled as a graph-based digital twin built from infrastructure data. The priority of each telecontrol is defined as the installed power that becomes unsupported when the device fails, which is obtained by analyzing changes in network connectivity. The method was validated using real data from the distribution network of Granada (Spain) through simulation experiments. Results reveal a strong heterogeneity in the impact of telecontrol failures and show that repair priorities depend on the current network configuration. The proposed approach provides a scalable tool to support maintenance decision-making and improve grid resilience.

Keywords: Power Grid Topology · Graph Theory · Telecontrols · Maintenance Prioritization · Smart Grid Resilience

1 Introduction

The reliability and resilience of electrical distribution networks are essential for maintaining the socio-economic stability of modern societies [10,11]. As power systems evolve toward the Smart Grid paradigm, the integration of monitoring, automation, and remote-control technologies has become increasingly widespread [5]. Among these technologies, telecontrol devices play a crucial role by allowing operators to remotely perform switching operations, isolate faults, and reconfigure network topology [1]. These capabilities contribute to improve service continuity and reduce reliability indicators such as the System Average Interruption Duration Index (SAIDI). However, telecontrol devices themselves may fail due to environmental conditions, equipment aging, or operational disturbances.

When multiple telecontrol devices become unavailable within a large-scale electrical distribution network, operators must determine the order in which repair actions should be carried out. Traditional maintenance strategies often

J. M. Ferrández Vicente et al. (Eds.): IWINAC 2026, LNCS 16575, pp. 359–368, 2026.
https://doi.org/10.1007/978-3-032-27317-8_34

rely on heuristic criteria or geographical proximity [4], which may not adequately reflect the actual structural impact of a device failure on the network. This situation highlights the need for advanced computational and data-driven approaches [6] capable of evaluating the operational criticality of grid components.

In this work, a graph-based methodology [2, 8, 9] is proposed to assess the importance of telecontrol devices within the electrical distribution network of the province of Granada (Spain). The infrastructure is modeled as an undirected graph where nodes represent substations, transformation centers, telecontrols, and connection points, while edges correspond to line stretches connecting these elements. This representation enables the identification of the transformation centers associated with each telecontrol and allows the computation of an importance metric based on the installed power that becomes unsupported when a device fails.

From the results obtained through the simulation experiments, a quantitative measure of the importance of each telecontrol device within the network is derived based on the marginal loss of controlled power when the device is out of service. In addition, the graph-based representation of the electrical distribution system enables the analysis of several structural and operational properties of the network.

2 Materials and Methodology

2.1 Data Sources and Network Architecture

The data used in this study consist of the nominal, geographical, and technical information describing the medium-voltage (MV) electrical distribution network in the province of Granada (Spain), provided by the distribution system operator e-Distribuciön. The dataset includes the hierarchical structure of the distribution infrastructure, covering high-voltage substations, medium-voltage lines, individual line stretches, transformation centers, and telecontrol devices.

For each element, the dataset provides standardized identifiers, geographical coordinates, and operational information such as the associated substation, electrical line, and responsible operational unit. In the case of transformation centers, additional technical parameters are included, such as installed power and installed power.

Electrical lines are represented as sequences of consecutive line stretches connecting substations with different nodes of the distribution network. Each stretch corresponds to the segment between two nodes and follows a systematic naming convention that identifies its origin and destination nodes. This nomenclature is consistently used across other infrastructure elements, including telecontrol devices and transformation centers, whose identifiers correspond to the nodes associated with the connected line stretches.

This consistent naming scheme enables the reconstruction of connectivity relationships between network components and facilitates the creation of graph-based digital representations of the electrical distribution infrastructure for subsequent analysis.

2.2 Graph Theory Background

Graph theory [3,12] provides a mathematical framework for representing interconnected systems. A graph is defined as $G = (V, E)$, where $V = v_1, v_2, \ldots, v_n$ is the set of vertices and $E \subseteq V \times V$ the set of edges connecting them.

In this work, the medium-voltage (MV) electrical distribution network is modeled as an undirected graph $G = (V, E)$, where each edge $e = u, v$ represents an unordered pair of vertices. This representation reflects the bidirectional nature of power flows in distribution systems. Vertices correspond to grid elements such as substations (S), transformation centers (T), telecontrols (TC), or connection points, while edges represent electrical line segments linking these components.

Connectivity is a key concept in graph theory. A path between two vertices $u, v \in V$ is a sequence $u = v_0, v_1, \ldots, v_k = v$ such that $v_{i-1}, v_i \in E$ for all i. A graph is connected if every pair of vertices is linked by a path. In general, however, graphs may consist of several connected components, defined as maximal subsets $C \subseteq V$ in which all vertices are mutually reachable. Accordingly, the vertex set can be partitioned as $V = C_1 \cup C_2 \cup \cdots \cup C_k$, where each $G[C_i]$ is a connected subgraph.

In MV distribution networks, connected components correspond to electrically isolated portions of the grid that may arise from switching operations, maintenance activities, or faults. Identifying these components is therefore essential for analyzing network topology and detecting isolated subnetworks. Representing the grid as a graph enables the application of graph-theoretic tools to study structural properties and support monitoring, optimization, and reliability analyses.

2.3 Telecontrol Controlled Power Computation

The relevance of a telecontrol device in an electrical distribution network can be interpreted as a multivariate function of several correlated variables, including the installed and installed power of the associated transformation centers, the number of connected distribution lines, the criticality of the supplied infrastructure (e.g., hospitals or industrial facilities), and the maintenance history of the device. In this work, the prioritization is simplified by considering only the installed power that becomes unavailable when a telecontrol device fails, which serves as a proxy for the operational impact of the failure on the grid following the experts' advice.

When a telecontrol device fails, its identifier and the list of previously failed devices are provided to the prioritization system. Using datasets describing line segments, transformation centers, and telecontrols, the algorithm builds a graph-based digital twin of the network with NetworkX library, where nodes represent grid elements and edges represent electrical connections. After constructing the graph G, nodes corresponding to previously failed telecontrols (TC^*) are removed and all substations are linked to a source node (S), representing the network state prior to the new failure. The node corresponding to the newly failed device (tc) is then removed to simulate the updated configuration.

The transformation centers that lose control due to this failure are identified by comparing the nodes connected to the source before and after removing tc:

$$\mathcal{T}(tc \cup TC^*) = (G\backslash(tc \cup TC^*)[\mathcal{S}] - G\backslash TC^*[\mathcal{S}]) \cap T.$$

The repair priority of the telecontrol device tc is defined as

$$\mathcal{P}(tc; TC^*) = \sum_{t \in \mathcal{T}(tc \cup TC^*)} \mathscr{P}(t), \tag{1}$$

where $\mathscr{P}(t)$ is the installed power of transformation center t. Thus, the priority corresponds to the additional installed power that becomes unsupported after the new failure.

Because failures can alter the topology of the meshed distribution network and modify the impact of other failed devices, the algorithm dynamically recalculates the priorities of all telecontrols after each new failure. Finally, all failed devices are stored in a file containing their identifiers, associated information, and computed priority, producing a ranked list of repair actions to guide maintenance resource allocation.

3   Results and Discussion

After constructing the graph representation of the medium-voltage (MV) electrical distribution network in the province of Granada, a geographical visualization was generated prior to computing the repair priorities of telecontrol devices. As shown in Fig. 1, the 24900 nodes and 25463 line segments are plotted according to their geographical coordinates, providing an intuitive view of the spatial extent and structural organization of the grid. The resulting graph reveals two connected components, each representing an independent portion of the distribution network. Consequently, electrical connectivity is preserved within each component but not shared between them, meaning that faults occurring in one component cannot directly affect the other due to the absence of physical line connections.

The histograms in Fig. 2 highlight the structural heterogeneity and robustness of the distribution network. In most cases, grid elements are connected to substations through multiple telecontrols and line stretches, so the failure of a single device typically results in a limited loss over the control of supplied power (Fig. 2A). However, certain configurations, such as rings or branching nodes connected through a single telecontrol, can still produce small but non-negligible losses. In contrast, telecontrols located at structurally critical points may control large portions of the network, and their failure can disconnect substantial amounts of installed power, explaining the observations in the upper ranges of unsupported load.

This heterogeneity is also reflected when only one telecontrol remains operational in the grid, as it may still manage a significant fraction of power to transformation centers, as shown in Fig. 2B.

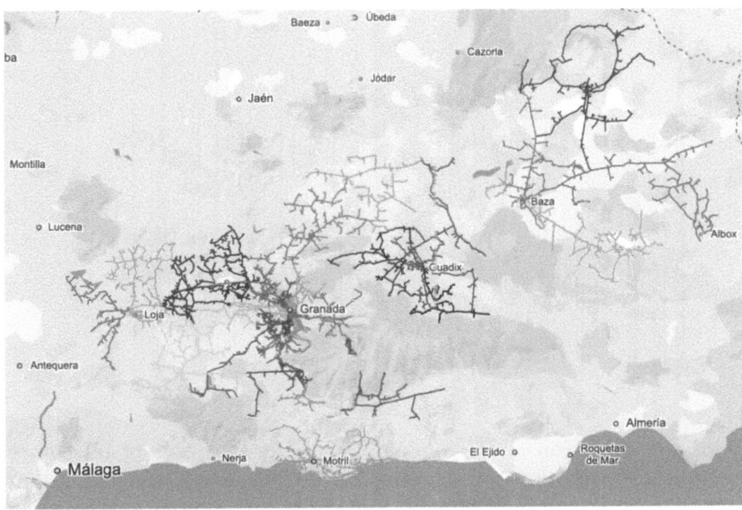

Fig. 1. Geographical representation of the MV electrical distribution network in the province of Granada. Lines are colored according to the substation to which they belong. The network is composed of two connected components.

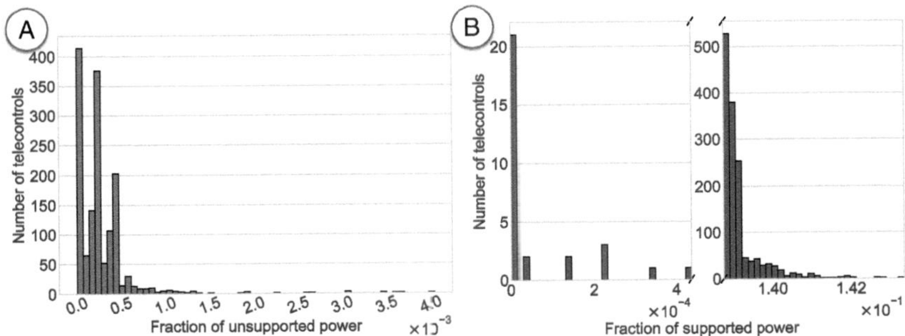

Fig. 2. (A) Histogram of the fraction of unsupported installed power when a single telecontrol fails. (B) Histogram of the supported installed power when only one telecontrol is present in the grid. The total installed power in the network is 2 896 380 MVA.

From an operational perspective, these distributions highlight the need for repair prioritization mechanisms, as addressing failures solely in chronological order could allocate resources to low-impact devices while more critical ones remain unresolved. The presence of a small number of high-impact telecontrols also indicates that network resilience is strongly influenced by specific nodes, whose identification is valuable for infrastructure planning and preventive maintenance.

To evaluate the proposed prioritization algorithm, a simulation experiment was performed using a subset of telecontrols from the Loja operational unit (161

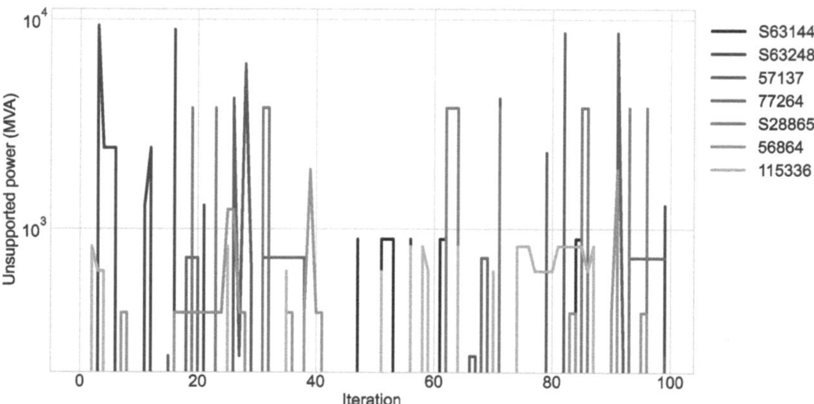

Fig. 3. Temporal evolution of the repair priority for a subset of telecontrol devices during the first 100 iterations of the simulation. The horizontal axis represents the iteration number, while the vertical axis indicates the amount of unsupported installed power associated with each failed device.

devices). Their operational state was randomly updated over 1500 iterations, transitioning between "Working" and "Out of service" with probabilities of 0.1 and 0.7 for failure and repair, respectively. At each iteration, the algorithm computed the repair priority for the devices that were out of service.

Figure 3 illustrates the evolution of repair priority for a subset of telecontrols during the simulation. The priority associated with a given device is not constant over time but fluctuates as the operational status of other telecontrols changes. This behavior reflects the interdependent nature of the distribution network: the impact of a single failure depends not only on its topological location but also on the current configuration of the remaining devices. Consequently, repair priorities must be dynamically recalculated according to the instantaneous operational state of the network.

Using the simulation results, additional properties of the network behavior were analyzed. Although it could be expected that the amount of unsupported power increases proportionally with the number of failed telecontrols, Fig. 4A shows that this relationship is neither linear nor strictly proportional. Instead, the results reveal a heterogeneous structure in which certain telecontrols produce significantly larger impacts on the network than others. This property is also confirmed in Fig. 4B, in which the most probable value for the fraction of unsupported power in the simulation is around 0.02 and in the 95% of the cases that fraction is lower than 0.04. For example, more than 80% of the devices control less than 10 000 MVA of supplied power each one. In the rest of simulations, the uncontrolled power is higher due to the failure of some of those important nodes.

To identify structurally important devices within the network, two complementary indicators were analyzed: an index (IP) related to the telecontrol repair

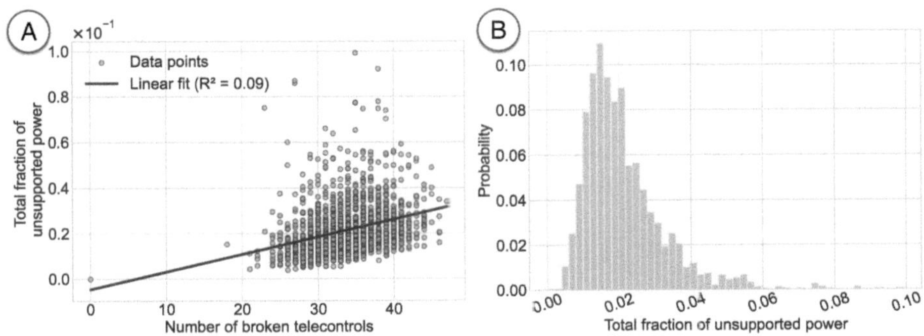

Fig. 4. (A) Total unsupported power versus the number of failed telecontrols for each iteration. Linear regression was conducted on the data, with a near-zero R^2 value. (B) Probability of each interval of the fraction of uncontrolled power in the grid in the simulation.

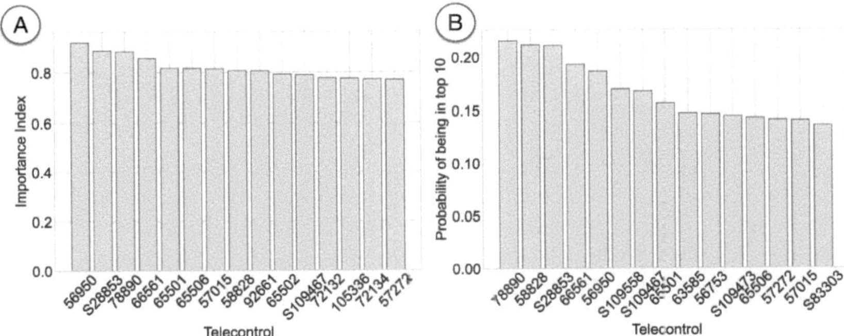

Fig. 5. (A) Value of the importance index for the top-15 devices with highest impact in the simulation. (B) Probability of appearing in the top-10 highest-priority repairs for the top-15 telecontrols during the simulation.

priority, and the probability that a device appears among the top-10 highest-priority repairs during the network simulation. The IP for a telecontrol i is defined as follows:

$$IP(i) = \sum_{s=1}^{M} \frac{\mathcal{P}(i; s)}{M_i T_s},\tag{2}$$

where $\mathcal{P}(i; s)$ is the priority of the telecontrol i in simulation s, M_i is the number of simulations in which that telecontrol is out of service, T_s is the number of broken telecontrols in simulation s and M is the total number of simulations.

Figure 5 shows the values of these metrics for the 15 telecontrols with the highest impact. In both analyses, some devices consistently appear among those producing the largest losses of managed power.

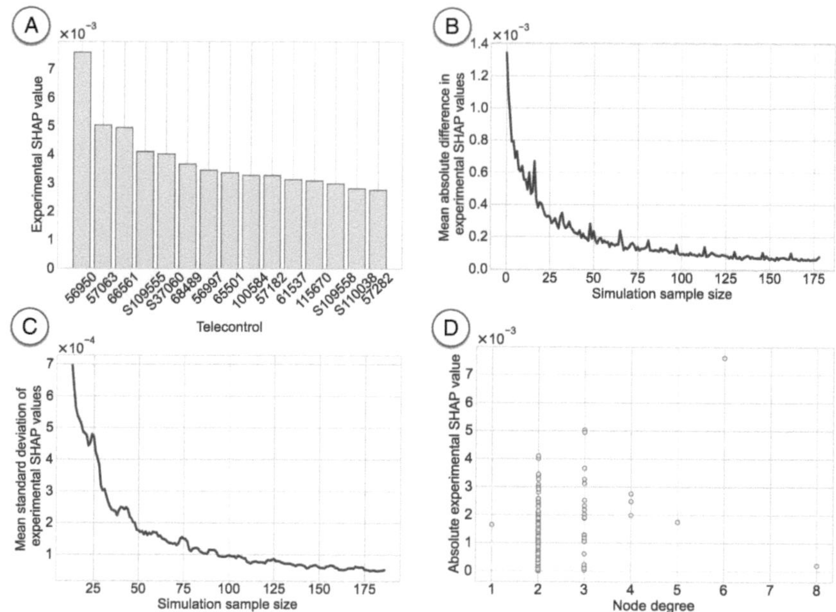

Fig. 6. (A) Estimation of the SHAP value for the top-15 highest-impact telecontrols using a sample size $N = 200$ for each state of the device. (B) Evolution of the mean across all telecontrols of the absolute difference between consecutive values of the experimental SHAP values for increasing values of the sample size. (C) Evolution of the mean across all telecontrols of the standard deviation of the experimental SHAP values computed using a sliding window equal to 5 for an increasing sample size. (D) Relationship between the absolute value of the estimated SHAP values and the corresponding node degree.

Additionally, a third indicator was computed for each telecontrol device as the difference between the mean unsupported power when the device is out of service and when it is operational (while other failures may still occur in the network) in a sample of the simulation. This quantity can be interpreted as an approximation of marginal contribution similar to SHAP (empirical SHAP), a well-established approach in Explainable Artificial Intelligence [7], since it measures the average marginal contribution of each telecontrol failure to the total unsupported power. Figure 6A shows these values for the 15 most influential telecontrols using a sample size of $N = 200$. Although the comparison is not performed between identical grid configurations differing only in the state of a single telecontrol, the mean values obtained from sufficiently large samples provide a reliable approximation of the true marginal contribution. Indeed, as N increases, the mean absolute difference between these experimental SHAP estimates across devices decreases and tends toward zero (Fig. 6B). Similarly, Fig. 6C shows the evolution of the standard deviation of the experimental SHAP as N increases, with a decreasing behavior. Most devices identified through this approach coincide with those highlighted by the previous indicators. Together, these metrics consistently identify the telecontrols whose failures produce the largest disruptions in terms of unsupported installed power, offering valuable insights for maintenance planning, resource allocation, and the development of more effective repair prioritization strategies.

Finally, the relationship between the importance and the degree of the corresponding node was analyzed in Fig. 6D. Most telecontrol nodes exhibit low degrees, typically between two and three connections, while higher degrees are uncommon. Although the most critical node (telecontrol 56950) has degree six, a wide dispersion of marginal impact values is observed for nodes lower degrees, particularly for degree two. This result indicates that the operational importance of telecontrol devices is determined not only by their local connectivity but also by their global position within the network topology, highlighting the limitations of simple structural metrics such as node degree to measure the importance in the grid.

4   Conclusions

The results obtained in this work show that modeling electrical distribution networks as graphs provides a useful framework for analyzing the impact of telecontrol failures and supporting repair prioritization. By evaluating the loss of control of the installed power associated with device failures, the proposed approach enables the identification of telecontrols whose malfunction produces the greatest disruption in the network.

Simulation experiments reveal a strong heterogeneity in the impact of telecontrol failures. While most devices cause relatively small losses of supported power, a limited subset of telecontrols is responsible for substantially larger disruptions due to their structural position within the grid. Different indicators, including the probability of appearing among the highest repair priorities and the marginal contribution to uncontrolled power, consistently identify these critical devices. The analysis also shows that repair priorities are dynamic and depend on the operational state of other devices, highlighting the interdependent nature of electrical distribution networks. Moreover, the weak relationship observed between node degree and failure impact suggests that simple local metrics are insufficient to characterize device importance, emphasizing the need for topology-aware prioritization methods.

Overall, these results demonstrate that graph-based analysis combined with simulation can provide valuable insights for maintenance planning and resource allocation in electrical distribution systems. Future work will focus on extending the methodology to larger electrical grids, incorporating additional operational factors that may influence device criticality, and integrating the proposed approach into real-time network management systems to support dynamic repair prioritization.

Acknowledgments. This work is funded by Universidad de Granada and Endesa Distribución under the Endesa-UGR chair in Artificial Intelligence. Besides, this research is part of the PID2022-137451OB-I00 and PID2022-137629OA-I00 projects, funded by the CIN/AEI/10.13039/501100011033 and by FSE+, and the C-ING-183-UGR23 project, cofunded by Consejería de Universidad, Investigación e Innovación and by the European Union under the Andalusia ERDF Program 2021–2027.

References

1. Conti, S., Rizzo, S.A., El-Saadany, E.F., Essam, M., Atwa, Y.M.: Reliability assessment of distribution systems considering telecontrolled switches and microgrids. IEEE Trans. Power Syst. **29**(2), 598–607 (2014)
2. Das, H., Jena, A.K., Rath, P.K., Muduli, B., Das, S.R.: Grid computing-based performance analysis of power system: a graph theoretic approach. In: Jain, L.C., Patnaik, S., Ichalkaranje, N. (eds.) Intelligent Computing, Communication and Devices. AISC, vol. 309, pp. 259–266. Springer, New Delhi (2015)
3. Diestel, R.: Graph Theory, Graduate Texts in Mathematics, vol. 173. Springer, Heidelberg (2025)
4. Endrenyi, J.: The present status of maintenance strategies and the impact of maintenance on reliability. IEEE Power Eng. Rev. **21**(12), 68 (2001)
5. Falvo, M.C., Martirano, L., Sbordone, D., Bocci, E.: Technologies for smart grids: a brief review. In: 2013 12th International Conference on Environment and Electrical Engineering, pp. 369–375. IEEE, Wroclaw (2013)
6. Górriz, J.M., et al.: Artificial intelligence within the interplay between natural and artificial computation: advances in data science, trends and applications. Neurocomputing **410**, 237–270 (2020)
7. Górriz, J.M., et al.: Computational approaches to explainable artificial intelligence: advances in theory, applications and trends. Inf. Fusion **100**, 101945 (2023)
8. Haynes, T.W., Hedetniemi, S.M., Hedetniemi, S.T., Henning, M.A.: Domination in graphs applied to electric power networks. SIAM J. Discret. Math. **15**(4), 519–529 (2002)
9. Holmgren, A.J.: Using graph models to analyze the vulnerability of electric power networks. Risk Anal. **26**(4), 955–969 (2006)
10. Mishra, D.K., Ghadi, M.J., Azizivahed, A., Li, L., Zhang, J.: A review on resilience studies in active distribution systems. Renew. Sustain. Energy Rev. **135**, 110201 (2021)
11. Morris, K., Kim, D.S., Wood, A., Woodward, G.: Reliability and resiliency analysis of modern distribution grids using reliability graphs. In: 2018 IEEE International Conference on Communications Workshops (ICC Workshops), pp. 1–6. IEEE, Kansas City, MO, USA (2018)
12. Yadav, S.K.: Advanced Graph Theory. Springer, Cham (2023)

"Explainable, Robust and Trustworthy Machine Learning and its Applications"

Trustworthy AI for Neonatal Facial Monitoring in Real NICU Environments

Nuria Velasco[1(✉)] [iD], Nuño Basurto[1] [iD], Juan Arnaez[2,3] [iD], Álvaro Herrero[1] [iD], and Daniel Urda[1] [iD]

[1] Grupo de Inteligencia Computacional Aplicada (GICAP),
Departamento de Digitalización, Escuela Politécnica Superior, Universidad de
Burgos, Av. Cantabria s/n, 09006 Burgos, Spain
{nuriavp,nbasurto,ahcosio,durda}@ubu.es
[2] Neurología Neonatal, Fundación NeNe. Calle Eloy Gonzalo, 3, 28010 Madrid, Spain
juan.arnaez@neurologianeonatal.org
[3] Unidad Neonatal, Hospital Universitario de Burgos, Avda Islas Baleares 3,
09006 Burgos, Spain

Abstract. Automatic analysis of neonatal facial behavior in real Neonatal Intensive Care Unit (NICU) environments is challenged by high data variability, visual noise, and the need for interpretable models suitable for clinical use. Facial expressions are a core component of neonatal pain, discomfort, and alertness assessments; however, their evaluation remains largely subjective in routine practice. In this study, a dataset of neonatal video recordings acquired under routine NICU conditions was analyzed, comprising 991 annotated videos after preprocessing. An attention-based convolutional neural network was employed for the frame-level binary classification of three clinically relevant facial traits: eye opening, eye frowning, and mouth opening. To address interpretability requirements in safety-critical settings, a dual explainability framework combining intrinsic attention mechanisms and post-hoc SHAP analysis was adopted. The proposed approach achieved strong performance, particularly for eye-related traits, despite challenging acquisition conditions. Explainability analyses showed that predictions were driven by anatomically meaningful facial regions, supporting model transparency and trustworthiness for clinical deployment.

Keywords: Neonatal Intensive Care Units · Computer Vision · Explainable Artificial Intelligence

1 Introduction

Neonates admitted to Neonatal Intensive Care Units (NICUs) are frequently exposed to stressful and painful stimuli during a critical period of brain development. In this context, clinicians rely on indirect indicators (such as physiological signals, behavioral cues, and facial expressions) to assess clinically relevant states, including pain, discomfort, alertness, and attention [7,8,11]. Among these

J. M. Ferrández Vicente et al. (Eds.): IWINAC 2026, LNCS 16575, pp. 371–380, 2026.
https://doi.org/10.1007/978-3-032-27317-8_35

indicators, facial expressions constitute a particularly informative and noninvasive source of information and are explicitly incorporated into several validated neonatal pain and discomfort scales [11]. However, their interpretation remains largely subjective and observer-dependent, which may introduce inter-observer variability and limit reproducibility across clinicians and care settings [8].

Beyond episodic clinical observation, continuous monitoring of neonatal facial traits enables the quantification of dynamic indicators related to pain intensity and attentional engagement, supporting timely interventions and early detection of neurological dysfunction. Altered facial behavior has been associated with adverse outcomes, such as neonatal encephalopathy [6,11]. Although objective physiological monitoring tools based on autonomic nervous system activity can complement clinical assessments, they do not directly capture facial behavior, which remains central to the evaluation of neonatal pain and alertness [9]. In this context, automated facial analysis using Artificial Intelligence (AI) offers a complementary approach to reduce subjectivity and improve the objectivity and reproducibility of facial assessments.

Recent advances in computer vision and Deep Learning (DL), particularly Convolutional Neural Networks (CNNs), have enabled accurate automatic analysis of facial expressions by learning hierarchical spatial representations. Several studies have demonstrated the feasibility of applying CNN-based approaches to neonatal pain assessment and behavioral monitoring, enabling near real-time or bedside deployment in NICU settings [4,7]. However, despite their strong performance, these models are typically treated as *black boxes*, providing limited insight into the underlying decision-making process, which poses a major barrier to clinical adoption in safety-critical environments [5]. To address this limitation, eXplainable Artificial Intelligence (XAI) has emerged with a variety of methods that can be broadly divided into post-hoc explainability techniques (e.g., saliency maps or Shapley) and intrinsic interpretability approaches (e.g., attention mechanisms) [4,10,12–14].

In this study, trustworthiness was addressed through a dual explainability framework, subject-aware validation, and robustness analysis under real NICU variability conditions using a dataset of 991 stimulation-aligned video clips acquired from 81 neonates during routine early neurological examinations under heterogeneous clinical acquisition settings. In particular, this framework combines attention-based CNNs with SHAP-based post-hoc analysis to interpret three clinically relevant facial traits (open eyes, open mouth, and pucked eyes), bridging the gap between high-performance models and the interpretability requirements of neonatal clinical practice.

The remainder of this paper is organized as follows. Section 2 describes the dataset acquisition protocol and preprocessing pipeline. Section 3 details the proposed methodology and outlines the experimental design and validation strategy. Section 4 presents the quantitative results and qualitative explainability analyses. Finally, Sect. 5 concludes the paper and discusses future research directions.

2   Dataset

The dataset used in this study consists of video recordings acquired from 81 neonates admitted to the NICU of the *Hospital Universitario de Burgos* (Spain). Recordings were obtained under real NICU conditions during routine early neurological examinations performed within the first days of life, following standard clinical protocols aimed at assessing neonatal alertness, responsiveness, and neurological integrity. These videos include variability in illumination, camera angle, infant positioning, and the presence of medical devices, which introduce significant challenges to automated analysis. During these examinations, neonates were exposed to controlled sensory stimuli that elicited a wide range of spontaneous and stimulus-driven facial expressions.

Preprocessing was applied to standardize facial inputs while preserving the natural variability of the NICU. The following steps were performed:

- Videos were first segmented into short clips corresponding to individual stimulation events during the neurological examination, ensuring temporal alignment between facial responses and clinical stimuli, resulting in 991 clips.
- RGB frames were extracted from each clip at the uniform sampling rate of 3 frames per second (fps).
- Automated neonatal face detection was applied independently to each extracted frame. When multiple detections were present, the facial bounding box with the highest confidence score was selected.
- To reduce temporal redundancy, only the frame with the highest face-detection confidence per second (1 fps) was retained.
- Detected faces were cropped using a square region centered on the face and resized to a standardized spatial resolution compatible with CNN inputs.
- Pixel intensity normalization was applied to all facial crops in order to mitigate variability caused by changes in illumination and camera exposure.
- Finally, a final manual curation step was performed, independently for each of the three facial analysis tasks, to remove frames affected by extreme motion blur, complete facial occlusion, or severe loss of facial visibility, ensuring that task-specific visibility requirements were satisfied.

Importantly, frames exhibiting partial occlusions, moderate head pose variations, and non-uniform illumination were deliberately preserved, as such conditions are common in real NICU environments and are necessary to evaluate model robustness under clinically realistic scenarios. The selected facial traits (eye opening, eye frowning, and mouth opening) were aligned with the objectives of early neurological examinations, which aim to assess neonatal alertness and responsiveness to nociceptive stimulation through observable behavioral markers.

After facial preprocessing, task-specific datasets were constructed from the same pool of facial frames with independent frame-level annotations for each facial trait. Clinically, eye opening is considered a marker of alertness, although some neonates may present with open eyes without adequate reactivity to stimulation, highlighting the need for objective quantification. Mouth opening is also a

Table 1. Task-specific dataset composition (by frames) after preprocessing, reporting the number of samples per class for each facial analysis task.

Task	Positive class	Negative class	Total
Eye Opening	Open: 2454 *(33.22%)*	Closed: 4934 *(66.78%)*	7388
Eye Frowning	Pucked: 1387 *(24.77%)*	Relaxed: 4213 *(75.23%)*	5600
Mouth Opening	Open: 1779 *(36.87%)*	Closed: 3046 *(63.13%)*	4825

relevant indicator of stimulation response and potential discomfort; however, it is not exclusively associated with pain because infants may exhibit an open mouth during calm states or normal respiration [3]. Moreover, respiratory support and oral secretions may introduce visual artifacts that affect automated recognition. Although each trait was analyzed individually in this study, together they represent clinically meaningful components of neurological assessment. The resulting datasets exhibit different sizes and natural class imbalance, reflecting realistic NICU conditions, as summarized in Table 1.

3 Methodology and Experimental Design

3.1 CNN for Facial Tasks Classification

Each facial analysis task considered in this study was formulated as an independent binary classification problem and addressed using a dedicated CNN trained from scratch. A lightweight architecture was deliberately designed to accommodate the limited size of neonatal datasets and the variability inherent to real NICU environments while reducing the risk of overfitting and facilitating interpretability. The network consists of three convolutional blocks, each composed of 3×3 convolutions, followed by batch normalization, ReLU activation, and max-pooling operations, enabling the progressive extraction of spatially meaningful facial features. These blocks are followed by a fully connected classification head with dropout regularization, which produces a probabilistic output that indicates the presence or absence of a target facial trait. Separate models were trained for each task to allow task-specific feature learning.

3.2 Explainability Mechanisms

To enhance model transparency, both intrinsic and post-hoc explainability mechanisms were employed.

- **Attention-Based Intrinsic Explainability.** Spatial attention mechanisms were integrated into the CNN to enable intrinsic interpretability by explicitly modeling the relevance of different facial regions during inference. Attention blocks were inserted after each convolutional block, allowing the network to emphasize the task-relevant spatial features associated with each facial trait. The resulting attention maps are directly accessible as intermediate outputs, facilitating intuitive visualization of the regions driving the model predictions without relying on gradient-based approximation methods.

- **Post-hoc Explainability Using SHAP Values.** To complement the intrinsic attention analysis, SHAP was employed as a post-hoc explainability method to independently assess feature relevance at the input level. SHAP-based explanations provide spatial attribution maps that highlight image regions that contribute positively or negatively to a given prediction. In this study, SHAP was used exclusively for model interpretation and validation purposes, enabling comparison with attention maps and supporting the clinical plausibility and robustness of the learned representations.

3.3   Experimental Design

All experiments were conducted at the frame level, treating eye opening, eye frowning, and mouth opening as independent binary classification tasks, each of which was addressed using a dedicated attention-based CNN. A subject-aware five-fold cross-validation (5-CV) strategy was employed to ensure robust performance estimation and prevent subject-level data leakage. All frames belonging to the same neonate were assigned to a single fold, guaranteeing strict separation between the training, validation, and test sets. In each CV iteration, three folds were used for training, one for validation, and one for testing.

The class imbalance was addressed by computing the class weights from the training data of each fold and incorporating them into the loss function. The models were trained using the Adam optimizer with binary cross-entropy loss. Data augmentation was applied exclusively to the training set to improve the robustness to variability in illumination, pose, and facial appearance commonly observed in NICU recordings. Early stopping based on the validation performance was used to reduce overfitting, and the model parameters corresponding to the best validation performance were retained.

Model performance was evaluated at the frame level by comparing the predicted probabilities with the corresponding ground-truth annotations. A task-specific decision threshold was selected using the validation data within each cross-validation fold. Given the imbalanced nature of the datasets, the performance was quantified using complementary metrics, including accuracy, F1-score, and geometric mean, which jointly reflect the classification performance in terms of sensitivity and specificity. The reported results correspond to the average performance across the 5-CV folds, ensuring that all metrics reflect generalization to unseen subjects.

4   Results and Discussion

4.1   Frame-Level Classification Metrics

The frame-level classification performance of the proposed model was evaluated across three facial analysis tasks using a subject-aware cross-validation protocol.

Table 2 summarizes the average frame-level classification performance of the proposed attention-based CNN across the three facial analysis tasks. For each task, the reported metrics corresponded to the mean values across cross-validation folds.

Table 2. Frame-level classification performance and inference time of the proposed attention-based CNN for the three facial analysis tasks. Acc: accuracy; F1: F1-score; G: geometric mean; AU-PR: area under the precision–recall curve; AU-ROC: area under the receiver operating characteristic curve; Time (s): training time.

Task	Acc	F1	G	AU-PR	AU-ROC	Time (s)
Eye Opening	0.931	0.899	0.929	0.933	0.973	164.2
Eye Frowning	0.923	0.723	0.826	0.793	0.899	153.9
Mouth Opening	0.643	0.777	0.232	0.760	0.645	100.3

The eye opening task achieved the strongest overall performance, with high accuracy, F1-score, and discriminative metrics, indicating reliable detection of ocular state despite illumination variability and partial occlusions. Eye frowning yielded slightly lower F1 and AU-PR values, which was expected given the subtle and localized nature of brow tension. However, the AU-ROC scores confirmed stable discrimination. This task also presented a higher number of false positives, reflecting the visual ambiguity between relaxed and mildly contracted brow configurations.

Mouth opening represents the most challenging scenario, as reflected by the lower accuracy and AU-ROC values. This behavior is largely attributable to increased intraclass variability and frequent occlusions caused by pacifiers or medical devices. Nevertheless, the competitive F1-score and AU-PR values indicate that the model remains effective at identifying clinically relevant mouth opening events. The inference times across tasks remained within a comparable range, supporting the feasibility of the proposed approach for near real-time frame-level analysis in NICU environments.

4.2 Explainability Analysis of CNN Predictions

As mentioned previously, the primary objective of this explainability analysis is to verify that the proposed CNN bases its predictions on anatomically and clinically meaningful facial regions, thereby supporting the validity of the quantitative performance metrics reported in Table 2. The subjects shown in Fig. 1 were selected as illustrative examples, as they are representative of both the correct model behavior and typical challenges that may lead to misclassifications of the model proposed in real NICU scenarios.

For the eye opening task, the model correctly classified seven of the eight frames, as indicated by the green borders in Fig. 1 (subjects A and B). Both XAI methods consistently highlight the periocular region when an event is present,

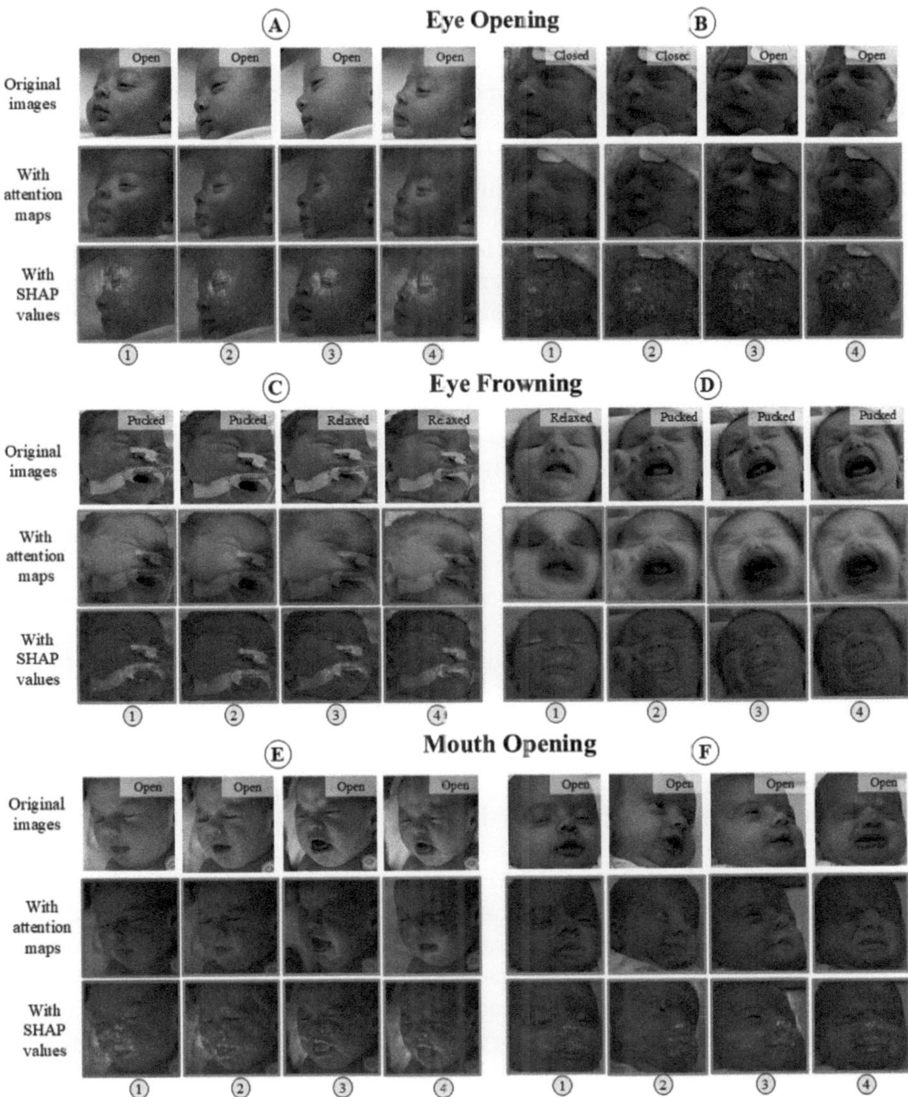

Fig. 1. Qualitative explainability results for the three facial analysis tasks. Two neonates per task (A-F) are shown with four consecutive frames (1–4). The first row displays the original images with ground-truth labels; the second and third rows show attention and SHAP maps, where yellow indicates a higher positive contribution. Green borders denote correct predictions and red borders indicate misclassifications. (Color figure online)

indicating that eye-related features contribute most strongly to the prediction. The only misclassified frame corresponds to frame 3 of subject B, where the neonate begins to slightly open the eyes after the previous closed-eye frames. At this stage, the narrow visible gap may be visually indistinguishable from the surrounding periocular wrinkles, leading to an ambiguous interpretation. Notably, frame 4 of subject B, in which eye opening became more evident, was correctly classified, suggesting temporal consistency in the model's behavior.

Additional sources of visual heterogeneity can be identified in this task. In subject A, one eye was partially occluded due to head pose, and attention maps assigned relevance to nearby anatomical regions, such as the nose or mouth, possibly as a compensatory mechanism for missing visual information. In contrast, subject B exhibited less common periocular anatomical features, including pronounced wrinkles, which likely explains the more spatially dispersed attribution patterns observed in both the attention and SHAP maps.

For the eye-frowning task, all frames of subject D were correctly classified, with the model successfully capturing the transition from a relaxed brow to a frowning expression between frames 1 and 2. In contrast, all frames of subject C were classified as frowning, with frames 3 and 4 (highlighted in red) corresponding to a relaxed state. This error can be partially explained by the SHAP maps, which revealed that the model assigned high relevance to the feeding or monitoring tube present in all four frames of subject C. This artifact introduces visual noise that appears to dominate the attribution patterns, reducing the sensitivity to subtle changes in brow configuration.

For the mouth opening task (subjects E and F), most frames were correctly classified, and both attention and SHAP maps showed highly localized and intuitive focus on the oral region. The only misclassified example corresponds to frame 1 of subject E, where the neonate presents a partially open mouth with slight tongue protrusion. In this case, the absence of a clearly visible dark oral cavity may explain why the model failed to detect the event. In subsequent frames, where mouth opening becomes more pronounced, predictions are correct, and attribution maps remain strongly concentrated on the mouth.

It is important to note that some misclassifications observed in this study may be attributable to clinically relevant sources of variability rather than purely to model failures. For example, eye closure can result from transient periorbital edema or sleep states rather than reduced alertness, and mouth opening may reflect baseline behavior or respiratory patterns rather than discomfort [3]. Furthermore, the frequent use of adhesive tapes, fixation materials, and respiratory support devices in NICUs may partially occlude facial regions, altering visual appearance and confounding automated recognition, as previously reported in real-world neonatal facial analyses [15]. These factors underscore the intrinsic complexity of translating nuanced clinical interpretations of neonatal facial behavior into robust automated systems.

Finally, the robustness of the explainability analysis was assessed by following the sanity-check principles [1]. Additional experiments confirmed that moderate variations in model parameters did not produce substantial changes in attention or SHAP attribution patterns when predictive behavior remained stable. In addition, as shown in Fig. 1, consecutive frames from the same subject often yield highly similar explanations, supporting the stability of the applied explainability techniques and suggesting that the highlighted regions reflect genuine decision-driving features rather than spurious artifacts.

5   Conclusion

This work addressed the automated frame-level analysis of neonatal facial actions in real NICU environments, emphasizing interpretability as a prerequisite for clinical applicability. An attention-based CNN was proposed to classify three clinically relevant facial traits, achieving strong performance under challenging acquisition conditions. A dual explainability framework combining intrinsic attention and post-hoc SHAP analyses confirmed that predictions are driven by anatomically meaningful facial regions, reinforcing confidence in the reported metrics and model transparency. Importantly, these findings highlight the feasibility of deploying interpretable AI models in realistic NICU environments while preserving clinically meaningful variability.

Despite these promising results, this study had some limitations. The dataset reflects the high heterogeneity of real NICU recordings, including variations in head pose, illumination, facial anatomy, and the presence of medical artifacts such as tubes or adhesive sensors. These sources of variability are not merely technical constraints but represent clinically relevant conditions, including ambiguous facial cues and partial occlusions inherent to routine neonatal care. Although more controlled recording setups could theoretically reduce visual variability, such constraints are often impractical in clinical practice and may limit scalability and multicenter deployment. In addition, the analysis was performed at the frame level, which may not fully capture the temporal dynamics of facial actions and can introduce ambiguity in transitional states. Nevertheless, the overall performance suggests that the trained model remains robust and generalizable under realistic conditions, which is particularly important in contexts where early recognition of altered alertness is critical, such as neonatal encephalopathy [2].

Future work will focus on further refining the dataset by reducing the influence of non-facial artifacts and evaluating the model behavior on cleaner subsets of data, enabling a more controlled analysis of facial dynamics. In addition, the use of more complex classification models, including pretrained architectures, will be explored, as they may improve the performance for more challenging facial actions such as eye frowning and mouth opening, which involve subtler and more complex facial patterns. From an explainability perspective, additional robustness analyses and the integration of temporal explainability strategies could further enhance the understanding of model behavior over time.

References

1. Adebayo, J., et al.: Sanity checks for saliency maps. Technical report
2. Arnaez, J., et al.: Usefulness of video recordings for validating neonatal encephalopathy exams: a population-based cohort study. Arch. Disease Childhood - Fetal Neonatal Edition **106**(5), 522–528 (2021)

3. Janet, L.: Brown: states in newborn infants. Merrill-Palmer Q. Behav. Dev. **10**(4), 313–327 (1964)
4. Carlini, L.P., et al.: A convolutional neural network-based mobile application to bedside neonatal pain assessment. In: Proceedings - 2021 34th SIBGRAPI Conference on Graphics, Patterns and Images, SIBGRAPI 2021, pp. 394–401. Institute of Electrical and Electronics Engineers Inc. (2021)
5. Doran, D., Schulz, S., Besold, T.R.: What Does Explainable AI Really Mean? A New Conceptualization of Perspectives (2017)
6. El-Dib, M., et al.: Neuromonitoring in neonatal critical care part I: neonatal encephalopathy and neonates with possible seizures (2023)
7. Ferreira, L.A., et al.: Disclosing neonatal pain in real-time: AI-derived pain sign from continuous assessment of facial expressions. Comput. Biol. Med. **189** (2025)
8. Howard, V.A., Thurber, F.W.: The interpretation of infant pain: physiological and behavioral indicators used by NICU nurses. Technical report (1998)
9. Kolek, F., Jonas, J., Vymazal, T.: Detection of nociceptive stimuli using the newborn infant parasympathetic evaluation index in children aged from 3 to 18 years. Paediatr Anaesth. **35**(9), 747–752 (2025)
10. Li, J., Jin, K., Zhou, D., Kubota, N., Ju, Z.: Attention mechanism-based CNN for facial expression recognition. Neurocomputing **411**, 340–350 (2020)
11. De Melo, G.M., et al.: Pain assessment scales in newborns: integrative review. Technical report 4 (2014)
12. Ornek, A.H., Ceylan, M.: Explainable artificial intelligence (XAI): classification of medical thermal images of neonates using class activation maps. Traitement du Signal **38**(5), 1271–1279 (2021)
13. Paoletti, M.E., Moreno, S.A., Xue, Y., Haut, J.M., Plaza, A.: AAtt-CNN: automatic attention-based convolutional neural networks for hyperspectral image classification. IEEE Trans. Geosci. Remote Sens. **61** (2023)
14. Raghavan, K., Balasubramanian, S., Veezhinathan, K.: Explainable artificial intelligence for medical imaging: review and experiments with infrared breast images. Comput. Intell. **40**(3) (2024)
15. Velasco-Pérez, N., Lozano-Juárez, S., Basurto, N., Arnaez, J., Herrero, Á., Urda, D.: Comparative evaluation of deep learning architectures for detecting neonatal alertness in early clinical assessments. Logic J. IGPL, in press

Evaluating Privacy Preservation in Regression Models for a Small Medical Dataset

Caroline König[1]([⊠]) , Pedro Jesús Copado[1] , Cecilio Angulo[2] ,
Àngela Nebot[1] , and Alfredo Vellido[1]

[1] Soft Computing Research Group (SOCO) at Intelligent Data Science and Artificial Intelligence (IDEAI-UPC) Research Centre, Universitat Politècnica de Catalunya (UPC Barcelona Tech), Jordi Girona 1–3, 08034 Barcelona, Spain
ckonig@cs.upc.edu
[2] Knowledge Engineering Research Group (GREC) at Intelligent Data Science and Artificial Intelligence (IDEAI-UPC) Research Centre, Universitat Politècnica de Catalunya (UPC Barcelona Tech), Jordi Girona 1–3, 08034 Barcelona, Spain

Abstract. The growing use of machine learning in healthcare requires careful consideration of patient privacy, particularly when models are trained on small medical datasets where the risk of re-identification is heightened. This study analyzes how regression models operate under privacy-preserving constraints and assesses their susceptibility to privacy leakage. A stability-based membership-inference framework quantifies how much model outputs reveal about individual training samples. Noise-injection techniques are applied to reduce this risk, and their effects on privacy and predictive accuracy are evaluated. Experiments on a small real-world medical dataset show a trade-off between model utility and privacy, identifying conditions in which regression models remain reliable while limiting exposure to membership-inference attacks.

Keywords: Privacy · Membership Inference · Stability · Regression · Medical data

1 Introduction

Artificial Intelligence (AI) systems are increasingly used in healthcare and medical applications [5], particularly in the field of personalized medicine [25], where treatments are tailored to individual patient needs using machine-learning (ML) models trained on health-related data. Beside achieving high predictive performance it is important to address also regulatory requirements. The EU AI Act [6] considers medical applications as *high-risk* applications and establishes additional requirements related to fairness, transparency, safety and the protection of personal data [4].

This study evaluates the privacy-preserving properties of the ML models of the prototype predictive platform developed in the framework of the European

J. M. Ferrández Vicente et al. (Eds.): IWINAC 2026, LNCS 16575, pp. 381–390, 2026.
https://doi.org/10.1007/978-3-032-27317-8_36

ERAPERMED 2022-292 research project "Towards a Personalized Medicine Approach to Psychological Treatment of Psychosis", hereafter referred to as PERMEPSY (www.permepsy.org). This project involves a consortium that comprises five clinical partners, namely Parc Sanitari Sant Joan de Déu (PSSJD, Spain; project coordinator), University Medical Center Hamburg-Eppendorf (UKE, Germany), the Polish Academy of Sciences (PAoS, Poland), Universidad de Valparaíso (UV, Chile), and University Hospital of Strasbourg (Inserm, France) as well as Universitat Politècnica de Catalunya (UPC, Spain) as the technical partner. The project aims to personalize Metacognitive Training (MCT) for individuals with psychosis, a psychological intervention designed to reduce positive symptoms by targeting cognitive biases [18,19,21]. A prototype of an AI-based predictive platform has been developed during the first phase of the project as a decision-support system to assist clinicians in tailoring Metacognitive Training (MCT) treatment plans for individuals with psychosis [12]. This platform incorporates eight ML models that predict how different type of symptoms are expected to evolve in response to MCT. These models were trained on a harmonized retrospective database on treatment effectiveness [15], which integrated clinical data from patients who previously received MCT [13]. A prototype of the platform is currently being evaluated in a controlled clinical trial within the scope of the project [16]. The trial aims to assess the usability of the web-based decision-support system in clinical practice and to validate the predictive accuracy of the underlying ML models. Future development cycles are expected to advance the platform toward a higher technological readiness level and ensure compliance with the non-functional requirements of the EU AI Act and medical-device regulations, particularly regarding safety, robustness, and transparency.

In this study, the prototype is further extended by evaluating privacy preservation of the ML models, with particular attention to their vulnerability to membership inference attacks. These attacks constitute a form of black-box privacy leakage in which an adversary tries to find out whether specific data records were used for model training. Such risks are especially relevant in the medical domain, where training data contains highly sensitive personal health information and where privacy violations are a major concern. Related work has shown that medical AI systems can be susceptible to privacy leakage due to small dataset sizes or heterogeneous data distributions [22,26]. To assess this risk, a prediction stability's evaluation procedure is applied. This method examines whether differences in prediction stability can be used to distinguish training samples from previously unseen data points, based on the assumption that models often produce more consistent outputs for instances seen during training [24]. Detecting such differences is essential for evaluating compliance with emerging regulatory frameworks such as the EU AI Act requiring privacy, robustness, and data-protection mechanisms for AI systems deployed in healthcare.

The remainder of the article is organized as follows. Section 2 presents the data and ML models under study. Section 3 describes the approach used to evaluate the risk of membership-inference attacks and the corresponding mitigation techniques, and Sect. 4 discusses the experimental results and Sect. 5 concludes with final remarks about directions for future work.

2   Materials

At the beginning of the PERMEPSY project in 2023, several ML models were developed to predict different type of symptoms using a harmonized dataset containing psychological, sociodemographic, and diagnostic variables [15]. These models estimate how a patient's symptoms are expected to evolve under Metacognitive Training (MCT). The input features include sociodemographic information (e.g., gender, age), living habits, substance-use indicators, diagnostic categories, and illness duration (i.e., time since diagnosis). As described in [12], the best-performing models identified during the modeling phase were selected for deployment in the web-based predictive platform. Specifically, Random Forest (RF) models [3], an ensemble-learning method, were chosen for predicting the severity of several type of symptoms.

The ML models aim to predict symptom levels measured by different clinical scales, including schizophrenia-related positive symptoms [10], the severity of delusions and hallucinations [8], self-esteem [20], and cognitive insight [2]. As a result, seven regression models were trained using a dataset comprising 559 patients for training and 140 for testing derived from a 80/20 split of the harmonized dataset. Prediction performance was evaluated with the Root Mean Square Error (RMSE) on the test set. Baseline approaches such as Decision Tree Regressors (DT) and Linear Regression (LR) were evaluated alongside more advanced ensemble methods, including Random Forest (RF), XGBoost (XB), and LightGBM (LB) Regressor [11]. Such ensemble models combine multiple weak learners to form a stronger predictor. While RF applies a bagging strategy to aggregate multiple decision trees in parallel, XB and LB rely on boosting, sequentially refining weak models to improve predictive performance [23].

3   Methods for Assessing Risk of Privacy Leakage

This section describes the experimental procedure used to evaluate whether the previously developed ML models show signs of privacy leakage focusing on vulnerability to membership-inference attacks. The analysis consists of two main steps: (1) a stability-based evaluation of the original models, and (2) the application of a noise-injection mitigation technique inspired by differential-privacy mechanisms [9].

3.1   Stability-Based Membership-Inference Evaluation

The first step evaluates the originally trained models using a prediction-stability test. Stability is assessed by generating perturbed versions of each input sample and examining the variability of the resulting predictions. For every instance in both the training and test sets, $K = 50$ perturbed samples are generated by adding Gaussian noise with variance 0.01 to each feature. The model is then evaluated on each perturbed sample, producing a set of perturbed predictions $\{\hat{y}'_1, \ldots, \hat{y}'_K\}$.

Two stability metrics are computed for each instance. The first is the *prediction variance*, defined as $\mathrm{Var}(x) = \mathrm{Var}(\hat{y}'_1, \ldots, \hat{y}'_K)$, which measures the variability of the perturbed predictions for an instance. The second is the *mean absolute deviation (MAD)*, defined as $\mathrm{MAD}(x) = \frac{1}{K} \sum_{j=1}^{K} |\hat{y}'_j - \hat{y}|$, which quantifies the average deviation of the perturbed predictions from the original prediction $\hat{y}$.

To determine whether the model behaves differently on training versus unseen data, the distributions of per-sample variances are compared using Levene's test for equality of variances [7], with a significance threshold of $\alpha = 0.05$. Significant differences indicate risk of the model to reveal membership information. While predictive performance is evaluated exclusively on the test set using RMSE, prediction stability is assessed on both the training and test sets to detect such discrepancies.

3.2 Noise-Injection Mitigation

To reduce stability differences that may reveal membership, a noise-injection mitigation strategy is applied. This approach introduces small stochastic perturbations into the input space during training, fostering the model to generalize better. Each numerical feature value x_{ij} is perturbed by adding independent Laplace noise, where $\epsilon_{ij} \sim \mathrm{Laplace}(0, \mathrm{scale})$ and the perturbed input is computed as $x'_{ij} = x_{ij} + \epsilon_{ij}$. The scale parameter was set to 0.01 in this experiment. This differential-privacy inspired technique [1] aims to produce models with more uniform prediction stability both for the training and test samples, thereby reducing susceptibility to membership-inference attacks. After applying noise injection, both prediction stability and predictive performance are evaluated to assess changes in privacy preservation and model accuracy.

4 Results and Discussion

Table 1 reports the performance of the regression models in predicting symptom levels across the different psychological scales. For each target variable and model, the table shows the prediction error (RMSE) for both the original dataset and the dataset augmented with Laplacian noise as a privacy-preserving mitigation strategy (models trained on the perturbed data are marked with the suffix L). The comparison confirms that RF models achieve the best performance for most symptom scales. Interestingly, in several cases the dataset perturbed with Laplacian noise leads to improved generalization, resulting in lower RMSE values. LB and LR also achieve comparable performance for some of the target variables.

Table 1. Performance of models in target variable prediction in RMSE. Best results for each target variable highlighted in bold.

Target	RF	RF_L	DT	DT_L	LR	LR_L	XB	XB_L	LB	LB_L
$PANSS\_P$	6.62	**6.56**	9.71	10.05	6.64	6.62	7.08	6.99	6.99	5.12
A_DEL	**2.05**	2.46	3.80	2.73	2.48	6.15	2.59	2.73	2.54	2.72
PSY_H	6.92	6.88	9.01	8.48	6.80	6.82	7.35	7.72	7.17	**6.71**
PSY_D	**4.56**	4.61	7.28	6.61	4.90	4.89	4.84	4.86	4.58	4.79
$RSES$	**6.20**	6.43	7.38	7.73	11.70	11.81	11.80	10.79	10.39	9.18
$BCIS\_R$	3.62	**3.59**	5.02	5.34	3.76	3.74	3.91	3.96	3.93	3.88
$BCIS\_C$	**2.73**	2.74	4.50	3.92	2.85	2.91	2.85	3.03	2.90	2.831

Table 2 summarizes the results of the stability analysis performed on the seven regression models using the original training setup, that is, without applying Laplacian noise. The table reports the variability of the perturbed predictions for the test and training sets, denoted as Vte and Vtr, respectively. It also includes the mean absolute deviation of the perturbed predictions from the original prediction, reported as $MADte$ and $MADtr$. The metric Vp corresponds to the p-value of Levene's test comparing the distributions of Vte and Vtr. P-values below the significance threshold of 0.05 are highlighted in bold.

The results in Table 2 show that, for most models, the variance of the test set exceeds that of the training set, which aligns with generalization theory. Moreover, the LR and RF models exhibit extremely high stability, with both Vtr and Vte values close to zero. LB also shows relatively low prediction variance, whereas DT and XB reveal higher instability. The Vp metric quantifies whether the difference in stability between training and test samples is statistically significant. According to these results, RF and DT show significant variance differences in four and two target variables, respectively. Such findings indicate a potential risk of membership inference, as stability discrepancies between training and test samples can be exploited in black-box attacks.

Regarding the mean deviation metrics (MADte and MADtr), these values cannot be directly exploited in a black-box membership-inference attack, since the true prediction is not observable by an adversary. Nonetheless, the MAD statistics reveal consistently lower deviations for RF models, while higher deviation is observed for the remaining models.

Table 3 presents the stability results for the models retrained on the dataset perturbed with slight Laplacian noise. The predictive performance of these retrained models is shown in Table 1. In most cases, performance remains comparable to that of the models trained on the original dataset, and in some cases (particularly for DT) generalization even improves. The stability analysis on the Laplace-perturbed dataset shows that overall stability decreases across all models, with LR now appearing more stable than RF. Importantly, the Vp values indicate that none of the models exhibit significant stability differences between training and test samples after noise injection. This suggests that the retrained

Table 2. Stability metrics and significance tests for target variables and models on the original dataset.

Target	Model	MADte	MADtr	Vtr	Vte	Vp
PANSS_P	DT	1.91	2.28	0.40	0.80	0.56
PANSS_P	LR	1.81	1.71	0.000415	0.000404	0.73
PANSS_P	LGBM	1.33	2.03	1.06	0.97	0.52
PANSS_P	XGB	1.65	2.72	1.60	1.20	0.10
PANSS_P	RF	0.47	0.56	0.000979	0.02	**0.000314**
PSY_D	DT	2.09	2.19	0.03	1.20	**0.00161**
PSY_D	LR	1.07	1.21	0.000890	0.000878	0.66
PSY_D	LGBM	1.04	1.23	0.18	0.19	0.63
PSY_D	XGB	1.73	2.03	0.72	0.83	0.56
PSY_D	RF	0.35	0.36	0.001692	0.00	**0.00344**
PSY_H	DT	0.93	0.61	0.02	0.13	0.13
PSY_H	LR	2.74	2.62	0.001127	0.001163	0.24
PSY_H	LGBM	0.95	1.03	0.12	0.13	0.98
PSY_H	XGB	1.15	1.10	0.73	1.10	0.38
PSY_H	RF	0.49	0.41	0.002141	0.00	0.18
A_DEL	DT	1.03	1.07	0.01	0.02	0.45
A_DEL	LR	0.94	0.94	0.000070	0.000073	0.47
A_DEL	LGBM	0.67	0.82	0.08	0.12	0.04
A_DEL	XGB	0.81	1.26	0.33	0.33	0.80
A_DEL	RF	0.23	0.26	0.04	0.04	0.06
BCIS_R	DT	1.39	1.48	0.03	0.12	**0.01**
BCIS_R	LR	1.25	1.21	0.002232	0.002291	0.41
BCIS_R	LGBM	1.08	1.41	0.13	0.14	0.82
BCIS_R	XGB	1.16	1.74	0.51	0.57	0.48
BCIS_R	RF	0.30	0.37	0.000556	0.000853	0.29
BCIS_C	DT	1.77	1.58	0.02	0.02	0.97
BCIS_C	LR	1.13	1.14	0.000035	0.000037	0.83
BCIS_C	LGBM	0.86	1.24	0.09	0.08	0.48
BCIS_C	XGB	1.19	1.71	0.34	0.34	0.86
BCIS_C	RF	0.22	0.31	0.000322	0.001181	**0.00114**
RSES	DT	1.42	2.82	0.25	0.81	0.20
RSES	LR	3.22	2.83	0.20	0.19	0.14
RSES	LGBM	2.12	2.54	0.45	0.48	0.98
RSES	XGB	2.17	3.18	8.33	9.91	0.85
RSES	RF	0.45	0.66	0.001321	0.02	**0.000358**

Table 3. Stability metrics and significance tests for target variables and models on the dataset perturbed with Laplacian noise.

Target	Model	MADte	MADtr	Vtr	Vte	Vp
PANSS_P	DT	3.56	3.67	18.19	17.79	0.85
PANSS_P	LR	1.83	1.73	0.013711	0.013644	0.53
PANSS_P	LGBM	1.63	1.80	1.90	1.68	0.09
PANSS_P	XGB	2.05	2.36	3.23	3.26	0.97
PANSS_P	RF	0.56	0.67	0.29	0.25	0.26
PSY_D	DT	1.89	1.50	5.27	6.25	0.35
PSY_D	LR	1.08	1.23	0.03	0.03	0.39
PSY_D	LGBM	1.14	1.23	1.04	0.97	0.68
PSY_D	XGB	1.65	1.60	2.26	2.21	0.49
PSY_D	RF	0.56	0.62	0.44	0.41	0.40
PSY_H	DT	1.23	1.66	12.90	8.94	0.25
PSY_H	LGBM	1.30	1.23	1.28	1.46	0.39
PSY_H	XGB	1.44	1.22	3.06	4.16	0.09
PSY_H	RF	0.78	0.91	2.31	2.38	0.32
A_DEL	DT	1.30	1.57	2.21	2.13	0.56
A_DEL	LR	0.96	0.95	0.001385	0.001395	0.67
A_DEL	LGBM	0.66	0.74	0.29	0.29	0.83
A_DEL	XGB	0.87	0.91	0.39	0.41	0.97
A_DEL	RF	0.23	0.26	0.04	0.04	0.06
BCIS_R	DT	2.18	2.21	5.27	5.16	0.96
BCIS_R	LR	1.26	1.20	0.008373	0.008012	0.62
BCIS_R	LGBM	1.17	1.18	0.64	0.60	0.35
BCIS_R	XGB	1.32	1.46	1.10	1.12	0.62
BCIS_R	RF	0.46	0.48	0.20	0.20	0.64
BCIS_C	DT	2.50	2.55	3.51	3.24	0.58
BCIS_C	LR	1.12	1.12	0.06	0.06	0.94
BCIS_C	LGBM	0.97	1.03	0.39	0.42	0.30
BCIS_C	XGB	1.24	1.32	0.82	0.80	0.51
BCIS_C	RF	0.43	0.43	0.10	0.13	0.08
RSES	DT	3.64	4.50	20.06	14.39	0.36
RSES	LR	3.86	3.32	2.24	2.21	0.28
RSES	LGBM	2.31	2.70	6.15	3.43	0.14
RSES	XGB	2.38	2.54	14.14	15.02	0.94
RSES	RF	0.76	0.99	1.48	1.25	0.64

models are more robust from a privacy-preserving perspective, reducing the risk of membership inference.

5 Conclusion

The study evaluated the risk of the PERMEPSY regression models to privacy leakage due to membership-inference analyzing the stability of their predictions under controlled input perturbations. The results show that in the original training configuration, several models (most notably RF and DT) had significant differences in the prediction variance comparing training samples with unseen data. Notably, even for very stable models (such as RF) there were still significant differences between train and test distributions. This behavior can be explained by the fact that some models learn partial memorization of training samples so that stability based membership inference could be feasible for these models in a black-box setting. LR and LG, in contrast, displayed more uniform stability, suggesting a lower inherent privacy risk. Adding Laplacian noise to the training data altered the prediction stability so that the retrained models showed an increase in prediction variance, but importantly no statistically significant differences between the training and test samples were found. This indicates that mild noise injection can reduce stability-based leakage without substantially degrading predictive performance and in some cases even improving generalization. These findings highlight the potential of lightweight perturbation strategies as practical privacy-preserving mechanisms in clinical ML applications.

In future work more elaborated noise-injection schemes, such as feature-adaptive noise or sensitivity-based calibration could be explored [14,17]. Such methods could provide stronger protection while minimizing performance loss. These results confirm the importance of systematically assessing privacy leakage in predictive clinical models and demonstrate the effectiveness of computational simple mitigation techniques to reduce the risk of exposing sensitive patient information.

Acknowledgments. The authors would like to acknowledge the contributions of all PERMEPSY GROUP members: Susana Ochoa, Maria Lamarca, Belen Ramos Josemaria, Judith Usall, Regina Vila Badia, Raquel Lopez Carrilero, Trini Pelaez Martinez, Irene Birulés, Claudia Requejo; Partner 1 members Steffen Moritz, Rabea Fischer, Merle Schlechte, Annika Schmueser, Antonia Meinhart, Jakob Scheunemann; Partner 2 members Fabrice Berna, Adrien Goncalves; Partner 3 members Łukasz Gawęda, Marytna Krezolek, Hania Gelner, Adrianna Aleksandrowicz, Justyna Piwinska; Partner 4 members Caroline König, Pedro Copado, Ángela Nebot, Alfredo Vellido, Cecilio Angulo, Marc Larroda; Partner 5 members Vanessa Acuña and Alvaro Cavieres.

Funding Information. This work is part of the European ERAPERMED 2022-292 call for international collaboration projects of the 20212023 Strategic Action in Health funded by European Union - Next Generation EU resources under the Recovery, Transformation and Resilience Plan, supported as grant AC22/0010 by the Instituto de Salud Carlos III (ISCIII) in Spain. The PERMEPSY project was supported under the frame of ERA PerMed by: Instituto de Salud Carlos III (ISCIII), Spain, Grant numbers AC22/00010 & AC22/0053; German Federal Ministry of Education and Research (BMBF), Germany, Grant number 01KU2306; Agence Nationale de la Recherche (ANR), France, Grant number ANR-22-PERM-0009-05.; National Centre for Research and Development (NCBR) Grant number: PerMed/V/82/PERMEPSY/2023, Poland; Agencia Nacional de Investigación y Desarrollo (ANID), Chile, Grant number REC+ERAPERMED2022-292.

Conflict of interests. The authors declare not to have any potential conflicts of interests.

References

1. Abadi, M., et al.: Deep learning with differential privacy. In: Proceedings of the 2016 ACM SIGSAC Conference on Computer and Communications Security, pp. 308–318 (2016)

2. Beck, A.T., Steer, R.A., Brown, G.: Beck depression inventory-II. Psychol. Assess. (1996)

3. Breiman, L.: Random forests. Mach. Learn. **45**, 5–32 (2001)

4. Busch, F., et al.: Navigating the European union artificial intelligence act for healthcare. NPJ Digit. Med. **7**(210) (2024). https://doi.org/10.1038/s41746-024-01213-6

5. Egger, J., et al.: Medical deep learning—a systematic meta-review. Comput. Methods Programs Biomed. **221**, 106874 (2022)

6. European Union: Artificial Intelligence Act (2024). https://www.europarl.europa.eu/doceo/document/TA-9-2024-0138_EN.pdf, adopted by the 27 EU member states in March 2024

7. Glass, G.V.: Testing homogeneity of variances. Am. Educ. Res. J. **3**(3), 187–190 (1966)

8. Haddock, G., McCarron, J., Tarrier, N., Faragher, E.: Scales to measure dimensions of hallucinations and delusions: the psychotic symptom rating scales (PSYRATS). Psychol. Med. **29**(4), 879–889 (1999)

9. Iyengar, R., Near, J.P., Song, D., Thakkar, O., Thakurta, A., Wang, L.: Towards practical differentially private convex optimization. In: 2019 IEEE Symposium on Security and Privacy (SP), pp. 299–316. IEEE (2019)

10. Kay, S.R., Fiszbein, A., Opler, L.A.: The positive and negative syndrome scale (PANSS) for schizophrenia. Schizoph. Bull. **13**, 261–276 (1987)

11. Ke, G., Meng, Q., Finley, T., Wang, T., Chen, W.: LightGBM: a highly efficient gradient boosting decision tree. In: Advances in Neural Information Processing Systems, vol. 30 (2017)

12. König, C., et al.: An artificial intelligence-based platform for personalized predictions of metacognitive training effectiveness. Comput. Struct. Biotechnol. J. **28**, 281–293 (2025)

13. König, C., Guendouz, W., Copado, P., Angulo, C., Nebot, À., et al.: Group discovery in a clinical database of patients with psychosis who have undergone metacognitive training. In: International Meeting on Computational Intelligence Methods for Bioinformatics and Biostatistics, pp. 269–280. Springer, Cham (2024)

14. Kulynych, B., Gomez, J.F., Kaissis, G., du Pin Calmon, F., Troncoso, C.: Attack-aware noise calibration for differential privacy. Adv. Neural. Inf. Process. Syst. **37**, 134868–134901 (2024)

15. König, C., et al.: Data harmonization for the analysis of personalized treatment of psychosis with metacognitive training. Sci. Rep. **15**(10159) (2025). https://doi.org/10.1038/s41598-025-94815-3

16. Lamarca, M., et al.: Permepsy: a multicentre, randomized, double-blind proof-of-concept trial of personalised metacognitive training for adults with psychosis. a study protocol. Front. Psych. **17**, 1711659 (2026)

17. Ma, C., et al.: Adaptive feature representation learning for privacy-fairness joint optimization. Appl. Sci. **15**(24), 13031 (2025)

18. Moritz, S., Menon, M., Balzan, R., Woodward, T.S.: Metacognitive training for psychosis (MCT): past, present, and future. Eur. Arch. Psychiatry Clin. Neurosci. **273**(4), 811–817 (2023)

19. Moritz, S., Woodward, T.S., Balzan, R.: Is metacognitive training for psychosis effective? Expert Rev. Neurother. **16**, 105–107 (2016)

20. Rosenberg, M.: Rosenberg self-esteem scale (RSE): acceptance and commitment therapy. measures package, 61. Society and the Adolescent Self-Image (1965)

21. Schlechte, M., Moritz, S., Veckenstedt, R., König, C., Berna, F.: Metakognitives training für psychose. Die Psychotherapie, pp. 1–6 (2025)

22. Shokri, R., Stronati, M., Song, C., Shmatikov, V.: Membership inference attacks against machine learning models. In: 2017 IEEE Symposium on Security and Privacy (SP), pp. 3–18. IEEE (2017)

23. Sutton, C.D.: Classification and regression trees, bagging, and boosting. Handb. Statist. **24**, 303–329 (2005)

24. Ying, Z., Zhang, Y., Liu, X.: Privacy-preserving in defending against membership inference attacks. In: Proceedings of the 2020 Workshop on Privacy-Preserving Machine Learning in Practice, pp. 61–63 (2020)

25. Zhang, S., Bamakan, S.M.H., Qu, Q., Li, S.: Learning for personalized medicine: a comprehensive review from a deep learning perspective. IEEE Rev. Biomed. Eng. **12**, 194–208 (2018)

26. Ziller, A., Usynin, D., Braren, R., Makowski, M., Rueckert, D., Kaissis, G.: Medical imaging deep learning with differential privacy. Sci. Rep. **11**(1), 13524 (2021)

Interpretable MobileNetV3 for Early and Late Blight Detection in Andean Potato Leaves

Lorena Guachi-Guachi[1][(✉)], Esteban Gavilánez[1], Jeffrey Guerrero[1],
Victor Osejo[1], Robinson Guachi[1], Wilman Suárez-Zambrano[2],
and D. H. Peluffo-Ordóñez[2,3]

[1] Faculty of Digital Engineering and Emerging Technologies,
Universidad Internacional del Ecuador, Av. Simon Bolivar, 170411 Quito, Ecuador
{lorena.guachi,fagavilanezmu,jeguerrerope,viosejoal,
roguachigu}@uide.edu.ec
[2] School of Mathematical and Computational Sciences, Yachay Tech,
Urcuqui, Ecuador
{wsuarez,dpeluffo}@yachaytech.edu.ec
[3] SDAS Research Group, Ibarra, Ecuador
{diego.peluffo}@sdas-group.com
https://sdas-group.com/

Abstract. Potato leaf blight remains one of the most destructive leaf diseases affecting potato crops in the Andean region, posing a significant threat to food security and the livelihoods of smallholder farmers. This work presents a computer vision framework for the automated detection of early blight (Alternaria solani) and late blight (Phytophthora infestans) in native Andean potato varieties using RGB imagery. Two datasets were employed: a localized dataset (2,766 images) and an extended-localized dataset incorporating additional distractor images that closely resemble those from localized dataset (3,666 images). Three convolutional neural network (CNNs) architectures, a custom CNN, EfficientNetB0, and MobileNetV3, were evaluated for classification performance and interpretability. MobileNetV3 achieved 100% accuracy on the localized dataset and 98.67% on the extended dataset. Grad-CAM visualizations revealed that, under increased variability, MobileNetV3 maintained spatially distributed attention over leaf regions while minimizing reliance on background artifacts, outperforming compared architectures in robustness and interpretability. These results demonstrate that lightweight CNNs trained on localized data augmented with distractor images can effectively mitigate dataset bias and enable the development of efficient, deployable disease detection tools for small-scale agriculture.

Keywords: Potato Leaf Blight · Convolutional Neural Networks · Andean Potato · Lightweight Deep Learning

J. M. Ferrández Vicente et al. (Eds.): IWINAC 2026, LNCS 16575, pp. 391–399, 2026.
https://doi.org/10.1007/978-3-032-27317-8_37

1   Introduction

The potato (Solanum tuberosum) is a crop of major agronomic and cultural importance in the Andean highlands, where native varieties contribute significantly to food security, biodiversity and rural economies [1]. Potato production in such region is severely limited by leaf diseases, particularly early blight and late blight, which can spread rapidly under the cool, humid conditions characteristic of high-altitude environments and can lead to substantial yield losses. Timely and accurate diagnosis of these diseases is therefore essential to inform effective interventions and minimize economic impact. Nevertheless, smallholder farmers in the Andes often lack access to specialized agronomic expertise due to geographic, economic, and infrastructural limitations. This gap has driven growing interest in automated disease detection systems based on computer vision and machine learning as scalable and accessible tools for plant health monitoring in resource-constrained agricultural contexts [2–4].

The application of deep learning to plant disease recognition has grown substantially in recent years. Early studies demonstrated that convolutional neural networks (CNNs) trained on large-scale datasets such as PlantVillage could achieve high classification accuracy across multiple crops and diseases types [5–7]. Several works employing deeper architectures, including VGG and ResNet variants, further improved performance under controlled imaging conditions [8,9]. Recent research investigated efficient, lightweight architectures suitable for mobile and edge deployment. Models such as MobileNet and EfficientNet have demonstrated strong performance while significantly reducing computational requirements [10,11]. These architectures have been successfully applied to crop disease detection, including potato blight detection, achieving competitive accuracy with lower inference cost [12,13]. Such efficiency is particularly relevant for agricultural applications in resource-constrained environments.

Despite these advances, empirical evidence remains limited regarding how lightweight CNNs attend to disease-relevant leaf regions in localized datasets. CNN-based plant disease classifiers frequently exhibit dataset bias and shortcut learning, where models rely on background artifacts rather than disease-specific visual features, thereby limiting generalization to field conditions [2,3,12]. This limitation is particularly relevant for underrepresented crops, such as native Andean potato varieties. Therefore, model selection should prioritize not only accuracy but also interpretability, ensuring predictions rely on meaningful visual evidence.

This work addresses this gap by evaluating three lightweight CNN architectures on localized and extended-localized datasets of native Andean potato leaves, combining accuracy analysis with Grad-CAM-based interpretability to inform model selection for equitable and deployable precision agriculture solutions.

2   Methodology

The proposed methodology for automated detection of potato leaf health conditions is illustrated in Fig. 1. The workflow integrates dataset preparation, convolutional feature extraction, and final classification using CNN-based architectures in both training and inference stages. The proposed approach was designed to operate effectively under limited data conditions while maintaining robustness and computational efficiency.

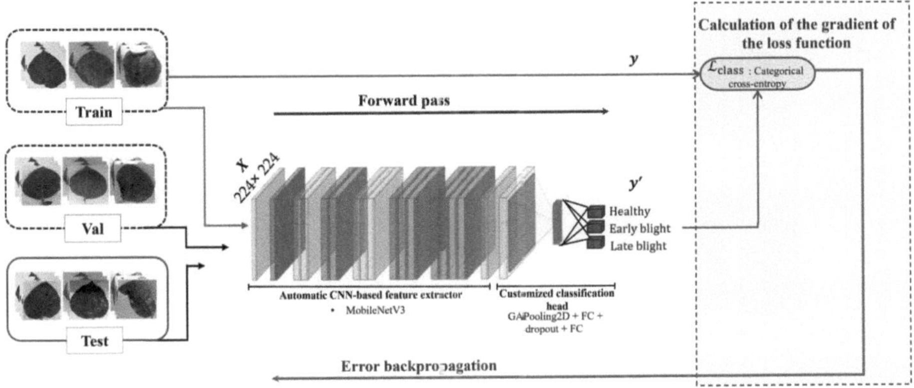

Fig. 1. Overview of the proposed methodology to identify potato leaf health condition. The workflow includes dataset preparation, followed by convolutional feature extraction and classification using CNN-based architectures.

2.1 Dataset

The localized dataset (LD) comprised 2,766 images of native Andean potato leaves (*Solanum tuberosum* subsp. *andigena*). All images were acquired under controlled lighting conditions with uniform backgrounds, ensuring that each leaf was centrally positioned. Of these, 2,466 images were used for training (666: healthy; 900 early blight; 900: late blight), while 150 images (50 per leaf health condition) were allocated for validation and the remaining 150 images (50 per condition) were allocated for testing. Native Andean potato varieties exhibit high genetic diversity at the plant level, which may result in increased morphological variability across samples; however, such variability is not necessarily visually distinguishable at the level of individual leaf images.

The extended localized dataset (ELD) consisted of 3,366 RGB images categorized into the same three classes: healthy, early blight, and late blight. This dataset was constructed by augmenting the training subset of the LD with 900 images from the publicly available Potato Leaf Disease Dataset [14], which primarily includes leaves from commercial potato cultivars of *Solanum tuberosum* grown under diverse agronomic and environmental conditions. These commercial cultivars tend to be more homogeneous as a result of selective breeding and adaptation to specific—often European—growing environments. Representative samples from both sources are illustrated in Fig. 2.

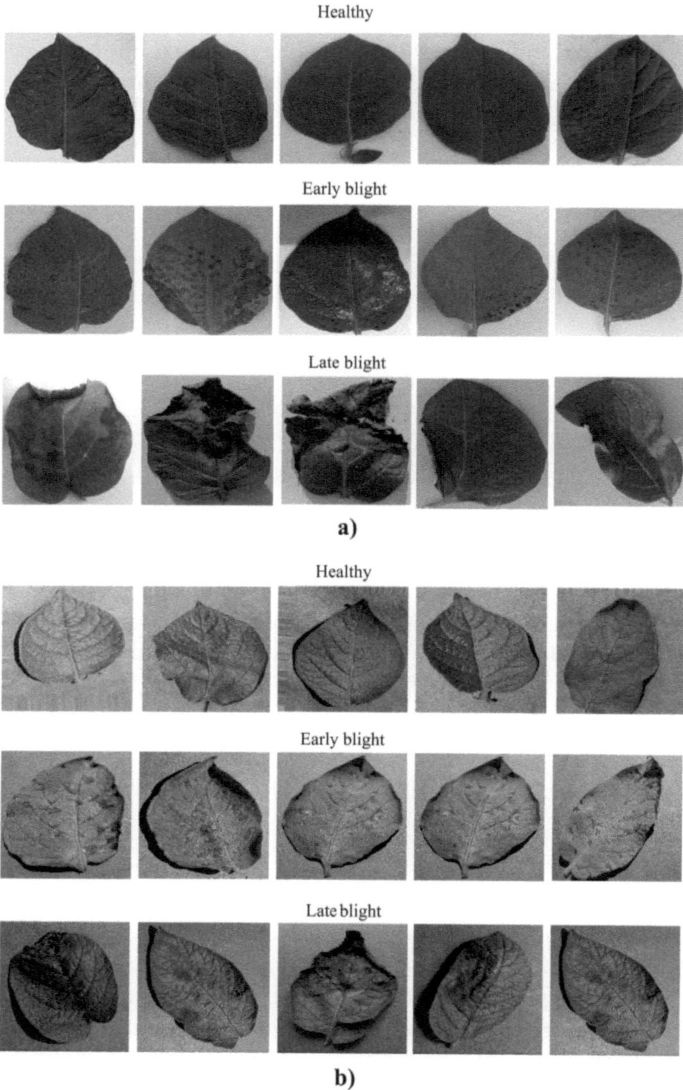

Fig. 2. Representative samples from the two data sources used in this study: a) locally collected Andean potato leaves and b) publicly available Potato Leaf Disease Dataset [14].

All images were resized to 224 × 224 pixels. During training, data augmentation based on linear transformations was applied to enhance generalization and mitigate overfitting. Such transformations included a random zoom-in operation centered on the leaf region (with height and width factors ranging from −0.1 to 0.0), simulating variations in camera distance while preserving the region of interest. Additionally, random contrast adjustment ($\pm15\%$) and brightness variation ($\pm10\%$) were introduced to account for illumination changes often encountered in real-world image acquisition scenarios.

2.2 Automatic Detection of Potato Leaf Health Conditions

The automatic detection task was formulated as a supervised multi-class classification problem. RGB images of individual leaves were input to a CNN-based feature extractor, which produced hierarchical representations subsequently classified into healthy, early blight, or late blight categories (Fig. 1).

Convolutional layers learn increasingly abstract visual patterns: early layers capture low-level features such as edges, color variations, and local texture irregularities, while deeper layers encode complex high-level features such as disease-specific traits, including leaf morphology, blight distribution, and spatial severity cues associated with disease progression. The resulting feature maps were then processed by a custom classification head consisting of a global mean pooling layer, a fully connected dense layer with 128 units and ReLU activation, and a dropout layer (rate = 0.4) to reduce overfitting. Finally, a softmax output layer with three units produced the class probabilities corresponding to the target categories.

The CNN-based architectures were trained by minimizing loss in $L_{\text{class}} = -\sum_{i=1}^{C} y_i \log\left(y_i'\right)$, using Adam optimizer [15] from Tensorflow 2.19 deep learning framework. Batch sizes and number of epochs were respectively set at 16 and 20 respectively.

3 Experimental Results and Discussion

Three CNN-based architectures were trained and evaluated for detecting potato leaf health conditions under different dataset configurations: a custom CNN, EfficientNetB0 [11], and MobileNetV3 [16]. During training stage, for CNN-based feature extraction, EfficientNetB0 and MobileNetV3 were initialized with pre-trained weights learned from the ImageNet data.

As shown in Table 1, MobileNetV3 achieved the highest performance across all metrics (100%) on the localized dataset (LD), outperforming both EfficientNetB0 and the custom CNN. On the extended-localized dataset (ELD), MobileNetV3 maintained strong performance with 98.67% accuracy across all evaluation metrics, demonstrating robustness to increased variability. Despite this slight decrease, MobileNetV3 continued to outperform the custom CNN and remained competitive with EfficientNetB0. Qualitative analysis using Grad-CAM revealed that MobileNetV3 exhibited more spatially distributed attention across the leaf surface when trained and evaluated on the ELD (Fig. 3). In contrast, heavier architectures, as well as MobileNetV3 trained exclusively on the LD, often focused partially or entirely on background regions, highlighting the importance of model selection and dataset diversity for learning relevant disease features.

EfficientNetB0 also demonstrated strong numerical performance, achieving 99.67% across all metrics for both LD and ELD. However, Grad-CAM visualizations indicate that EfficientNetB0 frequently concentrated on dominant blight pixels (Fig. 3), potentially reducing sensitivity to smaller or less prominent blicht pixels. Nonetheless, its overall high precision and recall indicate that it is highly reliable for aggregate detection tasks.

The custom CNN exhibited a marked decline in performance when transitioning from LD to ELD, with accuracy decreasing from 87.67% to 77.33% and comparable reductions in precision, recall, and F1-score. This decrease underscores the model's limited generalization capacity and sensitivity to dataset variability. The reduced performance likely reflects reliance on specific or spurious features, including background regions. Grad-CAM visualizations supported this observation, showing scattered and inconsistent attention across the entire image, indicating a risk of focusing on irrelevant artifacts (Fig. 3).

These findings suggest MobileNetV3 as the most suitable model for detecting blight on potato leaves in smallholder farming contexts, effectively mitigating dataset bias while maintaining both interpretability and computational efficiency.

Table 1. Overall performance of the CNN-based models for automatic detection of potato leaf health conditions under different data configurations. Metrics were computed on test subset. LD: Localized dataset; ELD: Extended-localized dataset.

Architecture	Accuracy [%]		Precision [%]		Recall [%]		F1-Score [%]	
	LD	ELD	LD	ELD	LD	ELD	LD	ELD
BlightNet	87.67	77.33	87.85	77.26	87.67	77.33	87.61	77.14
EfficientNetB0	99.67	99.67	99.67	99.67	99.67	99.67	99.67	99.67
MobileNetV3	**100.00**	**98.67**	**100.00**	**98.67**	**100.00**	**98.67**	**100.00**	**98.67**

CNN-based models have been proposed for plant disease detection and diagnosis, including potato leaf disease identification, using images of healthy and diseased leaves [2], where high classification accuracy has been reported. In contrast, the present study focuses on model robustness using data from native Andean potato varieties, aiming to balance predictive accuracy with attention-based interpretability. While authors in [18] demonstrated the effectiveness of EfficientNet and MobileNet architectures for generic plant disease classification and highlighted the efficiency of EfficientNet using Grad-CAM visualizations, our work extends this approach by incorporating data augmentation with additional distractor images that closely resemble the localized dataset. This strategy addresses data scarcity and allows for a systematic evaluation of attention distribution under increased dataset variability. Previous research [19] has highlighted the prevalence of shortcut learning in plant disease datasets. Our findings are consistent with these observations, providing empirical evidence that lightweight

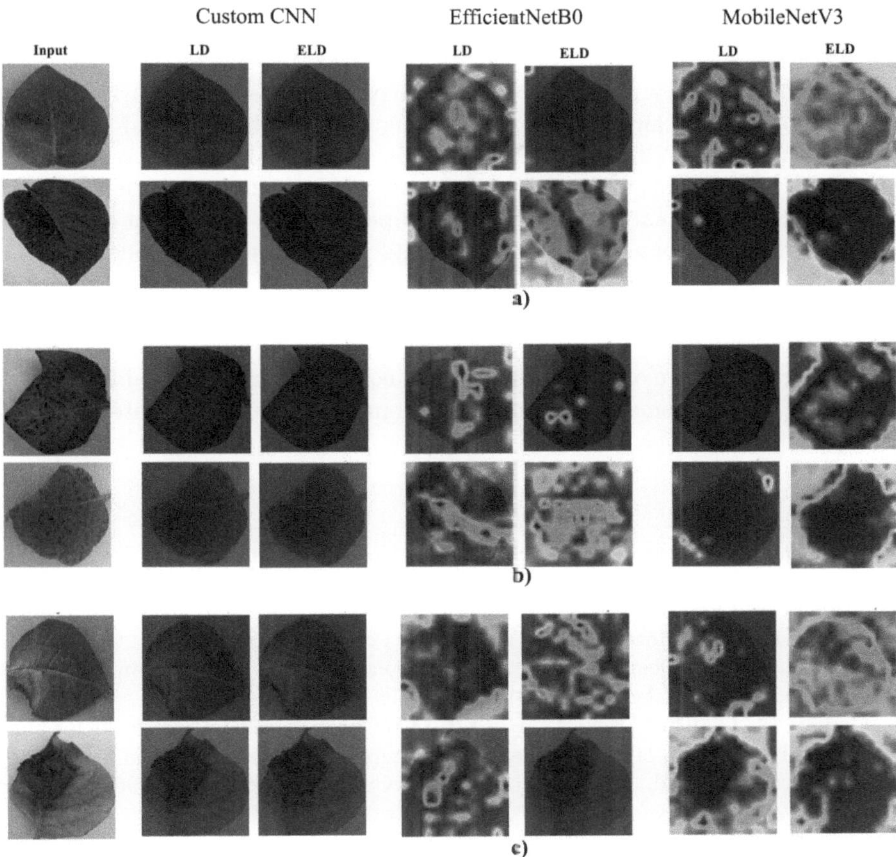

Fig. 3. Examples of the visual comparison of the attention map given by CNN-based architectures for automated detection of potato leaf health conditions: a) healthy; b) early blight; and c) late blight. Grad-CAM technique [17] was used to visualize the attention maps during inference, highlighting the regions that influenced the model's decision. Images represent examples of the test set used in this study.

architectures such as MobileNetV3, when trained on localized data, can mitigate background bias more effectively than heavier models.

The dataset, although localized and extended, remains limited in size and geographic scope. Seasonal variations, severe occlusions, and extreme illumination conditions in natural environments were not captured. Moreover, this study focuses on the presence of blight disease (early and late) rather than on quantifying disease severity. Therefore, further research addressing these limitations is needed to enable direct applicability for precise treatment recommendations.

4   Conclusion

This study presented a computer vision framework for detecting Early and Late Blight in native Andean potato varieties using localized datasets and lightweight CNN architectures. While MobileNetV3 achieved optimal accuracy on the localized dataset and slightly reduced performance under increased dataset variability, attention-based analysis demonstrated superior focus on relevant leaf regions and reduced background bias. These results underscore that model selection should consider not only numerical accuracy but also robustness and interpretability. By demonstrating effective disease detection using limited and underrepresented data, the proposed approach contributes to addressing data scarcity and supports the development of accessible, equitable, and deployable precision agriculture tools for smallholder and underrepresented farming contexts.

References

1. Food and Agriculture Organization of the United Nations. International Year of the Potato 2008: New light on a hidden treasure: An end-of-year review. Food and Agriculture Organization of the United Nations, Rome, Italy, 2009. FAO end-of-year review of the International Year of the Potato 2008
2. Ferentinos, K.P.: Deep learning models for plant disease detection and diagnosis. Comput. Electron. Agric. **145**, 311–318 (2018)
3. Caluña, G., Guachi-Guachi, L., Brito, R.: Convolutional neural networks for automatic classification of diseased leaves: the impact of dataset size and fine-tuning. In: Gervasi, O., et al. (eds.) ICCSA 2020. LNCS, vol. 12249, pp. 951–966. Springer, Cham (2020). https://doi.org/10.1007/978-3-030-58799-4_68
4. Raki, H., et al.: Crop classification using deep learning: a quick comparative study of modern approaches. In: International Conference on Applied Informatics, pp. 31–44. Springer, Cham (2022)
5. Kumar, S., Chaudhary, V., Chandra, S.K.: Plant disease detection using CNN. Turkish J. Comput. Math. Educ. **12**(12), 2106–2112 (2021)
6. Biswas, S., Saha, I., Deb, A.: Plant disease identification using a novel time-effective CNN architecture. Multimed. Tools Appl. **83**(35), 82199–82221 (2024)
7. Mondal, A., Chatterjee, A., Avazov, N.: A hybrid CNN-transformer model with adaptive activation function for potato leaf disease classification. Scientific Reports (2026)
8. Verma, A., Koundal, D., Jain, S., Doegar, A., Ranjan, R.: uvanet: a deep learning framework for precise detection of potato leaf diseases in sustainable agricultural production. Potato Research, pp. 1–30 (2025)
9. Trivedi, A.K., Mahajan, T., Maheshwari, T., Mehta, R., Tiwari, S.: Leveraging feature fusion ensemble of vgg16 and resnet-50 for automated potato leaf abnormality detection in precision agriculture. Soft. Comput. **29**(4), 2263–2277 (2025)
10. Howard, A.G.: Mobilenets: efficient convolutional neural networks for mobile vision applications. arXiv preprint arXiv:1704.04861 (2017)
11. Tan, M., Le, Q.: Efficientnet: rethinking model scaling for convolutional neural networks. In: International Conference on Machine Learning, pp. 6105–6114. PMLR (2019)

12. Nazir, T., Iqbal, M.M., Jabbar, S., Hussain, A., Albathan, M.: Efficientpnet–an optimized and efficient deep learning approach for classifying disease of potato plant leaves. Agriculture **13**(4), 841 (2023)
13. Sangar, G., Rajasekar, V.: Potato leaf disease classification using pre trained deep learning techniques -a comparative analysis. In: 2024 5th International Conference for Emerging Technology (INCET), pp. 1–6 (2024)
14. Putra, M.A.: Potato leaf disease dataset (2020). https://www.kaggle.com/datasets/muhammadardiputra/potato-leaf-disease-dataset. Kaggle dataset. Accessed Jan 2026
15. Jais, I.K.M., Ismail, A.R.: Adam optimization algorithm for wide and deep neural network. Knowl. Eng. Data Sci. **2**(1), 10 (2019)
16. Koonce, B.: Mobilenetv3. In: Convolutional Neural Networks with Swift for Tensorflow: Image Recognition and Dataset Categorization, pp. 125–144. Springer, Cham (2021)
17. Selvaraju, R.R., Cogswell, M., Das, A., Vedantam, R., Parikh, D., Batra, D.: Grad-CAM: visual explanations from deep networks via gradient-based localization. In: Proceedings of the IEEE International Conference on Computer Vision, pp. 618–626 (2017)
18. Bui, T., Hanh, H., Van Manh, N.-V.: Nguyen: Enhancing the performance of transferred efficientnet models in leaf image-based plant disease classification. J. Plant Dis. Prot. **129**(3), 623–634 (2022)
19. Noyan, M.A.: Uncovering bias in the plantvillage dataset. arXiv preprint arXiv:2206.04374 (2022)

"Crisp and Fuzzy Intelligent Systems (CFIS)"

From Adversarial Attacks to Demonstrations for Robust NLP Systems

Natalia Madrueño[(✉)] , Óscar Soto-Sánchez , Daniel Palacios-Alonso ,
Alberto Fernández-Isabel , and Isaac Martín de Diego

Escuela Técnica Superior de Ingeniería Informática, Universidad Rey Juan Carlos,
C/ Tulipán S/N, 28933 Móstoles, Spain
`{natalia.madrueno,oscar.soto,daniel.palacios,alberto.fernandez.isabel,`
`isaac.martin}@urjc.es`

Abstract. Once deployed in production Natural Language Processing
(NLP) models may receive adversarial inputs that lead to erroneous
or unintended predictions. These inputs contain textual perturbations
that may appear benign to humans but cause models to fail. An effective defense for improving robustness against such textual data without requiring model retraining is adversarial purification. The approach
transforms input text to mitigate the influence of adversarial perturbations before they reach the end prediction models. To this end, this
paper introduces a novel adversarial purification method for textual data
using Large Language Models (LLMs). Specifically, the proposed method
leverages decoder-based LLMs and their in-context learning capabilities to guide the transformation of input text. First, a set of adversarially perturbed examples is automatically generated from a collection
of benign texts. These benign-adversarial pairs are then used as few-
shot demonstrations within an LLM instruction prompt to guide the
transformation of new input texts and reduce the impact of adversarial
perturbations. Experiments were conducted to assess the effectiveness
of the proposed method and demonstrated an advantage over several
well-known LLM-based defense approaches. Specifically, the proposed
method demonstrates robustness improvement by up to 10% relative to
the best zero-shot purification defenses. It corrects many previously misclassified adversarial examples while preserving benign accuracy. Overall,
the proposed approach paves the way for safer NLP systems in real-world
deployments.

Keywords: Adversarial Purification · Adversarial Defense ·
Adversarial Example · Large Language Model · In-context Learning ·
Few-shot Learning

1 Introduction

Organizations often possess vast volumes of textual data that are infeasible to
analyze manually. In this context, Artificial Intelligence (AI) and NLP models

J. M. Ferrández Vicente et al. (Eds.): IWINAC 2026, LNCS 16575, pp. 403–412, 2026.
https://doi.org/10.1007/978-3-032-27317-8_38

and techniques facilitate the automated processing of such information [17,25]. They enable automated analysis of human language and support the extraction of knowledge from unstructured data [16].

Once in a production environment, these models may receive inputs whose characteristics differ from those observed during training [7]. Such distributional shifts can reduce prediction quality and increase the likelihood of producing unreliable outputs [22].

Automatically generated adversarial examples are among the most harmful inputs models can receive. They can induce misclassification by introducing small perturbations into benign text while preserving its meaning from a human perspective [13,26]. They also resemble perturbations that can naturally occur in production, such as transcription errors or poorly written human text [23].

Consequently, mitigating the impact of such perturbations is essential. Robustness to adversarial perturbations is often addressed through training-time defenses, such as adversarial training [1]. However, retraining is often impractical, especially for recent Large Language Models (LLMs). In this scenario, adversarial purification is an effective alternative [5,20]. It transforms input text to enhance robustness without requiring access to the model training pipeline.

This paper presents a novel adversarial purification method that improves robustness at inference time. It acts as a preprocessing step that reduces the impact of harmful perturbations before they reach downstream NLP models. Unlike prior work that relies on LLMs with zero-shot prompting [5,20], the proposed approach uses few-shot demonstrations. They guide the transformation of harmful adversarial inputs back into a benign form.

Specifically, the proposed method consists of an adversarial generator and a few-shot purifier. First, the adversarial generator creates adversarially perturbed examples from a set of benign texts. Then, these adversarial-benign pairs are introduced as few-shot demonstrations to an LLM acting as a purifier. They guide the transformation of new inputs into a benign version that better aligns with those expected by downstream prediction models.

The advantage of the proposed method lies in leveraging the text generation and in-context learning capabilities of recent LLMs for adversarial purification. By using adversarial-benign pairs as few-shot demonstrations, robustness to adversarial perturbations is improved at inference time while preserving performance on benign text.

Experiments were conducted to assess the validity of the proposal on two binary sentiment classification datasets. Benign sentences and their adversarially perturbed counterparts were analyzed, with each sentence labeled according to its positive or negative sentiment. Multiple LLMs were used both as purifiers and as end classification models. They transformed their own inputs before producing a final prediction.

The rest of the paper is organized as follows. Section 2 reviews related work. Section 3 describes the proposed adversarial purification method. Section 4 presents the experiments conducted to validate the proposal and examines their results. Finally, Sect. 5 concludes and outlines future work.

2   Related Work

NLP models deployed in production can receive unexpected inputs that harm prediction quality [7]. One of the most harmful cases is adversarial examples, which contain subtle perturbations introduced to deceive target models while remaining similar to the original text from a human perspective [13,26]. For this reason, robustness to such perturbations is commonly studied. Popular approaches include generating adversarial attacks and defense mechanisms that mitigate their impact.

The specific strategy most suitable for generating adversarial examples depends on the level of knowledge an attacker has regarding a victim model [4,21]. In white-box attacks, attackers have access to the internals of target models [8,29]. In black-box attacks, attackers cannot access these model internals [9,27]. To mitigate the impact of such attacks, adversarial training is a widely used strategy [1,2]. It trains models on adversarial examples to improve their robustness. Nevertheless, doing so is not always feasible. In that scenario, adversarial purification emerges as an effective approach at inference time [6]. It modifies input text to mitigate the impact of harmful perturbations, producing a new benign version that preserves semantic meaning.

Early text adversarial purification methods relied on dictionary-based and heuristic corrections to restore corrupted tokens [30]. However, they were limited to narrow perturbation types and often struggled with more complex perturbations. Later, neural approaches broadened coverage, spanning from recurrent models that infer intended tokens to BERT-based methods that use the masked language modeling objective to progressively recover corrupted sequences [10,24]. Nevertheless, these methods can still fail under attacks at multiple text levels. More recent work uses LLMs with zero-shot prompting for adversarial purification. These include basic prompting, explicit prompt rules that address common attacks [14,20], and sometimes prior detection of harmful inputs [5]. However, these approaches do not fully exploit the capabilities of recent LLMs.

In particular, recent LLMs have shown exceptional out-of-the-box capabilities in several downstream tasks. These include strong text generation and in-context learning capabilities [12,28]. Through prompt and context engineering, they can effectively address multiple NLP tasks [18,19]. Although they have demonstrated strong performance in zero-shot settings, where no training examples are provided [11], they typically improve their prediction capabilities in few-shot settings. In this scenario, a small number of in-context examples is included in the LLM instruction prompt [3]. Consequently, these improvements through few-shot prompting could be used to enhance adversarial purification.

This paper proposes a new adversarial purification method that acts as a preprocessing component. It leverages recent LLMs and their in-context learning capabilities. LLMs learn adversarial purification patterns by providing a sequence of adversarial-benign text pairs in a few-shot prompt. These demonstration pairs illustrate how adversarial inputs can be transformed back into a benign form, mitigating the impact of harmful perturbations. It strengthens the predictions of deployed NLP models without requiring their modification.

3   Proposed Method

This section presents the key elements of the proposed adversarial purification method. The core strength of the proposal lies in the use of adversarial-benign textual pairs as few-shot demonstrations within an LLM instruction prompt. These demonstrations illustrate how new input texts can be transformed to mitigate the impact of potentially harmful perturbations.

The proposed method consists of two components. First, an *adversarial generator* produces a sequence of adversarial-benign demonstration pairs by applying adversarial attacks to a set of benign texts. Then, a *few-shot purifier* embeds these demonstrations into a few-shot prompt to produce purified versions of new incoming texts. Such purified versions serve as the new inputs for end prediction models. Figure 1 provides an overview of this adversarial purification process.

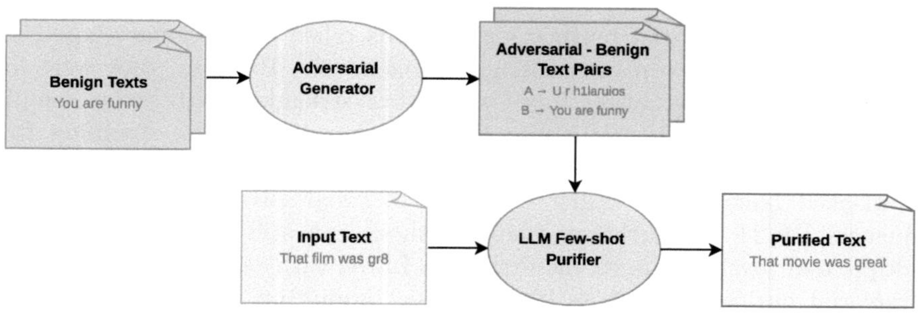

Fig. 1. Workflow of the proposed text adversarial purification method.

3.1   Adversarial Generator

The proposed adversarial purification method starts by using an adversarial generator. It constructs demonstrations that show how adversarially perturbed inputs should be transformed back into benign forms. The objective is to generate a sequence of adversarial-benign pairs that illustrate the purification pattern.

To do this, a sequence of benign texts $B = (X_1, X_2, \ldots, X_n)$ is first selected. For each benign text $X_i \in B$, an adversarial attack is applied, generating an adversarially perturbed version X_i' from X_i. The perturbations introduced in X_i' are designed to deceive downstream prediction models while remaining semantically similar to X_i from a human perspective.

By generating an adversarial counterpart for each $X_i \in B$, the sequence of adversarial-benign pairs $D = ((X_1', X_1), (X_2', X_2), \ldots, (X_n', X_n))$ is established as the set of demonstrations that illustrate the purification pattern. Each pair (X'_i, X_i) encodes a transformation from an adversarial text to a benign form. This demonstration set D is then fed into a few-shot purifier to reduce the impact of harmful textual perturbations during inference.

3.2 Few-Shot Purifier

Once the sequence of adversarial-benign demonstration pairs has been generated, it is incorporated within a few-shot purifier. An LLM uses a few-shot prompt to systematically transform input texts into purified versions that mitigate the impact of harmful inputs.

For this purpose, a purification prompt is constructed by concatenating LLM instructions I, a sequence of demonstration pairs D, and the new input text Q. In this few-shot prompt, each pair $(X'_i, X_i) \in D$ provides an explicit example of how an adversarially perturbed text should be transformed into a benign counterpart. Then, at inference time, an LLM acts as a purifier for potentially harmful inputs. It receives the composed prompt and generates a purified version of the incoming text, denoted as Q'. This output text Q' is expected to reduce or mitigate the effects of harmful perturbations while maintaining the intended semantic meaning of the original input text Q.

Consequently, this few-shot purifier acts as a plug-and-play preprocessing step that can be integrated into deployed pipelines. It improves robustness to harmful perturbations while avoiding the need to modify underlying models.

4 Experiments

4.1 Datasets

Two datasets were used to assess the quality of the evaluated adversarial purification approaches. Specifically, sentence-level binary sentiment classification was used, classifying each sentence by its positive or negative sentiment.

The first dataset is composed of the original sentences from the Binary Stanford Sentiment Treebank (SST-2) validation split. It is referred to as the *Original* dataset and consists of 872 single-sentence movie reviews extracted from Rotten Tomatoes[1]. The second dataset is composed of an adversarially perturbed version of this *Original* dataset. Starting from its benign sentences, at most one successful adversarial example was generated for the instruct versions of Gemma 2 9B, Llama 3.1 8B, Qwen 2.5 7B, and Yi 1.5 6B. The attack settings presented in [15] were used to generate these examples, and its setup was replicated exactly.

The adversarial examples produced for these LLMs incorporate perturbations generated with Generative Pre-Trained Transformer 4 Omni Mini (GPT4o mini) at the character-, word-, and sentence-level. They include paraphrases, typos, synonyms, and word insertions, as well as all pairwise, triple, and full combinations of these four perturbation types. For each instruct model and original

---

[1] https://www.rottentomatoes.com/.

sentence, an attack configuration was selected at random. The resulting dataset is referred to as the *Adversarial* dataset.

The *Original* and *Adversarial* datasets were divided into training and test splits. The training splits contain the first 500 original sentences of the SST-2 dataset and their adversarially perturbed versions. They were used to select the demonstrations for the few-shot purification proposal. Similarly, the test splits contain the remaining 372 original sentences and their adversarial counterparts.

4.2 Model Setup

Instruct versions of Gemma 2 9B, Llama 3.1 8B, Qwen 2.5 7B, and Yi 1.5 6B were used both as LLM-based purifiers and as end binary sentiment classification models. Note that these models were also previously used to generate the adversarial examples in the *Adversarial* dataset. For each model, purification is first applied as a preprocessing step that mitigates the effect of harmful perturbations. Then, the same instruct model predicts the sentiment label from its own purified text.

Multiple LLM-based purification strategies were tested with these instruct models. Previous state-of-the-art approaches rely on zero-shot prompting, including manual design of LLM instructions and metaprompting with teacher models. They include a straightforward instruction prompt for transforming text, denoted as *Baseline*, as well as guidelines for common adversarial attacks, referred to as *Guidelines*. Likewise, prompts generated via metaprompting using OpenAI o3 and Gemini 2.5 Pro are also considered for baseline comparison. They are denoted as *OpenAI o3* and *Gemini 2.5 Pro*.

Conversely, the proposed purification strategy relies on few-shot prompting. For each $n \in 2, 5, 10, 20, 50$, n demonstration pairs were sampled without replacement from the training split and appended to the Baseline prompt. To capture sampling-related variability, 10 different prompt variants were created for each n. These proposed few-shot purification prompts are denoted as *Random*.

4.3 Evaluation Metrics

The evaluation focuses on classification accuracy, calculated for the final sentiment label predicted after purification. It measures how well purifiers mitigate the impact of adversarial perturbations while preserving correct predictions on benign inputs. For the proposed few-shot purification prompts, results are reported using the prompt mean accuracy and standard deviation (Standard Deviation (SD)), as multiple prompt variants were considered.

Table 1 shows the accuracy of end sentiment classification models after applying the evaluated purifiers on the *Original* dataset. The best zero-shot and few-shot purifiers achieve accuracy values close to those obtained without purification. This suggests that they largely preserve the original prediction accuracy. Specifically, Guidelines keeps accuracy high, with scores of 0.93, 0.93, 0.93, and 0.92 across the four end classification models. However, other evaluated zero-shot prompts reduce accuracy for certain models. Baseline, OpenAI o3, and

Gemini 2.5 Pro yield values of 0.89, 0.88, and 0.89 on the instruct version of Yi 1.5 6B, indicating a drop in classification accuracy. Meanwhile, the strongest configurations of the proposed few-shot purification strategy consistently retain high accuracy scores. They achieve accuracy values of 0.93 ± 0.01, 0.94 ± 0.01, 0.93 ± 0.01, and 0.92 ± 0.00 across the evaluated classification models.

Likewise, Table 1 reports accuracy on the *Adversarial* dataset. In this scenario, the proposed approach yields markedly better predictive performance. Among zero-shot purifiers, Baseline reaches accuracy values of 0.74, 0.72, 0.74, and 0.72. This matches or surpasses Guidelines and metaprompted alternatives, whose top scores are 0.73, 0.71, 0.74, and 0.73. OpenAI o3 and Gemini 2.5 Pro tend to lag behind handcrafted zero-shot prompts. For instance, for the instruct version of Llama 3.1 8B, their peak accuracy values are 0.68 and 0.64, respectively. In comparison, the proposed few-shot purification method achieves markedly higher accuracy. Its best configuration obtains values of 0.81 ± 0.01, 0.79 ± 0.01, 0.80 ± 0.01, and 0.78 ± 0.01 across the four end classification models.

Table 1. Accuracy (mean $\pm$ SD) of the adversarial purification strategies

	Type	Purification	Gemma	Llama	Qwen	Yi
Original	zero-shot	Baseline	**0.93**	0.93	**0.94**	0.89
		Guidelines	**0.93**	0.93	0.93	0.92
		OpenAI o3	0.89	0.91	0.92	0.88
		Gemini 2.5 Pro	0.91	0.89	0.93	0.89
	few-shot	Random (n = 2)	0.93 ± 0.01	0.90 ± 0.09	0.93 ± 0.01	0.91 ± 0.01
		Random (n = 5)	0.92 ± 0.01	0.93 ± 0.00	0.93 ± 0.01	0.92 ± 0.01
		Random (n = 10)	0.92 ± 0.01	**0.94 ± 0.01**	0.93 ± 0.01	0.92 ± 0.00
		Random (n = 20)	0.92 ± 0.01	0.93 ± 0.01	0.93 ± 0.01	0.92 ± 0.00
		Random (n = 50)	0.91 ± 0.01	0.93 ± 0.01	0.93 ± 0.01	0.92 ± 0.01
	–	None	**0.93**	0.93	0.93	**0.93**
Adversarial	zero-shot	Baseline	0.74	0.72	0.74	0.72
		Guidelines	0.73	0.71	0.74	0.73
		OpenAI o3	0.72	0.68	0.74	0.70
		Gemini 2.5 Pro	0.67	0.64	0.68	0.62
	few-shot	Random (n = 2)	0.76 ± 0.02	0.76 ± 0.02	0.76 ± 0.01	0.75 ± 0.01
		Random (n = 5)	0.78 ± 0.01	0.77 ± 0.02	0.77 ± 0.01	0.76 ± 0.01
		Random (n = 10)	0.79 ± 0.01	0.78 ± 0.01	0.78 ± 0.01	0.77 ± 0.01
		Random (n = 20)	**0.81 ± 0.01**	**0.79 ± 0.01**	0.79 ± 0.01	**0.78 ± 0.01**
		Random (n = 50)	**0.81 ± 0.01**	**0.79 ± 0.01**	**0.80 ± 0.01**	**0.78 ± 0.01**
	–	None	0.58	0.49	0.55	0.51

Consequently, the proposed purification strategy is shown to be an effective defense against adversarial inputs. It surpasses previous state-of-the-art purification approaches that rely on zero-shot prompts provided to an LLM. By transforming input texts to mitigate the impact of harmful perturbations, it correctly classifies adversarially perturbed examples that were previously misclassified, while maintaining correct classifications for benign inputs. Even though the best zero-shot approaches also preserves accuracy on the *Original* dataset, the proposed method yields substantially larger accuracy gains on the *Adversarial* dataset.

5   Conclusions

This paper presents a new adversarial purification method that enhances robustness against adversarial inputs at inference time. It acts as a preprocessing step that transforms textual inputs back into a benign form before they are processed by downstream prediction models.

The proposed strategy comprises an adversarial generator and a few-shot purifier based on LLMs. It produces pairs of benign and adversarially perturbed examples that serve as demonstrations for the adversarial purification process. These demonstration pairs guide the transformations produced by LLMs. They reduce the impact of harmful perturbations while preserving the intended original semantic meaning.

The proposed purification approach has been empirically validated on two binary sentiment classification datasets involving single sentences. The experiments evaluate classification accuracy on both benign inputs and adversarially perturbed variants. Results show that incorporating few-shot demonstrations within the purification prompt notably increases robustness against adversarial perturbations without compromising predictions on benign texts. Moreover, the proposal demonstrates superior performance compared to previously analyzed state-of-the-art purification strategies relying on LLMs.

These findings indicate that the proposed adversarial purification strategy can be applied to reduce the impact of harmful inputs in deployed models. This could include real-time sentiment analysis and content moderation pipelines. By adding adversarial purification as a preprocessing step before inference, the robustness of downstream NLP models can be increased without requiring model retraining.

Future work could refine the selection of few-shot demonstrations, including harmful examples that naturally occur in real-world deployments. Retrieval-Augmented Generation (RAG) techniques could also be used to dynamically retrieve demonstrations that are most relevant to each incoming input. Finally, the proposed method could be evaluated across a wider range of NLP tasks and models. This includes downstream tasks such as machine translation and question answering, as well as scenarios in which the LLM used for purification differs from the end prediction model.

Acknowledgments. This work has been partially funded by the XMIDAS project (PID2021-122640OB-I00) and the project Explainable Approach for Detecting Advanced Facial Attacks for Security Enforcement (PID2021-124176OB-I00).

References

1. Alsmadi, I., et al.: Adversarial machine learning in text processing: a literature survey. IEEE Access **10**, 17043–17077 (2022). https://doi.org/10.1109/ACCESS.2022.3146405
2. Bai, T., Luo, J., Zhao, J., Wen, B., Wang, Q.: Recent advances in adversarial training for adversarial robustness. In: 30th International Joint Conference on Artificial Intelligence, pp. 4312–4321 (2021). https://doi.org/10.24963/ijcai.2021/591
3. Brown, T., et al.: Language models are few-shot learners. In: 34th International Conference on Neural Information Processing Systems, vol. 33, pp. 1877–1901 (2020). https://doi.org/10.5555/3495724.3495883
4. Chakraborty, A., Alam, M., Dey, V., Chattopadhyay, A., Mukhopadhyay, D.: A survey on adversarial attacks and defences. CAAI Trans. Intell. Technol. **6**(1), 25–45 (2021). https://doi.org/10.1049/cit2.12028
5. Chen, M., He, G., Wu, J.: ZDDR: a zero-shot defender for adversarial samples detection and restoration. IEEE Access **12**, 39081–39094 (2024). https://doi.org/10.1109/ACCESS.2024.3356568
6. Costa, J.C., Roxo, T., Proença, H., Inacio, P.R.M.: How deep learning sees the world: a survey on adversarial attacks & defenses. IEEE Access **12**, 61113–61136 (2024). https://doi.org/10.1109/ACCESS.2024.3395118
7. Gupta, K.D., Dasgupta, D.: Adversarial attacks and defenses for deployed AI models. IT Prof. **24**(4), 37–41 (2022). https://doi.org/10.1109/MITP.2022.3180330
8. Han, X., Zhang, Y., Wang, W., Wang, B.: Text adversarial attacks and defenses: issues, taxonomy, and perspectives. Secur. Commun. Netw. **2022**(1), 6458488 (2022). https://doi.org/10.1155/2022/6458488
9. Hu, X., et al.: Fasttextdodger: decision-based adversarial attack against black-box NLP models with extremely high efficiency. IEEE Trans. Inf. Forensics Secur. **19**, 2398–2411 (2024). https://doi.org/10.1109/TIFS.2024.3350376
10. Keller, Y., Mackensen, J., Eger, S.: BERT-defense: a probabilistic model based on BERT to combat cognitively inspired orthographic adversarial attacks. In: Findings of the Association for Computational Linguistics, pp. 1616–1629 (2021). https://doi.org/10.18653/v1/2021.findings-acl.141
11. Kojima, T., Gu, S.S., Reid, M., Matsuo, Y., Iwasawa, Y.: Large language models are zero-shot reasoners. In: 36th International Conference on Neural Information Processing Systems, vol. 35, pp. 22199–22213 (2022). https://doi.org/10.48550/arXiv.2205.11916
12. Li, J., et al.: Fundamental capabilities and applications of large language models: a survey. ACM Comput. Surv. (2025). https://doi.org/10.1145/3735632
13. Li, Y., Cheng, M., Hsieh, C.J., Lee, T.C.M.: A review of adversarial attack and defense for classification methods. Am. Stat. **76**(4), 329–345 (2022). https://doi.org/10.1080/00031305.2021.2006781
14. Lin, G., Tanaka, T., Zhao, Q.: Large language model sentinel: LLM agent for adversarial purification (2024). https://doi.org/10.48550/arXiv.2405.20770
15. Madrueño, N., Fernández-Isabel, A., Fernández, R.R., Martín de Diego, I.: Advancing text adversarial example generation using large language models. Knowl.-Based Syst. **329**, 114361 (2025). https://doi.org/10.1016/j.knosys.2025.114361
16. Mah, P.M., Skalna, I., Muzam, J.: Natural language processing and artificial intelligence for enterprise management in the era of industry 4.0. Appl. Sci. **12**(18) (2022). https://doi.org/10.3390/app12189207
17. Mariani, M.M., Machado, I., Magrelli, V., Dwivedi, Y.K.: Artificial intelligence in innovation research: a systematic review, conceptual framework, and future

research directions. Technovation **122**(1), 102623 (2023). https://doi.org/10.1016/j.technovation.2022.102623

18. Marvin, G., Hellen, N., Jjingo, D., Nakatumba-Nabende, J.: Prompt engineering in large language models. In: Jacob, I.J., Piramuthu, S., Falkowski-Gilski, P. (eds.) ICDICI 2023. Algorithms for Intelligent Systems, pp. 387–402. Springer, Singapore (2023). https://doi.org/10.1007/978-981-99-7962-2_30

19. Mei, L., et al.: A survey of context engineering for large language models (2025). https://doi.org/10.48550/arXiv.2507.13334

20. Moraffah, R., Khandelwal, S., Bhattacharjee, A., Liu, H.: Adversarial text purification: a large language model approach for defense. In: Yang, D.N., Xie, X., Tseng, V.S., Pei, J., Huang, JW., Lin, J.CW. (eds) PAKDD 2024. LNCS, vol. 14649, pp. 65–77. Springer, Singapore. h (2024). https://doi.org/10.1007/978-981-97-2262-4_6

21. Pelekis, S., Koutroubas, T., Blika, A., Berdelis, A., Karakolis, E., Ntanos, C., Spiliotis, E., Askounis, D.: Adversarial machine learning: a review of methods, tools, and critical industry sectors. Artif. Intell. Rev. **58**(8), 226 (2025). https://doi.org/10.1007/s10462-025-11147-4

22. Pelosi, D., Cacciagrano, D., Piangerelli, M.: Explainability and interpretability in concept and data drift: a systematic literature review. Algorithms **18**(7) (2025). https://doi.org/10.3390/a18070443

23. Qiu, S., Liu, Q., Zhou, S., Huang, W.: Adversarial attack and defense technologies in natural language processing: a survey. Neurocomputing **492**, 278–307 (2022). https://doi.org/10.1016/j.neucom.2022.04.020

24. Sakaguchi, K., Duh, K., Post, M., Van Durme, B.: Robsut wrod reocginiton via semi-character recurrent neural network. In: AAAI Conference on Artificial Intelligence, vol. 31, no. 1 (2017). https://doi.org/10.1609/aaai.v31i1.10970

25. Suryadevara, C.K.: Transforming business operations: harnessing artificial intelligence and machine learning in the enterprise. Int. J. Creat. Res. Thoughts **5**(2), 931–938 (2023)

26. Waghela, H., Sen, J., Rakshit, S.: Saliency attention and semantic similarity-driven adversarial perturbation. In: Nanda, S.J., Yadav, R.P., Gandomi, A.H., Saraswat, M. (eds) ICDSA 2024. LNNS, vol 1237, pp. 431–444. Springer, Singapore (2025). https://doi.org/10.1007/978-981-96-1185-0_33

27. Xu, X., et al.: An LLM can fool itself: a prompt-based adversarial attack. In: 12th International Conference on Learning Representations (2024). https://openreview.net/forum?id=VVgGbB9TNV

28. Yenduri, G., et al.: GPT (generative pre-trained transformer)—a comprehensive review on enabling technologies, potential applications, emerging challenges, and future directions. IEEE Access **12**(1), 54608–54649 (2024). https://doi.org/10.1109/ACCESS.2024.3389497

29. Zeng, G., et al.: OpenAttack: an open-source textual adversarial attack toolkit. In: 59th Annual Meeting of the Association for Computational Linguistics and the 11th International Joint Conference on Natural Language Processing: System Demonstrations, pp. 363–371 (2021). https://doi.org/10.18653/v1/2021.acl-demo.43

30. Zukarnain, N., Abbas, B.S., Wayan, S., Trisetyarso, A., Kang, C.H.: Spelling checker algorithm methods for many languages. In: 2019 International Conference on Information Management and Technology, vol. 1, pp. 198–201 (2019). https://doi.org/10.1109/ICIMTech.2019.8843801

Patch-Based Explainability for CNN Classification Models

Guido Bologna$^{(\boxtimes)}$ [iD], Jean-Marc Boutay, Damian Boquete, Deniz Köprülü, and Ludovic Pfeiffer

University of Applied Sciences and Arts of Western Switzerland, Rue de la Prairie 4, 1202 Geneva, Switzerland
Guido.Bologna@hesge.ch

Abstract. This work presents a rule-based approach for explaining the predictions of neural network classifiers, with a particular focus on Convolutional Neural Networks (CNNs). The FidexGlo algorithm was used to explain CNN decisions not at the pixel level but through patch-based conditions, where each antecedent expresses the average intensity of an image patch. Experiments were conducted on three standard benchmarks of grayscale images: MNIST, Fashion-MNIST, and EMNIST (letters). A ResNet-50 architecture was fine-tuned for each dataset. FidexGlo was then applied to the average values of image patches to extract rules closely aligned with the CNN's behaviour. Qualitative visualisations demonstrate that the extracted rules identify meaningful discriminative regions—such as holes in digits, or shape boundaries. Overall, the study shows that our explainability method enables efficient, interpretable rule extraction from CNNs using patch-based explanations, offering a human-understandable view of deep model decisions. FidexGlo is available at https://github.com/Jean-Marc-B/dimlpfidex_Hepia.

Keywords: Model Explanation · Rule Extraction · Convolutional Neural Networks

1 Introduction

In the previous IWINAC-24 congress we presented the FidexGlo algorithm that generates propositional rules from several models [3]. Currently, XAI (explainable AI) is an important research domain [1], with an increasing number of works. FidexGlo was initially applied to small tabular datasets, and has since been extended to Convolutional Neural Networks (CNNs) [2]. The key idea behind FidexGlo is the precise identification of discriminating axis-parallel hyperplanes. This is achieved by imposing structural constraints on the neural model such as sparse connectivity and quantisation by a staircase activation function that approximates a sigmoid. These mechanisms enable the network to translate its learned decision boundaries into interpretable propositional rules.

Very few works have tried to generate propositional rules from deep models, as popular explainability techniques are feature relevance methods and methods

J. M. Ferrández Vicente et al. (Eds.): IWINAC 2026, LNCS 16575, pp. 413–422, 2026.
https://doi.org/10.1007/978-3-032-27317-8_39

that produce heatmaps, such as GradCam [8], which highlight general regions for classification. Feature relevance methods, such as Shapley values [5] and LIME [7], assess the contribution of each input feature to a specific prediction.

In this work, we used FidexGlo to interpret CNN responses. Rather than obtaining rules involving image pixels, our aim was to explore the possibility of obtaining rule conditions that express the presence of patches. A patch corresponds to a small square. Using patches rather than pixels means fewer inputs have to be provided to the rule extraction algorithm, resulting in faster execution time. We applied FidexGlo to three benchmark classification problems, illustrating the characteristics of the generated rules with several explanatory examples. In the following sections we present the used models and algorithms, then the experiments, followed by a conclusion.

2   Models and Methods

2.1   Axis-Parallel Hyperplanes

Creating propositional rules requires the localisation of axis-parallel hyperplanes. We achieve this through the use of sparse connectivity and quantisation. Specifically, for a Multi Layer Perceptron (MLP), let us denote $x^{(0)}$ as a vector for the input layer. For layer $l+1$ $(l \geq 0)$, the activation values $x^{(l+1)}$ of the neurons are

$$x^{(l+1)} = \sigma(W^{(l)}x^{(l)} + b^{(l)}). \tag{1}$$

$W^{(l)}$ is a matrix of weight parameters between two successive layers l and $l+1$; $b^{(l)}$ is a vector called the bias and $\sigma(x)$ is a sigmoid activation function:

$$\sigma(x) = \frac{1}{1 + \exp(-x)}. \tag{2}$$

When $W^{(0)}$ is a diagonal matrix and the activation function in the first hidden layer is the step function $t(x)$ given below, we obtain axis-parallel hyperplanes; one for each input neuron [4].

$$t(x) = \begin{cases} 1 \text{ if } x > 0; \\ 0 \text{ otherwise.} \end{cases} \tag{3}$$

To train an MLP efficiently using axis-parallel hyperplanes, the step function is replaced with a staircase activation function which approximates a sigmoid. Each step of this function creates a potential axis-parallel hyperplane [2]. Creating axis-parallel hyperplanes is achieved in CNNs by adding a layer with sparse connectivity (via a diagonal matrix of weights) and by quantisation [2]. This layer is frozen during training, as its weights depend on the averages and standard deviations of the training data for each input neuron [2].

2.2   FidexGlo Rule Extraction Algorithm

Two algorithms are central to the methodology: Fidex, a local rule-extraction method, and FidexGlo, its global extension that generates a ruleset covering all training samples [2]. FidexGlo applies Fidex to each training instance, yielding an initial set of rules, and then selects a minimal subset that covers the training dataset. In this work, FidexGlo is used to explain CNN decisions not at the pixel level but through patch-based conditions, where each antecedent expresses the presence or absence of an image patch. This reduces the input dimension and allows the rules to capture semantically meaningful local patterns.

Fidex constructs a local rule through an iterative process that maximizes fidelity, defined as the agreement between the model's and the rule's predictions. At each iteration, it determines the hyperplane that involves the highest increase of fidelity. The execution time can be accelerated by considering two dropout parameters: p and q. Essentially, p determines at each step the proportion of input variables that will not be taken into account. The parameter q is similar, but concerning excluded hyperplanes. Fidex computational complexity grows linearly with the dimensionality of the problem, the number of training samples, the maximum number of antecedents per rule, and the number of steps in the staircase function.

3   Experiments

Our purpose was to generate rules involving patches that explain CNN responses. We applied the FidexGlo rule extraction algorithm to three classification problems in the public domain. The corresponding datasets are:

- MNIST hand-written digits (60000 samples for training and 10000 for testing with ten classes).
- Fashion-MNIST (60000 samples for training and 10000 for testing with ten classes).
- EMNIST hand-written letters (124800 samples for training and 20800 for testing with 26 classes).

All the samples are pictures of size $28 \times 28 (= 784)$ pixels. For all the datasets we fine-tuned the Resnet-50 neural network [6]. Moreover, 10% of the training samples selected randomly were used for early-stopping during the learning phase. The frozen quantisation layer before the Resnet model used a staircase activation function approximating a sigmoid with 200 steps. Finally, at each iteration, our algorithm attempted to maximise fidelity using two dropout parameters: one to exclude variables, and the other to exclude hyperplanes. These parameters were set to 0.8.

In the next Tables the results of the experiments include several features: patch size; explainability ratio; fidelity; prediction accuracy of the rules (denoted as Acc. R. a); prediction accuracy of the rules when rules and model agree (Acc. R. b); number of extracted rules; average number of rule antecedents; and average rule coverage.

The explainability rate is the proportion of samples in the testing dataset for which we can find one or more rules that either all agree on the same class, or include the class given by the model among several rules. Fidelity is calculated on the testing set and is the degree to which the generated rules match the model. Specifically, if there are P samples in the testing set and Q samples for which the classification of the rules corresponds to that of the model, then the fidelity is Q/P. For training samples, the fidelity is 100%. The prediction accuracy of the rules when the rules and the model agree is the proportion of the testing samples that activate a rule predicting the same class as the model. Finally, average rule coverage represents the mean number of covered samples for each rule.

3.1 MNIST Hand-Written Digits

Table 1 illustrates the results for different patch sizes. Note that the final row shows the average results obtained from ten trials using patches of size 1×1 (i.e. single pixels). The best results are provided with patches of size 4×4 and a stride of two pixels (s2). The explainability rate for the test samples is 94.69%, meaning that just over 5% of the test data has no explanation.

Put simply, almost 95% of the test data can be explained using the rules extracted from the training set. Any remaining samples that cannot be explained can always be explained by running the Fidex algorithm. For the best performance, the fidelity on the test set was 97.03% (the fidelity on the training set was set to 100%). Additionally, the accuracy when rules agreed with the model was 99.75%. We obtained the fewest rules (5125), the fewest conditions per rule (an average of 5.28) and the highest average coverage per rule (94.0).

Table 1. Rule extraction results on the hand-written digits involving different sizes of patches. The fine-tuned ResNet model achieved a predictive accuracy of 99.46%.

Patch Size	Expl.	Fid.	Acc. R. (a)	Acc. R. (b)	Nb. R.	Avg. Nb. Ant.	Avg. Cov.
2×2	93.75	96.29	95.95	99.69	5673	6.58	87.8
4×4	92.79	95.60	95.28	99.71	6595	6.90	69.9
4×4 (s2)	**94.69**	**97.03**	**96.69**	**99.75**	**5125**	**5.28**	**94.0**
5×5 (s3)	93.93	96.77	96.52	99.73	5560	5.34	84.9
1×1 [2]	—	96.10	96.40	99.62	6064	5.6	—

Figure 1 illustrates, on the left, a centroid representing 1013 samples that activate a rule of class "0". This centroid calculated by summing all the pixels and dividing by the number of samples covered. On the right, the same centroid representation is shown with the addition of coloured squares (i.e. patches). Green squares represent rule antecedents given as $a_i > t_i$, where a_i is a rule antecedent and t_i is a constant. Similarly, red squares indicate rule antecedents given as $a_j \leq t_j$. Here, a_i represents the average pixel intensity of a patch.

This intensity is represented in the pictures by different degrees of greenness or redness. Interestingly, three dark red patches of size 4×4 appear in the hole in the number, and two green patches appear in the light area on the left. Nine samples activating the previous rule are shown in Fig. 2.

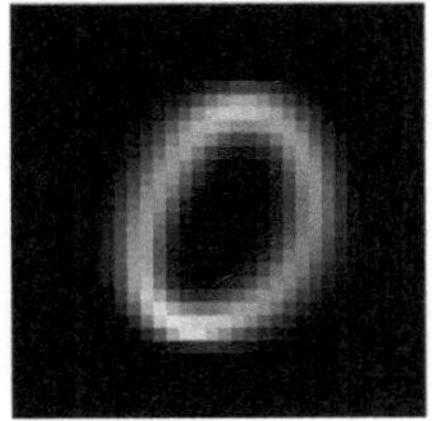
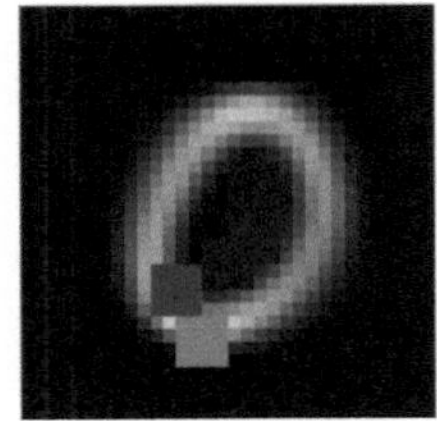

Fig. 1. Centroid of the samples covered by a rule of class "0" (left); same centroid with the addition of coloured squares that represent rule antecedents (right).

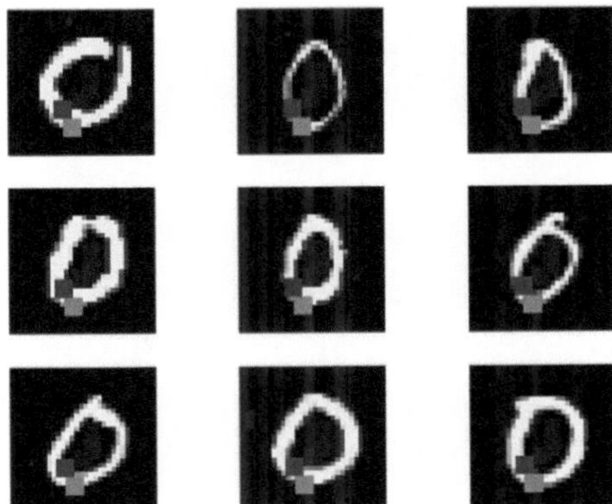

Fig. 2. Examples of samples that activate a rule of class "0".

Figure 3 illustrates, on the left, a centroid representing 162 samples that activate a rule of class "8". The coloured squares on the right represent the rule conditions (two red patches and five green patches). Note a dark red patch in the upper part of the hole, which clearly reflects a characteristic of this digit. We can also see a light green patch in the centre of the digit. In the lower part of this digit, we see a dark green patch and another dark red patch on the right, which delimit this centroid. Figure 4 shows nine samples activating this rule.

Figure 5 illustrates, on the left, a centroid representing 383 samples that activate a rule of class "3". To the right of this figure, there is a green patch in the centre, near three red patches. This reflects a key feature of the digit. Additionally, there are green patches in the upper and lower parts of the digit. Finally, Fig. 6 shows nine samples activating this rule.

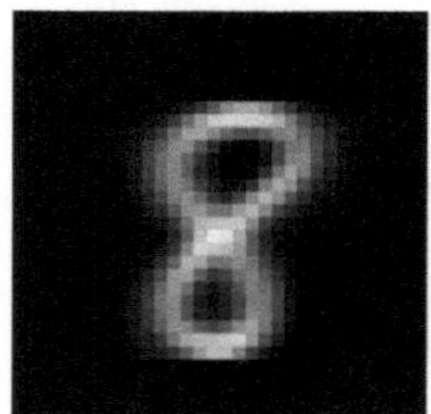 

Fig. 3. Centroid of the samples covered by a rule of class "8" (left); same centroid with the addition of coloured squares representing rule antecedents (right).

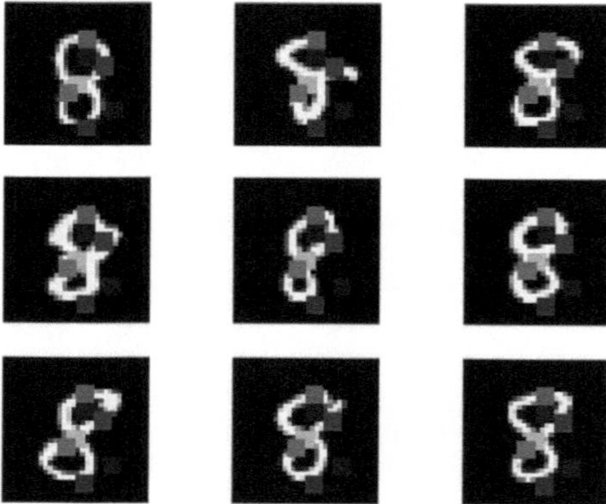

Fig. 4. Examples of samples that activate a rule of class "8".

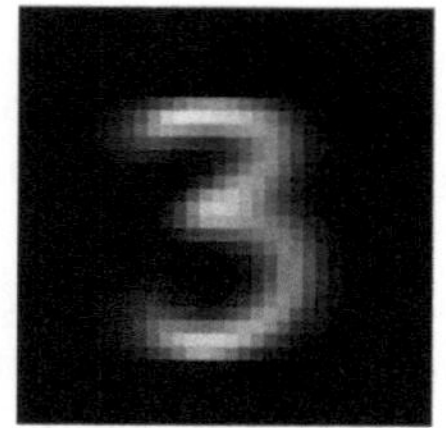 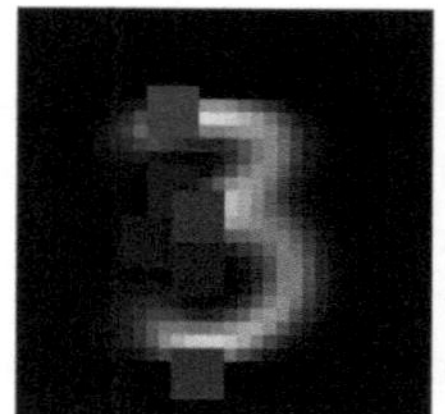

Fig. 5. Centroid of the samples covered by a rule of class "3" (left); same centroid with the addition of coloured squares representing rule antecedents (right).

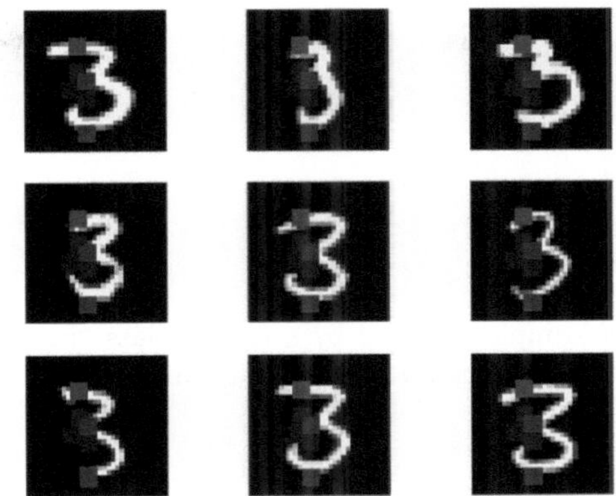

Fig. 6. Examples of samples that activate a rule of class "3".

3.2 Fashion-MNIST Dataset

Table 2 illustrates the results obtained with the Fashion-MNIST dataset. For these experiments, we limited ourselves to patches measuring 4×4 pixels and a stride of two pixels. Almost 90% of the test data can be explained using the rules extracted from the training set. Furthermore, the fidelity on the test set was 92.99% and the prediction accuracy when rules agreed with the model was 95.91%. Finally, FidexGlo generated 9,693 rules, each with an average of 5.5 antecedents, and with an average coverage of 52.3 samples.

Table 2. Rule extraction results on the Fashion-MNIST dataset with patches of size 4×4 and a stride of two pixels. The fine-tuned ResNet model achieved a predictive accuracy of 92.79%.

Patch Size	Expl.	Fid.	Acc. R. (a)	Acc. R. (b)	Nb. R.	Avg. Nb. Ant.	Avg. Cov.
4×4 (s2)	89.88	92.99	88.94	95 91	9693	5.5	52.3

Figure 7 illustrates, on the left, a centroid representing 810 samples that activate a rule of class "bag". On the right, we can see two green patches marking the main part of the bag (one patch at the bottom and the other at the top). Then, on the handle of the bag, we have a green patch, whereas in the dark area we have a red patch that is delimited by the handle. Finally, Fig. 8 shows nine samples activating this rule.

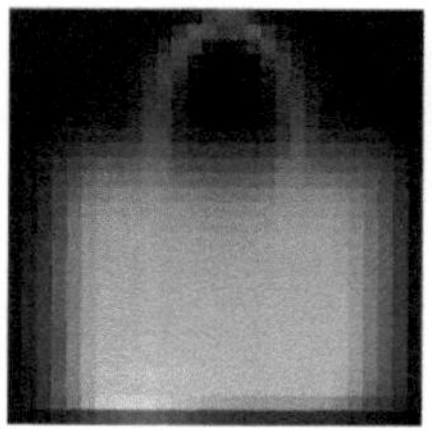 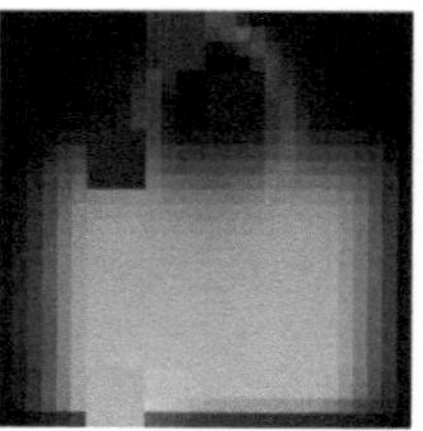

Fig. 7. Centroid of the samples covered by a rule of class "bag" (left); same centroid with the addition of coloured squares representing rule antecedents (right).

3.3   Letters-MNIST Dataset

The results obtained with the Letters-MNIST dataset are illustrated in Table 3. Here the explainability rate was lower, with a value of 81.58%. However, the accuracy of the rules was 96.43% when the activated rules agreed with the model. Using FidexGlo, we generated 30358 rules, each with an average of 6.1 conditions and an average coverage of 19.9 samples. Therefore, compared to previous datasets, we obtained more rules and less coverage. This was probably due to the increased number of classes (26).

Table 3. Rule extraction results on the Letter-MNIST dataset with patches of size 4×4 and a stride of two pixels. The fine-tuned ResNet model achieved a predictive accuracy of 94.77%.

Patch Size	Expl.	Fid.	Acc. R. (a)	Acc. R. (b)	Nb. R.	Avg. Nb. Ant.	Avg. Cov.
4×4 (s2)	81.58	89.37	85.89	96.43	30358	6.1	19.9

Figure 9 illustrates a centroid representing 114 samples that activate a rule of class "X". The patches of the rule are shown on the right. In the centre, we can see a green patch, with another slightly above it and two more in the branches of the "X" at the bottom. Furthermore, a red patch appears in the dark area between the two upper branches of the "X" at the top.

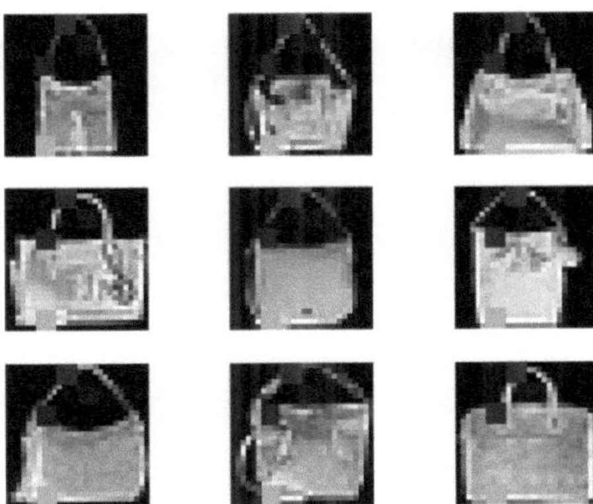

Fig. 8. Examples of samples that activate a rule of class "bag".

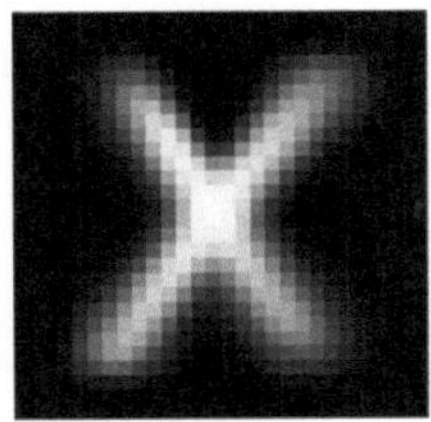

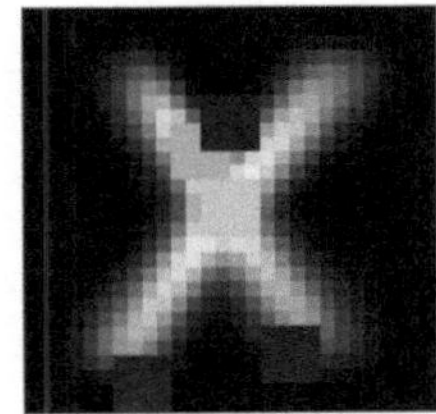

Fig. 9. Centroid of the samples covered by a rule of class "X" (left); same centroid with the addition of coloured squares representing rule antecedents (right).

4 Conclusion

In this study, we proposed a method for extracting propositional rules based on pixel patches. The extracted rules for classifying handwritten digits had similar characteristics to those obtained using the pixel-based approach in terms of number, fidelity and accuracy of rules. On hand-written digits, the best configuration used 4×4 patches with stride 2, achieving 94.7% explainability, 97.0% fidelity, and 96.7% rule accuracy. A significant advantage of this new approach was reduced computation time, since grouping new variables into pixel groups reduced the number of inputs provided to FidexGlo.

We obtained rules that are very easy for humans to understand, allowing us to identify the regions of the image that the model uses to differentiate between classes. Thus, by observing the rules, we could be able in the future to find biases in the datasets and improve the training. Our method can be used in many fields and for many datasets, enhancing model interpretability and enabling further optimisation.

Acknowledgments. This work was conducted in the context of the Horizon Europe project PRE-ACT (Prediction of Radiotherapy side effects using explainable AI for patient communication and treatment modification). It was supported by the European Commission through the Horizon Europe Program (Grant Agreement number 101057746), by the Swiss State Secretariat or Education, Research and Innovation (SERI) under contract number 2200058, and by the UK government (Innovate UK application number 10061955).

Competing Interests. The authors have no competing interests to declare that are relevant to the content of this article.

References

1. Adadi, A., Berrada, M.: Peeking inside the black-box: a survey on explainable artificial intelligence (XAI). IEEE Access **6**, 52138–52160 (2018). https://doi.org/10.1109/ACCESS.2018.2870052
2. Bologna, G., Boutay, J.M., Boquete, D., Leblanc, Q., Köprülü, D., Pfeiffer, L.: Fidex and fidexglo: from local explanations to global explanations of deep models. Algorithms **18**(3) (2025). https://doi.org/10.3390/a18030120. https://www.mdpi.com/1999-4893/18/3/120
3. Bologna, G., Boutay, J.M., Leblanc, Q., Boquete, D.: Fidex: an algorithm for the explainability of ensembles and SVMs. In: International Work-Conference on the Interplay Between Natural and Artificial Computation, pp. 378–388. Springer, Cham (2024). https://doi.org/10.1007/978-3-031-61137-7_35
4. Bologna, G., Pellegrini, C.: Constraining the MLP power of expression to facilitate symbolic rule extraction. In: 1998 IEEE International Joint Conference on Neural Networks Proceedings. IEEE World Congress on Computational Intelligence (Cat. No. 98CH36227), vol. 1, pp. 146–151. IEEE (1998). https://doi.org/10.1109/IJCNN.1998.682252
5. Chen, H., Lundberg, S., Lee, S.I.: Explaining models by propagating Shapley values of local components. In: Explainable AI in Healthcare and Medicine: Building a Culture of Transparency and Accountability, pp. 261–270 (2021). https://doi.org/10.1007/978-3-030-53352-6_24
6. He, K., Zhang, X., Ren, S., Sun, J.: Deep residual learning for image recognition. In: Proceedings of the IEEE Conference on Computer Vision and Pattern Recognition (CVPR), pp. 770–778 (2016)
7. Ribeiro, M.T., Singh, S., Guestrin, C.: Why should I trust you?: explaining the predictions of any classifier. In: Proceedings of the 22nd ACM SIGKDD International Conference on Knowledge Discovery and Data Mining, pp. 1135–1144. ACM (2016)
8. Selvaraju, R.R., Cogswell, M., Das, A., Vedantam, R., Parikh, D., Batra, D.: Gradcam: visual explanations from deep networks via gradient-based localization. In: Proceedings of the IEEE International Conference on Computer Vision, pp. 618–626 (2017). https://doi.org/10.1109/ICCV.2017.74

Hybrid SAT-Based Decision Trees

Marco Perrotta[ID], Guido Sciavicco[✉][ID], and Simona Tenasini[ID]

Department of Mathematics and Computer Science, University of Ferrara,
Ferrara, Italy
{marco.perrotta,guido.sciavicco,simona.tenasini}@edu.unife.it

Abstract. While the research in machine learning tends towards sub-symbolic methods, symbolic ones are still capturing the interest of certain parts of the community. Tree-based methods for learning patterns from data, in particular, are still celebrated as the ideal compromise between performance, computational effort, and explainability of the results. Decision trees have been around for over forty years, and their properties are well-known. The fact that learning optimal decision trees is an NP-complete problem pushed researchers and practitioners towards the use of greedy, sub-optimal learning algorithms, which are today the gold standard. Motivated by the recent advances in the field of SAT-solvers, in the past few years several SAT-based encodings of the problem of learning an optimal decision tree from a dataset have been proposed; however, the experiments on such implementations suggest that the practical usefulness of SAT-based decision tree learning is yet to be demonstrated. With the goal of filling the gap between the two approaches, in this paper we propose, design, implement and test an hybrid decision tree learning algorithm. We embed our open-source solution in an end-to-end framework for learning and reasoning, and we report on the results of several experiments, which seem to suggest that learning decision trees with an hybrid algorithm allows one to obtain noticeably smaller – still well-performing – trees than those obtained with a standard algorithm, while being able to deal with datasets with tens of thousands instances in reasonable time.

Keywords: Greedy decision tree learning · SAT-based decision tree learning · Hybrid decision tree learning

1 Introduction

Despite the fact that the modern approach to artificial intelligence is mostly sub-symbolic, symbolic techniques are still considered to have an important role. For tabular data, for example, recent results indicate that symbolic ensembles still outperform neural networks in simple tasks such as classification [7,13,17].

Focusing on classification, the simplest and most fundamental symbolic learning model is the *Decision Tree* (*DT*), the idea of which dates back to [5]. DTs were later brought to existence in several famous algorithms such as AID, THAID,

© The Author(s), under exclusive license to Springer Nature Switzerland AG 2026
J. M. Ferrández Vicente et al. (Eds.): IWINAC 2026, LNCS 16575, pp. 423–432, 2026.
https://doi.org/10.1007/978-3-032-27317-8_40

CHAID and finally CART, introduced in 1984. The modern version of DTs was proposed by Quinlan [12], with his algorithm universally known as *C4.5*; this is the basis of currently available implementations in well-known suits and frameworks, such as *SciKit-learn*[1] (in Python) and *MLJ*[2] (in Julia). Even today, decision trees are considered fundamental in many ways; for example, they are the cornerstone of modern ensemble systems such as *Random Forests* (*RF*s) [2] or *Boosted Trees* (*BT*s) [3,6] and they are used as sandbox for exploring more-than-propositional extensions of symbolic learning [4].

Decision trees are a very natural technique for extracting patterns from tabular data. However, producing small decision trees is a computationally hard problem; in particular, producing the smallest tree that classifies perfectly a given training dataset is a NP-hard problem [8,14]. This justifies the popularity of greedy, sub-optimal algorithms such as the already mentioned C4.5, which do not guarantee the minimality of the extracted trees.

Since the smallest tree problem is also NP-complete, recently a certain amount of effort has been directed towards encoding the problem as a SAT problem, therefore allowing the use of SAT solvers to this end. The first serious attempt at encoding decision trees as a SAT problem is probably due to Bessiere et al. [1]; their solution, however, has been shown to scale only for small-size examples and only for decision trees of fixed structure and size. Narodytska et al. [10] proposed a different encoding which improved on the previous limits; nevertheless, the resulting SAT-based trees can only handle binary features, and when facing bigger datasets (i.e., with a few hundreds instances), their solution too becomes computationally expensive, forcing the authors to employ sampling techniques that produce, in fact, only approximate trees. Schidler and Szeide's proposal [15] promised to overcome some of the obstacles that previous attempts had found, being able to handle several thousands instances. On the other hand, Schidler and Szeide's is not a decision tree learning method, but, rather, a SAT-based technique to refine and reduce a previously learnt tree, which is a different problem; moreover, this solution too is limited to binary data and involves non-trivial manipulations of trees, making it not immediate to implement. The most advanced SAT encoding for decision trees was proposed by Shati et al. [16]; in their work, the authors show that their solution handles binary and non-binary features and scales relatively well to non-toy datasets, although they still limit their experiments to datasets with less than two thousand instances.

It appears clear that the take-home message is that SAT-based learning is hard; even today, it is generally believed that learning optimal decision trees is impractical except for very small examples; to make the situation worse, industrial-level implementations of SAT-based learning of decision trees face non-trivial solver/machine-learning integration problems that result into a *de-facto* unavailability of SAT-based learning algorithms in popular learning suites.

Towards tackling the above problems, in this paper we consider a hybrid approach to DT learning. In particular, we propose a hybrid version of C4.5

---

[1] https://github.com/scikit-learn/scikit-learn.
[2] https://github.com/JuliaAI/MLJ.jl.

temp.	press.	pain	rash	survived?
37.5	115	3	1	0
39.5	120	2	0	1
41.2	110	4	1	0
. . .	. . .	. . .	. . .	. . .

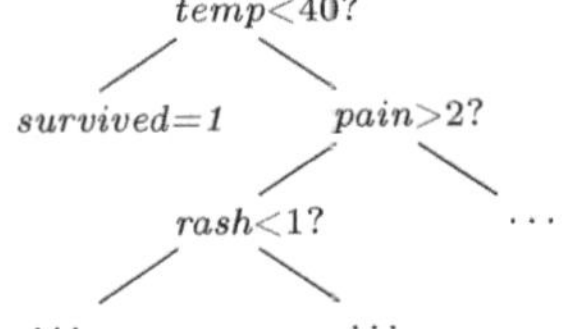

Fig. 1. An example of tabular dataset (left) and decision tree (right).

(*HybridSATC4.5*) based on a very simple idea: learn a greedy decision tree until
the number of instances falls below a threshold, then complete the learning with
a SAT-based tree. This strategy turns out to be very versatile: thresholds can
be fixed, dynamic, or even learnt on-the-fly, and the SAT-based module can
be seen as a parameter of the algorithm, allowing experimenting with different
solutions without modifying the structure. However, it requires a seamless integration of the learning algorithm and a SAT-solver, which is far from trivial. Our
solution is designed as part of the package $SOLE^3$, which is a logic and learning
framework that integrates and extends MLJ. Our experiments include a range of
public datasets, ranging from a few hundreds to several thousands instances and
beyond, and indicate that hybrid trees can learn quite accurate and relatively
small trees, with a very limited computational effort; the main goal of hybrid
trees is to be almost as performing as greedy trees but with using less decisions,
while remaining computationally affordable during the learning phase.

Hybrid decision trees open up a wide set of possibilities; to mention but two,
hybrid trees can now be used as atomic constructs in ensembles and boosted
trees, and can also be dynamically monitored during the learning phase to identify the most problematic areas of the training dataset, offering the user relevant
information beyond a well-performing model.

2 Preliminaries

We consider a set of *features* $\mathcal{F} = \{f_1, \ldots, f_K\}$, all of which are assumed to be in
$\mathbb{R}$; non-real attributes can always be encoded into real numbers with standard
techniques. A *supervised dataset for binary classification* is a set of *instances* (or
samples) $\mathcal{E} = \{e_1, \ldots, e_n\}$ partitioned in two *classes* $\mathcal{E}^+$ (*positive* samples) and
$\mathcal{E}^-$ (*negative* samples). Non-binary classification problems can be encoded as
binary ones. An example of dataset can be seen in Fig. 1, left. The *binary perfect
classification* problem *from the dataset* $\mathcal{E}$ is the problem of learning a function
$\tau : \mathbb{R}^n \to \{0, 1\}$ such that given a tuple $(x_1 \ldots, x_n)$, if $(x_1, \ldots, x_n, y) \in \mathcal{E}$ for
some y, then $y = f(x_1, \ldots, x_n)$; such a function τ is usually called *classifier*; a
binary decision tree is a possible classifier. A *binary decision tree* on the features
$\mathcal{F}$ is a full binary tree $\tau = (V, E)$, where V is the set of vertexes, E is the set of
edges, and $V_l \subseteq V$ is the set of leaves, associated with an *edge labeling function*

---

[3] https://github.com/aclai-lab/Sole.jl.

$e : E \rightarrow \{(f_i \bowtie r) \mid f \in \mathcal{F}, r \in \mathbb{R}, \bowtie \in <, \geq\}$ such that, for every pair of edges $(u, v), (u, v')$ it is the case that $e(u, v) = f < r$ if and only if $e(u, v') = f \geq r$, and a *leaf labeling function* $l : V_l \rightarrow \{0, 1\}$. Given a binary decision tree τ, identified by its root, we denote $left(\tau)$ (resp., $right(\tau)$) its left (resp., right) child. Given a decision tree τ and an edge (u, v) in it, and given an instance $e = (x_1, \ldots, x_n)$, we say that e *satisfies* $l(u, v) = (f_i \bowtie r)$, and we denote it by $e \models l(u, v)$, if and only if it holds that $x_i \bowtie r$. The class assigned by a binary decision tree τ to an instance $e = (x_1, \ldots, x_n)$ is denoted by $\tau(e)$, and it is computed as follows:

$$\tau(e) = \begin{cases} l(\tau) & \text{if } \tau \text{ is a leaf,} \\ left(\tau)(e) & \text{if } \tau \text{ is not a leaf and } e \models (e, left(\tau)), \\ right(\tau)(e) & \text{if } \tau \text{ is not a leaf and } e \models (e, right(\tau)). \end{cases}$$

An example of decision tree can be seen in Fig. 1, right.

The main purpose of learning a classifier from a dataset $\mathcal{E}$ is to apply it to a unsupervised different dataset $\mathcal{E}'$; in some cases, it makes sense to extract information from the classifiers, such as (total or partial) rules, or other characterizations of the concepts (i.e., the class) in $\mathcal{E}$. In any case, the value of such an information is proportional to the ability of the classifier to correctly label previously unseen instances; it is well-known that shorter trees tend to generalize better. Unfortunately, finding a decision tree that minimizes the average number of tests necessary to classify an example is NP-hard [14]. Thus, all practical approaches for learning decision trees are heuristic; the most famous one, which is paradigmatic of essentially all existing implementations, is the algorithm *C4.5* [12].

Motivated by the performances of modern SAT-solvers, learning optimal (in the sense of number of nodes and/or height) decision trees has been posed as a SAT problem in recent work [1,10,15]. The resulting encodings proved to have different drawbacks, from being able to handle only binary features to revealing themselves not performing enough, in terms of learning time, to be of any practical use. Among them, Shati et al. [16] proposal stands out as the most promising one. Briefly, the structure of the encoding is based on the following (sets of) propositional letter(s): $[a_{t,j}]$, representing whether feature j is chosen for the split at the branching node t, $[s_{i,t}]$, representing whether the instance i is directed towards the left child, if it passes through branching node t, $[z_{i,t}]$, representing whether the instance i ends up at leaf node t, and $[g_{t,c}]$, represents whether the label c is assigned to leaf node t. In the language expressed by such propositional letters, the decision problem *does a decision tree smaller than a given height h exists that represents a given dataset?* is formulated using the clauses in Table 1. In this way, the problem of extracting the minimum decision tree that classifies perfectly a given training dataset can be solved by attempting the previous one with increasing height until a solution is found (Fig. 2).

Table 1. General SAT Encoding Clauses (Numerical and Categorical Features)

	Clause	Condition
(1)	$(\neg a_{t,j},\ \neg a_{t,j'})$	$t \in \mathcal{T}_B,\ j \neq j' \in F$
(2)	$\left(\bigvee_{j \in F} a_{t,j} \right)$	$t \in \mathcal{T}_B$
(3)	$(\neg a_{t,j},\ s_{i,t},\ \neg s_{i',t})$	$t \in \mathcal{T}_B,\ j \in F,\ (i,i') \in O_j(X)$
(4)	$(\neg a_{t,j},\ \neg s_{i,t},\ s_{i',t})$	$t \in \mathcal{T}_B,\ j \in F,\ (i,i') \in O_j(X),\ x_i[j] = x_{i'}[j]$
(5)	$(\neg z_{i,t},\ s_{i,t'})$	$t \in \mathcal{T}_L,\ x_i \in X,\ t' \in A_l(t)$
(6)	$(\neg z_{i,t},\ \neg s_{i,t'})$	$t \in \mathcal{T}_L,\ x_i \in X,\ t' \in A_r(t)$
(7)	$\left(z_{i,t},\ \bigvee_{t' \in A_l(t)} \neg s_{i,t'},\ \bigvee_{t' \in A_r(t)} s_{i,t'} \right)$	$t \in \mathcal{T}_L,\ x_i \in X$
(8)	$(\neg g_{t,c},\ \neg g_{t,c'})$	$t \in \mathcal{T}_L,\ c \neq c' \in C$
(9)	$(\neg a_{t,j},\ s_{\#^1_j,t})$	$t \in \mathcal{T}_B,\ j \in F$
(10)	$(\neg a_{t,j},\ \neg s_{\#^{|X|}_j,t})$	$t \in \mathcal{T}_B,\ j \in F$
(11)	$(\neg z_{i,t},\ g_{t,\gamma(x_i)})$	$t \in \mathcal{T}_L,\ x_i \in X$

Algorithm 1. $HybridSATC4.5()$ for inducing an hybrid decision tree.

Require: dataset D
Require: set of features F
Require: feasibility parameter set Θ
Require: threshold $\theta \in (0,1)$
Ensure: feature tree T with labelled leaves
1: **if** $StoppingCondition(D)$ **then**
2:     **return** $Label(D)$
3: **end if**
4: **if** $Feasible(D, \Theta)$ **then**   ▷ Switch to SAT-based optimal subtree
5:     **return** $SATTree(D, F)$
6: **end if**
7: $S \leftarrow BestSplit(D, F)$
8: split D into subsets D_i according to the literals in S
9: **for** each i **do**
10:     $T_i \leftarrow HybridSATC4.5(D_i, F, \Theta)$
11: **end for**
12: **return** a tree whose root is labelled with S and whose children are T_i

---

3   Hybrid Decision Trees

The idea of hybrid decision trees is motivated by the following observations: first, SAT-based trees optimize the training performances, but this does not always translate to extremely good test performances; second, even with the most modern encoding and using an highly optimized SAT-solver, one cannot hope to use SAT-based learning for real, practical cases.

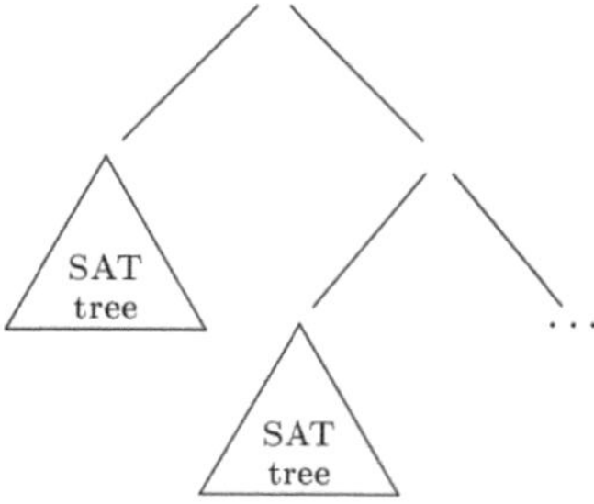

Fig. 2. The general structure of an hybrid tree: when the SAT-based learning becomes feasible, learning switches to SAT-based, and decisions become optimal.

Hybrid tree work in a very simple way: they are essentially greedy trees up to a certain point, and then become SAT-based. A greedy tree is recursively learned by checking a stopping condition (e.g., homogeneity of the dataset, cardinality of the dataset, amount of information that can be gained with a next step is applied), and if the check fails, then an information-based greedy step is applied to obtain a decision and split the dataset in smaller parts, on which the recursive call is performed. Learning an hybrid tree proceeds exactly in the same way, except when the algorithm decides that a new call is necessary, a feasibility condition on the current dataset is checked: if it the condition is met, then a SAT-based tree learning procedure is launched; otherwise, the algorithm simply applies a greedy step as in the standard case, obtaining smaller datasets on which the recursive call is performed.

A high-level pseudo-code of HybridSATC4.5 is shown in Algorithm 1; it obviously closely follows a standard version of C4.5. In the code, *StoppingCondition()* checks if the current dataset can be turned into a leaf, and, in that case, decides which label to assign with *Label()*. *Feasible()* checks the feasibility condition which allows the algorithm to decide whether to switch to the SAT-based learning strategy or to continue the learning with greedy step. In the former case, *SATTree()* is invoked. In the latter case, S is assigned to a decision via *BestSplit()*, and the recursive calls are performed.

Interestingly, *Feasible()* can be implemented in several ways, which correspond to different learning strategies with different computational effort/result tradeoffs. Three basic strategies can be immediately outlined, respectively based on the dataset absolute cardinality, on the remaining fraction of dataset, and on the allowed timeout. In the first case, we may decide that *SATTree()* is invoked as soon as the number of instances falls below a predetermined constant (e.g., 100 instances); while a low number of instances alone does not guarantee that *SATTree()* will perform well, it is usually a good proxy. In the second case, the algorithm bases the decision to switch on the fraction (in terms of number of instances) of the original dataset to which the current one corresponds (e.g., 0.5% of the original instances); in this case too there is no guarantee that the performances will be acceptable, but unlike the previous case the computational effort is strongly linked to the size of the problem. In the third case, the algorithm allocates a predetermined amount of time to a SAT-based learning attempt (e.g., 15 min), as well a maximal height to the SAT-based tree that is searched for at any given moment, and if the SAT problem cannot be solved within that time threshold, a smaller one will be attempted later; while this strategy has the most undeterminable behaviour, it guarantees that a certain experiment will not take more that a certain amount of time.

4   Experiments

We considered 31 datasets, all publicly available from the UCI webpage. We have chosen datasets spanning from 4 to 54 features and up to 17000 instances, and grouped them by size in terms of number of instances: size XS (extra small) contains datasets up to 200 instances; size S (small), between 200 and 1000; size M (medium), between 1000 and 2000; size L (large), between 8000 and 10000; finally, size XL (extra large), over 10000 (in our case, up to 20000).

We executed all algorithms in 5-fold cross-validation mode, and the presented results are the average of 5 individual executions; in every individual execution, we learned a decision tree on the training section (80%) and tested it on the remaining instances (20%). For each dataset and fold, we first ran the standard C4.5 algorithm, to obtain a benchmark result in terms of both test accuracy and tree height. Then, we ran the pure SAT-based approach; having set a timeout of 15 min per fold, the SAT-based learning algorithm was able to converge within the timeout only a handful of times. Finally, we ran three different parametrizations of HybridC4.5, at different degrees of aggressiveness, driven by the threshold used for the function $Feasible()$; for different groups of datasets, the parametrizations were different, to maximize the chance of termination within the set timeout. In particular, in this experiment we set HybridC4.5 to switch to SAT-based learning when the recursive call takes place on a portion of the original dataset determined by a parameter $p \in (0, 1] \subset \mathbb{R}$. The purpose of this experiment was to prove that HybridC4.5 is able to deal with real datasets, while still offering some of the benefits of SAT-based learning. In our experiments, $SATtree()$ implements Shati et al. [16]'s SAT-based decision tree learning algorithm. Our implementation, that employs the Microsoft SAT-solver Z3 [9], is embedded in the end-to-end, open-source learning and reasoning framework SOLE.

All results are in Table 2, ordered by group size from top to bottom; the average performances of each model are expressed using F1-score, to overcome potential unbalancing-related issues. Several considerations emerge immediately. First, in the group XS all algorithms were able to finish within the allocated time. The problems represented by datasets in this group are very simple, and this is witnessed by the fact that greedy trees and SAT-based ones differ only slightly in length. However, some differences emerge already in this group, as in *breast-tissue* and *breast-cancer-wis*, with a difference in depth of over 50–60%. Learning SAT-based trees in these cases is already very computationally

Table 2. Experiment's results. Performances are expressed in terms of F1-score. ∗: not all folds terminated within the timeout; †: no fold terminated within the timeout; -: elapsed time less than 0.001 s.

Dataset	C4.5			HybridC4.5 p = #2			p = #3			p = #4			SAT		
	F1	Time	Depth	F1	Time	Depth	F1	Time	Depth	F1	Time	Depth	F1	Time	Depth
balloons1	1.000	–	2.0	1.000	–	2.0	1.000	–	2.0	1.000	–	2.0	1.000	000.248	2.0
balloons2	1.000	–	2.0	1.000	–	2.0	1.000	–	2.0	1.000	–	2.0	1.000	000.209	2.0
balloons3	1.000	–	2.0	1.000	–	2.0	1.000	–	2.0	1.000	–	2.0	1.000	000.210	2.0
balloons4	0.747	–	3.2	0.747	000.042	3.2	0.747	001.041	3.2	0.747	000.334	3.2	0.547	000.666	3.0
lung-cancer	0.407	–	3.8	0.499	000.001	3.8	0.499	001.072	3.8	0.440	007.218	3.8	0.414	011.194	3.0
ces-small1	0.550	–	8.4	0.550	000.180	8.4	0.580	000.636	7.6	0.607	001.837	5.8	0.592	004.239	4.0
soybean-small	0.911	–	2.0	0.911	–	2.0	0.911	–	2.0	0.911	000.951	2.0	0.986	003.338	2.0
cervical-cancer-beh.-risk	0.707	–	4.0	0.777	000.032	4.2	0.777	000.055	4.2	0.761	002.178	3.8	0.740	006.713	2.8
immunotherapy	0.648	–	6.8	0.600	000.242	6.8	0.638	001.520	6.0	0.614	002.425	5.4	0.589	012.290	4.0
cryotherapy	0.851	–	6.6	0.873	000.163	6.2	0.898	000.386	5.2	0.885	002.507	4.4	0.816	010.501	3.8
breast-cancer-coimbra	0.717	–	7.4	0.674	000.539	7.4	0.645	002.146	6.6	0.666	008.116	5.6	0.634	014.570	4.0
iris	0.918	–	4.4	0.923	000.135	4.4	0.923	000.104	4.4	0.918	002.418	4.4	0.931	009.840	3.4
divorce	0.975	–	2.6	0.950	000.440	3.0	0.950	000.452	3.0	0.950	003.656	3.0	0.950	016.867	2.0
breast-tissue	0.606	–	8.0	0.601	000.859	7.6	0.641	002.530	7.0	0.528	007.943	5.8	0.579	029.781	4.6
breast-cancer-wis.	0.543	000.002	9.0	0.516	005.588	8.6	0.519	015.635	7.4	0.544	058.592	5.6	0.593	817.615	4.0
Mean	0.782 ±0.172	– ± –	5.200 ±2.809	0.775 ±0.189	000.548 ±1.416	4.773 ±2.488	0.782 ±0.184	001.705 ±3.939	4.427 ±2.085	0.771 ±0.194	006.545 ±14.668	3.920 ±1.500	0.779 ±0.181	060.306 ±195.729	3.162 ±0.901
seeds	0.875	–	6.2	0.900	002.541	5.8	0.900	000.951	5.6	0.900	000.904	5.6	0.893	026.613	4.0
statlog	0.754	000.001	9.4	0.753	015.324	7.2	0.746	018.687	7.2	0.716	019.086	6.6	†	†	†
penguins	0.963	–	5.2	0.962	000.956	5.0	0.962	000.585	5.0	0.959	001.415	4.8	†	†	†
ionosphere	0.880	000.002	8.8	0.873	016.497	8.0	0.850	019.736	7.8	0.845	022.802	7.4	†	†	†
dermatology	0.924	000.001	10.0	0.921	014.118	9.6	0.907	028.054	8.8	0.899	037.703	8.0	†	†	†
house-votes	0.949	–	8.8	0.939	040.118	6.0	0.939	030.514	6.0	0.939	030.545	6.0	†	†	†
*diabets**	0.665	000.002	16.0	0.693	569.099	9.3	0.704	281.061	9.4	0.712	310.999	9.4	†	†	†
tictactoe	0.860	000.001	11.6	0.908	364.520	8.4	0.898	523.663	8.4	†	†	†	†	†	†
Mean	0.816 ±0.135	000.001 ±0.001	11.660 ±5.591	0.869 ±0.089	127.897 ±202.550	7.413 ±1.586	0.863 ±0.086	112.906 ±178.078	7.275 ±1.500	0.853 ±0.094	060.493 ±103.057	6.829 ±1.448	0.893 ±0.000	026.613 ±0.000	4.000 ±0.000
heart	0.997	000.002	9.8	0.997	023.500	8.6	0.997	048.763	8.4	0.997	069.459	7.4	†	†	†
banknote	0.987	000.001	6.4	0.984	003.565	6.0	0.984	002.226	6.0	0.984	006.027	6.0	†	†	†
car	0.947	000.029	12.0	0.924	253.460	11.0	0.900	549.987	10.8	0.901	644.244	10.6	†	†	†
Mean	0.977 ±0.025	000.011 ±0.015	9.400 ±2.286	0.968 ±0.019	093.508 ±128.736	8.533 ±2.082	0.960 ±0.041	200.325 ±284.003	8.400 ±1.960	0.961 ±0.041	239.910 ±338.015	8.000 ±2.160	†	†	†
*beed-bangalore-eeg-epilepsy**	0.882	000.046	32.8	0.886	635.030	32.0	0.874	731.540	30.0	†	†	†	†	†	†
mushroom	1.000	000.006	6.0	1.000	001.169	6.0	1.000	036.730	6.0	1.000	030.660	6.0	†	†	†
occupancy	0.990	000.006	11.8	0.989	014.194	11.0	0.989	011.718	11.0	0.988	020.581	10.2	†	†	†
Mean	0.937 ±0.059	000.019 ±0.020	17.200 ±10.994	0.958 ±0.051	216.798 ±295.783	16.333 ±11.264	0.954 ±0.057	259.996 ±333.588	15.667 ±10.339	0.994 ±0.006	025.620 ±5.040	8.100 ±2.100	†	†	†
dry-bean	0.910	000.107	20.8	0.903	870.780	17.0	†	†	†	†	†	†	†	†	†
occupancy-estimation	0.987	000.089	10.8	0.988	019.158	10.2	0.985	026.594	9.2	0.986	040.038	8.0	†	†	†
Mean	0.948 ±0.004	000.098 ±0.030	15.800 ±1.980	0.945 ±0.404	444.969 ±530.867	13.600 ±3.400	0.985 ±0.000	026.594 ±0.000	9.200 ±0.000	0.986 ±0.000	040.038 ±0.000	8.000 ±0.000	†	†	†

expensive; in the case of *breast-cancer-wis* the average computation time takes over 13 min. Hybrid trees behave exactly as expected: already with the most conservative parametrization, the hybrid tree for *breast-cancer-wis* shows a 5% reduction in size compared with the greedy one, with similar test performance , which becomes around 15% in the middle configuration and around 40% in the most aggressive one, which still takes less than a minute to be learnt, in average. As we move towards harder problems, this behaviour becomes clearer. The S group is characterized by datasets on which SAT-based learning is still possible, but almost never within the set timeout (in fact, the SAT-based procedure was able to terminate in one out of eight cases). On the other hand, the hybrid version terminated its computation in about one minute in average, and less than 10 min in the worst case; as it can be seen, the average depth reduction goes from 30% to 40%, with no relevant performance loss (in fact, performances in the hybrid case are even superior, in average, to those of greedy trees). The remaining groups are characterized by datasets on which no SAT-based learning is possible, either because the computational time is unacceptable, or because the encoding produces too long formulas. As it can be seen, the pattern repeats: hybrid trees are considerably smaller than greedy ones, with improvements up to 20%, as in *dry-bean*, for which trees go from an average depth of 20.8 to an average depth of 17 in the least aggressive hybrid mode (the more aggressive combinations of hybrid mode were already computationally unaffordable for this dataset, indicating the need of a careful fine-tuning), with no test performance loss, and within the set timeout in almost all cases.

As a final observation, it is of notice that SAT-based trees do not always perform better than greedy ones. In fact, studying the behaviour of the hybrid version one realizes that SAT-based learning is beneficial up to some point, after which the performances tend to plateau. This explains why hybrid trees seem to be a convenient compromise.

5   Conclusions

SAT-based decision trees learning algorithms are a class of machine learning algorithms based on the idea of reducing the decision tree learning problem to a SAT problem, and then resort to an efficient SAT-solver. Despite the recent advancement in the field of SAT-solvers, pure SAT-based decision tree learning proved to be infeasible for all practical purposes; while there exist previous attempts to hybrid solutions, such as [15], previous literature does not offer approaches to SAT-solvers aided decision tree learning. In this paper we theorised, designed, implemented, and tested a novel form of hybrid decision trees combining standard greedy learning with SAT-based learning. Our results proved that hybrid learning is possible and is able to learn decision trees from datasets that would not be possibly dealt with a pure SAT-based encoding. By carefully tuning the learning parameters, we were able to extract trees from dataset containing up to several thousands instances. As it turns out, our trees are generally shorter than those learned with the greedy approach, while showing little or no degradation in test performance.

Albeit exploratory, this work opens up a wide range of possibilities, precluded to pure SAT-based learning. To mention a few, hybrid trees can be combined into ensembles, even with varying learning parameters, to obtain potentially very performing classifiers. Similarly, the idea of hybrid learning can be converted into a boosting technique, in light of our results that seem to indicate that SAT-based tree show a performance peak around the tens or low hundreds instances, after which tend to plateau. Finally, the hybrid learning idea can be combined with more elaborate encodings and deeper notions of feasibility, such as in [11].

References

1. Bessiere, C., Hebrard, E., O'Sullivan, B.: Minimising decision tree size as combinatorial optimisation. In: Proc. of the 15th International Conference on Principles and Practice of Constraint Programming. LNCS, vol. 5732, pp. 173–187 (2009)
2. Breiman, L.: Random forests. Mach. Learn. **45**, 5–32 (2001)
3. Chen, T., Guestrin, C.: XGBoost: a scalable tree boosting system. In: Proc. of the 22nd ACM SIGKDD International Conference on Knowledge Discovery and Data Mining (KDD), pp. 785–794 (2016)
4. Della Monica, D., Pagliarini, G., Sciavicco, G., Stan, I.: Decision trees with a modal flavor. In: Proc. of the 21st International Conference of the Italian Association for Advances in Artificial (AIxIA). LNCS, vol. 13796, pp. 47–59. Springer (2022)
5. Fisher, R.: Contributions to mathematical statistics. Biometrika **38**(1–2), 257–259 (1951)
6. Friedman, J.: Greedy function approximation: a gradient boosting machine. Ann. Stat, 1189–1232 (2001)
7. Grinsztajn, L., Oyallon, E., Varoquaux, G.: Why do tree-based models still outperform deep learning on typical tabular data? In: Proc. of the 35th Annual Conference on Advances in Neural Information Processing Systems (NeurIPS) (2022)
8. Hancock, T., Jiang, T., Li, M., Tromp, J.: Lower bounds on learning decision lists and trees. Inf. Comput. **126**(2), 114–122 (1996)
9. Moura, L.D., Nikolaj, B.: Z3: an efficient SMT solver. In: Proc. of the 14th International Conference on Theory and Practice of Software (TACAS), pp. 337–340 (2008)
10. Narodytska, N., Ignatiev, A., Pereira, F., Marques-Silva, J.: Learning optimal decision trees with SAT. In: Proc of the 27th International Joint Conference on Artificial Intelligence (IJCAI), pp. 1362–1368 (2018)
11. Ordyniak, S., Szeider, S.: Parameterized complexity of small decision tree learning. In: Proc. of the 35th AAAI Conference on Artificial Intelligence (AAAI), pp. 6454–6462 (2021)
12. Quinlan, J.: Induction of decision trees. Mach. Learn. **1**(1), 81–106 (1986)
13. Ramdani, F., Furqon, M.: The simplicity of XGBoost algorithm versus the complexity of random forest, support vector machine, and neural networks algorithms in urban forest classification. F1000Research **11**, 1069 (2022)
14. Rivest, R.: Learning Decision Lists. Mach. Learn. **2**(3), 229–246 (1987)
15. Schidler, A., Szeider, S.: SAT-based decision tree learning for large data sets. J. Artif. Intell. Res. **80**, 875–918 (2024)
16. Shati, P., Cohen, E., McIlraith, S.: SAT-based approach for learning optimal decision trees with non-binary features. In: Proc. of the 27th International Conference on Principles and Practice of Constraint Programming (CP). LIPIcs, vol. 210, pp. 50:1–50:16 (2021)
17. Shwartz-Ziv, R., Armon, A.: Tabular data: deep learning is not all you need. Inf. Fusion **81**, 84–90 (2022)

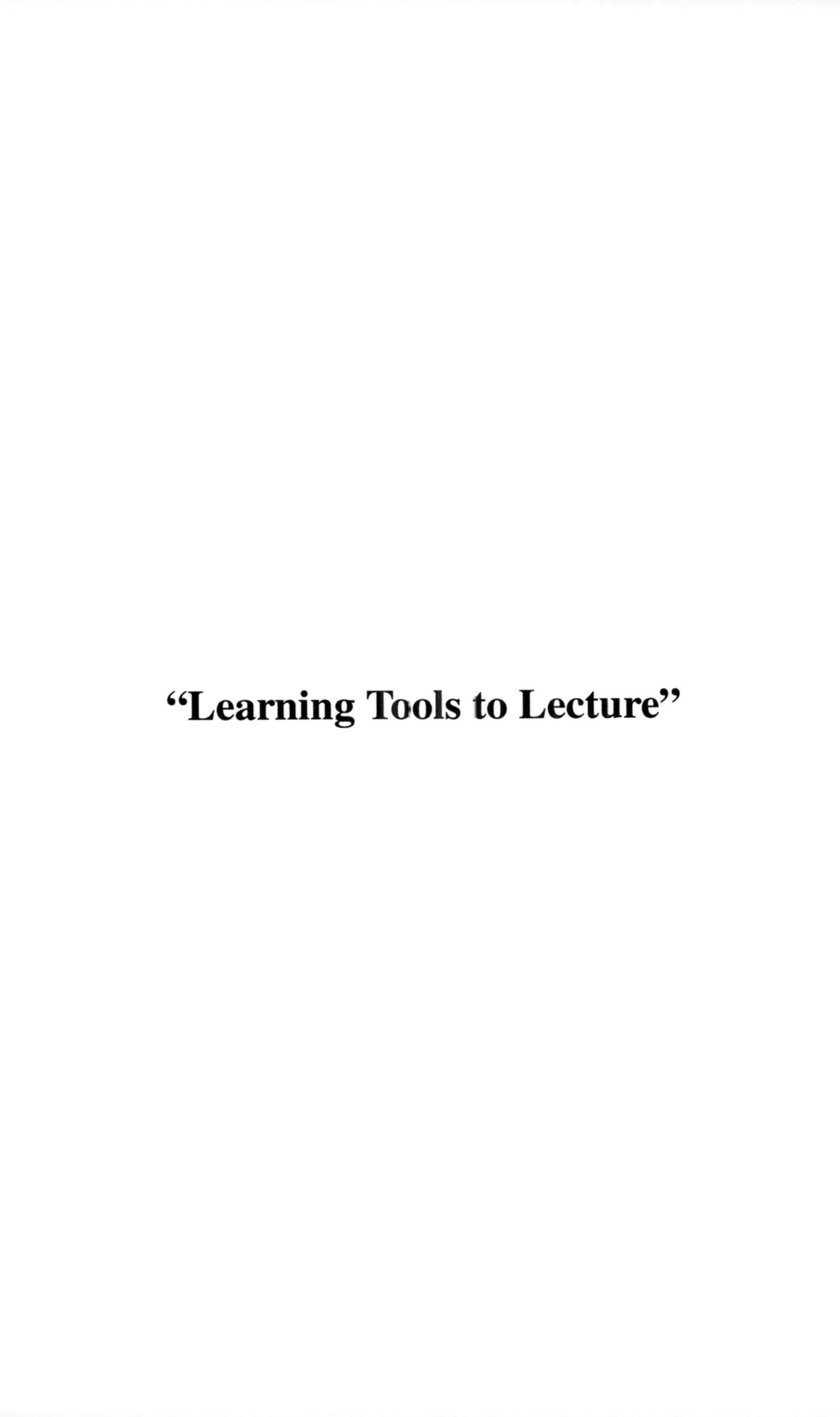

"Learning Tools to Lecture"

Teaching Embodied Artificial Intelligence to Children Through Computer-Based Simulation: The TEACH E-AI 2C Robotic Farm

Clara Nobile[1,2], Alessio Manfredini[2]([✉]), Davide Marocco[2], Onofrio Gigliotta[2], and Michela Ponticorvo[2]

[1] Department of Education, Cultural Heritage and Tourism, University of Macerata, Macerata, Italy
[2] NAC Lab, Department of Humanistic Studies, University of Naples "Federico II", Naples, Italy
`alessio.manfredini2@unina.it`

Abstract. Teaching Artificial Intelligence concepts to younger generations remains challenging due to the abstract and computational nature of many AI principles. Traditional instructional approaches often fail to provide learners with a conceptual understanding of AI-related mechanisms such as perception, decision-making, and adaptation.

This paper presents the TEACH E-AI 2C project, a computer-based educational framework designed to introduce Embodied Artificial Intelligence concepts to children through simulation-based and interactive learning activities. The structure of the educational framework, the software game, and the activities implemented are described, highlighting their role as computer-based laboratories for learning complex systems. Design considerations are discussed, along with challenges related to technology and future directions.

Keywords: Simulation-based learning · AI Literacy · Embodied AI · Educational Robotics · Evolutionary Robotics

1 Introduction

Artificial Intelligence (AI) is spreading in educational settings, both as a pedagogical tool and as a subject of instruction [33]: proposing AI literacy from an early age has become a key challenge for contemporary education. Introducing AI concepts to children and young adolescents can already be difficult due to the abstract, computational, and often opaque nature of many intelligent systems [13]. In addition, AI systems are rapidly changing and evolving [6] so that traditional instructional approaches to AI education do not satisfy all the needs. Frequently, AI instructional methods rely on passive learning modalities, such as algorithm-driven and block-based approaches, and these risk oversimplifying the

J. M. Ferrández Vicente et al. (Eds.): IWINAC 2026, LNCS 16575, pp. 435–444, 2026.
https://doi.org/10.1007/978-3-032-27317-8_41

underlying mechanisms of intelligent behavior, or conversely, children may perceive AI as overly hard [4], or "even magical" [1]. Although these approaches can increase familiarity with AI-related terminology or introduce programming skills, they might fail to support a deeper conceptual understanding [17]. Recent educational research highlights the importance of hands-on and experiential learning approaches, suggesting that understanding emerges more effectively when cognitive processes are grounded in action and perception [9,10]. For AI education, this implies moving beyond abstract descriptions toward learning experiences in which students can observe artificial agents in action, experiment with their behavior, and reflect on the relationship between internal mechanisms and external outcomes.

In this perspective, simulation environments can function as virtual laboratories, allowing students to explore and play with complex AI systems at work. Indeed, computer-aided simulation environments offer promising opportunities by allowing learners to interact with dynamic systems, modify parameters, and observe the consequences of their actions. These tools can support active learning, agency, and the construction of meaningful mental models [8,32].

Within this framework, the TEACH E-AI 2C Robotic Farm was developed as a computer-based educational game that introduces Embodied Artificial Intelligence (E-AI) concepts to children through simulation-based and interactive learning activities. The development of the Robotic Farm software lies in the TEACH E-AI 2C project [19], which integrates theoretical explanations with computer-aided simulation and hands-on activities, enabling learners to acquaint themselves with basic AI concepts and then explore the behavior and evolution of artificial agents with genetic algorithms. This can help to connect abstract AI principles with observable phenomena.

This paper presents the structure of the TEACH E-AI 2C project framework, describes its computer-based tools and simulation activities, and discusses its role as a pedagogical solution for teaching complex AI-related concepts in learning contexts.

2 Educational and Psychological Background

2.1 Constructionism and Learning by Doing

The educational framework of the TEACH E-AI 2C project is grounded in constructionist learning theories [12], which are particularly relevant in the context of K-12 AI education [14]. According to constructionism, learners' difficulties in understanding complex concepts often arise not from the intrinsic difficulty of the notions themselves, but from the absence of appropriate representational resources that can render them concrete and accessible [21]. Within constructionism, such resources are conceptualized as objects-to-think-with, namely physical or digital artifacts that function as cognitive tools, supporting manipulation and experimentation [12]. By interacting with these artifacts, students can connect abstract ideas to concrete experiences, facilitating deeper conceptual understanding. This learning-by-doing process is particularly effective in promoting understanding of complex systems, as it encourages learners to externalize their thinking, reflect on system behavior, and revise their assumptions accordingly.

Simulation-based learning environments provide a powerful means to operationalize constructionist principles in AI education. By enabling learners to modify system parameters, test hypotheses, and observe resulting behavioral changes in artificial agents, simulations support the gradual development of mental models of how AI systems operate. The interactive and artifact-centered nature of these environments allows abstract AI concepts to be concretized through hands-on experimentation and reflective activity, promoting understanding that goes beyond surface-level familiarity with terminology or algorithms [22].

2.2 Embodied Cognition and Embodied Artificial Intelligence

A key strategy within constructionist learning is embodied learning, which provides a meaningful bridge between abstract computational concepts and learners' everyday, experience-based practices [5, 34]. Embodied cognition posits that cognitive processes are deeply grounded in bodily experiences, including perception, sensorimotor activity, and ongoing interaction with the environment [2, 26].

The TEACH E-AI 2C project builds on these principles by introducing AI concepts through a biological metaphor. From this perspective, the functioning of artificial intelligence systems can be understood in terms of perceptionaction cycles and feedback loops between an artificial (as well as natural) agent and its dynamically changing environment. Thus, the so-called E-AI [3] offers a particularly suitable framework for translating these ideas into educational practice, as it conceptualizes intelligence as emerging from the interaction between an agent's embodied structure, its control mechanisms, and the environment it inhabits, in line with principles observed in natural evolutionary processes [23].

2.3 Gamification

The cognitive demands of simultaneously managing new tasks and integrating diverse skills can result in sensory overload, frustration, or disengagement among learners [11]. Strategies that scaffold this complexity in supportive and motivational environments are particularly important in AI teaching settings. Educational games provide structured goals, feedback, and challenges that render complex content more accessible while cultivating emotional investment in young learners by supporting engagement, motivation, and sustained participation [24, 25].

Gamification represents a further key component of the Robotic Farm development, adopting game-like elements to encourage curiosity and iterative experimentation, allowing learners to explore AI concepts at their own pace while maintaining a sense of agency and control.

3 The TEACH E-AI 2C Framework

The TEACH E-AI 2C project proposes an educational framework designed to support the teaching of basic concepts of AI in childhood and early adolescence with little or no prior knowledge of AI, and is intended for use in formal educational contexts, such as school classrooms [19,20]. The framework was developed to simplify core AI mechanisms for this audience, following the instructional design principles of the 4C/ID model [31]. According to this model's instructions, an educational implementation should provide four components: (1) permanent theoretical material that can be consulted at any time (Supportive Information); (2) related tasks spaced out by increasingly difficult (Learning tasks); (3) an in-depth practice on a specific and prominent topic (Part-task Practice); and (4) "how-to" checklists as instructions (Procedural Information) [31]. In the TEACH E-AI 2C framework, these components were developed respectively as (1) theoretical Learning Units, (2) paper and pencil activities, (3) a simulation software, and (4) practical procedures.

While the 4C/ID model guided the instructional design, the educational contents were developed following an E-AI approach. The integration of these two frameworks resulted in several key pedagogical outcomes. First, the proposed approach moves beyond a strictly algorithm-driven perspective, which may be inappropriate and potentially confusing for children encountering AI concepts for the first time. Instead, it promotes a more intuitive and experience-based understanding of intelligent systems. Second, the learning process is set on understanding how biological systems operate and has inspired artificial ones, enabling learners to anchor these novel concepts to prior ones acquired in school (e.g., brain and neuron structure, the five human senses). Third, students are introduced to the foundational principles underlying intelligent behavior and are guided in applying these principles to artificial agents that interact with the physical world. This process is supported through direct observation of simulated and real robots, allowing learners to witness intelligent behavior in action rather than as an abstract computational process.

3.1   Learning Units (Supportive Information)

The primary educational goal of TEACH E-AI 2C is to promote a conceptual understanding of key AI-related mechanisms rather than procedural or algorithmic knowledge. The E-AI approach leads to the biological-artificial parallelism, connecting AI to natural word processes. These Learning Units (LUs) aim to support learners in understanding:

a. **Artificial Intelligence**, such as how artificial agents perceive information from their environment, how internal decision-making processes influence agent behavior, and how agents adapt their actions in response to environmental changes.
b. **Artificial Neural Networks (ANNs)**, particularly the basic structure along with human brain neural networks, Supervised learning, Reinforcement learning, and Unsupervised learning.
c. **Embodied AI**, introduced with Robotics, Evolutionary robotics, along with Genetic Algorithms, explained with Darwin's Theory.

3.2   Paper-and-Pencil Activities (Learning Tasks)

A secondary goal is to promote student engagement and motivation through interactive and exploratory learning activities. By encouraging experimentation and hypothesis testing, the framework seeks to position learners as active participants in the learning process, rather than passive recipients of information. The TEACH E-AI 2C framework is organized in modular educational units. Each follows a structured sequence composed of three main phases: a concept introduction, daily life examples, and a paper-and-pencil activity.

At the end of the first LU, focused on the concept of Artificial Intelligence, students were provided with a decision-based flow chart designed to guide them through a series of reflective questions about digital machines. This activity aimed to support learners in distinguishing between AI-based systems and non-AI systems, promoting early critical thinking about what characterizes intelligent behavior in artificial artifacts.

At the end of the second LU, dedicated to ANNs, students were presented with a set of simple problem scenarios that could potentially be solved using AI. For each scenario, learners were asked to identify and select the most appropriate learning paradigm (i.e., supervised, unsupervised, or reinforcement learning), thus reinforcing their understanding of how different types of learning mechanisms are applied to specific problem structures.

During the third LU, a paper-and-pencil activity was introduced midway through the instructional sequence to further support conceptual integration. Students were first asked to design a robot of their own imagination. In order to qualify as a "real" robot, the design was required to incorporate at least one sensory system for environmental perception and one actuator system for environmental interaction. In a subsequent activity, learners were provided with a simplified schematic representation of a feedforward shallow artificial neural network, which served as a scaffold. Students were then asked to color and map the nodes of the network according to the sensory and motor components they had included in their robot design, explicitly linking perception, processing, and action.

3.3   "How-to" and "step-by-Step" Instructions (Practical Information)

The Robotic Farm laboratory was preceded by a conceptual revision, in which core AI concepts are introduced using age-appropriate language and visual supports. During the simulation exploration, learners were instructed about how to critically observe and manipulate artificial agents. At the end of the virtual simulation and evolution process, the final virtual robot was chosen and its ANN uploaded to a real robot. At this point, a brief reflection and discussion moment followed, aimed at supporting the interpretation of observed behaviors and linking them to the underlying AI mechanisms. This modular structure allows the framework to be adapted to different educational settings, time constraints, and learner profiles. Educators can select and combine units according to their instructional goals and the level of complexity appropriate for the target group.

4   The *Robotic Farm* (Part-Task Practice)

The Robotic Farm is a key component of the TEACH E-AI 2C framework. It is an integrated hardwaresoftware system developed for Thymio robots [16], grounded in principles of Evolutionary Robotics and Genetic Algorithms. This software simulates an environment in which learners interact with embodied artificial agents in a controlled and observable setting. Designed for laptops and tablets, its early version is only available on Windows operating systems. The software's perceived usability among children was evaluated in a previous study, which was found to be "Good" [20].

The simulation tool allows students to modify parameters, observe the evolution of agent behavior over time, and explore the relationship between internal mechanisms and external actions. Students were engaged with the Robotic Farm during the third learning unit on evolutionary AI, following a brief recap of Darwin's Theory and the three fundamental processes of selection, reproduction, and mutation. After a demonstration of the software interface, the students were tasked with "breeding" a population of digital robots. The objective is to train the agents to explore the environment and to develop obstacle avoidance behaviors.

Within the simulation environment, nine digital agents designed as Thymio robots are placed in an arena as the first generation (Fig. 1). Each agent moves controlled by an internal ANN with randomly assigned weights, producing distinct behavioral patterns (Fig. 2). Students observe these varied behaviors as the agents navigate the space. At the end of each generation cycle, students proceed to the selection phase, which operates in two modes. In user-guided selection, students critically evaluate agent performance and manually select three parents for reproduction. In computer-guided selection, the system automatically selects the three agents that explored the greatest percentage of space. The system then clones the selected ANNs and introduces random mutations to a small percentage of their weights, creating the next generation.

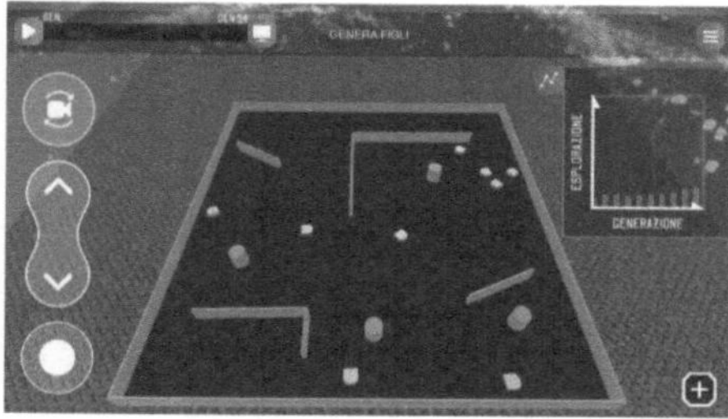

Fig. 1. Exploration percentage tracking graph and obstacles.

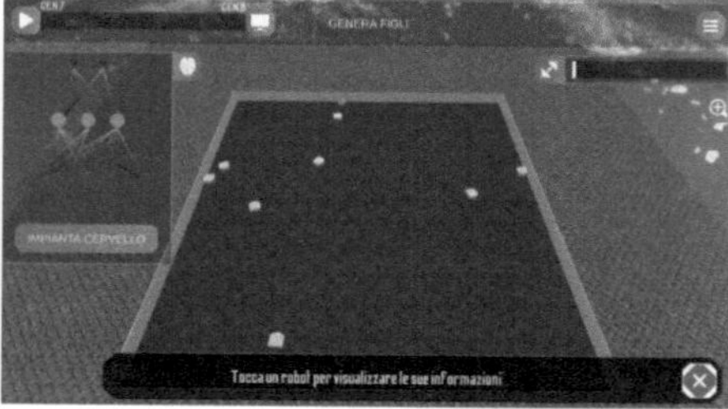

Fig. 2. ANN and Fitness function of the selected robot.

Through iterative cycles of observation, selection, reproduction, and mutation across at least 35 generations, students witness the evolution of agent behavior. At the conclusion of the laboratory activity, each group selects its best-performing robot, and its ANN is uploaded to a physical Thymio robot to observe its behavior in the real environment. This transition from virtual to physical reinforces the connection between simulated and embodied systems.

By functioning as a virtual laboratory, the Robotic Farm enables students to test hypotheses and observe outcomes without the technical complexity typically associated with physical robotic systems. Feedback is conveyed through visual and behavioral cues displayed by the artificial agents, allowing learners to directly associate their actions with observable outcomes. The simulation-based approach addresses practical constraints related to hardware availability, costs, and classroom logistics, offering a scalable solution for AI education.

Lastly, the virtual laboratory model supports scalability and adaptability across different educational contexts and technological platforms, offering flexibility for implementation in classrooms, workshops, or informal learning environments.

5   Educational Observations and Design Considerations

The implementation of the TEACH E-AI 2C framework provided valuable insights into the design and use of computer-based simulation tools for teaching AI concepts to children. Although the primary focus of the project is pedagogical design rather than quantitative evaluation, several educational observations emerged during the implementation of the activities. From an educational perspective, simulation-based activities support high levels of student engagement. Learners showed curiosity toward the behavior of artificial agents and actively participated in exploring the simulation environment, as suggested by previous research [7,15]. The possibility to manipulate parameters and immediately observe the resulting changes in agent behavior encouraged experimentation and sustained attention throughout the activities. Another relevant observation concerns the role of visualization and feedback in supporting conceptual understanding. Visual representations of agent behavior helped learners to connect abstract AI mechanisms with observable outcomes, facilitating discussion and reflection during guided sessions. The virtual laboratory format also supported collaborative interactions among students, who often engaged in shared exploration and collective problem-solving, consistent with prior findings in the field [18,28].

Alongside these educational benefits, several design considerations and challenges were identified. One key challenge relates to the balance between system complexity and accessibility. While richer simulations allow for more realistic representations of intelligent behavior, excessive complexity may increase cognitive load and reduce usability for younger learners [27,29]. Designing age-appropriate interfaces and gradually introducing system features emerged as essential considerations. Technological constraints also influenced the design of the framework. Issues related to hardware availability, computational resources, and platform compatibility highlighted the importance of adopting scalable and lightweight solutions. These limitations reinforce the value of computer-based simulation environments as alternatives to physical robotic systems, particularly in educational settings with limited resources [30].

Overall, these observations informed iterative refinements of the framework and highlighted the importance of aligning pedagogical goals with technological design choices. This experience suggests that simulation-based virtual laboratories can effectively support the introduction of E-AI concepts, provided that careful attention is paid to usability, feedback, and learner-centered design.

6   Conclusions

The TEACH E-AI 2C framework proposes a novel solution for AI education in K-12 settings. Short lessons, paper-and-pencil tasks, practical instructions, and computer-based simulations of robotic behaviors enable children not only to understand what neural networks are and how they work, but also to experiment hands-on with agentic AI systems, thereby overcoming the limitations of traditional, algorithm-driven approaches. Furthermore, the feedback provided by the physical robot allows children to experience first-hand the outcomes of the selection and evolution processes they have guided.

While this framework has achieved promising outcomes - such as high engagement, sustained attention, and collaborative interaction among students in problem-solving and decision-making tasks - several challenges remain to be addressed. Future work should focus on empirical evaluations across diverse educational contexts and age groups, and the expansion of platform compatibility to enhance scalability. Additionally, adaptation of the framework to non-formal educational settings and integration with broader AI literacy curricula warrant further investigation.

In conclusion, the TEACH E-AI 2C framework demonstrates the potential of simulation-based, embodied approaches to render E-AI concepts accessible and meaningful to young learners, contributing to the ongoing effort to prepare future generations for an increasingly AI-integrated world.

Acknowledgment. Thanks to Fondazione Compagnia di San Paolo and Cassa Depositi e Prestiti for funding the AI-LEAP project (D13C23001280007), which includes the Teach E-AI 2C sub-project.

References

1. Absalon, M., Deneux, T.: AlphAI: Teaching AI algorithms to K-12 by training learning robots and visualizing how they work. In: Proceedings of the AAAI Conference on Artificial Intelligence, vol. 39, no. 28, pp. 29096–29103 (2025). https://doi.org/10.1609/aaai.v39i28.35181
2. Barsalou, L.W.: Grounded cognition. Annu. Rev. Psychol. **59**, 617–645 (2008)
3. Brooks, R.A.: Intelligence without representation. Artif. Intell. **47**(1–3), 139–159 (1991)

4. Casella, M., et al.: Not only ChatGPT: educational approaches for embodied artificial intelligence. In: Proceedings of the 1st International Workshop on Education for Artificial Intelligence, Co-located with the 23rd International Conference of the Italian Association for Artificial Intelligence (AIxIA 2024), Bozen-Bolzano, Italy, pp. 54–64 (2024)
5. Dai, Y., Lin, Z., Liu, A., Wang, W.: An embodied, analogical, and disruptive approach to AI pedagogy in upper elementary education: an experimental study. Br. J. Educ. Technol. 55(1), 417–434 (2024)
6. Damioli, G., Van Roy, V., Vertesy, D., Vivarelli, M.: Is artificial intelligence leading to a new technological paradigm? Struct. Change Econ. Dyn. 72, 347–359 (2025). https://doi.org/10.1016/j.strueco.2024.12.006
7. Di Natale, A.F., Repetto, C., Riva, G., Villani, D.: Immersive virtual reality in K-12 and higher education: a 10-year systematic review of empirical research. Brit. J. Educ. Technol. 51(6), 2006–2033 (2020). https://doi.org/10.1111/bjet.13030
8. Engeness, I., Gamlem, S.M.: Agency in digital education: empowering students and teachers in technology-rich learning environments. Educ. Sci. 15(8), 1051 (2025). https://doi.org/10.3390/educsci15081051
9. Gennari, R., Melonio, A., Pellegrino, M.A., D'Angelo, M.: How to playfully teach AI to young learners: A systematic literature review. In: Proceedings of the 15th Biannual Conference of the Italian SIGCHI Chapter (CHItaly 2023), Article 1, pp. 1–9. Association for Computing Machinery, New York (2023). https://doi.org/10.1145/3605390.3605393
10. Gigliotta, O., Ponticorvo, M., Chinzer, E., Nobile, C., Giorgini, D., Vitanza, A.: Educational robotics: from computational to complexity thinking. In: Carletti, T., Njougouo, T.S., Tuci, E. (eds.) Artificial Life and Evolutionary Computation (WIVACE 2024). CCIS, vol. 2532, pp. 250–260. Springer, Cham (2025). https://doi.org/10.1007/978-3-031-93631-9_20
11. Gong, X., Wu, Y., Ye, Z., Liu, X.: Artificial intelligence course design: iSTREAM-based visual cognitive smart vehicles. In: Proc. IEEE Intelligent Vehicles Symposium (IV), pp. 1731–1735. IEEE (2018). https://doi.org/10.1109/IVS.2018.8500457
12. Harel, I., Papert, S. (eds.): Constructionism. Ablex Publishing, Norwood (1991)
13. Jia, K., Yu, J.: Technologies for children's AI learning: design features and future opportunities. In: Proceedings of the 2025 CHI Conference on Human Factors in Computing Systems, Article 1196, pp. 1–22. ACM, New York (2025). https://doi.org/10.1145/3706598.3713443
14. Lin, Z.X., Dai, Y., Ng, O.: Constructionism in K-12 AI literacy education: a systematic review of pedagogical designs, student outcomes, and learning mechanisms. J. Educ. Comput. Res. 63, 1748–1781 (2025)
15. Maas, M.J., Hughes, J.M.: Virtual, augmented and mixed reality in K–12 education: a review of the literature. Technol. Pedagog. Educ. 29(2), 231–249 (2020). https://doi.org/10.1080/1475939X.2020.1737210
16. Mondada, F., Bonani, M., Riedo, F., Briod, M., Pereyre, L., Retornaz, P., Magnenat, S.: Bringing robotics to formal education: the Thymio open-source hardware robot. IEEE Robot. Autom. Mag. 24(1), 77–85 (2017). https://doi.org/10.1109/MRA.2016.2636372
17. Morales-Navarro, L., Kafai, Y.B.: Unpacking approaches to learning and teaching machine learning in K-12 education: transparency, ethics, and design activities. In: Proceedings of the 19th WiPSCE Conference on Primary and Secondary Computing Education Research (WiPSCE 2024), pp. 1–10 (2024). https://doi.org/10.1145/3677619.3678117

18. Murray, G., Du, X., Zhu, M., Wang, W.: Building K-12 students' robotics skills through collaborative hands-on learning. In: Proceedings of the 2025 IEEE Integrated STEM Education Conference (ISEC), pp. 1–5. IEEE (2025). https://doi.org/10.1109/ISEC64801.2025.11147399

19. Nobile, C., Marocco, D., Gigliotta, O., Ponticorvo, M.: Teaching embodied artificial intelligence to children (Teach E-AI 2C): an educational proposal for young learners. In: Proceedings of the 2024 IEEE International Conference on Metrology for eXtended Reality, Artificial Intelligence and Neural Engineering (MetroXRAINE). IEEE Press (2024). https://doi.org/10.1109/MetroXRAINE62247.2024.10797080

20. Nobile, C., Diano, F., Manfredini, A., Gigliotta, O., Marocco, D., Ponticorvo, M.: Evaluating the usability of Teach E-AI 2C robotic farm: an educational software for introducing young learners to embodied artificial intelligence. In: Proceedings of the 2025 IEEE International Conference on Metrology for eXtended Reality, Artificial Intelligence and Neural Engineering (MetroXRAINE), IEEE Press (2025). https://doi.org/10.1109/MetroXRAINE66377.2025.11339919

21. Papert, S.: Mindstorms: Children, Computers, and Powerful Ideas. Basic Books, New York (1980)

22. Papavlasopoulou, S., Giannakos, M.N., Jaccheri, L.: Exploring children's learning experience in constructionism-based coding activities through design-based research. Comput. Hum. Behav. **99**, 415–427 (2019)

23. Ponticorvo, M., Walker, R., Miglino, O.: Evolutionary robotics as a tool to investigate spatial cognition in artificial and natural systems. In: Artificial Cognition Systems, pp. 210–237. IGI Global Scientific Publishing (2007)

24. Ponticorvo, M., Di Ferdinando, A., Marocco, D., Miglino, O.: Bio-inspired computational algorithms in educational and serious games: some examples. In: Verbert, K., Sharples, M., Klobučar, T. (eds.) EC-TEL 2016. LNCS, vol. 9891, pp. 636–639. Springer, Cham (2016). https://doi.org/10.1007/978-3-319-45153-4_80

25. Robson, K., Plangger, K., Kietzmann, J.H., McCarthy, I., Pitt, L.: Is it all a game? Understanding the principles of gamification. Bus. Horiz. **58**(4), 411–420 (2015)

26. Shapiro, L.: Embodied Cognition. Routledge, New York (2011)

27. Sigayret, K., Blanc, N., Tricot, A.: Should we use educational robots to introduce students to computational thinking? Insights from two experimental studies. J. Comput. Assist. Learn. **41**(4), e70074 (2025). https://doi.org/10.1111/jcal.70074

28. Sun, Y., Chang, C.H., Chiang, F.K.: When life science meets educational robotics: a study of students' problem solving process in a primary school. Educ. Technol. Soc. **25**(1), 166–178 (2022)

29. Sweller, J., van Merrienboer, J.J.G., Paas, F.G.W.C.: Cognitive architecture and instructional design. Educ. Psychol. Rev. **10**(3), 251–296 (1998)

30. Tselegkaridis, S., Sapounidis, T.: Simulators in educational robotics: a review. Educ. Sci. **11**(1), 11 (2021). https://doi.org/10.3390/educsci11010011

31. Van Merriënboer, J.J., Kirschner, P.A.: Ten Steps to Complex Learning: A Systematic Approach to Four-Component Instructional Design. Routledge, Oxon (2013). https://doi.org/10.4324/9781003322481

32. Wahyuni, N.T., Ariyanto, G.: Empowered learners in a digital age: the critical nexus of engagement, agency, interest, and motivation. Muslim Educ. Rev. **3**(2), 304–330 (2024). https://doi.org/10.56529/mer.v3i2.261

33. Wang, S., Wang, F., Zhu, Z., Wang, J., Tran, T., Du, Z.: Artificial intelligence in education: a systematic literature review. Expert Syst. Appl. **252**, 124167 (2024). https://doi.org/10.1016/j.eswa.2024.124167

34. Weisberg, S.M., Newcombe, N.S.: Embodied cognition and STEM learning: overview of a topical collection in CR:PI. Cogn. Res. Princ. Implic. **2**, 38 (2017)

Embodied Reading: Enhancing Digital Reading Comprehension Through Lectoentreno System

Mabel Urrutia[✉], Michael Villanueva, Pamela Guevara, Karina Fuentes, Pedro Salcedo, Esteban Pino, and Geoffrey Hecht

Facultad de Educación, Universidad de Concepción, Concepción, Chile
{maurrutia,mvillanueva2019,pguevara,kafuente,psalcedo,estebanpino,
ghecht}@udec.cl

Abstract. Purpose: This study presents the design, implementation, and evaluation of Lectoentreno, a web-based software developed to enhance reading comprehension in university students through embodied cognition strategies and text manipulation. The research addresses the global decline in literacy competencies, which is particularly critical in the Chilean context. Methodology: The software architecture follows a Model-View-Controller (MVC) pattern, integrating a Vue.js frontend and a Laravel back-end. A 15-session intervention program was conducted with university students. The impact was assessed through the System Usability Scale (SUS) and electrophysiological measures, specifically focusing on the modulation of N400 and post-N400 Event-Related Potentials (ERPs) during reading tasks. Results: Quantitative analysis revealed high usability scores (SUS = 89.3 for professors; 81.25 for students). Electrophysiological data indicated that the intervention effectively modulated neural activity in the N400 and post-N400 windows, particularly in conditions requiring high inferential effort. Compared to traditional methods, the experimental group showed more efficient construction and updating of mental models. Conclusion: Lectoentreno proves to be a superior tool for advanced reading instruction by successfully modifying neurocognitive processes associated to reading comprehension. By aligning pedagogical practices with modern neuroscientific evidence, the system provides a robust framework for monitoring student progress and fostering deep learning in higher education.

Keywords: Reading Comprehension · Educational Technology · Lectoentreno Software · ERP · N400 · Higher Education

1 Introduction

According to UNESCO (2014, 2020), 35% of reading failure is attributable to a lack of opportunities to access quality education. Consequently, proficient reading development entails improved academic performance, reduced dropout rates,

© The Author(s), under exclusive license to Springer Nature Switzerland AG 2026
J. M. Ferrández Vicente et al. (Eds.): IWINAC 2026, LNCS 16575, pp. 445–451, 2026.
https://doi.org/10.1007/978-3-032-27317-8_42

better access to competitive wages, and greater social mobility, thereby ensuring the active participation of proficient readers in modern societies (McGeown et al., 2015; Miller, 2015; Sánchez, García, & Rosales, 2010). Results from the 2023 Programme for the International Assessment of Adult Competencies (PIACC), conducted across 32 countries, reveal a global 6-point decline in reading comprehension since the previous assessment. This alarming situation also extends to Chile, which ranks last; specifically, 53% of Chilean adults aged 16 to 65 lack sufficient reading comprehension competencies, exhibiting a low level of performance (Aroyo y Valenzuela, 2018).

Furthermore, the adoption of new technologies has transformed information access, with global adult internet usage rising from 76% in 2012 to 93% in 2023. Conventional written reading is yielding to digital reading linked to social media. In Chile's case, reading comprehension difficulties are more pronounced in digital formats; Chileans ranked second to last among 19 countries in the OECD (2011) survey, where 37.7% scored at the lowest levels and only 1.1% reached the highest levels. According to the 2018 PISA assessment, although students prefer digital reading, they exhibit lower proficiency in it. In contrast to this reality, the development of artificial intelligence has reached a point where it could potentially answer approximately 80% of the literacy questions administered in the PIACC test- figures that differ significantly from the average performance of OECD students (OECD, 2023).

Consequently, AI-derived tools could contribute to the assessment of specific reading competencies, automating results and supporting teaching practices. They could also shift the relevance of certain literacy aspects, contributing to implicit comprehension levels and helping to resolve the ambiguity inherent in situation models derived from specific contexts (OECD, 2023). A significant number of commercial educational apps are currently on the market. Most focus exclusively on speed-reading techniques based on decoding rather than text comprehension, such as Reader Pro. Many claim to assist with memory, attention, or dyslexia, as seen with the Galexia app. Others even include 'neural accelerator' modules, such as the Speed Reading app; however, none of these provide scientific evidence regarding the effectiveness of their training, particularly within the field of neuroscience.

The overall objective of this article was to design and implement software that improves reading comprehension among university students through reading and manipulating texts by training them in certain verbal and lexical strategies. To achieve this, the project was developed in three stages: a) Design and implementation of software aimed at improving the reading comprehension of university students; b) Experimental validation of the software through unit tests, integration tests, and tests with real users; and c) Analysis and interpretation of the results.

2   Methodology

2.1   Software Description

Lectoentreno is a web platform designed to improve students' reading comprehension through pedagogical activities. By logging in, users access a school environment where students complete personalized reading activities within courses. The platform allows teachers to monitor their students' comprehension levels through detailed activity data, enabling them to identify areas for improvement and provide targeted support. In addition, the system collects and organizes educational data, enabling scientific studies on reading strategies and their effectiveness.

2.2   Software Architecture

Lectoentreno's software architecture is designed following the Model-View-Controller (MVC) pattern, integrating a frontend developed in Vue.js, a back-end based on an API built with Laravel 8 in PHP, and a database managed3 with MySQL. The software architecture at the container level is illustrated in Fig. 1. using the C4 model [1]. For context, the actors within the system are:

- Teachers: Primary actors who have access to create courses, texts, activities, and diagnostics. Additionally, they can perform detailed tracking of student progress.
- Students: Users who interact with the system to complete reading activities and diagnostics, improving their reading comprehension through strategies implemented in the platform.
- External email system: Used to send emails to users, facilitating password recovery.

  The system is composed of three containers:

- Web Application (Frontend): Built using Vue.js version 2, this interface allows users to interact with the system intuitively. It includes specific views for teachers and students, adapted to their respective needs.
- API (Backend): Developed with Laravel 8, it manages communication between the frontend and database. It implements controllers for core functionalities and ensures security through PHP middleware and JWT tokens.

Database: Uses MySQL to store and organize essential data, such as user information, activities, diagnostics, texts, and results.

2.3   Software Functionalities

The Lectoentreno platform provides specific tools for both students and teachers to easily use the system. Below are the main functionalities in the activity workflow, although survey-type diagnostics can also be integrated, not all system functions can be demonstrated:

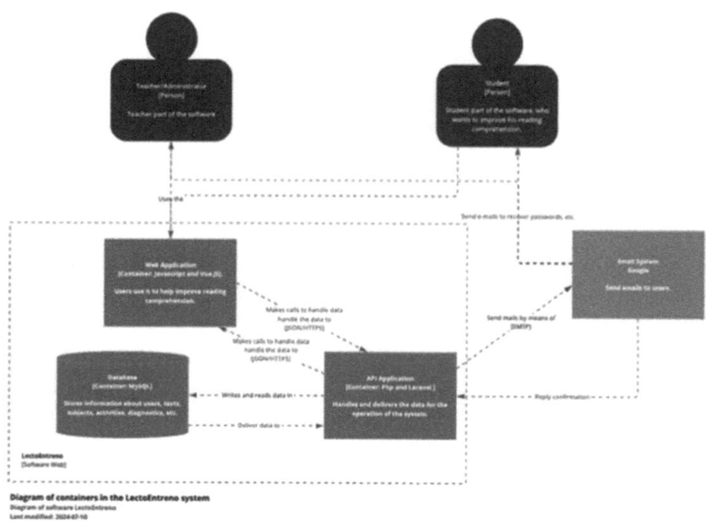

Fig. 1. Diagram of containers in the Lectoentreno system

User Profiles

To interact with the system, users must create a profile and authenticate through a login. Students can register directly on the website, while teachers can only be added by an administrator, who is a teacher with corresponding permissions. This distinction ensures proper control over system access and role assignment.

Course Creation

Once teachers log into the platform, they can create courses to organize their students, activities, and diagnostics. Students can be added to each course in two ways: manually, by selecting existing students in the system, or through bulk upload from an Excel file, which automatically registers student profiles in the system with a random password sent to their registered email.

Text Creation

Before creating activities or diagnostics, teachers must create a base text with its respective paragraphs, to later add related questions that will be used in activities, as well as integrate elements such as images associated with words.

Activity Creation

Activities are part of a course, so they are created within one, always being associated with it. The activity has 2 parts: reading and questions. During creation, teachers must integrate a previously added text with its respective questions for this activity, indicating the description and deadline. They can optionally include a maximum time to complete the activity and incorporate 2 mini-games: "The Image Mini-game" where students must associate the corresponding image with the read paragraph, and the "Paragraph Ordering Mini-game" where they have to read the paragraphs and order them to form the complete text.

Activities in the Student View
When completing an activity, students must first read the associated text, which includes extras added by the teacher, as well as mini-games. It also allows them to save words, highlight them, search words in the RAE dictionary, and manage font size. After finishing the reading, students answer the text questions, and once completed, they receive immediate feedback on their performance and are shown the correct answers.

Data Analysis for Teachers
The system provides teachers with tools to analyze the results of activities and diagnostics in a course so that teachers can see student progress or identify if anyone needs help improving. For this purpose, each course has a section showing all created activities and another section for associated diagnostics:

When selecting an activity, an interactive dashboard is displayed that includes:

1. General Summary: Shows the total score, average score obtained, average total time students spent on the activity, as well as average reading and response time.
2. Results by Activity Question: Details of each question, showing correct and incorrect answers along with a side bar graph indicating which was most selected by students.
3. Individual Performance: List of students with their individual scores, completion times, reading and response times, with access to details of each activity.
4. Summary Graphs: Includes a bar graph that classifies students according to percentage ranges, allowing teachers to quickly identify those with high or low scores. Also, a donut chart illustrating the percentage of students who completed and did not complete the activity.

These sections are designed to offer teachers a practical experience, facilitating data interpretation and thus enabling informed educational decision-making.

3   Results

To assess the functionality and usability of the Lectoentreno software in real life scenarios, we employed the System Usability Scale (SUS), a validated and widely adopted instrument to measure perceived system usability.

Prior to completing the SUS questionnaire, participants were provided with a structured set of instructions to explore system functionalities without time constraints. The evaluation was carried out with two different groups of users: university professors (n = 4) aged 35 to 45 years and university students (n=8) aged 20 to 28 years.

The evaluation methodology consisted of distributing evaluation forms to the professors, who subsequently shared them with students interested in participating in the evaluation activity. Both cohorts received identical forms containing procedural instructions and the standardized items of the SUS questionnaire.

For the teacher, the assessment protocol required participants to perform a sequence of system operations, they were asked to create a course in the system and perform all the steps necessary to implement a reading activity, including creating a text, creating the activity, and then analyzing it using the data dashboard. The student was tasked with system registration, participation in professor-created activities, completion of assigned readings, and response to associated assessment questions. The student had to register in the system, participate in the activities created by the teacher, complete the reading using the functions available here and then answer the associated assessment questions.

Upon completion of the prescribed tasks and achieving familiarization with the software platform, participants completed the SUS questionnaire. The quantitative analysis revealed mean SUS scores of 89.3 for professors and 81.25 for students.

In accordance with established SUS evaluation criteria, both scores indicate an "Acceptable" level of usability, validating the system's effectiveness across user groups. While these results demonstrate positive usability metrics, the evaluation process also identified minor operational issues and potential areas for enhancement, which will inform subsequent software iterations.

4   Intervention and Impact

The intervention consisted of a structured 15-session reading training program using Lectoentreno software (45 min per session). A reading assessment was performed before and after the intervention using the electrophysiological technique ERP (Event-Related Potential). Participants were assigned either to the experimental group, which received an embodied strategy intervention, or to the control group, which received training based on traditional reading strategies. Both programs were delivered in small groups and followed a standardized instructional protocol to ensure methodological consistency across sessions.

5   Conclusion

The results demonstrate that the intervention selectively modulated neural activity in the N400 (300–500 ms) and, more prominently, the post-N400 (500–800 ms) time windows, particularly in conditions that required greater inferential effort. This implies that participants were sensitive to context and showed greater negativity in stories with greater semantic complexity than in contexts with less difficulty after the intervention.

The experimental group showed clearer preâĂŞpost differentiation among contextual conditions than the control group, especially in contrasts involving less familiar contexts, suggesting that the intervention influenced processes involved in maintaining coherence when contextual support was reduced.

In regards to the training involving Lectoentreno software, the experimental group's verbal, visual, and multisensory simulation strategies facilitated more efficient construction and updating of mental models compared to the paraphrasing and rereading techniques used by the control group.

The findings have direct implications for teacher education, as participants were college students preparing for instructional roles. Developing the ability to construct and update coherent situation models is essential for both academic success and effective teaching practice where the use of technology enhances teaching practices and promotes the development of reading comprehension in university students. The present results suggest that embodied, simulation-based strategies can modify the neurocognitive processes that support comprehension and may therefore offer advantages over traditional approaches in higher-education reading instruction.

Acknowledgments. Supported by ANID/FONDECYT Regular Project No. 1241145.

Disclosure of Interests. The authors have no competing interests to declare that are relevant to the content of this article.

References

1. Aroyo, C., Valenzuela, A.: PIAAC: competencias de la población adulta en Chile, un análisis al sistema educativo y mercado laboral. Nota Técnica No. 5, CNEP (2018)
2. McGeown, S.P., Duncan, L.G., Griffiths, Y.M., Stothard, S.E.: Exploring the relationship between adolescents' reading skills, reading motivation and reading habits. Read. Writ. **28**(5), 745–760 (2015). https://doi.org/10.1007/s11145-015-9543-6
3. Miller, B.W.: Using reading times and eye-movements to measure cognitive engagement. Educ. Psychol. **50**(1), 31–42 (2015). https://doi.org/10.1080/00461520.2015.1004068
4. OECD: Education at a Glance 2011: OECD Indicators. OECD Publishing (2011). https://doi.org/10.1787/eag-2011-en
5. OECD: Is Education Losing the Race with Technology?: AI and the Future of Skills. Educational Research and Innovation. OECD Publishing, Paris (2023). https://doi.org/10.1787/73105f99-en
6. Sánchez, E., García, R., Rosales, J.: La lectura en el aula: qué se hace, qué se debe hacer y qué se puede hacer. Graó, Barcelona (2010)
7. UNESCO: Estrategia de educación 2014–2021 (2014). https://unesdoc.unesco.org/ark:/48223/pf0000231288_spa
8. UNESCO: Liderar el OSD4- Educación 2030 (2020). https://es.unesco.org/themes/liderar-ods-4-educacion-2030

GUI-Based Tools to Lecture Data Analytics: An Exploratory Data Analysis Scenario

Kelsy Cabello-Solorzano[1], Alejandro Bautista-Juárez[2], Luís Correia[3], Sung-Bae Cho[4], and Antonio J. Tallón-Ballesteros[5(✉)]

[1] International University of Andalusia, Huelva, Spain
kelsy.cabellosolorzano@estudiante.unia.es
[2] University of Huelva, Huelva, Spain
alejandro.juarez@alu.uhu.es
[3] LASIGE, Faculdade de Ciências, Universidade de Lisboa, Lisbon, Portugal
luis.correia@ciencias.ulisboa.pt
[4] Department of Computer Science, Yonsei University, Seoul, Korea
sbcho@yonsei.ac.kr
[5] Department of Electronic, Computer Systems and Automation Engineering, University of Huelva, Huelva, Spain
antonio.tallon@diesia.uhu.es

Abstract. This paper analyses various tools that are appropriate as teaching resources for data science or engineering at undergraduate or postgraduate levels. A comparison is performed between fsQCA, the online EDA (Exploratory Data Analysis) module within Nets4Learning and Minitab. We describe the functionalities of those frameworks and also the installation and running procedure. A visual tour is provided to showcase the main available tasks in these tools and to encourage other researchers or lecturers to introduce them in laboratory classes or as a complement for any theoretical lesson.

Keywords: Visual tools · Lecture · Data Analytics · Data Pre-processing · Data Post-processing

1 Introduction

Information is power. This is not only true in agriculture productivity as a recent sample [10] but also in Health, according to one of the root sources [4], and, in general, in any scientific branch such as Education Sciences [6]. Data Analytics or analytics of data [5] is older than a contemporary term like Google [2]; in recent times the usual term is Big Data Analytics [3]. BMD and BMDP (Bio-Medical Data Package) were introduced in the fifties of the previous century as statistical tools and had text-based interfaces. At that time computers were provided with a keyboard and a few years later the mouse was introduced in personal computers. Other classical programs like SPSS [7] incorporated a Graphical User Interface

J. M. Ferrández Vicente et al. (Eds.): IWINAC 2026, LNCS 16575, pp. 452–462, 2026.
https://doi.org/10.1007/978-3-032-27317-8_43

(GUI) from the nineties of the previous century. This research describes some visual tools such as EDA within Nets4Learning, fsQCA and Minitab. The first framework is available to operate online through a browser with internet connection via HyperText Transfer Protocol (HTTP), whereas the latter should installed on the host operating system through the installer. Visual frameworks to lecture are a key point of the digital society that we are living from a long time ago. Data analytics may be important to be applied both in the data pre-processing and post-processing to learn about the data in the former case and to assess data mining methods in the latter one [1].

This article aims to introduce some visual tools that could be extremely handy to lecture subjects related with Data Analytics or Intelligent Data Engineering in the umbrella of undergraduate or postgraduate degrees. The rest of this paper is organized as follows: Sect. 2 describes fsQCA; Sect. 3 introduces EDA module within Nets4Learning; Sect. 4 goes into Minitab; finally, Sect. 5 states the concluding remarks.

2   fsQCA

Charles Ragin developed a tool called Fuzzy-Set/Qualitative Comparative Analysis (fsQCA) [11]. As the name suggests, this framework accepts fuzzy sets. However, this paper introduces the application in order to operate on (crisp) data analysis as an initial step to any Knowledge Discovery in Databases (KDD) project. The installation of fsQCA should be done only using the suitable installer for the operating system at hand. Figure 1 shows the screen that initially appears and is similar to any basic suite application with a few additional menus to File such as Variables, Cases, Analyze and Graphs one. The first step to operate is to load a File using the File menu as Fig. 2 shows. The example displays the Pima problem from the University of California at Irvine (UCI) Machine Learning repository which nowadays is maintained by Markelle Kelly, Rachel Longjohn, and Kolby Nottingham; there are eight variables or features and one class label. Once the data set is loaded, to conduct the exploratory analysis, we tap on the Analyze menu, open the entry menu called Statistics and then click on Descriptives. Figure 3 represents this step. Next, the variables of interest will be chosen with the interface provided; there the user ticks the suitable features in order to perform the analysis. Be aware that the class label is not available for this study. The previous step result is displayed in Fig. 4. As we can see this data set has 576 instances.

3   Nets4Learning

Nets4Learning [9] is a powerful framework for Machine Learning including Tabular classification, Regression, Image classification and Object identification. This is a web-based tool developed by the University of Jaén for designing and testing deep learning models. However, given that our goal is to show tools covering the Exploratory Data Analysis, we will only explain the EDA tab. The steps

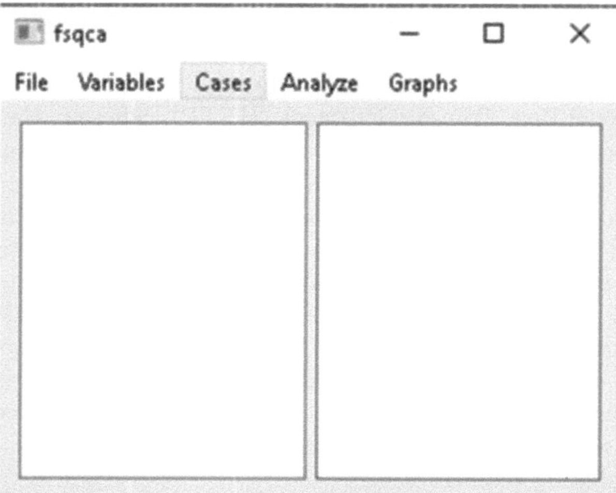

Fig. 1. Starting fsQCA

to operate with it are as follows: First, we go to Upload data set (as Fig. 5 shows) clicking on the rectangular action textbox; then it will appear the message window to locate the local CSV file, once you select a file you will Accept to do the request in this case to load the file within the framework. You can view the original data frame without any processing as Fig. 6 depicts (section is called DataFrame—Original). There are options that allow you to select the columns to be transformed based on the label, and you can also specify a destination column where the results generated after processing the data frame will be added. To analyze the dataset, the tool offers a view of the dataframe in its original format and the processed dataframe; it also includes submenus listing the transformations that were performed. We skip here the transformations. The statistical summary of the dataframe displays the variables selected for analysis as Fig. 7 displays. The box plots show the data distribution and outliers, and also allow for comparison of the variables under study. In the same way, a correlation matrix is generated to help identify unnecessary variables and select better features (see Fig. 8). It may also provide information about relationships between data points for metalearning purposes.

4   Minitab

Minitab contemporary versions [8] have been written in C++ programming language although the initial versions were coded in FORTRAN IV [12]; this paper covers the version 18. Minitab [13] is a multiple language framework and during the installation you can choose one of the eight possible human languages from different continents such as America, Europe and Asia; there are at least a couple of options from each of these regions. After starting Minitab (as Fig. 9

x0	x1	x2	x3	x4	x5	x6	x7	Class
0.352941	0.46	0.508197	0.32	0.148936	0.4769	0.002989	0.416667	y0
0.117647	0.505	0.47541	0.35	0.106383	0.324888	0.032878	0.016667	y0
0.294118	0.66	0.655738	0	0	0.399404	0.046114	0.8	y0
0.294118	0.775	0.688525	0.44	0.644208	0.576751	0.230999	0.216667	y0
0.117647	0.47	0.622951	0.18	0.078014	0.470939	0.243809	0.033333	y0
0.411765	0.405	0.639344	0.4	0.056738	0.695976	0.078138	0.35	y0
0.235294	0.475	0.57377	0.32	0	0.47839	0.22801	0.05	y0
0.117647	0.45	0.57377	0.17	0	0.406855	0.002989	0.016667	y0
0.235294	0.575	0.590164	0	0	0.4307	0.127242	0.416667	y1
0.882353	0.68	0.57377	0.32	0.130024	0.552906	0.032024	0.366667	y1
0.411765	0.92	0.688525	0.33	0	0.529061	0.118275	0.333333	y1
0.117647	0.495	0.491803	0.17	0.189125	0.545455	0.16012	0	y0
0.117647	0.585	0.737705	0.19	0.083924	0.375559	0.100342	0	y0
0.058824	0.63	0.491803	0	0	0.448584	0.115713	0.433333	y1
0.411765	0.795	0.540984	0	0	0.453055	0.130231	0.25	y1
0.176471	0.85	0.52459	0.37	0.265957	0.514158	0.118702	0.15	y1
0.117647	0.455	0.508197	0	0	0.406855	0.190863	0.016667	y0
0.176471	0.535	0.508197	0.13	0.056738	0.341282	0.256191	0.033333	y1

Fig. 2. fsQCA: loading a file (CSV format)

displays), we see the worksheet and also lot of menus with the names File, Edit, Data, Calc, Stat, Graph, Editor, Tools, Windows to mention a few of them. The first stage to work with this framework is to manually create the data set or to load from an MTW (MiniTab Worksheet) file which is the Minitab native format. Figure 10 shows the Azalea. MTW file which is an add-on sample. It is not defined as a supervised machine learning task and hence instances have only features and no labels. Figure 11 represents the detail of Calc menu and entry menu call Column Statistics... is very handy for Data Analysis; clicking there it will appear a window entitled Display Descriptive Statistics where we will select the variables to be studied. Next we press Ok and the computations will be done; Fig. 12 shows the result. The number of non-missing and missing values for any attribute is represented in columns labelled N and N*, respectively.

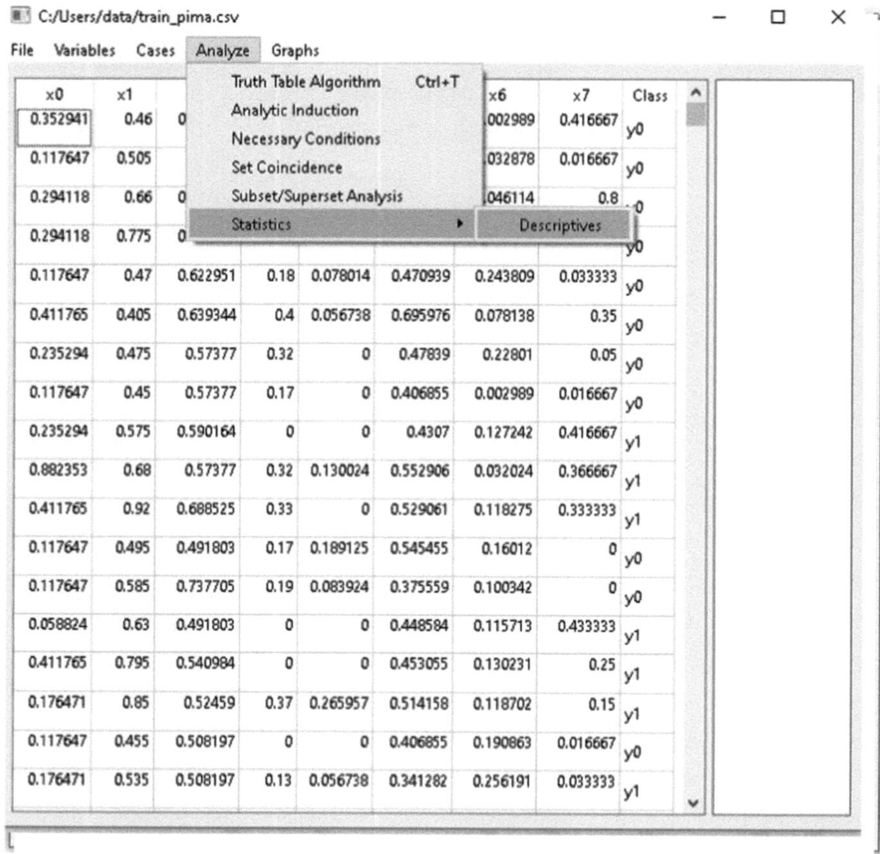

Fig. 3. fsQCA: preparation for a data analytics task

Fig. 4. fsQCA: data analytics task output

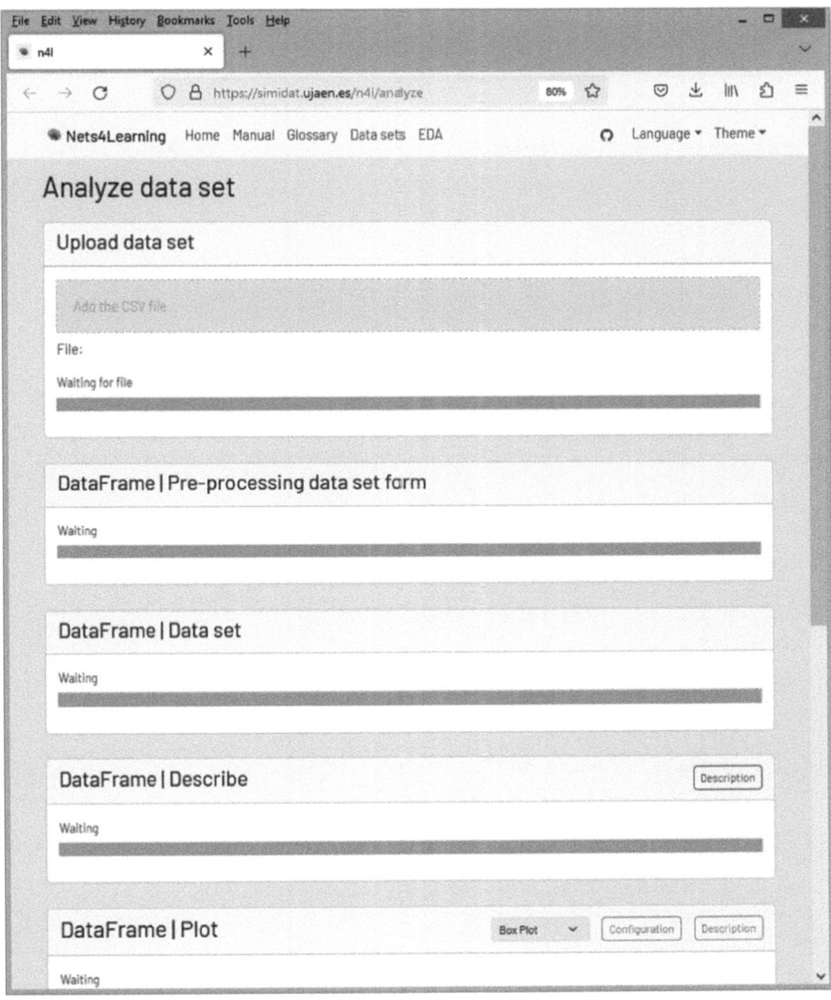

Fig. 5. Starting EDA module within Nets4Learning

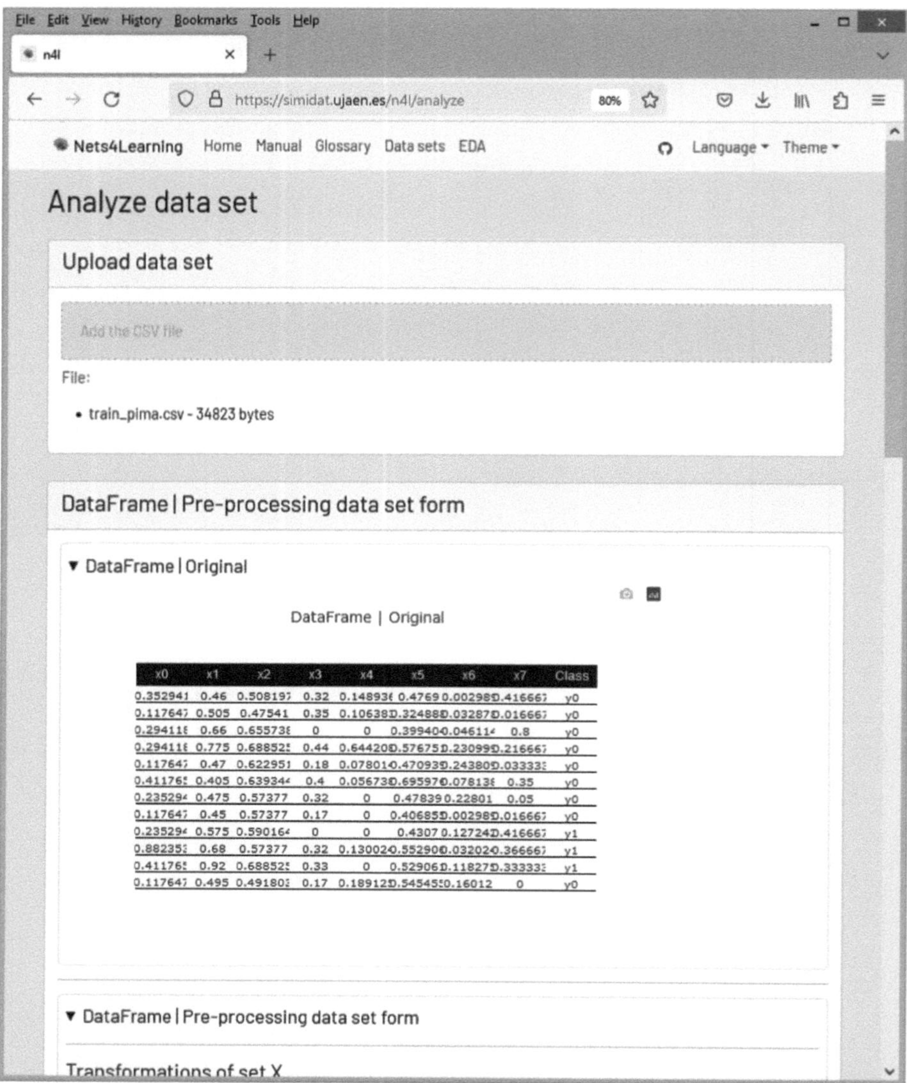

Fig. 6. EDA: loading a file (CSV format)

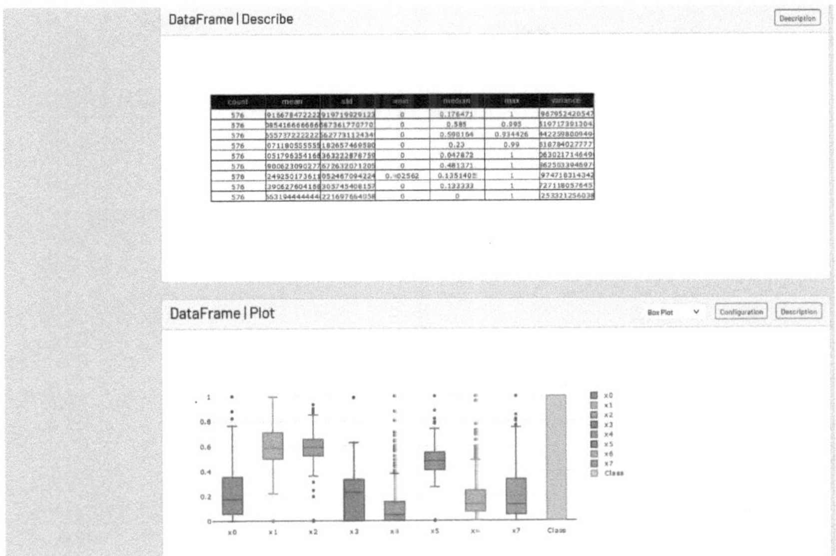

Fig. 7. EDA: data analytics task numerical results

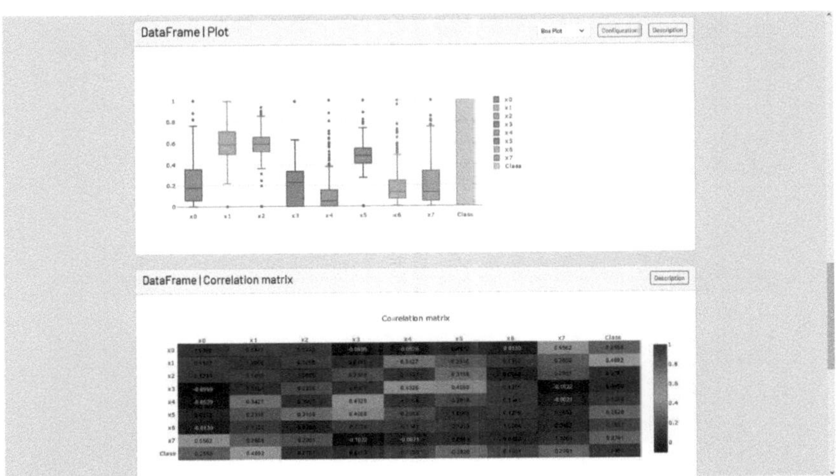

Fig. 8. EDA: data analytics task graphical output

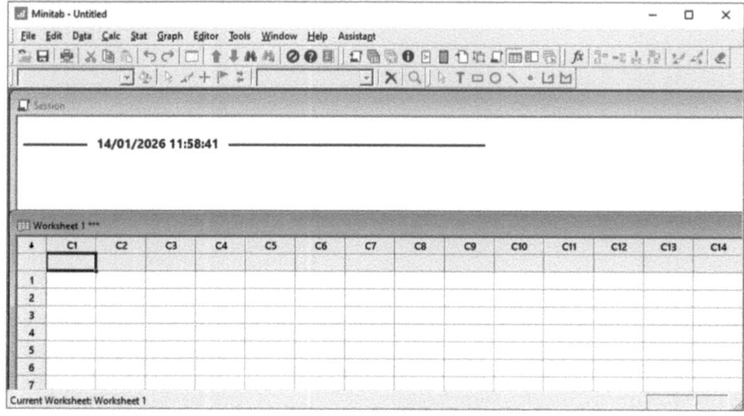

Fig. 9. Starting Minitab

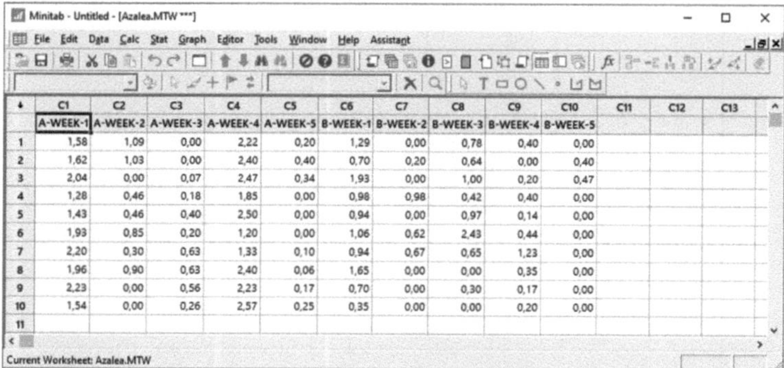

Fig. 10. Minitab: loading a file (MTW format)

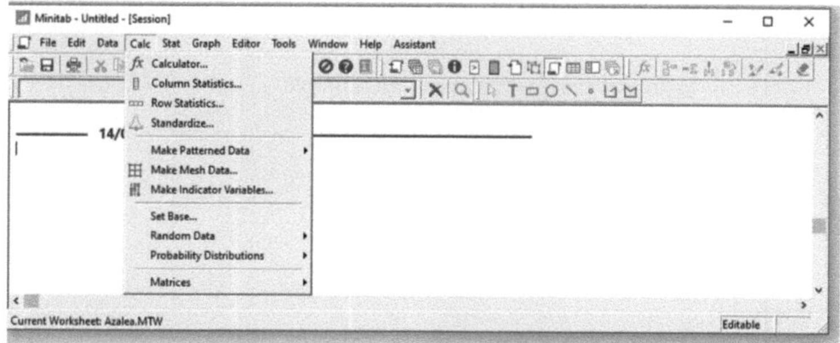

Fig. 11. Minitab: preparation for a data analytics task

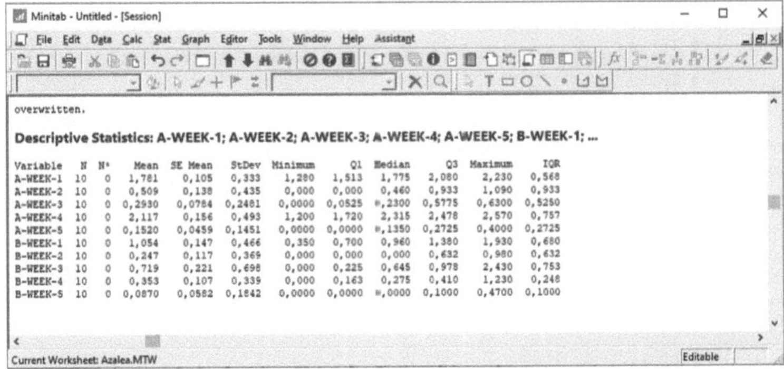

Fig. 12. Minitab: data analytics task output

5   Conclusions

This study explored and compared three GUI-based tools for teaching data analytics: fsQCA, EDA module within Nets4Learning, and Minitab. Minitab and the EDA module stands out for their ease in performing descriptive analyses and quick, dynamic visualizations, making them ideal for introducing basic statistical concepts. As for fsQCA, although it allows for unique qualitative comparative analyses, it is observed that its use can be more complex for researchers learning the tool, especially when working with datasets containing a larger number of variables. In conclusion, combining these tools in the classroom allows students to focus on interpreting results and the logic of data analysis, reducing the barrier to entry that learning programming languages alone can sometimes pose in the early stages.

References

1. Bruha, I.: Pre- and post-processing in machine learning and data mining. In: Paliouras, G., Karkaletsis, V., Spyropoulos, C.D. (eds.) ACAI 1999. LNCS (LNAI), vol. 2049, pp. 258–266. Springer, Heidelberg (2001). https://doi.org/10.1007/3-540-44673-7_13
2. Busby, M.: Learn Google. Wordware Publishing Inc. (2004)
3. Fisher, D., DeLine, R., Czerwinski, M., Drucker, S.: Interactions with big data analytics. Interactions **19**(3), 50–59 (2012)
4. Hardcatle, P.: Information is power. Curationis **6**(2), 19–21 (1983)
5. Kanyongo, W., Ezugwu, A.E., Moyo, T., Dombeu, J.V.F.: Informatics in medicine unlocked (2000)
6. Lewis, E.: Science instruction and information literacy: information is power. Scan: J. Educat. **18**(1), 49–53 (1999)
7. Milovanović, M., Perišić, J.: Advantages and limitations of using SPSS in teaching statistics. In: MEFkon 2020 Innovation as an Initiator of the Development "innovations in the Function of Development", p. 274 (2020)
8. INC Minitab. Minitab statistical software. Minitab Release, 13 (2000)

9. Mudarra, A., Valdivia, D., Ducange, P., Germán, M., Rivera, A.J., Pérez-Godoy, M.D.: Nets4Learning: a web platform for designing and testing ANN/DNN models. Electronics **13**(22), 4378 (2024)
10. Negi, D.S., Rao, R., Chakraborty, A.: Information is power: ICT and agricultural productivity. Perspectives **7**(2) (2025)
11. Ragin, C.C.: Fuzzy sets: calibration versus measurement (2007)
12. Ryan, T.A., Joiner, B.L., Ryan, B.F.: Minitab II Reference Manual: Preliminary Edition. Statistics Department, Pennsylvania State University (1976)
13. Nur Shaziayani, W., Sarimah, S., Norsyiha, F., Omar, M.: Engineering students' perception of minitab in learning statistics (2025)

"Other Applications"

Visual Analytics of Lung Cancer Risk in a Virtual Research Environment

Delia Aminta Moreno-Perdomo[1], Virginia González-Diez[1],
Antonio Jesús Díaz-Honrubia[1,2], Lucía Prieto-Santamaría[1,2],
Guillermo Vigueras[1,2], Alejandro Rodríguez-González[1,2],
and Paloma Tejera-Nevado[1(✉)]

[1] Centro de Tecnología Biomédica, Universidad Politécnica de Madrid, Madrid, Spain
{da.moreno,virginia.gonzalezd,antoniojesus.diaz,lucia.prieto.santamaria,
guillermo.vigueras,alejandro.rg,paloma.tejera}@upm.es
[2] ETS de Ingenieros Informáticos, Universidad Politécnica de Madrid, Madrid, Spain

Abstract. Lung cancer remains one of the leading causes of cancer-related mortality worldwide and represents a major public health concern. Although extensive research has identified numerous risk factors associated with this disease, further investigation is still required, particularly with respect to its underlying biological mechanisms. In prior work, a biological ontology was introduced to organize and harmonize heterogeneous biological data related to lung cancer and its subtypes. Nevertheless, lung cancer is inherently multifactorial, as biological processes interact with environmental and contextual factors that are commonly represented across disparate and unconnected data sources. To address this limitation, the present work extends the existing ontology to include both biological and environmental factors within a unified platform, which is embedded in a visual analytics tool. This approach enables the visualization and exploration of lung cancer–related risk factors and associated information across multiple heterogeneous data sources. By supporting cross-domain queries that integrate biological, environmental, and additional previously unconnected data, the proposed solution provides more functional and comprehensive access to knowledge relevant to lung cancer research.

Keywords: Visual Analytics Risk Factors · Lung Cancer · Knowledge Integration

1 Introduction

1.1 Lung Cancer

Lung cancer remains the leading cause of oncological mortality and the most frequently diagnosed cancer globally, with an estimated incidence of 2.48 million new cases annually [1]. In Spain alone, projections estimated over 34,500 new diagnoses for 2025, reflecting a persistent upward trend, particularly among women [2]. Histologically, the disease is classified into two major categories:

J. M. Ferrández Vicente et al. (Eds.): IWINAC 2026, LNCS 16575, pp. 465–474, 2026.
https://doi.org/10.1007/978-3-032-27317-8_44

Non-Small Cell Lung Cancer (NSCLC), comprising approximately 85% of cases, including adenocarcinoma and squamous cell carcinoma, and Small Cell Lung Cancer (SCLC), an aggressive neuroendocrine subtype primarily linked to heavy tobacco use [3]. While active smoking remains the dominant etiological factor, recent evidence highlights a complex interplay between biological predispositions, such as EGFR and KRAS mutations, and environmental exposures. Notably, long-term inhalation of fine particulate matter ($PM_{2.5}$) and indoor radon gas are now recognized as critical drivers of lung cancer in never-smokers, promoting carcinogenesis through sustained pulmonary inflammation [4,5]. Given this multifactorial landscape, there is a critical need for advanced visualization tools that can integrate geospatial environmental data with biological risk markers to identify high-risk clusters and inform precision public health strategies.

1.2 Risk Factor Analysis

In the contemporary landscape of precision medicine, the state of the art in disease risk factor analysis has transitioned from isolated variable assessment to the sophisticated integration of heterogeneous data. For complex pathologies like lung cancer, disease etiology emerges from an intricate interplay between biological susceptibility and the environmental exposome [6,7]. While multi-omics technologies and environmental sensors provide the raw data for these insights, the inherent diversity of these datasets, ranging from molecular pathways to geographic pollution indices, requires a unifying semantic layer to be clinically actionable. Consequently, modern research has moved toward the use of formal ontologies and knowledge graphs to provide a structured vocabulary that maps the relationships between disparate risk factors [8].

This shift is exemplified by current large-scale initiatives like the LANTERN study (2024–2025), which utilizes shared common ontologies to create "Digital Human Avatars" that integrate omics-based variables with established clinical factors [9]. Similarly, the LUng Cancer-related risk factors and their Impact Assessment (LUCIA) [10] project uses knowledge graphs to harmonize clinical databases, genomic repositories, and environmental monitoring records. This enables researchers to query complex semantic connections, such as identifying specific genes associated with both tobacco exposure and lung cancer susceptibility. Lung cancer remains a major contributor to cancer-related deaths worldwide, underscoring the need for continued research, particularly on its biological determinants. Although extensive biological data on lung cancer and its subtypes exist, heterogeneity in structure and format limits their effective integration and use in artificial intelligence applications. Ontologies and semantic technologies mitigate these limitations by enabling the creation of interoperable knowledge graphs. Lung-CABO is a lung cancer-specific ontology developed to support the construction of knowledge graphs for risk factor analysis and AI-driven research. Its modular architecture facilitates reuse and future extension, including the integration of additional data domains [11].

The utility of these ontologically-mapped datasets is realized through advanced visualization tools that bridge the gap between data complexity and clinical decision support. Tools like SCAN360 [12] and the Louisiana Tumor Registry Knowledge Graph [13] demonstrate how semantic interoperability allows for the visual deconstruction of risk.

1.3   Previous Work

A foundational component is the biological ontology titled LUNG-CABO, which was originally published as a structured representation of biological knowledge relevant to lung cancer [11]. LUNG-CABO captures detailed relationships among genes, proteins, molecular pathways, and disease phenotypes, providing a formal framework for querying and reasoning over biological risk factors, as exemplified by integrative resources such as DisGeNET[1] [14].

Subsequent efforts extended LUNG-CABO to incorporate environmental factors, resulting in a complementary environmental ontology integrating chemical exposure records, European demographic registries on lung cancer incidence and mortality, and additional environmental datasets (unpublished data). The integration of these heterogeneous data sources allows the ontology to provide a rich semantic representation of both intrinsic biological factors and extrinsic environmental determinants of disease. The biological and environmental ontologies share several nodes and semantic entities, enabling interoperability and cross-domain reasoning. These shared nodes support queries linking biological risk factors with environmental exposures and allow SPARQL queries spanning both ontologies to retrieve integrated information on lung cancer risk factors from biological, demographic, and environmental perspectives.

Together, these ontologies served as the primary knowledge base for the development of the Visual Analytics Risk Factors (VARF) tool. By leveraging the semantic structure of both LUNG-CABO and the extended environmental ontology, VARF platform is able to support interactive exploration, analysis, and visualization of risk factors, combining biological and environmental perspectives within a unified visual analytics framework. This integration represents a significant advance in the ability to query, correlate, and interpret multi-domain data relevant to lung cancer risk assessment.

2   Methodology

2.1   Conceptual Framework

The VARF framework is a conceptual approach that supports the identification, exploration, and interpretation of biological and environmental risk factors using semantic technologies and visual analytics. It combines ontology-based knowledge representation, formal query mechanisms, and interactive visualization to enable systematic analysis of complex, interrelated risk factors across

---

[1] https://www.disgenet.com/.

heterogeneous data sources. Biological and environmental risk factors are modeled with RDF (Resource Description Framework) ontologies, explicitly representing entities, attributes, and relationships that characterize risk dynamics, exposure pathways, and contextual dependencies. SPARQL is used as the primary query language, allowing precise, reproducible analyses over semantically enriched data.

A key feature of VARF tool is its emphasis on visual analytics, conceptualizing query results as interactive analytical objects rather than static outputs. Tabular views support detailed inspection and validation of individual risk factors, while graph-based representations reveal relational structures, dependencies, and propagation patterns. This multimodal visualization strategy is essential for uncovering latent relationships and enabling exploratory risk analysis.

2.2 Implementation

VARF system is implemented as a web-based tool to facilitate the application of Visual Analytics Risk Factors. The system follows a client–server architecture in which a Flask-based backend mediates communication between authenticated users and a Virtuoso-hosted RDF triple store. The semantic repository serves as the authoritative source of biological and environmental risk factor data, exposed via an SPARQL endpoint.

User interaction is facilitated through a web interface that includes a SPARQL query editor, execution controls, and dedicated containers for result visualization. Queries defined by users are transmitted to the backend using structured HTTP requests and executed against the SPARQL endpoint. The backend processes and normalizes the results into a consistent JSON format, decoupling semantic query execution from visualization logic and supporting extensibility.

Visualization constitutes a core component of the VARF implementation. Query results can be explored through both tabular and graph-based views, depending on the analytical objective. Tabular visualizations support precise examination of risk factor attributes and values, whereas graph-based visualizations emphasize semantic relationships, co-occurrence patterns, and interdependencies among risk factors, which are critical for understanding complex risk scenarios.

Graph generation and interactive visualization are implemented on the client side to ensure performance and scalability. Graph structures are created and managed using the Graphology[2] JavaScript library, which provides efficient data structures for handling nodes, edges, and associated risk-related metadata. Node positioning is computed using the ForceAtlas2[3] force-directed layout algorithm, allowing meaningful spatial organization based on relational strength and connectivity. To maintain user interface (UI) responsiveness when handling large or

---

[2] https://graphology.github.io/.

[3] https://graphology.github.io/standard-library/layout-forceatlas2.html.

dense graphs, layout computations are executed within a Web Worker, preventing blocking of the main UI thread.

Graph rendering and user interaction are handled by Sigma.js[4], which enables high-performance visualization and extensive customization. The library supports interactive features such as tooltips that display detailed information about individual risk factors when hovering over nodes, as well as dynamic highlighting of adjacent nodes and edges to emphasize local neighborhoods and relational context. These interaction mechanisms enhance interpretability and support both global overviews and detailed, localized risk analysis.

Access to the system is provided through two complementary deployments. A secured deployment integrates an OpenID Connect–based authentication layer with Keycloak, requiring user authentication to access the interface and execute SPARQL queries, thereby restricting interaction with the semantic risk knowledge base to authorized users and reinforcing compliance with security, data governance, and reproducibility best practices. In parallel, a publicly accessible deployment is made available to allow open exploration of the system without authentication, facilitating transparency and broader dissemination of the results. From an infrastructural perspective, the implementation emphasizes portability and reproducibility, enabling deployment across different environments and facilitating adaptation to diverse institutional contexts through configurable parameters.

The complete implementation of the VARF system is openly available to support transparency, reproducibility, and reuse. The source code of the application is accessible at https://medal.ctb.upm.es/internal/gitlab/lucia/varf. In addition, a fully operational instance of the VARF system has been deployed and is publicly accessible online at https://medal.ctb.upm.es/lucia/, allowing users to directly interact with the system, execute SPARQL queries over the underlying semantic infrastructure, and explore biological and environmental risk factors through the provided visual analytics capabilities.

3 Results

3.1 Integration of Biological and Environmental Data

The VARF platform also establishes explicit connections between biological and environmental data. Specifically, the Malignant Neoplasm of Lung disease class links biological information to environmental risk factors. Biomarker–Disease Associations connect this disease to relevant biomarkers, while Chemical–Disease Associations link various diseases to chemicals. Additionally, Chemical–Gene Associations connect specific genes to environmental chemical exposures. These integrated links allow users to explore the interactions between genes, biomarkers, chemicals, and environmental factors in the context of lung cancer, supporting a more comprehensive and comparative analysis of risk determinants.

---

[4] https://github.com/jacomyal/sigma.js.

Within the VARF platform, users can access information on: Gene–Disease Associations, Disease and Gene Fusions, Disease and Chromosomal Rearrangements, Variant–Disease Associations, Pathway–Disease Associations, Disease–Gene Pathways, Chemical–Evidence Associations, Biomarker–Disease Associations, Chemical–Location Associations, and Disease Demographics and Vital Statistics. The interface continues to be organized into a three-part workflow: query configuration on the left, an interactive network graph in the center, and a structured data table at the bottom. On the left side of the screen, the configuration panel serves as the technical entry point for researchers. For each selected query, a set of filters is available to refine results. Predefined SPARQL queries are provided for rapid execution, but users can also run queries manually. Query results are displayed both as rendered graphs and as tables, which can be downloaded in CSV format.

3.2   Use Case in a Biological Context

For the Pathway-Disease Association use case, VARF tool integrated multi-omics data to help researchers link genetic information to clinical disease classifications, enabling exploration through semantic queries, interactive knowledge graphs, and structured data tables (see Fig. 1). The system functions by pulling data through the SPARQL query interface on the left, which serves as the engine of the tool. In this specific execution, the researcher has queried the "Pathway Disease Association". The query leverages standardized biological prefixes, such as WikiPathways (WP) [15] and the National Cancer Institute Thesaurus (NCIT)[5], to ensure that the results are based on internationally recognized biomedical ontologies.

The core of the visualization is the interactive knowledge graph. This network visually maps the intersection between Non-small cell lung cancer and Small cell lung cancer. Each large central node acts as a "hub" for a specific disease, while the smaller teal nodes represent Gene Products or Pathways. This visual representation allows a researcher to immediately identify shared genetic drivers that might not be as obvious in a standard spreadsheet. The tabular results at the bottom provide the specific evidence for the visual graph.

For example, in the running example of Fig. 1, the table shows that AKT1 is associated with NSCLC (C0007131, WP4255) and SCLC (C0149925, WP4658). By linking the pathway IDs directly to these disease identifiers, VARF platform enables researchers to trace a gene's role across different lung cancer subtypes, supporting the identification of potential multi-purpose therapeutic targets.

---

[5] https://ncithesaurus.nci.nih.gov/.

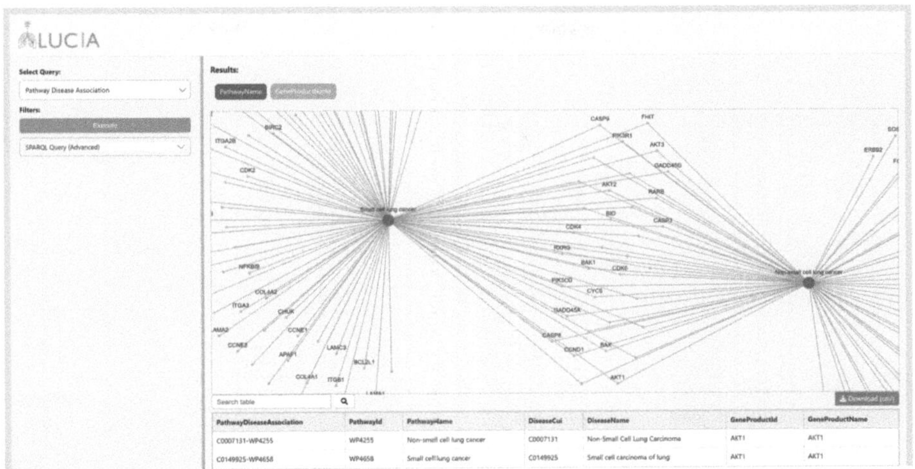

Fig. 1. Use case of the VARF tool in the biological field for Pathway-Disease Association. This interface demonstrates the integration of complex genetic data with clinical disease classifications to support lung cancer research. The left panel shows the execution of a SPARQL query that pulls standardized data from biological ontologies. The central visualization features a knowledge graph where central nodes represent specific clinical pathologies, NSCLC and SCLC, connected to teal satellite nodes representing shared gene products.

3.3 Use Case in an Environmental Context

The second use case implemented in this study focuses on Chemical Evidence Association, shifting the analytical lens toward the smoking-related exposome. A dropdown menu is set to "Chemical Evidence Association", which has triggered the generation of a complex SPARQL query in the advanced editor below (see Fig. 2). The center of the interface is dominated by a large, interactive radial network graph that visualizes the "smoking" exposome. A central node labeled "smoking" acts as a hub from which dozens of gray association lines radiate outward like spokes on a wheel. A two-color classification system is utilized to distinguish between different types of data: light blue nodes represent specific chemical entities, while yellow nodes designate corresponding evidence markers. This dual-color coding highlights a massive constellation of exposures radiating from the central smoking node, including heavy metals such as cadmium, cobalt, tin, and manganese. Furthermore, the graph maps critical metabolic fingerprints and biomarkers essential for understanding the biological impact of tobacco smoke. Notable nodes include cotinine, the primary metabolite of nicotine, and biomarkers of polycyclic aromatic hydrocarbon exposure such as 1-hydroxypyrene. The yellow evidence nodes such as 1-naphthol exposure, visually link these substances to their measured occurrence in human exposure data.

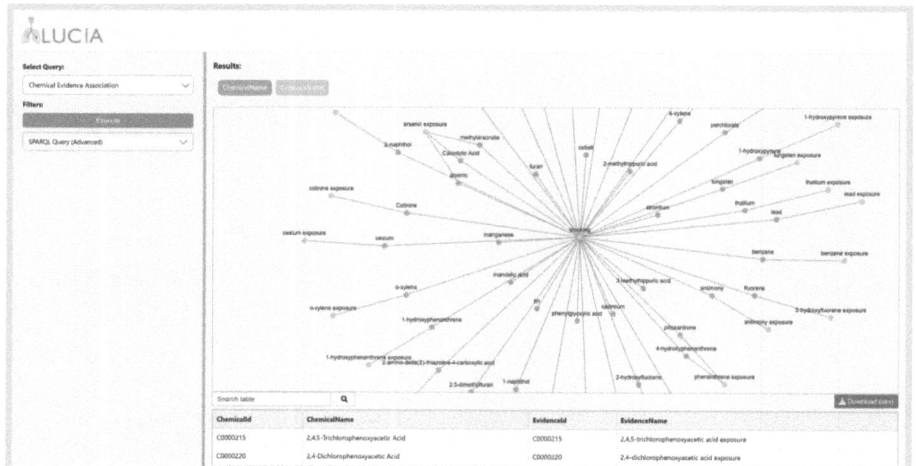

Fig. 2. Interface visualization of the smoking-related exposome: use case in an environmental context.

The tool completes this data integration by translating the visual network into a structured results table at the bottom of the interface. This table provides granular details, including Chemical IDs and Evidence IDs for substances like 2,4,5-Trichlorophenoxyacetic acid and 2,4-Dichlorophenoxyacetic acid. A search utility allows for the rapid filtering of specific environmental factors, while a dedicated download feature enables the export of these curated associations into CSV format for further epidemiological modeling and statistical analysis.

4   Discussion

Understanding lung cancer risk requires not only identification of relevant factors but also careful comparison of the strength of evidence supporting each association. Visual analytics offer an effective means of synthesizing complex epidemiological data, enabling clearer comparison across multiple risk and protective factors. In this discussion, we focus on comparative visual approaches that contextualize lung cancer risk within the broader cancer prevention evidence base, supporting more informed interpretation of relative risk and uncertainty.

The Interactive Cancer Risk Matrix from the World Cancer Research Fund (WCRF) provides a concise visual framework for comparing cancer risk factors and the strength of supporting evidence. Using an interactive bubble chart, it allows users to assess both associations and evidence levels across cancers [16]. In the case of lung cancer, the matrix shows that factors such as retinol intake are linked to only a limited-suggestive decreased risk, underscoring the relatively weak evidence base compared with stronger associations observed for other cancers. This comparative visual approach supports more nuanced interpretation of lung cancer risk within the broader prevention literature.

These findings are consistent with the multidimensional risk perspective exemplified by platforms such as SCAN360, which promote a '360-degree view' of cancer determinants. By integrating region-specific datasets, such as the Louisiana Tumor Registry Knowledge Graph, these approaches illustrate that cancer risk is a dynamic interplay of genetics, environment, and lifestyle rather than a fixed metric. While modifiable behaviors, including diet and physical activity, account for roughly one-third of common cancers, our results reinforce the SCAN360 principle that environmental and contextual factors significantly influence patient outcomes, including survival and quality of life [12]. This perspective underscores the value of combining biological, behavioral, and environmental data in both research and clinical decision-making for lung cancer.

Cancer InFocus is a data aggregation and visualization platform designed to streamline the assessment of cancer burden across geographic regions through a rapid and repeatable process for creating analytical tools. Developed by the Community Impact Office at the University of Kentucky Markey Cancer Center, the platform is accessible for broader use via CancerInFocus.org for data downloads and through a no-cost licensing agreement for access to its data collection and application development tools. In a discussion context, Cancer InFocus exemplifies how structured, reproducible visual analytics can support comparative evaluation of risk factors, highlight regional variations, and facilitate targeted public health interventions, reinforcing the broader importance of integrating diverse datasets for cancer risk assessment [17].

5   Conclusion and Future Work

The VARF tool translates the principles of Visual Analytics Risk Factors into a practical system for the interactive exploration and analysis of complex biological and environmental risk data hosted in Virtuoso-based semantic infrastructures. Through its integrated SPARQL query interface, the VARF platform facilitates, for example, the cross-referencing of fusion events and genomic variants with clinical phenotypes, ensuring that researchers can trace a molecular alteration from its raw data source to its clinical significance. By leveraging the VARF tool, researchers can systematically map documented chemical constituents to clinical evidence of exposure. This is particularly vital in lung cancer research, where the synergistic effects of various airborne toxins and heavy metals contribute significantly to disease progression. This tool allows for the identification of complex chemical profiles that are often obscured in traditional flat-data formats.

Looking ahead, this platform is being extended to support the integration of AI-driven models that combine clinical data with population-level risk factors. This ongoing development aims to enable the identification of previously unrecognized lung cancer risk factors and to advance understanding of the disease's underlying mechanisms. As these capabilities mature, they are expected to support more comprehensive, data-driven analyses, improved risk stratification, and deeper insight into the interactions between clinical, biological, and environmental determinants of lung cancer.

Acknowledgments. This work is supported by the project LUCIA - Lung Cancer-related risk factors and their Impact Assessment, funded by the European Union Horizon Europe Programme, that is being developed under grant 101096473.

Disclosure of Interests. The authors have no competing interests to declare that are relevant to the content of this article.

References

1. Bray, F., et al.: Global cancer statistics 2022: GLOCOCAN estimates of incidence and mortality worldwide for 36 cancers in 185 countries. CA Cancer J. Clin. **74**, 229–263 (2024)
2. Sociedad Española de Oncología Médica (SEOM). Las cifras del cáncer en España 2025. Sociedad Española de Oncología Médica/REDECAN. [Official report on Spanish epidemiology] (2025)
3. Siddiqui, F., Vagar, S., Siddiqui, A.H.: Lung Cancer. StatPearls (2025)
4. World Health Organization (WHO). WHO Handbook on Indoor Radon: A Public Health Perspective (2009). PMID: 23762967
5. Hill, W., et al.: Lung Adenocarcinoma promotion by air pollutants. Nature **616**, 159–167 (2023)
6. Young, A.S., et al.: The need for a cancer exposome atlas: a scoping review. JNCI Cancer Spectrum **9**(1), pkae122 (2024)
7. Argentieri, M.A., et al.: Integrating the environmental and genetic architectures of ageing and mortality. Nat. Med. **31**, 1016–1025 (2025)
8. Contreiras Silva, M., et al.: Ontologies and knowledge graphs in oncology research. Cancers **14**(8), 1906 (2022)
9. Loroco, F., et al.: Lung cancer multi-omics digital human avatars for integrating precision medicine into clinical practice: the LANTERN study. BMC Cancer **23**, 540 (2023)
10. LUCIA Homepage. https://luciaeuproject.technion.ac.il/. Accessed 20 Jan 2026
11. Moreno-Perdomo, D.A., et al.: Lung-CABO: lung cancer concepts association biological ontology. In: 38th IEEE International Symposium on Computer-Based Medical Systems (CBMS), pp. 660–663. Universidad Politécnica de Madrid, Spain (2025)
12. SCAN 360 Homepage. https://www.scan360.com/. Accessed 20 Jan 2026
13. Shamimui Hassan, S.M., et al.: Knowledge graph-enabled cancer data analytics. IEEE J. Biomed. Health Inform. **24**(7), 1952–1967 (2020)
14. Pinero, J., et al.: DISGENET: accelerating data-driven discovery in disease genomics and therapeutic development. bioRxiv (2026). 697749
15. Agrawal, A., et al.: WikiPathways 2024: next generation pathway database. Nucleic Acids Res. **52**(D1), D679–D689 (2024)
16. Interactive Cancer Risk Matrix Homepage. https://www.wcrf.org/research-policy/interactive-cancer-risk-matrix/. Accessed 20 Jan 2026
17. Cancer InFocus Homepage. https://www.kycancerneeds.org/maps/. Accessed 20 Jan 2026

An Offline Handwriting Approach
to Parkinson's Disease Detection

Daniel Corredor, José F. Vélez(iD), and Ángel Sánchez(✉)(iD)

Departamento de Informática y Estadística, Universidad Rey Juan Carlos,
28933 Móstoles, Madrid, Spain
angel.sanchez@urjc.es
https://www.gavab.es/

Abstract. Most research on Parkinson's Disease detection using handwriting relies on the online approach (i.e., digital tablets and smart pens) rather than the offline one (i.e., scanned paper documents), primarily because it captures dynamic temporal features that reveal early motor symptoms. However, offline handwriting presents some notable advantages, such as: its lower cost, fewer technical barriers especially for older adults who more frequently suffer from this disease, access to more historical data from patients, and easier clinical integration, among others. This paper describes a study to discriminate handwriting from healthy and Parkinsonian patients using offline handwriting images reconstructed from the online data contained in the PaHaW dataset. For this purpose, we perform a collection of experiments that have produced F1-Score prediction results above 62% for some writing tasks.

Keywords: Parkinson's Disease · Offline Handwritten Text Analysis · Deep Neural Networks · Online-to-Offline Handwriting Conversion · PaHaW Dataset

1 Introduction

Parkinson's disease (PD) is a progressive neurological disorder characterized by several motor manifestations—such as bradykinesia, tremor, muscle stiffness, gait abnormalities, and postural instability—as well as numerous non-motor issues [1,2]. Although the precise origins of PD remain unclear, it is thought to arise from a multifaceted interplay between genetic predisposition and life-long exposure to environmental agents, including pesticides, industrial solvents, and air pollutants. Globally, the disability and mortality linked to PD are rising faster than those associated with any other neurological condition.

Automatic handwriting analysis refers to the application of computational techniques and algorithms to assess and interpret handwriting patterns from diverse domains, including forensic biometrics and medical imaging, among others [3]. In recent years, deep learning approaches have significantly advanced handwriting recognition performance [4].

© The Author(s), under exclusive license to Springer Nature Switzerland AG 2026
J. M. Ferrández Vicente et al. (Eds.): IWINAC 2026, LNCS 16575, pp. 475–485, 2026.
https://doi.org/10.1007/978-3-032-27317-8_45

Handwriting has become an important approach for the early identification and tracking of PD [5]. Its usage in Parkinson's detection focuses on some characteristic motor deficits caused by the PD condition, which are reflected in the writing behavior. Several studies have shown that handwriting analysis offers a non-invasive, affordable, and dependable strategy for early PD screening [6,7]. Longitudinal handwriting evaluation (i.e., examining a person's handwriting over time to observe and analyze changes or stability) can also support the monitoring of disease progression and treatment effectiveness.

The distinction between offline and online handwriting acquisition is fundamental for the analysis of motor alterations associated with PD. Online handwriting captures the dynamics of the writing process, including parameters such as velocity, pressure, trajectory, and temporal patterns, using digital tablets. In contrast, offline handwriting consists solely of the final static image of handwriting on paper, usually obtained through scanning or photography. Based on the available research, online handwriting is more widely used than the offline alternative for PD detection [8]. Although offline data lack the kinematic information of online data, they offer several methodological and clinical advantages that make them highly suitable for large-scale assessment of PD. One of the main benefits of offline handwriting is its accessibility and cost-effectiveness. It requires only basic materials (paper, pen, and a scanner or smartphone) thus eliminating the need for specialized devices. Another relevant aspect is the availability of historical offline handwritten documents that have existed for much more years and patients that online ones, thus allowing for longitudinal analysis of PD evolution. Offline handwriting is also less intrusive and more natural for patients, particularly the older ones, who represent the majority of individuals affected by PD. Writing on paper is a familiar action that does not introduce technological anxiety or modify motor behavior, whereas digital tablets can impose constraints or induce behavioral changes that bias the results. Another advantage of the offline modality is its robustness in real-world contexts. In summary, offline handwriting analysis offers a practical approach for the detection, monitoring and evolution of PD.

The rest of the manuscript is organized as follows. In Sect. 2 we summarize some recent work related to the problem analyzed in this document. Section 3 describes the PaHaW dataset used in the experiments. The proposed method to solve the considered PD text detection is presented in Sect. 4. Section 5 describes and analyzes the different experiments performed, as well as the metrics used to evaluate the results. Finally, Section presents the conclusions and outlines future work.

2   Related Work

Handwriting analysis has become an important area of research in understanding and diagnosing Parkinson's disease (PD) [5,9]. Digital pens equipped with various sensors are used to capture detailed handwriting dynamics, including pressure, speed, and pen-tip position [10]. These devices can provide comprehensive data that are analyzed to detect subtle changes in handwriting, which are indicative of motor impairment in PD patients [7].

Machine learning algorithms are applied to handwriting data to distinguish between PD patients and healthy subjects. These algorithms can identify patterns and features in patients' handwriting that are not easily detectable by human observation [11]. Techniques such as Support Vector Machines (SVM), neural networks, and, more recently, deep learning architectures have shown a high accuracy when predicting PD based on handwriting samples [12].

Some characteristic features present in the handwriting of patients with PD, such as tremors or micrographia can be quantified through advanced image processing techniques. Studies have shown that these patients often exhibit these features distinctly when compared to healthy individuals [13].

It is also possible to monitor the progression of PD by periodically capturing handwriting samples [14]. The changes in handwriting characteristics can correlate with the severity of motor symptoms [10], thus providing a non-invasive method for tracking disease progression and also for analyzing the effectiveness of treatments [15].

There is a growing trend towards integrating handwriting analysis into clinical practice [1]. Tools and platforms are being developed to aid neurologists in the early diagnosis and personalized management of PD. These tools provide a standardized method to assess motor symptoms and can be used alongside other diagnostic criteria.

A paper by Casademunt et al. [16] investigates how PD causes distortions and fluency degradation in handwriting and aims to automatically detect these alterations by identifying which textual elements show the strongest Parkinsonian traits. Using a convolutional neural network trained on the PaHaW database, the authors perform multiple prediction experiments on handwritten samples and report an accuracy above 65%, demonstrating the potential of automatic handwriting analysis to support clinical diagnosis.

Regarding the use of offline handwriting in the detection of PD, a very recent work by Bensefia and collaborators [17] uses a CNN-based model to analyze Archimedean spiral images from the HandPD and NewHandPD datasets confirming the suitability of deep learning for this task. Their results demonstrate promising diagnostic performance, validating the potential of offline handwriting as a reliable indicator of PD.

In summary, the integration of digital technology and advanced computational methods in handwriting analysis represents a significant advancement in the early detection and management of PD. It offers a non-invasive, cost-effective, and accessible means to support clinical decision-making and improve patient outcomes.

3   PaHaW Dataset

The Parkinson's Disease Handwriting Database (PaHaW) [5,12] consists of multiple handwriting samples from 37 parkinsonian patients (19 men/18 women), and 38 gender and age matched controls (20 men/18 women). The average length of patients with PD in this dataset is 8.38 years. The database was acquired in cooperation with the Movement Disorders Center at the First Department of Neurology, Masaryk University and St. Anne's University Hospital in Brno, Czech Republic.

Figure 1 illustrates a snippet of a spreadsheet containing the data provided by PaHaW for each person in the dataset. In particular, the following information is present: subject ID, Nationality, Sex, Disease (i.e., 'PD' for sick people and 'H' for healthy ones, respectively), PD status (it provides information similar to the previous column: if the value is 'ON', the subject has PD; if it has no value, it is a control subject), Age (where the mean age of the individuals is 65.82 years and the median is 65), Dominant hand (where all the subjects in this dataset are right-handed), LED (acronym for "Levodopa Equivalent Dose": the administration of a drug that produces the same Antiparkinsonian effects as 100 mg of levodopa drug), UPDRS V (i.e., the most commonly used scale for estimating the severity of Parkinson's disease), and, finally, Length of PD (number of years of PD, where subjects have been suffering from the disease for an average of 8.38 years, respectively).

ID	Nationality	Sex	Disease	PD status	Age	Dominant hand	LED	UPDRS V	Lenght of PD
0001	Czech	F	PD	on	86	r	1115	2	6
0002	Czech	F	PD	on	78	r	2110	2	8
0003	Czech	F	PD	on	69	r	1556.6	2	7
0004	Czech	F	PD	on	79	r	1691	2	12
0005	Czech	F	PD	on	69	r	600	2	2
0006	Czech	F	PD	on	57	r	1271.66	2	9
...									

Fig. 1. Data provided by PaHaW on each of the subjects.

Each database subject was asked to complete a collection of handwriting exercises, called "tasks", according to the prepared filled template. The completed template was shown to the subjects; and no restrictions about the number of repetitions of syllables/words in the tasks or their height were given.

A tablet was overlaid with an empty paper template (containing only printed lines and a square box specifying the area for the Archimedean spiral), and a conventional ink pen was held in a normal fashion, allowing for immediate full visual feedback. The signals were recorded using the Intuos 4M (Wacom technology) digitizing tablet with a 150 Hz sampling frequency.

Digitized signals were acquired during the movements executed while exerting pressure on the writing surface and during the movements above the writing surface. These signals were denoted as "on-surface movements" and "in-air movements", respectively. The perpendicular pressure exerted on the tablet surface was also recorded. The recordings started when the pen touched the surface of the digitizer and finished when the task was completed. The tablet captured the following dynamic features (i.e., time-sequences): x-coordinate; y-coordinate;

time stamp; button status; pressure; tilt; and elevation. Button status is a binary variable, being '0' for pen-up state (in-air movement) and '1' for pen-down state (on-surface movement).

Figure 2 shows the template used by the subjects during the creation of the PaHaW database. It contains a total of eight handwriting tasks to be performed by all the subjects in the dataset.

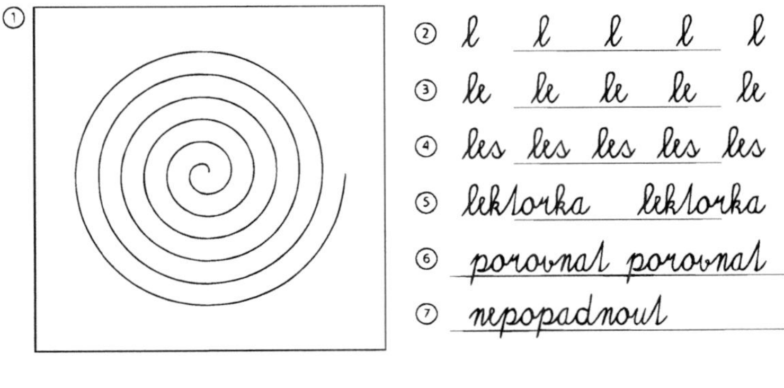

Fig. 2. Writer's template used in the PaHaW database.

For each one of the tasks executed by each individual (healthy or Parkinsonian), PaHaW provides a text file containing online data corresponding to the sequence of points captured when handwriting the task. The information for each point is in a text line, and the initial line contains the variable number of points required to complete the task. Moreover, for each point in the given task, the following information is sequentially stored in this order:

- Y-coordinate,
- X-coordinate,
- *Timestamp*: time at which the coordinate point was generated (in milliseconds),
- *Status*: '1' (writing device on the surface) or '0' (writing device in the air),
- *Azimuth*: inclination of the projection of the pen on the surface with respect to the north of the surface,
- *Height*: angle of inclination of the pen with respect to the horizontal of the surface, and
- *Pressure*: pressure exerted by the pen on the surface.

PaHaW dataset provides a comprehensive, relevant, and validated resource for developing predictive models for PD based on handwriting analysis [18,19].

4   Proposed Method

Figure 3 illustrates, with a handwriting sample of a patient (corresponding to Task 2 of PaHaw dataset), the successive preprocessings carried out on the online image to convert it into an offline one and to prepare it for neural model training. First, the sequence of online (X, Y) point coordinates corresponding to a given text task, together with their associated pressure and altitude signals, are only considered (being the remaining online information discarded). We track the sequence of points and use pressure information to simulate pixel intensities of corresponding offline text and altitude to simulate the thickness of strokes, respectively. After that, a simple data augmentation is applied by randomly selecting one among three possible image transformations: dilate, shear and rotate, respectively. These augmented offline samples are then padded to remove empty spaces between successive writing components (e.g., letters, syllables or words). Finally, the samples of text overlapped patches, to train the neural architecture, are generated using a sliding window procedure.

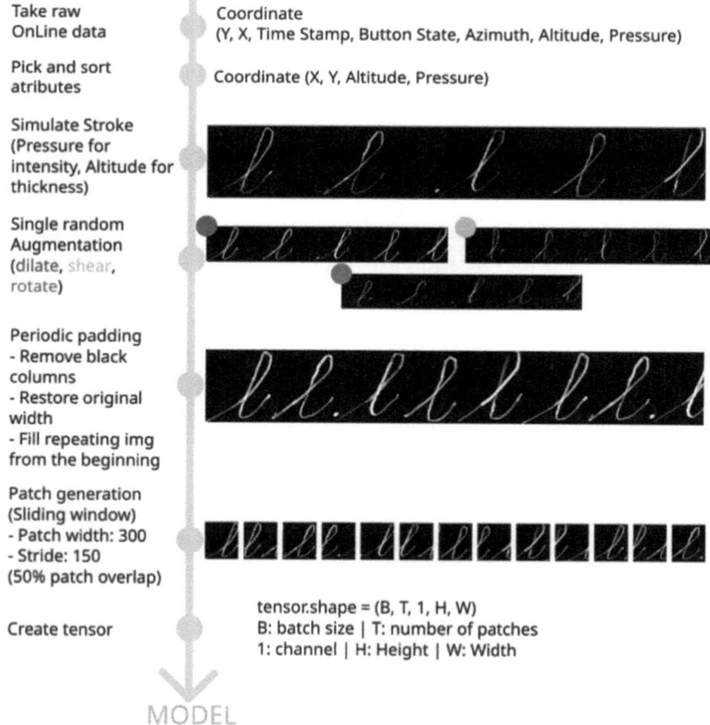

Fig. 3. Successive preprocessings to convert an online handwriting task to corresponding offline one and to prepare the samples for training.

Figure 4 shows the neural model used in our experiments. This model is a hybrid CNN–RNN architecture designed to capture both spatial patterns (i.e., local handwriting shapes) and temporal structure (i.e., stroke evolution). It processes a handwriting image as a sequence of patches, embeds each patch with a CNN, then models the sequence with an LSTM before producing the final prediction of the presented text as "healthy" or "Parkinsonian".

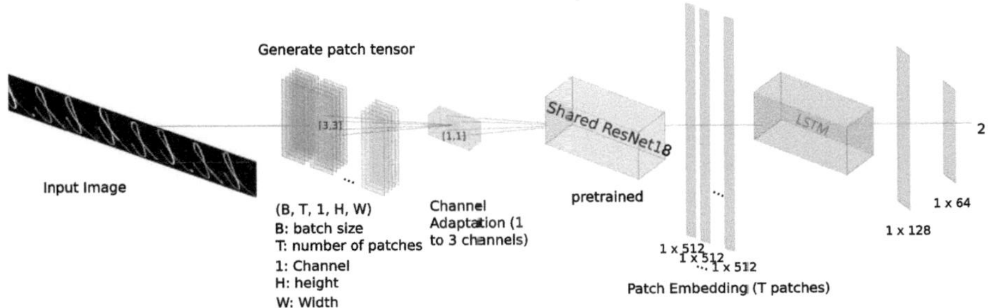

Fig. 4. Deep neural architecture to predict offline samples as corresponding to healthy or Parkinsonian patients.

5   Experiments

This section summarizes the evaluation metrics and the PD prediction experiments carried out. The following system hardware was employed for the experiments performed: the operating system was Ubuntu 22.04.5 LTS; the CPU used was AMD Ryzen Threadripper PRO 7945WX with 64 GB of RAM; the GPU was NVIDIA RTX A4000, CUDA 12.6; and the IDE employed was Visual Studio Code. For model training, the software stack was primarily based on PyTorch, which was used to implement and train the neural network architectures. A ResNet backbone pre-trained was employed as a feature extractor. Image loading and preprocessing operations were performed using OpenCV (cv2) and NumPy. Evaluation metrics were computed using scikit-learn.

Table 1 summarizes some important training model hyperparameter values used in the experiments. These values were determined by experimentation.

In our experiments, we have partitioned all the 75 PaHaW patients into training and test ones (i.e., their corresponding complete handwritten tasks). Due to insufficient sample size for training the model, a Leave-One-Subject-Out (LOSO) cross-validation procedure was applied on the three presented experiments, and corresponding results are reported next.

Model evaluation is the process of assessing how well a machine learning model performs on unseen data. In our context of handwritten text prediction over the tasks performed by the involved subjects, we first compute the values of True Positives (TP), False Positives (FP), False Negatives (FN) and True

Table 1. Training hyperparameters for Parkinson's detection

Parameter	Value
Training Epochs	100
Batch Size	2
Optimizer	AdamW
Learning rate	1.00×10^{-3}
Momentum	0.7
Decay	1.00×10^{-4}

Negatives (TN), respectively. Next, the confusion matrices (CM) are computed. Finally, the *Accuracy*, *Precision*, *Recall*, *Specificity* and $F1-score$ metrics are then calculated as follows:

$$Precision = \frac{TP}{TP + FP} \; ; \; Recall = \frac{TP}{TP + FN} \; ; \; Specificity = \frac{TN}{TN + FP} \quad (1)$$

$$Accuracy = \frac{TP + TN}{TP + FP + TN + FN} \; ; \; F1\text{-}score = 2\,\frac{Precision \times Recall}{Precision + Recall} \quad (2)$$

5.1   Experiment 1: Training Using Samples from Individual Tasks

In this experiment, we trained the network of Fig. 4 for each of the seven considered tasks of PaHaW dataset (Tasks from 2 to 8 of Fig. 2) using only the text samples of the corresponding task. Table 2 shows the respective metrics for each task, where the column *CM* stands for "Confusion Matrix". Best global results were achieved for Task 6.

Table 2. Metrics for each task (in %): Single Task Train LOSO-Cross Validation

Task	CM(TP,FN/FP,TN)	Accuracy	Precision	Recall	Specificity	F1-Score
2	19,22/18,16	46.67	51.35	46.34	47.06	48.72
3	10,22/27,16	34.67	27.03	31.25	37.21	28.99
4	17,19/20,19	48.00	45.95	47.22	48.72	46.58
5	19,11/18,27	61.33	51.35	63.33	60.00	56.72
6	25,22/12,16	54.67	67.57	53.19	57.14	**59.52**
7	19,14/18,24	57.33	51.35	57.58	57.14	54.29
8	17,19/20,19	48.00	45.95	47.22	48.72	46.58

5.2   Experiment 2: Training Using Samples from Multiple Tasks

In this second experiment, we trained the network of Fig. 4 for each of the seven tasks considered of PaHaW dataset (Tasks from 2 to 8 of Fig. 2) using the training samples of all the seven tasks considered. Table 3 shows the metrics for each considered task. Best global results were achieved for Task 8.

Table 3. Metrics for each task (in %): Multitask Train LOSO-Cross Validation

Task	CM(TP,FN/FP,TN)	Accuracy	Precision	Recall	Specificity	F1-Score
2	11,15/26,23	45.33	29.73	42.31	46.94	34.92
3	13,11/24,27	53.33	35.14	54.17	52.94	42.62
4	24,16/13,22	61.33	64.86	60.00	62.86	62.34
5	14,7/23,31	60.00	37.84	66.67	57.41	48.28
6	19,15/18,23	56.00	51.35	55.88	56.10	53.52
7	20,9/17,29	65.33	54.05	68.97	63.04	60.61
8	26,20/11,18	58.67	70.27	56.52	62.07	**62.65**

5.3   Experiment 3: Discriminating PD at Early Stages

In the last experiment, we analyze the discriminating ability of our model when separating healthy patients from those ones with PD at an early stage (i.e., with less than five years after diagnosis of PD). A set of 18 patients was used in this experiment (9 "healthy" ones randomly selected and the only 9 available ones in PaHaW with early PD). We trained the network of Fig. 4 for each of the seven tasks considered of PaHaW dataset (Tasks from 2 to 8 of Fig. 2) using the training samples of all the seven tasks considered. Table 4 shows the respective metrics for each considered task. Best global results were achieved for Task 4.

Table 4. Metrics for each task (in %): Early PD LOSO-Cross Validation

Task	CM(TP,FN/FP,TN)	Accuracy	Precision	Recall	Specificity	F1-Score
2	2,7/7,2	22.22	22.22	22.22	22.22	22.22
3	3,6/5,4	38.89	37.50	33.33	44.44	35.29
4	6,3/4,5	66.67	60.00	66.67	55.56	**63.16**
5	2,7/2,7	50.00	50.00	22.22	77.78	30.77
6	1,8/8,1	11.11	11.11	11.11	11.11	11.11
7	4,5/8,1	27.78	33.33	44.44	11.11	38.10
8	5,4/5,4	50.00	50.00	55.56	44.44	52.63

6   Conclusion

We have presented an experimental study on the application of an offline handwriting approach to discriminate between handwriting samples from healthy and Parkinsonian patients. We described a procedure to convert online handwriting into offline images, and applied it to the public PaHaW dataset. Using the obtained offline images, we trained a proposed neural architecture and conducted a series of experiments to evaluate its performance. The best prediction results were achieved on tasks with longer handwritten texts, with some F1-scores above 62%. As future work, we aim to extend our experiments using new public handwriting datasets.

Acknowledgments. This research was supported by the Spanish Research Project no. PID2021-124064OB-I00 and Comunidad de Madrid grant no. M3600-6611/PEJ-2024-AI/COM-33538.

References

1. Postuma, R.B., et al.: MDS clinical diagnostic criteria for Parkinson's disease. Mov. Disord. **30**(12), 1591–1601 (2015)
2. Olanow, C.W., Schapira, A.H.V.: Therapeutic prospects for Parkinson's disease. Ann. Neurol. **74**(3), 337–347 (2013)
3. Plamondon, R., Srihari, S.N.: Online and off-line handwriting recognition: a comprehensive survey. IEEE Trans. Pattern Anal. Mach. Intell. **22**(1), 63–84 (2000)
4. Ruiz-Parrado, V., et al.: A bibliometric analysis of off-line handwritten document analysis literature (1990–2020). Pattern Recognit. **125**, 108513 (2022)
5. Drotár, P., et al.: Analysis of in-air movement in handwriting: a novel marker for Parkinson's disease. Comput. Methods Programs Biomed. **117**(3), 405–411 (2014)
6. Cascarano, G.D., et al.: Biometric handwriting analysis to support Parkinson's disease assessment and grading. BMC Med. Inform. Decis. Mak. **19**, 252 (2019)
7. Rosenblum, S., et al.: Handwriting as an objective tool for Parkinson's disease diagnosis. J. Neurol. **260**(9), 2347–2351 (2013)
8. Białek, K., et al.: Analysis of handwriting for recognition of Parkinson's disease: current state and new study. Electronics **13**, 3962 (2024)
9. Thomas, M., et al.: Handwriting analysis in Parkinson's disease: current status and future directions. Mov. Disord. Clin. Pract. **4**(6), 806–818 (2017)
10. Eichhorn, T.E., et al.: Computational analysis of open loop handwriting movements in Parkinson's disease: a rapid method to detect dopamimetic effects. Mov. Disord. **11**(3), 289–297 (1996)
11. Impedovo, D., Pirlo, G.: Dynamic handwriting analysis for the assessment of neurodegenerative diseases: a pattern recognition perspective. IEEE Rev. Biomed. Eng. **12**, 209–220 (2019)
12. Drotár, P., et al.: Evaluation of handwriting kinematics and pressure for differential diagnosis of Parkinson's disease. Artif. Intell. Med. **67**(3), 39–46 (2016)
13. Tamás, G., Illyés, G., Várkonyi, T.: Computerized handwriting analysis in Parkinson's disease. Comput. Biol. Med. **100**, 127–137 (2018)
14. Senatore, R., et al.: Distinctive handwriting signs in early Parkinson's disease. Appl. Sci. **12**, 12338 (2022)

15. Sauzeon, H., Roussel, N., Reversat, D.: Longitudinal assessment of handwriting in Parkinson's disease. J. Mot. Behav. **52**(6), 679–688 (2020)
16. Casademunt, A., et al.: A study on automatic analysis of handwriting alterations due to Parkinson's disease. In: Santos, M.F. (ed.) EPIA 2024. LNCS, vol. 14968, pp. 62–73. Springer, Cham (2025). https://doi.org/10.1007/978-3-031-73500-4_6
17. Bensefia, A., Djeddi, C., Hannousse, A., Diaz, M.: Parkinson's disease detection through offline handwriting analysis: a CNN-based approach. Int. J. Online Biomed. Eng. (iJOE) **22**(1), 133–146 (2026)
18. Gazda, M., Hireš, M., Drotár, M., P.: Multiple-fine-tuned convolutional neural networks for Parkinson's disease diagnosis from offline handwriting. IEEE Trans. Syst. Man Cybern. Syst **52**(1), 78–89 (2022)
19. Gupta, U., Bansal, H., Joshi, D.: An improved sex-specific and age-dependent classification model for Parkinson's diagnosis using handwriting measurement. Comput. Methods Programs Biomed. **189**(105305) (2020)

An Exhaustive Ordinal ECOC Framework for Ordinal Classification

Francisco Bérchez-Moreno[1]([✉]) [iD], Victor M. Vargas[2] [iD], Alberto Suárez[3] [iD],
Lorena Álvarez-Pérez[4] [iD], and Pedro A. Gutiérrez[1] [iD]

[1] Departamento de Ciencia de la Computación e Inteligencia Artificial,
Universidad de Córdoba, Córdoba, Spain
{fberchez,pagutierrez}@uco.es
[2] Departamento de Teoría de la Señal y Comunicaciones,
Universidad de Alcalá, Madrid, Spain
victor.vargas@uah.es
[3] Department of Computer Science, Universidad Autónoma de Madrid,
Madrid, Spain
alberto.suarez@uam.es
[4] Centro de Innovación Experimental del Conocimiento (CEIEC),
Universidad Francisco de Vitoria, Madrid, Spain
lorena.alvarez@ufv.es

Abstract. Error-Correcting Output Codes (ECOC) decompose multi-class problems into a set of simpler subproblems, providing robustness through redundancy. In ordinal classification, however, standard ECOC designs may violate the natural order structure of the labels. In this work, we introduce an exhaustive ordinal ECOC framework that systematically generates all monotone partitions of the ordered class set. The proposed construction is obtained by considering every non-empty subset of admissible threshold positions, thereby deriving the complete family of contiguous ordinal groupings. The resulting coding matrix preserves ordinal consistency while increasing structural redundancy in a principled manner. Experimental evaluation on 46 benchmark ordinal datasets, using logistic regression as base learner and 30 independent runs, shows that the proposed method consistently outperforms both a nominal ECOC baseline and strong ordinal competitors. Statistical analysis confirms that the improvements are significant across datasets. These results demonstrate that exploiting the full space of monotone ordinal decompositions yields richer structural information than classical ordered partitions.

Keywords: Ordinal classification · Error-correcting output codes · Multiclass classification

1 Introduction

Classification is a central task in Machine Learning (ML) and has been extensively studied in the literature [6]. Depending on the number of classes involved,

J. M. Ferrández Vicente et al. (Eds.): IWINAC 2026, LNCS 16575, pp. 486–495, 2026.
https://doi.org/10.1007/978-3-032-27317-8_46

classification problems are commonly categorised into binary and multi-class tasks. In binary classification tasks, if the classes are encoded using a single numerical value (say 0 for one of the classes, 1 for the other one) there are no formal differences between ordinal and nominal problems.

In multi-class problems, the relationships among classes play a crucial role. From this perspective, classification tasks can be divided into nominal classification, where no intrinsic ordering exists among classes, and Ordinal Classification (OC), in which class labels exhibit a natural ordering [13]. Representative applications of OC include, among others, disease severity assessment [5], and quality control [18]. In such problems, the ordinal structure provides additional information that can be explicitly exploited to improve predictive performance, which is typically evaluated using order-aware performance metrics [13].

ECOC [9] constitute a well-established framework for addressing multi-class classification problems by decomposing them into a set of binary classification tasks and combining their outputs through a decoding stage [10]. Beyond random or predefined designs, several works have highlighted the importance of problem-dependent code construction. For example, a discriminant ECOC design strategy that adapts the coding matrix to the underlying class structure [16] demonstrated that structured codebooks can significantly improve performance. In this sense, while ECOC methods have shown strong performance and robustness in nominal multi-class scenarios [1], most existing approaches do not explicitly incorporate information on the natural ordering of the classes in the coding and decoding stages, which means that the learning model cannot take advantage of this structure.

To overcome these limitations, this paper proposes a novel ordinal ECOC framework based on an exhaustive coding strategy. Instead of restricting the codes to binary ones, we use ordinal multiclass codes, where the number of possible values is always lower than in the original problem. Contrary to sparse or randomly generated code designs, the proposed method relies on a deterministic construction that exploits all non-trivial ordinal partitions of the label space. This approach allows ordinal relationships among classes to be implicitly embedded within the ECOC framework while providing the maximum possible level of redundancy for a given number of classes. The effectiveness of the proposed ordinal ECOC design is validated through an extensive experimental evaluation conducted on multiple benchmark datasets using order-aware performance metrics.

The remainder of this paper is organised as follows. Section 2 introduces the problem of OC and explains how ECOC is used to tackle standard classification problems. The proposed methodology is detailed in Sect. 3. Experimental settings and evaluation protocols are described in Sect. 4, while results and statistical analyses are presented in Sect. 5. Finally, conclusions are drawn in Sect. 6.

2   Background

This section presents the relevant background required to position the contributions of this work. First, it introduces the formal definition of OC and discusses its distinguishing characteristics. Then, it reviews standard ECOC methodologies, with particular emphasis on the Binary Complete Coding (referred to as Exhaustive Coding in [9]), analysing their general inability to exploit the ordinal information inherent to OC problems.

2.1   Ordinal Classification

In a supervised learning problem, the goal is to build a predictor from $\mathcal{D} = \{(\mathbf{x}_i, y_i)\}_{i=1}^{N}$, a dataset consisting of N labelled samples. The i-th sample in this set is characterised by $\mathbf{x}_i \in \mathcal{X} \subseteq \mathbb{R}^d$, a vector of d attributes, and y_i the corresponding class label. In a multi-class classification problem $y_i \in \{C_1, \ldots, C_J\}$ with $J \geq 3$.

In OC problems [13], the set of output classes is characterised by an intrinsic ordering imposed by the underlying problem domain, in contrast to nominal classification scenarios where no such order exists. This ordinal structure is commonly expressed as $C_1 \prec C_2 \prec \cdots \prec C_J$, where the relation $\prec$ indicates relative order between classes. Given a trained classifier, the prediction process yields a set of estimated labels $\{\hat{y}_1, \hat{y}_2, \ldots, \hat{y}_N\}$.

To facilitate the computation of ordinal performance measures, class labels are frequently mapped into their corresponding positions along the ordinal scale through the function $O(\cdot)$. In particular, each category C_j is assigned the numerical value $\mathcal{O}(C_j) = j$, such that $O(y_i) = j$ whenever $y_i = C_j$, for $1 \leq j \leq J$. This allows prediction errors to be quantified in a manner that takes into account the natural ordering of the classes. Throughout this paper, ordinal labels will be referred to interchangeably by their symbolic form C_j or by their numerical representation $\mathcal{O}(C_j) = j$, depending on the context.

2.2   Error-Correcting Output Codes

ECOC provide a general framework for addressing multi-class classification problems by decomposing them into a set of binary sub-problems. The framework consists of two main stages: coding, where a code matrix is defined, and decoding, where the outputs of the classifiers are combined to obtain a final prediction.

In the coding stage, a binary code matrix $M \in \{0,1\}^{J \times L}$ is constructed, where J denotes the number of classes and L the number of classifiers. Each row represents the codeword assigned to a class, while each column defines a binary partition of the class space used to train a classifier. Among the various coding strategies proposed in the literature, Binary Complete Coding [9] includes all non-trivial partitions of the class set, maximising the Hamming distance between codewords. Under this strategy, the number of classifiers grows exponentially with the number of classes, yielding strong error-correction capabilities when the base learners perform better than random guessing.

Once the ensemble of binary classifiers has been trained, the decoding stage assigns a label to a new instance by comparing the vector of classifier outputs with the predefined codewords. The most widely used decoding rule relies on the Hamming distance, which measures the number of mismatches between the predicted code and each class codeword. This decoding scheme is known for its robustness, as errors from binary classifiers can be compensated by the code redundancy.

To reduce computational complexity in problems with a large number of classes, several problem-independent ECOC designs have been proposed, including One-versus-All, One-versus-One, and random coding strategies [13]. Although effective in nominal settings, class labels are treated as unordered categories and therefore fail to exploit the intrinsic ordering present in OC problems.

3   Proposed Ordinal ECOC Design

This paper proposes a novel ordinal ECOC framework designed to exploit the exhaustive partitioning of the label space while directly addressing the limitations of standard binary decoding in ordinal contexts. By considering more than two classes for the base classifiers, ordinality is incorporated into their training process. The methodology is divided into two phases: the construction of the ordinal exhaustive code matrix and the voting-based decoding strategy.

3.1   Phase I: Ordinal Exhaustive Coding Matrix

Let $\mathcal{C} = \{1, \ldots, J\}$ be an ordered set of J classes. Denote by $\mathcal{B} = \{1, \ldots, J-1\}$ the set of admissible cut positions between consecutive classes. Each non-empty subset $B \subseteq \mathcal{B}$ induces an ordinal partition of $\mathcal{C}$. Specifically, if we use the integer representation of ordinal labels, we can define the mapping $f_B : \mathcal{C} \to \{1, \ldots, |B|+1\}$ as $f_B(j) = 1 + \sum_{b \in B} \mathbb{1}(j > b)$, where $\mathbb{1}(\cdot)$ denotes the indicator function.

This construction increases the group index each time a selected cut position is crossed. By definition, f_B satisfies the monotonicity constraint $i < j \Rightarrow f_B(i) \leq f_B(j)$, ensuring that only contiguous ordinal groupings are produced (the original ordinality is respected). We derive below the exhaustive ordinal coding matrix, $\mathbf{M} \in \mathbb{N}^{J \times L}$, which is obtained by considering all non-empty subsets of $\mathcal{B}$:

$$\mathbf{M} = \left[f_B(j) \right]_{\substack{j=1,\ldots,J \\ B \subseteq \mathcal{B},\, B \neq \emptyset}}. \tag{1}$$

Since the number of non-empty subsets of a set of size $J - 1$ is $L = 2^{J-1} - 1$, the resulting matrix contains all possible ordinal partitions of the class set, resulting on the complete family of monotone partitions of the ordered label set. As an example, for $J = 4$, where $\mathcal{B} = \{1, 2, 3\}$, the exhaustive matrix is:

$$\mathbf{M}(4) = \begin{pmatrix} 1\,1\,1\,1\,1\,1\,1 \\ 2\,1\,1\,2\,2\,1\,2 \\ 2\,2\,1\,3\,2\,2\,3 \\ 2\,2\,2\,3\,3\,3\,4 \end{pmatrix} \tag{2}$$

Columns associated with larger subsets B correspond to increasingly refined ordinal decompositions obtained by jointly encoding multiple threshold partitions. Subsets of cardinality one recover individual binary decompositions of the classical $J-1$ *Ordered Partitions* decomposition [11,13]. Consequently, the proposed framework can be interpreted as a generalisation of *Ordered Partitions*, where increasing the cardinality of B yields progressively finer ordinal encodings while preserving the classical formulation as a minimal instance. In this way, the proposed construction can be interpreted as the ordinally-constrained analogue of the Binary Complete design, where admissible partitions must be monotone.

3.2 Phase II: Voting-Based Decoding Strategy

We implement a majority voting decoding strategy, instead of minimising a distance metric. This approach treats each classifier's output as a "vote" for the original class. The predicted class $\hat{y}$ is determined by the class that accumulates the highest number of agreements across the ensemble:

$$\hat{y} = \arg\max_{j \in \{1,...,J\}} \sum_{l=1}^{L} \mathbb{1}(y_l = \mathbf{M}_{j,l}) \tag{3}$$

where y_l is the prediction of the l-th classifier, $\mathbf{M}_{j,l}$ is the matrix entry for class j, and $\mathbb{1}(\cdot)$ is the indicator function. Furthermore, this voting strategy is a generalisation of the binary decoding; for standard binary matrices, majority voting yields the same results as Hamming decoding, ensuring a fair comparison between the different approaches.

4 Experimental Settings

This section presents the experimental setup designed to validate the proposed ordinal ECOC framework. The study's empirical evaluation is structured as follows: we first introduce the 46 datasets selected to ensure a comprehensive assessment; then, we define the performance metrics used to quantify the model's predictive accuracy; finally, we detail the specific training and evaluation protocols. To facilitate reproducibility, all experiments were implemented using the open-source `dlordinal` Python library [3], which is publicly available on GitHub[1].

4.1 Datasets

The empirical assessment is conducted over the TOCUCO repository [2], including 46 datasets. This repository is publicly hosted by the AYRNA research group[2]. TOCUCO incorporates 24 datasets derived from discretised regression tasks and 22 datasets containing inherent ordered categorical variables.

---

[1] https://github.com/ayrna/dlordinal.
[2] https://www.uco.es/grupos/ayrna/materials/tocuco/.

4.2   Evaluated Methodologies

To ensure a rigorous experimental comparison, the choice of the base classifier is the same across all strategies. Both the proposed ordinal framework and the baseline BinaryECOC methods employ the Logistic All-Threshold (LogAT) model [14] as the base classifier: a linear logistic regression model generalised to tackle OC problems. Furthermore, to mitigate the impact of unbalanced data, all LogAT classifiers are always trained using class-balancing weights.

Moreover, the proposed ordinal ECOC framework is compared with a set of ordinal and nominal classification techniques. Table 1 summarises the main characteristics of each method, highlighting the model type and whether it exploits the ordinal information of the problem.

Table 1. Summary of evaluated methodologies.

Method	Model Type	Ordinal
Ridge [15]	Multi-output regression	No
LogAT [14]	Logistic All-Threshold classifier (CLM)	Yes
MLP [6]	Multi-Layer Perceptron (softmax)	No
MLP-CLM [17]	MLP with CLM output layer	Yes
MLP-Triang [19]	MLP with triangular soft labelling loss function	Yes
BinaryECOC [9]	Binary Complete ECOC	No
OrdinalECOC	Ordinal exhaustive ECOC	Yes

4.3   Models Training

The experimental procedure ensures statistical robustness and reproducibility across the 46 TOCUCO datasets. Each model configuration is evaluated over 30 independent runs with different random seeds. We use the holdout partitions provided with TOCUCO [2] (70% training, 30% testing). For each run, hyperparameters are optimised via grid search on a stratified sub-sample of the training set (Table 2) guided by the Average Mean Absolute Error (AMAE) metric [12].

4.4   Model Evaluation

Three evaluation metrics are considered to assess the performance of the methodologies compared in this work. The metrics considered in this study are:

- Quadratic Weighted Kappa (QWK) [4] is an ordinal performance measure based on the Cohen's Kappa statistic (κ). It incorporates a quadratic weighting scheme that assigns larger penalties to prediction errors occurring between classes that are further apart in the ordinal scale.

Table 2. Hyperparameter values used for cross-validation of each methodology.

Method	Hyperparameter	Values
Ridge, LogAT	Regularisation strength	$\{10^{-3}, 10^{-2}, 10^{-1}, 10^{0}, 10^{1}, 10^{2}, 10^{3}\}$
	Maximum iterations	$\{1000, 1500, 3000, 5000\}$
MLP, MLP-CLM, MLP-Triang	Hidden units	$\{5, 8, 10, 15, 20, 50, 100\}$
	Maximum iterations	$\{1000, 1500, 3000, 5000\}$
	Learning rate	$\{10^{-5}, 10^{-4}, 10^{-3}\}$
MLP-Triang	Adjacent class probability	$\{0.01, 0.05, 0.10\}$
	Smoothing factor eta	$\{0.8, 1.0\}$
MLP-CLM	Minimum distance	$\{0.0, 0.1, 0.2\}$
BinaryECOC, OrdinalECOC	Regularisation strength	$\{10^{-3}, 10^{-2}, 10^{-1}, 10^{0}, 10^{1}, 10^{2}, 10^{3}\}$

– AMAE [12] is an ordinal metric that averages the mean absolute error of each category, making it suitable for imbalanced datasets.
– Maximum Mean Absolute Error (MMAE) [7] is an ordinal metric that computes the MAE separately for each class and then reports the maximum value. It is particularly useful in imbalanced problems.

5   Results

This section reports the experimental results using the performance measures described in Sect. 4.4. The average test-set rankings are summarised in Table 3, comparing all methods across datasets and random seeds. Each mean ranking averages the results on the 46 datasets, which are based on 30 runs (i.e. it is based on 1380 models). The complete experimental results are available at[3].

Table 3. Ranking results of each method and evaluation metric (Mean and Standard Deviation, Mean$_{\text{SD}}$). The best result is shown in bold and the second best one in italics.

Methodology	Ranks AMAE	Ranks MMAE	Ranks QWK
Ridge	$5.565_{1.530}$	$5.326_{1.863}$	$5.478_{1.457}$
LogAT	$2.728_{1.775}$	$2.272_{1.397}$	$2.174_{1.165}$
MLP	$3.511_{1.240}$	$3.641_{1.214}$	$4.370_{1.424}$
MLP-CLM	$4.326_{1.477}$	$4.283_{1.530}$	$3.728_{1.587}$
MLP-Triang	$4.435_{1.377}$	$4.620_{1.313}$	$5.261_{1.467}$
BinaryECOC	$5.815_{1.525}$	$5.870_{1.424}$	$5.185_{1.617}$
OrdinalECOC	$\mathbf{1.620_{1.121}}$	$\mathbf{1.989_{1.551}}$	$\mathbf{1.804_{1.352}}$

---

[3] https://www.uco.es/grupos/ayrna/materials/ecoc-iwann26/.

The results in Table 3 show that OrdinalECOC achieves the best overall performance among all methods, consistently outperforming nominal classifiers (MLP, Ridge), the BinaryECOC strategy, and the standalone LogAT model, which yields the second-best results. These findings demonstrate the effectiveness of the OrdinalECOC coding design in improving a strong OC baseline. This suggests that exploiting higher-order ordinal partitions provides complementary structural information beyond classical cumulative modelling. They also indicate that OrdinalECOC behaves consistently across a diverse set of datasets.

An AMAE boxplot across the 46 datasets is shown in Fig. 1. OrdinalECOC achieves the lowest median and mean values among all methods. The method also shows a compact interquartile range and lower extreme values than BinaryECOC and Ridge, which exhibit higher variance and more outliers. Compared with the competitive LogAT model, OrdinalECOC maintains a tighter distribution with fewer severe errors, indicating greater stability.

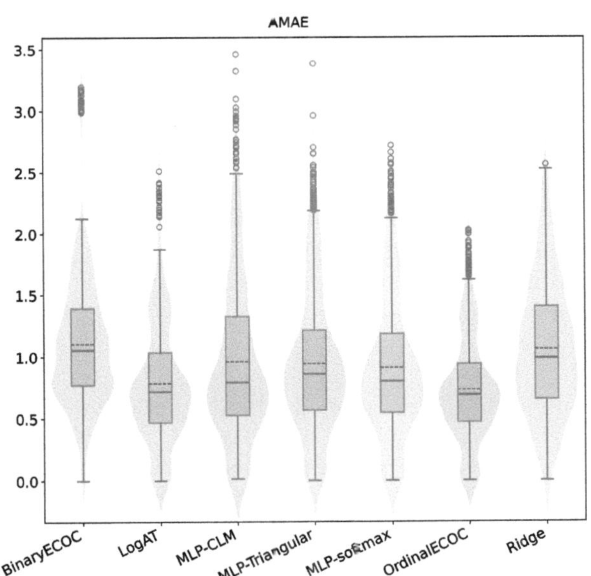

Fig. 1. AMAE boxplot comparing all methodologies. The solid black line indicates the median, while the dashed red line represents the mean for each boxplot. (Color figure online)

A critical difference diagram [8] based on the mean AMAE ranks across all datasets is shown in Fig. 2. Statistical significance was assessed using a Wilcoxon test with $\alpha = 0.05$, followed by a Holm correction, and the resulting cliques are indicated in the diagram. From this analysis, OrdinalECOC achieves the best average rank, significantly outperforming LogAT, which presents the second-best performance, and the remaining nominal and ordinal methods. The gap between

OrdinalECOC and BinaryECOC further highlights the benefit of exploiting ordinal coding in these tasks.

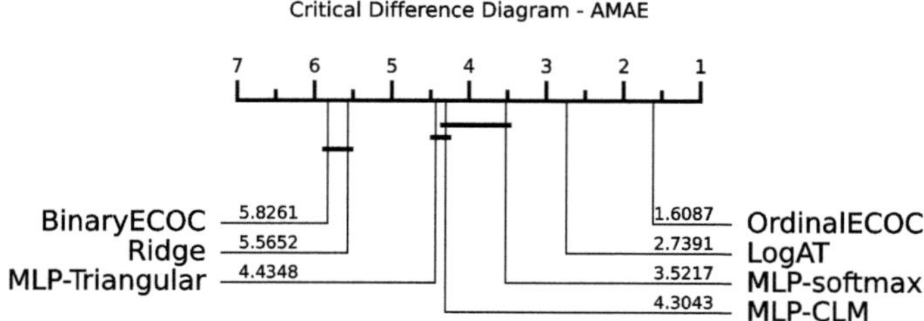

Fig. 2. Critical difference diagram using Wilcoxon test for AMAE metric.

6   Conclusions

This work introduced an exhaustive ordinal ECOC framework that incorporates class-order information in the coding and decoding stages. By leveraging all non-trivial ordinal partitions of the label space and using majority voting for decoding, OrdinalECOC addresses the limitations of standard BinaryECOC designs for ordinal problems. Experiments on 46 TOCUCO datasets show that OrdinalE-COC outperforms nominal and ordinal methods across order-aware metrics, with statistically significant improvements. These results support exhaustive ordinal coding as an effective strategy for OC.

Acknowledgments. The present study has been supported by the "Agencia Estatal de Investigación (España)" (grant ref.: PID2023-150663NB-C22/AEI/10.13039/501100011033), and by the University of Córdoba and the Junta de Andalucía (grant ref.: PP2F_L1_15). Francisco Bérchez-Moreno has been supported by "Plan Propio de Investigación Submodalidad 2.2 Contratos predoctorales" of the Universidad de Córdoba. Víctor Manuel Vargas has been supported by the Ministerio de Ciencia, Innovación y Universidades, the Agencia Estatal de Investigación and the European Social Fund Plus (grant ref.: MICIU/AEI/10.13039/501100011033, JDC2024-054787-I).

References

1. Allwein, E.L., Schapire, R.E., Singer, Y.: Reducing multiclass to binary: a unifying approach for margin classifiers. J. Mach. Learn. Res. **1**, 113–141 (2000)
2. Ayllón-Gavilán, R., et al.: Toc-uco: a comprehensive repository of tabular ordinal classification datasets (2025). https://arxiv.org/abs/2507.17348
3. Bérchez-Moreno, F., et al.: dlordinal: a python package for deep ordinal classification. Neurocomputing **622**, 129305 (2025). https://doi.org/10.1016/j.neucom.2024.129305

4. Berchez-Moreno, F., Fernandez, J.C., Hervas-Martinez, C., Gutierrez, P.A.: Fusion of standard and ordinal dropout techniques to regularise deep models. Inf. Fusion **106**, 102299 (2024). https://doi.org/10.1016/j.inffus.2024.102299

5. Bérchez-Moreno, F., et al.: Knee osteoarthritis severity grading using soft labelling and ordinal classification. In: International Work-Conference on Artificial Neural Networks, pp. 522–533. Springer, Hervás-Martínez, C. (2025). https://doi.org/10.1007/978-3-032-02725-2_41

6. Bishop, C.M.: Pattern Recognition and Machine Learning (Information Science and Statistics). Springer-Verlag, New York (2006)

7. Cruz-Ramírez, M., Hervás-Martínez, C., Sánchez-Monedero, J., Gutiérrez, P.A.: Metrics to guide a multi-objective evolutionary algorithm for ordinal classification. Neurocomputing **135**, 21–31 (2014). https://doi.org/10.1016/j.neucom.2013.05.058

8. Demšar, J.: Statistical comparisons of classifiers over multiple data sets. J. Mach. Learn. Res. **7**, 1–30 (2006)

9. Dietterich, T.G., Bakiri, G.: Solving multiclass learning problems via error-correcting output codes. J. Artif. Intell. Res. **2**, 263–286 (1994). https://doi.org/10.1613/jair.105

10. Escalera, S., Pujol, O., Radeva, P.: Separability of ternary codes for sparse designs of error-correcting output codes. Pattern Recogn. Lett. **30**(3), 285–297 (2009). https://doi.org/10.1016/j.patrec.2008.10.002

11. Frank, E., Hall, M.: A simple approach to ordinal classification. In: De Raedt, L., Flach, P. (eds.) ECML 2001. LNCS (LNAI), vol. 2167, pp. 145–156. Springer, Heidelberg (2001). https://doi.org/10.1007/3-540-44795-4_13

12. Gómez-Orellana, A., Guijo-Rubio, D., Gutiérrez, P., Hervás-Martínez, C., Vargas, V.: ORFEO: ordinal classifier and regressor fusion for estimating an ordinal categorical target. Eng. Appl. Artif. Intell. **133**, 108462 (2024). https://doi.org/10.1016/j.engappai.2024.108462

13. Gutiérrez, P.A., Perez-Ortiz, M., Sanchez-Monedero, J., Fernandez-Navarro, F., Hervas-Martinez, C.: Ordinal regression methods: survey and experimental study. IEEE Trans. Knowl. Data Eng. **28**(1), 127–146 (2015). https://doi.org/10.1109/TKDE.2015.2457911

14. Pedregosa, F., Bach, F., Gramfort, A.: On the consistency of ordinal regression methods. J. Mach. Learn. Res. **18**(55), 1–35 (2017)

15. Pedregosa, F., et al.: Scikit-learn: machine learning in python. J. Mach. Learn. Res. **12**, 2825–2830 (2011)

16. Pujol, O., Radeva, P., Vitriá, J.: Discriminant ecoc: a heuristic method for application dependent design of error correcting output codes. IEEE Trans. Pattern Anal. Mach. Intell. **28**(6), 1007–1012 (2006). https://doi.org/10.1109/TPAMI.2006.116

17. Vargas, V.M., Gutierrez, P.A., Hervas-Martinez, C.: Cumulative link models for deep ordinal classification. Neurocomputing **401**, 48–58 (2020). https://doi.org/10.1016/j.neucom.2020.03.034

18. Vargas, V.M., Gutiérrez, P.A., Rosati, R., Romeo, L., Frontoni, E., Hervás-Martínez, C.: Deep learning based hierarchical classifier for weapon stock aesthetic quality control assessment. Comput. Ind. **144**, 1–13 (2023). https://doi.org/10.1016/j.compind.2022.103786

19. Vargas, V.M., Gutiérrez, P.A., Barbero-Gómez, J., Hervás-Martínez, C.: Soft labelling based on triangular distributions for ordinal classification. Inf. Fusion **93**, 258–267 (2023). https://doi.org/10.1016/j.inffus.2023.01.003

Glucose Variability and its Association with Short-Term Glucose Prediction in Type 1 Diabetes

Andrea Hongn[1,2](✉) [iD], Javier Garrigós[3] [iD], and Paula M. Bonomini[2,4] [iD]

[1] Universidad de Buenos Aires, Facultad de Ingeniería, Instituto de Ingeniería Biomédica (IIBM), Buenos Aires, Argentina
ahongn.ext@fi.uba.ar
[2] CONICET, Instituto Argentino de Matemática "Alberto P. Calderón" (IAM), Buenos Aires, Argentina
[3] Universidad Politécnica de Cartagena, Cartagena, Spain
[4] Instituto Tecnológico de Buenos Aires (ITBA), Buenos Aires, Argentina

Abstract. Short-term glucose forecasting has become a central research topic in Type 1 Diabetes Mellitus management. In this work the relationship between glucose variability and short-term CGM-based prediction performance using a segment-based modeling strategy is analyzed. Simple univariate models, including linear regression and ensemble models (Random Forest, LightGBM and XGBoost), were evaluated for a 30-min prediction horizon in two independent datasets (n = 11). Among participants, prediction performance was strongly associated with glucose variability in the evaluation segments. Individuals with lower variability consistently achieved lower errors, whereas higher variability segments resulted in increased prediction error across all models (lowest vs highest RMSE: 16.1 mg/dL vs 24.3 mg/dL; lowest vs highest MAE: 11.7 mg/dL vs 18.5 mg/dL). These findings indicate a potential association between segment-level glucose variability and short-term prediction performance. Rather than model complexity alone, metabolic stability may contribute substantially to the observed forecasting accuracy, highlighting the value of incorporating patient-specific and state-aware perspectives in future studies.

Keywords: Type 1 diabetes mellitus · glucose variability · glucose forecasting · continuous glucose monitoring

1 Introduction

Type 1 Diabetes Mellitus (T1DM) is a chronic autoimmune condition characterized by the destruction of pancreatic β-cells, leading to a deficiency of endogenous insulin. Consequently, patients must rely on exogenous insulin administration through multiple daily injections, insulin pumps, or closed-loop systems. In all cases, strict glucose monitoring is required to ensure proper dosing and prevent acute complications such as hypoglycemia and hyperglycemia [1].

J. M. Ferrández Vicente et al. (Eds.): IWINAC 2026, LNCS 16575, pp. 496–506, 2026.
https://doi.org/10.1007/978-3-032-27317-8_47

Continuous Glucose Monitoring (CGM) systems have become the standard technology for glucose assessment. These minimally invasive devices provide interstitial glucose measurements (IG) at frequent intervals, typically every five minutes. The increasing availability of high-resolution glucose data, combined with information from insulin pumps and wearable sensors, has driven significant research efforts toward short-term glucose forecasting using artificial intelligence techniques [2].

Most studies focus on tuning complex machine learning and deep learning architectures, with Long Short-Term Memory (LSTM) networks emerging as particularly promising approaches [2–5]. Although some work relies on univariate forecasting models [5], others incorporate multiple physiological and contextual features to improve predictive performance [4,6], as factors such as food intake, physical activity, and acute mental stress can induce sudden variations in glucose levels and can be captured through wearable-derived features [7,8]. In general, model development has largely emphasized reducing numerical prediction errors through architectural sophistication and feature engineering.

However, a question remains open: to what extent is short-term glucose predictability associated with the intrinsic dynamics of the glycemic profile? Beyond model complexity, metabolic stability could contribute to differences in forecasting performance across individuals.

The primary objective of this study is therefore not to maximize predictive accuracy through complex architectures, but to investigate the relationship between glycemic excursions and short-term glucose predictability. Using a segment-based modeling strategy and simple univariate models, we analyze whether individual glucose variability patterns influence forecasting performance. By doing so, we aim to better understand how intrinsic glycemic dynamics shape the limits of short-term prediction.

2 Materials and Methods

2.1 Data Description

The data used in this work come from two independent cohorts of individuals with T1DM, as described below.

Own Observational Study: HIBA Dataset. Five TDM1 patients participated in an observational study that lasted one month and in which they wore a wearable device for physiological recording and a CGM system for interstitial glucose monitoring. In addition, participants completed structured supervised sessions of physical activity and mental stress tests. They were also asked to report similar activities occurring in their daily lives, as well as food intake, through the Insumate app [9], which was connected to the CGM sensor to enable remote real-time glucose monitoring and facilitate data annotation.

The study was designed and conducted in collaboration with researchers from CONICET, Universidad Nacional de La Plata, Instituto Tecnológico de Buenos

Aires, and Hospital Italiano de Buenos Aires. The protocol was approved by the Ethics Committee of the Hospital Italiano de Buenos Aires (HIBA) (Registration Code No. 11719).

For the present work, only CGM data were used. Glucose levels were measured using the Dexcom One CGM sensor, which provides interstitial glucose readings every 5 min. All participants were treated with insulin pump therapy.

External Validation Dataset: OHIO T1DM. For external validation, the publicly available OHIO T1DM dataset [10] was used. This dataset includes CGM, wearable sensor and annotation data from 12 individuals with T1DM monitored for approximately eight weeks. Participants belong to two cohorts (2018 and 2020). In this work, only the 2018 cohort was considered (n = 6).

Participants from the 2018 cohort used the Medtronic Enlite CGM sensor, which provides glucose measurements at 5-min intervals, matching the sampling frequency of our observational study.

Final Study Population. In total, this work includes data from 11 individuals with T1DM: five participants from our observational study (P1-P5), and six participants from the OHIO 2018 dataset (P559, P563, P570, P575, P588, P591).

Descriptive statistics for both datasets are presented in Tables 1 and 2, respectively. Glycemic metrics were computed according to the 2026 American Diabetes Association (ADA) recommendations [11]. The following indicators were calculated:

- Mean glucose: Mean of glucose values
- Glucose coefficient of variation (CV): Spread of glucose values
- Time Above Range (TAR):
  - TAR >250 mg/dL: Percent of time in level 2 hyperglycemia (TAR_1)
  - TAR >180 mg/dL: Percent of time in level 1 hyperglycemia (TAR_2)
- Time In Range (TIR) 70–180 mg/dL: Percent of time in range
- Time Below Range (TBR):
  - TBR <70 mg/dL: Percent of time in level 1 hypoglycemia (TBR_1)
  - TBR <54 mg/dL: Percent of time in level 2 hypoglycemia (TBR_2)

Due to CGM connectivity issues and sensor replacements, there are missing data gaps in both datasets. Missing data were computed as the difference between the theoretical number of glucose samples and the observed number of measurements.

The theoretical number of glucose readings was computed assuming consecutive glucose readings every five minutes between the first and the last available CGM timestamp for each participant.

2.2   Data Processing

Missing data was one of the main challenges in both datasets. Data gaps occurred due to different causes: connectivity losses, sensor disconnections, and CGM

Table 1. Descriptive CGM data for each participant: HIBA Dataset.

Variable	P1	P2	P3	P4	P5
Gender	M	F	F	F	M
Samples	7630	7632	7536	7042	7438
Missing data (%)	1.78	1.36	0.79	9.17	2.34
Mean value (mg/dL)	191.34	165.27	157.19	149.84	157.14
Standard deviation (mg/dL)	66.38	60.45	53.55	48.63	54.63
CV (%)	34.69	36.58	34.07	32.45	34.77
Median value (mg/dL)	177.00	158.00	153.00	144.00	151.00
Maximum value (mg/dL)	401.00	401.00	356.00	401.00	370.00
Minimum value (mg/dL)	62.00	39.00	39.00	42.00	43.00
TAR_1 (%)	48.17	35.6	32.50	22.35	30.56
TAR_2(%)	18.49	8.57	4.76	3.08	5.55
TIR (%)	51.77	62.43	64.16	75.77	67.36
TBR_1 (%)	0.07	1.97	3.34	1.87	2.08
TBR_2 (%)	0.00	0.48	0.96	0.21	0.27

replacements. Consequently, the duration of these gaps ranged from brief interruptions (approximately 10 min) to several hours.

To avoid introducing artificial patterns or smoothing effects, no interpolation or imputation techniques were applied. Instead, a segment-based strategy was adopted to preserve the intrinsic glucose dynamics. This decision was further motivated by the planned integration of physiological signals in future work, where discontinuities are also common and sampling frequencies differ substantially from the 5-min CGM interval.

Although CGM devices nominally provide measurements every 5 min, timestamps are not always perfectly aligned due to discrepancies in seconds and milliseconds. Therefore, timestamps were standardized within each segment to ensure a consistent 5-min spacing before model training.

2.3   Segment Based Modeling

Since the objective of this study is short-term glucose forecasting (30-min prediction horizon, corresponding to 6 future steps), using a historical window of 12 previous samples (60 min), a valid segment was defined as a continuous CGM period containing at least 18 consecutive samples (12 input steps + 6 forecast steps).

To ensure a realistic forecasting scenario and prevent information leakage, data were split using a strictly temporal 80/20 scheme. Specifically, for each participant, the first 80% of the chronological data was assigned to the training set, while the remaining 20% was reserved for testing. This approach mirrors

Table 2. Descriptive CGM data for each participant: OHIO 2018 Dataset

Variable	P559	P563	P570	P575	P588	P591
Gender	F	M	M	F	F	F
Samples	13310	14694	13727	14456	15431	13607
Missing data(%)	11.01	6.93	5.26	8.63	3.47	12.78
Mean value (mg/dL)	167.23	149.80	192.95	143.34	166.82	153.75
Standard deviation (mg/dL)	69.91	49.75	64.09	60.40	50.33	56.94
CV (%)	41.80	33.21	33.21	42.14	30.17	37.03
Median value (mg/dL)	159.00	144.00	195.00	133.00	163.00	147.00
Maximum value (mg/dL)	400.00	400.00	388.00	400.00	400.00	397.00
Minimum value (mg/dL)	40.00	40.00	46.00	40.00	40.00	40.00
TAR_1 (%)	39.68	26.21	58.02	24.18	37.22	31.18
TAR_2 (%)	12.61	2.74	20.67	5.78	4.96	6.20
TIR (%)	56.71	71.79	40.49	68.22	61.98	64.89
TBR_1 (%)	3.61	1.99	1.49	7.60	0.80	3.93
TBR_2 (%)	0.77	0.24	0.10	2.02	0.16	0.97

the predefined split provided in the OHIO dataset and ensures methodological consistency across cohorts.

After the temporal split, segmentation was applied independently within the training and testing sets. Consequently, both subsets consisted of multiple continuous valid segments of varying lengths, depending on the occurrence and duration of missing data gaps.

Models. Forecasting experiments were implemented using the Darts time series library, which facilitates structured time series modeling through its TimeSeries object abstraction [12]. This framework enabled consistent handling of multiple independent CGM segments.

Although deep learning approaches such as Long Short-Term Memory (LSTM) networks have demonstrated strong performance in glucose forecasting tasks [2,4,5], the primary objective of this study was not to enhance predictive performance through complex architectures, but rather to understand the relationship between glycemic excursions and short-term glucose predictability. Therefore, we restricted the analysis to standard regression-based models without hyperparameter tuning.

Consequently, global regression models such as Linear Regression (LR), Random Forest (RF), XGBoost (XGB) and LightGBM (LGBM) were utilized in this study. All models were trained using lagged CGM values as input features. Specifically, for each time step t, the input vector consisted of the previous 12 glucose samples (corresponding to 60 min of history), and the target corresponded to the next 6 time steps (30-min prediction horizon).

Each model was trained using all available training segments. The evaluation of the test set was performed using a historical forecasting strategy (rolling forecast), where the predictions were generated iteratively one step forward at a time without model retraining. This configuration reflects a real-world deployment scenario, where models trained on historical data are evaluated on future unseen glucose trajectories.

Performance metrics were computed for each test segment, and final reported values correspond to the average across all test segments.

2.4   Evaluation

Evaluation Metrics. Mean Absolute Error (MAE) was selected for its robustness to outliers and its direct interpretability in clinical units (mg/dL). MAE applies a linear penalty to prediction errors, making it particularly suitable for glucose forecasting, where extreme deviations may arise from physiological variability or sensor-related noise rather than systematic model failure.

In line with prior studies in glucose prediction and time-series forecasting, Root Mean Squared Error (RMSE) was also reported to enable direct comparison of results [3,5]. Like MAE, RMSE is expressed in clinical units (mg/dL), facilitating interpretability.

Clarke Error Grid. Clarke Error Grid (CEG) was designed to evaluate clinical implications of patient-generated blood glucose values, inspired for blood glucose systems evaluation [13]. However, the CEG remains widely used for clinical assessment in glucose prediction models [2,4,6,14].

The error grid analysis defines the x-axis as the reference blood glucose (CGM data) and the y-axis as the value generated by the monitoring system (predicted IG values). The grid is divided into five zones of varying degrees of accuracy and inaccuracy of glucose estimation. Zones A and B are clinically acceptable, whereas values in zones C, D, and E are potentially dangerous and therefore are clinically significant errors.

As well as model metrics, Clarke Error Grid analysis was performed by aggregating all out-of-sample predictions obtained during each test segment evaluation, ensuring a clinically meaningful evaluation of prediction safety.

3   Results

Different regression models were trained and evaluated on both datasets. The predictive performance, expressed in terms of MAE and RMSE (mean $\pm$ standard deviation across test segments), is reported in Tables 3 and 4 for the HIBA and OHIO cohorts, respectively.

To contextualize prediction performance [5], each table also reports the average glucose variability computed across the training and testing segments. Glucose variability was quantified as the proportion of consecutive glucose differences

Table 3. Prediction performance (mean ± standard deviation across test segments) for the HIBA dataset.

	P1	P2	P3	P4	P5
Segment Variability (%)					
Train	11.83	6.41	10.42	8.00	7.00
Test	12.00	10.69	4.05	5.76	9.14
RMSE (mg/dL)					
LR	30.1 ± 7.6	23.7 ± 5.1	17.1 ± 2.4	20.9 ± 8.8	23.8 ± 0.0
RF	30.7 ± 6.5	24.9 ± 5.4	18.8 ± 2.2	21.9 ± 10.1	26.9 ± 0.0
LGBM	30.0 ± 4.3	25.5 ± 6.1	19.1 ± 2.7	18.8 ± 5.3	26.3 ± 0.0
XGB	30.0 ± 5.0	29.7 ± 5.5	18.8 ± 2.7	19.8 ± 6.0	26.6 ± 0.0
MAE (mg/dL)					
LR	22.4 ± 6.5	17.6 ± 3.6	13.1 ± 1.5	18.0 ± 9.8	16.9 ± 0.0
RF	23.2 ± 6.0	18.3 ± 3.8	14.3 ± 1.2	19.2 ± 10.6	19.2 ± 0.0
LGBM	22.7 ± 4.4	18.8 ± 4.1	14.4 ± 1.5	15.7 ± 4.0	19.1 ± 0.0
XGB	22.8 ± 5.0	21.3 ± 4.9	14.2 ± 1.6	16.5 ± 5.2	19.1 ± 0.0

exceeding 10 mg/dL within each segment. This threshold was selected to capture abrupt glycemic excursions, reflecting rapid changes in glucose dynamics.

In the HIBA dataset, the best predictive performance was observed for participant P3, with an RMSE of 17.1 mg/dL and an MAE of 13.1 mg/dL. This participant also exhibited the lowest segment-level variability in the test split (4.05%). In contrast, the worst performance corresponded to participant P1, with an RMSE of 30.1 mg/dL and an MAE of 22.4 mg/dL, who also presented the highest segment variability in the test split (12.00%). Reported metrics correspond to the Linear Regression model.

Similarly, in the Ohio 2018 dataset, participant P570 achieved the best predictive performance (RMSE = 16.1 mg/dL; MAE = 11.7 mg/dL) and the lowest test segment variability (2.70%). Conversely, participant P591 exhibited the poorest performance (RMSE = 24.3 mg/dL; MAE = 18.5 mg/dL), alongside the highest segment variability (7.25%). All reported metrics correspond to the Linear Regression model.

Clarke Error Grid zone distributions are presented in Table 5 for both datasets. These results correspond to the Linear Regression model, which achieved the most consistent predictive performance across participants.

The Clarke Error Grid analysis showed that more than 97% of predictions fell within clinically acceptable regions (Zones A and B) for all participants.

In the HIBA dataset, participant P4 achieved the highest proportion of clinically acceptable predictions (A+B = 99.85%). In contrast, participant P3 exhibited the largest proportion of predictions falling within non–clinically acceptable zones (D = 2.92%).

Table 4. Prediction performance (mean ± standard deviation across test segments) for the OHIO 2018 dataset.

	P559	P563	P570	P575	P588	P591
Segment Variability (%)						
Train	9.84	3.26	3.90	6.70	7.56	8.76
Test	4.67	4.63	2.70	7.10	5.88	7.25
RMSE (mg/dL)						
LR	18.8 ± 5.6	20.8 ± 7.0	16.1 ± 2.2	21.5 ± 9.9	19.8 ± 2.0	24.3 ± 7.7
RF	20.2 ± 6.8	20.3 ± 4.3	17.7 ± 2.6	21.8 ± 9.4	20.8 ± 2.5	23.5 ± 5.7
LGBM	20.0 ± 6.3	20.7 ± 4.7	17.5 ± 2.6	21.5 ± 9.8	20.7 ± 2.5	24.1 ± 6.0
XGB	20.2 ± 6.5	21.0 ± 4.6	18.0 ± 3.0	21.5 ± 9.6	20.8 ± 2.7	23.7 ± 5.8
MAE (mg/dL)						
LR	14.0 ± 4.6	14.0 ± 2.8	11.7 ± 1.3	15.7 ± 6.3	14.7 ± 1.8	18.5 ± 5.5
RF	14.9 ± 5.7	14.4 ± 2.1	12.8 ± 1.9	15.6 ± 6.3	15.3 ± 2.2	18.2 ± 4.4
LGBM	14.7 ± 5.2	14.5 ± 2.2	12.7 ± 1.7	15.5 ± 6.5	15.2 ± 2.1	18.7 ± 4.7
XGB	14.9 ± 5.5	14.6 ± 2.2	12.9 ± 2.1	15.5 ± 6.5	15.2 ± 2.4	18.4 ± 4.7

In the Ohio dataset, participant P588 showed the highest proportion of clinically acceptable predictions(A+B = 99.85%), whereas participant P591 presented the largest proportion of predictions within Zone D(D = 2.80%).

4 Discussion

Due to the relatively small sample size (six participants from the 2018 Ohio dataset cohort and five from the HIBA dataset), a formal statistical analysis was not feasible. Therefore, this study adopts a descriptive approach, emphasizing the importance of analyzing individual glycemic dynamics to better understand prediction performance.

In both datasets, the best predictive performance was consistently observed in participants with the lowest glucose variability in the test segments, while the worst performance corresponded to those with the highest variability. All evaluated models showed similar behavior in terms of RMSE and MAE. In the HIBA dataset, LightGBM consistently yielded the worst performance; however, differences between the best-performing models were minimal (approximately 0.3 mg/dL). These findings suggest that glucose variability in the evaluation segment has a stronger influence on prediction performance than the specific model architecture.

We further analyzed the ratio between variability in the training and test segments. Under the assumption of comparable test variability—considered the dominant factor—we hypothesized that a higher train-to-test variability ratio would be associated with improved performance. However, this relationship was not consistently observed across participants.

Table 5. Clarke Error Grid zone distribution (%) for the Linear Regression model on the HIBA and OHIO 2018 datasets. A+B represents the percentage of clinically acceptable predictions.

	CEG (%)					
	Zone A	Zone B	A+B	Zone C	Zone D	Zone E
P1	86.71	12.88	99.59	0.00	0.41	0.00
P2	87.94	11.72	99.66	0.14	0.20	0.00
P3	87.52	9.57	97.09	0.00	2.92	0.00
P4	89.10	10.75	99.85	0.00	0.15	0.00
P5	86.34	13.19	99.53	0.00	0.48	0.00
P559	90.78	8.23	99.01	0.00	0.99	0.00
P563	92.37	7.11	99.48	0.08	0.44	0.00
P570	95.26	4.43	99.69	0.00	0.31	0.00
P575	86.03	11.39	97.42	0.17	2.41	0.00
P588	90.69	9.16	99.85	0.00	0.15	0.00
P591	82.13	14.95	97.08	0.07	2.80	0.04

Regarding clinical relevance assessed through Clarke Error Grid (CEG) analysis, in the HIBA dataset the best results were associated with the participant exhibiting the highest Time in Range (TIR). However, this pattern was not replicated in the Ohio dataset, where better CEG zone distributions were observed in a participant with lower TIR. These results suggest that TIR alone may not directly determine short-term predictability.

It should be noted that discrepancies were observed between numerical performance metrics and clinical assessment through the Clarke Error Grid. Although participant P3 achieved the lowest RMSE (17.1 mg/dL) and MAE (13.1 mg/dL) in the HIBA dataset, this participant also presented the highest proportion of predictions in Zone D (2.92%), corresponding to clinically significant errors. In contrast, participant P4 exhibited slightly higher numerical errors (RMSE = 20.9 mg/dL; MAE = 18.0 mg/dL) but a substantially lower proportion of Zone D predictions (0.15%). These findings reinforce the importance of jointly evaluating statistical accuracy and clinical relevance when assessing glucose forecasting models.

Overall, TIR did not demonstrate a consistent relationship with prediction performance, whereas segment-level glucose variability emerged as a more robust explanatory factor.

Although only simple models were employed, RMSE values for participants P559, P570, and P575 were comparable to those reported by Martinsson et al. [5] using a complex LSTM-based architecture for a 30-min prediction horizon. For participants P588, P563, and P591, baseline models exhibited at least a one-point difference in RMSE compared to the reported LSTM results. Interestingly, while participant P575 presented the worst performance in Martinsson et al., in the present study participant P591 exhibited the highest prediction error, coinciding with the highest variability in the test segment. It should be noted that participant P575 also showed high test variability, closely approaching that of participant P591.

5   Conclusion

This study investigated the relationship between glucose variability and short-term CGM-based prediction performance using a segment-based modeling strategy. Across two independent datasets, prediction accuracy appeared to be more associated with patient-specific glucose dynamics than with model complexity.

Simple linear models achieved performance comparable to ensemble-based approaches in several participants. Moreover, all evaluated models consistently exhibited poorer prediction accuracy in individuals with higher glucose variability in the evaluation segments.

Segment-level variability emerged as a key factor conditioning predictability, with lower variability periods consistently associated with reduced forecasting errors. Importantly, despite differences in numerical error metrics, Clarke Error Grid analysis demonstrated that most forecasts remained within clinically acceptable regions across participants.

These findings suggest that short-term glucose predictability is linked to metabolic stability rather than exclusively to algorithmic sophistication. This highlights the importance of incorporating segment-aware and patient-specific modeling strategies in the development of future glucose forecasting systems.

Acknowledgments. This work was (partially) supported by Programa Iberoamericano de Ciencia y Tecnología para el Desarrollo (CYTED) (through Red [225RT0169]).

References

1. Lucier, J., Mathias, P.M.: Type 1 Diabetes. In: StatPearls [Internet]. StatPearls Publishing, Treasure Island (2025). https://www.ncbi.nlm.nih.gov/books/NBK507713/
2. Calzavara, A., Prendin, F., Cappon, G., et al.: Systematic review on deep learning algorithms for blood glucose forecasting in type 1 diabetes. IEEE J. Biomed. Health Inf. (2026)
3. Khadem, H., Nemat, H., Elliott, J., Benaissa, M.: Blood glucose level time series forecasting: nested deep ensemble learning lag fusion. Bioengineering **10**(4), 487 (2023)
4. Pikulin, S., Yehezkel, I., Moskovitch, R.: Enhanced blood glucose levels prediction with a smartwatch. PLoS ONE **19**(7), e0307136 (2024)
5. Martinsson, J., Schliep, A., Eliasson, B., et al.: Blood glucose prediction with variance estimation using recurrent neural networks. J. Healthc. Inf. Res. **4**, 1–18 (2020)

6. Huang, X., Schmelter, F., Uhlig, A., et al.: Comparison of feature learning methods for non-invasive interstitial glucose prediction using wearable sensors in healthy cohorts: a pilot study. Intell. Med. **4**(4), 226–238 (2024)

7. Hongn, A., Bosch, F., Prado, L.E., Bonomini, P.: Wearable physiological signals under acute stress and exercise conditions. Sci. Data **12**, 520 (2025)

8. Hongn, A., Bosch, F., Prado, L., Bonomini, P.: Wearable device dataset from induced stress and structured exercise sessions (version 1.0.0). PhysioNet (2025)

9. Garelli, F.: Solicitud No. 827774. Instituto Nacional de la Propiedad Intelectual (INPI), Argentina. INSUMATE. Marca tipo D (denominativa), clase 9 (2019)

10. Marling, C., Bunescu, R.: The OhioT1DM dataset for blood glucose level prediction: update 2020. CEUR Workshop Proc. **2675**, 71–74 (2020)

11. Committee, A.D.A.P.P.: Glycemic goals, hypoglycemia, and hyperglycemic crises: standards of care in diabetes—2026. Diab. Care **49**(Suppl. 1), S132–S149 (2026)

12. Herzen, J., Lässig, F., Piazzetta, S.G., et al.: Darts: user-friendly modern machine learning for time series. J. Mach. Learn. Res. **23**(124), 1–6 (2022)

13. Clarke, W.L., Cox, D., Gonder-Frederick, L.A., Carter, W., Pohl, S.L.: Evaluating clinical accuracy of systems for self-monitoring of blood glucose. Diabetes Care **10**(5), 622–628 (1987)

14. Bogue-Jimenez, B., Huang, X., Powell, D., Doblas, A.: Selection of noninvasive features in wrist-based wearable sensors to predict blood glucose concentrations using machine learning algorithms. Sensors **22**(9), 3534 (2022)

Towards Machine Learning–Enhanced Ad Hoc Networks for Disaster Scenarios

Wilman Suárez-Zambrano[1,2], Juan Pablo Astudillo-León[1,2],
Leticia Lemus-Cárdenas[2,5], Lorena Guachi-Guachi[4(✉)],
and D. H. Peluffo-Ordóñez[1,3]

[1] School of Mathematical and Computational Sciences, Yachay Tech, Urcuquí,
Ecuador
{wsuarez,jastudillo,dpeluffo}@yachaytech.edu.ec
[2] Communication Networks and Intelligent Services Research Group (ComNet
Innova YT), Yachay Tech University Urcuquí 100115, Ecuador
[3] SDAS Research Group, Ibarra, Ecuador
diego.peluffo@sdas-group.com
[4] Faculty of Digital Engineering and Emerging Technologies, Universidad
Internacional del Ecuador, Av. Simon Bolivar, Quito 170411, Ecuador
loguachigu@uide.edu.ec
[5] Departamento de Fundamentos del Conocimiento, Universidad de Guadalajara,
Guadalajara, Mexico
leticia.lemus@academicos.udg.mx
https://sdas-group.com/

Abstract. Reliable communication is one of the main challenges in disaster scenarios, where conventional infrastructure is often unavailable and mobile nodes exhibit highly dynamic behavior. This paper presents an artificial intelligence–based approach to enhance communication in wireless ad hoc networks under such conditions. A dataset was generated from scratch by integrating the **ns-3** network simulator with **BonnMotion** to model realistic human mobility in disaster environments. From these simulations, two key features—*channel utilization factor* and *queue packet size*—were extracted and used to train a supervised learning model with the **CatBoost** algorithm. The model was validated with accuracy, precision, and F1-score, and then reintroduced into the simulation to support real-time decision-making. Experimental results show that the AI-enhanced strategy achieves substantial improvements in **Packet Delivery Ratio (PDR)**, **Throughput**, and **End-to-End Delay** compared to a baseline without Quality of Service (QoS). These findings demonstrate the feasibility of integrating machine learning into communication layers to increase the resilience and efficiency of ad hoc networks for disaster response applications.

Keywords: Disaster scenarios · Machine learning ns-3 · BonnMotion

1 Introduction

Natural and human-made disasters—such as earthquakes, hurricanes, wildfires, and targeted attacks on critical infrastructure—often disable conventional

J. M. Ferrández Vicente et al. (Eds.): IWINAC 2026, LNCS 16575, pp. 507–517, 2026.
https://doi.org/10.1007/978-3-032-27317-8_48

telecommunications networks within minutes [1,2]. In such contexts, rapid and autonomous communication becomes essential for coordinating rescue operations, sharing aerial imagery, and transmitting sensor data. Mobile Ad Hoc Networks (MANETs) provide a compelling solution, as each device simultaneously acts as a router and a terminal, enabling the deployment of infrastructure-free meshes within minutes [3]. Field experiences, such as the 2017 Puebla earthquake, demonstrated the potential of MANETs but also exposed significant limitations, including latency and packet loss due to chaotic mobility and signal shadowing [4].

To mitigate these challenges, researchers have incorporated **artificial intelligence (AI)** into the protocol stack. Machine learning (ML) models can predict link failures, balance load, and adjust transmission power in real time [5,6]. Reinforcement learning strategies have shown superior performance over classical routing protocols [7], while unsupervised clustering reduces signalling overhead in dense and heterogeneous scenarios [8]. Yet, many of these advances rely on synthetic mobility patterns, often neglecting the real dynamics of disaster-stricken populations, which leads to overly optimistic quality-of-service estimates [9]. Recent work has thus focused on realistic simulators, such as BonnMotion's Disaster Area Mobility Model (DA-MM) [10], obstacle-shadowing extensions in **ns-3** [11], as well as empirical traces from real evacuations [12]. These advances emphasize not only technical improvements but also ethical principles, with guidelines highlighting the importance of transparency, fairness, and robustness in AI for safety-critical applications [13].

In this paper, we address these issues by: (i) designing and simulating datasets that characterize communication under disaster conditions; (ii) implementing supervised ML models to reduce latency and packet loss without sacrificing throughput; and (iii) validating performance using standard QoS metrics such as packet delivery ratio and end-to-end delay. This contribution aims to advance toward resilient and privacy-preserving communication systems capable of sustaining emergency response when conventional infrastructure collapses.

2   Background and Foundations

Ad Hoc Networks in Disaster Response: *Ad hoc* networks are considered the fastest alternative to re-establish communications when conventional infrastructure becomes unavailable. Their behaviour, however, is strongly influenced by factors such as unpredictable mobility, obstacles that cause shadowing, and interference from the environment. To account for these effects, researchers combine disaster–specific mobility models—most notably the *Disaster Area Mobility Model* (DA-MM) from BonnMotion—with discrete–event simulators such as **ns-3**. In these settings, obstacle–attenuation or shadow–fading modules are typically coupled to the simulator to avoid overestimating network performance [9–11].

Mobility Models and Simulation Workflow. The DA-MM reproduces the trajectories of victims and responders across shelters, command posts, and rubble zones [10]. When exported from BonnMotion into formats readable by `ns-3`, these traces allow the topology to evolve consistently with the simulated scenario. By incorporating appropriate propagation models, the system corrects the overly optimistic results produced by generic random mobility patterns, leading to more reliable evaluations of packet–delivery ratio (PDR), end-to-end delay, and throughput [9,11].

Machine Learning for Adaptive Networking: In recent years, ML has been increasingly applied to enable *ad hoc* networks to adapt autonomously to dynamic topologies. Reported contributions include selecting more stable routes, adjusting medium–access parameters, and prioritising critical flows in real time [7]. These approaches contribute to the self–organising character of the network, allowing it to redistribute resources under adverse conditions. Nevertheless, their effectiveness depends critically on the representativeness of the training data and on the realism of the simulated mobility and channel models [8].

A Typical Disaster-Area Scenario: The **Disaster Area Mobility Model** (DA-MM), included in BonnMotion 3, was designed to *accurately reproduce* the movements of victims and first responders after a catastrophic event [10]. Unlike random-waypoint models, DA-MM partitions the scene into *functional zones*: debris fields, command posts, evacuation routes, and safe areas. Each zone enforces specific speed limits, turning angles, and congestion probabilities, so that node trajectories capture both physical obstacles and the tactical logic of search-and-rescue operations.

The scenario considered in this study is an introductory example and is based on a large-scale disaster drill presented in [14]. The exercise took place in May 2005 in Cologne, Germany, as part of the preparations for World Youth Day 2005 and the FIFA World Cup 2006. The underlying assumption was that a catastrophe in an event hall had injured more than 250 people [14].

The different zones involved in this scenario are: Incident location (IL), Patients waiting for treatment area (PWFTA), Casualties clearing stations (CCS), Ambulance parking point (APP), and Technical operational command (TEL). The overall area spans approximately 350×200 m. The incident location is the event hall; directly in front of it lies the zone where patients wait for treatment. Injured individuals are transported to four casualty-clearing stations. In addition, a technical operational command centre and an ambulance parking point are provided.

3   Methodology

Figure 1 illustrates the overall workflow for implementing artificial intelligence in disaster scenarios. To simulate human mobility in post-disaster environments, we used the **BonnMotion** simulator, which generates realistic movement patterns of individuals in dynamic and chaotic conditions. For modeling communication between individuals, we employed the **ns-3** network simulator, configuring it to represent ad hoc wireless networks in infrastructure-less settings. During the simulation process, we collected relevant communication parameters, including the *channel utilization factor* and the *queue packet size*, which serve as the primary input features for our AI model.

In the data processing phase, the collected information was labeled to construct a supervised learning dataset. We trained a machine learning model using this dataset, incorporating *hyperparameter optimization techniques* to improve model performance. The trained model was then evaluated using standard machine learning metrics. Finally, the resulting model was exported and integrated back into the **ns-3** simulation environment, allowing us to test its performance under new disaster-driven communication scenarios. Additional details about each component of the methodology are presented in the following subsections.

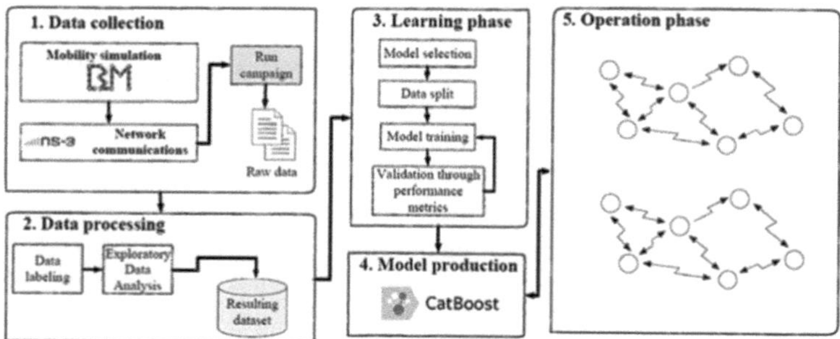

Fig. 1. Overview of the proposed methodology for integrating AI into disaster scenarios.

3.1 Data Collection

In the data collection phase, we used the **BonnMotion** tool to simulate the mobility of individuals in a disaster scenario. This tool allows the generation of realistic human movement patterns, which are essential to model behavior in chaotic environments. The main parameters configured in BonnMotion for this study are summarized in Table 1.

To simulate communication between individuals, we used the **ns-3** simulator, configuring a wireless ad hoc network without fixed infrastructure. The network layer employed the **OLSR** (Optimized Link State Routing) protocol, which is suitable for highly dynamic topologies typical in disaster situations. At the transport layer, the **UDP** protocol was used. Packet sizes followed an **exponential distribution** with an average of approximately 200 bytes, reflecting the variability in message lengths common in emergency communications. Additionally, we used the **IEEE 802.11a** standard to model the physical layer of the wireless network. The main simulation parameters are as follows: Mobility Model: Disaster Mobility Model, Number of Nodes: 50, Simulation Duration: 300 s, Speed Range: 0.5 to 1.5 m/s, and Pause Time: 0 s.

To improve the diversity and robustness of the dataset, multiple simulation runs were performed with different random seeds. This approach enabled the collection of a wide range of communication scenarios and mobility patterns. The simulation outputs were stored and organized to compute key performance metrics, including *channel utilization* and *queue packet size,* which serve as input features for the machine learning model.

Table 1. NS-3 Simulation Configuration Parameters

Parameter	Value/Description
Network Protocol	OLSR (Optimized Link State Routing)
Transport Protocol	UDP
Packet Size Distribution	Exponential (mean: 200 bytes)
PHY/MAC Standard	IEEE 802.11a
Channel Bandwidth	20 MHz
Simulation Time	300 s
Number of Nodes	50
Seed Variations	Multiple seeds for robustness
Application Traffic	[Constant Bit Rate or On-Off model

3.2 Data Processing

After the simulation phase, a large volume of raw data was collected from multiple network runs. These data represent low-level information related to node behavior, packet transmissions, queue dynamics, and channel access events. To prepare the dataset for machine learning, it was necessary to apply specific feature extraction techniques to derive meaningful indicators of network status.

For our study, we focused on two key features that characterize the state of the network at any given time:

- **Channel Utilization Factor**: This metric estimates the level of congestion in the wireless medium. It is calculated by monitoring the percentage of time the channel is sensed as busy versus idle. To smooth temporal fluctuations and capture recent behavior trends, we applied an *Exponential Weighted Moving Average (EWMA)* over the raw channel activity measurements.
- **Queue Packet Count**: This metric reflects the number of packets queued for transmission at each node. A high queue occupancy may indicate potential congestion, which could lead to packet drops or increased delays. The queue

management policy used was the default *FIFO* (First-In-First-Out) policy provided by the **ns-3** simulator.

These two features were extracted at regular time intervals throughout each simulation and paired with the corresponding network outcomes. In particular, each data instance was labeled according to whether a packet successfully reached its destination or not, under the prevailing network conditions. This labeled dataset forms the basis for training our machine learning model, enabling it to learn how network metrics influence packet delivery success in disaster-driven ad hoc environments.

3.3   Model Training and Evaluation

The classification task in this study is binary in nature: given the current network conditions, the model must predict whether a packet will be successfully delivered to its destination or not. Various supervised learning algorithms could be applied to this type of problem; however, we chose to employ an ensemble-based approach using the **CatBoost** classifier.

CatBoost, developed by Yandex, is a high-performance gradient boosting algorithm based on decision trees. It is specifically designed to handle categorical data efficiently and reduce overfitting by implementing advanced techniques such as ordered boosting. One of its main advantages lies in its efficient handling of decision splits through symmetric trees and histogram-based processing, which makes it especially suitable for deployment on resource-constrained devices.

To train the CatBoost model, we focused on tuning the most critical hyperparameters: the **tree depth**, set to values between 6 and 10, and the **number of trees**, which varied up to 5000 estimators. In order to determine the optimal combination of these hyperparameters, we performed an exhaustive **Grid Search**. This method was selected over more lightweight alternatives due to the availability of sufficient computational resources, allowing for a comprehensive evaluation of the hyperparameter space (Table 2).

The final trained model was validated using a hold-out portion of the dataset and evaluated using standard classification metrics, as discussed in the next section. The performance of the trained CatBoost model was evaluated using standard machine learning metrics for binary classification: **accuracy, precision, recall**, and the **F1-score**. These metrics provide a comprehensive view of the model's ability to distinguish between successful and unsuccessful packet deliveries under varying network conditions.

The model achieved an *accuracy* of **0.888**, indicating a high proportion of correct predictions across the entire dataset. To assess reliability, *precision* was measured at **0.883**, reflecting the model's consistency when predicting successful deliveries. Furthermore, the *recall* reached **0.888**, and the *F1-score*—the harmonic mean of precision and recall—was **0.885**. This balanced assessment is particularly relevant given its robustness against potential class imbalances. These results, computed on a held-out test set, demonstrate strong generalization capabilities and suggest that the model is well-suited for real-time deployment in simulated disaster communication environments.

Table 2. Main hyperparameters tuned for CatBoost training.

Hyperparameter	Value Range	Description
`depth`	6–10	Maximum depth of each decision tree; controls model complexity
`iterations`	up to 5000	Number of boosting iterations (trees) to build the ensemble
`learning_rate`	0.01–0.3	Step size shrinkage used to prevent overfitting
`12_leaf_reg`	1–10	Regularization term applied to leaf values to improve generalization
`border_count`	32–254	Number of splits for continuous features (histogram-based)
`bagging_temperature`	0–1	Controls the intensity of Bayesian bootstrap; higher values add more randomness
`eval_metric`	Accuracy, F1-Score	Metrics used to evaluate classification performance

4   Numerical Results

After training the artificial intelligence model using the custom-built dataset and validating its performance through machine learning metrics, the final model was exported and integrated into the **ns-3** simulator. The aim was to evaluate its effectiveness in a simulated disaster scenario by comparing network performance in two different settings: one without Quality of Service (QoS) mechanisms and another enhanced with the AI-driven decision-making process.

To quantify the benefits of the proposed approach, we evaluated both scenarios using key network performance indicators. These include the **Packet Delivery Ratio (PDR)**, which represents the percentage of packets successfully delivered to their destinations; the **Throughput**, which measures the effective data rate achieved by the network; and the **End-to-End Delay**, which quantifies the average time taken for packets to traverse the network from source to destination.

4.1   Packet Delivery Ratio (PDR)

Figure 2 presents the evaluation of the Packet Delivery Ratio (PDR) across four applications in a disaster scenario. Human mobility patterns were generated using the BonnMotion simulator, and wireless ad hoc communication was modeled using ns-3. The experiment compares three QoS strategies: a baseline scenario without congestion control (NO_CC), a traditional approach using EDCA (EDCA_CC), and an AI-driven method (ML_CC) based on a CatBoost model trained on relevant network features. As depicted in the figure, the AI-based

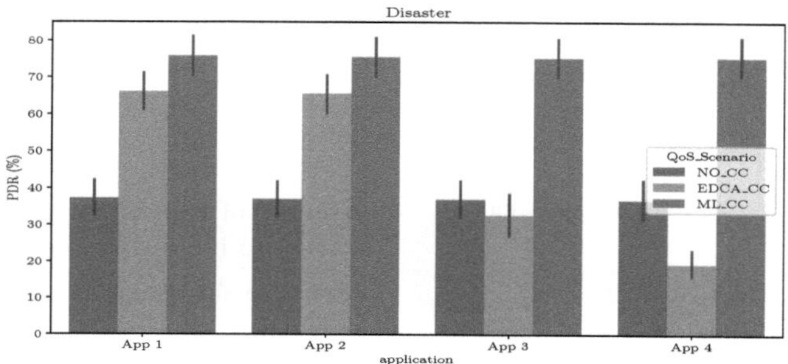

Fig. 2. Comparison of Packet Delivery Ratio (PDR) under three QoS scenarios in a disaster environment: no congestion control (NO_CC), EDCA-based control (EDCA_CC), and machine learning-based control (ML_CC).

solution (ML_CC) consistently outperforms the other two approaches in terms of PDR. While the EDCA mechanism provides moderate improvements over the NO_CC scenario in certain applications, its performance degrades significantly under specific conditions, particularly in App 4. In contrast, the ML_CC approach demonstrates robustness and adaptability by maintaining high PDR across all applications. These results suggest that the AI-enhanced strategy is better equipped to handle the dynamic and congested conditions typical of disaster environments. By leveraging real-time features such as channel occupancy and queue length, the model is able to make informed decisions about packet transmission, thereby improving reliability and overall QoS performance.

Throughput, defined as the rate of successfully received data at the destination (in kbps), is a critical metric for assessing the efficiency of communication in disaster-prone ad hoc networks. These environments are highly dynamic, with frequent topology changes, variable signal conditions, and intense channel contention—making high throughput difficult to sustain.

Figure 3 illustrates the throughput performance of the three QoS strategies evaluated: the baseline without congestion control (**NO_CC**), the EDCA-based mechanism (**EDCA_CC**), and the machine learning-based control (**ML_CC**) using the **CatBoost** algorithm.

Overall, the **ML_CC** approach achieves comparable or higher throughput than the other scenarios, particularly in applications where traditional methods struggle. For example, in **App 4**, **ML_CC** significantly outperforms both **EDCA_CC** and **NO_CC**, highlighting its ability to adapt under high congestion or degraded channel conditions. While **EDCA_CC** shows slight improvements over the baseline in some applications (Apps 1 and 2), it suffers in others due to its static nature and lack of predictive capabilities.

These findings reinforce the value of intelligent, data-driven control mechanisms that can dynamically adjust to real-time network states. The increased throughput seen with **ML_CC** aligns with the improvements observed in **Packet Delivery Ratio (PDR)**, and further demonstrates the effectiveness of machine

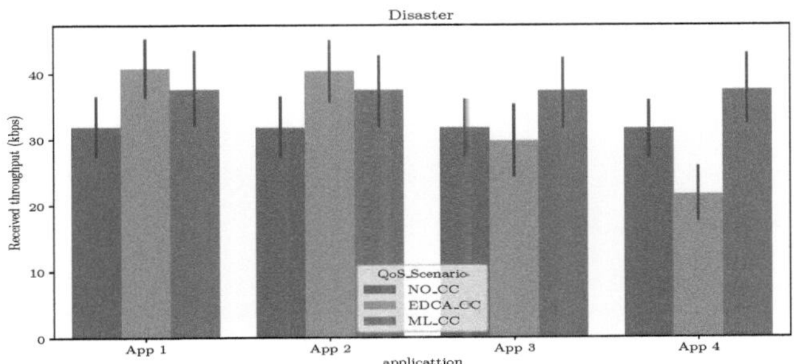

Fig. 3. Comparison of received throughput across three QoS strategies (**NO_CC**, **EDCA_CC**, and **ML_CC**) in a simulated disaster scenario.

learning in reducing retransmissions, optimizing packet scheduling, and improving overall communication efficiency in critical scenarios.

4.2 End-to-End Delay

End-to-End Delay refers to the average time a data packet takes to travel from the source to the destination node. In highly dynamic and unpredictable disaster scenarios, reducing delay is essential for enabling prompt communication, especially in applications that involve safety-critical or emergency data.

Figure 4 displays the end-to-end delay observed under three different Quality of Service (QoS) strategies: no congestion control (**NO_CC**), EDCA-based control (**EDCA_CC**), and machine learning-based control (**ML_CC**) using the **CatBoost** algorithm.

The results show a significant reduction in delay for the **ML_CC** scenario across all applications. While the EDCA approach achieves moderate improvements over the baseline, it fails to maintain low delay under more congested or variable conditions (e.g., **App 4**). In contrast, the **ML_CC** strategy exhibits consistent low latency, indicating its effectiveness in avoiding transmission under unfavorable conditions such as high queue occupancy or busy channels.

These findings demonstrate that AI-driven strategies can dynamically adapt to the network state, minimize queuing and processing delays, and ultimately enhance responsiveness in wireless ad hoc environments affected by disaster-induced mobility and interference.

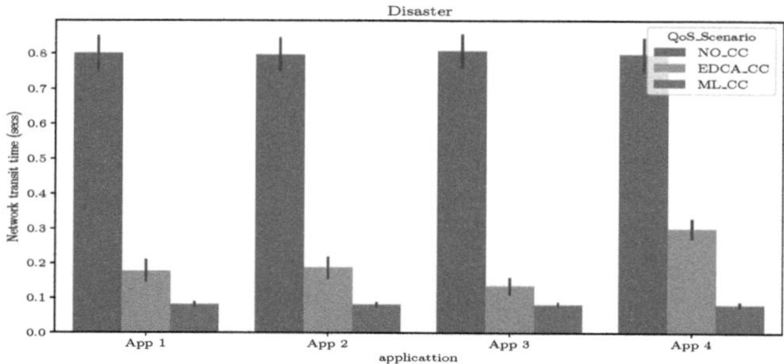

Fig. 4. Comparison of end-to-end delay under three QoS strategies (**NO_CC**, **EDCA_CC**, and **ML_CC**) in a disaster scenario.

5   Conclusion

This work proposed an intelligent approach to enhance communication in ad hoc wireless networks for disaster scenarios. Using **BonnMotion** and **ns-3**, a custom dataset was generated, capturing key indicators such as *channel utilization factor* and *queue packet size*. These features were used to train a **CatBoost** binary classification model. The model was validated with standard metrics (accuracy, precision, and F1-score) and reintegrated into the simulation environment for real-time decision-making. Results showed clear improvements over the baseline (without QoS), particularly in **Packet Delivery Ratio (PDR)**, **Throughput**, and **End-to-End Delay**.

Overall, the findings highlight the potential of AI-driven, adaptive communication strategies in dynamic environments. Future work will explore multi-class models, additional network features, and real-time deployment on embedded platforms.

References

1. Alexander, D.: Resilience and disaster risk reduction: an etymological journey. Nat. Hazard. **13**(11), 2707–2716 (2013)
2. Federal Communications Commission. 2023 communications lifeline report (2023). https://www.fcc.gov/document/communications-lifeline-report-2023. Accessed 24 June 2025
3. Corson, S., Macker, J.: Mobile ad hoc networking (manet): routing protocol performance issues and evaluation considerations. In: IETF RFC 2501 (1999)
4. Garcia, L., Romero, M.: Rapid manet deployment after the 2017 puebla earthquake. In: IEEE Global Humanitarian Technology Conference, pp. 1–6 (2020)
5. Mao, S., Chen, M., Guo, S.: A survey on machine learning for networking: algorithms, applications and open issues. IEEE Commun. Surv. Tutor. **21**(4), 2633–2670 (2018)
6. Sun, S., Li, X., Li, Y.: Dynamic resource management in 5g network slicing using deep reinforcement learning. IEEE Trans. Netw. Serv. Manag. **17**(4), 2062–2076 (2020)

7. Jin, Z., Huajian, X., Kong, Z.: A resilient routing strategy based on deep reinforcement learning for urban emergency communication networks. Comput. Netw. **257**, 110898 (2024)
8. Suh, B.K., Ismatov, A., Park, Y.B.: A resilient routing protocol to reduce update cost by unsupervised learning and deep reinforcement learning in mobile ad hoc networks. Electronics **14**(1), 166 (2025)
9. Mahiddin, N.A., Fatin, F., Affandi, M., Mohamad, Z.: A review on mobility models in disaster area scenario. Int. J. Adv. Technol. Eng. Explorat. **8**(80), 848–864 (2021)
10. Aschenbruck, N., Gerhards-Padilla, E., Martini, P.: Bonnmotion: a mobility scenario generation and analysis tool. In: Proceedings of 3rd International ICST Conference on Simulation Tools and Techniques (SIMUTools), pp. 51–60 (2010)
11. Carpenter, S.E., Sichitiu, M.L.: An obstacle model implementation for evaluating radio shadowing with ns-3. In: Proceedings of the 2015 Workshop on ns-3 (WNS3), pp. 17–24 (2015)
12. Liu, L., Zhang, X., Jiang, S., Jiang, S.-P., Zhao, X., Zhao, X.: Hurricane evacuation analysis with large-scale mobile device location data during hurricane ian. Transp. Res. Part D: Transp. Environ. **139**, 104559 (2025)
13. High-Level Expert Group on Artificial Intelligence. Ethics guidelines for trustworthy AI. European Commission (2019). https://digital-strategy.ec.europa.eu
14. Aschenbruck, N., Gerhards-Padilla, E., Martini, P.: Modeling mobility in disaster area scenarios. Perform. Eval. **66**(12), 773–790 (2009)

Automatic Detection of Methane Emissions in Urban Landfills Using Hyperspectral Imaging and Machine Learning

José Manuel Alcántara Pérez[1][iD], María Gema Carrasco-García[2][iD],
Javier González-Enrique[3][iD], Juan Jesús Ruiz-Aguilar[2(✉)][iD],
and Ignacio J. Turias[3][iD]

[1] ARCGISA, 11379 Los Barrios, Cádiz, Spain
`josemanuel.alcantara@arcgisa.es`

[2] Department of Civil and Industrial Engineering, University of Cádiz, 11202 Algeciras, Spain
`{maria.carrasco,juanjesus.ruiz}@uca.es`

[3] Department of Computer Science, University of Cádiz, 11202 Algeciras, Spain
`{javier.gonzalezenrique,ignacio.turias}@uca.es`

Abstract. This study proposes a data-efficient framework for the automatic detection of methane (CH_4) emissions in urban landfill environments using hyperspectral satellite imagery and machine learning. Given the limited availability of labeled data, restricted to two hyperspectral cubes acquired by the EnMAP mission, a synthetic data augmentation strategy was developed to expand the training manifold by combining soil spectral signatures with controlled methane absorption patterns. Shallow Artificial Neural Networks (ANNs), optimized through Bayesian hyperparameter tuning, were employed to model the spectral response of methane while mitigating overfitting risks associated with deep architectures. The methodology was evaluated under both inter-scene generalization and intra-scene validation scenarios using repeated cross-validation. Results demonstrate that the proposed approach achieves high predictive accuracy and strong generalization across different temporal acquisitions, with robust detection of methane-related spectral features. Spatial prediction maps further confirm the model's capability to localize methane plumes and distinguish them from background materials. The findings highlight the effectiveness of combining spectral feature engineering, data augmentation, and shallow learning models for environmental monitoring under data-scarce conditions, offering a scalable and computationally efficient solution for methane detection in real-world scenarios.

Keywords: Hyperspectral image (HSI) · ANNs · methane emissions · urban landfill

1   Introduction

Methane (CH_4) is a potent greenhouse gas with a global warming potential approximately 28 times greater than that of CO_2 over a 100-year period. Urban landfills are among the most significant anthropogenic sources of methane emissions, contributing substantially to local air pollution and climate forcing. Monitoring these emissions is therefore essential for implementing mitigation strategies and supporting environmental compliance. Rapid methane mitigation is one of the most effective pathways to curb global warming due to its high short-term global warming potential and relatively short atmospheric lifetime [1–4]. Among anthropogenic sources, municipal solid waste (MSW) landfills account for 13–18% of global methane emissions and have been identified as localized "super-emitters" with high potential for cost-effective mitigation [5–7]. In recent years, advances in hyperspectral remote sensing have enabled the detection of methane plumes by identifying their unique absorption features in shortwave infrared (SWIR) spectral bands. However, the use of hyperspectral imagery in urban landfill monitoring remains limited due to the infrequent temporal coverage of satellite missions and the restricted availability of labeled datasets. The recent development of satellite-based hyperspectral and multispectral sensors (e.g., PRISMA, EnMAP, EMIT, GHGSat, Sentinel-2, TROPOMI) has enabled the detection and quantification of methane plumes at the facility scale in large urban landfills, revealing that actual emissions frequently and significantly exceed conventional bottom-up inventories [5,6,8,9]. However, global systematic monitoring remains constrained by the discontinuous coverage of hyperspectral sensors, quantification uncertainties, and the need for specialized processing pipelines [5,8–10].

Methane detection using remote sensing has gained substantial attention over the past decade due to the launch of hyperspectral and multispectral satellites. Early studies focused on physics-based approaches, exploiting radiative transfer models and matched filtering to identify methane absorption features near 2.3–2.4 μm. These methods, while accurate under controlled conditions, are highly sensitive to atmospheric variability and require precise calibration. Rapid advancements have been made in automated methane detection methods based on machine learning. For wide-swath multispectral data, deep networks (such as CNNs) have improved detection thresholds and noise robustness by one or more orders of magnitude compared to traditional thresholding and band-ratio approaches [1,2,11,12]. In hyperspectral imagery, architectures like U-Net, Mask R-CNN, and domain-specific segmenters have markedly reduced false positive rates and automated plume segmentation [3,10,13,14]. However, they typically require massive volumes of annotated data and tend to be highly overfitted with specific sensors [3,4,14,15]. This reliance on large training datasets constitutes a critical bottleneck in scenarios where only a few satellite images are available per landfill or region, a common limitation for hyperspectral sensors with low revisit frequencies or during pilot campaigns [3,9,10]. Therefore, when only a small number of scenes are available, data-driven deep architectures such as CNNs face major limitations, including overfitting and poor generalization to unseen spatial contexts. In such scenarios, shallow artificial neural networks (ANNs) can offer a more efficient alternative. Shallow networks require fewer parameters, are more robust to small datasets, and can still capture the key spectral signatures associated with methane absorption. By focusing on spectral-based feature extraction instead of spatial convolution, shallow ANNs can effectively leverage the limited data available from hyperspectral sensors to enable reliable methane detection in urban landfill environments.

In this study, we propose an automatic detection framework for methane emissions from urban landfills based on hyperspectral image analysis and shallow neural network modeling. Our approach aims to overcome the data scarcity challenge by prioritizing spectral decomposition and feature learning rather than deep spatial hierarchies. The method is evaluated using a set of hyperspectral scenes with known methane sources, and its performance is compared with CNN-based baselines under limited training conditions. The present work builds upon these insights by demonstrating that shallow ANNs, when properly tuned and combined with physical feature engineering, can achieve robust methane detection performance under data-sparse conditions. This approach contributes to the growing field of low-data machine learning for environmental monitoring, emphasizing generalizable, interpretable, and computationally efficient models. This contribution seeks to complement recent advancements in automated methane detection by providing a data-efficient alternative, which is particularly relevant for landfill monitoring programs in countries or municipalities constrained by low hyperspectral revisit frequencies and limited annotation resources.

This study contributes to the advancement of efficient and scalable solutions for environmental monitoring based on hyperspectral technology. Section 2 describes the methodology, including the models and the experimental procedure. Section 3 presents the main results and their discussion, while the conclusions of the research are summarised in Sect. 4.

2   Materials and Methods

To evaluate the proposed architectures, a hyperspectral image dataset was specifically created based on two hypercubes (scenes) recorded by EnMAP (a German hyperspectral satellite mission that monitors and characterizes Earth's environment) in January and June of 2024. Due to the inherent scarcity of labeled real-world methane plumes within the hyperspectral cubes, a targeted data augmentation strategy was implemented to provide the shallow ANNs with a robust and statistically significant training manifold. For the June 2024 scene (ENMAP01_L1B_20240616), a total of 160 ground hyperpixels were identified as baseline soil signatures. Similarly, 100 ground hyperpixels were extracted from the January 2024 scene (ENMAP01_L1B_20240102). These pixels represent the underlying "background" reflectance of the landfill surface, serving as the physical foundation for the synthetic expansion of the training sets.

The augmentation process utilized a stochastic mixing model where each original ground hyperpixel was used to generate 25 unique synthetic samples.

By blending the spectral characteristics of the landfill soil with varying concentrations and random perturbations of the reference CH_4 signature, the June database was expanded to a total of 4,000 synthetic samples (160×25), while the January database reached 2,500 samples (100×25). To guarantee the robustness of the training set, the synthetic sample generation was formulated to be strictly coherent with the Beer-Lambert law, accurately modeling the radiometric attenuation based on the physical principles of gas absorption. This procedure ensured that the Bayesian-optimized models were exposed to a wide variance of soil-gas interactions, effectively mitigating the risk of overfitting to the limited number of original samples and enhancing the network's ability to generalize across different temporal and atmospheric conditions.

2.1 Performance Analysis and Inter-Scene Generalization (Scenario 1)

In the first experimental scenario, the model was trained using the augmented dataset from one hyperspectral cube and subsequently evaluated on the second, completely independent scene. This setup was designed to test the spatial generalization of the proposed architecture. Despite the inherent variability between hyperspectral captures (e.g., atmospheric interference and lighting geometry), the shallow ANN demonstrated a robust capability to identify methane plumes. The successful labeling of hyperpixels based on the CH_4 absorption signature proved critical. By focusing on the physical spectral properties of the gas rather than scene-specific spatial features, the model avoided the common pitfall of "spectral-spatial leakage." The results indicate that the synthetic data augmentation effectively bridged the gap between the limited real samples, providing the network with enough variance to recognize the methane signature across different areas of the Cádiz landfill.

2.2 Intra-Scene Validation and Data Augmentation Impact (Scenario 2)

The second scenario, which used a hold-out test set comprising pixels from both hyperspectral cubes, yielded the highest performance across all metrics (MSE, MAE, R^2). This confirms that the data augmentation strategy successfully expanded the training manifold without introducing significant noise.

The use of Bayesian Optimization was a determining factor in these results. By iteratively refining the hyperparameters of the shallow ANN, the optimization process identified an architecture that balanced model capacity with the risk of overfitting. Specifically, the shallow network architecture, combined with Bayesian-derived regularization, ensured that the model remained effective even with the high dimensionality of the hyperpixels.

From a practical standpoint, the combination of shallow ANNs and Bayesian tuning offers a significant advantage for real-time environmental monitoring. Unlike deeper architectures that require massive datasets and high computational power, our approach is suited for deployment on edge-computing devices or aerotransportated (UAV) sensors. In this work, the use of shallow Artificial Neural Networks (ANNs) is motivated by the extremely limited availability of training data, consisting of only two hyperspectral cubes acquired from satellite observations. Under such data-scarce conditions, deep learning architectures such as Convolutional Neural Networks (CNNs) are prone to severe overfitting due to their large number of trainable parameters and their reliance on extensive datasets to effectively learn hierarchical spatial-spectral features. In contrast, shallow ANNs provide a more suitable bias-variance trade-off, as their reduced architectural complexity allows for more stable training and better generalization when the sample size is constrained. Moreover, in methane detection tasks, the discriminative information is often strongly linked to specific spectral signatures rather than complex spatial patterns, which further supports the use of models that prioritize spectral relationships over spatial feature extraction. Therefore, shallow ANNs constitute a robust and computationally efficient alternative in this context, enabling reliable detection performance while mitigating the risks associated with data scarcity and model overparameterization. To identify the optimal configuration of the network, a Bayesian optimization procedure was implemented to tune key hyperparameters, including the number of hidden neurons, learning rate, and regularization weights. Unlike traditional grid search methods, this probabilistic approach allowed for an efficient exploration of the parameter space, ensuring the selection of a model that minimizes the loss function while maintaining high generalization capabilities. To ensure the robustness and statistical significance of the results, a random resampling scheme was integrated with cross-validation. This entire experimental workflow was repeated 20 times, allowing for the derivation of comprehensive statistical distributions (mean and standard deviation) for all performance metrics evaluated on independent test sets.

3   Results and Discussion

Figures 1 and 2 present a comparative analysis between the theoretical methane signature (CH_4, solid blue line), incorporated as a reference baseline, and the hyperpixel profiles extracted from the EnMAP datasets (January and June scenes). The primary objective of this comparison is to verify the physical consistency of our labeling process. As observed in both figures, the Methane Hyperpixel Profiles (purple, green, and cyan lines) exhibit a high morphological correlation with the reference signature, particularly within the diagnostic SWIR window between 2300 nm and 2400 nm. The most significant alignment occurs at the characteristic absorption trough near 2370 nm, where the extracted pixels accurately replicate the molecular absorption drop of the CH_4 reference.

The distinction between these methane-labeled pixels and the environmental background is equally evident. The "Out-Landfill" and "In-Landfill" background signatures (orange and yellow lines) lack the specific absorption features of the gas, showing instead a relatively flat or ascending transmittance trend in the critical 2350–2380 nm range. This clear spectral separation, validated against the incorporated CH_4 reference, confirms that the synthetic data augmentation and the subsequent training of the shallow ANNs were based on genuine physical features rather than stochastic noise. The fact that this alignment persists across different temporal captures (Fig. 1 vs Fig. 2) underscores the robustness of the Bayesian-optimized model in identifying methane plumes under varying atmospheric and seasonal conditions. The classification of methane hyperpixels was performed using shallow ANNs, an architecture specifically selected to balance computational efficiency with the need to mitigate overfitting in high-dimensional hyperspectral data.

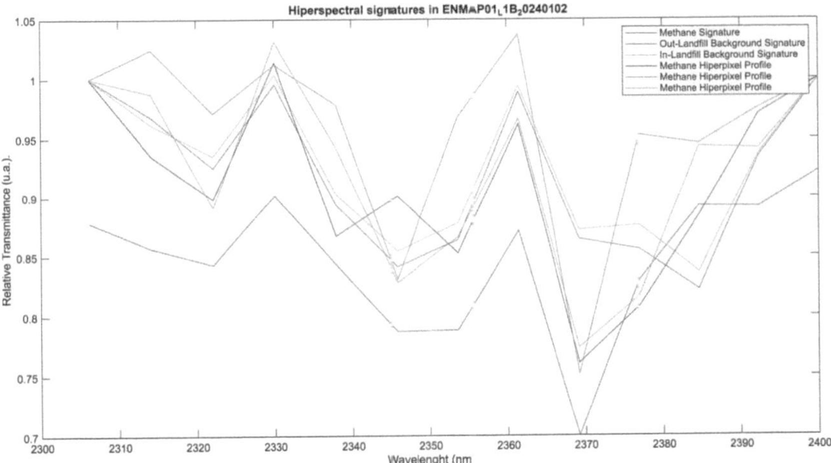

Fig. 1. Hyperspectral signatures on the Scene ENMAP01_L1B_20240102. (Color figure online)

For the annotation of the individual hyperpixels within the test scenes, the reflectance spectra underwent a trend removal process. Flattening the spectral baseline is a critical preprocessing step to suppress low-frequency background variations and enhance the specific high-frequency absorption bands of the target gas. Once flattened, each hyperpixel was evaluated against the theoretical hyperspectral signature of methane through the computation of the Pearson correlation coefficient, yielding the discrete labels used for model training and validation. To ensure the spectral integrity of the dataset, any spatial samples exhibiting a probability of cloud cover were systematically excluded from the analysis. This rigorous cloud-screening step is essential, as even minor cloud contamination or associated shadows can severely attenuate the target methane absorption features and introduce critical artifacts into the machine learning pipeline. Consequently, the network was trained and evaluated exclusively on highly reliable, clear-sky observations.

The quantitative performance of the Bayesian-optimized shallow ANNs is detailed in Table 1, focusing on inter-scene generalization. When the model

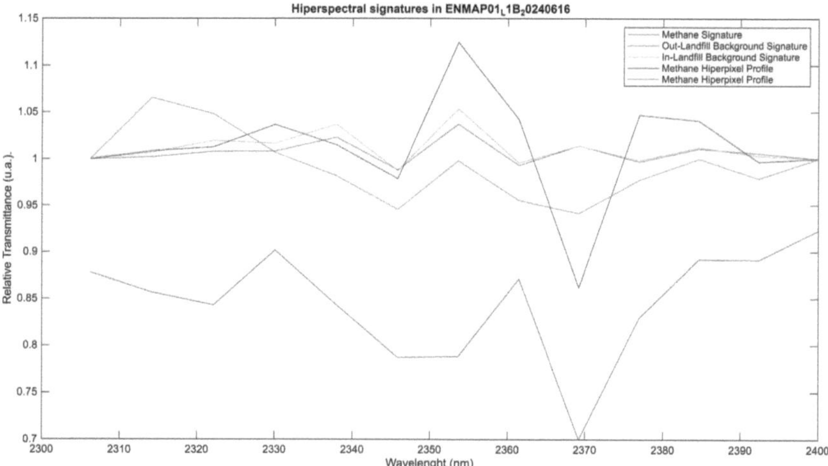

Fig. 2. Hyperspectral signatures on the Scene ENMAP01_L1B_20240616. (Color figure online)

was trained on the January synthetic database (DB1) and evaluated on the June scene, it achieved a mean RMSE of 0.0439 and a mean R^2 of 0.8566, with the optimal architecture identified. Interestingly, the model trained on the June dataset (DB2) and tested on the January capture showed a higher mean R^2 of 0.9309, despite a larger mean RMSE of 0.1332. This discrepancy suggests that while seasonal variations in atmospheric conditions and solar geometry between January and June influence the absolute error magnitude, the network maintains a high capacity for capturing the underlying spectral variance of the methane plumes across different temporal captures.

Table 1. Metrics of ANN-based models evaluated on Test Scene. DB1 is the synthetic database based on the ground hyperpixels of the Scene ENMAP01_L1B_20240102; the metrics are resulting from testing the ANN-based model on Test Scene ENMAP01_L1B_20240616. DB2 is the synthetic database based on the ground hyperpixels of the Scene ENMAP01_L1B_20240616; the metrics are resulting from testing the ANN-based model on Test Scene ENMAP01_L1B_20240102.

Metric on Test	rmse			mae			R^2			Best ANNs	
	max	mean	std	max	mean	std	max	mean	std	rmse min	Arch.
DB1	0.0578	0.0439	0.0052	0.0451	0.0260	0.0076	0.8915	0.8566	0.0321	0.0378	[30,23]
DB2	0.2485	0.1332	0.0452	0.1947	0.0980	0.0385	0.9604	0.9309	0.0196	0.0821	[30,16]

A further refinement of the model's capabilities is presented in Table 2, which incorporates unseen pixels from the training scene into the test set (Scenario 2). This configuration resulted in a significant improvement in the determination coefficients R^2, reaching mean values of 0.9695 for DB1 and 0.9409 for DB2. The reduction in the standard deviation of these metrics (e.g., 0.0085 for DB1 R^2 underscores the stability provided by the synthetic data augmentation strategy. These results demonstrate that the combination of Bayesian hyperparameter tuning and data augmentation allows the shallow ANNs to achieve high internal consistency and reliable detection, effectively bridging the gap between intra-scene precision and inter-scene spatial generalization.

Table 2. Metrics of ANN-based models evaluated on the Test Scene and the hyperpixels of the Training Scene unseen during training. DB1 is the synthetic database based on the ground hyperpixels of the Scene ENMAP01_L1B_20240102; the metrics are resulting from testing the ANN-based model on Test Scene ENMAP01_L1B_20240616 and the hyperpixels of ENMAP01_L1B_20240102 not used in the DB generation. DB2 is the synthetic database based on the ground hyperpixels of the Scene ENMAP01_L1B_20240616; the metrics are resulting from testing the ANN-based model on Test Scene ENMAP01_L1B_20240102 and the hyperpixels of ENMAP01_L1B_20240616 not used in the DB generation.

Metric on Test	rmse			mae			R^2		
	max	mean	std	max	mean	std	max	mean	std
DB1	0.0630	0.0482	0.0064	0.0433	0.0289	0.0057	0.9781	0.9695	0.0085
DB2	0.2205	0.1183	0.0401	0.1561	0.0795	0.0308	0.9665	0.9409	0.0178

The results suggest that for specialized tasks like methane detection in landfills, where emissions typically consist of a complex biogas mixture rather than pure methane, the quality and physical relevance of the training data (enabled here by spectral labeling and augmentation)are more important than model depth. This methodology provides a scalable framework for landfill monitoring in regions.

The predictive performance of the Bayesian-optimized shallow ANNs is further validated by the regression plots shown in Figs. 3 and 4, which compare the predicted CH_4 values (YPred) against the test ground-truth (YTest) for both temporal captures. In the June 2024 scene (Fig. 3), the model achieves an R^2 of 0.8915 and a remarkably low RMSE of 0.0378. The data points are tightly clustered around the 1:1 identity line, particularly for values below 0.15, indicating that the network could be highly sensitive to lower methane concentrations even under the atmospheric conditions typical of the summer season in Cádiz. While a slight underestimation is observed at the higher end of the scale (0.25–0.45), the overall linear fit remains robust, confirming the model's ability to maintain precision across the entire detected range. The results for the January 2024 scene (Fig. 4) demonstrate an even higher degree of correlation, with an R^2 of 0.9114. Although the RMSE increases to 0.0821, this is consistent with the broader dynamic range of methane values present in this specific capture compared to the June scene. The scatter plot shows a well-distributed alignment across the regression line, proving that the synthetic data augmentation effectively provided the model with the necessary variance to handle different scales of spectral intensity. The consistency of these high R^2 values (>0.89) across both winter and summer scenes underscores the spatial and temporal generalization of the proposed methodology. This stability is a direct result of the Bayesian hyperparameter tuning, which prevented the shallow architecture from overfitting to scene-specific illumination artifacts.

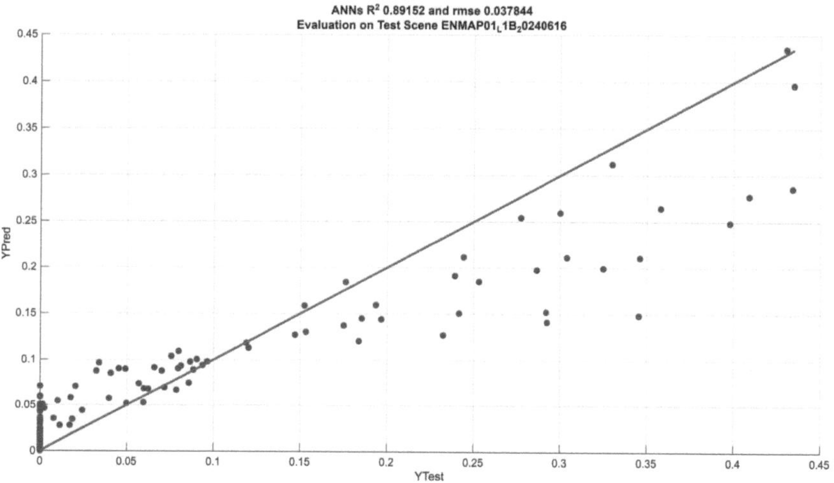

Fig. 3. ANN-based model trained with a synthetic database generated with Scene ENMAP01_L1B_20240102 and evaluated on Test Scene ENMAP01_L1B_20240616.

Figures 5 and 6 present the spatial prediction maps generated by the Bayesian-optimized shallow ANN models for the June and January EnMAP scenes, respectively. These maps provide qualitative validation of the model's ability to translate spectral predictions into coherent spatial patterns of methane presence. In both cases, the detected methane regions (class 1) and high-probability zones (class 2) exhibit clear spatial clustering, which is consistent with the expected behavior of gas emissions in landfill environments. The gradual transition from high-probability methane areas to low-probability regions (class 3) suggests that the model captures not only binary presence but also intermediate concentration gradients, reflecting a physically meaningful interpretation of methane dispersion. Importantly, the ground class (class 4) remains well separated from methane-related classes, confirming that the model does not confuse background spectral variability with gas absorption features.

A comparative analysis between both figures highlights the robustness of the proposed methodology under different temporal and environmental conditions. Despite variations in atmospheric composition, illumination geometry, and seasonal effects between the January and June acquisitions, the spatial distribution of predicted methane plumes remains consistent in terms of structure

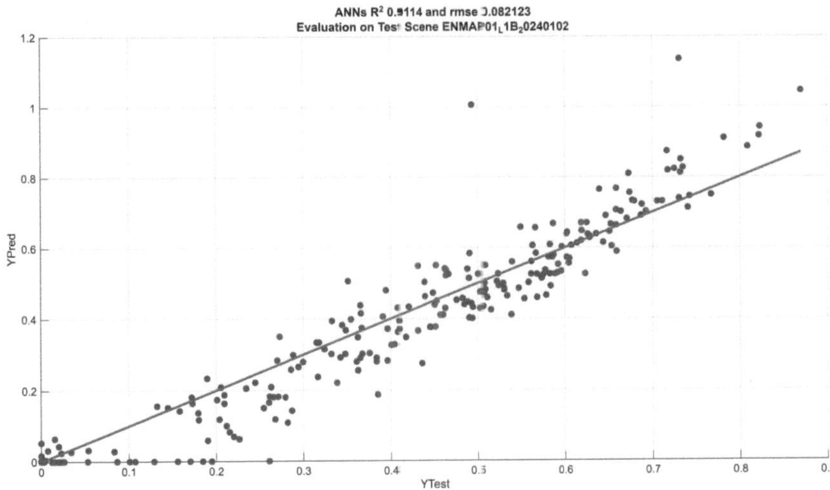

Fig. 4. ANN-based model trained with a synthetic database generated with Scene ENMAP01_L1B_20240616 and evaluated on Test Scene ENMAP01_L1B_20240102.

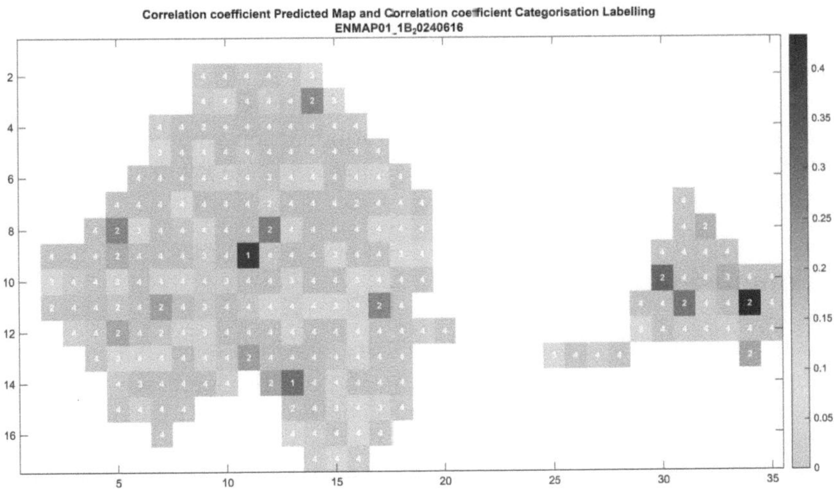

Fig. 5. Prediction map of Test Scene ENMAP01_L1B_20240616. The colors represent the prediction of the ANN-based model, and the numbers represent the labelling made with the correlation coefficients: (1) Methane; (2) High probability of methane, (3) Low probability of Methane, (4) Ground.

and localization. This stability reinforces the effectiveness of the spectral-based learning approach, which prioritizes methane absorption features over scene-dependent spatial characteristics. Moreover, the absence of significant spatial noise or random misclassifications indicates that the combination of synthetic data augmentation and Bayesian optimization successfully regularizes the model.

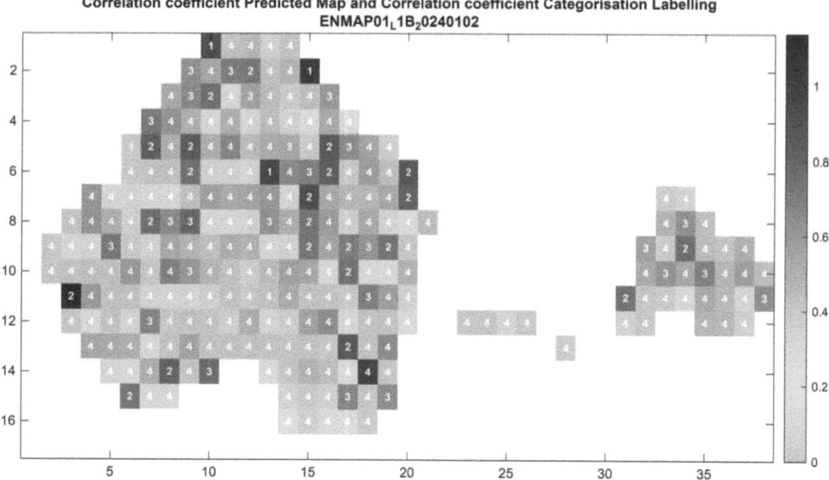

Fig. 6. Prediction map of Test Scene ENMAP01_L1B_20240102. The colors represent the prediction of the ANN-based model, and the numbers represent the labelling made with the correlation coefficients: (1) Methane; (2) High probability of methane, (3) Low probability of Methane, (4) Ground.

As a result, the generated prediction maps demonstrate that shallow ANNs can provide reliable and interpretable spatial outputs, even when trained on highly limited hyperspectral datasets, supporting their applicability in operational environmental monitoring systems.

4   Conclusions

This study demonstrates the feasibility of CH_4 detection in landfill environments using hyperspectral imaging, even when constrained by significant data scarcity. By leveraging the specific physical spectral signature of CH_4 for hyperpixel labeling and employing a synthetic data augmentation strategy, we successfully developed a robust training framework that overcomes the limitations of small sample sizes. The integration of Bayesian optimization was instrumental in refining the architecture of the shallow ANNs, ensuring an optimal balance between model complexity and generalization. The experimental results across two distinct scenarios, inter-scene generalization and intra-scene validation, confirm that the proposed methodology is not only accurate but also highly adaptable to varying environmental conditions.

Furthermore, it is essential to consider the role of satellite-based remote sensing in this context. While satellite platforms offer the advantages of large-scale coverage, global accessibility, and high temporal frequency for periodic monitoring, they often lack the spatial and spectral resolution necessary for the precise identification of localized methane plumes in topographically complex landfill sites. In contrast, the hyperspectral cubes utilized in this study provide the high-fidelity data required for accurate hyperpixel classification, despite their higher logistical acquisition costs. Furthermore, the computational efficiency of optimized shallow architectures makes this approach particularly suitable for real-time monitoring applications using aerotransportated sensors or edge-computing platforms. This research provides a scalable and cost-effective solution for landfill emissions monitoring, paving the way for more frequent and accessible environmental audits in regions where extensive hyperspectral datasets are not yet available.

Future work should investigate a multi-scale framework that leverages high-resolution aerial imagery to calibrate and improve the performance of satellite-based monitoring systems. This approach would involve deploying a hyperspectral imaging system on UAVs to acquire data in uncontrolled environments, subject to varying lighting and weather conditions. To support this, the imaging payload will be integrated into a UAV platform equipped with stabilization and georeferencing capabilities, enabling precise and reliable data collection during flight operations. In addition, on-board preprocessing methods will be explored to mitigate noise introduced by atmospheric disturbances and illumination variability. These efforts will be complemented by domain adaptation and transfer learning techniques to retrain and fine-tune models using field-collected datasets. Overall, this extended framework is intended to provide a more realistic evaluation of model robustness and generalization in operational contexts such as port environments, oil spill response, and industrial discharge monitoring.

Acknowledgments. This work is part of the technological contract OT2024/028, "Use of Hyperspectral Imaging and UAV in Smart Management of Urban Waste Landfills," supported by ARCGISA. Furthermore, the authors would like to thank the financial support provided by the Plan de ayudas para el Fomento de la Investigación y Transferencia de Conocimiento en el Campus Bahía de Algeciras (promoted by the Algeciras Technological Campus Foundation, University of Cádiz). Additional funding was provided by the Andalusia FEDER Operational Programme 2021–2027 under grant FEDER-UCA-2024-B2-07, titled "Spectral Imaging Technology and Deep Learning for Environmental Protection: Detection of Water and Air Pollution (DeepEnvSI)."

References

1. Rouet-Leduc, B., Hulbert, C.: Automatic detection of methane emissions in multispectral satellite imagery using a vision transformer. Nat. Commun. **15**(1), 3801 (2024)
2. Schuit, B.J., et al.: Automated detection and monitoring of methane super-emitters using satellite data. Atmos. Chem. Phys. **23**(16), 9071–9098 (2023)
3. Ruzicka, V., Mateo-García, G., Gómez-Chova, L., Vaughan, A., Guanter, L., Markham, A.: Semantic segmentation of methane plumes with hyperspectral machine learning models. Sci. Rep. **13**(1), 19999 (2023)
4. Tiemann, E., Zhou, S., Kläser, A., Heidler, K., Schneider, R., Zhu, X.X.: Machine learning for methane detection and quantification from space - a survey (2024)

5. Zhang, X., et al.: Global identification of solid waste methane super emitters using hyperspectral satellites. Environ. Sci. Technol. **59**(34), 18134–18145 (2025)
6. Zhang, S., Lei, M., Huang, X., Zhang, Y.: Evaluation of methane emission from MSW landfills in China, India, and the U.S. from space using a two-tier approach. J. Environ. Manage. **377**, 124705 (2025)
7. Cusworth, D.H., et al.: Using remote sensing to detect, validate, and quantify methane emissions from California solid waste operations. Environ. Res. Lett. **15**(5), 054012 (2020)
8. Maasakkers, J.D., et al.: Using satellites to uncover large methane emissions from landfills. Sci. Adv. **8**(32), eabn9683 (2022)
9. Bai, S., Li, F., Yan, Y., Huang, Q., Jiang, F., Chen, H., Zhang, Y.: Seasonal variations of methane emissions from a Urumqi landfill in China and its driving factors using hyperspectral satellite time-series observations. J. Geophys. Res. Atmos. **130** (2025)
10. Cai, X., Bao, Y., Huang, Q., Li, B.: Evaluation of methane emission from landfill based on EMIT. In: Gao, Z. (ed.) Third International Conference on Remote Sensing, Mapping, and Geographic Information Systems (RSMG 2025), vol. 13791, p. 137910D. International Society for Optics and Photonics, SPIE (2025)
11. Zortea, M., Almeida, J.L.D.S., Klein, L., Junior, A.C.N.: Detection of methane plumes using sentinel-2 satellite images and deep neural networks trained on synthetically created label data. In: 2023 IEEE International Conference on Big Data (BigData), pp. 3830–3839 (2023)
12. Zhao, S., Zhang, Y., Zhao, S., Wang, X., Varon, D.J.: A data-efficient deep transfer learning framework for methane super-emitter detection in oil and gas fields using the sentinel-2 satellite. Atmos. Chem. Phys. **25**(7), 4035–4052 (2025)
13. Ronald Albert de Araújo and Maciel Zortea: Learnable matched filter for methane plume segmentation in hyperspectral imagery. IEEE Geosci. Remote Sens. Lett. **22**, 1–5 (2025)
14. Si, G., Shiliang, F., Yao, W.: Unlocking the potential: multi-task deep learning for spaceborne quantitative monitoring of fugitive methane plumes (2024)
15. Jahan, I., Mehana, M., Matheou, G., Viswanathan, H.: Deep learning-based quantifications of methane emissions with field applications. Int. J. Appl. Earth Obs. Geoinf. **132**, 104018 (2024)

Modeling Non-linear Atmospheric Dynamics: A Comparative Study of Attention-Based CNN-LSTM and XGBoost for Ozone Forecasting

Javier González-Enrique[1]([✉]) [iD], María Gema Carrasco-García[2] [iD], Juan Jesús Ruiz-Aguilar[2] [iD], Paloma Rocío Cubillas Fernández[3] [iD], and Ignacio J. Turias[1] [iD]

[1] Department of Computer Science, University of Cádiz, Puerto Real, Spain
`javier.gonzalezenrique@uca.es`
[2] Department of Civil and Industrial Engineering, University of Cádiz, Algeciras, Spain
[3] Department of Thermal Engines and Machines, University of Cádiz, Puerto Real, Spain

Abstract. This study addresses the challenge of 24-h ahead tropospheric ozone forecasting in the complex atmospheric basin of Seville, Spain. To capture the highly non-linear dynamics of photochemical pollutants, a hybrid CNN-LSTM-Attention framework is proposed, utilizing a 72-h sliding window in a multivariate approach. To explicitly prevent temporal data leakage and ensure robust evaluation, a purged walk-forward cross-validation scheme with fold-isolated preprocessing was implemented. Furthermore, novel optimization strategies, including Stochastic Weight Averaging (SWA) and Bayesian hyperparameter tuning, were applied during training to enhance structural robustness and convergence stability. Evaluated on an unseen 2023 testing set, deep sequence models demonstrated clear hierarchical superiority over traditional tree-based baselines. The CNN-LSTM-Attention SWA model achieved the highest performance ($R^2 = 0.699$, MSE $= 368.30$), significantly mitigating the temporal lag and systematic amplitude damping observed in simpler architectures. Conversely, while XGBoost reduced computational overhead to a few minutes, it systematically underestimated ozone peak concentrations. Ultimately, the synergy between convolutional feature extraction, attention mechanisms, and SWA stabilization yields superior generalization. This establishes a robust foundation for early warning systems in Mediterranean environments, successfully capturing the amplitude and phase of diurnal ozone spikes where conventional models fail.

Keywords: Tropospheric Ozone Forecasting · Time Series Prediction · Deep Learning · Attention Mechanisms · SWA · LSTM

1   Introduction

The degradation of urban air quality is one of the main environmental and public health challenges of the 21st century. Among various air pollutants, tropospheric ozone (O_3) presents a particular complexity. Unlike primary pollutants, O_3 is a secondary pollutant that is not directly emitted into the atmosphere but rather is formed through complex photochemical reactions between nitrogen oxides (NO_x) and volatile organic compounds (VOCs) in the presence of solar radiation [10].

This strong dependence on meteorological variables makes its modeling highly non-linear. Specifically, conditions such as high temperatures accelerate the rate of photochemical reaction, while intense ultraviolet (UV) radiation drives the photolysis of nitrogen dioxide (NO_2). This problem is critically exacerbated in southern European regions. The city of Seville (Spain) in particular emerged as a severe photochemical hotspot during the summer months, where high precursor emissions from road traffic converge with extreme temperatures and intense solar radiation.

Predicting O_3 concentrations to trigger early warnings against extreme peaks is a vital public health requirement. As a highly reactive oxidant, elevated O_3 exposure induces severe oxidative stress, significantly increasing respiratory and cardiovascular mortality [11]. Consequently, developing accurate forecasting models transcends computational challenges, becoming essential to mitigate severe health risks.

1.1   Related Work

Historically, air quality forecasting has relied on classical statistical models (e.g., ARIMA) and deterministic Chemical Transport Models (CTMs). Although physically grounded, these transport models are computationally expensive and frequently struggle to capture the highly non-linear photochemical processes driving tropospheric ozone formation, especially in high-insolation regions such as Seville, in southern Spain.

In recent years, data-driven approaches have established a new paradigm. Machine Learning (ML) models, particularly tree-based ensembles like Random Forest and XGBoost, efficiently map the complex interactions between O_3 precursors and meteorological variables [1]. Furthermore, Deep Learning (DL) architectures, such as Long Short-Term Memory (LSTM) networks and hybrid spatiotemporal models (e.g., CNN-LSTM), have become the standard for retaining long-term dependencies and pushing the boundaries of predictive accuracy [7].

Despite these algorithmic advances, a critical operational gap remains. Standard ML and DL models are systematically trained to optimize global error metrics, such as Mean Squared Error (MSE) or Mean Absolute Error (MAE). This optimization strategy forces models to converge toward the mean of the target distribution, which inherently penalizes variance when dealing with imbalanced continuous data [2]. Consequently, state-of-the-art models systematically smooth the prediction curve and underestimate extreme O_3 peaks. Accurate forecasting of these rare and hazardous episodes remains a major challenge, but it is exactly the critical capability that public health and environmental administrations require.

1.2 Proposed Approach

To bridge this operational gap, predictive methodologies must shift from the conventional pursuit of global error minimization to peak-aware and domain-informed optimization strategies. In alignment with this necessary paradigm shift, this paper presents an advanced prediction framework for tropospheric ozone on a 24-h horizon ($T + 24$). The proposed methodology is evaluated on the Seville air quality network using recent data from 2018 to 2023, reserving the entire year of 2023 as an unseen testing set to ensure strict chronological validation.

Specifically, to capture the highly non-linear and transient nature of photochemical pollutants, we propose a hybrid CNN-LSTM-Attention architecture operating over a 72-h historical observation window. This deep sequence approach is systematically benchmarked against a highly optimized tree-based baseline (XGBoost). Furthermore, to guarantee methodological rigor and robust generalization, the framework integrates dynamic mRMR feature selection, a purged walk-forward cross-validation scheme to prevent temporal data leakage, and Stochastic Weight Averaging (SWA) to stabilize convergence toward flatter loss minima.

The remainder of the paper is organized as follows: Sect. 2 details the nature of the dataset and the preprocessing steps. The core algorithms are described in Sect. 3. Section 4 outlines the architecture of the proposed models and the experimental design. The empirical results and comparative analysis are presented in Sect. 5. Finally, the main conclusions and implications for public health management are drawn in Sect. 6.

2 Dataset and Preprocessing

2.1 Study Area and Data Acquisition

The dataset utilized in this study is derived from the official air quality monitoring network of Andalusia and was acquired through the European Environment Agency (EEA) data repository. Specifically, the data were collected at the Santa Clara monitoring station, located in the northeast sector of Seville, Spain. This location is particularly relevant for the analysis of tropospheric ozone due to its specific urban topology and its exposure to high levels of insolation, which drive complex photochemical reactions.

The temporal scope of the dataset spans six years, from January 1, 2018, to December 31, 2023, recorded at an hourly resolution. This extensive timeframe guarantees the inclusion of multiple seasonal cycles, long-term climatic variations, and anomalous extreme pollution events, providing a robust foundation for training complex Deep Learning architectures.

2.2 Chronological Splitting and Outlier Mitigation

To ensure strict chronological validation and prevent any form of temporal data leakage, a sequence of preprocessing steps is implemented. First, the dataset is strictly partitioned based on a temporal threshold: the data spanning five years from 2018 through 2022 are designated for the training and cross-validation phases, while the entire year of 2023 is strictly isolated as an unseen testing set to evaluate the final generalization capabilities of the models.

Following the chronological split, anomalous sensor readings and extreme isolated spikes are mitigated using a Hampel Filter [5]. This robust outlier detection mechanism is applied independently to the training and testing subsets.

2.3 Sequence Generation and Feature Engineering

To model the highly non-linear dynamics of O_3 in Seville, the forecasting problem is formulated as a multivariate sequential mapping. A sliding window approach is used to explicitly preserve the temporal autocorrelation of the series.

Given a multivariate time series $\mathbf{X} \in \mathbb{R}^{T \times M}$, where T is the total length of the series and M represents the number of engineered features, a fixed observation window of $w = 72$ h is defined. The objective of the predictive algorithms is to learn a mapping function f such that:

$$\hat{y}_{t+24} = f(\mathbf{x}_{t-w+1}, \ldots, \mathbf{x}_{t-1}, \mathbf{x}_t) \tag{1}$$

This parameterization allows the models to capture the essential short-term meteorological transitions and local emission dispersion cycles over a three-day historical period ($w = 72$ h). To construct the M-dimensional feature space $\mathbf{x}_t$ at each time step, a reduced and domain-informed configuration is engineered. The final array consists of three lagged historical variables and seven future contextual variables aligned with the prediction horizon:

- **Autoregressive and state variables (lagged):** To capture the immediate conditions and the chemical inertia of the system, three variables are extracted from the look-back window. These include the raw historical O_3 concentrations, the first-order derivative of the series to encode the rate of change and trend, and a boolean peak-alert flag designed to help the models explicitly track previous threshold-exceeding extreme events.
- **Cyclical and contextual variables (future horizon at $T + 24$):** To model the highly non-linear photochemical cycles without introducing external meteorological uncertainty, the future temporal context is mathematically encoded using seven variables. Time is transformed into a continuous cyclic space using sine and cosine functions for the hour, month and day of the week. This trigonometric encoding ensures that cyclical transitions (e.g., from 23:00 to 00:00) are smoothly represented in the mathematical space. Finally, a binary weekend flag is incorporated to account for the O_3 weekend effect, a phenomenon in NO_x saturated urban regimes where lower weekend NO emissions paradoxically increase O_3 levels.

3 Methodology and Techniques

Modeling tropospheric ozone concentrations is inherently challenging due to its strong seasonality, inherent stochasticity, and the complex non-linear dynamics of its precursors. To overcome these barriers, a hybrid forecasting framework that integrates deep sequence learning with dynamical systems analysis and information theory was implemented. The specific structural components and techniques comprising this methodology are detailed below.

3.1 Feature Selection

To evaluate the impact of dimensionality, the XGBoost baseline is deployed in two configurations: using the full feature space and a subset filtered by the Minimum Redundancy Maximum Relevance (mRMR) algorithm [13]. Unlike linear correlations, mRMR employs Mutual Information (I) to capture non-linear dynamics through the Mutual Information Difference (MID) formulation:

$$\max_{S \subset F, |S|=m} \left[I(S; y) - \frac{1}{|S|^2} \sum_{i,j \in S} I(i; j) \right] \tag{2}$$

where $I(S; y)$ maximizes relevance with the target y, while the second term minimizes redundant information among the selected predictors S.

3.2 Tree-Based Gradient Boosting: XGBoost

eXtreme Gradient Boosting (XGBoost) [3] is implemented as a high-performance tree-based competitor to evaluate non-linear dependencies without the inductive bias of recurrent architectures. This ensemble minimizes a second-order Taylor approximation of the loss function:

$$\mathcal{L}^{(t)} \simeq \sum_{i=1}^{n} \left[g_i f_t(x_i) + \frac{1}{2} h_i f_t^2(x_i) \right] + \Omega(f_t) \tag{3}$$

where g_i and h_i denote the gradient and Hessian, respectively. Structural complexity is controlled via the regularizer $\Omega(f_t) = \gamma T + \frac{1}{2}\lambda \sum_{j=1}^{T} w_j^2$, which penalizes the number of leaves T and their weights w. This configuration allows for a direct confrontation between gradient-boosted decision boundaries and the deep sequence learning approaches proposed in this study.

3.3 Deep Sequence Architectures: From Standard LSTM to CNN-Attention

In contrast to tree-based methods, deep sequence architectures are employed to bypass manual feature selection by directly mapping raw temporal dependencies. Two recurrent approaches are evaluated in this study to demonstrate the incremental value of local filtering and attention mechanisms.

The first approach serves as a recurrent benchmark, consisting of a sequence-to-scalar standard LSTM [6]. This configuration relies exclusively on internal gating mechanisms (input, forget and output gates) to manage temporal dependencies. To ensure a fair comparison, this baseline incorporates a stochastic noise injection layer, which applies Gaussian noise ($\sigma \in [0.01, 0.1]$) exclusively to chemical precursor features while preserving deterministic temporal variables.

The second, and more advanced configuration, integrates a 1D Convolutional Neural Network (CNN) [8] as a local pattern extractor:

$$H_{cnn} = \mathrm{Swish}(\mathrm{Conv1D}(X, k = 3)) \tag{4}$$

The CNN layer utilizes the Swish activation function [15], defined as $f(x) = x \cdot \mathrm{sigmoid}(\beta x)$. This function is preferred over ReLU for deep atmospheric modeling due to its smooth, non-monotonic profile, which helps maintain gradient flow across complex loss surfaces. With a kernel size of $k = 3$ h, this layer functions as a non-linear moving average, smoothing high-frequency instrumental noise before the signal reaches the LSTM backbone:

$$H_{lstm} = \mathrm{LSTM}(H_{cnn}) \tag{5}$$

The core of this study focuses on this hybrid CNN-LSTM-Attention architecture. The backbone features a flexible depth ($n \in \{1, 2\}$) and incorporates an asymmetric multi-head attention mechanism [16]. This technique designates the final hidden state $H_{lstm}^{(t-1)}$ as the Query (Q), representing the current atmospheric state, while the latent history acts as Keys (K) and Values (V). The block is stabilized by a residual skip connection and Layer Normalization to ensure robust feature propagation:

$$H_{out} = \mathrm{LayerNorm}(Q + \mathrm{Attention}(Q, K, V)) \tag{6}$$

3.4   Robust Optimization

The training process is driven by the AdamW optimizer [9] combined with Stochastic Weight Averaging (SWA) during terminal epochs. By maintaining a running average of the weights ($w_{SWA} = \frac{1}{n} \sum_{i=1}^{n} w_i$), SWA forces convergence toward flat local minima. This significantly reduces the model's sensitivity to stochastic shifts in ozone precursors, enhancing structural robustness and preventing overfitting to the training window.

Additionally, architectural and regularization hyperparameters (σ, δ, attention dimensionality) are not fixed, but dynamically tuned via Bayesian optimization [4]. This process employs a Gaussian Process surrogate model that maximizes the Expected Improvement (EI):

$$EI(x) = \mathbb{E}\left[\max(0, f_{best} - f(x))\right] \tag{7}$$

where f_{best} is the lowest observed validation error and $f(x)$ is the probabilistic prediction for the hyperparameter set x.

3.5   Generalization Metrics

To rigorously quantify the degree of overfitting and mathematically validate the efficacy of the regularization techniques utilized (SWA, Dropout), a customized Generalization Index ($\mathcal{G}$) was tracked. This dimensionless metric measures the stability of the model's performance when transitioning from the validation manifold to the unseen testing distribution:

$$\mathcal{G} = \frac{R^2_{test}}{R^2_{val}} \tag{8}$$

An optimal architecture should achieve a $\mathcal{G}$ score approaching 1.0, indicating a perfect transference of learned photochemical dynamics without memorization of the training noise.

4   Methodological Design and Experimental Procedure

To address the complex non-linear dynamics of ozone precursors described in Sects. 2 and 3, a hybrid forecasting framework was implemented in Python. Tree-based models were developed using Scikit-learn, while deep sequence architectures were built in TensorFlow/Keras. To manage the computational overhead of Bayesian optimization and attention mechanisms, all training was accelerated on an NVIDIA RTX 8000 GPU utilizing Mixed Precision (FP16), optimizing VRAM usage and convergence speed without compromising numerical stability.

4.1   Phase 1: Dynamic Phase Space Reconstruction

To capture the underlying non-linear dynamics of the atmospheric system, the one-dimensional time series is projected into a multidimensional space using a sliding window approach ($w = 72$).

4.2   Phase 2: Strategic Partitioning and Validation Protocol

Ensuring the generalizability of predictive models requires a partitioning schema that respects the arrow of time. Following the chronological split (2018–2022 for training/validation and 2023 for testing), internal model validation was conducted via a 5-fold walk-forward cross-validation scheme using TimeSeriesSplit.

To rigorously prevent data leakage stemming from the strong temporal autocorrelation of atmospheric variables, a purged cross-validation strategy was implemented [14]. Given the 72-h multivariate sliding window used for phase-space reconstruction, standard cross-validation would result in overlapping sequences between the training and validation sets. To address this, a temporal buffer (purging) was introduced between the splits within each fold. This gap strictly removes any overlapping samples, ensuring that the validation metrics reflect true generalization capabilities on unseen temporal dynamics rather than the memorization of boundary conditions.

4.3   Phase 3: Pipeline Integration and Fold-Isolated Preprocessing

To strictly prevent information leakage during the walk-forward validation, all preprocessing and feature selection steps are embedded within Python pipelines. This architectural design ensures that transformations are fitted independently on the active training subset of each fold, remaining completely blind to the validation data.

Numerical stabilization is managed via a ColumnTransformer. A RobustScaler [12] is applied exclusively to continuous predictors to mitigate extreme outliers, while cyclical and binary variables explicitly bypass scaling to preserve their strict mathematical bounds. Furthermore, to prevent data leakage, mRMR feature selection for the tree-based pipeline is computed dynamically within each isolated fold. Accordingly, the proportion of retained features is a parameter to be optimized by the Bayesian search.

4.4   Phase 4: Bayesian Hyperparameter Optimization

The structural complexity and learning dynamics of the models are governed by a set of configurable hyperparameters. To efficiently navigate this multi-dimensional search space, the training process employs Bayesian optimization via BayesSearchCV. This probabilistic approach iteratively samples the most promising parameter configurations (e.g., noise intensity σ, number of attention heads, CNN filter size, and the aforementioned mRMR feature retention percentage) guided by the EI criterion defined in Sect. 3, minimizing computational overhead while maximizing cross-validated performance.

The exact boundaries and sampling distributions defining the Bayesian search space for both the deep sequence architectures and the tree-based baseline are detailed in Table 1. Furthermore, it is important to note that the batch size for the deep sequence models was strictly fixed to 128 samples across all trials to maintain consistent gradient estimation during training.

4.5   Phase 5: Experimental Suite and SWA Stabilization

To evaluate the models clearly and rigorously, we designed a focused experimental setup using three core algorithms: a standard LSTM, a hybrid CNN-LSTM-Attention architecture, and XGBoost. The XGBoost model was tested in two ways: using all available features and using a reduced subset selected by the mRMR algorithm.

Additionally, every model was trained using a fixed short-term historical observation window ($w = 72$ h). To ensure a robust hyperparameter search, each model configuration underwent 50 independent iterations of Bayesian optimization.

To mitigate computational overhead, a parallelized 5-fold cross-validation scheme using ten jobs was implemented, enabling concurrent fold evaluation without compromising the sequential integrity of the Bayesian acquisition function.

Table 1. Condensed hyperparameter search space for Bayesian optimization.

Hyperparameter Group	Search Space/Range
Deep Sequence Architectures (LSTM & Attention)	
Regularization $(\delta, \sigma, \lambda)$	$\delta \in [0.1, 1.0], \sigma \in [0.01, 0.1], \lambda \in [10^{-5}, 10^{-2}]$
Architecture Depth & Size	$n \in \{1, 2\}$, Units $\in [16, 128]$
Dropout Rates (Base/Attn)	$[0.10, 0.35]^*/[0.05, 0.15]^\dagger$
Learning Rate	$[2 \cdot 10^{-4}, 1 \cdot 10^{-2}]$ (Log-Uniform)
Attention Config.† (Dim/Heads)	Dim $\in \{16, 32, 64\}$, Heads $\in \{1, 2, 4\}$
Tree-Based Baseline (Pipeline & XGBoost)	
Feature Selection (mRMR Retention %)	$[1, 100]$ (Integer)
Tree Structure (Depth/Estimators)	Depth $\in \{3, 4\}$, $N \in [100, 500]$
Learning & Regularization (η, α, λ)	$\eta \in [0.01, 0.1], \alpha \in [0.1, 50], \lambda \in [1, 100]$
Stochastic Params (Subsample/Colsample)	Sub. $\in [0.6, 0.8]$, Col. $\in [0.4, 0.6]$
Growth Control $(\gamma,$ Min. Child Weight)	$\gamma \in [0.1, 5.0]$, Weight $\in [5, 30]$

$^*, \dagger$: Specific to Attention-based CNN-LSTM architectures.

Deep sequence models were trained for 150 epochs, evaluating two optimization paradigms: a standard approach using Early Stopping with best-weight restoration, and an SWA approach integrating Stochastic Weight Averaging from epoch 60. To integrate both approaches, a custom conditional callback was engineered to bypass weight restoration during the SWA phase, preserving the moving average to favor flatter minima and superior generalization.

5   Results and Discussion

To rigorously evaluate the proposed architectures, the predictive performance was analyzed using the established 72-h historical observation window. The models were tasked with forecasting the tropospheric ozone concentration 24 h into the future, relying solely on the data captured within the previous three days. The following sections dissect the results from both a global statistical perspective (Table 2) and a detailed dynamic analysis through visual inspection of the best configurations for each family (Figs. 1, 2, and 3).

The empirical results reveal a clear performance hierarchy, with deep sequence models outperforming the tree-based baseline. The visual analysis of the prediction trajectories provides deep insights into the reason why certain architectures excel in this chaotic domain.

The CNN-LSTM-Attention SWA model achieved the highest global performance ($R^2 = 0.699$, MSE $= 368.3$). Visually, Fig. 1(A) confirms a dense alignment of points along the ideal 1:1 line (red dashed line). More importantly, the critical episode zoom (Panel C) demonstrates the attention module's specific contribution. The blue predicted trajectory tightly tracks the complex diurnal amplitudes of the black actual line (Local MAE $= 13.82$). While it slightly

Table 2. Predictive performance metrics for the 72-h temporal window evaluated on the 2023 testing set. Bold values indicate the best performance in each category.

Model Configuration	MAE	MSE	R^2	$\mathcal{G}$	Time (min)
Deep Sequence Architectures					
CNN-LSTM-Attention (SWA)	**14.61**	**368.30**	**0.6992**	0.94	399.10
CNN-LSTM-Attention (Std)	14.70	373.90	0.6946	**0.96**	409.45
Baseline LSTM (SWA)	15.03	379.49	0.6900	0.95	176.90
Baseline LSTM (Std)	15.12	379.45	0.6901	0.95	180.39
Tree-Based Baseline (XGBoost)					
XGBoost (Full Features)	15.62	404.71	0.6694	0.89	6.40
XGBoost (mRMR Selected)	15.65	405.43	0.6688	0.87	**5.00**

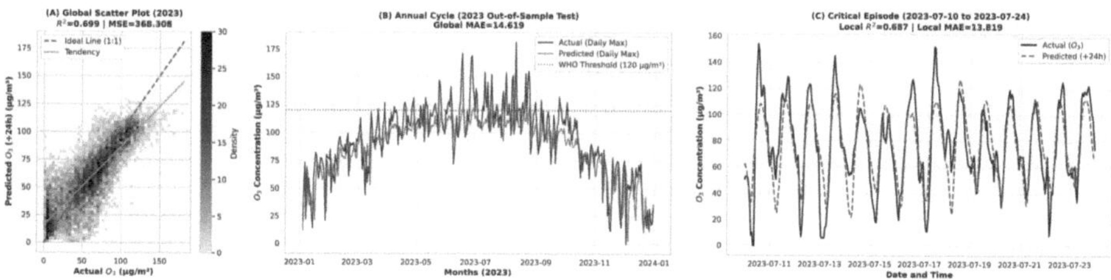

Fig. 1. Detailed performance evaluation for the best-performing architecture: hybrid CNN-LSTM-Attention equipped with Stochastic Weight Averaging (SWA). (A) Global scatter plot on 2023 test set showing high density correlation ($R^2 = 0.699$). (B) Annual cycle tracking daily maxima against the WHO health threshold (120 µg/m^3). (C) Zoomed critical summer episode highlighting the network's superior capacity to capture the amplitude and phase of non-linear diurnal O_3 peaks (Local $R^2 = 0.687$).

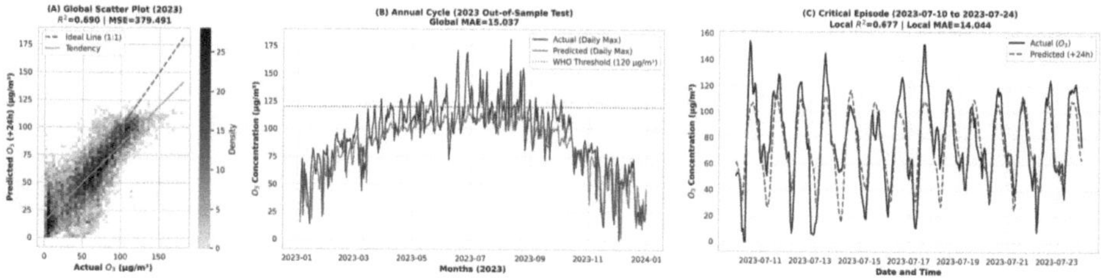

Fig. 2. Detailed performance evaluation for the deep baseline: standard LSTM with SWA stabilization. Compared to the attention mechanism, this architecture shows a slightly higher global MSE (379.49) and a reduced accuracy in capturing maximum amplitudes during critical episodes (Panel C, Local MAE increased to 14.04 µg/m^3).

underestimates the absolute maximum of severe spikes (e.g., July 14th), it accurately captures the phase and sharp rise of nearly every diurnal cycle, justifying the 11-point MSE reduction over the baseline LSTM. The attention mechanism

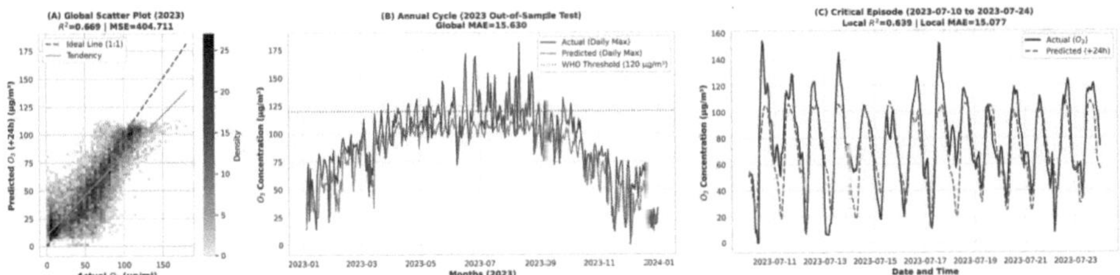

Fig. 3. Detailed performance evaluation for the tree-based baseline: XGBoost trained on full engineered features. The global metrics deviate from deep learning models ($R^2 = 0.669$). Panel (A) shows a shallower regression slope (orange line), and Panel (C) visually confirms a noticeable underestimation of peak values during highly dynamic atmospheric cycles. (Color figure online)

successfully weights the relevant historical conditions within the 72-h window, effectively modeling the non-linear photochemical activation lag.

While the standard LSTM with SWA remains statistically competitive ($R^2 = 0.690$), detailed analysis reveals greater temporal lag and reduced amplitude fidelity during severe ozone spikes (Local MAE $= 14.04\ \mu g/m^3$). This underscores that while recurrent layers adequately capture general chemical inertia, the integration of CNN feature extractors and attention mechanisms is vital for mitigating phase delays in non-linear transients. Furthermore, SWA optimization significantly lowered the hybrid model's MSE to 368.30, effectively stabilizing convergence toward flatter minima and ensuring robust generalization ($\mathcal{G} = 0.94$).

Conversely, despite its computational efficiency (< 7 min), XGBoost suffered from systematic peak underestimation ($R^2 = 0.669$) and noticeable amplitude damping. Even with mRMR feature optimization, the tree-based baseline remains structurally incapable of resolving the high-frequency photochemical dynamics required for reliable alerting.

Consequently, the superior phase tracking and amplitude fidelity of the deep sequence architectures justify their higher offline training footprint (399 min) as their online inference time remains negligible for real-time forecasting.

6   Conclusions

This study demonstrates that 24-h ahead ozone forecasting in complex urban environments requires architectures capable of modeling non-linear photochemical dynamics beyond simple temporal inertia. The hybrid CNN-LSTM-Attention model, stabilized with Stochastic Weight Averaging (SWA), emerged as the superior configuration ($R^2 = 0.699$, MSE $= 368.30$). The integration of multi-head attention proved essential to mitigate temporal lag and capture the full amplitude of diurnal O_3 spikes, significantly outperforming tree-based baselines.

A pivotal contribution of this research is the validation of the Generalization Index ($\mathcal{G}$). The CNN-LSTM-Attention SWA model achieved a score of $\mathcal{G} = 0.94$, proving that the synergy between attention mechanisms and SWA optimization forces convergence toward flatter minima. This ensures that the predictive performance is not a result of local overfitting to historical noise but a robust reconstruction of the underlying atmospheric dynamics. In contrast, while XGBoost optimized with mRMR offered extreme computational efficiency, its inability to process sequential autocorrelation led to amplitude dumping, rendering it unreliable for peak-exposure alerting.

Future research will focus on expanding the input space with NO_2 and $VOCs$ to better resolve precursor stoichiometry. Additionally, exploring State-Space Models (e.g., Mamba) could facilitate the assimilation of longer historical windows, such as full weekly cycles, without the quadratic computational overhead of standard attention, further refining the accuracy of operational early warning systems.

Acknowledgments. This work is part of the technological contract OT2024/028, "Use of Hyperspectral Imaging and UAV in Smart Management of Urban Waste Landfills", supported by ARCGISA. Furthermore, the authors would like to thank the financial support provided by the Plan de Ayudas para el Fomento de la Investigación y Transferencia de Conocimiento en el Campus Bahía de Algeciras (promoted by the Algeciras Technological Campus Foundation, University of Cádiz). Additional funding was provided by the Andalusia FEDER Operational Programme 2021–2027 under grant FEDER-UCA-2024-B2-07, titled "Spectral Imaging Technology and Deep Learning for Environmental Protection: Detection of Water and Air Pollution (DeepEnvSI)".

References

1. Aljanabi, M., Shkoukani, M., Hijjawi, M.: Ground-level ozone prediction using machine learning techniques: a case study in Amman, Jordan. Mach. Intell. Res. **17**(5), 667–677 (2020). https://doi.org/10.1007/s11633-020-1233-4
2. Branco, P., Torgo, L., Ribeiro, R.P.: A survey of predictive modeling on imbalanced domains. ACM Comput. Surv. (CSUR) **49**(2), 1–50 (2016). https://doi.org/10.1145/2907070
3. Chen, T., Guestrin, C.: XGBoost: a scalable tree boosting system. In: Proceedings of the 22nd ACM SIGKDD International Conference on Knowledge Discovery and Data Mining. KDD 2016, pp. 785–794. ACM, New York (2016). https://doi.org/10.1145/2939672.2939785
4. Golovin, D., Solnik, B., Kochanski, S., Young, G., Karro, T., Sculley, D.: Google Vizier: a service for black-box optimization. In: Proceedings of the 23rd ACM SIGKDD International Conference on Knowledge Discovery and Data Mining. KDD 2017, pp. 1487–1495. ACM, New York (2017). https://doi.org/10.1145/3097983.3098043
5. Hampel, F.R.: The influence curve and its role in robust estimation. J. Am. Stat. Assoc. **69**(346), 383–393 (1974). https://doi.org/10.1080/01621459.1974.10482962
6. Hochreiter, S., Schmidhuber, J.: Long short-term memory. Neural Comput. **9**(8), 1735–1780 (1997). https://doi.org/10.1162/neco.1997.9.8.1735
7. Huang, C.J., Kuo, P.H.: A deep CNN-LSTM model for particulate matter (PM2.5) forecasting in smart cities. Sensors **18**(7), 2220 (2018). https://doi.org/10.3390/s18072220

8. Kiranyaz, S., Avci, O., Abdeljaber, O , Ince, T., Gabbouj, M., Inman, D.J.: 1D convolutional neural networks and applications: a survey Mech. Syst. Signal Process. **151**, 107398 (2021). https://doi.org/10.1016/j.ymssp.2020.107398

9. Loshchilov, I., Hutter, F.: Decoupled weight decay regularization. In: International Conference on Learning Representations (2018)

10. Monks, P.S., et al.: Tropospheric ozone and its precursors from the urban to the global scale from air quality to short-lived climate forcer. Atmos. Chem. Phys. **15**(15), 8889–8973 (2015). https://doi.org/10.5194/acp-15-8889-2015

11. Nuvolone, D., Petri, D., Voller, F.: The effects of ozone on human health. Environ. Sci. Pollut. Res. **25**(9), 8074–8088 (2018). https://doi.org/10.1007/s11356-017-9239-3

12. Pedregosa, F., et al.: Scikit-learn: Machine learning in python. J. Mach. Learn. Res. **12**, 2825–2830 (2011). https://jmlr.csail.mit.edu/papers/v12/pedregosa11a.html

13. Peng, H., Long, F., Ding, C.: Feature selection based on mutual information criteria of max-dependency, max-relevance, and min-redundancy. IEEE Trans. Pattern Anal. Mach. Intell. **27**(8), 1226–1238 (2005). https://doi.org/10.1109/TPAMI.2005.159

14. López de Prado, M.: Advances in Financial Machine Learning. Wiley, Hoboken (2018)

15. Ramachandran, P., Zoph, B., Le, Q.V.: Searching for activation functions, arXiv:1710.05941 (2017)

16. Vaswani, A., et al.: Attention is all you need. In: Advances in Neural Information Processing Systems, vol. 30 (2017). https://proceedings.neurips.cc/paper/2017/file/3f5ee243547dee91fbd053c1c4a845aa-Paper.pdf

Author Index